BOTTOM LINE YEAR BOOK 2001

BY THE EDITORS OF

Bottom Line
PERSONAL

Contents

PART THREE: YOUR FINANCIAL FUTURE

11 • RETIREMENT PLANNING

12 • ESTATE PLANNING

PART FOUR: YOUR LEISURE

13 • TRAVEL CONFIDENTIAL

14 • MAKING THE MOST OF YOUR LEISURE TIME

15 • YOUR CAR

16 • YOUR FAMILY AND YOUR HOME

17 • THE WINNING EDGE

PART FIVE: YOUR LIFE

18 • BUSINESS AND CAREER SMARTS

19 • EDUCATION SMARTS

20 • SELF-DEFENSE

21 • VERY, VERY PERSONAL

1

Staying Healthy

Lifesaving Breakthroughs In Cancer Care

Each year, cancer specialists from around the globe gather for the annual meeting of the American Society of Clinical Oncology. Drawing more than 20,000 doctors, it's the largest meeting of its type in the world.

Recently, there was much excitement about potentially revolutionary new drugs that interrupt *angiogenesis*. That's the process by which tumors grow the new blood vessels they need to survive.

More recently, conferees got an update into research on antiangiogenesis drugs...and discussed breakthroughs on a number of other fronts...

BREAST CANCER

Researchers made headlines in 1999 when they announced that *tamoxifen* (Nolvadex)—a drug long used as a treatment for breast cancer—could also help prevent the disease.

Now research suggests that a related drug called *raloxifene* (Evista)—developed as a treatment for osteoporosis—has a role in breast cancer prevention.

In one recent study involving 7,700 osteoporosis patients, researchers were startled to find that raloxifene use not only increased bone density but also reduced the risk for breast cancer by 70%.

Given this and similar findings, raloxifene will soon be presented to the FDA for approval for use as a breast cancer preventive.

Breast cancer specialists are also discovering that the cancer-killing power of existing breast cancer drugs can be significantly enhanced by using them in various combinations.

Preliminary evidence suggests that chemotherapy plus the new drug *trastuzumab* (Her-

Derek Raghavan, MD, associate director and chief of medical oncology at the Norris Comprehensive Cancer Center of the University of Southern California School of Medicine in Los Angeles.

1

ceptin) may be more effective at treating breast cancer than chemotherapy given alone.

DIGESTIVE TRACT CANCER

Several experimental drugs have shown good results against digestive tract cancers—and so should come into clinical use within the next year.

•**Fludarabine** (FUDR) is proving to be highly effective against metastatic bowel cancer in the liver.

•**Irinotecan** seems to be effective against colon cancer.

•**Oxaliplatin** is proving to be effective against cancers of the colon and stomach.

Cancer surgeons are reporting important advances as well. In one study conducted recently at the University of Chicago's Pritzker School of Medicine, researchers found that rectal tumors can be removed without cutting into the anal sphincter. That's the circular muscle that controls bowel function.

Patients who undergo this procedure retain full control of their bowels after surgery. That isn't always assured with conventional surgery for rectal cancer.

KIDNEY CANCER

Doctors at New York Presbyterian Hospital have developed the first blood test for kidney cancer. For now, the test is being used in an experimental setting to determine whether a lump in the abdomen is kidney cancer...and to check for metastatic cancer in patients who have already had a cancerous kidney surgically removed.

As its accuracy is improved, experts hope that this test will permit screening of the general public. That's significant, since kidney cancer is among the most "silent" of all malignancies.

LIVER CANCER

Researchers at Memorial Sloan-Kettering Cancer Center in New York City have developed a better way to treat bowel cancer that has spread to the liver. In the study, all patients received traditional chemotherapy. Half of the patients also got the drug FUDR.

After two years, 85% of the FUDR group were still alive. Only 62% of the other group were alive.

In another development, doctors in Perth, Australia, have found that liver cancer patients undergoing chemotherapy live longer when tiny radioactive pellets are injected into the hepatic artery.

The pellets are carried by the blood to the tumor, where they release tumor-killing radiation.

PROSTATE CANCER

Conventional surgery for prostate cancer often causes nerve damage that leads to incontinence and/or impotence.

But better knowledge of how prostate cancers grow is enabling researchers to develop drugs that attack prostate tumors while leaving surrounding, healthy tissue unharmed. Among these drugs is *docetaxel* (Taxotere).

There is also early evidence of the effectiveness of gene therapy against localized prostate cancer.

In a recent study, copies of the p53 gene—which induces damaged cells to "commit suicide"—were injected into the prostates of 26 prostate cancer patients. Seven of the patients showed a marked reduction in tumor size.

SKIN CANCER

Although antiangiogenesis drugs may prove to be effective against many types of cancer, the first human trial of the drugs involved skin cancer.

In one recent study, conducted at the University of Southern California School of Medicine in Los Angeles, an experimental antiangiogenesis drug called *IM862* shrank tumors by more than 50% in patients with Kaposi's sarcoma. That's a form of skin cancer commonly seen in AIDS patients.

In light of this finding, there are now plans to test antiangiogenesis drugs against ovarian cancer and melanoma.

Best Cancer Fighters

Raspberries, strawberries and grapes contain the highest levels of the cancer-preventing compound *ellagic acid*.

This compound—found in slightly lower concentrations in nuts and other fruits—helps protect DNA by binding to and thereby deactivating chemical carcinogens. Such damage raises the risk for cancer.

Ellagic acid is also thought to reduce risk for stroke and heart attack.

Miriam Rossi, PhD, associate professor of chemistry, Vassar College, Poughkeepsie, NY.

Garlic vs. Cancer

Eating as little as half of a clove of raw garlic a day—finely chopped on salads, for example—seems to decrease the risk of intestinal cancer. Garlic contains *diallyl disulfide,* a compound that triggers synthesis of enzymes that help deactivate carcinogens in the gastrointestinal tract. *Bad news:* You'd have to eat about nine times as much cooked garlic to derive the same benefit.

Rex Munday, PhD, senior scientist, Ruakura Agricultural Centre, Hamilton, New Zealand.

Should You Put Medicine *On* You Instead of *In* You?

Timothy McCall, MD, a New York City internist and author of *Examining Your Doctor: A Patient's Guide to Avoiding Harmful Medical Care.* Citadel Press.

Each year, 100,000 Americans are killed by prescription medications *that have been prescribed—and taken—correctly.* That's the startling conclusion of a study published in *The Lancet,* the prestigious medical journal from England. This figure places medications just behind cancer, heart attack and stroke as a leading cause of death in the US. Of course, drugs also save countless lives. The trick is to maximize benefits while minimizing risks.

The most important principle for avoiding harm from drugs is to use them only when necessary. When a drug is needed, it's a good idea to pick the safest one available—and use

it in the safest possible way. If two drugs are equally effective, the one that causes fewer side effects is the better choice. This is one reason why doctors usually pick *acetaminophen* (Tylenol, etc.) over aspirin for fever and pain. And safety is the major reason that I advocate the use of topical medications instead of oral or injected ones whenever possible.

Consider capsaicin. For many arthritis sufferers, a salve made from this chili pepper extract soothes pain—with less risk of side effects than oral painkillers. The problem with arthritis pills is that they're absorbed into the bloodstream and circulated all over the body. This means that *ibuprofen* (Motrin, Advil, etc.) or another pill taken for a bum knee could wind up causing intestinal bleeding or kidney damage. Topical capsaicin isn't risk-free—it can irritate the skin. But it's safer than pills. The same is true for most topical medications.

In the case of sore throat, a couple of old-fashioned topical remedies are very effective at lessening the discomfort. The first is gargling with salt water. Dissolve one-half teaspoon of salt into a glass of warm water, and gargle for 20 seconds. Since you spit the water out, little salt is absorbed. You can repeat this several times a day.

Another sore throat remedy I like is slippery elm. Lozenges containing this herbal "demulcent" coat the mucous membranes of the throat, easing pain almost instantly.

This points up another advantage of topical treatments: Since they're applied directly to the affected area, they start to work very rapidly.

Another example of an effective topical treatment is inhaled drugs for asthma. These drugs are breathed directly into the bronchial tubes and lungs. Even though some of the medication is absorbed into the blood, these drugs are much safer than asthma pills like *theophylline,* which can cause side effects like insomnia and rapid heart beat.

Some topical medications, including vaginal creams containing estrogen, are so well absorbed that they're not much different than the same medication taken orally. In fact, skin patches, such as those used to administer nicotine and nitroglycerin, rely on absorption through the skin to bring the drug to the general circulation. I'm not saying that these drugs are bad, just that the risk of side effects may be just as great as if they were taken by mouth.

Several familiar remedies for minor ailments are topical treatments. If your muscles ache, you can soak in a hot bath. If you sprain an ankle, you can put ice on it. Ice also soothes lower back pain and arthritic joints.

One of my favorite topical treatments is massage. Studies have found it effective for everything from headache to depression to postsurgical pain. And it's nice to know that something that feels good is good for you, too.

Too Much Medicine Can Give You a Headache

Rebound headaches can be caused by taking headache medicine frequently. They can be worse than the original headache. Any pain medication, including over-the-counter pain relievers, can cause rebound headaches if taken too often. *Self-defense:* If your use of pain medication increases over time, consult your doctor.

Randolph W. Evans, MD, neurologist and clinical professor of neurology, University of Texas Medical School, Houston.

Eye Problems from Non-Eye Drugs

Many medications can affect the eyes. *Especially common:* Any corticosteroid— drugs ending in "sone," such as prednisone, cortisone and dexamethasone. They're prescribed for emphysema, arthritis and a wide range of other diseases. When taken over the course of several months, these drugs can cause cataracts and glaucoma.

Danger: With many other concerns about your condition, your doctor may not warn you of a drug's possible effects on your eyes.

Whenever you're given a new prescription to take for more than a month or two, educate yourself. Read the list of potential side effects in the patient information pamphlet and ask your pharmacist whether the drug could affect your eyes. If so, you may want to be under an ophthalmologist's care while taking the drug.

James F. Collins, MD, FACS, a practicing ophthalmologist and medical director of the Center for Eye Care in West Islip, NY.

SAM-e Is Here

S-adenosylmethionine (SAM-e) is a yeast-based dietary supplement that is now being sold in the US after having been used for more than 20 years in Europe. SAM-e has key advantages over prescription antidepressants and Saint-John's-wort. It works faster...and it doesn't cause sexual dysfunction or other side effects. Nor are there withdrawal symptoms when one stops taking it. *Bonus:* SAM-e boosts liver function. *Caution:* If depression lasts for more than two weeks or is accompanied by thoughts of suicide, see a doctor.

Richard Brown, MD, associate professor of clinical psychiatry, Columbia University School of Medicine, New York City. He is coauthor of *Stop Depression Now.* Putnam.

Heart Attack Survival

To survive a heart attack when you're alone, first take an aspirin...then expend as little energy as possible while waiting for help to arrive...and recline but do not lie flat. *Warning:* A widely circulated Internet message suggests that heart attack victims use "cough CPR"—coughing vigorously, breathing deeply, coughing vigorously, etc.—to maintain blood flow and restore cardiac rhythm. *However:* Cough CPR is just not known to work in this setting. Most important is early recognition of heart attack symptoms—particularly pain in the chest, arm and/or neck and shortness of breath—and then obtaining expert medical care as quickly as possible. Those at risk of heart attack should always carry aspirin in case of emergency.

Mara McErlean, MD, associate professor of emergency medicine, Albany Medical College, Albany, NY.

You Don't Have to Put Up With Fatigue Anymore

Erika T. Schwartz, MD, an internist in private practice in Armonk, NY. She is the author of Natural Energy: From Tired to Terrific in 10 Days. Putnam.

You've tried getting more sleep. You've tried exercising and taking other steps to control psychological stress. Yet you're still feeling tired and run down.

You know it's unwise to prop yourself up with caffeine. But what else can you do to boost your energy levels?

Once anemia, heart disease, thyroid disease, hepatitis, mononucleosis and other medical causes of fatigue have been ruled out, the average physician is at a loss as to what to do next.

"You'll just have to learn to live with it," he/she might say. Or, "Well, you *are* getting older."

Not true. *These nutrition-based strategies can be very effective...*

DRINK MORE WATER

Many cases of fatigue can be traced to the *mitochondria,* the microscopic "power plants" inside each cell of the body.

Mitochondria synthesize *adenosine triphosphate* (ATP), a high-energy molecule that's used throughout the body as a source of energy. But the chemical reactions that yield ATP also make free radicals and other toxins as by-products.

To flush out these toxins, the body needs at least 64 ounces of water a day. Less than that, and mitochondria are apt to become "clogged" with toxins, becoming inefficient at pumping out ATP.

RECONSIDER SALT

For many people with high blood pressure, salt deserves its status as a dietary no-no. But in healthy individuals, moderate salt intake boosts energy levels.

Salt helps the body hold onto the water it takes in. By boosting water retention, salt helps keep mitochondria free of toxins and functioning properly.

As long as your blood pressure is normal, it's safe to boost your intake of chicken stock, miso soup, salted nuts and other unprocessed sources of salt whenever you feel fatigued.

EAT SMALL, EAT OFTEN

Eating three big meals a day puts your blood sugar (glucose) levels on a roller coaster. Low glucose can cause fatigue.

Eating every three hours helps keep your energy up by steadying your glucose levels.

Your goal should be to consume a mix of protein and fiber at each meal. Because fiber- and protein-rich foods are digested slowly, they provide a steady, reliable source of energy.

Eat plenty of vegetables, brown rice, multi-grain bread, grilled chicken or fish, nuts and dried fruits.

ENERGY-BOOSTING SUPPLEMENTS

Three nutrients are of proven value in the treatment of chronic fatigue...

●**L-carnitine.** This amino acid helps transport fatty acids into mitochondria, where they're used to make ATP.

L-carnitine is found in lamb, beef and other meats, but you'd have to consume impossibly large amounts of these natural food sources to get the 1,000 mg of L-carnitine needed each day to boost your energy.

Ask your doctor about taking the prescription L-carnitine supplement *Carnitor.* The typical dosage is three or four 330-mg tablets a day.

●**Coenzyme Q10.** This antioxidant enzyme acts as a catalyst to "spark" synthesis of ATP.

Organ meats are the best source of co-enzyme Q, but you'd have to eat far too much to get the recommended 100 mg of coenzyme Q10 per day.

Coenzyme Q10 is sold over the counter in powder or gel form. The gel is more easily absorbed. The typical dosage is two 50-mg gel-caps a day.

•**Magnesium.** This mineral is needed for ATP synthesis. Unfortunately, chocolate, caffeine, soft drinks and highly processed foods tend to deplete the body of magnesium. As a result, magnesium deficiency is common in the US, and fatigue is a symptom of magnesium deficiency.

At special risk: Diabetics, people who consume lots of caffeine and people who take diuretic drugs.

Good sources of magnesium include wheat bran...brown rice...spinach...kale...chicken...turkey...pork...apricots...and curry powder.

Ask your doctor about taking a magnesium supplement, too.

Feel More Energetic! It's Easy!

Richard N. Podell, MD, clinical professor of medicine at Robert Wood Johnson Medical School in New Brunswick, NJ. Dr. Podell is one of several doctors nationwide who are conducting studies on Ampligen, an experimental drug for chronic fatigue syndrome. He is the author of four books, including *Doctor, Why Am I So Tired?* Fawcett.

Among older people, chronic fatigue is often symptomatic of diabetes, thyroid disease, anemia, hepatitis or another underlying illness.

In young people, it's more likely to be the result of psychological stress, anxiety or depression...or poor sleep, poor nutrition and/or a lack of exercise.

Up to 1% of American adults have chronic fatigue syndrome, a debilitating and as-yet incurable condition that's believed to be triggered by one or more viruses.

Whenever fatigue lasts for three weeks or longer—or interferes with your work or your enjoyment of life—see a physician. Simple blood tests can detect most of the common physical causes of fatigue.

Good news: For most fatigue sufferers, these changes in diet and lifestyle provide a substantial energy boost...

•**Eliminate sugar...**and cut back on carbohydrates. In some people, the body responds to sugar and carbohydrates by releasing too much insulin. This causes glucose levels to plummet, resulting in fatigue.

I often ask my patients suffering from fatigue to stop eating sugar and cut their daily consumption of carbohydrates to two slices of bread or one serving of pasta. These changes often trigger a dramatic rise in energy. You'll know within three weeks if the changes are going to make a difference for you.

•**Exercise four times a week.** Regular exercise causes the body to release energizing compounds called *endorphins*. It also boosts the flow of oxygen to the brain...and reduces stress and anxiety.

Start at a low level of exercise. Then increase the distance or pace by about 10% each week, as long as you don't feel worse.

While many people feel energized after each exercise session, others require several months of reconditioning before their fatigue dissipates.

•**Eliminate caffeine from your diet.** Despite its reputation as a stimulant, the caffeine in cola, coffee and black tea tends to exacerbate fatigue. *There are two reasons for this...*

•Caffeine is addictive. You need increasing amounts to feel "normal." When you fail to get your usual "dose" of caffeine, you feel tired.

•Too much caffeine causes anxiety, which can interfere with restful sleep.

If you drink caffeinated beverages, give them up for a week. See if you feel more energetic. Reduce your intake by one cup a day. This will help you avoid caffeine-withdrawal headaches.

•**Consume alcohol in moderation**—and *never* late at night. Alcohol disrupts sleep, especially when consumed after 7 pm. It also exacerbates the low blood sugar condition *hypoglycemia.*

If you're trying to boost your energy, one drink a day is the limit. Total abstinence is better.

●**Eat fruits and vegetables daily.** Green beans, broccoli, spinach, carrots, summer squash and certain other vegetables—and most fruits—are rich sources of potassium, magnesium and other key nutrients.

Having five servings each of vegetables and fruits helps ensure you're getting everything needed for optimal metabolism.

●**Have a daily "energy cocktail."** Most Americans are deficient in at least one essential nutrient. Such deficiencies interfere with energy production, causing fatigue.

Many of us would benefit from taking a multivitamin/multimineral supplement, along with daily supplements containing...

●Fish oil or primrose oil (1 g). These oils contain essential fatty acids that help the body produce beneficial prostaglandins.

●N-acetylcysteine (600 mg). This supplement supplies the body with a key antioxidant called glutathione.

●Bilberry or grape-seed extract (60 mg). These increase energy, speed up metabolism and improve circulation.

●B-complex (25 mg to 50 mg of each B vitamin). B vitamins are water-soluble, so they're depleted more quickly than other nutrients.

Women of childbearing age should take an iron supplement to replace iron lost during menstruation.

●**Take ginseng.** This stimulant herb, often taken in capsule form, isn't addictive the way caffeine is. For best results, ask your doctor about using ginseng intermittently for up to two weeks at a time. Follow label directions carefully.

●**Take naps.** Americans today sleep about an hour less than they did just 90 years ago. Sleeping an extra 45 minutes each night can bring big improvements in energy levels.

If you can't find the extra 45 minutes, take a 10- or 20-minute nap whenever you feel tired.

Trap: Excessive daytime napping interferes with nighttime sleep.

●**Discuss medications with your doctor.** Fatigue is a common side effect of *hundreds* of prescription and over-the-counter drugs.

Show your doctor or pharmacist a list of every drug you take. In many cases, switching to a slightly different drug eliminates fatigue.

Caution: Never change medications without first consulting your doctor.

●**Take frequent mental breaks.** Set aside five to 20 minutes at least once a day for quiet time. Use the time to practice deep breathing.

What to do: Sit comfortably. Inhale slowly through your nostrils until your lungs fill. Gently contract your stomach muscles and hold for a few seconds. Exhale slowly. Repeat the cycle until your quiet time is up.

A single deep breathing session can provide a surge of energy that lasts one hour or more.

Ten-Step Program for Chronic Pain Works Very, Very Effectively

Dharma Singh Khalsa, MD, founding director of the Acupuncture Stress Medicine and Chronic Pain Program at the University of Arizona College of Medicine in Phoenix. He is now president and medical director of the Alzheimer's Prevention Foundation in Tucson, Arizona, and is the author of *The Pain Cure.* Warner Books.

Twenty-five million Americans are bedeviled by some form of chronic pain—sciatica, migraine, arthritis, muscle pain, etc. There are effective ways to curb chronic pain, but these *aren't* the ways typically recommended by mainstream physicians.

In addition to surgery and narcotics, mainstream doctors often recommend nonsteroidal anti-inflammatory drugs (NSAIDs) like *ibuprofen* (Motrin) to their patients with chronic pain.

These drugs can be highly effective against acute pain, such as sprains or toothaches. But they're less effective against chronic pain. And—NSAIDs can cause bleeding ulcers and other side effects.

A new prescription drug called *celecoxib* (Celebrex) appears to stop chronic pain with less risk of side effects than NSAIDs. Still, it's not yet clear how effective celecoxib will be in the long run.

Here are 10 pain-relieving strategies that really work...

●**Eat more fish and poultry.** Doctors often prescribe *fluoxetine* (Prozac) for chronic pain. This prescription antidepressant helps curb pain by boosting levels of the neurotransmitter *serotonin* in the brain. Serotonin blocks synthesis of *substance P,* one of the main chemical messengers involved in chronic pain.

But many people can keep serotonin levels high simply by eating foods rich in *tryptophan,* an amino acid that the body converts into serotonin.

Two excellent sources of tryptophan are poultry and fish. If you have chronic pain, try eating three ounces of either one five days a week.

In addition to blocking substance P, serotonin helps make people less aware of pain by improving mood and regulating disturbed sleep cycles.

●**Eat a banana every day.** Most chronic pain stems from arthritis, muscle pain or another inflammatory condition, which invariably goes hand in hand with muscle spasms. These spasms contribute to chronic pain.

Eat one banana a day—along with a bit of the lining of the peel that you've scraped off with a spoon. Doing so will supply you with lots of magnesium and potassium. Both minerals help control spasms.

●**Get regular exercise.** Exercise triggers the synthesis of natural painkillers known as *endorphins.*

If you're experiencing severe pain, of course, you probably don't feel like doing vigorous exercise. That's fine. Endorphin synthesis can be triggered by any form of activity that pushes the body a bit harder than it's accustomed to.

If you've been sedentary for a long time, something as simple as rotating your arms for a few seconds can work. So can sitting in a chair and raising your legs a few times.

●**Take steps to control psychological stress.** Stress plays a central role in chronic pain. Meditation and other relaxation techniques

reduce muscle spasms, limit the release of pain-causing stress hormones and improve breathing. Each of these helps reduce pain intensity.

One recent study found that pain sufferers who meditated for 10 to 20 minutes a day visited a pain clinic 36% less often than did their nonmeditating peers.

What to do: Carve out at least 15 minutes of quiet time each day. If you aren't comfortable meditating, use the time to pray...visualize a tranquil scene...or sit quietly.

●**Avoid harmful fats.** Red meat and cooking oil stimulate production of *arachidonic acid,* a compound that the body converts into hormone-like substances that trigger inflammation. These substances are known as *prostaglandins.*

Chronic pain sufferers should avoid red meat entirely...and use cooking oil sparingly.

●**Take omega-3 fatty acid supplements.** Taking 1,000 mg to 3,000 mg of fish oil or flaxseed oil each day helps block synthesis of prostaglandins.

In addition to blocking prostaglandin synthesis, a type of omega-3 fatty acid known as *eicosapentaenoic acid* (EPA) improves circulation by making the platelets—cell-like structures that are responsible for blood clotting—less "sticky." This helps keep blood from pooling and causing inflammation and irritation.

Fatty acid supplements are unnecessary for individuals who eat cold-water, dark-flesh fish several times a week. Salmon, tuna, mackerel and sardines all fit the bill.

●**Take a vitamin B complex supplement.** Chronic pain is often accompanied by fatigue. When you feel more energetic, your pain is more manageable.

Ask your doctor about taking a daily supplement that contains at least 50 mg of B complex vitamins.

Vitamin B helps increase energy levels by facilitating the production of ATP, the high-energy compound found in mitochondria, the "power plants" inside cells.

●**Season food with turmeric.** Its primary constituent, *curcumin,* has been shown to be as effective at relieving pain as cortisone or ibuprofen—without any risk of side effects. A pinch or two a day is all you need.

•**Try acupuncture.** There's now solid evidence that acupuncture can be more effective than drug therapy for relieving many types of chronic pain.

Acupuncture that is done by a physician seems to be especially effective. So-called medical acupuncture often involves the application of electrical current to needles inserted into the skin. This variant of traditional acupuncture is called electroacupuncture.

For referral to an acupuncturist in your area, call the American Academy of Medical Acupuncture at 800-521-2262.

•**See a chiropractor or osteopath.** Most physicians rely upon drug therapy and surgery for controlling pain. Chiropractors and osteopaths incorporate physical manipulation into their treatments. For back pain especially, manipulation often works better than drugs or surgery.

Secrets Of Cataract Prevention... And Reversal

Robert Abel, Jr., MD, clinical professor of ophthalmology at Thomas Jefferson University School of Medicine in Philadelphia. He is the author of *The Eye Care Revolution*. Kensington.

Cataracts are the number-one cause of vision loss in the US, affecting nearly half of adults age 65 or over. But it's a mistake to think of cataracts as affecting only older people. The physical changes that cause them begin almost at birth.

Background: The transparent lens of the eye consists of proteins densely interwoven in a crystalline structure. When these proteins are damaged by free radicals—harmful oxygen molecules produced in the body, especially upon exposure to sunlight and cigarette smoke—the lens becomes cloudy or opaque.

Eventually this leads to vision loss, from reduced nighttime vision to blindness.

Good news: Even people who have already begun to form cataracts can often preserve their sight and forestall cataract surgery by blocking the effects of free radicals. *It even may be possible to reverse damage that's already been done...*

•**Protect the eyes from ultraviolet radiation.** Along with visible light, sunlight contains invisible ultraviolet (UV) light. Since the lenses of the eyes are transparent, UV light has no trouble getting in and sparking production of free radicals.

Everyone, children included, should wear sunglasses outside—even on cloudy days.

Most quality sunglasses block UV light. If you are not sure that yours do, you should have them tested by an optometrist.

If you wear prescription glasses, spend a little more for the anti-UV coating.

•**Take eye-protecting supplements.** The liver produces antioxidants that help block the action of free radicals. Taking antioxidant supplements—and eating antioxidant-rich foods—confer extra protection.

The main antioxidant for preventing lens damage is *glutathione*. The liver produces glutathione when you eat sulfur-containing foods, such as onions, garlic, asparagus and eggs. But this may not be enough to guard against cataracts.

Ask your doctor about taking a daily glutathione booster, such as *N-acetylcysteine* (NAC). NAC is converted into glutathione in the body.

NAC supplements—sold over the counter in drugstores and health-food stores—help prevent and even reverse cataracts.

Other eye-protecting antioxidants include...

•**Vitamin C.** Data from a recent Tufts University study suggest that taking 400 mg of vitamin C a day can reduce the risk for severe cataracts by 77%.

Other research has shown that people who eat lots of fruits and vegetables, which are high in vitamin C and other antioxidants, have a significantly lower risk.

Ask your doctor about taking 2,000 mg of vitamin C a day, divided into two doses.

Vitamin C supplementation is especially important for smokers. Cigarette smoke, including second-hand smoke, vastly increases levels of free radicals within the eyes. And each cigarette smoked destroys about 25 mg of vitamin C in the body.

●**Vitamin E.** This is another powerful antioxidant, one that's difficult to get from food sources. Ask your doctor about taking 400 international units (IU) of vitamin E in the form of mixed tocopherols once a day.

●**Quercetin.** This bioflavonoid antioxidant blocks the action of *aldose reductase,* an enzyme in the body that boosts the risk for cataracts. Ask your doctor about taking 1,000 mg a day.

Quercetin supplements are sold in health-food stores.

●**Magnesium.** This mineral helps dilate blood vessels in the eyes, helping the body flush out free radicals. Take 400 mg to 500 mg on an empty stomach at bedtime to increase blood flow to the eyes during sleep.

●**Carotenoids.** Take a daily vitamin that contains about 5,000 IU of vitamin A and 12 mg of lutein. These compounds have been shown to protect eye lenses from damage.

●**Drink six eight-ounce glasses of water a day.** Unlike most other tissues in the body, the lenses themselves have no blood vessels to regulate fluid levels. They depend on water that you consume to remove lactic acid and other protein-damaging toxins.

●**Eat less saturated fat.** People who are obese are at above-average risk for cataracts. That's because obesity tends to go hand in hand with consumption of saturated fat, which triggers formation of free radicals.

Read food labels carefully. Polyunsaturated and monounsaturated fats are okay in moderation. But over time, eating lots of saturated fat —along with hydrogenated or partially hydrogenated fat—will cause trouble for your eyes.

Good news: Eating less red meat, baked goods and full-fat dairy foods will automatically reduce the amount of saturated fat in your diet.

●**Ask your doctor about eucalyptus honey.** Preliminary research involving dogs suggests that eucalyptus honey eye drops can help reverse cataracts.

Also promising: MSM (methylsulfonylmethane) eye drops, which may prevent cataracts by increasing levels of sulfur in the lens.

IF SURGERY BECOMES NECESSARY

If you do wind up needing cataract surgery, rest assured that it's among the safest, most effective operations being done.

Typically, just a few minutes are needed to remove the damaged lens and replace it with an artificial lens. It's not uncommon for people to have cataract surgery and return to work the same day.

The standard technique for removing cataracts is *phacoemulsification.* The surgeon uses ultrasound to break up the damaged proteins in the lens. At this point, the proteins can be flushed with saline solution and removed from the eye. Then the surgeon inserts the artificial lens.

Some replacement lenses are *multifocal*— that is, they're designed to correct both near and distance vision.

It sounds like a great idea, but people with this type of artificial lens tend to have problems with glare at night. Most people prefer a single-vision implant.

Picking a surgeon: Make sure he/she has experience performing phacoemulsification. The more often a surgeon has performed the procedure, the more successful it is likely to be.

You'll want someone who does at least four cataract operations a week.

Grapefruit Juice Warning

Bruce Yaffe, MD, internist and gastroenterologist in private practice, 201 E. 65 St., New York 10021.

Grapefruit juice can kill when taken with the wrong prescription drugs. Grapefruit juice inhibits the liver from breaking down certain drugs as they pass through the body, and this can cause these drugs to build up to toxic—even fatal—levels.

Drugs affected: Calcium-channel-blocker heart drugs, such as Procardia and Verapamil SR...the cholesterol-reducing drugs Zocor, Mevacor and Pravachol...heart drugs Plendil and Sular...the blood thinner Coumadin...and others.

Note: The potency of the "grapefruit effect" varies greatly among individuals and according to specific circumstances. Consult your doctor for details.

More from Bruce Yaffe...

Do You Have Enough Protein?

Have your protein status checked at your next physical exam if you are in your 60s or older or have surgery scheduled. A simple blood test for *albumin* can indicate whether your body has enough stored protein. Adequate protein is important for fighting off postsurgical complications—particularly infection. *Cost:* Generally less than $10.

Best Ways to Use the Web for Better Health

Tom Ferguson, MD, adjunct associate professor of health informatics at the University of Texas Health Science Center in Houston and editor of *The Ferguson Report (www.fergusonreport.com)*, a free on-line newsletter covering the on-line health industry. He is the author of *Health Online: How to Find Health Information, Support Groups, and Self-Help Communities in Cyberspace.* Addison-Wesley.

It's no secret that the Internet is a terrific source of medical news and information. But getting the latest on specific diseases and treatments is just the most obvious of what health-minded people can do on-line.

Here are six other ways to use the Internet for better health—with a choice of the best sites...

CONSULT A PHYSICIAN

There's no substitute for a face-to-face meeting with a doctor. But you can get basic medical questions answered via on-line medical consultation services. *How it works:* A doctor answers queries that you type in while logged on.

●**AmericasDoctor.com** *(www.americas doctor.com)* offers free, real-time consultations with board-certified or board-eligible physicians 24 hours a day. All communications are private and one on one.

The physicians answer your questions and suggest reliable sources of information. They do not diagnose any condition or recommend treatment.

FIND A DOCTOR

Selecting a family doctor or specialist can be difficult. On-line referrals are a useful adjunct to referrals from family members, friends and other physicians.

●**Physician Select** *(www.ama-assn.org)*, operated by the American Medical Association (AMA), provides detailed information about virtually every physician licensed to practice in the US.

Listings include the physician's medical school and year of graduation, residency training and primary practice specialty. You can search by name, location, specialty, etc. To get to Physician Select, click on "Doctor Finder" on the AMA home page.

GET SUPPORT

Nowadays there's an on-line support group for virtually every ailment. These can be of great help to patients and their families alike.

●**Self-Help Sourcebook Online** *(www. mentalhelp.net/selfhelp)* offers links to more than 800 national and international self-help support groups. You can search by ailment or by keyword—cancer, depression, heart disease, etc. There's also guidance on starting your own group or linking up with a traditional off-line support group in your area.

MAINTAIN MEDICAL RECORDS

Having all your medical records in one place isn't just convenient. In an emergency, it can be a lifesaver. Some sites require you to do the work yourself. Others work with your doctor to keep records up to date.

● **PersonalMD.com** *(www.personalMD. com)* is a free service that acts as an electronic repository of your medical records, including details about your blood type, allergies, etc. These records can quickly be accessed from anywhere in the world via the Internet or fax. You are responsible for entering and maintaining data and can decide who gets access (through the appropriate password and personal identification number).

Electrocardiograms and other graphical documents can be faxed to the service to be scanned into your personal records.

FIND A CLINICAL TRIAL

Patients who have exhausted all standard treatment options or are interested in being on medicine's cutting edge may be able to enroll in clinical trials—studies of promising experimental treatments. On-line services help steer patients to these studies.

● **Drug Study Central** *(www.drugstudy central.com)* lets you search for trials by disease name, medical condition or geographic location. The site provides details of each study and sends E-mail alerts about new ones.

BUY HEALTH INSURANCE

On-line health insurance is no cheaper than health insurance obtained through traditional channels. But it's easier to compare policies on-line—and you don't have to deal with high-pressure salespeople.

● **Healthaxis.com** *(www.healthaxis.com)* sells health and prescription medicine coverage. It also provides instant quotes and insurance-buying advice.

Important: Not all policies are available in all states.

Too Much of a Good Thing

Too much vitamin A can cause osteoporosis. When vitamin A intake and bone mineral density of almost 70,000 European women were measured, researchers found that the higher a woman's intake of vitamin A, the lower her bone mineral density. For every 3,300 international unit (IU) rise in vitamin A consumption, risk of hip fracture rose by 68%. The recommended daily intake of vitamin A is 5,000 IU.

Special caution: Excessive vitamin A consumption by pregnant women can lead to birth defects.

Håkan Melhus, MD, department of internal medicine, University Hospital, Uppsala, Sweden.

Toothbrush Precaution

Toothbrushes can harbor germs that cause colds, flu and gum disease.

Self-defense: Rinse your toothbrush under running water for at least 15 seconds after each use…shake off excess water…and store it upright. If your bathroom has a "community" toothbrush holder, use a toothbrush cover. If you catch a cold, discard your toothbrush. Continuing to use your old brush can extend the length of your illness.

Howard S. Glazer, DDS, a dentist in private practice in Fort Lee, NJ, and a spokesman for the Academy of General Dentistry, Chicago.

Advice from Dermatologist Dr. Barney Kenet

Barney J. Kenet, MD, dermatologic surgeon at New York Presbyterian Hospital/Cornell Medical Center. He is author of *How to Wash Your Face: America's Leading Dermatologist Reveals the Essential Secrets to Youthful, Radiant Skin.* Simon & Schuster.

The secret of looking younger than your age begins with skin care. But the countless new products and procedures in advertising and magazines have left many people unsure about how to treat common skin problems.

Dr. Barney Kenet clears up the confusion...

Dr. Kenet, is there any way to reverse skin aging once wrinkles and age spots start to appear? Skin that has been overexposed to the sun's ultraviolet rays can be improved.

The first step is to limit further damage by using a sunscreen every day—in summer and winter, rain and shine—even if you are only outside intermittently during the day.

Reason: Ultraviolet exposure is cumulative. You may be in sunlight only five minutes a day. But that totals 35 minutes by the end of the week.

●**Use a sunscreen with an SPF of 15 on your face** and any exposed parts of your body every morning. Sunscreens not only protect your skin from harmful ultraviolet radiation, they also allow sun-damaged skin to repair itself.

Apply sunscreen-based moisturizer after washing your face, while your skin is still damp.

If you must be in the sun for an extended period of time, wear a broad-brimmed hat, long sleeves, slacks and sunglasses. Try to avoid the sun's peak hours between 11 am and 4 pm.

●**Apply creams that contain alpha hydroxy acid (AHA) every evening.** AHA is in many over-the-counter skin creams. It can have a positive effect on skin that has been overexposed to the sun.

No one has yet proven how or why AHA works. But research shows that when AHA products are used regularly, the skin's outer layers take on a more youthful fullness.

●**Use Retin-A or Renova daily** to improve wrinkling, skin texture and uneven pigment. Apply at night. Either skin product requires a prescription. Results take four to 12 months.

Side effects may include redness and irritation...but both can be reduced by adjusting the frequency and amount of the application. Discuss the application of these creams with your dermatologist.

What can be done about cellulite—that dimply skin on thighs, hips and buttocks? At the moment, there is no cure for cellulite. Many products promise to reduce or eliminate these ripples—but they don't actually deliver.

Anticellulite creams and lotions were the rage a few years ago, but they never lived up to their promises. And—a new dietary supplement has not demonstrated its effectiveness.

Endermologie—the process of rolling or kneading the skin with a massage machine—has no scientific data to prove effectiveness. Yet there are reports that some people find it beneficial.

If your skin is dry, massaging it with a lotion can make it look smoother for a while —but the effect doesn't last. Not even liposuction has much impact on cellulite.

Exercise and losing weight can provide some benefit—especially if the weight is lost in the areas where cellulite typically appears. But weight loss and exercise aren't the complete answers to making cellulite disappear.

What can be done for adults who have pimples? First determine your skin type by monitoring which factors contribute to your breakouts...

●**Environmentally sensitive.**

●**Hormonally reactive.**

●**Stress reactive.**

Men and women with occasional breakouts may be reacting to excessive stress. Constantly touching the face makes it worse.

When blemishes appear, use over-the-counter products that contain salicylic acid or benzoyl peroxide. Prevent breakouts during menstruation by applying AHA or salicylic products one week prior to menstruation.

Avoid caffeine, alcohol and spicy foods. They can make breakouts redder.

How does diet affect the skin? Eating right is critical for healthy-looking skin. A diet rich in vitamins and fiber can restore your body and even help correct the ravages of sun, dehydration and time. The most important nutrients for good skin are vitamins A, C and E.

The best way to get these nutrients is through foods—especially leafy or dark-colored vegetables, such as tomatoes and peppers. You can also get these vitamins in supplements—but they need to be taken throughout the day rather than all at once in order to be effective.

Topical creams containing these vitamins are of little benefit. In fact, applying vitamin E to a wound or scar has been shown to *slow* the healing process.

Drinking lots of water helps your skin. However, too much water *on* your skin can actually be drying.

Reduce your shower time to five minutes. Use medium-warm water, not hot. You may even want to skip your daily shower once or twice a week.

What is the best way to wash your face? The most important skin-care advice is *don't overwash.* Most adults over age 30 wash too often and too long, and the result is itchy, irritated skin.

Avoid deodorant soaps. They irritate your skin. I prefer soap-free cleansers in liquid form. Massage gently with your fingertips, and don't scrub with a washcloth. Rinse your face with tepid water—and gently pat dry.

What can be done about dandruff? Those itchy flakes are signs of an inflammatory condition called seborrheic dermatitis. Dandruff results from the overproduction of cells on the outer layer of the scalp. The cause is unknown, but you can treat it with shampoos that contain zinc pyrithione.

If you have a more oily scalp and hair, use tar-based shampoos.

Like all your skin, the scalp can become dry, especially during winter. Too much hair washing and showering, low humidity and wearing hats can contribute to scalp problems. Warm oil treatments once a week can help—drugstore products or homemade ones, using two tablespoons of olive oil.

Using shampoos that contain AHA once or twice a week also helps remove grime and retain moisture.

Self-Hypnosis... The Edge You Need to Overcome Bad Habits

C. Roy Hunter, a certified hypnotherapy instructor in Tacoma, WA. He is the author of *Master the Power of Self-Hypnosis* (Sterling) and *The Art of Hypnosis* (Kendall/Hunt).

Finding it hard to quit overeating? Smoking? Drinking? You're not alone. As we all know, the vast majority of people who try to break a bad habit fail at first. Many fail repeatedly.

You can remind yourself a hundred times a day that your habit is bad for you. Unfortunately, it's the *unconscious* mind that fuels bad habits. It doesn't care about logic. All it wants is the physical and emotional satisfactions your habit supplies.

Hypnosis helps you let go of the negative unconscious desires...and replace them with positive, habit-breaking emotions.

Hypnosis isn't magic. You will still have to work hard at breaking your bad habit. But hypnosis can give you the edge you need to succeed.

MYTH vs. REALITY

Hollywood has given hypnosis an unrealistic image. The hypnotic trance is not a mystical state in which you lose all self-control. You cannot be forced to quack like a duck or do other humiliating things when you're under hypnosis. In fact, you won't do anything you don't want to do.

The hypnotic trance is nothing more than a state of very deep relaxation.

This state is similar to the one that exists just before you fall asleep, when the beta brain waves that predominate during consciousness are replaced by alpha waves.

You're still fully conscious, but your rational mind is less active than usual...and your imagination is more active. This shift is critical because imagination is the language of the unconscious.

With practice, the emotions you generate during each hypnosis session become permanently embedded in your unconscious. That gives your willpower a much-needed boost.

DO IT YOURSELF

Many psychologists practice hypnosis, but it's also effective when done on your own. *Here's how to do it...*

● **Carefully consider the emotional benefits associated with breaking your habit.** Odds are you've already given a great deal of thought to the physiological benefits—reduced risk for heart attack, stroke, cancer, etc.

But you must also consider all the emotional reasons you have for changing. These might include feeling more in control...pleasing your family...having more energy...looking better.

● **Put yourself in a trance.** Find a comfortable and quiet place to lie down or sit. Unplug the phone and turn off the lights.

Take several deep breaths as you imagine your cares slipping away. Then imagine a beach at sunset, a mountain meadow or some other relaxing scene.

Tell yourself, "My toes are relaxed...my breathing is relaxed...I'm getting more and more relaxed."

You've entered a trance when you feel totally relaxed and your mind starts to wander. For most people, this takes about five minutes.

● **Imagine the pleasure you will feel upon successfully breaking your habit.** Once you've entered the trance, imagine that you have already reached your goal. Savor the emotions that thought triggers.

You might think, "My family is so proud of me"..."I look great"..."I feel so much better."

Over time, these feelings will become part of your unconscious...and will stay with you even when you're fully awake and going about your business.

● **Replace old "triggers" with new ones.** Still in the trance, imagine new ways of behaving.

Perhaps you tend to have a cigarette each time you relax with a cup of coffee. During the trance, imagine that having the coffee triggers a *different* response from you.

You might say, "I don't *really* want a cigarette with my coffee. I'd rather focus on reading that novel I just started."

Repeat this scenario again and again.

● **Come out of your trance.** Count slowly from one to five. When you reach five, say, "Fully awake."

Most people notice a diminution in their cravings after just a few sessions of self-hypnosis.

For the first three weeks, it's best to do self-hypnosis for about 20 minutes each day. After that, you can cut back to 20 minutes once or twice a month.

Of course, you can always intensify your self-hypnosis schedule if you find your resolve weakening.

How to Put the Healing Power of Sound Work for You

Mitchell L. Gaynor, MD, Director of Medical Oncology at the Strang-Cornell Cancer Prevention Center in New York. He is author of several books, including *Sounds of Healing: A Physician Reveals the Therapeutic Power of Sound, Voice, and Music.* Broadway Books.

Eight years ago, I discovered the greatest healing tool I have ever known outside the wonders of modern science—the healing powers of sound, music and your own voice.

Although I'm deeply entrenched in mainstream medicine, I've also studied and practiced complementary techniques for many years.

One day a patient of mine, a Tibetan monk, played a Tibetan singing bowl for me. These bowls are made of several metals designed to reverberate in a complex way like a quartet of musical saws.

As he moved a small wooden baton lightly around the rim of the bowl, he created a rich, deep note with a strong vibrato. The sound was so exhilarating that tears of joy sprang to my eyes. The vibration resonated through my body and made me feel—I do not exaggerate—in harmony with the universe.

Using a crystal bowl with attributes similar to those of the metal one, I have now taught the technique to thousands of patients with remarkable results. Aided by sound, many have quickly reached within to a part of themselves where they could no longer be afraid.

Before I began using the bowls, it typically took patients six months to a year to overcome their anxiety when diagnosed with cancer. Yet immediately after listening to the bowls, patients now walk out of my office with a sense of calm different from any they have ever known.

Response to these sounds and to exercises I have devised has been consistent and compelling.

Why: The human body is 70% water, which carries sound well. The body contains millions of cells that are constantly vibrating. We can respond physically and very deeply to tones and sounds. Everyone can benefit from the qualities of sound.

THE HEALING POWERS OF MUSIC

Doctors are finally learning what primitive healers have known for centuries. *Reputable scientific studies have demonstrated that listening to peaceful music can...*

- **Lower blood pressure.**
- **Strengthen the immune system.**
- **Boost natural painkillers** (endorphins).
- **Reduce the secretion of stress hormones** (cortisol and ACTH) during difficult diagnostic and surgical procedures.
- **Slow rapid heartbeats and breathing,** reducing anxiety.
- **Reduce complications after heart attacks.**
- **Reduce the need for anesthesia during surgery.**

Inner harmony takes us beyond fear and anguish. Chronic disharmony can lead to disease.

VIBES

When two pendulums of different sizes swing in the same room, the smaller one gradually assumes the speed of the larger. That phenomenon is called "entrainment." People do it unconsciously, entraining with a harmonious or disharmonious environment.

You can use sound to reach emotional and energetic equilibrium. Listen to calming sounds for brief periods every morning and evening. You will enhance your ability to ignore disharmonious noises that accost you. This will improve your sleep, and help put your mind and body in balance.

THE HEALING POWERS OF YOUR OWN VOICE

In traditional Chinese medicine, the life force, *chi,* comes into the body through the breath. To sing a long line of sound, you must first breathe in deeply. (Don't suck air in abruptly.) Make your in-breathing long, thin, slow and as deep as you can. This will strengthen your chi.

Incorporating this precept into your daily life can improve your health and the state of your mind. Sing in the shower, in the car, as you walk in the woods. Find the sound of your own uniquely harmonious voice. *Here's my three-part healing sound prescription...*

- **Life songs.** Your life song is a unique string of several one-syllable sounds to use as your "mantra," to be repeated over and over as your consciousness expands.

   Examples: "SOM MA TUM"..."TA KEE LA"..."TA ME HUM." Any combination of vowels and consonants will do. These primal sounds will resonate within you as a profound expression of who you are.

   Chanting your life song silently during stressful situations can supply inner peace and strength.

- **Sound meditation.** Use your voice plus the singing bowl or another sound source—a gong, a chime, a pitch pipe—to create a level of awareness beyond workday worries. Chanting your life song during sound meditation clears away negative thoughts, creating space for productive ones.

- **Energetic recreation.** In a quiet place, close your eyes and take deep breaths, concentrating on each breath.

Think positive thoughts: Infinite love... infinite peace...infinite wisdom...infinite harmony...infinite healing...infinite life...infinite light...infinite success...infinite possibility... infinite health...infinite hope...infinite energy ...infinite courage...infinite strength.

Experience your greatest fear of the future as a sound, such as "AAH," "RAH" or "HEE." This can mitigate the fear. Visualize your life force (chi) as a white light above your head. *Release* the sound of your fear by attaching "M"—a hum—to the end of the sound you're making. *For instance:* "AAH-MMMmmmmmmm" or "RAH-MMMmmmmmmm."

Pronounce the sound distinctly, drawing it over your entire exhalation five or six times. Alternate your sound with the transformed negative sound.

Chant with the bowl, feeling your fear of the future coming into harmony with your sense of trust. Your negative feeling will quickly lose its disharmonious emotional charge.

By giving voice to both the positive and negative sides of an emotional conflict, you will create blends of sound that help you to transcend these polarities.

Get to The Root of the Headache

Suffering from "mystery headaches"? Foods likely to trigger headaches include corn (a very common trigger)...any overripe fruit ...anything pickled, fermented or marinated...baked goods containing yeast, especially when hot from the oven.

Also watch out for: Preserved or processed meats—bologna, hot dogs, hard sausage, etc....ripened cheese...eggs...chocolate...beverages containing caffeine or alcohol...anything containing preservatives.

Robert Milne, MD, member of the American Academy of Medical Acupuncture, California State Homeopathic Medical Society, and author of *An Alternative Medicine Definitive Guide to Headaches.* Future Medicine Publishing.

New TB Scare

Beware: New strains of tuberculosis (TB) are highly contagious and drug-resistant. While the risk of contracting TB is low for most Americans—only 18,000 cases were recorded last year—the infection has reached epidemic proportions globally. TB is spread over a prolonged period—on average, it takes a few months—but that doesn't mean

you can't catch it on an eight-hour flight or in other closed environments. *Self-defense:* When on an airplane, if you are seated near someone who is coughing profusely, ask the person to cover his/her mouth and turn away. If he doesn't comply, ask for a new seat. If you suspect you've been exposed to TB, get the TB test. If diagnosed with TB, seek care from a TB expert and take the antibiotics for the full duration prescribed.

Lee B. Reichman, MD, MPH, executive director, New Jersey Medical School National Tuberculosis Center, Newark.

Eliminate Wrinkles Without Redness

New skin cream helps eliminate wrinkles without irritation. The prescription lotion *tretinoin* (Renova) can cause burning and peeling. So can nonprescription antiwrinkle creams containing *alpha hydroxy acids.* But *furfuryladenine* cream (Kinerase) improved skin appearance in all 87 people who used it for six months—and caused redness in only one person. The cream is sold over the counter.

Bruce Katz, MD, associate clinical professor of dermatology, Columbia University College of Physicians and Surgeons, New York City.

Ulcer Preventative

Polyunsaturated fats may help prevent stomach ulcers. Corn oil, sunflower oil, safflower oil and fish oil, all polyunsaturated fats, stopped the growth of the bacterium responsible for most stomach ulcers. However, saturated fats (coconut oil, butter) and monounsaturated fats (such as olive oil) did not. This result is consistent with the fact that people whose diets are high in polyunsaturated fats have a lower risk of stomach ulcers. Research suggests that substituting foods containing these oils for ones containing saturated fats may reduce the likelihood of developing ulcers, and possibly also cut the risk of stomach cancer.

Duane Smoot, MD, associate professor of medicine at Howard University College of Medicine, Washington, DC.

Blood Pressure Trap

If you take medication for high blood pressure, make sure your drug regimen controls your hypertension 24 hours a day.

Recent study: People with high blood pressure underwent psychological testing for hostility.

Those with high scores were found to have elevated blood pressure even while asleep. Ordinarily, blood pressure dips during sleep.

Those with low scores experienced a blood pressure dip at night but had sharp rises in blood pressure upon waking. These surges have been linked to early morning heart attack.

Implication: Hypertensives who tend to be hostile should generally take their antihypertensive medication at bedtime.

Those who are less hostile should generally take a slow-release pill in the morning.

In addition, hostile hypertensives should consider psychotherapy and/or relaxation techniques to help them curb their hostility.

Jogoda Pasic, MD, PhD, chief resident, department of psychiatry, University of Washington Medical Center, Seattle.

Better Breathing for a Much Healthier You

Increase stamina and overall health by breathing properly. The key is in the exhale.

Exercise: Stand facing straight ahead. Raise arms directly overhead. Force an exhale by squeezing the belly toward the spine until it hurts a little. Let the breath come in naturally and effortlessly.

When the breath is as big as it can get without forcing it, bend from the chest side to side like a metronome while simultaneously counting as fast as you can (like an auctioneer), clearly and softly but out loud, from one up to a maximum of 20.

Let the rest of any exhale occur as you lower your arms. Repeat up to 10 times several times a day.

When you are in stressful situations: Force out your belly breath, extending the exhale to at least four times the length of your inhale. Then let the deeper, longer inhale occur on its own.

This controls your stress response...lets you take in extra oxygen...and facilitates deeper relaxation for work, play and sleep.

Michael White, founder and executive director of Optimal Breathing, which teaches breathing techniques to singers, athletes and people with breathing problems, Bryson City, NC.

2

Doctors, Hospitals and You

Hospital Overcharge... Self-Defense...Keep Records...Keep Track... Keep at It

Ninety percent of hospital bills include mistakes—three-fourths of which favor the hospital. These aren't small errors, either. One study found that the average overcharge totals $1,400.

Overcharges affect your wallet even if your HMO or insurance company pays most of the bill. Your copayments mount up...and future premiums may rise as a result of the hospital costs you incur.

Here's how to avoid paying the hospital more than you owe...

●**Keep a treatment log.** During your hospital stay, list every doctor's visit, procedure and medication in a notepad kept within easy reach of your bed. This will give you a clear record to check later against your itemized bill.

If you're too ill to maintain the log—or too groggy from anesthesia or medication—ask a family member or friend to keep it for you.

●**Question any service you suspect isn't okayed by your attending physician.** While you're in the hospital, your attending physician—the doctor who admitted you or the specialist assigned to your case—is the only person authorized to approve consultations, procedures and medications.

Nonetheless, the hospital may initiate services on its own to boost revenues or reward affiliated doctors.

Examples: A quick "drop-by" visit from a staff psychiatrist...an "assistant surgeon" drawn from the hospital's roster...a visit from your own family doctor, who may bring the hospital many referrals.

Patients are legally entitled to refuse to pay for any such unauthorized services. But it's

---

Charles Inlander, president of the People's Medical Society in Allentown, PA. He is author of *This Won't Hurt (And Other Lies My Doctor Tells Me).* People's Medical Society.

usually easier to take preemptive action to prevent them in the first place.

While hospitalized, insist that your attending physician outline his/her treatment plan so you know what to expect.

If a nurse or another doctor announces an unexpected visit or procedure, ask to see the hospital record indicating the attending physician's approval. If you have any doubts at all, politely decline the service and insist on talking with the attending physician.

●**Insist on a fully itemized bill.** Don't settle for bills that list broad categories like "pharmacy" or "surgical charges." Hospitals are required to provide a detailed account of all charges. *The bill should list each...*

- ●Procedure you underwent.
- ●Doctor's visit to your hospital room.
- ●Dose of medicine that was given to you.
- ●Facility used—X-ray suite, operating room, etc.
- ●Supply provided for your care—bandages, IV lines, etc.

If you're hospitalized for two or more days, ask for a new itemized bill daily. That makes it easier to keep track of your charges and to start questioning any suspect items right away.

The hospital's operator can give you the number of the billing office. Call and request the update directly from the department head.

If he/she balks, talk with the hospital's patient representative (ombudsman). If this doesn't work—or if there's no patient rep—calling the hospital's chief administrator almost always brings a fast response.

●**Scrutinize your bill.** Even with the help of your detailed log, the abbreviations on the bill may be hard to decipher. If any items on it stump you, call the billing department for clarification.

Also check with your attending physician if any charges on the bill seem suspect.

The most common overcharges are for services and/or procedures that you didn't actually receive. The second most common overcharges are for duplications of service.

Examples: A charge for use of the radiology suite for an X-ray taken at your bedside...a charge for six blood tests when you actually had only three.

●**Have your bill audited.** If any of the listed charges seem erroneous to you, ask the billing department to check your bill against hospital records to make sure all itemized services really were performed.

The department should conduct this audit willingly and at no charge...and promptly correct all mistakes.

●**Alert your insurer.** If you dispute the billing department's finding, and the dispute can't be resolved, contact your insurance company or HMO.

Taking this action doesn't mean you're accusing anyone of a crime. But it is the surest way to get prompt action.

Your best bet is to contact the company's fraud division directly. Bypass the customer service department.

If you are covered by Medicare, contact the Inspector General of the Federal Health and Human Services Department at 800-447-8477.

For greatest efficiency when you call your insurer...

●**Have all pertinent documents on hand** when you call.

●**Be prepared to detail** exactly which charges you feel are fraudulent, and why.

If the insurance company agrees with you, it will generally take over and resolve the case. That might even involve going to court.

The bill typically goes on hold while matters are disputed.

The Importance of Your Medical History

Emergency medical care goes more smoothly when patients provide doctors with their medical histories. *What to do:* In your wallet or purse, keep a brief, up-to-date account that includes your doctor's name and phone number...all medications you take...diagnoses and treatments...results of major diagnostic tests...list of drug allergies you have...and—if you have heart trouble—a copy of a recent electrocardiogram. This information helps doctors pinpoint your problem rapidly. Parents should carry this information for their children—but children can carry their own, too.

Frank Rasler, MD, MPH, emergency room physician, Dekalb Medical Center, Atlanta.

How to Guard Against Medical Misinformation

Dean Edell, MD, host of the nationally syndicated radio talk program "The Dr. Dean Edell Show." He is author of *Eat, Drink & Be Merry.* HarperCollins.

Americans are setting records for good health and longevity—and are more worried about health than ever before. But much of this concern is misplaced. A great deal of medical misinformation is afoot, and it's scaring us needlessly...

Myth: **All germs are harmful.** Despite all the worried talk about the AIDS and Ebola viruses and flesh-eating bacteria, the vast majority of viruses and bacteria coexist peacefully with humans.

Some germs are beneficial. Human skin, for example, is covered with bacteria that help prevent illness by "crowding out" disease-causing bacteria.

The germs most likely to harm us are those that we worry about least. Food poisoning caused by *Salmonella* and *E. coli* is common. So is influenza. It kills 20,000 to 30,000 Americans each year.

Focus on germs that are likely to cause illness. Wash your hands frequently to reduce your risk of catching colds or flu. Regular soap is fine—no need for antibacterial varieties.

Food poisoning can usually be prevented by cooking meats thoroughly and taking care that raw meat juices don't come in contact with other foods.

Myth: **Cold weather causes colds.** No matter what conventional wisdom says, colds are caused by viruses. These viruses are with us during warm weather and cold.

Colds are more prevalent in winter because we spend more time indoors then—in close proximity to other people. The viruses that cause colds are spread mainly by droplets from sneezes and coughs of infected individuals.

Myth: **Herbal remedies are inherently safer than conventional drugs.** More than half of all conventional medications contain ingredients that are similar or identical to those found in herbs.

Getting these compounds in natural rather than synthetic form doesn't make them safer. Just the opposite may be true.

When you take a conventional drug, you're getting a single active ingredient. Herbal remedies often contain *thousands* of active ingredients. We don't always know which of these compounds are truly beneficial.

Herbal remedies are reasonable alternatives to conventional medical treatment only as long as they've been proven to work.

Reliable studies have shown that ginger prevents motion sickness and that feverfew is good for migraines.

Echinacea, on the other hand, does not seem to deserve its reputation as a cold-fighter.

Myth: **Salt causes high blood pressure.** The recommended upper limit for salt intake is 2,400 mg per day. Most Americans consume three to four times that much—and yet few of us have blood pressure problems.

Salt *does* elevate blood pressure in an estimated 30% of Americans who are "salt sensitive." Unfortunately, there's no way to predict who is sensitive.

The only prudent course of action is to have your blood pressure checked...and ask your doctor whether sodium restriction makes sense for you.

The biggest sources of sodium are *not* potato chips and other salty-tasting foods. Most sodium comes in the form of white bread, chocolate pudding and other foods that don't taste salty.

Myth: **Caffeine is harmful.** Caffeinated coffee—and to a lesser extent tea and soft drinks—can cause stomach upset. Too much caffeine can also be a problem for pregnant women and those prone to anxiety and insomnia. Otherwise, there's nothing wrong with it.

Caffeine is actually beneficial for people with asthma. It's chemically similar to the bronchodilating drug *theophylline* (Uniphyl).

To avoid insomnia and anxiety, limit your caffeine intake to about 250 mg a day. That's the equivalent of two cups of caffeinated coffee, six cups of black tea, eight cups of green tea or six 12-ounce cans of cola.

Otherwise, caffeine is one of life's little pleasures. Enjoy it.

Myth: **Infections should always be treated with antibiotics.** Viral infections, like colds and flu, should *never* be treated with antibiotics. Antibiotics have no effect on viruses—only on bacteria.

Since some infections are serious and require treatment, it's always smart to consult a doctor. But do *not* assume that antibiotics are called for.

If you think you have a cold and your doctor prescribes an antibiotic, ask why. Some doctors prescribe antibiotics because they think their patients expect them to.

Myth: **Sugar makes children hyperactive.** Controlled studies have shown that behavior problems are no more common among kids who are fed sugar than among kids fed an inert sugar substitute.

The "sugar myth" got started when parents noticed that kids tend to act up at birthday parties—where large amounts of sugar are consumed. But it's the excitement of the party that causes the misbehavior—not the cake and ice cream.

Myth: **Chocolate causes acne.** With the possible exception of seafood, no food has ever been shown to cause acne. Outbreaks occur when testosterone—found in females as well as males—stimulates glands in the skin to secrete oil (sebum). Excess sebum blocks pores, causing pimples.

Adolescents are prone to acne because of their changing hormone levels. In adults, psychological stress is often the culprit. It triggers a transient rise in testosterone levels.

If you're bothered by acne, do your best to avoid stress. Don't wash your face too often. Soap dries the skin, increasing flaking. That can block the pores.

Are You Getting Less Than the Best From Your Doctor?

Alan N. Schwartz, MD, assistant clinical professor of radiology at the University of Washington School of Medicine in Seattle, and director of the MRI clinic at Stevens Hospital in Edmonds, WA. He is coauthor of *Getting the Best from Your Doctor: An Insider's Guide to the Health Care You Deserve.* John Wiley & Sons.

Patients are generally all too aware of the most obvious of their doctors' shortcomings—running late for appointments, not listening carefully to their concerns and so on.

But few patients are adept at recognizing the more significant ways that doctors fail them...

●**Failing to prescribe the best medications.** Some doctors have trouble keeping up with the ever-growing list of drugs. Others do keep up, yet continue to prescribe outdated drugs again and again. Still other doctors are discouraged from prescribing certain medications by restrictive rules set up by health insurers.

Result: Patients often wind up taking one drug even when another works more reliably, with fewer side effects and/or with some other key advantage.

Example: Some doctors continue to recommend only calcium-containing antacids or another source of calcium for osteoporosis patients. Yet the combination of a calcium supplement and the new drug alendronate (Fosamax) is better at preventing bone loss.

Self-defense: If a doctor prescribes a particular drug, ask what it's for...whether it could cause side effects...whether it could interact with other drugs or certain foods...and how long it takes for the drug to work.

If you foresee any problems with using the recommended medication, ask if there are any alternatives.

● **Neglecting to order crucial diagnostic tests.** In the days before managed care, some doctors had a financial incentive to order diagnostic tests. Now there's often a financial incentive for doctors *not* to order tests. In some cases, this incentive keeps doctors from ordering tests that are clearly needed.

Example: Someone with chronic stomach pain should be tested for the ulcer-causing bacterium *H. pylori.* But some doctors simply prescribe *omeprazole* (Prilosec) or another acid-blocker. Acid-blockers do *not* eradicate H. pylori, so the underlying infection never gets treated. The ulcer recurs.

Self-defense: Ask your doctor if there is a test that would make him/her more confident in his diagnosis…or would change the course of treatment. Ask about side effects, the potential for pain and risks, too.

If your doctor seems unable to diagnose your ailment—or if a course of treatment is not yielding results—ask if there's a diagnostic test that might provide useful information.

● **Not referring patients to a specialist.** If a patient fails to respond to a treatment regimen, it's the doctor's responsibility to refer the patient to a specialist. This doesn't always happen. In some cases, the doctor simply wants a bit more time to sort out the problem. In others, he may be unaware that his approach is failing…or he may have a financial incentive not to refer patients to specialists.

Self-defense: When your doctor recommends a treatment, ask how long it will take to get results. If the treatment fails to produce results by the deadline you both agreed on, he should make the referral.

● **Performing surgery despite a lack of experience with a given procedure.** Study after study has shown that the more often a doctor performs a surgical procedure, the more likely his patients are to have a good outcome. A doctor who has scant experience with a particular procedure should admit this to his patients. Yet some doctors are too embarrassed to reveal their lack of experience.

Others keep their lack of experience secret because they want the experience or the income…or because they're pressured to do so by a health maintenance organization (HMO).

Self-defense: If a doctor offers to do surgery, ask him to name the doctor he would go to if he needed the procedure (excluding himself). Then ask both doctors how many times they have performed this procedure.

What constitutes a good minimum? For common operations such as appendectomy, 50 times is enough. For less common procedures, even the most experienced surgeon may have done no more than a handful.

To evaluate the skills of a surgeon, seek others' opinions of him.

● **Divulging confidential information.** Unless they have a patient's permission to do so, doctors are personally honor-bound not to reveal confidential medical information.

Self-defense: Ask your doctor about his policy regarding confidentiality. Can your records be accessed from outside his office? If so, why?

Insist that your doctor let you personally review any requests for information regarding your medical records. Ask to have those sections that you wish to remain private labeled: "Not to be released without my signature."

To learn more about privacy issues, contact the Electronic Privacy Information Center at 202-544-9240…or on the Web at *www.epic.org.*

Send E-mail to Your Doctor

It's a good way to handle routine matters such as referrals, billing questions, appointments, medication questions and prescription renewals. Many doctors are willing to communicate with patients through E-mail, if patients do not abuse the privilege by flooding the doctor with messages or using E-mail improperly. E-mail is not for diagnoses, complex questions or emergencies of any type. Ask your doctor if he/she uses E-mail or would be willing to try.

David Stern, MD, PhD, assistant professor of internal medicine, University of Michigan, Ann Arbor, quoted in *Prevention,* 33 E. Minor St., Emmaus, PA 18098.

If the Doctor Says Cancer...

C. Norman Coleman, MD, director of the radiation oncology sciences program and deputy director of the division of clinical sciences at the National Cancer Institute in Bethesda, MD. He is author of *Understanding Cancer: A Patient's Guide to Diagnosis, Prognosis and Treatment.* Johns Hopkins University Press.

Being given a diagnosis of cancer is inevitably an extremely stressful experience. But daily life—and treatment—should go more smoothly if the patient takes an active, informed approach to battling the disease.

Good news: Cancer rarely requires an immediate response. In most cases, it's okay to take several days or even a few weeks to learn about the specific type of cancer and various treatment options.

Helpful resource: The National Cancer Institute hotline. Call 800-422-6237.

OBTAINING A DIAGNOSIS

The patient's primary-care doctor should coordinate the steps necessary to confirm the initial diagnosis. That includes making plans for a biopsy and/or other necessary tests.

CONSULTING AN ONCOLOGIST

If tests confirm a malignancy, the primary-care doctor should refer the patient to a cancer specialist (oncologist).

There are three main kinds of oncologist...

• **Surgical oncologists** specialize in surgical removal of tumors.

• **Medical oncologists** specialize in chemotherapy.

• **Radiation oncologists** specialize in radiation therapy.

Several oncologists may eventually be involved in treating the cancer. To prepare for that possibility, it's best to select one primary oncologist to coordinate all tests and treatments.

It's also a good idea to ask the primary-care physician to weigh in on key decisions. Given his/her knowledge of the patient's medical history, he may be able to offer guidance that specialists are unable to offer.

STAGING STUDIES

Before treatment can be initiated, the exact nature and extent of the malignancy must be determined. This process—known as "staging"—enables the patient and his doctors to decide upon the best course of treatment. It also provides a benchmark that indicates just how effective any treatment is.

Staging studies include physical exams, biopsies, blood tests and diagnostic imaging procedures.

Oncologists use different scales to indicate cancer stage. Some use the numerals 1, 2, 3 and 4—or the Roman numeral equivalents. Others use the letters A, B, C and D. In each case, the higher the number or letter, the more severe the cancer.

Example: Stage 1 breast cancer is a small tumor, no bigger than 2 centimeters (cm) in diameter. Stage 2 is a tumor between 2 cm and 5 cm. Stage 3 is a tumor larger than 5 cm. Stage 4 means the cancer has spread (metastasized) to other sites in the body.

Some oncologists further describe cancers using the *TNM* system. The T grade indicates the size of the primary tumor. The N grade indicates the degree to which cancerous cells have been found in the lymph nodes. The M grade indicates whether the cancer has metastasized.

Example: A 3-cm breast tumor that involves one lymph node—but which hasn't spread to other sites in the body—would be designated T2N1M0.

EVALUATING TREATMENT OPTIONS

Once the cancer is staged, the patient should spend a few days or weeks amassing information about treatment options.

Helpful: A checklist should be prepared. It should be taken along each time the patient meets with any of his doctors. The checklist should include...

• **Patient's name, address, phone number and medical record** identification numbers.

• **Primary oncologist's name, address and phone number,** along with his speciality.

• **Names of all other doctors** involved in the treatment.

• **Type of cancer/tumor site.**

• **The cancer's stage,** along with results of staging studies.

•**Treatments being considered.** With each, list the duration of treatment, whether hospitalization is necessary and whether the patient will be able to pursue his normal activities.

•**Potential benefits and side effects** of each treatment.

•**Clinical trials of experimental treatments** in which the patient might want to enroll.

As the patient gathers information, he should touch base periodically with his primary-care physician and primary oncologist —to review the pros and cons of each treatment option.

If participation in a clinical trial of an experimental cancer treatment is being considered, the patient should find out exactly what is involved.

GETTING A SECOND OPINION

Since cancer is such a complex disease, it's usually best to consult several specialists before picking a treatment.

Second opinions are especially valuable when more than one type of treatment is available—for instance, if radiation therapy is being weighed against surgery or chemotherapy.

SELECTING A TREATMENT

Once all the information has been amassed, the patient should review his checklist with family and friends, then discuss each treatment with the primary oncologist to review the choice and formulate a specific plan.

Treatments Vary from Hospital to Hospital

Heart attack patients fare better when they're treated at a hospital that treats a high volume of heart attack patients.

The death rate among heart attack patients treated at a high-volume hospital was 17% lower than that for similar patients treated at a low-volume hospital, a recent study found. The difference is thought to reflect greater experience levels among staffers at high-volume hospitals—and better equipment.

Trap: In most cases, patients with chest pain are taken to the *nearest* hospital.

David R. Thiemann, MD, assistant professor of medicine, Johns Hopkins University School of Medicine, Baltimore. His review of medical records of 98,898 heart patients was published in *The New England Journal of Medicine*, 10 Shattuck St., Boston 02115.

How to Avoid Becoming A Medical-Error Statistic

Timothy McCall, MD, a New York City internist and the author of *Examining Your Doctor: A Patient's Guide to Avoiding Harmful Medical Care*. Citadel Press.

Medical errors are in the news again. Recently, the Institute of Medicine (IOM) issued a report estimating that mistakes by doctors and other health-care workers kill up to 98,000 Americans each year. That's more than twice as many deaths as are caused by breast cancer.

The IOM report focuses on what doctors and health-care institutions can do to reduce the error rate, but there's a lot patients can do, too.

•**Surgical errors.** These account for about half of all medical mistakes. I'm talking about everything from accidentally nicking a vital organ or failing to monitor anesthesia properly to amputating the wrong leg. Fearing that the doctor will do the right procedure on the wrong side of the body, some surgical patients are using markers to indicate the surgical site right on their bodies. Even some surgeons have started to do it.

What's far more important is to focus on the surgeon's credentials. Studies show that patients are safer in the hands of a surgeon who does the particular operation frequently. There's no magic number, but I'd certainly prefer a surgeon who had done a procedure hundreds of times over one who had done it 10 times. And be sure to get a second opinion for any elective operation—to make sure you truly need it.

It's also smart to consider the hospital where the surgery will be done. You want an institution that employs lots of registered nurses (RNs), as opposed to nurse's aides, who may lack adequate training. It's impossible to give an exact number of nurses to look for, but the hospital you pick should assign no more than a few postsurgical patients to each RN. Given rising cost-cutting pressures, it's now commonplace for hospitals to assign a dozen or more patients to each RN. Having family members stay with you in the hospital can also help ensure that you get the care you need.

●Drug errors. This category encompasses everything from giving the wrong medication or dose to forgetting to check for allergies. Because one doctor may not realize what another is prescribing, I recommend bringing a list of all your medications—or a bag containing the bottles—to each visit. Be sure to include vitamins and other over-the-counter pills. These can interact dangerously with prescribed drugs—and with each other.

Use common sense. If a pill looks different than usual, alert your doctor, nurse or the pharmacist. If you develop new symptoms after starting to take a medication, call promptly to ask whether they might be caused by the medication. Never leave the doctor's office until you know *exactly* what you're being given and why, how to take it and what side effects to watch out for.

●Missed or delayed diagnoses of cancer or another life-threatening condition. If you don't respond to treatment or have worrisome symptoms your doctor can't explain, consider getting a second opinion. You might have another pathologist review a biopsy specimen or another radiologist read a questionable mammogram, for example.

●Sloppy practice. In the rushed world of modern medicine, doctors sometimes forget to wash their hands or follow up on an abnormal X-ray. A doctor who's too busy to keep up with the medical literature may be unaware of a new life-saving treatment for your condition.

When it comes to countering doctors' sloppiness, there's no substitute for paying attention and being politely assertive. Scrutinize the quality of your physician's care. Switch if you're not satisfied. Good doctors shouldn't feel threatened by patients who take an active role in their care. They should welcome it, because two heads really are better than one.

 **More from Timothy McCall...**

Do You Know Who's Doing That X-Ray?

Cutting costs has become a mantra in health care. One of the main ways it's being accomplished is by replacing highly trained professionals with less-skilled substitutes. So the person who comes to your bedside after surgery may not be a registered nurse (RN) but an aide who literally may have been working in housekeeping the week before.

No matter how well-intentioned such aides may be, you simply cannot expect them to deliver the same high-quality care as the workers they have replaced. Perhaps more important, they may not recognize medical problems the way an experienced RN would.

In some of the clinics I've worked in, receptionists and nurses are enlisted to take X-rays. Yet studies have shown that non–X-ray technicians take lower-quality X-rays, expose patients to more radiation and have to repeat films more frequently—the result of poor technique.

Increasingly, pharmacies are employing technicians to do work that was once done only by licensed pharmacists. Technicians can count out pills as well as a pharmacist, but they can't be expected to educate you about the medications you take—or warn you if there's a potential conflict between one pill you're taking and another.

Now that surgery is commonly performed in doctors' offices rather than in hospitals, the issue of staffing has become especially important. Except for minor procedures, such as colonoscopy or the removal of a mole, it's important that an anesthesiologist (a medical doctor specializing in sedation during surgery) or a nurse anesthetist be on hand. Afterward, it's best if an RN provides your care.

In this age of managed care, even doctors are being replaced by nurse practitioners (NPs) and physician assistants. For physical exams and minor ailments like urinary tract infections or colds, these practitioners can deliver excellent care—sometimes even better than that provided by MDs. NPs in particular —because of their more holistic outlook, longer visits and emphasis on patient eduction —have higher patient satisfaction numbers than doctors. For serious problems, though, you're better off seeing a physician.

Sometimes the substitutions won't affect you that much—you'll do fine either way. At other times, less-skilled health workers could compromise your care. Here's how to protect yourself and your loved ones:

•**Don't assume that a white coat has any significance.** In hospitals and clinics, the garb worn by clerical workers and the people who transport patients may be indistinguishable from that worn by doctors and nurses.

When you're in a medical setting, make it a habit to look at the name tags of anyone who treats you. The tag should give not only the individual's name, but also his or her degree, such as MD or RN. Also acceptable are terms like "clinical nutritionist." Beware of titles like "clinical aide" or "patient care technician," which are essentially meaningless. If the hospital or clinic doesn't issue informative name tags to its workers, I'd complain.

•**Decide when qualifications matter.** It's fine if an aide measures your blood pressure during a routine clinic visit. But if you're seriously ill or are undergoing intensive treatment, ask your doctor or a hospital official to see that someone with appropriate credentials be assigned to care for you.

•**Vote with your feet.** If you feel that the lack of credentials among your caregivers is placing you or a loved one in jeopardy, you have every right to complain. If complaining doesn't help, take your business elsewhere.

What You Need to Know Before You Get a Blood Test

Hospital blood technicians routinely draw up to 10 times more blood than is needed to perform diagnostic tests. Blood draws can significantly reduce a patient's blood volume, causing anemia or other health problems. A generation ago, diagnostic equipment required large volumes of blood. But today's equipment is so sophisticated that only tiny samples are needed. Patients should request minimal blood draws.

Jocelyn M. Hicks, PhD, chair, department of laboratory medicine, Children's National Medical Center, Washington, DC.

Presurgery Precautions

Herbal remedies should be stopped at least two weeks prior to any surgical procedure. Saint-John's-wort, ginkgo biloba, feverfew, ginseng and other herbs can cause dangerous changes in heart rate and blood pressure.

John Neeld, MD, chair of anesthesiology, Northside Hospital, Atlanta, and president, American Society of Anesthesiologists, Park Ridge, IL.

How to Help Your Mind Help Your Body Prepare For Successful Surgery

William W. Deardorff, PhD, assistant clinical professor of medicine, University of California, Los Angeles, School of Medicine. He is coauthor of *Preparing for Surgery: A Mind-Body Approach to Enhance Healing and Recovery.* New Harbinger.

No matter what kind of operation you are facing, planning will minimize your risk for complications...and help ensure a speedy, uneventful recovery.

THE STRESS RESPONSE

Like any stressful event, surgery triggers the release of *cortisol, adrenaline* and other stress hormones. It's long been known that this stress response sends heart rate and blood pressure soaring. And now evidence shows that it impairs the body's self-healing process.

In a recent study conducted at Johns Hopkins University School of Nursing in Baltimore, researchers found that undergoing surgery can promote growth of cancer cells by suppressing activity of *natural killer cells.* These specialized cells are a key component of the immune system.

PAYOFFS OF PREPARATION

Preparing for surgery blunts the stress response, bringing faster recovery as well as...

●**Reduced risk for infection** and other complications.

●**Reduced need for painkilling medication** during surgery and afterward.

●**Less postoperative pain.**

If you need emergency surgery, of course, it's impossible to do any planning. But nowadays 80% of all operations are elective.

To ensure that you have time to prepare: Pick a date for surgery that's at least three weeks away.

THREE WEEKS BEFORE SURGERY

●**Learn all you can—or wish to learn— about your upcoming surgery.** Some people feel most relaxed when they know all the details. Others find that lots of information makes them anxious...and prefer not to know too much.

Whether you're an information seeker or avoider, it's important that you pose certain key questions to your surgeon before your operation...

●**How long will the procedure take?**

●**How intense will postsurgical pain be?**

●**How long will I be bedridden** following surgery?

●**How much help will I need** from family members once I leave the hospital?

If your surgeon seems too busy to answer your questions thoroughly, make arrangements to speak with his/her assistant or a nurse instead.

Helpful: Bring along a notepad and a friend or relative.

●**Speak with your anesthesiologist.** Tell him what medications you take, including over-the-counter and prescription drugs and herbal remedies. Also alert the anesthesiologist to any allergies you have...and to any reactions you've had to anesthetics or pain medications.

●**Practice deep breathing.** Pain causes muscle tension...which causes more pain... which causes more tension. Deep breathing helps break this vicious cycle.

Basic technique: Sit or lie comfortably. Close your eyes. Inhale slowly through your nose, silently counting to five. Then exhale slowly through your mouth, to a count of five.

Do deep breathing for five to 10 minutes, twice daily, each day leading up to surgery.

Patients who practice deep breathing experience less post-surgical pain than do similar patients who have not practiced deep breathing.

●**Take care of details.** Pre-cook two weeks' worth of meals and store them in your freezer ...prepay recurring bills...get written authorization for surgery, if necessary, from your health insurer...notify your employer of the date of your surgery and how long you'll be off work...arrange for disability payments.

Taking care of these mundane chores will help curb your pre-surgery jitters.

●**Give up bad habits.** Smoking, overeating, getting insufficient sleep, abusing alcohol, etc., negatively affect the outcome of surgery and recovery.

●**Think positively.** Negative thoughts lead to depression, which slows healing. *Try to avoid...*

●Catastrophizing, as typified by remarks such as, "What if I never get better?"

●Negative tunnel-vision, typified by, "Nothing helps."

●Overgeneralization, typified by, "I'll always be in pain."

Be realistic. Avoid the temptation to make dire predictions about your operation.

●**Prepare your home environment.** Tack down rugs. Clear away clutter that might cause you to trip and fall.

It may be necessary to order a special toilet seat, walker or hospital bed...or to schedule home nursing care. Ask your doctor what he recommends.

ONE WEEK BEFORE SURGERY

•**Complete your pre-op physical.** Your surgeon should tell you which laboratory tests, X rays, etc., are required.

•**Pack for the hospital stay.** Include clothing, books, toiletries, pajamas, slippers and a robe...as well as a list of medications, your insurance card, a notepad and pen.

Make sure the clothing you pack for your hospital stay is appropriate, given the procedure you'll be undergoing. If you are going to have surgery on your head, for example, pack a button-front shirt—not a pullover.

Music is a good distraction from pain, so you may want to pack tapes or compact disks of soothing music, along with a player and extra batteries.

Some patients find it helpful to listen to recorded music *during* surgery. Just be sure to clear it with your surgeon first.

Make certain, too, that your tape or CD player has an auto-reverse function. That way, the operating room staff won't be forced to keep turning over the tape.

•**Stop taking medications that might interfere with surgery.** Aspirin and other anti-inflammatory drugs should generally be discontinued a few days before surgery because of their blood-thinning action.

Find out from your doctor about other medications and herbs that should be stopped prior to surgery.

ONE DAY BEFORE SURGERY

•**Make arrangements for transportation to and from the hospital.**

•**Follow your surgeon's advice about what you should or should not eat or drink.** Your doctor may request that you avoid consumption of all food and liquids beginning eight hours before surgery.

•**Continue with deep breathing and positive thinking.**

DAY OF SURGERY AND AFTERWARD

•**Use deep breathing for relaxation and pain control.**

•**Continue positive thinking.**

•**Review your notes on what to expect during recovery.**

 # How to Recover From Surgery

Preparing for surgery improves recovery: Keep blood pressure up. Most patients who report awareness during surgery have below-average blood pressure. *Normal blood pressure range:* 130 to 139 over 85 to 89. Talk with your doctor about the best strategies for raising pressure that is too low. Eat a high-protein diet in the weeks leading up to surgery to boost strength. Eliminate caffeine. Get a bit of exercise daily—walking 20 minutes should be sufficient. Visualize the surgery going successfully.

Jeanette Tracy, PhD, founder of Awareness with Anesthesia Research Education (AWARE), 697 Sunningdale Dr., Oceanside, CA 92057. The group studies surgery awareness and advises patients on how to prepare for surgery.

Prevent Post-Op Hangover

More oxygen during surgery can prevent the postoperative anesthesia "hangover" many patients suffer. During surgery, patients breathe a mixture of 30% oxygen and 70% nitrogen. *Recent finding:* Boosting oxygen to 80% of the total—and breathing the mix for two hours in recovery—cut postsurgical nausea and vomiting nearly by half. It's not known why more oxygen helps, but the finding is especially important as the trend toward outpatient surgery continues.

Daniel I. Sessler, MD, professor of anesthesia, University of California, San Francisco, School of Medicine. His study of 231 surgical patients was published in *Anesthesiology,* 6546 JCP, 200 Hawkins Dr., Iowa City, IA 52242.

Even the Best Doctors Make Dangerous Errors

Richard N. Podell, MD, internist at Podell Medical Center, New Providence, NJ. Dr. Podell is a specialist in chronic fatigue syndrome and fibromyalgia. He is author of several books, including *The G-Index Diet*. Warner.

Physicians now face time and financial pressures that make it impossible to spend as much time as they want to with each patient. And most patients are too timid or embarrassed to ask for more time—even if they need it.

In their rush to see as many patients as possible, some doctors are making big mistakes. *Here's how to deal with a doctor's mistakes and make sure your medical needs are fully met...*

Mistake: **Not asking if you have any questions.** A good doctor won't be offended if you question him/her or ask for an explanation of something he has said or is about to do.

Key: At the beginning of your visit, tell your doctor exactly what topics you want to discuss while you're there.

A verbal outline prepares the doctor for the likelihood of your questions along the way and keeps him from viewing your questions as challenges.

As a doctor, I find it frustrating when a patient brings up a major concern while I'm wrapping up the consultation. When you mention all your concerns at the outset, you and your doctor can pace the available time to make sure everything is covered.

Mistake: **Failing to ask what vitamins, minerals and herbs you are taking.** Many of these supplements can interact with the drugs you're taking or affect your symptoms.

Examples: Ginkgo biloba can thin blood —and is particularly dangerous for patients taking blood thinners. Licorice root can cause potassium loss.

If your doctor doesn't ask, it's your responsibility to inform him.

Helpful: Before you visit the doctor, prepare a list of all the vitamins, minerals, herbs and prescription and nonprescription drugs you're taking. Even if you mentioned them during a previous visit, remind him again. Your prescription regimen or health may have changed since your last visit.

Mistake: **Not ordering a biopsy for a breast lump that doesn't disappear after a menstrual period.** Even if a mammogram has shown no evidence of cancer, any persisting lump has the potential to be malignant.

Most lumps are not, but looking at a mammogram or feeling the lump can't tell you for certain if a lump is cancerous.

Roughly 15% of breast cancers don't show up on mammograms. Any new lump that doesn't disappear with a menstrual cycle must be biopsied or the patient should be referred to a specialist—regardless of mammogram results.

Mistake: **Failing to prescribe potassium supplements for patients who are taking thiazide-type diuretics.** Thiazide diuretics, such as Hydro-DIURIL, are used to lower blood pressure by decreasing fluid retention.

These drugs increase the outflow of potassium and magnesium in the urine. That raises the risk of dangerous heart-rhythm abnormalities.

What to do: If you're taking a thiazide diuretic, potassium levels should be monitored within one month of starting the medication...and then every three to six months thereafter. Also ask whether you need to be taking potassium or possibly magnesium supplements. Magnesium levels can also fall when taking diuretics, although measuring blood levels does not always reveal this.

Don't try to stabilize potassium levels yourself by taking over-the-counter supplements. Potassium levels need to be monitored carefully by your doctor. Besides, over-the-counter supplements don't have enough potassium to be effective in this situation.

Mistake: **Missing signs and symptoms of depression.** Depression is extremely common, but many people who suffer from it don't realize they have it. The primary mental symptom of depression is loss of pleasure in things you used to enjoy. Depression also manifests as vague physical symptoms, such as fatigue, headache, backache, etc.

Self-defense: Mention any troublesome symptoms to your doctor and that you suspect you may be depressed. Otherwise, your doctor may not take the kind of history necessary to properly diagnose depression.

Psychological therapy and antidepressant drugs are among the effective treatments for depression. But the problem can't be treated unless it's diagnosed.

Mistake: **Not asking how you're sleeping.** Insufficient sleep is a major contributor to both physical and mental illness. Yet doctors rarely ask patients about their sleep patterns. Not all doctors realize that sleep is one of the body's most powerful natural healing processes.

Tell your doctor if you are not sleeping well. There are specific disorders that can disrupt rest—and they can usually be treated with drugs and/or behavioral therapy.

Examples: Periodic leg movement disorder, in which small muscles twitch throughout the night...sleep apnea, in which the individual stops breathing for brief moments throughout the night.

The New World of Office Surgery: Eight Questions That Could Save Your Life

Ervin Moss, MD, executive medical director of the New Jersey State Society of Anesthesiologists, Princeton Junction and clinical professor of anesthesiology at Robert Wood Johnson Medical Center, New Brunswick, NJ.

S urgery has moved outside the hospital surgical suite and into a doctor's office near you.

Thirteen percent of all surgical procedures are now done in doctors' private offices. By 2005 that figure is expected to rise to 20%. That's almost 10 million operations a year. These include cataract surgery...biopsies...ear tube insertions...cosmetic and plastic surgery ...and hernia repairs.

Office surgery costs less than similar procedures done in hospitals or outpatient surgical facilities. It can be more convenient and "patient friendly," too. But office surgery also poses potential risks.

Even the best-equipped doctor's office lacks the state-of-the-art surgical suites and extensive support staffs found in hospitals. Some in-office surgeons lack the training required of their hospital counterparts. And office surgery generally isn't regulated by state or national agencies.

That's not to say that surgical procedures can't be done safely in doctors' offices. *But before bypassing the hospital, patients should ask the surgeon...*

●**Do you have hospital privileges to perform this procedure?** Surgeons earn hospital privileges—the right to operate in the hospital—by undergoing intensive scrutiny. Only surgeons who provide exemplary care get the privileges.

Surgeons who work in office settings may not have those privileges. And if they have a high rate of poor outcomes, they normally aren't required to report it.

Also important: Ask your doctor if he/she is board-certified for the type of surgery to be done. Certification means that the surgeon has passed written tests and keeps up with developments in his specialty through continuing medical education courses.

●**How many similar procedures have you performed?** Surgeons get better with practice. A surgeon who has done only a few dozen procedures is still learning. Patients should choose surgeons who have performed many operations similar to the one they will undergo.

●**Who will administer the anesthetic?** The person administering the anesthetic should be a board-certified anesthesiologist or a certified nurse-practitioner-anesthetist. That's a registered nurse (RN) who has had two years of specialized training in anesthesiology.

States have standards regarding the types of anesthetic that nurse-anesthetists can administer in the hospital and the circumstances under which they can do so. These standards vary among states. Ask your doctor which standards his hospital follows. His in-office surgical practice should follow the same standards.

●**Is your office prepared for emergencies?** Are resuscitation and life-support equip-

31

ment and medicine on hand in case things go wrong during surgery?

At a minimum, this equipment should include a "crash cart" with a defibrillator and airway resuscitation equipment.

●**Do you have an ongoing relationship with an ambulance company?** The drivers should know exactly where the office is…the best routes to get there and from there to the hospital…and which entries and exits are large enough to accommodate a stretcher.

●**Who staffs your office?** The doctor's office should employ at least one RN who, like the surgeon and anesthesiologist, has training in advanced cardiac life support. All nurses assisting during surgery should be RNs specializing in operating room procedures. And—all RNs caring for patients after surgery should be specialists in post-anesthesia recovery.

●**Has your facility been accredited?** Several agencies inspect physicians' offices, protocols and procedures to certify that they meet standards for quality in-office surgery.

The most demanding agency is the Joint Commission on Accreditation of Healthcare Organizations (JCAHO).

Facilities offering in-office surgery aren't required to be JCAHO-accredited, but some go through the procedure voluntarily. Ask to see the accreditation certificate. It assures you that the facility is well-run and up-to-date.

●**How long will my procedure take?** In-office surgery is safest when it does not exceed four hours. Any operation lasting longer should be done in a hospital.

Is Vision-Correcting Laser Eye Surgery for You?

Douglas D. Koch, MD, professor of ophthalmology at Baylor College of Medicine in Houston. He is associate editor of *The Journal of Cataract and Refractive Surgery*, 4000 Legato Rd., Suite 850, Fairfax, VA 22033.

If your eyesight is less than perfect, you may be wondering whether you should have vision-correcting eye surgery.

Hundreds of thousands of Americans have undergone the most popular form of the surgery, known as *laser in situ keratomileusis* (LASIK). That number will certainly continue to grow in the coming years.

A 15-minute outpatient procedure that costs about $2,500 per eye, LASIK has proven highly effective at correcting nearsightedness (myopia) and certain other vision problems. But it's not without drawbacks.

●**How effective is LASIK?** It's very effective for people with mild to moderate myopia, farsightedness (hyperopia) or astigmatism. Among people with one of these problems, 90% of those who undergo LASIK wind up with vision of 20/40 or better. Fifty percent to 60% achieve perfect 20/20 vision.

LASIK cannot correct cataracts, glaucoma or macular degeneration. Nor can it correct *presbyopia*, the aging-related vision problem that necessitates the use of reading glasses.

●**How safe is it?** As with any invasive procedure, there is a slight risk for infection. Ordinarily, infection caused by LASIK can be eradicated with antibiotics. But in rare cases, the infection leaves the patient with mild vision loss.

In extremely rare cases—fewer than one in 10,000—someone whose vision had been correctable with eyeglasses winds up legally blind after LASIK.

Altogether, about 1% of people who undergo LASIK experience complications either during surgery or afterward.

●**Who is a candidate for LASIK?** Anyone with mild to moderate myopia, hyperopia or astigmatism who would prefer not to wear contact lenses or eyeglasses.*

The main consideration is this—*would it dramatically enhance your life to be able to see clearly without corrective lenses?* If not, it makes no sense to assume even the tiny risk that your eyesight could be harmed.

●**Who is *not* a candidate?** Anyone with

---

*Vision problems are measured in *diopters*. In general, LASIK should not be used for myopia of more than 12 diopters…hyperopia of more than six diopters…or astigmatism of more than four diopters. With advances in technology, it may soon be possible to treat more severe vision problems.

dry eyes, severe diabetes, an immune system disorder, glaucoma or another ailment that might affect the healing process. LASIK is also off-limits to people who have had previous eye surgery…who have unusually thin corneas…or who have *keratoconus*. That's a condition in which the cornea develops a conical shape.

Federal regulations require that LASIK patients be at least 18. There is no upper age limit.

●**Exactly what does LASIK involve?** The patient, who might be given a mild sedative like *diazepam* (Valium), reclines on a chair or gurney. The eyelashes are taped back, and a speculum is used to hold the eye open.

Using a special cutting device known as a *microkeratome*, the ophthalmologist slices a thin flap of cornea. That's the transparent "window" at the front of the eye. This flap is folded, hinge-like, back from the eye.

Next, the ophthalmologist uses an excimer laser to vaporize portions of the cornea, reshaping it to alter its refractive power. That's the extent to which it bends light rays that enter the eye.

The corneal flap is folded back into its original position and the eye is treated with antibiotic drops.

Some patients recover within 24 hours. Others take several weeks. Typically, an eye patch is worn for several hours after surgery, and then at night for a few days.

●**Is LASIK performed on both eyes at once?** Most patients like to take care of both eyes at once. But I sometimes prefer to do one eye and then the other eye a week or so later—to make sure that the patient is recovering well from the surgery.

●**What's the best way to pick a LASIK surgeon?** Get a referral from your ophthalmologist or family doctor…or from the head of the ophthalmology department at a local teaching hospital or medical school.

You'll want to select a board-certified ophthalmologist who has performed at least 100 LASIK procedures.

If You Have High Blood Pressure…

High blood pressure isn't being treated aggressively enough. Treatment should bring blood pressure down to 140/90 or lower. Yet in a recent study, only 7% of hypertensives whose readings were consistently above that level got additional treatment. *Self-defense:* If your readings remain elevated despite treatment, ask your doctor if your dosage should be increased…or if you should be switched to another blood pressure drug.

Dan R. Berlowitz, MD, MPH, associate director, Center for Health Quality, Outcomes and Economic Research, Veterans Affairs Hospital, Bedford, MA, and associate professor of medicine, Boston University School of Medicine.

Biopsy Alert

Susan L. Blum, former editor, *Bottom Line/Health*, 55 Railroad Ave., Greenwich, CT 06836.

Recently, pathologists at Johns Hopkins University School of Medicine took a second look at more than 6,000 biopsy samples previously analyzed at other institutions. The results were shocking. Almost two of every 100 analyses were erroneous, they found. Nearly 25% of the misdiagnoses mistook a benign growth for a cancer.

Scary: Six percent gave patients an "all clear" when in fact they had cancer.

As a result of these errors, some healthy patients underwent grueling cancer treatment —unnecessarily. And some cancer patients failed to receive needed treatment.

Why so many potentially life-threatening errors? Jonathan L. Epstein, MD, professor of pathology at Johns Hopkins and lead author of the study, told me that the trend is the ironic result of medical progress.

New, less invasive techniques such as needle biopsies are easier on patients, since they remove less tissue. But that gives pathologists smaller samples to examine—which means signs of disease may be missed.

Also, earlier biopsies are now the norm, thanks to cancer screening procedures like blood tests and mammograms. But early biopsies are more likely to be ambiguous ...and the potential for "false positives" greater.

To protect yourself, Epstein advises, have biopsy samples double-checked by a pathologist specializing in the tissue type under scrutiny.

If you've had a prostate biopsy, for instance, find a prostate cancer expert. Ask your doctor for help in locating the right specialist. The sample can be sent anywhere in the country. A second opinion will take about a week and cost about $125 to $175. The answer may be priceless.

The Importance of Follow-Up Testing

Follow-up tests are crucial for patients who test positive for hidden blood in the stool —a possible sign of colon cancer. Patients who are screened for colon cancer and who test positive for hidden blood in the stool should have either a colonoscopy...or a flexible sigmoidoscopy to check the colon internally and also a barium-enema X-ray exam. *Troubling:* Only about one-third of patients who initially test positive undergo both recommended follow-up procedures.

Jon Lurie, MD, MS, assistant professor of medicine, Dartmouth Medical School, Hanover, NH, and leader of a study of the records of more than 24,000 people age 65 and older who were screened for colon cancer in 1995.

Pre-Dental Surgery Preparation

Control dental surgery pain with non-steroidal anti-inflammatory drugs (NSAIDs). These drugs—including aspirin and ibuprofen—are often more effective than codeine or synthetic narcotics.

Best: Use NSAIDs *before* your appointment, so they will be effective at suppressing the body's pain response when the dentist begins working. Then take at regular intervals for the rest of the day after surgery.

Caution: NSAIDs cannot be used by people who are allergic to aspirin...have a history of bleeding ulcers or clotting problems...have renal problems...or are pregnant. They are best taken with food in your stomach.

Alan Winter, DDS, Park Avenue Periodontal Associates, New York.

Prepare Questions Before Doctor Visits

Get better answers from your doctor by organizing your questions before your visit. Decide on a reasonable number of questions—no more than two for each 10 minutes with the doctor. Prioritize the questions and group related topics together. Write down the questions and make a copy for him/her. When you do not understand an answer, ask him to clarify.

Frederic Platt, MD, clinical professor of medicine, University of Colorado, Denver, quoted in *American Health,* 28 W. 23 St., New York 10010.

3

Simple Solutions to Common Health Problems

Wisest Ways to Treat Home Medical Emergencies

I t is difficult to stay calm when you are confronted with a health emergency, such as a bad cut...a serious allergic reaction...or sudden and debilitating back pain. *Don't panic.* Even if you are waiting for an ambulance or driving to the emergency department, taking the appropriate action right away—and avoiding common mistakes—will improve the chances of a complete and fast recovery.

The most common home emergencies—and what you should do for them immediately...

ALLERGIC REACTIONS

Some people suffer a life-threatening allergic reaction called anaphylaxis. It can follow insect bites or stings...eating certain foods...or taking a medication to which you are sensitive.

Prime symptoms: Difficulty breathing, dizziness, nausea or a sudden and severe rash.

Do: Take Benadryl (diphenhydramine) right away. Follow dosage recommendations on the label. If you have a known allergy and carry an epinephrine self-injector, use it right away. Then get to an emergency department.

Don't: Wait for a serious allergic reaction to go away on its own. It can escalate very, very quickly.

HEAD INJURIES

Head trauma is responsible for more than two million emergency department visits a year. If you or someone you're with loses consciousness—even briefly—following a head injury, get emergency treatment. There could be a concussion or other type of brain damage.

Do: Be alert for symptoms like lethargy or sleepiness...nausea...weakness...changes in vision, etc. These are signs of brain injury that require immediate attention.

Don't: Assume the worst. Most people recover quickly from head injuries. As long as

---

Ted Christopher, MD, chief of the division of emergency medicine at Thomas Jefferson University Hospital in Philadelphia.

you're not feeling dazed, weak or disoriented, you can treat the discomfort at home with an ice pack and by taking acetaminophen. Do not take aspirin or ibuprofen, which may increase bleeding.

HEART ATTACK

Chest pain, often accompanied by sweating, shortness of breath or nausea, is the most common symptom of a heart attack. Call an ambulance if the discomfort doesn't go away promptly or if you have a history of heart problems.

Do: Take an aspirin at the first sign of symptoms. It can help prevent heart damage.

Don't: Wait to get medical attention, even if the discomfort improves. Prescription medications that are used to dissolve blood clots are most effective when given within just a few hours of symptom onset.

DEEP CUTS

Get help right away for any cut that is longer than one inch or in which you can see underlying tissue.

Do: Use a lot of water pressure when cleaning deep cuts. It spreads the tissues apart and provides more thorough cleaning. Use cool or tepid water, and flood the cut for two to three minutes. Wash with soap (regular bath soap is fine) to prevent infection. Apply pressure with gauze or a clean cloth to stop the bleeding.

Don't: Wash cuts with hot water. It dilates blood vessels and may increase bleeding. And don't use hydrogen peroxide to disinfect cuts—it can damage the tissue.

Warning: If the area surrounding the wound is numb or turns blue, a nerve or major blood vessel may have been damaged. Get to an emergency department right away.

PUNCTURE WOUNDS

Cuts from animal bites or stepping on a nail and other puncture wounds are always serious. The wounds are narrow and deep—they are difficult to wash and there is little bleeding—so bacteria can get trapped inside.

Do: Get to an emergency department quickly. Puncture wounds have a high infection rate. You'll probably need prescription antibiotics and a tetanus shot.

Don't: Remove nails, pencils, etc. that have penetrated deeply into the body. Pulling them out may increase the damage.

Better: Fasten the object in place with a clean bandage and tape...and get to an emergency department.

SUDDEN BACK PAIN

Most cases of back pain are caused by muscle strains. Acting quickly can mean the difference between a fast recovery and spending days—or even weeks—in bed.

Do: Take aspirin, ibuprofen or acetaminophen right away. These medications block the action of prostaglandins—chemicals in the body that cause inflammation after an injury. However, seek medical attention immediately for back pain associated with fever or loss of control of your bladder or bowels. Do not self-medicate.

Do: Apply a cold pack or ice cubes wrapped in a cloth to the area for at least 20 minutes, every few hours. The cold will constrict blood vessels and help prevent swelling.

Don't: Apply heat right after a back injury—it may increase swelling. After 24 hours, however, applying heat may help relax muscle spasms.

Warning: Back pain is rare in children. In the absence of an obvious injury, it may be a symptom of a more serious illness. Get it checked out right away.

Also, persistent back pain in the elderly should be checked by a physician. It could be a symptom of a serious medical problem.

HEAT BURNS

Even small burns can be slow to heal, and infections are common.

Do: Flood the area with cool water for five minutes. It lowers the temperature in the skin and helps prevent damage from residual heat. Cool water also acts as an anesthetic to reduce the pain.

Pat the area dry, and apply a triple antibiotic ointment. Then loosely cover with a gauze pad.

To reduce swelling and pain, take aspirin or ibuprofen.

Don't: Apply ice or very cold water to burns —extreme cold damages the skin. Also, don't "protect" the burn with petroleum jelly or butter. The oils trap heat and restrict air circulation. Do not pop burn blisters intentionally. Intact blisters help prevent infection.

POISONING

If you or someone you're with has ingested a toxic substance (including a large amount of over-the-counter or prescription medicine), get to an emergency department right away.

Do: Call an emergency department or your local poison control center for advice while you're waiting for help. If possible, have the product container in front of you so you can describe exactly what was taken.

Don't: Induce vomiting without medical advice. Many substances will cause additional damage on the way back up. There's also the risk that the vomit will be aspirated into the lungs.

Home Remedies For Common Conditions

· Doug Dollemore, who has written on the subject of aging for 15 years. Mr. Dollemore is author of many books, including *The Doctor's Book of Home Remedies for Seniors.* Rodale Press.

There's much we can do to maintain our own health and manage our own care as we age. *Here are some home remedies for common conditions...*

CLUMSINESS

If you're constantly tripping over your own feet, or can't wash the dishes without breaking one, you might try changing the way you do things. *Strategies...*

•**Stay physically fit.** Fitness will help you maintain your balance, especially when you reach out to grab something.

•**Get regular eye checkups**—to keep your corrected vision at its best.

•**Don't rush.** It's better to take a little extra time on a task than to have an accident—and possibly be injured.

•**Sit while doing chores that you can just as easily do seated.** This way, you can concentrate on the task without worrying about your balance.

•**Get a better handle on things.** Buy coffee mugs and other handheld items with thick handles. Wrap cork tape (used on bicycle handles and available in most bicycle shops) around the handles of spoons, knives, tools, etc., for a better grip.

•**Wear rubber gloves when washing the dishes.** You'll be better able to handle slippery glasses and plates.

MEMORY LOSS

As you age, you may find your memory is not as good as it used to be. *But—there are a number of simple strategies that help keep your mind sharp and your memory working to capacity...*

•**To-do lists** are a valuable way to remind yourself of things you have a tendency to forget. But don't rely on written lists exclusively. At least once a week, exercise your memory skills by relying on a mental list.

•**Aerobic exercises** such as brisk walking and swimming can improve memory 20% to 30%.

•**Get enough sleep** to keep your brain in top shape.

•**Keep your things organized.** If you always put everything in its place, you will know where to find it.

•**Talk to yourself as you do a task** to focus your attention on what you are doing and make it easier to remember later.

DESIRE

Sex can be enjoyed throughout life. (If you're having physical problems, see a doctor. They are generally correctable.) *To rekindle desire...*

•**Treat sex as play.** Use hugs, kisses and gentle caresses to show tenderness—emotional rewards are as fulfilling as physical ones.

•**Be romantic.** A moonlit walk...a single blossom left on your spouse's pillow...bathing together by candlelight.

●**Be creative.** Planting a garden, baking bread, building a piece of furniture—or any creative activity—can rev up your sex drive.

FOOT PAIN

For quick, temporary relief of most types of foot pain, take ibuprofen or other over-the-counter NSAIDs...but not for more than a few weeks at a time.

For longer-lasting relief, wear sneakers or running shoes, or put heel cups and/or other cushioned inserts in your shoes. And lose weight to reduce the pressure on your feet.

Two ways to relieve foot pain by stretching your Achilles tendon: *Do these stretches before going to bed and before getting up in the morning...*

●**Sit or lie down, bend your leg until you can reach your toes** and use both hands to pull your toes toward your shin. Hold for 20 seconds.

●**Place your hands on the wall and lean forward** with your feet flat on the ground, keeping your back straight and knees locked. Repeat 10 times, holding each stretch for 30 seconds.

You can relieve foot pain by rubbing your feet with capsaicin cream...reduce swelling by soaking them in warm water with Epsom salts (one tablespoon per quart).

Eating a half teaspoon of ground fresh ginger daily also reduces swelling.

OSTEOPOROSIS

Diet and lifestyle are the keys to avoiding bone loss that leads to fragility. *Most important...*

●**Get enough calcium.** 1,000 milligrams (mg) per day for people under age 65 and 1,200 mg per day for those age 65 and older and all postmenopausal women not taking estrogen.

Sources: Two-and-a-half to three glasses of fat-free milk daily...or two-and-a-half cups of fat-free yogurt...or five ounces of no-fat cheese.

Non-dairy sources: Sardines with bones ...tofu...collard greens...calcium-fortified orange juice. Calcium is absorbed most effectively when taken with vitamin D.

Sources of vitamin D: Exposure to sunlight combined with milk and certain breakfast cereals.

●**Protein should make up 30% to 40% of your diet.**

●**Strengthen bones with weight-bearing exercises,** but avoid those that require bending and twisting motions that strain joints and risk breaking bones. The recommended 20 to 30 minutes a day of aerobic exercises—like walking and weight lifting—three times a week can be made up from smaller chunks of time.

Another helpful exercise: Stand up straight against a wall with your spine as straight as possible...squeeze your shoulder blades.

Also: Don't smoke...or consume more than one and a half ounces of hard liquor...or more than 12 ounces of beer...or more than five ounces of wine...or more than three caffeinated drinks...or more than 2,400 mg of sodium per day.

HIGH BLOOD PRESSURE

To minimize the risk of heart disease or stroke, aim to keep your blood pressure reading below 120/80. It may be possible for you to accomplish this without medication by making two simple changes—losing weight and keeping your sodium intake below 2,400 mg a day.

Reduce sodium intake by eating low-sodium foods...adding spices instead of salt.

Also—eat enough fruits and vegetables to bring your potassium intake up to 3,500 mg per day (e.g., a medium-sized banana has 467 mg of potassium and a four-ounce baked potato without skin has 607 mg)...take a brisk 30-minute walk every day...get 1,200 mg of calcium and 400 IU of vitamin D per day. And if you don't have any heart or kidney problems, get 400 mg of magnesium daily.

SNORING

Snoring occurs while inhaling during sleep. The soft tissues of the throat vibrate against your tongue or the back of the throat. *To quiet snoring...*

●**Sleep on your side or stomach,** not your back. *Helpful:* Sew a tennis ball into the back of your pajamas.

●**Spray your nose with Nasalcrom spray** before going to sleep to clear your nasal passages and improve breathing.

●**If your nostrils get sucked in** as you breathe, tape Breathe Right nasal strips over your nose before going to bed.

●**Avoid alcohol and sleeping pills.** Don't smoke.

●**Humidify the bedroom.**

Apnea: Severe snoring may be caused by *sleep apnea*. It occurs if the passage of air is completely blocked many times each night during sleep. This condition causes a dangerous increase in blood pressure and can result in heart failure, depression and mental clouding. If loud snoring persists despite all your prevention techniques, consult a physician specializing in sleep disorders.

Aspirin Isn't Just For Headaches

Peter Elwood, MD, professor of epidemiology at the University of Wales College of Medicine in Cardiff.

Over the past 25 years, more than 140 studies have shown that aspirin can help prevent heart attack and stroke. Recent research suggests that it may cut risk for other diseases as well.

To learn about the latest research on this remarkable medication—and to find out who should and who should not be taking it—we posed several questions to Peter Elwood, MD, lead author of a landmark 1974 study that was the first to link aspirin with reduced heart disease risk...

●**Just how effective is aspirin at preventing heart attack and stroke?** In studies involving men who had already sustained a heart attack or stroke, low-dose aspirin therapy—typically one tablet or less a day—cut the risk for heart attack and stroke by 30% to 40%.

The vast US Physicians' Health Study indicates that aspirin reduces heart attack risk in healthy men as well as in male heart patients. However, since healthy, nonsmoking men (and presumably women) have an extremely low risk for heart attack, the actual benefit to these individuals is probably too small to make daily aspirin therapy worthwhile.

But for people at high risk for heart attack —older people, smokers, those with high blood pressure or elevated cholesterol and/or a family history of heart disease—aspirin therapy is often worthwhile.

Aspirin prevents heart disease by reducing the "stickiness" of platelets. Those are the cellular fragments that clump together to start a blood clot.

●**Doesn't aspirin also play a role in heart attack treatment?** Absolutely. Taking an aspirin tablet as soon as symptoms become apparent may substantially boost the chance of survival, studies have shown.

The more promptly aspirin is taken, the better the odds for survival.

Since heart attack can kill within minutes, anyone at risk for heart disease should always carry a pillbox containing aspirin...and take a tablet at the first sign of chest pain.

To get aspirin into the bloodstream as quickly as possible, *chew* the tablet before you swallow it.

●**Which other conditions can aspirin help prevent?** Preliminary evidence suggests that aspirin can help prevent Alzheimer's disease.

Evidence is much stronger that aspirin helps prevent *vascular dementia*, a form of cognitive impairment associated with transient ischemic attacks (TIAs) and strokes.

Researchers now believe that TIAs and strokes caused by blood clotting cause about half of all cases of dementia. Since there's little downside to aspirin therapy, anyone who shows signs of mental deterioration suggestive of vascular dementia should probably be taking aspirin.

There is also good evidence that aspirin can help prevent certain forms of cancer. Three large-scale studies and many smaller ones found that patients who take aspirin on a daily basis face a reduced risk for colon cancer.

Cancers of the rectum, stomach and esophagus also may be prevented by aspirin use, according to recent studies.

Regular use of aspirin also seems to reduce the risk for cataracts...and to prevent the potentially blinding diabetes-related condition known as *diabetic retinopathy.*

●**Can't aspirin cause stomach trouble and other side effects?** About 8% of people on a low-dose aspirin regimen report nausea and/or stomach pain. Taking aspirin *after* a meal helps alleviate these symptoms.

Some people notice that they bruise more easily after going on aspirin therapy. This is nothing to worry about. Rarely, aspirin causes acute bleeding—vomiting blood or blood in the stool. This is a medical emergency.

To be safe, consult a doctor before taking aspirin—especially if you have a peptic ulcer... if you're taking an anticoagulant, such as *warfarin* (Coumadin)...or if you're allergic to aspirin.

●**What dosage of aspirin is appropriate?** When it comes to preventing illness, low dosages work fine. The World Health Organization now recommends 100 mg per day to prevent heart attack. This dosage is probably appropriate for preventing other illnesses as well.

A standard aspirin tablet contains 325 mg. Some manufacturers have begun making 100-mg aspirin tablets. But it's okay to take half of a 325-mg tablet...or one 81-mg children's aspirin.

●**Does the type of aspirin make a difference?** Plain aspirin is fine for use in daily aspirin therapy...as well as for treating a suspected heart attack.

Enteric-coated aspirin bypasses the stomach and dissolves in the small intestine. It was developed to minimize gastrointestinal effects in chronic pain patients and other individuals who take large doses of aspirin. Since aspirin therapy involves low dosages, there's no reason to prefer enteric-coated over plain aspirin.

How to Stop Migraine Pain

Alexander Mauskop, MD, associate professor of clinical neurology at the State University of New York in Brooklyn, and director of the New York Headache Center in New York City. He is author of *The Headache Alternative.* Dell.

New painkilling medications have brought welcome relief to millions of migraine sufferers. But medications aren't the only effective weapons against migraine.

Many alternative therapies, from acupuncture to nutritional supplements, can enhance the effectiveness of migraine drugs. In some cases, they eliminate the need for drugs altogether.

STRESS MANAGEMENT

Psychological stress can trigger migraines. Some migraineurs get headaches during periods of intense stress. Others get "letdown" headaches after stress has subsided.

By retraining your nervous system, biofeedback can be extremely effective at countering psychological stress.

It doesn't have to be conventional biofeedback, in which the patient—hooked up to electrodes—monitors his/her anxiety level via visual or audible signals. Almost any relaxation technique can work—including meditation, yoga, self-hypnosis, progressive relaxation or tai chi.

ELIMINATING CAFFEINE

In small amounts, caffeine eases migraine pain. Not surprisingly, many aspirin-based painkillers contain caffeine...and migraineurs often gulp coffee at the first sign of pain.

But among those who consume more than the equivalent of two cups of coffee a day, skipping a cup can cause caffeine withdrawal. That can trigger migraine.

Lesson: Migraineurs who drink lots of caffeinated coffee, tea or cola—or eat lots of chocolate, which also contains caffeine—can benefit by giving up their habit.

DIETARY TRIGGERS

Headache frequency and severity can be reduced by avoiding certain food triggers...

●**Aged cheese, red wine, pickled food, bananas, figs and other foods containing the amino acid *tyramine*.**

●**Yogurt, beer, freshly baked bread and other fermented foods.**

●**Dried fruit.** Most contain sulfites, preservatives that can trigger headaches. Raisins contain a red pigment that can trigger migraine.

●**Foods containing nitrites and/or monosodium glutamate (MSG).**

●**Bread and pasta made from wheat.** Although true wheat sensitivity is rare, some migraineurs find that avoiding wheat helps curb their headaches.

SLEEP HABITS

Migraines can be triggered by getting too little sleep—or too much. Aim for eight hours of sleep a night. Do not try to "catch up" by sleeping late on weekends. Take short naps during the day instead.

VITAMINS AND MINERALS

Magnesium plays a key role in brain function. Among other things, it influences blood vessel dilation and serotonin levels—each of which is a factor in migraine pain.

Up to 50% of migraineurs have a magnesium deficiency, according to recent research.

Spinach and other dark-green, leafy vegetables are rich in magnesium. But other good magnesium sources—including nuts and beans—contain compounds that can trigger migraines. For this reason, it's hard to correct a magnesium deficiency through diet alone.

Better: Ask your doctor about taking a supplement containing 300 mg to 600 mg of magnesium per day.

Also helpful: Vitamin B-2 (riboflavin) supplements. A double-blind study published last year in the journal *Neurology* found that taking 400 mg a day significantly reduced migraine frequency.

You may have to take B-2 supplements for up to four months before you notice any effect.

FEVERFEW

Feverfew, an herb related to chamomile, has been used against migraine for centuries. Recent studies have found that daily use of feverfew reduces migraine frequency by up to 25%.

Feverfew is sold at health-food stores. The usual dosage is 100 mg a day.

ACUPUNCTURE AND MASSAGE

Acupuncture can be quite effective at relieving migraine pain. You might try one 20- to 30-minute session a week for 10 weeks as a preventive measure…plus periodic "touch-ups" if headaches recur.

For the name of an acupuncturist in your area, contact the American Academy of Medical Acupuncture at 800-521-2262.

Massage fights migraine indirectly, by relieving stress. But certain forms of massage seem to do more to relieve migraine than simply relieve stress.

These migraine-fighting massage techniques—described by Toru Namikoshi in his 1985 classic *Shiatsu and Stretching*—have proven to be particularly effective…

●**Place your thumbs on each side of the spine,** in the hollows between the neck muscles just below the base of the skull. Tilt your head back. Press firmly for two to three minutes, breathing deeply as you do.

●**Press the web between your thumb and forefinger with the thumb and index finger of your opposite hand.** Press hard for one minute, breathing deeply. Repeat with the other hand.

WHEN MEDICATION IS NEEDED

The 1993 introduction of *sumatriptan* (Imitrex) was hailed as a breakthrough for migraine sufferers—and no wonder.

Taken at the first sign of migraine, this prescription medication constricts dilated blood vessels, relieving not only pain but also the nausea and sensitivity to light and noise that often accompany migraine headaches.

Sumatriptan can be taken orally or—for faster relief—sprayed into the nose or injected.

Unfortunately, sumatriptan can cause unpleasant side effects, including chest pressure and a transient rise in blood pressure.

Sumatriptan and the newer "triptans," including *zolmitriptan* (Zomig), *rizatriptan* (Maxalt) and *naratriptan* (Amerge), are off limits for most heart patients and individuals at risk for heart disease.

Other drugs proven effective in preventing migraine include…

- **Anticonvulsants,** such as *valproic acid* (Depakote) and *gabapentin* (Neurontin).

- **Antidepressants.** Tricyclics, such as *nortriptyline* (Pamelor), *imipramine* (Tofranil) and *desipramine* (Norpramin), are most effective.

- **Beta-blockers,** such as *propranolol* (Inderal) and *atenolol* (Tenormin).

Cherries Kill Pain

Experiments conducted at Michigan State University in East Lansing suggest that, ounce for ounce, cherries pack painkilling power comparable to aspirin.

The compounds that make cherries red—known as *anthocyanins*—are effective at blocking the enzymes that trigger the inflammatory process underlying arthritis and many forms of pain.

Michigan State University.

Five Steps to Fight Awful Arthritis

Harris McIlwain, MD, rheumatologist, Tampa, FL, and author of *The Super Aspirin Cure for Arthritis.* Bantam Books.

Use moist heat on affected joints twice a day. *Examples:* Warm shower or bath… hot tub…warm, moist towels.

- **Exercise joints** to improve flexibility and strengthen muscles.

- **Take the right medicine.** Get samples of new medicines from your doctor, or fill enough of a prescription for a week or two. Buy a full supply only when you find a medicine that works.

- **Eat a healthful, varied diet,** with plenty of vegetables, fruits and whole grains. Maintain a normal weight.

- **Eliminate foods that sometimes trigger arthritis,** such as alcohol, eggs and milk.

Set up tests of possible triggers with your doctor.

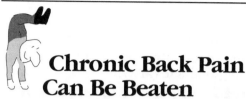

Chronic Back Pain Can Be Beaten

Art Brownstein, MD, assistant clinical professor of medicine at the University of Hawaii's John A. Burns School of Medicine in Honolulu, and medical director of the Princeville Medical Clinic in Princeville. He is author of *Healing Back Pain Naturally.* Harbor Press.

I suffered from debilitating back pain for more than 20 years, starting in the early 1970s. Surgery didn't help. The pain got so bad I became hooked on painkillers…and plunged into a deep depression.

Out of desperation, I spent five years studying with healers in the US and the Far East, exploring alternatives to conventional medical treatment for back pain. *What I learned…*

- **Surgery is rarely the answer.** It is appropriate in certain cases, such as when there's a cyst on the spine or a congenital spine abnormality. But for most back problems, surgery only weakens the spine.

- **Back pain originates in the muscles.** Doctors and patients often think of back pain as a skeletal problem. In fact, the spine's curvature, alignment and movement are all governed by the surrounding back muscles.

Tight muscles and muscle spasms in the back squeeze the vertebrae. This compresses the disks between the vertebrae, and an X-ray of the back shows an apparent disk problem.

The real source of the trouble, however, is the muscles.

One major contributor to back pain is sitting. Sitting causes the back muscles to shorten, stiffen and grow weaker. That leaves them vulnerable to injury.

- **Psychological stress plays a key role.** My first serious episode of back pain occurred during medical school, a notoriously stressful environment.

In the four years leading up to my surgery, I had lost four family members…and my wife was dying of cancer.

At the time, I didn't connect any of these stressors with my back pain. But I learned that the brain is "hardwired" to the back muscles, and that psychological stress inevitably causes these muscles to contract.

This can throw the back out of alignment. It can also constrict blood vessels, choking off the blood supply to the back.

The holistic approach I learned during those five years worked wonders. I now surf, teach yoga and run a busy medical practice—all without pain.

Here are the strategies you can use to beat back pain...

STRETCHING

Daily stretching decompresses the spine, improving its flexibility and boosting blood flow to the back muscles.

It also helps reverse muscle atrophy caused by a sedentary lifestyle. *Some simple, safe stretches...*

•**Gluteal squeezes.** Lie on your back with your knees bent and your feet flat on the bed or floor. Squeeze the muscles in your buttocks as tightly as you can, then slowly relax.

•**Knee raises.** Lie on your back. Slowly raise your right knee to your chest. Place your hands on your right shin, and gently pull your leg closer to your chest.

Notice the expansion of your chest and abdomen and the stretching in your hip, knee and lower spine. Lower your right knee and repeat with your left knee.

•**Cat/horse stretch.** Get on your hands and knees, with your weight distributed equally from front to back and side to side. Slowly arch your spine like a cat. Lower your head, and relax the muscles in your neck and shoulders.

Hold this position for several breaths, feeling your back muscles stretch. Then slowly release the arch and let your back droop like an old horse's. Raise your head and look up, extending your buttocks upward and feeling the stretch in your neck, upper back and spine.

Caution: Don't force yourself into any position that's painful. Breathe smoothly and slowly throughout each stretch.

The best overall stretching program for the back is yoga. Unfortunately, yoga classes offered by health clubs are often too vigorous for people with back trouble.

Before signing up, make sure the instructor has experience working with back patients.

STRENGTHENING

Once you've been doing daily stretches for a month or two, add a program of walking, swimming or another gentle form of exercise to further strengthen your back muscles.

Important: Pay attention to how your back feels as you move.

Caution: If you ride a bicycle, avoid the bent-over position. It can exacerbate back pain.

STRESS REDUCTION

Meditation and other relaxation techniques —practiced for 20 minutes or so each day— are very effective at alleviating stress.

Easy relaxation technique: Sit comfortably with your eyes closed. Notice your back moving slightly with each breath. Also notice the gentle pulling on your spine that occurs with each breath.

As you relax, visualize your back as strong, healthy and flexible. See yourself bending and moving with grace and vigor.

Leisure activity—play—is perhaps the most effective way to alleviate the stress that can cause back pain. Spend time on your hobbies. Listen to music. Pursue your favorite sport—but be sure to protect your back.

Crucial: Avoid the win-at-all-costs mentality. Learn to play for the joy of the game.

UNDERSTANDING PAIN

Like me, many of my patients have found it helpful to have an "internal dialogue" with their back pain.

What to do: Close your eyes. Imagine that your pain has taken the form of an animal, cartoon character or anything else that occurs to you. *Ask your pain...*

•**Why are you here?**

•**Why do you hurt so much?**

•**How can I get rid of you?**

To conclude the dialogue, express your gratitude and slowly open your eyes. Repeat this process once or twice a day.

Cayenne Pepper Can Prevent Dysentery

Cayenne increases the intestine's resistance to *enterococci* and other microbes that cause the severe abdominal pain, fever and diarrhea. If you're traveling in tropical climates or anywhere with poor sanitation, sprinkle enough pepper on one meal a day to make it very spicy.

Andrew L. Rubman, ND, director, Southbury Center for Traditional Medicines, Southbury, CT.

Cataract Control

Vitamin C may prevent cataracts. At least 10 studies show that taking 300 milligrams (mg) of vitamin C a day decreases risk of age-related cataracts—but the recommended dietary allowance is only 60 mg/day.

Good food sources of vitamin C are fresh fruits and vegetables, including citrus fruits, tomatoes, brussels sprouts and spinach. People over age 50 should consider taking vitamin supplements to be sure they get enough Vitamin C.

Vitamin C supplements are especially important for smokers (and those who live with smokers) because they tend to develop cataracts 10 years earlier than others.

Stuart Richer, OD, PhD, chief of optometry, DVA Medical Center, North Chicago, IL.

Tonic Water Fights Leg Cramps

If you get cramps during the day, try drinking tonic water before bedtime. It contains quinine—a muscle relaxant that can be effective against leg cramps. An eight-ounce glass of tonic water contains 27 mg of quinine—enough to relieve cramps in many people. Add orange juice or lemon to tonic water to make it taste less bitter.

Paul Davidson, MD, associate clinical professor of medicine, University of California, San Francisco.

Quick Varicose Vein Treatment

Large varicose veins in the legs can now be removed without surgery. A 20-minute outpatient procedure known as *endovenous radiofrequency vein closure* involves only a one-quarter-inch incision in the thigh. A catheter tipped with a radiotransmitter is threaded through this incision and into the problem vein. High-intensity radio waves emitted by the catheter tip seal off the vein. Patients can resume normal activity the next day. With conventional surgery, recovery takes up to seven days.

Mitchel P. Goldman, MD, associate clinical professor of dermatology, University of California, San Diego, School of Medicine.

4

Diet, Nutrition and Exercise

How Nutritionists Shop for Groceries

Grocery shoppers are overwhelmed by choice. The average supermarket now stocks 25,000 items, and these products are packaged, promoted and displayed so as to encourage us to buy them whether they are healthful or not.

Here's the smart way to shop for food...

●**Ignore the front of the box.** This is where manufacturers trumpet information that exploits our desires. We gravitate to items labeled "NO CHOLESTEROL," "LOW-FAT" or "LIGHT" because we think these are good for our health.

Those words are often misleading. Plant-based foods *never* contain cholesterol, since cholesterol is found only in animal products. And potato chips, margarine and other foods that are labeled "CHOLESTEROL-FREE" may be very rich in fat—and fat promotes synthesis of cholesterol in the body.

Similarly, many items labeled "low-fat" may be high in calories. So eating these foods may do little to help you control your weight.

Self-defense: Read the ingredients list and Nutrition Facts box before putting any item into your shopping cart.

●**Examine the *order* of ingredients.** Ingredients are listed in descending order of weight. To judge how healthful a particular food is, consider the first four ingredients.

Example I: If you want to buy whole wheat bread, the first ingredient should be whole wheat flour, not enriched white flour.

Example II: If you pick up a bottle of "juice" that has water and sugar among the first ingredients, it's not really juice.

●**Watch for ingredient "aliases."** Fat, salt and sugar have many names. If you need to

---

Ramona Josephson, registered dietitian and nutritionist (RDN), codirector of the outreach program of the British Columbia Lipid Clinic and a dietitian in private practice, both in Vancouver. She is author of *The HeartSmart Shopper: Nutrition on the Run.* Douglas & McIntyre.

watch your intake of these nutrients, you must be able to identify them in all their forms...

●**Fat** can be listed as lard, shortening, hydrogenated vegetable oil, coconut or palm oil, tropical oil, tallow or monoglycerides or diglycerides.

●**Salt** can be listed as monosodium glutamate (MSG), baking soda, baking powder, brine, kelp, soy sauce or a variety of names containing the word "sodium."

●**Sugar** can be listed as honey, molasses, dextrose, sucrose, fructose, maltose, lactose, dextrin, maltodextrin, maple syrup, corn syrup or malt syrup.

●**Avoid trans fats.** When it became clear that butter and saturated fat were harmful to the heart, food manufacturers started using vegetable oil instead.

But vegetable oil is often chemically altered —via a process known as *hydrogenation*—to render it more solid. Hydrogenation causes formation of trans fatty acids, which are now thought to be even more deleterious to heart health than saturated fat.

Hydrogenated or partially hydrogenated oils are used to make french fries, donuts, margarine and many baked goods, including crackers and cookies.

Self-defense: If hydrogenated or partially hydrogenated oil is among the first four items in a food's ingredient list, choose another product.

●**Pay attention to serving size.** The Nutrition Facts label explains, among other things, just how much of the particular food constitutes a single serving. This is the quantity on which all the other nutrition information is based.

Serving sizes are often confusing. A serving of yogurt may be one-half cup, for example, yet the container may hold three-quarters of a cup. In some cases, similar cereals made by the same manufacturer have different serving sizes.

Example: One serving of Post Great Grains is two-thirds of a cup, while a single serving of Post Cranberry Almond Crunch is one cup.

Self-defense: When comparing products for fat grams, calories and nutrients, take serving size into account.

●**Beware fantasy thinking.** Food ads would have us believe that we can be transformed by eating certain foods. Not true.

The term "granola" might sound as if eating it would turn us into vigorous outdoors people, but granola bars are often high in fat and sugar.

And while athletes use sports drinks, you won't become more athletic if you drink them. In fact, sports drinks can be high in calories. Nonathletes who use them often gain unwanted weight.

Self-defense: Base food purchases on ingredients, *not* on seductive advertising.

●**Pay attention to product placement.** Food manufacturers pay a premium to have their products shelved at eye level. These are often heavily promoted products—and are not necessarily the most healthful.

Cast your eyes higher and lower on the shelves to discover other healthful options.

●**Scrutinize impulse items.** Items at the ends of aisles and at checkout counters are placed there because these positions are conspicuous. The idea is for you to buy something you hadn't planned on buying.

Think twice before adding these items to your basket.

●**Avoid the snack food aisle.** Don't think you're being health-conscious by buying baked chips instead of regular potato chips. While they're less fatty, baked chips aren't much more healthful than fried ones.

Snack foods should be healthful mini-meals, not chips and other nutritionally empty foods.

Good snack choices: Raw vegetables, yogurt, fruit or mini-pizzas with low-fat mozzarella and tomato sauce.

Fat-Free Trap

Going fat-free can backfire. In a recent study, men were fed a lunchtime shake made with either skim or whole milk, then monitored to see what they ate later in the day. They didn't know which shake they got.

Result: The men who drank the skim-milk shake tended to eat more fat later in the day than did the other men.

Implication: Eating meals containing a little fat will help you avoid fatty foods all day.

John Allred, PhD, professor of nutrition, Ohio State University, Columbus.

Weight-Loss Help

If you're having trouble losing weight, ask a doctor about taking *bupropion* (Wellbutrin).

In a study of 50 nondepressed women on a calorie-restricted diet, those who took this prescription antidepressant lost four times more weight than those who took a placebo.

The drug, which is also used in smoking cessation, works by enhancing the activity of *dopamine.* That's a brain chemical involved in producing feelings of pleasure.

Patients who take bupropion say it helps them feel satisfied when they eat less. *Only side effect:* Dry mouth.

Caution: People with an eating disorder or seizure disorder should not take bupropion.

Kishore Gadde, MD, assistant professor of psychiatry, Duke University Medical Center, Durham, NC.

Six Ways to Lose That Too-Big Potbelly

Garry Egger, PhD, MPH, director of the Centre for Health Promotion and Research in Sydney, Australia, and adjunct professor of health sciences at Deakin University in Melbourne, Australia. He is coauthor of *Gut-Buster: Waist Loss Guide.* Allen & Unwin.

Whether it's called a potbelly or a spare tire, fat deposits concentrated around the middle of a man's body have long been the butt of jokes.

But mid-body fat is no laughing matter. It raises the risk for heart disease, diabetes, high blood pressure, back pain, knee problems, snoring and even impotence.

Almost every man develops at least a bit of a paunch as he grows older. How can you tell if yours is reason for concern?

Do *not* rely on your bathroom scale—either to check yourself now or to monitor weight loss later on. A scale can tell you if you weigh more than most men your height. But muscular men are sometimes overweight without being fat.

Your waist measurement is a more reliable indicator of potential health problems. Any man whose waist spans 39 inches or more should take immediate steps to lose the belly.

To find your waist size: Place a tape measure around your waist at the level of the navel. Do not suck in your gut. That will only give you an artificially small number—reassuring, perhaps, but dangerously misleading.

SIX WAYS TO SHRINK A BELLY

The good news for men is that it's not especially difficult to lose a potbelly. Abdominal fat tends to be more "mobile" than weight deposited at the hips and thighs—as women's fat often is.

Follow these guidelines, and you should lose an inch of fat in your waist measurement every two to three weeks…

●**Cut fat consumption *dramatically*.** Most health experts continue to recommend getting about 30% of total calories in the form of fat. But it's not really the percentage of dietary fat that counts. It's the total *amount* of fat that you eat that controls how fat your body is.

Important: Eat no more than 40 g of fat per day. Pick up a fat-count book, such as Karen Bellerson's *The Complete & Up-to-Date Fat Book* (Avery).

Recent research suggests that dietary fat is actually addictive—the more you eat it, the more you crave it. Stop eating fatty foods for just two weeks, and you should lose most, if not all, of your craving.

Helpful: Pay attention to your eating. Do you tend to snack while watching television? Do you eat in your car? At your desk? Many men are surprised to discover that they can break these bad habits—and cut down on unconscious eating—simply by paying attention to their eating habits.

●**Eat small, frequent meals.** Doing so boosts your metabolic rate, speeding the rate at which the body burns calories and helping you avoid the hunger that sometimes leads to uncontrolled eating.

Never go more than four hours without eating. Do *not* skip breakfast. If you have no appetite upon rising, start the day with toast and juice.

●**Focus simply on moving more—not necessarily getting more exercise.** Vigorous exercise is unnecessary. Your goal should be simply to boost the amount of time you spend in motion—going up stairs, walking the dog, mowing the lawn, etc.

Helpful: Use a pedometer to count how many steps you take each day. At least 7,500 steps are necessary to lose weight, but 10,000 to 12,000 steps per day are better.

Stomach exercises do firm the abdominal muscles. But they have no special magic against belly fat. Walking is actually more effective, since it's a more efficient way of burning calories.

●**Cultivate a caffeine habit.** Too much coffee or any other caffeinated beverage can cause health problems, including anxiety. But it's now clear that a little caffeine each day constitutes a safe way to speed your metabolism and lose weight.

Because the body quickly develops a tolerance to caffeine, drinking coffee, cola, etc., is most effective after a period of abstinence.

If you're a habitual coffee, tea or cola drinker, go "cold turkey." After two weeks, gradually reintroduce caffeine into your diet. Limit consumption to two cups of coffee—or four cups of tea or cola—per day.

If you're not much of a caffeinated beverage drinker right now, start slowly. Have one-half cup of coffee in the morning and one-half cup in the afternoon.

●**Season your food with hot peppers.** *Capsaicin*, the compound that makes hot peppers hot, fights body fat in two ways. It boosts your metabolism...and helps reduce the amount of food eaten at each meal. It does the latter by curbing your appetite.

Sources of capsaicin: Red and green chili peppers, cayenne pepper, Tabasco sauce and jalapeños.

●**Observe your drinking habits.** Contrary to popular belief, alcohol is not a significant contributor to a potbelly. It's the chips, cheese, etc., that you eat while drinking alcohol that add on the pounds.

If you already drink, it's okay to continue having up to four drinks per day. Just cut down on your eating while you drink.

What if you're a teetotaler? At least as far as your belly is concerned, there is no reason to start drinking.

Watch What You Eat —Literally

People who watch themselves eating in a mirror tend to eat less unhealthful food than people away from mirrors. *Possible reason:* Mirrors help people compare actual behavior with internal standards. Failing to match the standard of eating well makes people uneasy, so they eat well when watching themselves. *Worth a try:* A mirror on the refrigerator door.

Brad Bushman, PhD, associate professor of psychology, Iowa State University, Ames.

The Strang Center's Nutritional Approach To Cancer Prevention

Mitchell L. Gaynor, MD, director of medical oncology at Strang Cancer Prevention Center, an affiliate of New York Presbyterian Hospital in New York City. He is co-author of *Dr. Gaynor's Cancer Prevention Program* (Kensington) and author of *The Sounds of Healing: A Physician Reveals the Therapeutic Power of Sound, Voice and Music* (Broadway Books).

At some point during their lives, one in three Americans will be diagnosed with cancer. *Most of us already have a pretty good idea of what we need to do to minimize our risk…*

- **Don't smoke.**
- **Stay out of the sun.**
- **Avoid consumption of saturated fat.**
- **Eat lots of fresh fruits and vegetables.**
- **Exercise regularly.**
- **Get regular cancer screening tests.***

In recent years, nutrition researchers have gone far beyond these basic strategies. They've shown that certain naturally occurring compounds have potent anticancer properties.

By boosting your consumption of the foods that contain these *phytochemicals*, you can drive your risk for cancer even lower…

- **Carotenoids,** including beta-carotene and lycopene. Found in fruits and orange, red and leafy, green vegetables. These powerful antioxidants fight cancer by neutralizing free radicals.
- **Isoflavones.** Found in tofu, soy milk, veggie burgers and other soy products. Among other effects, isoflavones block *angiogenesis*. That's the process by which new blood vessels form to bring nutrients to cancerous growths.
- **Sulforaphane.** Found in broccoli, kale, brussels sprouts and cabbage. It activates anticancer enzymes in the body.
- **Epigallocatechin gallate.** Found in green tea. This potent antioxidant—200 times more powerful than vitamin C—helps block the effects of nitrosamines and other carcinogens. Green tea should be drunk *without milk*, which reduces antioxidant activity.
- **Omega-3 fatty acids.** Found in salmon, haddock, cod, tuna, halibut, mackerel and sardines. These acids block the synthesis of *prostaglandins*, natural body compounds that promote tumor growth.

Other sources of omega-3 fatty acids include flaxseed oil (two tablespoons a day) or fish oil capsules (700 mg to 1,000 mg, three times a day).

*Women: Mammogram for breast cancer (age 40 to 49, every one to two years…50 or over, every year). Pap test for cervical cancer (18 or over, every year). *Men:* PSA blood test for prostate cancer (50 or over, every year). *Colon cancer screening for men and women:* Digital rectal exam (40 or over, every year)…fecal occult blood testing (50 or over, every year)…flexible sigmoidoscopy (50 or over, every three years).

- **Ginger.** It contains *gingerol* and 13 other antioxidant compounds, each more potent than vitamin E. Recent studies involving mice showed that consumption of ginger can prevent skin tumors.

Each day, drink two or three cups of ginger tea…or take one 550-mg ginger capsule.

- **Rosemary.** This popular herb contains *carnosol*, which is a compound that deactivates carcinogens and helps curb the effect of prostaglandins in the body. In recent tests, tumors shrank by 85% in mice that were fed large quantities of rosemary.

Human studies have yet to be done. However, given the fact that rosemary is safe, there is no downside to eating it on a regular basis. It's sold in tea form or as an extract, which can be added to green tea.

FITTING IT ALL IN

Nutritionists often say that five servings of fruits and vegetables each day are enough to maintain good health. But for maximum anticancer benefit, it's better to have six to eight daily servings (including at least one cruciferous vegetable and one tomato).

One serving equals one-half cup of vegetables…or one piece of fruit.

Problem: Even conscientious eaters often find that they have trouble fitting in all of these fruits and vegetables.

If you're having trouble getting your daily quota, consider juicing. Buy a quality juicing machine, such as those sold by Omega and Juiceman. Spend time experimenting with fruit and vegetable combinations.

Two tasty combinations…

- **Juice #1:** One head of cabbage, two carrots and one beet.
- **Juice #2:** One-third cup broccoli, two carrots, one apple and one cucumber.

Even with juicing, it's hard to get adequate amounts of certain anticancer nutrients from foods alone. *It's a good idea to take supplements containing…*

- **Alpha-lipoic acid.** This antioxidant helps replenish stores of vitamin E in the body and may prevent activation of certain cancer genes. Take 60 mg to 200 mg a day.

●**Vitamin E.** This antioxidant has been shown to reduce prostate cancer by up to one-third. Take 200 international units (IU) to 400 IU a day.

●**Selenium.** This mineral has been shown to reduce the risk for colon cancer by roughly 60%. Take 100 micrograms (mcg) to 200 mcg daily.

THE IMPORTANCE OF RELAXATION

Stress, depression and pessimism depress the immune response, leaving the body vulnerable to cancer. To reduce your cancer risk, learn to relax.

Forget TV. Focus on practicing meditation, yoga, tai chi or another relaxation technique.

One easy and highly effective tool for relaxation is *toning*.

What to do: Inhale through your nose, then release the breath through your mouth while making one sustained sound.

Toning can be done as often as you like—anytime, anywhere.

Beta-Carotene Prevents Breast Cancer

Sweet potatoes, carrots, apricots, spinach and other foods rich in beta-carotene help prevent breast cancer. In a recent study, breast cancer risk was 68% lower in women who consumed the highest quantities of beta-carotene than in those who consumed the least.

Prevention, 33 E. Minor St., Emmaus, PA 18098.

Cut Your Risk of Cancer By Two-Thirds

J. Robert Hatherill, PhD, a research scientist in the environmental studies program at the University of California in Santa Barbara. He is author of *Eat to Beat Cancer*. Renaissance Books.

Can changing your diet eliminate your risk of developing cancer? That proposition—the centerpiece of a book called *The Breast Cancer Prevention Diet* (Little, Brown)—caused a firestorm of controversy several months ago.

Critics of the book, written by television correspondent Bob Arnot, MD, argue that nothing can eliminate the danger of cancer altogether. They're right. No diet, supplement or drug can *guarantee* you won't get cancer. But you can do a great deal to protect yourself.

Diet is now believed to be a factor in approximately 60% of all malignancies, with smoking, heredity and viral infections accounting for the rest.

Theoretically, an effective anticancer diet should be capable of cutting your cancer risk by roughly two-thirds.

NO QUICK FIX

The most compelling demonstrations of cancer risk reduction come from *population studies*. These experiments compare the incidence of certain diseases among different groups of people.

More than 200 such studies have been completed. Among other things, these studies show that cancer rates are much lower in developing nations than in the US.

Citizens of developing nations tend to eat very differently than the average American does. The average American eats lots of fatty and/or highly processed foods. In developing countries, people eat mostly fruits, vegetables and grains.

WHAT TO AVOID

It is now well established that eating less dietary fat can cut your cancer risk. Dietary fat clearly raises the risk for breast, colon and prostate cancers. *In addition, you must avoid foods known to raise cancer risk—and boost consumption of foods that lower the risk...*

●**Minimize consumption of beef, pork, poultry and fish.** These foods can be concentrated sources of dioxin, polychlorinated biphenyls (PCBs) and other potent carcinogens.

These compounds sap the body's cancer-fighting ability...and trigger genetic mutations that can lead to cancer.

●**Wash produce thoroughly.** If peeling is not an option, use VegiWash or another produce wash. Whenever possible, buy organic.

• **Drink more water.** Drinking eight eight-ounce glasses of water a day helps flush carcinogens out of the body.

• **Consume more dietary fiber**—in the form of fresh fruits, vegetables and whole grains. Fiber speeds the passage of feces through the intestines, reducing the amount of time any carcinogens present in the body remain in contact with body tissues.

• **Avoid processed foods.** Potato chips, baked goods and other processed foods tend to contain lots of trans fatty acids, refined sugar and/or sodium. Animal studies have linked each of these substances to cancer.

A SHIELD AGAINST CANCER

From the standpoint of cancer avoidance, virtually all fruits, vegetables and grains are beneficial. But certain plant foods are special—because they contain cancer-preventing compounds.

Eight plant foods are particularly rich sources of these *phytochemicals*. They should be eaten every day.

• **Onions and garlic.** The same sulfur compounds that give these herbs their characteristic aromas protect cells against oxidative damage. That's the first step in the cancer process. Onions and garlic also block the formation of *nitrosamines*. These potent carcinogens are formed in the stomach following consumption of cured meats and other nitrate-containing foods.

• **Crucifers.** Broccoli, cauliflower, cabbage and brussels sprouts are rich sources of potent anticancer compounds known as glucosinolates.

Crucifer consumption has been linked with reduced risk for lung and colon cancer.

• **Nuts and seeds.** In addition to antioxidants, nuts and seeds contain *protease inhibitors*. These compounds help block the growth of blood vessels that tumors need to obtain nutrients from the bloodstream.

• **Whole grains.** Oats, wheat and other grains contain fiber that helps isolate cancer-causing compounds and remove them from the body.

Flaxseed, rye and millet are rich in *lignans*. These compounds act as weak estrogens, helping stymie the growth of breast cancer and other malignancies that are often estrogen-dependent.

• **Legumes.** Beans, peas and lentils are rich in fiber and *saponins,* compounds that block tumor growth by inhibiting DNA synthesis. Soybeans are the most potent anticancer legume.

• **Fruits.** In addition to vitamin C—a potent antioxidant—citrus fruits contain cancer-fighting compounds known as *monoterpenes* and *glutathione. Ellagic acid*—in blackberries, strawberries and raspberries—binds to carcinogens and thereby deactivates them.

• **Tomatoes.** Tomatoes get their red color from *lycopene,* a phytochemical that blocks the formation of carcinogens. Lycopene appears to be especially effective at preventing prostate cancer.

Important: Lycopene is more easily absorbed from cooked tomatoes than from raw tomatoes.

• **Umbellifers.** Carrots, parsley, celery and the spices cumin, anise, caraway and coriander are rich sources of phytochemicals. The *carotenoids* in carrots are strong antioxidants. Compounds found in celery boost the action of the carcinogen-deactivating enzyme *glutathione S-transferase.*

How to Use the New "Functional" Foods...What Works...What Doesn't Work

Clare M. Hasler, PhD, nutritionist and executive director of the functional foods for health program at the University of Illinois in Urbana-Champaign and Chicago.

Not long ago, it was enough that food provided nourishment. Now we clamor for so-called *functional* foods that protect us against serious illness.

We eat broccoli because it contains *glucosinolates,* compounds that reduce the risk for cancer. We drink green tea because it contains polyphenols, which inhibit tumor growth. And we favor soy foods because they contain heart-protective protein.

That's not all. There are now cholesterol-lowering margarines...and memory-boosting candy bars. Even ketchup is now being touted as cancer-protective.

WHY FUNCTIONAL FOODS? WHY NOW?

A functional food is any food or food ingredient that provides specific health benefits beyond simple nutrition.

Some functional foods occur naturally—broccoli, for example. But consumers seem to be especially excited about functional foods that contain special added ingredients.

Why the recent excitement over functional foods? For starters, people are more health-conscious than ever. As the population ages, there's greater interest in disease prevention. And it's increasingly clear that eating well has a dramatic impact on health and longevity.

In addition, federal regulations that govern labeling of prepared foods have been relaxed. It's now easier for food manufacturers to make health claims for their products. The terms "functional food" and "health food" aren't regulated *at all*. These monikers can be tacked onto anything from cereal to donuts—simply to boost sales.

Functional foods can be beneficial to your health. But not everything touted as healthful truly is. Some functional foods confer no special benefit. Others actually sabotage good nutrition.

SPECIFIC HEALTH CLAIMS

Specific disease-prevention benefits can be mentioned on food labels *only* if there is solid scientific evidence to support the purported benefits.

If a product carries such a label, it also means that a standard serving contains *enough* of the food component in question to make a meaningful difference.

The FDA has approved functional food claims for...

- **Oats.** Certain oat-containing products now bear labels saying they may reduce the risk of heart disease.

These products must contain at least 0.75 g of soluble fiber per serving. That's one-fourth of the amount that has been shown to lower cholesterol levels when consumed on a daily basis.

- **Psyllium.** Psyllium seed husks—a source of soluble fiber that's been shown to lower cholesterol levels—are found primarily in breakfast cereals. Any such food that contains at least 1.7 g of soluble fiber per serving can claim on the label that it reduces heart disease risk.

- **Soy protein.** Studies show that eating 25 g of soy protein daily lowers cholesterol enough to reduce heart disease risk by 9%. The FDA permits tofu, tempeh and other soy foods containing at least 6.25 g of soy protein per serving to indicate this fact on the label.

HEALTHY MARGARINE?

Last year saw the introduction of two cholesterol-lowering margarines. They're called *Benecol* and *Take Control.*

These products contain *plant stanol* or *sterol esters,* compounds proven to lower cholesterol significantly. Three servings daily of these margarines cut total cholesterol by 10% to 14%. The FDA permits these products to bear the claim that they "promote healthy cholesterol levels."

GENERAL CLAIMS

The FDA permits certain other foods to claim health benefits even with no proof that the benefits are real. How can you tell these foods from those with proven health benefits?

Again, *check labels.* Instead of specifying disease prevention, the labels refer in more general terms to body parts or physiological functions.

Example: A food label might mention "improves memory"..."for a healthy prostate"... "promotes a strong immune system."

There may be some truth to these claims. But even if there is, there's no guarantee that there's *enough* of the active ingredient to make a difference.

WHAT ABOUT HERBS?

Anyone who has gone food shopping in recent months has probably seen *ginkgo* candy bars (for better memory)…*echinacea-fortified* juice (for prevention of colds)…and corn chips containing *kava kava,* which are said to promote relaxation.

Before you purchase these foods, keep in mind that…

•**Medicinal herbs generally must be taken for weeks or months** to be effective. Even then, they don't always provide any benefit.

•**The amount of the herb in such products** is usually too small to allow for any significant effect.

•**Candy bars and chips typically contain large amounts of unhealthful sugar,** salt and/or fat.

If you want to take ginkgo, kava kava, etc., supplements are a better bet than snack foods.

USING FUNCTIONAL FOODS

Even those functional foods with a strong claim to health benefits are beneficial *only* if they're part of a healthful diet. That means little fat, lots of dietary fiber and five to 11 servings of fruits and vegetables daily.

No matter how appealing the special ingredient may be, keep the big picture in mind. Ketchup contains the natural pigment *lycopene,* which seems to reduce the risk for prostate cancer. But slather it on a jumbo order of fries, and the net effect on your health is negative.

Ultimately, functional foods should be thought of as an adjunct to other health-promoting strategies and treatments that you employ for optimal well-being.

Peanuts May Be Heart-Healthy After All

Health-conscious individuals have long shunned peanuts because of their high fat content.

New finding: Levels of LDL (bad) cholesterol and triglycerides were lower among healthy men and women who regularly ate peanuts, peanut butter or peanut oil than among people who ate a low-fat diet but didn't eat peanut products.

Theory: Like olive oil, peanuts are a good source of heart-healthy monounsaturated fat.

Penny Kris-Etherton, PhD, RD, professor of nutrition, Pennsylvania State University, University Park.

Heart Attack Prevention Secrets: Low-Tech Strategies Are Highly Effective

David Heber, MD, PhD, director of the Center for Human Nutrition at the University of California, Los Angeles, School of Medicine. He is author of *Natural Remedies for a Healthy Heart.* Avery.

Even with all the recent advances in cardiology, natural strategies continue to be useful tools for preventing heart attack—and often the only ones needed.

LOWERING CHOLESTEROL

Atorvastatin (Lipitor) and other cholesterol-lowering "statin" drugs are highly effective at lowering elevated cholesterol levels.

But statins can cause nausea, muscle aches, insomnia and other side effects. For this reason, it's a good idea to explore dietary strategies for keeping cholesterol levels down.

Some of the cholesterol in our bodies comes from eggs, whole milk, meat and other animal food sources. But most is produced by the body itself.

What determines how much cholesterol your body makes? Dietary fat is key. The more fat you consume—particularly saturated fat—the more cholesterol your body makes.

CUTTING OUT THE FAT

The average American gets 40% of his/her calories in the form of fat. The American Heart Association recommends cutting this back to 30%. *But for most people, that's still too high to reduce cholesterol.*

To have a significant impact on cholesterol levels, you must get no more than 20% of your total calories from fat. *To do this, take steps to eliminate fatty foods from your diet...*

●**Oil-based salad dressings.** Switch to a mixture of mustard and balsamic vinegar, rice vinegar or wine vinegar.

●**Butter, margarine and mayonnaise.** Use broth or wine for sautéing. Use cooking spray to keep food from sticking to pans.

Whenever possible, eat bread while it's still warm. That way, it's moist even without a fatty spread. Spread jam or roasted garlic on your toast instead of butter.

●**Red meat.** Substitute white-meat chicken or turkey...or give up meat altogether. Recent studies show that replacing animal proteins with tofu, tempeh and other soy foods can reduce cholesterol levels by up to 8%. That translates into a 16% reduction in heart attack risk.

●**Farm-raised fatty fish, including catfish, trout and salmon.** Substitute low-fat fish, such as snapper, halibut, shellfish or tuna packed in water.

●**Whole or low-fat milk and cheese.** Choose skim milk. While reduced-fat cheeses are available, it's better to avoid even these varieties. They often contain up to 70% of the fat found in ordinary cheese.

●**Egg noodles.** Use rice or pasta instead.

●**Baked goods.** Commercially baked cookies, pies and crackers tend to be high in fat. Better to stick with homemade baked goods made with applesauce instead of oil. Applesauce can be substituted cup for cup for oil.

THE IMPORTANCE OF FIBER

The undigestible part of fruits and vegetables, fiber helps lower cholesterol levels by promoting excretion of cholesterol-rich bile acids. You should be getting 25 g to 35 g of dietary fiber each day. That's 15 g to 25 g more than the average American gets.

To boost your fiber intake...

●**Have a bowl of oatmeal or another high-fiber cereal as part of each breakfast.** Look for cereals that contain at least 8 g of fiber per bowl.

●**Consume five to 11 servings of fruits and vegetables a day.** Good choices are brussels sprouts, broccoli, carrots, tomatoes, bananas, oranges and berries.

SUPPLEMENTS

Cholesterol forms artery-obstructing deposits in the coronary arteries only if it has been oxidized. Antioxidant nutrients such as vitamins C and E interrupt the oxidation process.

It's hard to get enough antioxidants from diet alone. For this reason, it's a good idea to take 400 international units (IU) of vitamin E each day, plus 500 mg of vitamin C.

Folic acid serves primarily to lower levels of *homocysteine*, an amino acid now thought to be a risk factor for heart disease. Consider taking 400 micrograms (mcg) of folic acid each day.

Garlic seems to cut cholesterol and lower blood pressure, too. Consider taking two to four 500-mg garlic capsules each day.

WHEN STATINS ARE NEEDED

If your total cholesterol remains above 240 after 12 weeks of this natural heart-health plan, you may need to take a statin. Ask your doctor.

If your cholesterol is between 200 and 240, however, you may be better off taking *Cholestin*. This over-the-counter remedy—derived from a yeast that grows on rice—is a modern formulation of an ancient Chinese remedy called *Xuezhikang*.

Cholestin is chemically similar to *lovastatin* (Mevacor). Like lovastatin, it is quite effective at lowering cholesterol levels.

In a study done at four Beijing hospitals, 324 patients taking Xuezhikang saw an average cholesterol reduction of 23%. This finding has been corroborated by researchers in the US.

Unlike lovastatin and other statins, Cholestin is unlikely to cause side effects. Only 3% of the people who use it report even minor discomfort, and less than 1% discontinue Cholestin because of adverse effects.

Bonus: Cholestin costs about $20 for a one-month supply. A one-month supply of lovastatin runs about $185.

Caution: Cholestin should not be taken by women who are pregnant or nursing. If you have heart disease or liver disease—or if you are taking any medication regularly—consult your doctor.

STRESS REDUCTION

Stress spurs the release of adrenaline-like chemicals that raise blood pressure and make the heart beat faster. This extra workload raises the risk for heart attack, even if your cholesterol level is low. *That's why stress reduction is a crucial part of any heart-health program...*

●**Avoid stressful situations.** Keep a diary of the stressors in your life. Think about how you could change each situation—or your response—to ease the wear on your cardio-vascular system.

Example: To avoid heavy traffic, you might try leaving for work earlier...or listening to relaxing music as you drive.

●**Find ways to refresh yourself between stressful episodes.** Gardening, reading, yoga or even something as simple as stopping briefly to breathe deeply when tension builds can be very effective.

In addition to stress relief, regular workouts bring marked reductions in cholesterol levels and blood pressure. They promote weight loss, too, helping to reduce the heart's workload even more.

Exercise needn't be strenuous. One brisk 30-minute walk per day is enough to reap most of the benefits. Check with your doctor before starting an exercise program.

Dressings Made with Soybean Oil Can Help Reduce Risk of Heart Attack

Conclusion from the ongoing health study of more than 76,000 nurses: Those who consumed more than five tablespoons a week of soy-oil-based salad dressing had only half as many fatal heart attacks as those who rarely used dressing. Researchers believe that the reason for the lower number of heart attacks is the protective effect of alpha-linolenic acid, an omega-3 fatty acid found in soybean oil, a key ingredient in most salad dressings.

Walter Willett, MD, chairman of the Department of Nutrition, Harvard University School of Public Health, Boston.

OJ for Your Cholesterol

Drinking orange juice can increase the amount of "good" (HDL) cholesterol in your body. When researchers gave people with high blood cholesterol levels orange juice daily for three months, increasing the amount until they were drinking three glasses a day in the third month, they found that the amount of HDL cholesterol in their blood increased by more than 21%. Five weeks later, when the subjects were back on their original diets, their HDL was still at the elevated level.

Elzbieta M. Kurowska, PhD, a research associate in the department of biochemistry at the University of Western Ontario in London.

Chocolate Boosts Longevity

Men who eat just a few pieces each month live nearly a year longer than those who don't. Antioxidant compounds in chocolate—similar to those found in red wine—get the credit, say researchers.

British Medical Journal.

 # Does Your Cookware Boost Your Intake of Iron?

Stainless steel cookware boosts the iron content of some foods an average of 14%.

Recent study: Iron leached into scrambled eggs, hamburgers, stir-fried chicken breast and pancakes...but not into rice, green beans or medium-thick white sauce.

Six percent of Americans are believed to have too little iron in their bodies, while 1% are believed to have too much. Either condition can be dangerous. If you're unsure of your iron status, ask a doctor about getting tested.

Helen C. Brittin, PhD, professor of food and nutrition, Texas Tech University, Lubbock.

Sugar-Free Soda

Sugar-free diet soda harms your teeth. Diet soda is highly acidic and can eat away tooth enamel over time. People who sip sugar-free soft drinks all day can damage their teeth to the point where they need significant repair. *More damaging:* When they sip drinks without eating food, or have an otherwise dry mouth. *Reason:* Acid residue from the soda stays on the teeth longer. *Antidote:* Rinse with water after drinking any soda.

Sheldon Nadler, DMD, a dentist in private practice in New York.

Eye Self-Defense

Macular degeneration risk is higher in individuals whose diets are low in *lutein* and *zeaxanthin.*

Foods rich in these carotenoids include eggs, grits, corn bread, orange juice, spinach, broccoli, orange peppers, squash, pumpkin, kiwi fruit and red grapes.

A breakdown of cells in the retina, macular degeneration is a leading cause of blindness in individuals age 40 or older.

Alan C. Bird, MD, professor of clinical ophthalmology, University College, London. His study of the carotenoid content of foods was published in the *British Journal of Ophthalmology,* University of Aberdeen Medical School, Foresterhill, Aberdeen, Scotland AB25 2ZD.

All About Genetically Engineered Foods

Sheldon Krimsky, PhD, professor of urban and environmental policy at Tufts University in Medford, MA. He is author of *Hormonal Chaos: The Scientific and Social Origins of the Environmental Endocrine Hypothesis* (Johns Hopkins University Press) and *Agricultural Biotechnology and the Environment* (University of Illinois Press).

Some nutrition experts and geneticists have expressed concern that genetically engineered foods will have unintended, and dangerous, side effects.

To learn more about the potential dangers, we spoke at length with biotechnology specialist Sheldon Krimsky, PhD…

●**What exactly is genetic engineering?** It's a technique for snipping individual genes from one organism—plant, animal or microbe—and slipping them into another. This is done to introduce new traits or to enhance existing traits in crops.

One common goal of genetic engineering is to render crops resistant to attack by insects and the herbicides applied to control weeds.

Another goal is to lengthen the timespan that fruits and vegetables stay fresh. The *Flavr Savr* tomato, which made headlines when it was introduced in 1993, contained a gene that suppresses *polygalacturonase,* an enzyme that causes ripening.

●**Are genetically engineered foods safe to eat?** There's no evidence to suggest that genetically altered foods are harmful—or that they're less nutritious than their unaltered counterparts.

However, there is no compelling evidence that they're safe either. That's because food producers are not required to conduct safety tests on genetically engineered foods which they deem to be equivalent to the natural foods from which they are derived.

Perhaps of greatest concern is the use of genetically engineered *bovine growth hormone* (BGH), which is widely used in the dairy industry to increase cows' milk production.

Cows given BGH are more likely than other cows to develop mastitis, an infection of the udders.

Preliminary research involving animals suggests that drinking milk from cows treated with BGH causes high levels of *insulin-like growth factor* (IGF-1), which are linked to higher cancer risk.

Also, since infections are more common among cows that have been given genetically engineered BGH, they receive more antibiotics.

If dairy farmers could ensure that these powerful drugs didn't get into the human food supply, this might not matter. But antibiotics do slip through.

Widespread use of antibiotics—by doctors as well as food producers—has contributed to the surge in antibiotic-resistant streptococcal infections and other bacterial infections.

●**What can I do to protect myself?** Given what we now know, it's prudent to buy dairy products from producers who don't use BGH.

This information is sometimes included on carton labels. I look for it when I buy milk.

●**Which other foods are likely to have been genetically modified?** Today, nearly 60% of soybeans sold in the US have been genetically modified using gene-splicing techniques.

Other crops whose DNA has been altered include apples, broccoli, cranberries and peanuts. These are not yet on the market, but may be soon.

Except for soybeans, corn and some varieties of tomatoes and potatoes, few "whole" foods on the market have been genetically modified.

It's difficult to avoid genetically modified soybeans because they're an ingredient in so many different products. I don't even bother looking for it on the label.

I do try to avoid genetically engineered foods when doing so is feasible. I buy organic produce because I know that organic trade organizations do not certify foods that have been genetically modified. And I buy free-range chicken because I know that it hasn't been treated with hormones.

If you don't have access to organic foods—or prefer not to pay the premium price—consider buying produce at a local farmers' market.

Small farms are less likely than large growers to use genetically modified seeds.

●**Isn't gene-swapping a problem for those with food allergies?** It can be. The FDA now requires food producers to alert consumers when a genetically engineered food contains a known allergen.

In one highly publicized case, a company was considering transferring a gene from a Brazil nut into a soybean. Then a study showed that individuals allergic to Brazil nuts also became allergic to the genetically modified soybeans. Ultimately, the company did not market the soybean.

Currently, there is no required testing for new allergens created by genetically modified foods. Consequently, as genetic engineering becomes more common, people may find themselves experiencing allergies to foods that never gave them problems before.

●**Do genetically engineered foods taste different?** Food producers say there's no difference, but I'm not so sure.

Once I asked my students to do a blindfolded taste-test on two tomatoes, one of which had been genetically modified. The genetically engineered tomato looked fantastic, but it wasn't nearly as tasty. Some students said it tasted like cardboard.

With other foods, you may never notice the difference.

Secrets from Hollywood For Getting in Shape Fast

Greg Isaacs, director of corporate fitness at Warner Bros. Movie Studios, Burbank, CA. He is author of *The Ultimate Lean Routine*. Summit.

As a trainer who works with actors and actresses—some of the most body-conscious people in the world—I have found that they aren't very different from you and me.

Like average people, actors eat out of emotion…have sedentary jobs…often dislike exercising…have crazy work schedules…and are frequently exposed to tempting, high-calorie foods.

What makes them different is that their jobs depend on being fit and trim. That gives them a very special incentive to get in shape and stay that way.

You don't have to be a celebrity to have a body like one. You just have to be willing to work out like one. I recommend the following exercises to all of my clients.

Important: For each exercise, do three sets of eight to 12 repetitions. Perform each of the exercises slowly. You'll strengthen your muscles faster and with fewer repetitions this way. Increase the weight of your dumbbells as soon as an exercise becomes easy for you to perform.

SCULPTED ARMS AND SHOULDERS

Do push-ups. Position yourself on all fours on the floor. Keep your upper body and your elbows straight and your hands beneath your shoulders.

Either bend your legs at the knees and cross your ankles—the easiest way to do push-ups—or balance on your toes for the greatest benefit.

Lower your chest to the floor using only your arms. Then raise your chest off the floor using only your arms until your elbows are straight again—but not locked. Repeat.

BULGING BICEPS

Do a biceps curl using an eight- to 10-pound weight. Stand or sit. Stick your chin up and your chest out. Keep your elbows in—close to your sides—palms forward. Don't cheat by letting your elbow swing back and forth as you lift the weight or by leaning forward to begin a lift. Curl up one weight with a "one-two" count. Pause briefly. Lower and repeat with the other arm.

WELL-DEFINED CHEST

Do the dumbbell fly. Lie on your back on a flat bench with your feet on the floor and an eight- to 10-pound dumbbell in each hand.

Slightly bend your arms, and place them directly out to your sides. Keep your palms up and the dumbbells in line with your chest. Let the dumbbells pull your arms down so you feel a slight stretch.

In an arcing motion, bring both the dumbbells together over your upper chest with your palms facing together. Slowly lower the dumbbells, and then repeat.

RIPPLING BACK

Do a one-arm dumbbell row with the weights described for the biceps curl.

Lean over a flat bench, and place your left knee on the bench and your left hand at the top with your fingers curling over the side of the bench. Position yourself so your back is flat. Place your right foot securely on the floor. Hold a dumbbell in your right hand.

Fully extend your arm down with your palm facing your foot. Pull the dumbbell up to your hip, rotating your palm inward as you do so. Bring your elbow as far upward as you can. Slowly return to the starting position. Repeat on each side.

WASHBOARD STOMACH

Do leg lifts. Lie on the floor on your back, and place your hands behind your head to elevate it. Lift your legs up to a 75° to 90° angle. Using your abdominal muscles, roll your buttocks off the floor, keeping your legs up.

Pull your elbows in toward your knees. Do *not* jerk your neck. Then slowly ease your buttocks back to the ground.

Simpler: If you can't lift your buttocks with your legs held up, do the exercise with your knees at a 45° angle.

FIRM BUTTOCKS

Squats are the answer. Stand against a wall. Elevate your heels on a book (or books) two inches thick. Bend your knees and slide down until you reach a sitting position. Keep your back straight. Hold for a few seconds. Slowly come back up.

Squeeze your buttocks muscles as you return to the starting position. Don't lock your knees. Repeat.

STRONG THIGHS

Do pliés—the ballet exercise. They'll also tone your abdominal muscles. Stand with your legs shoulder-width apart, toes pointed outward—what's known in ballet as second position.

Keeping your back, buttocks and hips aligned, bend your knees and go down as far as you can without lifting your heels off the floor.

As soon as you reach the bottom of your plié, slowly return to the starting position. Squeeze your inner thighs as you raise your body.

SHAPELY LEGS

Do walking lunges down a hallway or outside. Stand erect. Take a large step forward. Bend your knees and lower your body. Keep the knee of your forward leg above the ankle, and let the rear knee almost touch the floor.

Return to an upright position, and drag the trailing leg forward. Press the heel of your front leg down as you come up, and squeeze your buttocks together as your bring your legs back to the starting position.

Repeat on each leg.

DROP POUNDS FAST

The basic fundamentals of weight loss never change. You have to expend more calories than you consume. This becomes harder as you age because your metabolic rate slows.

Best: Jump-start your day with 45 minutes or more of cardiovascular exercise. You'll not only burn calories, you'll also work off some of your stored energy so it won't be converted to fat.

And…do strength-training exercises twice a week. As you build muscle, you'll raise your metabolic rate and burn more fat—even when you're resting—since muscle cells burn more calories than fat cells do.

Important: Don't be lured by fad diets, such as the currently popular high-protein plans. The best way to lose pounds fast, safely and for good is to follow a diet high in fruits, vegetables and whole grains…and low in fat.

Start with one set of 10 to 15 crunches. Gradually build up to two sets, and wean yourself from supporting your neck.

Amazing: You may feel yourself getting stronger within one week.

Warning: Do crunches slowly to protect your back. If you are prone to back or neck problems, see a physician first.

Bob Greene is an exercise physiologist, certified personal trainer and best-selling author. His latest book is *Keep the Connection: Choices for a Better Body and a Healthier Life.* Hyperion.

Beware: Caffeine And Exercise

Consuming caffeine before exercising can be dangerous. Systolic blood pressure (the first number in a reading) jumps an average of seven points—and sometimes much more—from the caffeine in two six-ounce cups of coffee or 36 ounces of cola. Moderate walking transiently increases systolic blood pressure 12 to 18 points. Combined, these increases may cause trouble for people with high blood pressure.

Self-test: Take your blood pressure just before having a caffeinated beverage and again 30 minutes later. If the systolic reading jumps 10 or more points, ask your doctor if you should avoid caffeine before working out—or altogether.

Leonard A. Kaminsky, PhD, professor of physical education, Ball State University, Muncie, IN.

For Great Abs

Important exercise to do every day—abdominal crunches. They strengthen the muscles in the abdomen, back and neck…and help align the spine. Floor exercises are best—abdominal rolling machines don't exercise the neck.

Step-by-step: Lie on the floor—or a mat or a rug—with knees bent, feet flat on the floor. Slowly raise your head about six inches, supporting your neck with one or both hands …gently lower your head back to the floor.

If You Think Osteoarthritis Is Inevitable, You're Wrong! Read On…

Brenda D. Adderly, MHA, coauthor of *The Arthritis Cure Fitness Solution.* Lifeline Press.

Experts now believe that osteoarthritis (OA) of the hands, hips, knees and other joints is actually brought on by a chemical change in the cartilage of the affected joint, caused in part by important nutrients being flushed out of the cartilage.

This makes the cartilage less spongy and more vulnerable to inflammation.

One way to reverse this chemical change is to take two specific food supplements—glucosamine and chondroitin sulfate—on a daily basis. These over-the-counter nutritional supplements (available in pharmacies and nutrition stores everywhere) help promote the growth of healthy cartilage tissue, reversing arthritic symptoms.

In addition to a daily dose of these two supplements, the main thing you can do to ward off the symptoms of OA is to exercise…

• **Exercise helps you maintain a healthful weight,** which puts less stress on your joints as you stand and walk.

• **Exercise encourages the flow of nutrient-rich lubricating fluids** into the cartilage tissue of the joints—helping to repair arthritis-related damage caused by the loss of nutrients.

• **Exercise also strengthens the muscles around your joints,** providing added support and cushioning for the joints themselves.

My *Arthritis Cure Fitness Plan* has three parts to its exercise program—stretching, strength building and cardiovascular workouts.

STRETCHING

Most people with osteoarthritis have limited flexibility and range of motion in the affected joints. This makes it easy to strain adjoining muscles, and puts more stress on other parts of the body that compensate for the inflexible areas.

That's why stretching exercises, done five days a week, should be the first step in your fitness program.

Try starting with just one of the stretches listed below. Do it for a couple of days, then add a stretch or two…then more.

You'll find these exercises improve your flexibility and reduce the discomfort of muscle exertion.

Chest stretch: In standing position, clasp your hands together behind your back. Next, pull back your shoulders while lifting your hands a few inches higher, as though you wanted to flaunt your favorite necklace or necktie. Your chest will automatically expand. Hold for 10 to 30 seconds.

Back and torso stretch: Lie flat on your back, with your lower back pressed to the floor. Bend both knees, and then lower them both slowly to your left side, so your right knee and ankle rest on top of your left knee and ankle.

Spread both arms out to either side, pushing your shoulders as flat as possible, and turn your head in the opposite direction from your knees.

Relax and hold this position for 30 seconds, feeling the stretch in your back and legs. Then switch sides and repeat.

Upper arm and back stretch: Cross your right arm over your chest and rest the upper part of it on your left palm, so that your left hand completely supports your right arm.

Hold the "lazy arm" and gently pull it across your body until you feel a stretch in your upper right shoulder. Hold for 10 to 30 seconds, then switch sides and repeat.

Hamstring stretch: Sit on the edge of a sturdy chair with your hands on your hips. Straighten your right leg in front of you, keeping your left leg bent.

Lean forward from the hips, pushing your chest toward your knee until you feel a good stretch in the back of your right thigh, knee and calf. Hold for 10 to 30 seconds, then switch sides and repeat.

Buttocks stretch: Lying flat on the floor, grasp your right leg behind the knee with both hands, keeping your left leg straight.

Gently and slowly pull the knee as close to your chest as possible, feeling the stretch in your lower back and buttocks. Hold 10 to 30 seconds, then switch legs and repeat.

Calf stretch: Step forward with your left leg as if you're about to start a running race. Keeping your right leg straight and your right heel flat on the floor, bend your left knee slightly and shift your weight onto your left leg. You should feel a stretch in your right calf as you lean forward. Hold 10 to 30 seconds, then switch legs and repeat.

STRENGTH BUILDING

Developing better muscle strength is the most important part of the Arthritis Cure Fitness Plan. Strong muscles take weight off arthritic joints and also act as shock absorbers, reducing pain when you move about. Muscle strengthening has the added benefit of building bone mass.

The following exercises can be done with or without weights. You'll know you're at the right resistance level when you feel a slight burning sensation in the muscle you're working after about 10 repetitions.

For best results, these exercises should be done at least three times a week.

Shoulder and biceps: Holding dumbbells or full cans of food in each hand (or with your hands empty, if cans are too heavy), bend your elbows so your fists are even with your shoulders. Slowly raise both arms straight over your head. Do eight to 10 repetitions of this movement.

Shoulders and triceps (back of upper arms): Sitting in a sturdy armchair, grasp both arms of the chair and push yourself up until you're half-standing, using only your arms—no leg power.

Repeat this "chair pushup" eight to 10 times.

This exercise should be avoided by people with arthritic hands or wrists.

Quadriceps I (front of the thighs and lower back): Lie on your back with both knees bent. Pushing from your feet, raise your buttocks three or four inches off the floor. Hold this position for 10 seconds, then slowly release and lie flat for five seconds. Repeat eight to 12 times.

Quadriceps II (front of the thighs): Sit in a chair and place the handles of a plastic grocery bag containing one or two full cans of food over your right ankle.

Lift your right leg straight out in front of you, lifting the bag off the ground, and hold for a count of five. Slowly lower your leg back down to the ground, then repeat up to 10 times, if possible. Switch legs and repeat.

CARDIOVASCULAR WORKOUTS

Cardiovascular (aerobic) workouts don't merely strengthen your heart and circulatory system—they also bring sinovial fluid into the joints and build muscular strength and endurance. They also give additional support to your joints. They're the best way to keep your weight at a healthful level.

Begin by doing whatever you can, even just a block or two of walking at a comfortable pace (slow is fine). Add a small increment of distance each time you work out, until you're up to a half hour or more.

Cardiovascular workouts should be done two or three times a week, alternating day to day with strength-building workouts. *Aerobic activities...*

●**Walking.** Especially good for those with arthritis in the hips, knees and ankles.

●**Swimming.** Good for improving flexibility and decreasing arthritis-related pain—also recommended for people with OA who are overweight.

●**Water aerobics.** This can be as simple as walking in the shallow end of the pool. Many people with arthritis find it beneficial to alternate a few minutes of water aerobics with a few minutes of easy swimming.

●**Bicycling.** This activity is especially good for people with arthritis in the knees.

●**Aerobics classes.** Good for arthritis in all parts of the body.

●**Ballroom dancing.** Good for arthritis in all parts of the body.

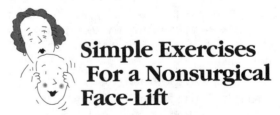

Simple Exercises For a Nonsurgical Face-Lift

Judith Olivia, national spokesperson for Advanced Dermatology Care, an organization that lectures to medical professionals on advancements in the field, and creator of the videos *Face Aerobics and Advanced Face Aerobics.* Available through her company, Judith Olivia Inc., Box 181706, Casselberry, FL 32718.

Face-lifts make the skin tighter, but the benefits are often temporary because the underlying muscles continue to sag.

Then a second—or even a third—face-lift is often necessary.

Free and painless alternative: Strengthen and firm the facial muscles. Facial exercises pull the muscles *upward* so that the skin looks firm and youthful.

These exercises hit the main trouble spots. Do each exercise once a day for two weeks. After that, weekly workouts are fine. Facial muscles are small, so you'll see improvements quickly.

UNDER-EYE BAGS

Using both hands, gently place one forefinger under each eye, just below the lower lid. Use the muscles of the lower lids to try to lift the weight of your fingers. Do this exercise 20 times, twice a day.

SAGGING JOWLS

Lift your bottom lip so it covers the top lip. Tilt your head up slightly, and smile toward the tops of the ears. Hold for a count of 10, then relax. Repeat five times.

You'll know you're doing it right when you feel a tingle in the muscles of the jaw and throat.

Male advantage: Men move their faces around almost every day when they are shaving, so this exercise is less important for men than it is for women.

DOUBLE CHIN

Lie on your back, with your knees slightly bent and feet flat on the floor. Slowly raise your head and tuck your chin against your chest. Hold this position for a second, then slowly lower your head. Try to repeat it 10 times at first...and gradually work up to 50 repetitions.

DROOPY EYELIDS

Using both hands, put a forefinger on each eyebrow, exerting enough pressure so the eyebrows won't move easily. Try to close your eyes, working against the resistance of your fingers. Don't scrunch your forehead—just try to push the upper lashes into the lower ones as hard as you can. Repeat between five and 20 times, holding for a count of five each time.

FOREHEAD LINES

Cover your forehead with the palm of one hand, holding it firmly. Try to push the forehead muscle toward the top of the head, pushing against the resistance of your hand. Hold for a second, then relax. Repeat 10 times.

Bonus: This exercise not only tightens skin on the forehead—it also helps smooth frown and worry lines. It trains the forehead muscles to work together, instead of rippling.

LOOSE THROAT

Flex throat muscles—as a weight lifter's neck would look straining to lift weights. Hold for a minute, then relax.

Smarter Outdoor Exercise

Where and when you exercise might be more important than the exercise itself. High ozone levels make it unhealthful to breathe outdoor air for more than one hour. Those levels are highest between 7 am and 9 am...and 4 pm and 7 pm. *Best:* Exercise outdoors at other times. *The 12 cities with the highest ozone levels:* Los Angeles, Houston, New York, Chicago, Baltimore, Philadelphia, Milwaukee, Boston, El Paso, Washington, DC, Atlanta, San Francisco.

Lawrence Schwartz, registered nutritional adviser and certified personal trainer, Dallas, and author of *The Professional's Guide to Fitness.* Taylor.

5

Natural Healing

Norman Ford Tells How to Age-Proof Your Body...Naturally

 ur bodies are designed by nature to age at a very slow pace. We should stay strong and healthy well into our 80s and beyond. *But three aspects of our modern lifestyle speed up the process...*

- **Sedentary living.**
- **A high-fat, low-fiber diet.**
- **Worry, anxiety and stress.**

If you begin to address these three core areas, you can maintain a biological age that's many years younger than your chronological age. Scientists now believe that chronological age is actually irrelevant. An 80-year-old can have the body of a 40-year-old—and be virtually disease-proof—by adopting a healthy, active, stress-free lifestyle.

In fact, when researchers at the Human Nutrition Research Center (HNRC) at Tufts University established a number of "biomarkers" to measure aging, they concluded that declines in every biomarker were caused primarily by a high-fat diet and lack of aerobic and strength training exercise.

Fortunately, they also found these declines could be easily reversed in a fairly short time, simply by changing diet and lifestyle.

AEROBIC EXERCISE

Many people think it's "natural" to lose strength and fitness as they get older. But this decline has nothing to do with age...it starts the minute we put our feet up and start to take life easy.

Only about 10% of Americans exercise enough to improve their health. The rest have abandoned all strenuous exercise, and a slow, inexorable decline is under way.

But this decline isn't inevitable. At any age, a program of regular exercise will lower your

---

Norman D. Ford, writer, fitness enthusiast and anti-aging expert. At age 78, he is a dedicated long-distance cyclist. He is author of many health books, including *18 Natural Ways to Look & Feel Half Your Age*. Keats Publishing.

biological age in a few short months—even if you haven't exercised for years.

Example: The human cardiovascular system has evolved to the point where it can function in top condition for at least 100 years. Studies have shown that a healthy 90-year-old heart can pump blood just as effectively as the heart of a 20-year-old. Yet without exercise, the average 65-year-old has lost 30% to 40% of his/her aerobic capacity.

To begin restoring the health of your heart, lungs and arteries—and maintaining it—I recommend doing some aerobic exercise every other day. This could be walking, swimming, bicycling or other brisk, rhythmic movement.

Start by doing 20 minutes, and build up until you're doing four to five miles of walking, or an hour of swimming or cycling. This will take a few weeks to a few months.

When you exercise, move briskly, but don't push yourself so hard that you feel fatigued.

You can begin this age-proofing technique —and start reaping benefits—immediately.

Hundreds of studies have shown that regular aerobic exercise reduces the risk of type II diabetes, raises your HDL ("good") cholesterol while lowering dangerous LDL cholesterol, reduces brain neuron loss, increases bone density and lowers the risk of breast or prostate cancer. It also creates tremendous increases in energy, stamina and endurance. And the more out of shape you are, the more rapid your progress.

STRENGTH TRAINING

Until the early 1990s, most exercise physiologists focused on aerobics as the principal anti-aging exercise. But they now believe that strength training may be even more important than aerobics because strength training builds more muscle mass in a way that aerobics can't.

Above everything else, this muscle mass is the key to youthfulness. After scores of tests and surveys, the HNRC concluded that loss of muscle mass and strength is the underlying cause of almost every sign of aging. Muscle mass is also the key to shedding fat, since large, strong muscles burn more calories—24 hours a day, even when you're not exercising.

A thrice-weekly schedule of strength training—done on the days between your aerobic workouts—should be at the core of your anti-aging program.

Join a health club that has weight machines and instructors who can show you the right exercises.

I recommend doing nine exercises, focusing on these muscle groups: Biceps, pectorals, triceps, abdominals, lower back, quadriceps, upper back, shoulders and hamstrings.

For each exercise, find the maximum amount you can lift one time, then use 80% of that weight and lift it smoothly, up to eight or nine times in a row. It's OK if you can only do three or four repetitions. Once you can lift a weight 10 times or more, you'll need to increase the weight.

Begin with one exercise per muscle group, then gradually add an additional set or two as you gain strength and stamina.

EAT A LOW-FAT DIET WITH LOTS OF FRUITS AND VEGETABLES

Scientists now believe that most premature aging is caused by disease, mainly due to free radicals—electrically charged particles that wreak havoc on our cells by causing toxic chain reactions. Wrinkled skin, clogged arteries and weak immune response have all been linked to free-radical damage.

One of the main causes of free-radical build-up is a high-fat diet. Fat molecules produce free radicals as they're oxidized. If you eat too many fat molecules, these free radicals cause plaque to build up in your arteries, and can lead to heart disease, cancer and other diseases.

Fortunately there's a natural antidote. Fruits and vegetables contain hundreds of compounds called phytochemicals, which work to prevent free-radical formation (which is why they're often called antioxidants).

The Framingham Heart Study found that increasing the amount of fruit and vegetables you eat greatly reduces your risk of heart attack.

These foods also tend to be high in fiber, which speeds digestion and may have anti-cancer benefits.

On the other hand, animal products—beef, eggs, fish, poultry, dairy products, etc.—contain no antioxidants, no fiber and no cancer-preventing chemicals. To age-proof your body against disease, cut down on these foods and increase your intake of fruits and vegetables.

FREE YOUR MIND

Whatever you can do to eliminate stress will also help stop the aging process. One way is to practice forgiveness. Being unable to forgive is a major cause of stress. *Other stress-busters...*

●**Progressive muscle relaxation.** Lie on a rug in semidarkness with a pillow under your head. Tense each muscle group in turn for about six seconds, then relax. You can cover your whole body in about 90 seconds with this method. Next, concentrate on mentally warming your hands. With practice, you can increase the blood flow to your body in just a few minutes.

●**Watch TV as little as possible.** Television is the most passive, useless activity in which you can engage—yet half the US population sits hypnotized by the tube for up to four hours a day.

●**Use your mind actively and creatively.** The more you exercise your mind, the healthier and more alert you will be. Mental activity can even help speed up your physical reflexes!

Dr. Leo Galland Makes It Easy to Strengthen Your Body's Ability To Heal Itself

Leo Galland, MD, director of The Foundation for Integrated Medicine, 133 E. 73 St., Suite 308, New York 10021. He is author of *Power Healing*. Random House.

Unscientific as they were by modern standards, the ancients can teach us a lot about health.

The Greeks and others focused less on specific diseases than on harmony between the mind and body. Maintaining mind/body balance, they knew, keeps us strong. When it is disrupted, we fall prey to illness.

Today, we can have the best of both worlds —the insights of ancient wisdom bolstered by 20th-century science.

Power healing: The four key aspects of my concept of well-being are *relationships, diet, environment* and *detoxification*.

Strengthening these four pillars of healing will maintain the balance and harmony that protect against illness. If you're ill, these factors will work together with medical care to help you get better.

RELATIONSHIPS

In recent decades, evidence has grown that strong relationships are a potent force for health. *Example*: A California study found that marriage, close friendships and membership in church or community organizations lowered the overall death rate, as well as the risk of death from cancer, heart disease and stroke.

Good relationships strengthen your ability to deal with stress. The heart is under less strain and the immune system fights off disease and cancer better when you feel supported by friends and loved ones.

Social support makes you feel capable of doing positive things for yourself and your health.

The first step in strengthening this pillar of healing is to become aware of its importance. *How...*

●**Take stock.** How much time and energy do you devote to others? What can you do to nurture more gratifying relationships?

●**Make an effort to help others.** Volunteering (at a soup kitchen, hospital, school, museum) reduces stress and eases health problems. By giving to others, you give to yourself.

DIET AND LIFESTYLE

It should come as no surprise anymore that what you eat has great impact on your health, and that the standard American diet—high in fats, low in vegetables—is a recipe for serious illness.

You can strengthen this pillar of healing dramatically with *one simple step*. Eliminate— or at least *sharply reduce*—your consumption of the junk foods that make up 30% of the average American's calorie intake.

By avoiding processed foods—whose nutrients have been replaced by sugar, salt and shortening—you reduce the risk of heart disease and high blood pressure.

Healthful snacks: When you snack, choose raw vegetables, nuts and seeds rather than junk food.

Two nutrients deserve special attention...

•**Omega-3 fatty acids** have a positive impact on virtually every aspect of cell function. Their gradual disappearance from modern diets has been linked to diseases ranging from arthritis to depression.

Fish that are rich in omega-3s include salmon, albacore tuna and sardines. Flaxseed oil and flaxseed flour are the best vegetable sources.

•**Magnesium** regulates the enzyme reactions that support life in virtually every cell, but two-thirds of Americans don't get enough in their diets. Advancing age depletes the body of this mineral, as does stress. You probably need more magnesium if you suffer from irritability...palpitations...muscle tension or spasms.

Green vegetables (especially broccoli), beans, seeds and nuts are good sources of magnesium.

Lifestyle includes regular physical activity. You don't need to go to a gym. Just incorporate activity into your routine—by walking instead of driving the car, for instance.

ENVIRONMENT

Chemical and biological pollutants wreak havoc with the body, suppressing the immune system, damaging lungs and raising cancer risk, as well as causing minor health problems. Air pollution and toxic dumps are big culprits, *but the risk of exposure is greatest indoors...*

•**Don't permit anyone to smoke in your home.** Second-hand tobacco smoke increases cancer and heart disease risk and aggravates asthma. Carcinogenic tars cling to curtains and furniture.

•**Leave your shoes at the door.** Pesticides and other toxic wastes come in with you off the street, and are collected by carpets.

•**Fight molds.** They can cause allergy symptoms, eczema and asthma, as well as fatigue, joint pain and headache. Some secrete toxins that suppress the immune system. Use a dehumidifier to keep humidity below 50%...discard moldy food...ventilate basement and attic.

•**Ventilate your stove, heater and dryer properly.** These appliances produce toxic gases (carbon monoxide, nitrogen dioxide and formaldehyde). *Helpful*: A carbon monoxide detector. *Cost:* $50 to $80.

DETOXIFICATION

Your body has natural defenses against environmental pollutants as well as toxic substances produced by normal cell processes. The liver breaks these pollutants down, at which point they are excreted by the bowels and kidneys. *To enhance and support your body's detoxification efforts...*

•**Avoid over-the-counter medications when possible.** Many common drugs impair the liver's ability to break down toxic chemicals. Use natural substitutes.

Examples: *Acetaminophen* (Tylenol) depletes the body of *glutathione*, a key detoxification chemical that protects against cancer and boosts immune function. If you take Tylenol daily, work with your doctor to remedy the source of pain, rather than just treating the symptom. Avoid alcohol, which further depletes glutathione from the liver.

Cimetidine (Tagamet), *ranitidine* (Zantac) and similar drugs widely taken for heartburn impair liver function. Instead, learn strategies to avoid heartburn altogether—eat small, low-fat meals, at least three to four hours before lying down...take chewable calcium with each meal ...avoid alcohol and coffee.

•**Actively boost your body's natural detoxification capability.** Do this by consuming foods that neutralize carcinogens and other chemicals that damage cells.

Helpful: *Cruciferous* vegetables (such as broccoli, cabbage, brussels sprouts, cauliflower) and those containing *carotenoids* (such as carrots, sweet potatoes, tomatoes).

The herb milk thistle protects and improves the liver's efficiency.

The most toxic environment in your body is the digestive tract. Help your intestines expel toxins by eating fiber (fruits, vegetables, whole grains)...and add fermented foods (such as yogurt) to your diet, to maintain the healthy bowel bacteria that break down toxins.

Getting the Most Out of Herbal Medicines

Timothy McCall, MD, a New York City internist and author of *Examining Your Doctor: A Patient's Guide to Avoiding Harmful Medical Care*. Citadel Press.

Herbal medicine is going mainstream. Americans now spend $4 billion a year on herbal remedies, medical journals are publishing studies on herbs, and three pharmaceutical giants—including the manufacturer of One-A-Day vitamins—have launched their own lines of the remedies. Even Harvard is getting into the act. Recently, I traveled to Boston to attend a Harvard Medical School conference on alternative medicine, and it included lots of information about herbs.

I applaud these developments. It's true that a few herbs, including chaparral and comfrey, are too risky to be taken internally. In general, though, herbal remedies are safer than prescription drugs. Herbs also tend to cost less than conventional drugs, and many appear to be effective. But as with drugs, herbs must be used carefully. *Here's what I suggest:*

•**Get diagnosed first.** It's fine to try an herbal remedy for a minor ailment like the common cold or for chronic illnesses like arthritis that aren't life-threatening. But if you've begun experiencing a new symptom like fatigue or weight loss—either of which could point to a serious medical condition—it's best to see a physician to get a diagnosis first. Then you can make an informed decision about treatment.

•**Alert your doctor—and your pharmacist—before taking any herbal medicine.** That way, they can warn you about side effects and possible interactions with other treatments. Remember, herbs are essentially natural forms of conventional drugs. They have side effects and can interact with foods, other herbs and prescription and over-the-counter medications. Ginkgo biloba combined with aspirin, for example, increases the risk for internal bleeding.

•**Read labels carefully.** The Food and Drug Administration now requires every dietary supplement to have a "Supplement Facts" box on its label. This box makes it easier to compare products.

I recommend looking for "standardized" extracts. A standardized extract promises to deliver a specified amount of active ingredient. Since the FDA doesn't regulate ingredients in herbal products, the promise is only as good as the company that makes it. That's why it's important to buy herbal remedies made by a reputable manufacturer.

You should also look for the words "clinically proven" on the label. That assures you that the ginkgo, for example, is the same preparation that was found effective in studies. Be sure to consider what ailment the herb is clinically proven for. St. John's wort seems to be effective against mild to moderate depression. But there's no evidence that it works for weight loss.

•**Avoid herbs if you're pregnant—or might become pregnant.** This is especially critical during the first trimester. That's when the baby's internal organs are developing.

•**Do your own research.** Many doctors and pharmacists are doing their best to get up to speed on herbal medicine, but many remain uninformed.

If you take herbs with any regularity, it pays to invest in a book such as *Tyler's Honest Herbal* (Haworth Press) or the *Physicians' Desk Reference for Herbal Medicines* (Medical Economics). Another good resource is the Web site of the American Botanical Council at *www.herbalgram.org.*

The more you know about herbs, the more effectively you'll be able to use them. You might even be able to teach your doctors a thing or two that they didn't learn in medical school.

Herbal Remedies Help Control Asthma And Allergies

Combinations of various herbs—such as saiko, mao and others—are currently included in the national asthma-management guidelines in Japan. *In the US:* See a traditional Japanese or Chinese herbalist, most of whom practice under the title *Licensed Acupuncturist*

(LAC) or *Doctor of Oriental Medicine (OMD).* Talk to your doctor before taking any herbal therapy.

Satoshi Yoshida, MD, FACP, a physician and research fellow, department of pulmonary and critical care medicine at Harvard Medical School, Boston.

Herbal Cold Fighter

B*est herb for fighting off colds:* Larix, a powdery substance extracted from larch trees and available at health-food stores.

How to use: At the start of a cold or other upper-respiratory infection, drink one teaspoonful of Larix dissolved in juice or water. *Frequency:* Two or three times daily until symptoms disappear. There are no known side effects, but check with your doctor if you have a suppressed immune system.

Andrew Rubman, ND, associate professor of clinical medicine at College of Naturopathic Medicine, University of Bridgeport, CT.

Breathing Your Way To Better Health

Robert Fried, PhD, director of the Stress and Biofeedback Clinic of the Albert Ellis Institute in New York City. He is author of six books, including *Breathe Well, Be Well.* John Wiley & Sons.

E*veryone* knows that taking a deep breath is a great way to cool off when you're angry.

And any woman who has used Lamaze breathing during childbirth is aware that focusing on one's breath provides a welcome distraction from severe pain.

But few people realize that how you breathe day in and day out plays a key role in triggering—or preventing—chronic conditions. Among the conditions affected by breathing are high blood pressure...heart disease...migraines...and Raynaud's syndrome, a chronic circulatory disorder marked by uncomfortably cold hands and feet.

THE BREATH–BODY CONNECTION

The world is divided into two types of breathers...

•**Belly breathers** take slow, deep breaths, letting their abdomens rise with each inhalation and fall with each exhalation.

This form of breathing is ideal, but relatively few adults breathe this way.

•**Chest breathers** take rapid, shallow breaths. This form of breathing causes the body to expel too much carbon dioxide, adversely affecting how the blood carries oxygen to the organs and tissues.

To find out which kind of breather you are, sit comfortably and place your left hand on your chest, your right hand over your navel. Breathe normally for one minute. Note the movement of each hand as you inhale and exhale.

If your left hand is virtually motionless while your right hand moves out when you inhale and in when you exhale, you're a belly breather.

If your left hand rises noticeably—or if both hands move more or less simultaneously in a shallow motion—you're a chest breather.

Being a chest breather does *not* mean you're going to keel over anytime soon. But eventually, your health will suffer.

Reason: Chest breathing is less effective than belly breathing at introducing fresh, oxygenated air into the lower reaches of the lungs. That's where the tiny air sacs (alveoli) that absorb oxygen are most concentrated.

Less air reaching the alveoli means that less oxygen gets into the bloodstream with each breath. To get enough oxygen to meet the body's needs, these people must breathe rapidly.

Rapid breathing upsets the blood's normal acid-base balance (pH), which is measured on a scale that runs from zero to 14.

Ordinarily, blood has a pH of 7.38 (slightly alkaline). When blood pH climbs above that level, arteries constrict, impairing blood flow to all parts of the body.

Result: Increased susceptibility to high blood pressure...insomnia...anxiety...phobias ...Raynaud's syndrome...migraines...and, for heart patients, angina.

HOW TO BREATHE RIGHT

No matter how poor your current breathing habits may be, it's reassuring to know that each of us was born knowing how to breathe properly. And—it's surprisingly easy to re-learn proper breathing habits. *The keys...*

●**Stop sucking in your gut.** A flat stomach may be attractive, but clenching the abdominal muscles inhibits movement of the diaphragm. That's the sheetlike muscle separating the abdomen from the chest cavity.

Since the movement of the diaphragm is what causes the lungs to fill and empty, proper breathing is possible only if it can move freely.

●**Avoid tight clothing.** Like clenching your abdominal muscles, wearing overly tight clothing can restrict movement of the diaphragm.

●**Breathe through your nose.** Doing so makes hyperventilation almost impossible. The only time you should breathe through your mouth is during vigorous exercise.

●**Practice belly breathing.** At least twice a day—for about four minutes each time—sit in a comfortable chair with your left hand on your chest, your right hand on your abdomen.

As you inhale, use your left hand to press lightly against your chest to help keep it from rising. Allow your right hand to move outward as air fills your belly.

With each exhalation, slowly pull your abdomen back in as far as it will go without raising your chest. With practice, your body will find its own natural rhythm.

Good idea: Practice belly breathing when you're stuck in traffic, waiting in line, etc.—whenever and wherever you can. It's a good use for time that would otherwise be wasted. Once you get the hang of it, practice belly breathing without using your hands.

You may want to augment the effects of these practice sessions by combining belly breathing with...

●**Classical music.** Stick with slow compositions, such as Pachelbel's *Canon* or Bach's *Jesu, Joy of Man's Desiring.* As you breathe, imagine that you are inhaling the music...and that it is filling every space in your body.

●**Muscle relaxation.** Imagine that the tension in the muscles in your forehead is flowing out of your body with each exhalation. Do the same thing, breath by breath, with your jaw, neck, shoulders, arms, hands, legs and feet.

●**Imagery.** Close your eyes, and imagine yourself standing on a sunny beach. Feel the warmth of the sun. As you inhale, imagine the surf rolling toward your feet. As you exhale, picture the surf rolling back out to sea.

●**Do on-the-spot breathing therapy.** Once you've mastered belly breathing, you're ready to start using breathing as an instant feel-better tool.

A few deep belly breaths can dissipate anxiety...ward off an impending panic attack or migraine...restore circulation to cold, numb fingers and toes...and help ease you to sleep if you're experiencing insomnia.

If you're diligent about practicing belly breathing, there's a good chance it will become second nature. For most people, the change takes about six weeks.

Caution: Breathing exercises are safe for most people. But if you've recently suffered an injury or had surgery, check with a doctor.

Certain disorders, such as heart disease, kidney disease and diabetes, lead to rapid breathing to compensate for chemical changes in the body. If you suffer from one of these ailments, slow breathing may be unsafe.

Controlling Anxiety Without Antianxiety Drugs

Harold H. Bloomfield, MD, a psychiatrist in private practice in Del Mar, CA. He is the author of 17 books, including *Healing Anxiety Naturally.* HarperCollins.

Each year, millions of Americans reach for a prescription medication to curb feelings of anxiety. Unfortunately, the *benzodiazepine* tranquilizers doctors often prescribe can cause foggy thinking, memory loss and sleep disturbance...and are highly addictive.

Putting up with the long-term consequences of stress involves its own risks. Each period of anxiety triggers the release of stress hormones, such as *adrenaline* and *cortisol*. *Chronically high levels of these hormones...*

...damage artery walls, creating crevices where fatty deposits adhere. These deposits can trigger heart attack.

...raise levels of clotting factors, thereby raising the risk for blood clots that can cause stroke or heart attack.

...constrict arteries, increasing blood pressure.

...suppress immunity, raising the risk for infection and cancer.

...cause premature aging of brain cells.

Daily exercise and a low-fat, nutrient-dense diet help fortify the body against the effects of stress. So do getting plenty of sleep and practicing a relaxation technique, such as yoga or meditation.

If these measures fail to keep anxiety in check, ask your doctor about herbal remedies. Often, they're a better choice than prescription antianxiety drugs.

KAVA

For occasional anxiety, kava offers both immediate and long-term benefits. Made from the root of a Polynesian pepper tree, this non-addictive herb has proven to be just as effective as benzodiazepines—but without the unwanted side effects.

In clinical trials, 100 mg of a standardized kava extract taken three times a day reduced mild to moderate chronic anxiety without causing any side effects. At this dosage, kava appears to be safe even for long-term use.

Kava can be used on an intermittent basis for acute anxiety. If you're anxious about getting on a plane or giving a presentation, for example, you can take three 100-mg capsules of kava extract one hour beforehand.

Caution: Kava accentuates the effects of alcohol and benzodiazepines. Avoid drinking or taking a benzodiazepine within 24 hours of taking kava.

ST. JOHN'S WORT

For individuals whose emotional state alternates between anxiety and depression, St. John's wort (*Hypericum perforatum*) is often a better choice than kava.

A common perennial plant with yellow flowers, this herb has proven to be just as effective as prescription antidepressants against mild to moderate depression. Since depression and anxiety often go hand in hand, the herb is widely recommended for anxiety—and for sleep disorders, too.

St. John's wort lowers levels of cortisol and enhances the activity of *gamma-aminobutyric acid* (GABA), a naturally occurring tranquilizer in the brain.

But you must be patient. The antianxiety effect can take four to six weeks to kick in.

Caution: Do *not* take St. John's wort within four weeks of taking a monoamine oxidase (MAO) inhibitor antidepressant, such as *phenelzine* (Nardil) or *tranylcypromine* (Parnate). This combination can trigger a dangerous rise in blood pressure, along with severe anxiety, fever, muscle tension and confusion.

Most studies of St. John's wort extract have involved dosages of 300 mg three times per day. At this level, side effects are mild.

St. John's wort does make the skin more sensitive to sunlight. People with fair skin should use extra sun protection, and those prone to cataracts should wear wraparound sunglasses.

VALERIAN

Valerian—derived from a large perennial plant native to India—is often helpful when chronic anxiety interferes with the ability to fall asleep or sleep through the night.

Like *triazolam* (Halcion) and other popular sleeping pills, valerian reduces the length of time it takes to fall asleep. Unlike these drugs, valerian produces an entirely "natural" sleep ...and is nonaddictive.

The typical dosage of valerian is 900 mg taken one hour before bedtime. If you have chronic insomnia, valerian can take up to two weeks to provide relief.

SHOPPING FOR HERBS

Herbal remedies are sold over the counter in drugstores and health-food stores. For optimum benefit, check labels carefully, and choose only *standardized* herbal extracts. A standardized extract delivers the active ingredient or ingredients in precise amounts...

●**Kava.** Look for a product standardized to 70% *kavalactone.* That's the active ingredient.

●**St. John's wort.** Look for a product standardized to 0.3% *hypericin.*

●**Valerian.** Look for a product standardized to 0.8% *valerenic acid.*

Stick with reputable brands. These include *Enzymatic Therapy, Murdock Madaus-Schwabe* and *Sunsource.*

Caution: Check with your doctor and/or pharmacist before taking any herbal remedy. Ask about potential side effects...and about any precautions that should be taken.

If you are pregnant, over age 75, in frail health or taking multiple prescription drugs, take herbal remedies only under close medical supervision.

Music and Healing

Postoperative pain can be minimized by listening to soft, soothing music.

Surgical patients who listened to music for as little as 15 minutes a day while recovering reported significantly less pain than did those who relied only on painkillers.

Also helpful: Relaxation techniques such as slow, rhythmic breathing. Music and relaxation should be considered adjuncts to painkilling medication—not replacements for it.

Marion Good, PhD, RN, associate professor of nursing, Case Western Reserve University School of Nursing, Cleveland. Her study of 500 surgical patients was published in *Pain,* 666 W. Baltimore St., Rm. 5E-08, Baltimore 21201.

How to Build Strong Bones The Natural Way

Annemarie Colbin, MA, CCP, CHES, food therapist and founder of The Natural Gourmet Institute for Food and Health in New York. She is author of *Food and Our Bones—The Natural Way to Prevent Osteoporosis.* Plume Books.

If you're worried about preventing osteoporosis, as most people are, you're probably trying to consume several servings of milk products each day.

Problem: Concentrating just on dairy products is not the best way to build strong bones. Statistics show, for example, that the countries that consume the most dairy products (including the US) have the *highest* rates of osteoporosis. *Reasons...*

●**Calcium is not the only nutrient** needed for strong bones.

●**Magnesium, phosphorus and sodium are also important**—and these are found mostly in vegetable sources of calcium, such as green leafy plants. People who consume a lot of dairy products tend to eat fewer of these vegetables.

●**Heavy milk drinkers tend to eat more animal protein, and more refined flour and sugar**—all foods that make the bloodstream slightly acidic temporarily, causing the bones to release calcium to restore the normal pH balance of the blood.

●**Vegetables, on the other hand, make the blood alkaline,** encouraging calcium to be stored in the bones.

Bottom line: A diet that is high in animal proteins and refined flour and sugar will actually encourage bone loss.

Better way: Get your calcium from the same places that cows and horses get theirs—plants.

A DIET FOR STRONG BONES

●**Eat vegetables, vegetables, vegetables.** For maximum calcium retention, you should eat at least two vegetables with every meal (either raw or cooked).

While virtually all vegetables and beans contain calcium, I recommend trying to eat high-calcium plants whenever possible—including kale, collards, mustard greens, arugula, bok choy, parsley, watercress, broccoli, cabbage, carrots and acorn or butternut squash.

Avoid spinach and swiss chard, though— they're high in oxalates, chemicals that interfere with the body's absorption of calcium.

Recommended: Organically grown vegetables, which tend to be higher in mineral content.

●**Moderate your protein intake.** Some dietary protein is essential for strong bones— collagen, a tough web of protein, makes up about one-third of your bone mass and is essential for keeping your bones flexible and resistant to fracture.

But too much concentrated animal protein, as was just explained, will temporarily upset the pH balance of your blood, increasing the risk of bone loss.

I recommend limiting your intake to two or three servings a day of any of the following protein foods—fish, organically raised fowl or meat, organic eggs, beans (including lentils, split peas, kidney beans, navy beans and black beans), nuts (almonds, cashews, walnuts), sesame seeds (which are also high in calcium) and sunflower or pumpkin seeds.

●**Eat soy products occasionally.** Eating soy foods, such as tofu, unpasteurized miso and tempeh, two or three times a week will provide another source of protein, as well as phytoestrogens, which may help prevent bone loss.

I don't recommend highly processed soy products, such as textured vegetable protein, however.

●**Eat whole grains.** For a good source of fiber, B vitamins and complex carbohydrates, eat two or three servings a day of brown rice, barley, buckwheat or kasha, millet, quinoa, oats, cornmeal or whole wheat.

●**Eat sardines—bones and all.** The soft fish bones in sardines are an excellent source of calcium and other nutrients.

●**Make soups using vegetable, chicken or beef stock.** Boiling soup bones or vegetables for an extended period of time is another superb way to extract key nutrients.

●**Avoid calcium-draining foods and other substances.** Refined flour and sugar products top this list, since they acidify your blood the same way too much protein does.

This includes all pasta and any nonwhole-grain breads, muffins and rolls, as well as sugared drinks, candy, pastries, ice cream and any other sweet dessert.

Excessive caffeine will also deplete your calcium stores. Drinking two cups of coffee a day over a lifetime has been linked to reduced bone density later in life, unless the coffee drinkers also drink a daily glass of milk (which appears to blunt the calcium-draining effect).

BONE-BUILDING RECIPES

Sardine Spread

1 can (about 4⅜ oz.) sardines with skin and bones, packed in oil or water
1 tablespoon fresh lemon juice
1 tablespoon grated onion
¼ teaspoon sea salt
1 tablespoon tahini (optional)
1½ tablespoons chopped fresh parsley
Freshly ground pepper

Open the can of sardines partway and drain out the oil or water. Then place the sardines, lemon juice, onion, salt, tahini and parsley in a bowl and mix with a fork until well blended. For extra flavor, top with freshly ground pepper. Makes about two-thirds of a cup. Can be eaten as part of a light lunch or an appetizer. Spread on whole-rye crackers or whole-grain bread.

Basic Garlic Greens

½ pound kale, collards or mustard greens
1 teaspoon extra virgin olive oil
2 garlic cloves, chopped
1 to 1½ cups vegetable or chicken stock (or water)
1 pinch of sea salt
1 pinch of grated nutmeg

Cut off the stems of the greens, then wash the remaining leaves and cut them into bite-sized pieces. Next, heat the oil gently in a saucepan, and add the garlic. Stir for a minute, then add the greens and the stock, using a wooden spoon to push the greens under the surface of the liquid. Simmer uncovered for 15 to 20 minutes. Then add the salt and nutmeg and stir for another two minutes. Drain. (Drink the cooking liquid if there is any left or save it for soup.) Serves four.

Crispy Baked Small Fish

> *1 pound fresh small whole fish, such as*
> *anchovies, smelts or whitebait*
> *½ cup cornmeal*
> *½ teaspoon sea salt*
> *½ teaspoon pepper*
> *½ cup olive oil*
> *4 to 6 lime or lemon wedges*

Have the fish cleaned, but leave the heads and tails on. Wash the fish in several changes of water, then pat dry with paper towels. Place the cornmeal, salt and pepper in a plastic or paper bag and shake until mixed. Add the fish to the bag and shake well until the fish is covered with the mixture.

Next, put the olive oil in a soup plate and dip the fish in it briefly. Then put the fish into a metal baking pan lined with parchment paper and bake at 400°F. for 30 to 40 minutes (depending on the size of the fish) until the fish is crisp but not overbrowned. Fish four inches or longer should be turned over once halfway through cooking. Serve with lime or lemon wedges. Serves three to four.

Beef Stock

> *2 pounds beef marrow bones*
> *4 quarts water*
> *1 large carrot, cut up*
> *1 medium onion, cut into quarters*
> *2 celery stalks, cut up*
> *3 garlic cloves, peeled*
> *2 tablespoons olive oil*
> *½ cup parsley stems*
> *1 cup red or white wine, or 2 tablespoons*
> *wine vinegar*

Place the bones and water in a six- to eight-quart stockpot. Bring to a boil, then simmer for 10 minutes. Skim the top of the liquid, then add the vegetables, oil, parsley and wine to the pot. Simmer on very low heat for two or three hours with the cover ajar, skimming occasionally.

When done, strain the liquid, then chill it. Remove all congealed fat. Makes two quarts.

Simple Ways to Prevent Heart Disease

Jamison Starbuck, ND, a naturopathic physician in family practice and a lecturer at the University of Montana, both in Missoula. She is past president of the American Association of Naturopathic Physicians and a contributing editor of *The Alternative Advisor: The Complete Guide to Natural Therapies and Alternative Treatments.* Time Life.

Not long ago, I had dinner with my friend Sarah. Knowing my fondness for vegetarian, heart-healthy fare, Sarah had gone to great lengths to prepare a meal I would like. The table was laden with steamed vegetables, roasted garlic, brown rice and kidney bean salad.

On sampling the beans, I noticed that they tasted unusually sweet. Sarah denied adding sugar but admitted that the beans had come from a can. "There couldn't be any sugar in them, could there?" she asked. "I looked for plain beans."

We checked the can. The label indicated that the beans were free of salt. But there, in tiny print, sugar was listed as the third ingredient—after beans and water.

Scientists now know that sugar is almost as big a culprit in heart disease as dietary fat. Sugar raises levels of blood fats and LDL (bad) cholesterol. It also damages the linings of blood vessels, raising the risk for stroke, heart attack and high blood pressure.

What exactly is meant by the term "sugar"? I tell my patients that it means not only the sucrose in white table sugar but also fructose, brown sugar, corn syrup, corn sweetener, honey, molasses and maple syrup. It does not mean natural, unprocessed sources of sugar or carbohydrates, such as fruits and vegetables or grains.

I urge you to scan food labels before buying. Avoid sweetened versions of ketchup, frozen fruit, sauces and canned foods. Shun granola, "energy bars" and sweetened cereals, too. Pass up salad dressing and beverages—including fruit juices—that have been sweetened. Be especially wary of fat-free and salt-free products. They're often loaded with sugar.

If you keep this hidden sugar out of your diet, the occasional sugary dessert is nothing to worry about.

If sugar is an often-overlooked cause of heart trouble, water is an often-overlooked means of prevention. In a recent six-year study, heart disease risk was 51% lower in men who had at least five glasses of water a day than in men who had fewer than two glasses a day. Among women, drinking lots of water reduced heart disease risk by 35%. I urge my patients to consume at least 64 ounces of water each day.

If heart disease runs in your family, you should probably be taking a daily multivitamin that contains 400 international units of vitamin E, 400 micrograms (mcg) of folic acid, 400 mcg of vitamin B-12, 100 mg of vitamin B-6 and 1,000 mg of vitamin C. These nutrients improve blood vessel health, in part by breaking down *homocysteine*, a compound known to cause arterial damage. For best absorption, take vitamins with food.

If you already have heart disease, ask your doctor about adding a daily dose of hawthorn (*Crataegus oxyacantha*). Like the grapes used to make red wine, the berries and flowers of this common tree are rich in heart-protective compounds known as flavonoids. Hawthorn also boosts blood flow to the heart, defending it against damage caused by lack of oxygen.

Hawthorn is also effective against potentially dangerous heart rhythm disturbances known as arrhythmias...and in improving strength and circulation in people with congestive heart failure.

I prefer the solid extract of hawthorn. This jellylike substance is sold in health-food stores. A typical dose is one-half teaspoon daily.

More from Jamison Starbuck...

There Are Better Ways to Treat Arthritis

More than 40 million Americans suffer from osteoarthritis, the chronic disease in which cartilage degeneration leads to joint pain and stiffness. Sadly, few of these people are receiving the best possible care.

Doctors tend to treat osteoarthritis with *nonsteroidal anti-inflammatory drugs* (NSAIDs) such as ibuprofen, naproxen and the newly released *celecoxib* (Celebrex). NSAIDs do curb pain. But they also inhibit formation of new cartilage. That can lead to further joint destruction. And NSAIDs can damage the intestines and cause peptic ulcers. Experts estimate that up to 30% of all bleeding ulcers are caused by NSAIDs taken for chronic pain. Millions of dollars "officially" spent on arthritis care are actually spent on treating the side effects of NSAID use.

Recently, I treated a patient suffering severe side effects of NSAID use—diarrhea, dizziness, fatigue, shortness of breath, iron-deficiency anemia and a bleeding ulcer. She survived. But each year, hundreds of Americans die as a result of complications from NSAIDs.

The good news is that osteoarthritis can usually be controlled safely and effectively with naturopathic remedies—as long as the condition is caught before significant joint damage has occurred. Consider the case of my patient-friend Sue. When Sue first told me about her arthritis, her fingers were so painful that she was unable to hold a magazine. But last March—after I had been treating her arthritis for some time—Sue and I spent an entire day cross-country skiing. Even at the end of the day, Sue was still pain-free.

When treating people who have osteoarthritis, I typically recommend these steps...

●**Eliminate the *source* of inflammation, not just inflammatory symptoms.** In many cases, osteoarthritis is caused by an allergy or sensitivity to a particular food. A blood test to measure levels of IgG and IgE antibodies to common foods can pinpoint foods that cause inflammation. Likely culprits include wheat, corn, dairy foods and nightshade vegetables (potatoes, tomatoes, eggplant and peppers). The test can be ordered by your doctor. It costs less than $200.

●**Eat foods known to decrease inflammation.** Substitute fish for meat at meals several times each week. Eat dark purple fruits such as blueberries, blackberries, cherries and plums instead of fatty desserts. Boost your intake of sulfur-rich veggies, such as garlic, onion, cabbage and brussels sprouts. Add a tablespoon of freshly ground flaxmeal to your breakfast cereal.

•**Take joint-protective nutritional supplements.** My two favorites are *glucosamine sulfate* and an anti-inflammatory herb called Indian frankincense (*Boswellia serrata*).

Glucosamine helps curb pain by restoring the shock-absorbing ability of damaged cartilage. I typically recommend 1,500 mg a day. Results are generally evident within eight weeks. Glucosamine is sold over the counter in health-food stores and some drugstores.

Boswellia offers pain relief within a few days of using it. It can be used for pain management while joint health is restored with glucosamine and dietary changes. I usually recommend to my patients 900 mg daily to start, then cut the dose to 300 mg—or stop it completely—once symptoms improve. Boswellia is sold in health-food stores.

Vitamin E Reverses Eye and Kidney Problems

Eye and kidney abnormalities associated with diabetes may be reversible with vitamin E.

Recent study: Diabetics at risk for the potentially blinding eye disorder retinopathy and/or the kidney disorder *nephropathy* took 1,800 international units (IU) of vitamin E a day for four months.

Result: Blood tests revealed that their risk for the two conditions was diminished. The greater the risk for eye or kidney trouble, the greater the benefit.

Sven-Erick Bursell, PhD, investigator, eye research section, Joslin Diabetes Center, Boston.

Minerals for Better Health

For the best absorption of iron supplements, take them with orange juice or with a meal containing meat or poultry...and avoid tea or coffee when taking iron. For the best absorption of calcium, take half in the morning and half in the evening. Take iron and calcium supplements at different times of the day—calcium can block the absorption of iron. *Not necessary:* Chelated minerals, which are sold in health-food stores. Chelation describes a type of chemical bond. It's no better for the body than standard mineral supplements.

James Fleet, PhD, director, graduate program in nutrition, University of North Carolina at Greensboro.

Best Supplements for Boosting Energy, Strength And Stamina

Edmund R. Burke, PhD, professor of exercise science and director of the exercise science program at the University of Colorado in Colorado Springs. He is coauthor of *Sports Nutrition Almanac*. Avery.

If you've ventured into a health-food store or a drugstore recently, you've probably seen shelves lined with creatine, DHEA and other "performance enhancing" products.

Which of these over-the-counter products really enhance athletic performance? Which ones are safe? *Here's a product-by-product rundown...*

CREATINE

Of all the products that purportedly have a strength-building effect, creatine is the top contender. There's ample scientific evidence to support creatine's effectiveness.

This protein-like substance—made up of three amino acids found naturally in meat and fish—is not a substitute for exercise. It does not build muscle or boost strength on its own. But it can help boost the muscle-building effect of weight-lifting workouts. It can also put more power in your tennis serve... and make you a faster runner. It's safe, too.

Creatine may also be effective at preventing and even reversing the muscle loss that typically accompanies aging. This condition is known as *sarcopenia.*

Typical dosage: 2 g to 3 g per day, preferably with a meal or carbohydrate-rich beverage, such as Gatorade.

GLUCOSAMINE

If your joints and muscles often feel sore after exercise, consider taking *glucosamine.* This amino acid supplement promotes repair of cartilage and ligaments.

Typical dosage: 500 mg to 750 mg in the morning and again at night.

RECOVERY DRINKS

Endurox R4, Metabolol Endurance and other "recovery drinks" really can help people bounce back from hard workouts. Drink them within 30 minutes of exercising. The carbohydrates and protein act to restore energy and prevent sore muscles later.

If you regularly exercise vigorously for more than one hour, recovery drinks probably make sense for you.

VITAMIN SUPPLEMENT

A multivitamin/mineral tablet is perhaps the most important overall performance enhancer you can buy. It's also the safest and cheapest.

Take a supplement that contains a minimum of 100% of the RDA for most vitamins and minerals every morning with your breakfast.

ANDROSTENEDIONE

Andro is said to stimulate muscle growth by boosting testosterone levels. It's been touted as a natural alternative to anabolic steroids, the dangerous drugs used by many bodybuilders.

There is no scientific evidence that andro builds muscle mass or strength. Research has shown that it increases testosterone for less than one hour, even when taken in large doses. Increased testosterone could raise the risk for prostate cancer in men and of acne or excessive body hair in women.

If you still choose to take andro, take it only under medical supervision so that your prostate-specific antigen (PSA) level—a marker for prostate cancer—can be monitored.

DHEA

Dehydroepiandrosterone is naturally produced by the adrenal glands and ovaries.

DHEA is supposed to build muscle mass and increase strength. But as with andro, there's no evidence that it does either. It may also carry the same risks and side effects as andro.

DHEA is beneficial only for men whose blood tests have shown chronically low levels of testosterone.

It should be taken under a doctor's supervision so that testosterone levels and PSA levels can be monitored.

GINSENG

Ginseng is purported to boost energy and endurance…and to help reverse fatigue. Russian athletes have used it for years. Yet there's little scientific evidence to back up these claims.

If you want to try ginseng anyway, the usual dosage is 100 mg, two to four times daily.

Caution: Ginseng can raise blood pressure. Do not take it if you have that condition.

Oils That Improve Health

Eucalyptus is an antibacterial that soothes acne and relieves sinus congestion.

Geranium soaks up facial oiliness and also can tighten skin temporarily.

Lavender soothes tension headaches and migraines.

Rose hydrates and soothes sensitive, dry, itchy or inflamed skin.

Tea tree fights athlete's foot, dandruff, insect bites, cold sores and acne.

Caution: Except for lavender and tea tree, don't apply full-strength oils directly to skin. Dilute in a vegetable carrier oil such as almond oil or grape seed oil.

Victoria Edwards, founder, Aromatherapy Institute & Research, Fair Oaks, CA, quoted in *Self,* 350 Madison Ave., New York 10017.

Psychotherapy For Psoriasis

Psoriasis and other skin disorders respond remarkably well to psychotherapy. So say researchers at Kent and Canterbury Hospital in London. They found that an hour with a shrink could be beneficial even to people whose skin conditions were resistant to conventional drug therapy. The theory is that if strong emotions can bring on these skin conditions, talking through these feelings helps clear them up.

Postgraduate Medical Journal.

Writing Can Help Ease Serious Health Problems

In a recent study, people suffering from asthma or arthritis spent 20 minutes a day for three days writing about the most stressful experience they'd ever had. When these individuals were examined four months later, 47% showed marked improvement in their condition. Only 24% of nonwriters had improved.

Theory: Writing alleviates stress that exacerbates illness.

Joshua Smyth, PhD, assistant professor of psychology, North Dakota State University, Fargo.

Natural Ways to Control Premenstrual Syndrome

Michelle Harrison, MD, a lecturer and consultant in Highland Park, NJ. She is coauthor of *Self-Help for Premenstrual Syndrome*. Random House.

Premenstrual syndrome (PMS) has been controversial for decades. Women know from personal experience that it exists, but scientists still don't know exactly how the hormonal changes that occur during the menstrual cycle trigger the symptoms of PMS.

One thing researchers do know is that PMS is *not* a specific set of specific symptoms. Rather, it's an "amplification" of what women experience at other times of the month.

Example: Emotional women become even more so, and women who get migraines get them more frequently. Women who tend to overeat binge, and those prone to mood swings become depressed.

Whatever the symptoms of PMS—anger, crying, insomnia, bingeing, urinary difficulties, acne, fatigue or headaches, to name a few—certain strategies can bring welcome relief…

DIETARY CHANGES

Foods have long been known to affect mood, and changing what you eat can help minimize PMS symptoms.

•**Avoid sweets.** Sugary foods alter blood sugar levels. That can exacerbate depression, headache, anxiety and fatigue. Even artificial sweeteners can have this effect, so it's best to avoid anything that tastes sweet.

•**Avoid alcohol.** In addition to creating a sugar "high," alcohol acts as a depressant. Women are especially sensitive to alcohol just before the menstrual period.

•**Avoid caffeine.** It can cause anxiety. If you cannot give up coffee or tea completely, at least avoid drinking these beverages on an empty stomach.

As you may know, giving up caffeine can cause lethargy and headaches. To make the transition easier, give up caffeine the week after your period. That way, you won't have to put up with caffeine withdrawal and PMS symptoms simultaneously.

Contrary to popular belief, there's no need for PMS sufferers to limit their salt intake. Premenstrual bloating is caused by a redistribution of water within the body—no matter how much salt is consumed.

•**Eat six small meals a day.** If you go too long without food, blood sugar drops. That can exacerbate anxiety, headache and fatigue.

It can take up to three months for these changes to make a noticeable difference in symptoms. Changes must be maintained all month—not just when symptoms are present.

VITAMINS AND MINERALS

Some women find that nutritional supplements help ease PMS symptoms. Various vitamins and minerals—including calcium and magnesium—have been identified as "the answer" for PMS. In fact, no single nutrient is a PMS cure. The key is to take vitamins and minerals in the proper balance.

Several over-the-counter (OTC) supplements, including *Optivite* and *ProCycle*, are formulated specifically to provide this balance. These supplements should be taken on a daily basis all month—not just during the days leading up to menstruation.

EXERCISE AND STRESS REDUCTION

It doesn't matter what kind of exercise you do—as long as you do it for 30 minutes a day. Pick something you find pleasurable. Your goal isn't weight loss or cardiovascular fitness —although those are important goals. It's to enjoy your workouts.

You can never totally eliminate stress from your life, but you can learn to control your reaction to it. Meditation, deep breathing, yoga, massage and keeping a journal are all good ways to relax. Pick something that works for you...and practice it for 20 to 30 minutes a day.

COMPLEMENTARY TREATMENTS

Recent studies suggest that certain alternative remedies are effective at controlling PMS...

●**Evening primrose oil.** Sold over the counter in health-food stores, this oil contains essential fatty acids that seem to relieve breast tenderness.

●**St. John's wort.** This herb can be helpful at relieving PMS-related depression.

Caution: St. John's wort should not be taken by anyone who is already taking a prescription antidepressant.

●**PMS teas and beverages.** These remedies haven't been scientifically proven to work, but some women swear by them. Supposedly, they alleviate symptoms by boosting levels of the neurotransmitter *serotonin*. Low levels of serotonin have been blamed for depression.

Caution: If you take any OTC remedy for premenstrual syndrome, follow directions carefully. Any woman who is already taking medication should consult a doctor before taking any OTC preparations.

HORMONE THERAPY

If diet, supplements, exercise and stress reduction fail to relieve symptoms of PMS, ask your doctor about taking natural progesterone during the second half of your menstrual cycle.

Available by prescription only, natural progesterone comes in many forms. Long-acting tablets seem to work best.

If you experience drowsiness, dizziness, a delay in the onset of menstruation or a slight flushing, ask your doctor about reducing the dosage.

Wild yam cream, sold over the counter, contains little if any natural progesterone. If you prefer cream to pills, ask your doctor about using natural progesterone cream instead of wild yam cream.

Caution: Natural progesterone differs greatly from synthetic progesterone, such as that found in birth control pills. Synthetic progesterone can actually exacerbate PMS symptoms.

How to Beat Back Pain Without Surgery

Stephen Hochschuler, MD, chairman of the Texas Back Institute in Plano. His most recent book is *Treat Your Back without Surgery*. Hunter House.

Sooner or later, we're all likely to develop lower back pain. Four out of five Americans do. In the vast majority of cases, the culprit is a sedentary lifestyle.

Chronic inactivity weakens back muscles, making them vulnerable to strain. It also loosens the ligaments and tendons that support the spine...and causes spinal discs to deteriorate.

Caution: See a doctor at once for back pain accompanied by loss of bladder or bowel control...sudden onset of weakness in the arms or legs...loss of weight or appetite...blood in the urine or stool...or continuous pain at night. These symptoms suggest serious illness.

FIRST STEPS

Back pain usually resolves on its own within 48 hours. To dull the pain during that time, apply ice to the affected area.

Cold reduces pain by helping to curb swelling and inflammation.

Fill a plastic bag with ice cubes, then wrap the bag in a moist towel. Place the wrapped bag on your back, and leave in place for five minutes. If you leave the ice bag on longer than that, the cold temperature might damage your skin.

For back pain that persists beyond 48 hours, heat from a heating pad or hot shower or bath works better than cold. It dilates blood vessels, boosting circulation and speeding nutrients to damaged tissues.

What about painkillers? *Acetaminophen* (Tylenol), *ibuprofen* (Advil), *naproxen* (Aleve) and aspirin are equally effective.

Caution: If you experience stomach upset, nausea or diarrhea after taking an over-the-counter painkiller, stop taking it at once.

PHYSICAL ACTIVITY

Until about 15 years ago, bed rest was the treatment of choice for back pain. Now we know that inactivity is one of the worst things you can do.

A fitness regimen consisting of aerobic exercise, strength training and stretching helps treat and prevent back pain. If you're temporarily hobbled by back pain, even a brief walk can be helpful. So can these pain-relieving exercises...

•**Back extension.** Lie on your stomach with your hands flat on the floor by your chest. Press up so your chest and back arch slightly. Hips should remain flat on the ground. Hold for 10 seconds, then repeat several times.

•**Lumbar flexion.** Get on your hands and knees, then arch your back upward slightly. Hold for 10 seconds, then repeat several times.

BODY MECHANICS

Everyone knows that it's best to lift heavy objects using the legs, not the back. The idea is to let your strongest muscles do the work...and protect the back from needless strain.

Other smart moves...

•**Push objects rather than pull them.** Pulling a heavy object is more likely to strain your back muscles than pushing.

•**Distribute carried weight evenly across your body.** Do not heft a heavy object on one hip.

•**When unloading a car trunk,** place a knee or foot on the bumper to improve your leverage.

Good body mechanics is also about what to do when you're *not* moving. Sitting still for too long "starves" the back by decreasing circulation.

To avoid trouble: Get up and take a brief walk every 20 minutes. If that's impossible, shift your seating position...stretch...and/or do Kegel exercises.

To do Kegels, repeatedly tighten your pelvic floor muscles—the ones you use to stop urine in midstream—for five seconds.

MASSAGE

In addition to relaxing tense, painful muscles, massage improves circulation and raises levels of *endorphins,* the body's natural pain-killing compounds.

Massage from a partner can be helpful, but it's better to seek the services of a professional massage therapist. A one-hour session runs $50 to $60. You may need up to three sessions a week for two to three weeks.

To find a massage therapist in your area, contact the American Massage Therapy Association at 847-864-0123.

ACUPUNCTURE AND MAGNETS

If you still think of acupuncture as "far-out," think again. In 1997, the National Institutes of Health—famous for its skepticism regarding alternative therapies—issued a report acknowledging that acupuncture can be helpful against lower back pain.

The procedure is relatively painless. Five to 15 thin needles inserted in specific locations on the body stimulate the release of endorphins.

An initial consultation with an acupuncturist costs about $100. Follow-up visits run $35 to $75.

To find an acupuncturist near you, call the National Certification Commission for Acupuncture and Oriental Medicine at 703-548-9004.

Magnets have become popular for treating back pain, especially among athletes. Worn in belts or taped across the back, they're inexpensive and unobtrusive.

There's still no good scientific evidence that magnets really work. But given their safety, they may be worth trying if nothing else works.

PERSISTENT PAIN

If the pain persists for more than a week, it's time to consult a chiropractor or physician.

Chiropractors and physicians take different approaches to relieving back pain. But both approaches—spinal manipulation by chiropractors and use of prescription painkillers or injections of muscle relaxants or steroids by physicians—are of proven effectiveness.

To find a chiropractor, contact the American Chiropractic Association at 800-986-4636.

Surgery should be considered only if pain remains unbearable after all other options have been exhausted.

To find a back surgeon in your area, contact the North American Spine Society, 6300 N. River Rd., Suite 500, Rosemont, IL 60018. 847-698-1630.

Magnets vs. Diabetes

Many diabetics develop peripheral neuropathy, a condition that causes numbness or tingling in the feet. This can progress into severe and disabling pain.

Good news: In a preliminary study, specially designed magnetic insoles relieved pain significantly in nine of 10 diabetics who wore them consistently.

The magnets used in the study were made by New Magnetics, Inc. (800-572-9651).

Michael I. Weintraub, MD, clinical professor of neurology, New York Medical College, Valhalla.

Beware of Chromium Picolinate

This over-the-counter nutritional supplement is supposed to build muscles and reduce body fat. But a new study suggests that it triggers chemical reactions that may lead to cancer.

John B. Vincent, PhD, associate professor of chemistry, University of Alabama, Tuscaloosa.

HupA Delays Memory Loss

Memory-boosting herb delays progression of age-related memory loss and Alzheimer's disease. *Huperzine A* (HupA), a compound derived from *Huperzia serrata* moss, has been used in China for centuries to reduce fever and inflammation. *Now:* Research demonstrates that it blocks breakdown of *acetylcholine,* a neurotransmitter that plays a critical role in memory. *Recent finding:* HupA improved mental function in 58% of those who took it, as compared with 36% who took a placebo.

HupA, sold over the counter, should be taken under medical supervision.

Alan Kozikowski, PhD, professor of neurology, Georgetown University, Washington, DC.

Drug-Free Ways To Fight Depression

Hyla Cass, MD, assistant clinical professor of psychiatry at the University of California, Los Angeles, School of Medicine. She is author of *St. John's Wort: Nature's Blues Buster* (Avery) and *Kava: Nature's Answer to Stress, Anxiety and Insomnia* (Prima). Her Web site is *www.cassmd.com.*

Symptoms of depression—sadness, hopelessness, suicidal feelings, etc.—are usually caused by reduced levels of neurotransmitters such as *dopamine, serotonin* and *norepinephrine*. These are the mood-controlling molecules that mediate thoughts and emotions in the brain.

Prescription antidepressants—such as *fluoxetine* (Prozac), *amitriptyline* (Elavil) and phenelzine (Nardil)—elevate one or more of these messenger molecules.

But the drugs are no panacea. Three out of 10 people don't respond to antidepressants. When the drugs do work, they often become less effective over time. They can also cause unpleasant side effects such as nausea...fatigue...and sexual dysfunction.

Antidepressants certainly aren't a cure when depression is symptomatic of a medical condition, such as hypothyroidism, diabetes or anemia.

In a recent study, most people hospitalized for depression were found to have an undiagnosed physical illness that was causing their symptoms.

If you have symptoms of depression, it's essential to see your doctor. If the diagnosis is depression, together you may decide to explore alternatives to prescription antidepressants.

Some options...

●**See a psychotherapist.** Therapy allows depressed individuals to confront painful issues of self-esteem, anger and troubled relationships. Resolving these issues directly affects the levels of neurotransmitters within the brain.

●**Rethink your diet.** Depression is often caused by a deficiency of amino acids, vitamins or other nutrients the body needs to make neurotransmitters. Although slight, the deficiencies may be enough to alter brain chemistry and affect mood.

To restore the balance...

●**Eat adequate amounts of protein.** Fish, chicken, turkey, meat, tofu and dairy products provide the raw materials for neurotransmitter production.

Bonus: Salmon, mackerel and other fatty fish are also rich sources of the omega-3 fatty acids known to improve nerve signaling in the brain—enhancing mood and memory.

●**Eat more complex carbohydrates.** Complex carbohydrates are long chains of sugar molecules strung together. Because complex carbohydrates are digested slowly, they help prevent fluctuations in blood sugar levels that can cause depression. Whole grains, beans, peas and vegetables are all good sources of complex carbohydrates.

Bonus: Complex carbs help to elevate serotonin levels.

Foods to avoid: Donuts, cookies and other sugary snacks trigger insulin release, which lowers blood sugar levels and makes mood and energy plummet.

●**Limit alcohol intake.** Like sugary foods, alcohol temporarily raises blood sugar, then makes it plunge.

Limit intake to one glass of wine or beer or one cocktail daily. Drink it only with meals to slow its absorption.

●**Take supplements.** To boost mood without prescription drugs, you might take...

●A high-potency multivitamin/mineral complex that contains about 50 mg of each of the B vitamins. This supplies "co-factors" needed to manufacture neurotransmitters.

●*S-adenosylmethionine* (SAM-e). This bioactive form of the amino acid methionine enhances neurotransmitter activity. More than 100 double-blind, placebo-controlled studies have suggested that SAM-e is effective in alleviating depression.

Typical dosage: One 200-mg capsule once a day. After a week, it may be necessary to increase to two daily capsules.

Trap: SAM-e supplements are unstable in high temperatures. Buy enteric-coated supplements. Or choose supplements that have been refrigerated at the store...and refrigerate them at home.

●**Try herbs.** *Natural mood-enhancers include...*

●St. John's wort. Dozens of studies, involving more than 5,000 patients, have been conducted on this herb. The research shows that, on average, 70% of depressed people who take it report a significant decrease in symptoms and an increase in feelings of well-being.

St. John's wort appears to reduce the rate at which brain cells take up serotonin. That means more of it stays in synapses—the tiny gaps between brain cells—where it's needed to ferry mood-enhancing nerve impulses.

Dosage: The average dose is 300 mg three times a day, but some people get results with 300 mg only twice a day. Others may require 300 mg up to four times daily.

Full effects may not be felt for up to three weeks.

Warning: Do not take St. John's wort within four weeks of taking a monoamine oxidase (MAO) inhibitor antidepressant such as phenelzine (Nardil) or tranylcypromine (Parnate). This drug combination can raise your blood pressure dangerously.

Recent studies also indicate that St. John's wort can reduce the effectiveness of drugs used for AIDS and organ transplantation.

St. John's wort also increases sensitivity to sunlight. If you're fair-skinned, use extra sun protection. If you're at risk for cataracts, wear wraparound sunglasses.

• Ginkgo biloba. Reduced blood flow is a common cause of depression, especially in older people. A vasodilator, ginkgo improves blood flow to the brain. Ginkgo may also boost production of serotonin.

Consult your doctor before taking ginkgo if you're taking aspirin, *warfarin* (Coumadin) or another blood-thinning drug.

Typical dosage: 40 mg three times daily. Some people respond within four weeks. Others take several months. If you don't see a difference in four weeks, increase the dosage to 80 mg three times daily.

• **Get more sunshine.** Sunlight stimulates the brain's pineal gland to produce melatonin, a hormone that helps regulate sleep cycles and mood.

Exposure to light is especially vital for people who suffer from seasonal affective disorder (SAD). This form of depression is triggered by the lack of sunlight in fall and winter.

The treatment is sunlight. Thirty minutes each day often does the trick.

If you can't get out in daylight—or live in a dark, northern climate—consider buying special lights that mimic sunlight's effects.

Good source for the lights: Tools for Exploration catalog (800-456-9887).

• **Get aerobic exercise.** Walking, running, biking and swimming all reduce stress hormones and increase levels of endorphins. Those are the mood-boosting, painkilling brain compounds famous for the feel-good "runner's high."

Exercising aerobically as little as 20 minutes several times a week suffices.

How to Harness the Healing Power of Faith

Harold G. Koenig, MD, director of the Center for the Study of Religion/Spirituality and Health, and associate professor of psychiatry and behavioral sciences, both at Duke University Medical Center in Durham, NC. He is author of *The Healing Power of Faith: Science Explores Medicine's Last Great Frontier.* Simon & Schuster.

People who know the benefits of good nutrition, exercise and stress reduction often overlook another potentially very potent health factor—spirituality.

There's now compelling evidence that praying and participating in weekly worship services are associated with a reduced risk for serious illness and with an extended lifespan.

In fact, researchers now believe that religious faith may be roughly equivalent to not smoking when it comes to conferring health benefits.

I'm not talking about miracles, faith healing or divine intervention. Rather, the *thoughts* and *actions* of religious life seem to enhance health in ways that make scientific sense.

A LONG, HEALTHY LIFE

The best evidence for the power of faith is also the simplest—*religious people live longer.* There's plenty of solid evidence to back up this statement.

In one ongoing study, University of California researchers have followed 5,286 men and women in Alameda, California, for nearly 30 years.

What they've found: Individuals who attended worship services at least once a week were 36% less likely to die during the study than were those who went less often.

Even after researchers accounted for other factors that often go along with religious faith—lower alcohol consumption, better social support, etc.—the death rate among the religious people was 23% lower than that among their less religious peers.

This landmark study has been corroborated repeatedly. In one study involving 4,000 adults in North Carolina, religious observance was associated with a 28% reduction in the death rate.

Perhaps even more important, being religious can add vigor to these extra years. A study of 2,812 elderly Connecticut residents found that those who worshiped weekly were significantly more likely to live on their own and be free of disabilities.

RELIGION AND THE HEART

Faith may offer powerful protection against heart attack. In part, it may do so by helping keep blood pressure down.

The North Carolina study also found that high blood pressure was 40% less common among those who regularly attended religious services and prayed or read the Bible.

An Israeli study, appearing in the journal *Cardiology* in 1993, followed more than 10,000 men for 23 years. Researchers noted that there were 20% fewer deaths from heart attack among those who were most religious.

In another study that involved 232 patients, those who "lacked strength and comfort from religion" were more than three times more likely to die within six months following heart surgery.

RELIGION AND HOSPITALIZATION

Religious people are hospitalized less frequently than nonreligious people. And when religious people must be hospitalized, they tend to have shorter stays.

A survey of 542 men and women, average age 70, found that those who attended religious services regularly were almost half as likely to have been hospitalized during the previous year.

Hospital patients who identified themselves as being religious went home in half the time that it took similar patients with no religious affiliation.

WHAT FAITH CAN DO

Religion certainly doesn't guarantee good health. *But it does seem to promote...*

●**Good habits.** Religious people tend to exercise more and smoke less.

●**Social support.** Members of a congregation are part of a community. They're involved in the lives of others and feel cared about. Their marriages are more likely to last.

●**Reduced stress.** If you believe in a benevolent God, you probably see the world as being largely *on your side.* The problems that befall us—big and small—seem easier to bear.

In addition, the act of prayer has been shown to trigger what Harvard researcher Herbert Benson, MD, has dubbed the "relaxation response." That's a state of deep relaxation in which blood pressure, heart rate and breathing rate decrease.

IF YOU'RE ALREADY RELIGIOUS

Magnify the health-promoting power of your faith by making it a central part of your life...

●**Attend services more frequently,** and get involved in activities such as prayer or Bible study. Get to know your fellow congregants. Reach out to those who are in need of help.

●**Join other congregants in volunteer programs** that help the poor, homeless, etc.

●**Include private prayer or reflection in your daily schedule.** At bedtime, look back over the day's events, to understand them in the context of faith.

●**Take a few minutes each day to pray with your family.** While you're together, ask about conflicts in their lives.

●**Read inspiring passages from religious writings.** You'll find comfort and encouragement.

IF YOU'RE NOT RELIGIOUS

You can't simply "practice" religion for your health, the way you might start exercising or adopt a low-fat diet. But you can open your mind to the benefits of faith...

●**Be honest in your search for meaning in your life.** Discuss God with religious people whose principles, behavior and intelligence you respect.

•**If you've had negative experiences with religion, re-examine them.** Discuss your feelings with a trusted friend or counselor.

•**Read the writings of people of deep faith**—Martin Buber, Martin Luther King, Jr., Thomas Merton, Albert Schweitzer and any other people you find particularly inspiring.

•**Practice meditation.** Pausing for 30 minutes of introspection and reflection is deeply relaxing…and may open the door to spiritual experiences.

•**Attend religious services** at a church, synagogue or mosque that is truly alive and involved with its community. Speak with members of the congregation.

•**Do good deeds.** Volunteering, doing charity work, watching out for the well-being of others are helpful—and healthful—no matter what you believe in.

Look for the USP On the Label

If a vitamin supplement does not disintegrate in the digestive tract, it will provide little benefit.

The best guarantee that pills will disintegrate properly is to look for the letters "USP"

on the label. That means they meet the disintegration standards of US Pharmacopeia, an independent nonprofit pharmaceutical-testing organization. Generic vitamins approved by USP meet the same test standards as more expensive name brands.

Robert Russell, MD, associate director, USDA Human Nutrition Research Center on Aging, Tufts University, Boston.

Good News for CFS Sufferers

People with chronic fatigue syndrome can boost energy levels with NADH. NADH is a coenzyme found in body cells that helps them produce energy. A preliminary study found that when chronically fatigued men and women were given a daily dietary supplement containing 10 mg of an easily absorbed form of NADH, they reported higher energy. *Caution:* Consult a physician before trying NADH to make sure your cause of exhaustion is chronic fatigue syndrome.

Joseph A. Bellanti, MD, director of the International Center for Interdisciplinary Studies of Immunology at Georgetown University School of Medicine in Washington, DC.

Related Useful Sites

Alternative Health

☐ Alternative Health News Online
www.altmedicine.com

Best sources of information on alternative health solutions for longevity, mind/body control, diet, nutrition and more. Easy-to-read digest of the latest health/medical news.

Consumer

☐ Quackwatch
www.quackwatch.com

Consumer advocate physician's excellent site aids in identifying fraudulent alternative therapies. Scores of links to "questionable" advertisements, products and services and dubious sources of advice.

☐ PharmInfoNet
www.pharminfo.com

Valuable information on various diseases and medications. The *drug database* contains a searchable index of articles arranged by generic and brand names. Links to disease-related sites.

☐ MotherNature.com
www.mothernature.com

Great site for finding your way through the maze of vitamins and minerals and ordering what is right for you. Learn about supplements for you and your family.

☐ American Medical Association
www.ama-assn.org

The American Medical Association's (AMA) Web site allows users to check any doctor's educational and professional credentials or to pull up a list of specialists anywhere in the US.

Health Tips

☐ Your Health Daily
www. yourhealthdaily.com

Comprehensive rundown of the week's leading medical stories. Topics include AIDS, cancer and women's health, among many others. On-line discussion groups.

☐ HealthWorld Online
www.healthy.net

Great links to self-help health and medical sites, plus an on-line bookstore for health-related titles and a health-food store. Best of all, the ins and outs of health insurance.

☐ OnHealth
www.onhealth.com

Wellness Manager can be used to search for and save information specific to your individual needs. Extensive and easy-to-use *Conditions A-Z* for symptoms, causes and treatments; columns, daily and weekly health tips.

Women's

☐ Women's Health Issues
www.feminist.com/health.htm

This is probably the most comprehensive health sites we've seen on the Web. Categories: *General Health, Breast Cancer/Cancer, Reproductive Health,* and *Women and Aids* contain links to dozens of subcategories.

☐ Childbirth.org
www.childbirth.org

A wonderfully comprehensive site for parents-to-be. There's information on virtually every aspect of pregnancy from pre-conception to postpartum issues. Click on *Ask a Pro* and consult with a midwife, nurse, lactation consultant or fitness expert.

Diseases

☐ Centers for Disease Control and Prevention
www.cdc.gov

A comprehensive and informative site. Select *Health Information* links to information on diseases, injuries and disabilities, health risks, prevention strategies, etc. or Travelers' Health: disease outbreaks, geographic recommendations, cruise ship sanitation inspections, etc.

☐ Mayo Clinic Health Oasis
www.mayohealth.org

The world-renowned Mayo Clinic answers just about any health or medical question. Browse articles, consult the site's *major resource centers*, including cancer, diet and nutrition, heart health and more. Have your *questions about medicines answered*.

☐ Association of Cancer Online Resources, Inc.

www.acor.org

This site offers a full-text search engine for locating cancer-related resources on the Web as well as on-line support groups.

First Aid

☐ Active First Aid Online

www.parasolemt.com.au

An extremely comprehensive site that just may keep you out of the emergency room. Numerous links to handling medical crises: head injury, burn, fracture or epileptic seizure. Even instructions for performing *cardiopulmonary resuscitation*.

Nutrition

☐ Center for Science in the Public Interest

www.cspinet.org

Sensible, reliable information on nutrition and food safety from a respected source. There's an excellent section on *how to make your diet healthier,* the *Chow Club for Kids* and *Nutrition Quizzes*.

☐ International Food Information Council

www.ificinfo.health.org

A great resource for avoiding food-related health problems and learning about nutrition with sections on food additives, artificial sweeteners, child and adolescent nutrition and food allergies. Up-to-the minute nutrition news.

☐ LightLiving.com

www.lightliving.com

Offers loads of *low-fat recipes,* an opportunity to convert regular, *high-fat recipes to low-fat equivalents* and a new recipe each week.

Seniors

☐ Seniornet.com

www.seniornet.com

This is the premier lifestyle site for people over 50. It offers not just health and wealth information, but community, discussion boards and roundtables for people like you, who share your fears and interests, people you can talk to and learn from.

☐ Seniors-Site.com

www.seniors-site.com

For seniors and their families. Financial tips for seniors, self-help for Alzheimer's patients, people with hearing loss and other age-related medical concerns. Nifty on-line pen pals feature.

6
Better Money Management

Your Bank Is Still Ripping You Off...Best Ways to Beat Their New Tricks... And Old Ones

The average American family is paying far more than it should in bank fees, including ATM charges and mortgage interest. *Some of the latest bank rip-offs and how you can avoid them...*

LOAN RIP-OFFS

•**Interest rates.** Two customers walk into a bank and ask for loans. One has a great credit rating and a 20% down payment. The other has an okay credit rating and a 10% down payment. Which customer gets the better deal from the bank? Neither! Both get the same quote.

Banks will not offer below-standard rates without some prompting. But they generally will when good customers push.

The best customers have clean credit ratings, ongoing relationships with the lender and adequate collateral. These customers should ask for the loan rate to be lowered by one-half to one percentage point.

On a typical 30-year, $100,000 mortgage, that's a saving of up to $25,000 over the life of the loan.

•**Loan type.** When you're ready to accept the rate offered, tell the loan officer you want to borrow on a *simple-interest, single-payment note* that allows for monthly payments or an *installment note calculated by simple interest.* Do not take the standard front-end loaded installment note that is usually offered.

With a standard installment note, the borrower pays interest on the entire loan amount through the life of the loan—despite the fact that an increasing portion of the loan is paid

---

Edward F. Mrkvicka, Jr., former chairman of a national bank and current president of Reliance Enterprises, Inc., a national financial consulting firm, 22115 O'Connell Rd., Marengo, IL 60152. He is author of *Your Bank Is Ripping You Off.* St. Martin's Griffin.

off over time. With a simple-interest, single-payment note, you pay interest on only the amount of the loan outstanding.

Example: For a $10,000, four-year loan at 10.25% Annual Percentage Rate (APR), you'll save $140 by requesting a simple-interest note.

Also tell the loan officer that you don't want *Credit Life and Disability Insurance* on your loan. This coverage protects the bank's interests—not yours. While not required, such insurance is often slipped into the loan—increasing its cost—without the customer knowing or understanding that he/she could have refused coverage. The premium is then subject to hidden finance charges.

You can get better coverage at less cost from your insurance agent.

FEE RIP-OFFS

●**Overdraft checking.** With this type of account, if you write a check that exceeds your balance, the bank automatically lends you the money to cover it. But it's not as good as it sounds. The bank lends this money at a high interest rate, and these accounts often carry additional charges, such as transaction fees—even if you pay off the overdraft right away.

Better: Ask to have your checking account *red flagged*. Many banks—particularly small ones—allow such no-cost arrangements, under which customers are called if they overdraw. If the customer can cover the checks that day, the bank waives the overdraft fees.

●**Unadvertised account options.** Don't assume the checking and savings policies in a bank's literature are the only ones available.

Example: Free low-balance checking accounts often are available for senior citizens, students and the disabled—but only if you ask.

●**Bank consolidation.** The number of banks continues to fall, from a peak of nearly 15,000 in 1983 to roughly half that today. Less competition is never good for consumers. Large banks generally charge more and provide less than small banks. Whenever two banks merge, they inevitably adopt the fee structure and charges of the more expensive bank.

Better: If you're currently shopping for a new bank, consider a credit union. These institutions typically offer better rates than banks and are less likely to be taken over. Contact the Credit Union National Association (CUNA) to find credit unions in your area that you are eligible to join. 800-358-5710...or *www.cuna.org*.

CREDIT CARD RIP-OFFS

●**Disappearing grace periods.** Not long ago, credit card users could be relatively confident that if they paid off their bills within 30 days, they wouldn't pay interest. But more credit card companies are doing away with "grace periods" and charging interest from the moment of purchase.

Today, the top priority for those not carrying balances should be a grace period, not interest rates or special features.

●**Debit card downsides.** *Two problems to be aware of...*

●Debit cards withdraw funds from your account immediately.

●Married couples are more likely to incur overdraft fees when using debit cards. Before debit cards were introduced, if both partners wrote big checks on the same day, one could run to the bank with a deposit to cover the shortfall. But today the immediacy of debit cards means that overdrawn is overdrawn.

More from Edward Mrkvicka...

Smoother Switch to a New Bank

Set up the new account before closing the old one. Keep enough money in both accounts to meet the minimum-balance requirements. Start doing business in the new account while making sure everything clears in the old one—including outstanding checks and changes in direct-deposit instructions. Be sure to suspend automatic payments in the old account and switch them to the new one. Keep records of both accounts during the transition and report errors promptly.

Bill-Paying Magic

The key to easier bill paying is consistency —in who pays the bills...when...where... and how.

●**One person should pay all the bills.** But make sure the non-bill-paying spouse understands the system.

●**Pay bills twice a month,** on the same days every month.

●**Set up one file for the first half of the month** and another for the second. When bills come in, file by due date. If a bill has no due date, put it with the group to be paid first.

●**Choose a convenient place to pay your bills,** and use it routinely. A bill-paying kit— with checks, pens, envelopes, stamps and return-address labels—should be kept there.

●**Pay all bills of the same type in the same way.** *Example:* Charge all medical expenses—on the same card.

New opportunities: On-line payment saves time and stamps...programs such as *Quicken* can be used to print your own checks.

●**After paying a bill, put the date paid** and check number on the part that you retain. File by category—medical, taxes, etc. Keep only the current year's bills and one year back. *Important exception:* Bills you need for tax purposes.

Excellent for storage: Portable files from Decoflex. You can purchase them at most office supply stores.

Julie Morgenstern, president, Task Masters, professional organizing firm for individuals and businesses, New York, and author of *Organizing from the Inside Out.* Owl.

Simplify Your Financial Life

Consider why you have each account. There is no need for multiple money market or discount-brokerage accounts—most are pretty much the same. Also think about what you hold *in* the accounts. There is no reason to have several mutual funds with similar investment objectives...and a good mutual fund may be a better holding than a bundle of individual stocks you have bought over the years.

Eric Tyson, personal finance counselor and syndicated columnist, San Francisco, and author of *Personal Finance for Dummies.* IDG Books.

On-Line Banking Is Not for Everyone

Chris Musto, director of financial services at Gomez Advisors, Inc., independent consumer Internet research firm in Lincoln, MA. He also manages the Gomez Advisors Internet Scorecard, which helps consumers find on-line banks that best suit their needs. *www.gomez.com.*

Like traditional banks, most Internet banks provide a wide range of FDIC-insured banking products and services to consumers.

However, unlike traditional banks, which own branches, on-line banks cut costs by delivering these products and services exclusively through the Internet and other electronic channels.

OPPORTUNITIES

You're an ideal candidate for on-line banking if you...

●**Plan to keep at least several thousand dollars in an on-line account.** Many on-line banks now typically pay rates that are consistently better than the national average on all deposit accounts.

●**Want to pay your bills via your computer.** Electronic bill payment lets you "write" and send checks through your computer. You use an on-screen grid. You fill in the blanks and then send the checks. Before you sign up, be sure the institutions you pay each month accept electronic checks.

●**Use financial software, such as Quicken, to organize your finances.** Many on-line banks allow you to download account information, making it easy to integrate the data into your financial-planning software.

TRAPS

On-line banking is probably *not* for you if you...

● **Make frequent ATM withdrawals.** Because on-line banks do not have branches, you may be charged up to $1.50 per withdrawal at some ATMs.

Helpful: The Independent Community Bankers of America *(www.ibaa.org)* lists the ATMs in all 50 states that do not charge for withdrawals.

● **Want deposits to appear quickly in your checking account.** Because you must send any paper deposit through the mail, the amount takes longer to hit your account. And when you pay bills on-line with electronic checks, most on-line banks debit your account immediately. That could result in overdrafts if you're not careful.

TOP INTERNET BANKS

Before you sign up with any on-line bank, assess its hookup fees...monthly fees for electronic checking...and minimum balance requirements. *Leading on-line banks...*

● **Net.B@nk.** *www.netbank.com.*

● **Security First Network Bank.** *www. sfnb.com.*

● **Wells Fargo.** *www.wellsfargo.com.*

Odd CDs Payoff

O dd-term CDs pay more than ones with standard terms. Most banks offer odd-term certificates of deposit (CDs) because they do not want all their CDs to mature at the same time. To get customers to accept different maturities, banks pay higher interest on odd-term CDs.

Strategy: Decide what maturity you want —for instance, six months—and ask your bank for its interest rate. Then ask for the rate on odd-term CDs—for instance, five- or seven-month. The difference can be significant.

Stephanie Gallagher, personal-finance columnist, Washington, DC, and author of *Fabulous Bargains! Great Deals You Can Get for (Almost) Wholesale.* St. Martin's Griffin.

How to Get Your Money's Worth from Your Credit Cards

Robert McKinley, president of CardWeb, Inc., which tracks nationwide credit card rates, Gettysburg, PA.

N ow is an excellent time to get your credit card bills under control by changing to a card that best suits your needs. *My top choices in different categories...*

● **Balance below $2,000.** Look for a card with a very low interest rate and no annual fee.

● Capital One Bank (800-655-9116) has a 9.9% fixed interest rate, no annual fee.

● First USA (800-955-3050) has a 9.99% fixed interest rate, no annual fee.

● **Balance of $4,000 or more.** Look for a gold card with low rates but expect a higher annual fee.

● AFBA Gold Card (800-776-2265) has a 10.25% variable interest rate, $35 annual fee.

● **Charge a lot—pay your balance in full each month.** Select a credit card that has rebates or rewards for services you use.

● Southwest Airlines Rapid Rewards Visa (800-792-8472) offers a flight credit for every $1,000 spent—16 flight credits equal one free roundtrip ticket. 16.4% variable interest rate, $29 annual fee.

● **High credit limit.** Consider platinum cards. Expect interest rates in the mid-teens and credit limits of $25,000 to $100,000.

● AT&T Universal Platinum (800-662-7759) has a 16.5% variable interest rate, no annual fee and a credit line up to $25,000.

● Chase Platinum (800-324-4250) has a 15.15% variable interest rate, no annual fee and a credit line up to $100,000.

● **Debt transfer.** Look for credit cards with reasonable rates and high credit limits for consolidating your debts.

● NationsBank Visa Platinum (800-274-0877) has a 3.9% introductory fixed interest rate for six months when you transfer balances from other credit cards, then reverts to a 17.65% variable interest rate. No annual fee and a credit line up to $100,000.

●**Carry a high balance**—and want a lot of perks for it. Look for gold or platinum cards that offer perks you'll use.

●First USA Bank World Master-Card Platinum (888-467-5011) has a 15.99% fixed interest rate…$40 to $125 annual fee, depending on benefits. Each dollar earns one airline mile, good on most major domestic and international airlines (no blackout periods)…$1 million of travel accident insurance…credit card concierge makes reservations for you at restaurants, books tee times at golf courses, etc.

Closing a Credit Card

Gerri Detweiler, credit specialist and author of *Invest in Yourself: Six Secrets to a Rich Life.* John Wiley & Sons.

When you cancel a credit card, be sure it's listed as closed on your credit report. If the report still lists the account as open, your ability to borrow may be reduced. After canceling a card, ask for written verification that it has been canceled. A month later, ask for a copy of your credit report. If the report still shows the account as open, inform the credit bureau and send it a copy of the verification letter showing the account to be closed. By law, credit bureaus must verify disputed information with the source within 30 days.

More from Gerri Detweiler…

Dangers of Cosigning a Loan

You will be listed with credit bureaus as responsible for the loan—and your credit could be damaged if payments are missed. Since the amount of the loan appears as your debt, you may find it harder to qualify for a loan of your own. If payment trouble develops, you may not find out until the borrower has defaulted and your credit has been damaged.

Extra danger: Cosigning on credit cards. Since credit lines may be increased periodically, you may end up being responsible for much more than you planned.

Debt Payoff Is Getting Harder

Some credit card issuers are increasing interest charges for people in debt-workout programs. In the past, creditors reduced or eliminated interest for people working out debts, so they had a better chance of getting back their money. Now, card issuers are going in the opposite direction.

Self-defense: If you are getting into credit card debt trouble, switch as much of your balance as possible to an issuer that cuts rates for debtors or call your issuer and ask for a lower interest rate if you agree to a strict payment schedule.

Stephen Brobeck, executive director, Consumer Federation of America, Washington, DC.

Peter J. Strauss Makes the Use of Trusts In Medicaid Planning Much Simpler

Peter J. Strauss, Esq., a partner in the law firm Epstein Becker & Green, PC, 250 Park Ave., New York 10017. He is a fellow of the National Academy of Elder Law Attorneys and coauthor of *The Elder Law Handbook—A Legal and Financial Survival Guide for Caregivers and Seniors.* Facts on File.

The *average* cost of spending a year in a nursing home is about $50,000 now. But it's more than $100,000 a year in some places. Who's going to pay for this?

With the help of a good lawyer, you may be able to arrange your finances so you become eligible for Medicaid. Then the government will pay your nursing home costs.

Medicaid is a joint federal and state program that pays for the cost of a nursing home for those whose income and assets are below set amounts. To meet these limits, assets must be spent or transferred in such a way that you don't disqualify yourself for assistance. The rules are very tricky.

THE LOOKBACK RULES

Giving away your assets in order to qualify for Medicaid may seem like a smart thing to do.

Trap: When an application for Medicaid is submitted, all transfers of your assets for which you didn't receive full payment—gifts, in particular—within three to five years of the application, called a "lookback" period, are taken into account for qualification purposes.

Transfers within the lookback period may result in a penalty—a period of ineligibility for Medicaid.

The penalty on these transfers is figured by dividing the gifts by the average monthly nursing home costs in the person's area—a figure fixed by law.

Example: If, within the lookback period, a mother gives $80,000 to her children and the average nursing home cost in the area is $4,000 a month, the penalty is 20 months of ineligibility ($80,000 divided by $4,000).

The lookback periods are three years for most transfers...and five years for certain trust transfers.

USE OF TRUSTS

Different types of trusts are commonly used by older people to achieve certain objectives...

●**Revocable trusts.** Also called *living trusts,* these are trusts over which the grantor (the person setting up the trust) retains control. He/she can change beneficiaries, alter the terms of the trust or cancel it entirely.

Typically, revocable trusts are used for asset management—to empower someone to handle the funds in the event of the grantor's incapacity. These trusts are also used as will substitutes to avoid the costs and delays associated with probate.

●**Irrevocable trusts.** These are permanent trusts. Once they are set up, the grantor cannot change the terms or get the money back.

These trusts generally are used for estate planning purposes to give money to others, with strings attached.

Example: A parent may set up an irrevocable trust for the benefit of a child who is irresponsible in handling money. The trust will give the child income (in fixed amounts or at the discretion of a trustee who is not the grantor). Ulti-

mately, the money will pass to grandchildren or others under the terms of the trust.

●**Income-only trusts.** These are a type of irrevocable trust created with Medicaid eligibility in mind. The trust provides that all income is available for the grantor (who is the income beneficiary of the trust). But the assets that make up the principal of the trust can't be touched for the grantor.

The trustee has no discretion to use any principal for the benefit of the grantor. The trust funds (after any penalty period) are preserved for the next generation, which inherits the property when the grantor dies.

Note: Only trusts set up by the person who's applying for Medicaid are subject to the lookback rules. Trusts set up by third parties are not.

UNDERSTANDING TRANSFERS IN TRUST

Not all trust-related transfers are subject to the five-year lookback period nor do they necessarily result in a penalty period. *Here's a guide on trust-related transfers and their lookback periods...*

●**Transfers *to* a revocable trust.** Putting funds into a revocable trust (such as a living trust) where the grantor (the person who sets up the trust) keeps the right to cancel the trust are not subject to any lookback period.

Reason: The funds are still subject to the control of the grantor (there's been no gift), so they remain available for his/her medical care.

●**Transfers *from* a revocable trust.** Gifts made from a revocable trust are subject to a three-year lookback period. The transfers are treated as if the grantor withdrew the funds and then made the gift.

●**Transfers *to* an irrevocable trust.** Putting funds into an irrevocable trust (one that is permanent and in which the grantor cannot get back the money) are subject to the five-year lookback period as long as the grantor has no interest in the trust.

●**Transfers *from* an irrevocable trust.** There's no lookback period in this case. The lookbackperiod started to run from the time the funds were put into the trust (the date on which the gift was made).

● **Transfers *to* an income-only trust.** The five-year lookback period applies in the same manner as to any other irrevocable trust, even though the grantor only has an income interest.

● **Transfers *from* an income-only trust.** As with any other irrevocable trust, there is no lookback period, since it started to run from the time the funds went into the trust.

EXPERT ADVICE REQUIRED

Because the rules are complicated and the stakes for Medicaid eligibility are high, older people should not make sizable gifts without discussing their plans with an *elder law attorney*. Such an attorney will have expertise in Medicaid rules.

To get a free brochure about elder law attorneys, call the National Academy of Elder Law Attorneys at 520-881-4005.

Benefit of Paying Off Your Debt

Earn a high interest rate when rates are low by paying off credit card debt. Paying off a credit card balance accruing 18% interest provides the same benefit as investing at 18% —a rate *far* higher than you could get anywhere else.

Strategy: Compare your "debt portfolio" and your investment opportunities. If the interest cost on debt is higher than the after-tax gain from investments, pay off debt first.

Jonathan Pond, president, Financial Planning Information Inc., 9 Galen St., Watertown, MA 02472.

Baby Boomers' Planning Gap

Baby boomers are way ahead of their parents' generation in investing for their children's education and their own retirement. But they fall woefully short in key

legal/financial areas such as an up-to-date will…a durable power of attorney in case of incapacitation…disability insurance…written instructions for their survivors, such as a listing of their holdings and debts and the whereabouts of the key to the safe-deposit box.

Stuart Kessler, CPA, a partner in the accounting firm Goldstein Golub Kessler LLP, 1185 Avenue of the Americas, New York 10036.

Financial Planner's Wise Money Stretchers

Ross Levin, CFP, president of Accredited Investors, Inc., a financial advisory firm, 7701 France Ave. S., Suite 105, Edina, MN 55435.

The key to achieving long-term financial security is to be a smart spender. *To save more money without compromising your lifestyle…*

● **Use two checkbooks.** Most people use the amount in their checkbooks to pay for all types of expenses. But *two* checkbooks will force you to save for variable expenses. And—many banks allow you to open a second checking account for free. *How the system works…*

● Primary checkbook holds cash needed for necessities—mortgage, groceries, utilities, insurance premiums, etc.

● Second checkbook functions as a savings account and is used to pay for gifts, travel, unreimbursed health insurance costs and all other variable expenses.

The two-tiered checkbook approach will help you set saving priorities and encourage you to pay in full for major, luxury expenses rather than with a credit card.

● **Try the *painful* payment method.** The ideal way to pay for what you buy is not the one that makes you feel best. The more uncomfortable you feel when you pay, the more likely you will think about whether each purchase is really worth it. *Result:* You'll wind up spending less.

Example: If it hurts to pay cash, pay cash. If you hate writing checks, pay by check. Either method is far more annoying than using a credit card, which is the worst way to pay—because there are no feelings of restraint or guilt.

●**Forget about frequent-flier miles.** Credit cards that reward you with miles are terrible temptations. They encourage you to overspend because you think you'll get a bargain on airfare.

Reality check: Each mile you receive has a real-world value of about one cent. So if you spend $100 more at the mall than you should, your actual "reward" will be $1.

A Dollar Saved Is More Than a Dollar Earned

If you spend just a little less now on a home, a car or other high-ticket items, you will have *substantially* more money later, thanks to the miracle of compounding.

Example: You choose to save $100 a month—$3,600 over three years—by leasing a cheaper vehicle. If the money earns 9% annually, the $3,600 will compound into an astounding $28,000 after 24 years.

Rule of 72: To determine how long it will take to double your money, divide 72 by the interest rate. Money earning 9% annually will double in eight years…money earning 6% will double in 12 years.

Caution: When cutting costs, don't skimp. Planning for tomorrow should not keep you from enjoying life today.

Ed Mendlowitz, CPA, partner, Mendlowitz Weitsen, LLP, CPAs, New York.

Redeem E Bonds Or Lose Interest

You may have been given US Series E or EE Savings Bonds as an anniversary gift or when you were married. Or maybe you even bought them through a payroll savings plan at work many years ago.

You probably stashed the bonds in the back of a drawer and then forgot about them, as so many people do.

Problem: E and EE bonds stop paying interest when they reach their final maturity date. The Federal Reserve says there are now $7.39 billion worth of unredeemed savings bonds that are no longer paying interest.

What to do: Dig out your savings bonds and turn them in if they've matured. Put the money in something that pays interest.

E bonds issued before December 1965 have a 40-year final maturity, so a bond issued in December 1960 stopped paying interest in December 2000.

E bonds issued from December 1965 through June 1980 and EE bonds issued from January 1980 onward have a final maturity of 30 years, so an EE bond issued in March 1971 will stop paying interest in March 2001.

Deferring taxes: When you redeem the bonds, instead of paying tax on all the interest that has accrued, you can roll them over into US Government Series HH bonds.

HH bonds pay interest semiannually, but you will put off paying tax on your EE bonds until the HH bonds mature. HH bonds reach their final maturity after 20 years.

Barbara Weltman, an attorney with offices in Millwood, NY, and author of *J.K. Lasser's Tax Deductions for Your Small Business, Fourth Edition* (John Wiley & Sons) and *The Complete Idiot's Guide to Making Money After You Retire* (Macmillan).

Owning a Home Costs More for People With High Incomes

David S. Rhine, CPA, partner, national director of family wealth planning, BDO Seidman, LLP, New York.

Most homebuyers assume mortgage interest and property taxes are fully deductible for income taxes. But this is not true for taxpayers with "high" Adjusted

Gross Incomes. Above $128,950 most itemized deductions are reduced in 2000—up to as much as 80%. This effectively raises taxes for people above the limit—and increases the cost of owning a home.

More from David S. Rhine...

Some Ways to Give Noncash Gifts To Charity Are Better Than Others

Cash is the easiest gift to give to charity, but often not the best tax-wise. *Here are the best ways to get tax savings using noncash gifts to charity...*

●**Donate stock or fund shares.** If you own appreciated stock or mutual fund shares held for at least one year—so they qualify as long-term capital-gains property—consider donating them to charity instead of cash.

Reason: You'll get a deduction for their full market value without having to pay the capital-gains tax that would otherwise be due.

●**Unloading losers.** Don't donate shares that have declined in value to a charity. Instead, sell them and donate the proceeds. You'll realize a tax loss from the sale that you can use on your tax return.

●**"Stock bailout donation."** A stock donation can work even better if you're the owner of a privately held corporation. You can use it to have your company make a cash payment to a charity—which you deduct on your return.

How it works: Donate company shares to a public charity and have the company redeem the shares. The charity gets cash from the company. You'll get the charitable deduction on your personal tax return.

If you own 100% of the business before such a transaction, you will still own 100% after—and you will get a deduction for a payment made by the business.

Rule: When the gift is made, there can't be any enforceable agreement with the charity requiring the shares to be redeemed. Typically, the charity will want to redeem donated shares for cash.

●**Leave a retirement account to charity.** To make a charitable bequest in your will—and obtain a charitable deduction for your estate— the best donation may be a retirement account.

Reason: A retirement account, such as an IRA or a 401(k), is tax-favored while you're alive. But, after you die, account proceeds paid out to your heirs will be fully taxed at up to 39.6% on their federal returns. If you leave a retirement account to charity, your estate will get a deduction for its full value. No tax on the income will ever be paid.

Trap: If you have a qualified plan, don't bequeath appreciated assets, such as stocks, to charity under your will. Heirs inherit appreciated assets with "stepped-up basis"—the market value of the assets at your death which is treated as the cost of the assets to your heirs for tax purposes. This eliminates taxable gain.

Example: You have an IRA worth $100,000 and appreciated stock shares worth $100,000. By donating the shares to charity and keeping the IRA, your heirs pay up to $39,600 in income tax when they liquidate the IRA. Donate the IRA and bequeath the stock to heirs—they won't pay income or capital gains on the predeath appreciation.

Note: Federal law prohibits giving a retirement account away while you're alive.

●**Donate property rights to charity.** It's possible to get a no-cash-cost deduction by donating qualified property rights, known as a "conservation easement," to charity and still live on the property.

By donating property rights to a publicly supported qualified conservation group, you can bar the property's development, restrict its use and/or preserve the property's historic or scenic nature. You then can claim a charitable deduction for the amount by which the easement reduces the property's fair market value.

Pay Off a Mortgage Early? Good Question!

Making prepayments on a mortgage can be a powerful way to save—but there are drawbacks as well.

PROS
●**Gives you free-and-clear ownership of your home sooner.**

Example: A $100,000, 30-year mortgage at 8% interest carries a $734 monthly payment. Adding just a $50 prepayment monthly pays off the loan in 23 years and 11 months.

● **Saves thousands of dollars of interest expense.** The same $50 prepayment saves $39,900 of interest payments over the life of the loan.

● **Increases equity in your home,** so you'll receive more if you sell it. Halfway (15 years) through the same loan, the $50 monthly prepayments reduce your loan balance to about $59,500 compared with $76,800. So, if you then sell the home, you'll clear $17,300 more as a result of making prepayments that totaled $9,000.

CONS

● **Prepayments reduce your liquidity.** If you later need cash, you may be forced to take out a home equity loan that carries a higher interest rate than your mortgage. Moreover, home equity loan interest is deductible only on $100,000 of borrowing. So if you prepay your mortgage, you may never be able to take an interest-deductible loan against its full value again.

● **You may earn more by investing than by prepaying a mortgage.** If you are in the 28% tax bracket, an 8% mortgage costs only 5.6% after tax. If you can earn more than 5.6% in a tax-favored account or more than 8% in a taxable account, you'll be better off financially by doing so.

● **You probably are paying higher interest rates on other kinds of borrowing.** It doesn't make any sense to pay off a mortgage effectively costing 5.6% when you are paying rates near 18% on credit card loans.

Dennis Whicker, a CPA practicing in Salt Lake City.

Don't Use All Assets To Prepay

Do not pay down your mortgage until you have other investments and a contingency fund. Paying extra principal ties up more money in your house—and your home is not a liquid investment. If you are laid off or you hit bad economic times, you may need access to money quickly. You can use a contingency fund, or sell stocks or mutual funds, more easily than you can get cash out of your home.

Also: Paying down a mortgage reduces the amount of tax-deductible interest you pay—and you may want to keep the deduction.

Members of Ernst & Young personal financial counseling practice, authors of *Ernst & Young's Financial Planning Essentials.* John Wiley & Sons.

Found Money

Between $30 to $50 in loose change is in the pockets, purses and drawers of the average American. There is so much loose change lying around that some areas are experiencing a penny shortage—even though plenty of pennies have been minted. Before cashing in coins, check carefully for valuable ones—illustrated collectors' books are helpful.

Poll by Coinstar, Inc., a maker of coin-counting machines, Bellevue, WA.

New Income-Boosting Essentials

Barbara O'Neill, PhD, CFP, a professor of family and consumer sciences at Rutgers University. She is author of *Saving on a Shoestring* and *Investing on a Shoestring.* Dearborn Financial Publishing.

Yesterday's conventional wisdom held that as people neared or reached retirement age, they had to reduce risk by moving most of their savings into conservative investments, such as bonds.

Today's reality: You can't afford not to be invested in equities to some degree, even after you've retired. Stocks or stock mutual fund investments keep your income ahead of inflation. *Fact:* Stocks have outpaced inflation better than any other investment over time.

Best allocation: Keep at least 20% to 50% of your investments in stocks and stock mutual funds. The rest of your portfolio can be in less risky investments, such as bank CDs and government bonds.

For more conservative investments: Consider US Treasuries. Depending on how competitive bank rates are in your area, Treasury bills, notes and bonds will earn 1% to 4% more than bank savings products—particularly passbook accounts. And while earnings on Treasuries are subject to federal income tax like CDs, they are not subject to state and local income taxes. *Three kinds of Treasuries...*

● **Treasury bonds** are sold in $1,000 increments with maturities up to 30 years. These and other Treasury instruments are available from banks and brokerage firms for about a $50 transaction fee. Or you can purchase them directly from the Federal Reserve without a fee through a program called Treasury Direct. *For information:* 212-720-6619 or *www.ny.frb.org.*

● **Treasury bills** are sold in three-, six- and 12-month maturities and cost a minimum of $1,000 from Treasury Direct, with additional increments of $1,000.

● **Treasury notes** are sold in two- to 10-year maturities in $1,000 increments through Treasury Direct.

Strategy: "Ladder" maturities when buying CDs and Treasuries.

Instead of buying a single $10,000 CD, say, buy ten $1,000 CDs and stagger their maturities so that one comes due in year one, a second comes due in year two, a third in year three and so on.

Benefits: You won't tie up all your money in a single CD or bond—you will receive a regular check as each one matures—and you can more easily take advantage of changing interest rates.

How: If rates increase, you can move some of your money into a higher rate CD as soon as one matures, instead of having to wait until a longer term CD matures.

INVESTMENT APPROACHES

● **Never put your money in an investment product you don't completely understand.** Too many people, while chasing high yields, put money into investments only because they've been told they'll get a high return.

● **Follow the "four-year-old-kid rule."** Don't invest in anything you can't quickly and easily explain in a way that a four-year-old would understand.

● **Don't avoid an investment simply because it has a duration longer than your life expectancy.** Just because someone is age 70 doesn't mean he/she shouldn't buy a 30-year Treasury bond. These long-term investments generally produce higher returns than ones with shorter terms. Remaining principal will become part of your estate and will be passed on to your heirs.

● **Continue to set financial goals.** Reaching retirement doesn't mean you've reached your financial goals. You may need more money in retirement than you had planned. *Retirement expenses may include...*

● Travel, which can be expensive.

● Unanticipated health-care needs plus long-term-care insurance.

● Building up your estate to leave more to your heirs.

● Helping grandchildren pay for college.

● One or more new cars.

Expenses such as these may require you to shift assets to higher producing, riskier investments.

Required: A sound financial strategy to increase the odds that these new goals will be met.

CONTINUE TO WORK

There's a growing sentiment in this country that retirement is a dead end. More and more people say they don't want to retire—ever. They want to continue to work, at least part-time, as long as their health holds out, well past age 65. *If this is your intention...*

● **Check with former employers** about returning to work.

● **Get a part-time job.**

● **Split a full-time job** with somebody in a time-sharing arrangement.

● **Turn a hobby into a business.**

As you know, continuing to work after you've started receiving Social Security benefits can reduce the size of your benefit checks. *How Social Security cutbacks work for 2000...*

● **Those aged 62 to 65** can earn $10,080 before losing $1 of benefits for every $2 earned.

● **For those over 65,** there is no earnings limit. Social Security will not be cut back no matter what they earn.

CUT EXPENSES

One of the easiest ways to increase your retirement income is simply to spend less by cutting expenses. This will enable you to save more. *Some painless strategies for reducing costs include...*

● **Review your insurance policies** to make sure you're not paying for coverage you no longer need.

● **Play the "age card,"** and get a Senior ID through your local Office of the Aging. This card entitles you to a wide array of discounts.

● **Shift to a low-interest credit card.**

● **Join a co-op** to buy food in bulk.

● **Choose basic clothing styles** that can be dressed up or down. And build your wardrobe around a few colors that complement you.

● **Revive the lost art of letter-writing,** or better still, send E-mail, instead of making expensive long-distance telephone calls.

● **Call the local utility company** for an energy audit and take advantage of its cost-saving advice.

● **Consider low-cost entertainment options,** such as early bird dinners, college theater presentations and inexpensive adult education classes.

● **Swap services,** such as pet-feeding and house-sitting, with neighbors and friends.

ATM Self-Defense

To head off ATM problems, always keep the receipt—no matter what transaction you do at an automated teller machine. Deposit checks only at an ATM at the branch where you keep your account. Never deposit cash, which can be impossible to trace. Use ATMs only at banks you know. Double-check your end-of-month statements to be sure all credits and debits are correct.

If you find an error: Call or visit your local bank immediately. You have 60 days from the date of the problem to report it—but the sooner you do, the sooner you can stop possible fraudulent activity.

Barry Schreiber, PhD, professor of criminal justice, St. Cloud State University, St. Cloud, MN, and editor, *ATM Crime and Security Newsletter,* 26720 Highway 169, Zimmerman, MN.

Better On-Line Mortgage Shopping

Visit sites with *at least* 10 lenders. Sites with fewer than 10 may be set up to lead you to a particular lender, which may or may not offer the best deal. Sites with more than 10 lenders give you a wide enough choice so you should be able to find the best mortgage for you.

Examples: E-Loan *(www.e-loan.com)* has more than 60 lenders...iOwn.com *(www. iown .com)* has more than 30. One site, Real Estate.com *(www. realestate.com),* offers loan auctions. The borrower posts criteria and lenders bid for the loan.

Blanche Evans, author of *Homesurfing.net: The Insider's Guide to Buying and Selling Your Home Using the Internet.* Dearborn Financial.

7

Insurance Strategies

How to Outsmart Your Managed-Care Organization

Before the era of managed care, people who sought medical care were known as patients. Nowadays many of us are *customers* of a health-maintenance organization, preferred-provider organization or another managed-care organization (MCO).

Customers of MCOs don't always get what they pay for...

●**Some MCOs deny patients key diagnostic tests.**

●**Some MCOs refuse to pay for costly medications.**

●**Some MCOs push customers into surgery with a surgeon who has substandard training**—in a second-rate hospital.

There's really no need to be a victim of managed care. *Here's how to fight back...*

PLAIN FACTS ABOUT MCOs

Managed care is big business. Your doctor may focus on easing symptoms and healing disease, but MCOs inevitably focus on the *bottom line*. Whatever its fancy brochure says, its allegiance is to its shareholders—not to you.

Like all businesses, MCOs try to maximize revenues while minimizing expenditures. Raising premiums is one way MCOs cut costs. They also reduce the *medical loss ratio*. In plain English, that means delivering as little health care as possible.

CHOOSING A DOCTOR

In most MCOs, customers must choose a primary-care physician from a roster of participating doctors. These doctors are listed by medical specialty.

Bruce A. Barron, MD, PhD, associate professor of clinical obstetrics and gynecology at Columbia–Presbyterian Medical Center and a former senior medical director at Empire Blue Cross/Blue Shield, both in New York City. He is author of *Outsmarting Managed Care: A Doctor Shares His Insider's Secrets to Getting the Health Care You Want.* Times Books.

Trap: Just because a doctor is listed as an internist, cardiologist, etc., does not mean he/she has had the extra training and has passed the rigorous tests required for board certification.

It's common for MCOs to hire doctors who are not board-certified, even though board certification has long been considered a mark of medical expertise.

What to do: Call your MCO or the doctor's office to find out about board certification.

For a list of board-certified physicians in the US, consult the *Directory of Medical Specialists.* This book—available at most public libraries—also details doctors' training, experience, etc.

The American Medical Association offers similar information on its Web site, *www.ama-assn.org.* Or you can call the American Board of Medical Specialties at 800-776-2378.

Important: If a doctor you are considering practices as part of a group, check the credentials of his partners, too.

The doctor you select must be your ally. Will he help you fight for proper medical care? Will he help you get critical tests, treatments and referrals even if the MCO doesn't want to provide them? Ask at your first visit.

Although it is hard to know how a doctor will behave until a problem does arise, it is important to find out his general feelings on the subject.

GETTING FIRST-RATE CARE

Some doctors like to joke that managed care is fine—as long as you don't get sick.

Unfortunately, the joke contains a kernel of truth. And the more serious your illness, the harder it can be to get state-of-the-art medical care.

Example: An endoscopic examination of the stomach is often the best way to check for a peptic ulcer. But an MCO may refuse to cover endoscopy, arguing that this $1,200 procedure falls outside its "practice guidelines."

Each time you discuss treatment options with your doctor, ask whether his recommendations are constrained by rules set down by the MCO.

If so, ask what he *would* do—which tests, procedures, medications, etc., he would recommend—if there were no such constraints.

If this recommendation differs from his original one, ask that he explain his position *in writing.* That way, you'll have a record if you need to appeal an MCO decision.

If you need a specialist, do the ones affiliated with the MCO have the best qualifications? Or are there better specialists outside of the MCO's network?

If you need surgery, how do the surgical track records of hospitals affiliated with the MCO compare with the track records of hospitals unaffiliated with the MCO?

Death rates tend to be much lower in hospitals that do a high volume of a given procedure.

If you believe the MCO's rules will adversely affect your health, the MCO is required *by law* in some states to review your case. But you'll have a battle on your hands.

TAKING IT TO THE TOP

When you telephone the MCO to appeal a decision, you'll probably talk first to a "case manager." In many cases, this person is a nurse who simply explains the MCO's treatment guidelines.

If the case manager rejects your appeal, insist on speaking to a "medical director"—a doctor who works for the MCO.

Do *not* let yourself be intimidated. Non-physicians tend to be deferential around medical doctors. That's inappropriate here. You're dealing not with Marcus Welby, but with a representative of a giant corporation.

Find out the medical director's specialty. If he's a dermatologist and you have cancer, he may know less about your condition than you do. In such a case, ask to speak to a medical director who has training in oncology.

If this medical director rules against you, ask to speak with the MCO's "medical director for policy." This company official has greater power to help you.

Crucial: Each time you speak with a representative of the MCO, ask for a report of the conversation or ruling *in writing.* It's essential that you create a paper trail. That way, you'll have all the documentation needed if you choose to get an external review, in which an expert outside the MCO evaluates your case.

At some point as you make your way up the hierarchy, the MCO will probably give in to your demands.

If the MCO does not give in, file a complaint with the agency that regulates insurance companies. In most states, it's the department of consumer affairs.

Another option: Contact the media. When TV or newspaper reporters cover cases in which an MCO customer has been denied care, the MCO almost always capitulates.

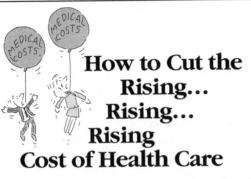

How to Cut the Rising... Rising... Rising Cost of Health Care

JoAnn E. Manson, MD, DrPH, professor of medicine at Harvard Medical School and chief of preventive medicine at Brigham & Women's Hospital, Boston.

Frank Darras, partner at Shernoff, Bidart, Darras & Dillon, 600 S. Indian Hill Blvd., Claremont, CA 91711, and coauthor of *Fight Back & Win: How to Get Your HMO and Health Insurance to Pay Up.* Capital Books.

Charles Inlander, president of People's Medical Society, 462 Walnut St., Allentown, PA 18102, and author of *The Over-the-Counter Doctor.* Andrews McMeel.

Health-care costs continue to escalate, by 5% during the past two years alone —that's twice the inflation rate. Health-care providers are frequently accused of caring more about their healthy profits than about healthy people.

Three experts from different aspects of health care give advice on how to beat these rising costs...

HEALTH SAVERS
JoAnn E. Manson, MD, DrPH

Prevention is the best antidote for escalating health-care costs—especially for chronic diseases, such as heart disease, stroke, adult-onset diabetes, cancer and osteoporosis. *Tried-and-true strategies...*

•**Don't smoke.** Avoid all forms of tobacco —including secondhand smoke.

•**Exercise moderately for at least 30 minutes a day.** After quitting smoking, physical activity is the most important thing anyone can do to preserve health. Also include resistance training to build muscle. This helps preserve strength, balance and mobility and will boost your metabolism—so you are less likely to gain weight as you age.

•**Eat a plant-based diet.** To help prevent heart disease, stroke and cancer, eat at least five servings of fruits and vegetables daily.

Lean toward whole-grain, unprocessed foods. Make sure that no more than 7% of your caloric intake is from saturated fats.

HEALTH INSURANCE
Frank Darras

There are many ways to limit what you spend on health care, from taking advantage of free services to challenging HMO denials. *Most important...*

•**Keep all your policy materials**—including the advertising that prompted you to subscribe...records of doctor visits...communications with the medical group and the plan. Gain a thorough understanding of benefits, policies and procedures of your plan and your medical conditions. Question your doctor to make sure you are getting proper treatment and quality of care promised.

•**Get prescreening and wellness tests.** Generally, the earlier a health problem is diagnosed, the easier and less expensive it will be to treat. Most plans include free wellness and prescreening services. Use them.

Included: Cholesterol, blood pressure, diabetes, mammograms, Pap smears and childhood immunizations.

•**Make sure prescriptions for chronic conditions are covered**—especially when considering a health plan switch. Look at the plan formulary—list of prescription drugs covered by a plan—and compare what is covered and the deductibles before changing plans. Inquire about generics if your name-brand prescription is not on the list.

•**Follow the grievance and appeal requirements to the letter** if you feel you aren't getting proper care or you've been denied or delayed access for testing, treatment or a specialty referral. The more thorough your appeal, the more prompt a response you'll receive.

Document what treatment was promised, why it should be covered and what effect the delay or denial of benefits is causing you.

It is always persuasive if your primary caregiver is advocating and supporting your benefit or authorization requests...so always be courteous and persistent.

Also complain in writing to the state's Department of Corporations or Department of Insurance. HMOs across the country are graded on the timeliness and delivery of their promised services and how easy they are to access...and they want their report cards to shine.

MEDICATION SAVERS
Charles Inlander

Medication isn't cheap, prescription or non-prescription. *To trim costs...*

●**Order medication for chronic conditions by mail or on-line.** It's often 10% to 15% cheaper. AARP has a mail-order service for its members, as do many health plans.

Check prices at local pharmacies as well. If the drug is cheaper on-line than at your local pharmacy, your pharmacist may match the lower price.

Leading on-line services: www.cvs.com... www.drugstore.com...www.planetrx.com... www.walgreens.com.

Never buy from pharmacies that aren't based in the US—you may not get the proper formulation of the drug.

●**Buy generic drugs whenever possible.** This can save between 50% and 75%. Generic formulations are not for everyone—ask your doctor.

●**Order only a few days' supply of a new prescription.** Prescription medications aren't returnable, so if you have a bad reaction to a drug, you are stuck. Take it for a day or two. If it works, you can fill the rest of the prescription.

Better: Ask your doctor for samples.

●**Try an over-the-counter medication instead of a prescription.** If you're paying for prescription drugs, an over-the-counter remedy may be just as effective and much less expensive. Again, ask your doctor first.

●**Regularly review your list of all medications with your doctor.** Include vitamins, over-the-counter drugs, herbal remedies and prescriptions.

First check for dangerous interactions. Then make sure you aren't wasting money on medications that are no longer necessary. The dosage might have changed as well—for instance, if you've lost weight.

More from Charles Inlander...

911 Danger?

Beware: Calling 911 can be very costly if you belong to an HMO. Some HMOs' membership materials purposely omit directing members to call 911 if they think they are having a heart attack or other major emergency. This may allow the HMO to refuse to pay for the cost of a 911 response—which can be as much as $1,000.

Troubling: Three-quarters of HMOs said they would deny a claim if a problem was determined not to be an emergency.

Self-defense: Know your HMO's policy on calling 911. If you are considering joining an HMO, find one that uses a *prudent layperson* rule for emergencies—meaning it will pay if a reasonable person would consider the situation an emergency.

Short-Term Health Insurance

This can protect you between jobs. It may also be suitable for recent college graduates who are no longer covered by their parents' insurance...and for Medicare beneficiaries traveling abroad and not covered by other policies. Cost depends on copays, deductibles and coverage limits. *Renewal is not automatic* —you must reapply at the end of each coverage period.

Limitations: Coverage may be limited to 180 days within a year...short-term policies do not cover maternity costs—except the cost of complications associated with birth...not all states allow the sale of short-term health insurance.

Roy Diliberto, president, Financial Planning Association, Denver.

Millions of Americans Must Buy Their Own Health Insurance... How to Choose Wisely

Bruce Pyenson and Jim O'Connor, principals with Milliman & Robertson, a consulting firm that works with insurance companies and health-care providers, 2 Pennsylvania Plaza, New York 10121. Mr. Pyenson is author of several books, including *J.K. Lasser's Employee Benefits for Small Business*. Prentice-Hall.

Most health insurance is provided through group policies in the workplace. But there are millions of people who are self-employed or between jobs who have to find individual coverage on their own. Medicare also offers different coverage options.

While there are plenty of good policies out there, finding one that fits your needs takes some digging.

SIZE UP YOUR NEEDS

The health-care needs of families with young children are different from those of singles starting new jobs...couples without children... and empty nesters. Families with infants want a full range of preventive care that covers everything from routine vaccinations to ear infections. Healthy singles may only need bare-bones coverage for unexpected catastrophes.

In these days of managed care, there are four basic types of coverage...

HEALTH MAINTENANCE ORGANIZATIONS (HMOs)

A very prevalent type of group coverage, HMOs provide comprehensive medical care through networks of physicians. Typically, you pay $5 or $10 per in-network doctor visit and don't have to fill out forms after each appointment or worry about meeting a deductible requirement.

If you have a special health problem, you typically must first consult your primary care physician—also known as the *gatekeeper*. This physician may treat you or may refer you to a specialist. If you decide to use an out-of-network specialist or hospital, coverage—if any— is limited.

With limited choice about which doctors and hospitals to use and limited access to specialists, these plans are usually the most economical. Your out-of-pocket costs are fairly low for the wide range of coverage you get.

Best for: People with children who are new to a community—they have no relationships with physicians or hospitals. Also good for people with children whose current physician and hospital are part of the HMO network.

PREFERRED PROVIDER ORGANIZATIONS (PPOs)

These types of policies—which are more expensive than comparable HMOs—give you the ability to go outside the plan network for your medical care. Most PPO plans don't have a gatekeeper system, so you usually don't need approval to see specialists.

If you see a physician within the network, you get one level of benefits (usually 80% of a claim is covered). If you see a physician outside the network, you get another, lower level of benefits (only 60% to 70% of the claim might be covered).

Best for: People who want more choice about health-care providers...and whose doctors are part of the PPO network.

INDEMNITY POLICIES

These plans pay benefits no matter what doctor or hospital you go to. Such traditional policies appeal to people who have lived in the same community for a long time and have established ties to physicians and hospitals. While they guarantee you the most latitude in terms of choosing your health-care providers, indemnity plans are also the most expensive. Sometimes people who want the flexibility of an indemnity policy opt for high deductibles of as much as $10,000 to reduce monthly premiums.

"ANY DOCTOR" POLICIES

These hybrid plans use a PPO approach for hospitals but allow you to see any licensed physicians you wish. They are cheaper than indemnity policies but more expensive than full-fledged PPOs.

Best for: People who feel comfortable with the hospitals in the PPO network but want the flexibility of using any doctor they choose.

FINDING THE BEST PLAN

●**Research what is available in your state.** Because each state regulates insurance, choices will be limited. Not all insurance companies offer policies in all states. And a company's policies may be different in different states.

If your car and homeowner's insurance is with a company that sells through a network of agents, start by calling your agent.

If you belong to a professional or trade group or a college alumni association, find out if these organizations offer special health policies for members. Such policies often cost less than individual policies but more than group policies. If you have chronic health problems, these policies can be a good deal since you may not be able to get an affordable policy on your own.

●**Determine what different types of policies will cost you.** Call two major companies that write health insurance nationwide.

For HMOs: Aetna (800-872-3862)…United Health Group (877-311-7848).

For PPOs, "Any Doctor" and indemnity: Fortis Health (800-211-1193)…Mutual of Omaha (800-775-6000).

Simplify your search by using the Internet. Two sites that provide up to 20 different premium quotes are *www.quotesmith.com* and *www.insweb.com.*

Be sure to get the answers to some crucial questions…

●**Does the plan cover maternity, mental health and substance abuse?**

●**What are the rules concerning preexisting conditions** (health problems you had before taking out the policy)?

●**Ask the insurer about rate increases.** You want to know how often and by how much insurers boost their premiums each year. Ask what the increases have been for the past several years. Some companies charge very low initial rates but then raise premiums by a large amount. Rate increases are currently running 10% to 15% a year. If your insurer is boosting rates by 30% or more annually, it's time to shop around.

●**Find out if customers are satisfied.** Get the names of current HMO members. Ask if they've experienced delays in obtaining membership cards, problems communicating with physicians, difficulty getting pharmacies to accept their coverage, trouble getting doctor's appointments quickly or trouble getting prompt referrals to specialists.

You can also call your state insurance or health department (they usually are listed in the state government pages of your telephone directory). Some states develop statistics that indicate complaint ratios of HMOs.

If you have an established doctor, you might also call him/her for feedback on the plan you are considering, particularly for HMOs.

Shrewder Long-Term-Care Insurance Buying

Terry-Ann Orman, CFP, financial planning specialist with the Wealth Management Group at Beers & Cutler PLLC, Washington, DC.

Best time to buy long-term-care insurance is in your early 60s. At that age, the premiums are relatively low and there is small chance of a health problem that could make it impossible to obtain coverage.

Waiting trap: Premiums may be twice as high if you wait until your 70s—if you can obtain coverage at all. *Note:* The probability of needing long-term-care insurance is less than 10% for people under age 65…and rises to 40% for people in their 80s.

Comparison shop before you buy…make sure your package gives broad coverage and includes protection against rising health-care costs.

When comparing insurers: Make sure that the insurance company is strong financially. Agencies such as Moody's Investor Service (*www.moodys.com*), A.M. Best Company (*www.ambest.com*) and Duff & Phelps (*www. dcrco.com*) make their ratings available to the public.

Ask questions until you thoroughly understand what the policy does—and does not—cover. Assuming good health, the basic policy premiums can range from $1,400 per year for a five-year benefit if the policy is purchased at age 60 to $2,900 per year if purchased at age 70.

How You Can Make the Most of Medicare Coverage

David S. Landay, Esq., president of NVR, Inc., a New York City company that provides financial counseling to people who have serious health conditions. He is author of *Be Prepared: The Complete Financial, Legal and Practical Guide to Living with Cancer, HIV and Other Life-Challenging Conditions*. St. Martin's Press.

As you may already know, Medicare has two key advantages over private health insurance. It costs little (or nothing) and is available to every US citizen or legal resident age 65 or older—even those with pre-existing conditions that would make them ineligible for private insurance.

Eligible people receive an enrollment form in the mail a few months before turning 65. Once they fill it out and send it back, they're in the program.

But like most federal programs, Medicare is enormously complex. David S. Landay, a lawyer specializing in counseling people with serious illness, explains how take full advantage of it…

•*I know that Medicare has two parts. Could you please explain them?*

Part A covers in-patient hospital care and—under some circumstances—home health care, treatment in a nursing facility and hospice care.

This part of the program is free to any Medicare enrollee who has accumulated—or whose spouse has accumulated—about 40 credits. That generally means 10 years of full-time work.

Part B covers doctors' fees, outpatient medical and surgical services, diagnostic tests and more. This part is optional. It costs $45.50 per month.

You'll automatically be enrolled in Part A if you complete the Medicare application. When you enroll in Part A, you're automatically enrolled in Part B, unless you check a box on the enrollment form.

•*Is Part B worth the expense?*

For most people, the answer is yes. Otherwise, unless you're covered by private insurance, you'll be responsible for paying doctors' fees as well as the costs of diagnostic tests. Compared with other insurance plans, the monthly premium is very reasonable.

Some people decline Part B because they're covered by a group insurance plan at work and feel they don't need additional coverage.

This may be unwise, particularly for people who have a medical problem or who come from a family with a history of medical problems, since Part B picks up many of the co-payments and deductibles.

•*Where does Medigap coverage fit in?*

Since Medicare doesn't cover everything, many people get additional coverage through a so-called Medigap policy.

Medigap policies are sold by private insurance companies, but the benefits they offer are standardized. This makes it easy to compare prices and coverage levels among companies.

There are 10 Medigap policies, designated by the letters A through J. Plan A provides the most basic coverage, Plan J the most comprehensive. Each policy covers some or all of Medicare's coinsurance payments. A few pay the deductibles as well.

Which plan makes sense for you depends upon your health, the cost of any prescription medications you take and, of course, what you can afford to pay in monthly premiums.

Medigap policies can be confusing, and there's a great deal of overlap among them. For free help in picking one, call your state health insurance assistance program. Look in your phone book in the state government section under "Insurance" or "Department of Insurance."

●*Can I switch Medigap policies if my health starts to decline?*

Yes, but try to do so within six months of the time you first enroll in the program. Otherwise, you'll have to pay a higher premium because of your preexisting condition.

By law, every Medigap policy comes with a money-back guarantee. If you're dissatisfied with the coverage, ask for a refund and switch to another insurer.

●*What's the best policy for covering prescription drugs?*

The most comprehensive Medigap policy, Plan J, pays 50% of the cost of prescription drugs up to an annual maximum of $3,000. Plans H and I also pay 50% of the cost, but the annual cap will be lower.

Except for medications you receive in the hospital and some cancer drugs, Medicare does not pay the cost of medications.

●*What is Medicare managed care?*

It's an arrangement whereby an HMO or another managed-care program provides Medicare coverage.

Signing your benefits over to an HMO typically extends your coverage to things not traditionally covered by Medicare—dental care, hearing aids, prescription medications, etc. And the fees with a Medicare HMO are more predictable than those in fee-for-service coverage.

The disadvantages with this arrangement are the same as those you would face in any managed-care organization. You'll have to choose a primary-care physician from the plan's roster, and you'll have to get all of your care within the plan. The plan—and not you—will be managing your care.

If you sign up for managed care and decide you're unhappy with your treatment, you can switch back to standard Medicare at any time.

●*How do I protect myself in case I need long-term care?*

Neither Medicare nor the various Medigap policies pay for indefinite nursing home care. Review your policies carefully to determine exactly what's covered, and then decide whether you need extra insurance. Consult a lawyer, social worker or your insurance broker if you need assistance.

A companion program to Medicare, Medicaid does provide long-term nursing care.

Ordinarily, only low-income people and those who meet certain financial criteria are eligible for Medicaid. But home owners and others with substantial financial assets who anticipate that they may need extended long-term care should consult a lawyer. In many cases, it's possible to take advantage of the Medicaid safety net without liquidating all of your assets.

Insurance Gap Trap

Your business insurance policies may not cover everything you think they do.

Example: Normal hazard insurance does not cover floods, earthquakes in California or hurricanes in Florida.

"Replacement value" insurance for structures may not cover upgrades in a replacement structure that are required by building codes.

Coverage for business equipment, particularly computers, may not cover the value of the information on the equipment, which may be far more valuable than the equipment itself.

Prudent: Ask your broker—and if possible, a second broker—to identify all the company's points of vulnerability…and give advice on how to fill any significant gaps.

Bernard Kulik, associate administrator for disaster assistance, US Small Business Administration, Washington, DC.

Compare Insurance Quotes

Comparison shopping for term-life insurance could lower your premiums. Rates for term-life insurance have been plummeting in recent years as insurers have become more competitive. To compare the rates you're paying now with the rates you could be paying if you bought a new policy today, visit the Web site *www.quotesmith.com*. It provides free policy quotes.

Caution: Don't drop your old policy until the new one is in place.

Jonathan Pond, president, Financial Planning Information, Watertown, MA, and author of *Your Money Matters*. Putnam.

Life Insurance Checkup

Persons who funded their estate plans with universal life insurance before 1991 may be facing a ticking time bomb.

Trap: Because interest rates were so much higher then than now, the "policy illustrations" used to determine the policy's performance may now provide a much smaller benefit than expected—leaving the estate short of funds.

When insurance is owned by a life insurance trust, there's an extra complication—coverage must be updated by the trustee rather than the insured.

Strategy: Ask the insurance company for an "in-force illustration." Make sure it shows the current state of the policy and projects future policy performance using today's rates—which may be one-third of original rates. This will tell you whether you need to increase your premium payments or change policies.

Marc J. Minker, partner, Personal Financial Counseling Group, Ernst & Young LLP, 433 Hackensack Ave., Hackensack, NJ 07601.

Life Insurance Is a Vital Tool for Protecting a Family's Financial Security

Lee Slavutin, MD, CPC, CLU, chairman of Stern Slavutin-2 Inc., an insurance and estate planning firm, 530 Fifth Ave., New York 10036. Dr. Slavutin is author of the recent *Guide to Life Insurance Strategies* (Practitioners Publishing Co.) and the AICPA course "Tax Planning with Life Insurance." He has also published more than 75 articles on insurance and estate planning.

The exact kind of insurance protection a family requires depends on particular circumstances. These guidelines can help determine what is right for you and your family. *Reasons to buy life insurance…*

● **To protect family income.** The most basic use of life insurance is to protect the family's income in the event of the death of the breadwinner. Yet many families—especially young families—are underinsured.

It's not difficult to estimate how much insurance you need. *How to do it…*

● Take the amount of your annual earnings and subtract from it the amount of income tax you pay and amount you save. This is the portion of your earnings that your family is living on.

● Determine the amount of principal your family will need to generate sufficient income to replace these earnings if they are lost. Thus, assuming a 5% after-tax return, $20,000 of principal will be needed to generate every $1,000 of income.

● Subtract from this principal the amount of any other savings or investments that may be available to produce income after your death.

The result will be the amount of life insurance proceeds needed to replace your earnings should you die.

Example: The family breadwinner annually earns $100,000, pays $25,000 in income tax, and saves $10,000. The family is living on $65,000. Assuming a net after-tax return of 5%, principal of $1.3 million would produce that much income. If the family has savings of $150,000 outside retirement plans, and another $150,000 in retirement plans, they need $1 million of insurance to close the gap.

Insurance needs can be gauged more exactly by taking into account the time duration of specific financial needs. In our example, the family may not have to make up $65,000 a year forever—for instance, after the mortgage is paid off and the children are grown, income needs may drop off. To estimate needs more precisely you should consult with an expert.

Best income-protection insurance: Term insurance often is best to protect family income because it is inexpensive.

Best: Seek a *level-premium* term policy to avert future premium increases. Make sure it is guaranteed 20 to 30 years—some companies offer only a five-year guarantee. Also, ask about your options to convert the policy to a *whole life, universal* or *variable policy* down the road.

Price outlook: In the near future, I expect there will be a leveling out or even an increase in term insurance premium prices, so now is the time to buy.

●**To protect family assets.** Many older people have accumulated substantial assets—a home, business, investments—that they want to pass on to heirs.

If these assets exceed the amount that can be passed on free of estate tax, life insurance may be needed to finance estate tax on the assets at rates that may reach as high as 55%.

Exempt amount: In 2000, an individual can leave $675,000 free of estate tax, and a couple that utilizes proper planning can leave up to $1.35 million.

Tax trap: If you make the mistake of owning the insurance policy that will be used to finance ·the tax on your estate, the policy proceeds will be part of the estate and be taxed themselves, rather than be available to pay tax.

So make sure the policy is owned by a third party—either a trust or perhaps your children. *Caution:* If a trust is to be the owner, the trust documents should be drawn up by a lawyer who specializes in trusts and estates, not by a general practitioner.

Never require the trust itself to pay estate taxes, or the IRS may hold that the policy actually is part of your estate. Rather, give the trustee discretionary authority to lend money

to the estate or buy assets from the estate, to finance the tax payments.

QPRTs and GRATs: Two devices often used in estate plans to pass assets to heirs on favorable tax terms are *qualified personal residence trusts* (QPRTs)…and *grantor retained annuity trusts* (GRATs).

Each can offer benefits if the grantor outlives the term of the trust. But if he/she dies during that term, the trust assets will be taxed as part of his estate. So purchasing insurance for the term of the trust can provide a safety net for this plan.

Option: A couple that needs life insurance to help cover a future estate tax liability may reduce the premium cost by buying a second-to-die policy that pays a benefit on the death of the longer-lived spouse.

●**To fund a charitable bequest.** It's possible to fund a gift to charity with life insurance. And the idea makes sense if you have life insurance that you no longer need.

Example: After the mortgage is paid off, the kids have grown up, and your retirement accounts are fully funded, you may no longer need the life insurance that you bought when you were younger to protect your family. By donating the policy to charity you may get a charitable income tax deduction for the policy's value (essentially what you paid in premiums over the years), plus further deductions for any premiums you continue to pay on it.

An even better idea may be to keep the life insurance policy to finance bequests to heirs, freeing up other property to be donated to charity. This arrangement works particularly well with qualified retirement plan accounts and IRAs. These retirement accounts can be subject to double taxation on death—first estate tax, then income tax when funds are withdrawn by heirs.

By donating such retirement accounts to charity, an estate can get a charitable deduction while heirs receive an income-tax-free death benefit from the insurance, instead of taxable funds from the retirement plan.

SMART BUYING

There are a lot of different insurance policies on the market and the cheapest is not necessarily a bargain. Get expert advice, ideally from *two* people—an insurance professional, and...an accountant or lawyer you trust, one who receives no insurance commission.

The combination of insurance and tax law is extremely complex. It is vital to get expert professional advice before acting.

More from Lee Slavutin...

Alternative to Canceling Life Insurance

To get out of a whole-life policy that does not fit your needs, consider letting it lapse. By not paying the premium—the insurer may then apply the cash value to term insurance with the same death benefit. Or declare the policy reduced and paid up to get a lower, lifetime death benefit based on the cash value.

Other alternatives: A tax-free exchange into an annuity. Consult your financial adviser. Or you may be able to sell the policy to a viatical settlement company.

Disability Insurance Trap

Some insurers are denying coverage under long-term-disability policies on the basis of a *Functional Capacity Evaluation* (FCE) conducted by physical therapists.

FCE tests are designed to simulate the demands on a person's body by requiring him/her to perform physically demanding, repetitive and stressful activities. But FCEs are unreliable.

Self-defense: Be sure your policy only requires examination by physicians and does not mention FCEs. Insist that the insurer adhere to the policy.

Richard Quadrino, partner, Quadrino & Schwartz, PC, attorneys specializing in insurance cases, 666 Old Country Rd., Garden City, NY 11530.

Beware Private Pension Plans

Private Pension Plans (PPPs) are just variable life insurance policies with fancy sales pitches. Brokers may highlight a PPP's big selling point—the ability to borrow from it tax-free.

What your broker won't tell you: Cash value is low in the early years due to high brokers' commissions—you'll lose money if you want to cash out. If you borrow, your money is effectively committed to *cash-value life insurance*—not always the best investment option.

Trap: If the loan lapses, you face a big tax bill—loans get added back to the cash value to determine taxable gain.

Better alternatives: Cheap, guaranteed, convertible, level-premium term insurance and no-load mutual funds, such as Vanguard's index funds (800-523-7731).

Glenn Daily, a fee-only insurance consultant in New York.

Shop Around For Car Insurance

Insurance rates have been dropping because cars are now safer, auto thefts are down and drunk-driving laws are stronger. Comparison shopping for insurance could cut your rate by even more—rates vary widely among insurers.

Caution: Your rate will go up, not down, if you buy a new, more expensive car or a vehicle that is more likely to damage others in a collision.

Robert Hunter, director of insurance, Consumer Federation of America, Washington, DC.

Advice About Appeals

You may be able to handle the early stages of a Medicare appeal yourself. But—if the claim is for what you consider to be a sizable amount, it's wise to retain a lawyer.

If Medicare loses, it has a right of appeal and you must continue to see things through.

There are several Medicare advocacy programs that provide free or low-cost counseling on the appeals process. *Among them...*

●**Center for Medicare Advocacy** (860-456-7790).

●**Medicare Rights Center** (212-869-3850).

Peter J. Strauss, Esq., partner in the law firm Epstein Becker & Green, PC, 250 Park Ave., New York 10017. He is a fellow of the National Academy of Elder Law Attorneys and coauthor of The Elder Law Handbook—A Legal and Financial Survival Guide for Caregivers and Seniors. *Facts on File.*

Beware of Too Much Insurance

If the kids are grown, the mortgage is paid off, retirement plans are fully funded and estate taxes are not a concern, you may no longer need life insurance—while the premiums you pay reduce your spendable cash.

Options: If you own a policy with cash value, cash it in or donate it to charity for a tax deduction. If you have a term policy, terminate it.

Caution: The tax and financial implications of cashing in a policy can be very complex, so review your situation carefully.

The Consumer Federation of America will run a computerized analysis of your policy and advise if you should keep it. Call 202-387-6121. *Fee:* $40 for the first report, $35 for each additional one.

Edward Mendlowitz, CPA, partner, Mendlowitz Weitsen, LLP, CPAs, 2 Pennsylvania Plaza, Suite 1500, New York 10121.

Renter's Insurance: A Must Have

Rental insurance is a must for people who live in apartments. Many people believe that a building's insurance covers their belongings in case of fire or other catastrophe. But that is not true—even in condominiums or co-ops. The only way to protect what you own, no matter where you live, is to have your own insurance policy. *And:* Apartment owners need insurance even if they rent out the apartment.

Robert Irwin, real estate investor and broker, Los Angeles, and author of The 90 Second Lawyer. *John Wiley & Sons.*

8

Tax Angles

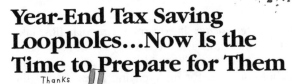

Year-End Tax Saving Loopholes...Now Is the Time to Prepare for Them

FOR INDIVIDUALS

Here's an incentive for you to spend some time in the last two months of the year cutting your 2000 tax bill—use the tax money you save on a millennium spree.

Loophole: Wipe out the tax on investment gains. Sell assets on which you have losses before the end of the year and use the losses to offset the capital gains you've taken earlier in the year, especially short-term capital gains which are taxed at up to 39.6%.

In addition to offsetting an unlimited amount of capital gains with capital losses, you can use an extra $3,000 of losses to offset salary and other income.

Capital losses you can't use on your 2000 return can be carried forward and applied against gains and up to $3,000 of salary in future years.

Planning ahead: Estimate capital gains distributions from mutual funds. Be sure to have enough losses on hand to offset these taxable distributions.

Loophole: Avoid the "wash sale rule." The wash sale rule bars investors from deducting losses when the same securities are purchased within 30 days before or after the stock is sold. But what if you need losses and want to keep the stock in your portfolio? Here's how. You can deduct the loss if you wait 31 days to buy back the shares.

Alternative: Double up the number of shares (buy an equal number of the same shares), wait 31 days, and then instruct your broker to sell the first lot.

Loophole: Donate appreciated long-term stock instead of cash to your favorite charities.

Edward Mendlowitz, CPA, partner, Mendlowitz Weitsen, LLP, CPAs, Two Pennsylvania Plaza, Suite 1500, New York 10121. He is author of eight books on taxes, including *IRA Distributions: What You Should Know.* Practical Programs, Inc.

When you do this, you get to deduct the full fair market value of the shares and you will owe no capital gains tax on the stock's buildup in value since you bought it.

Example: You own 100 shares of ABC stock, bought 10 years ago for $15 per share. When you donate the shares, now worth $50, to charity, you deduct the full $5,000 fair market value (not your $1,500 cost). You also avoid capital gains tax on the $3,500 appreciation in the shares.

Loophole: Fund a charitable remainder trust with appreciated securities. When you transfer appreciated securities to such a charitable trust, the trust can sell the securities tax free and buy higher yielding, more diversified investments.

The trust will pay you income for life and the charity receives the remainder after your death.

Tax impact: You get an immediate income tax deduction for the present value of the amount the charity will receive after your death. IRS tables are used to calculate the present value of the charity's postponed gift.

Loophole: Avoid a hefty penalty by taking the legally required minimum distribution from your IRA. You must begin minimum withdrawals from your IRA by April 1 of the year after the year you turn 70½. If you don't take a distribution, you'll owe the IRS a penalty of 50% of the amount you should have withdrawn but didn't. Once you are required to take distributions, they then must be taken by December 31 of each year.

Loophole: Plan the exercise of Incentive Stock Options (ISOs) very carefully. Many people wait until the last day possible to exercise their ISOs. However, the untaxed difference between the value on the date the ISO is exercised and the price paid is subject to the Alternative Minimum Tax (AMT), which is as high as 28%.

The right way to handle ISOs: Exercise just enough ISOs in 2000 so that your regular tax is equal to your AMT.

Note: The holding period for the stock starts when the options are exercised.

Extra note: You might be able to pay for the ISO stock by swapping company stock you already own.

Loophole: Consider converting a regular IRA to a Roth IRA. Why? So that you can ulti-

mately withdraw money from the account completely tax free. To be eligible to convert, your Adjusted Gross Income for the year must be $100,000 or less.

Downside: To gain this benefit of tax-free withdrawals from a Roth IRA, you must pay income tax on the money you take out of the regular IRA.

Loophole: Avoid penalties for underpayment of estimated tax. Review your withholding taxes to make sure you have paid the IRS at least 105% of last year's tax to avoid penalties for underpayment of estimated tax. Have additional amounts withheld from your pay, if necessary.

How to do it: If you are employed, arrange for your employer to deduct additional money from your final paychecks for the year. You will avoid underpayment penalties, because tax withheld is deemed to have been withheld ratably over the year's four quarters.

Caution: People who pay *estimated* taxes cannot simply add more money to their final estimated payment, because estimated taxes are not considered to be paid ratably throughout the year.

Alternative: If you own a regular IRA, take out money and ask the trustee to withhold sufficient tax so you will avoid any penalty you would otherwise owe for underpaying taxes. Repay the IRA withdrawal within 60 days in full including the withheld tax amount you did not receive.

Loophole: Consider taking a taxable distribution from your 401(k) plan. A tax-savvy way to get cash is to take distributions of company stock from your 401(k) plan.

Reason: The tax you owe on the distribution is based on the cost of the stock to the plan, not the fair market value of the stock you receive.

Note: This only applies to employee contributions.

401(k) reminder: Be sure to maximize your 401(k) plan contributions for 2000. You can contribute up to $10,500 this year.

Loophole: Minimize the impact of the AMT if you can't avoid it this year. Do everything you can to accelerate the receipt of income into 2000. The income will be taxed at the AMT rate, that is not more than 28%. Also, delay deducting state and local taxes and other expenses that are forfeited under AMT calculations.

FOR BUSINESSES

Consider implementing these tax-saving strategies before the end of the year if you own a business...

Loophole: Get deductions for contributions to retirement plans that are set up before year-end. Unincorporated businesses should set up Keogh plans, and incorporated businesses should set up pension or profit sharing plans before December 31.

If the plans are established before the end of the year, you have until the extended due date of the 2000 return to fund them. You'll still get 2000 deductions.

Saver: If you miss the December 31 deadline for establishing a traditional retirement plan, you can still get deductions by establishing a Simplified Employee Plan (SEP). As long as you set up the SEP by the due date of your 2000 tax return, contributions will be deductible. With a SEP, you can put away up to 15% of the earned income of each employee, including the owners, up to a maximum of $25,500 a year.

Opportunity: Companies that are making a lot of money should consider starting an age-weighted target benefit plan. Because contributions to such a plan are based on employees' ages, you can contribute as much as $30,000 for an older business owner and as little as $2,000 for younger employees.

Loophole: Accelerate advertising expenses to maximize your 2000 deductions. Amounts spent—or accrued—for general advertising by December 31 are fully deductible, even though the primary benefit occurs in the following year.

Example: Mail-order businesses might consider sending out a customer mailing by year-end.

Loophole: Mark down slow-moving inventory so that the business can take a write-off this year. Generally, you cannot write down slow-moving or excess inventory if you are still selling the inventory items for full price. To secure the deduction in 2000, offer the goods for sale at substantially reduced prices.

Loophole: Increase your bad-debt deduction by writing off uncollectible accounts receivable from your books. Businesses cannot get a deduction for additions to reserves for uncollectible accounts—they can only get the deduction when it is determined that all or part of a particular accounts receivable is uncollectible and that amount is written off the books.

Strategy: When you turn over accounts receivable to a collection agency that charges a fee based on a percentage of collections, you should write off the difference between the receivable and the maximum amount you would receive if the agency were 100% successful.

Loophole: Consider year-end charitable contributions of publicly traded stock. When your company owns publicly traded stock, it makes more sense tax-wise to contribute the appreciated shares to charity than to sell them and donate the proceeds.

Reason: The profit on the stock sales would be fully taxable to the company (there is no corporate capital gains rate). However, when you donate shares to charity, no gain is recognized and the company can deduct the full fair market value of the stock, subject to overall limits on charitable contributions.

Loophole: Give stock bonuses to key employees. Stocks are a tax-effective incentive because the company can deduct the full fair market value of the shares.

Loophole: Consider converting your company to an S corporation effective in 2001. S corporations generally pay no taxes themselves. Corporate income and losses are reported on the individual tax returns of the company's shareholders, creating many opportunities to save income, gift, and estate taxes.

Bonus: S corporation distributions are not subject to FICA or Medicare taxes.

Loophole: Make a capital contribution or loan to your S corporation if its 2000 losses exceed your basis to boost your deductible losses this year. *Reason:* You cannot deduct tax losses that exceed your basis in an S corporation (generally, the cash you invested in the company plus any loans you made).

Alternative: Skip the capital injection until January if you expect to be in a higher tax bracket next year, to maximize the value of the deductible loss.

Loophole: Hire your kids for the holidays for your sole proprietorship (or husband-wife partnership). You don't owe Social Security, Medicare, or unemployment taxes on wages paid to your children who are under 18.

Catch: You must run your business as a sole proprietor or husband-wife partnership, not a corporation, to get this benefit.

Bonus: Your children can shelter up to $4,400 of income earned in 2000 with their standard deduction. Each child can put up to $2,000 of salary into a Roth IRA and never pay taxes on the accumulation.

Loophole: Boost productivity and employee morale with low-cost subsidized meals. Your company can deduct the entire cost of meals provided to employees on the company's premises, as long as more than half the employees benefit and the meals are for the convenience of the employer. This includes in-house meals during the holiday season so employees can leave early to prepare for the holiday.

Loophole: Cash-basis businesses can defer income by delaying billings into January. Accelerate deductible expenses into 2000 if the business will be in the same or lower tax bracket next year.

Strategy: Deductible expenses that are charged on general-use credit cards by December 31 are deductible this year even if you don't pay off the charges until next year.

Trap: Items charged on a retailer's own store card are not deductible until the charges are paid.

Self-defense: Send last-minute checks by certified mail to prove the payment was a 1999 expense should the IRS inquire.

More from Edward Mendlowitz...

Tax Return Filing Loopholes

S lash your tax bill and reduce the odds of an audit by using these smart strategies for preparing and filing your tax return...

Loophole: Ask for an automatic extension of time to file your return. Returns for 2000 are due on April 16, but you can extend the due date for filing to October 15 by getting two extensions from the IRS. The first extension gives you four months to file and is granted automatically. The second, which is not given automatically—you must provide a plausible reason for filing late—is at the discretion of the IRS.

Forms to file: File Form 4868, *Application for Automatic Extension of Time to File,* by April 16 to get four months. And file a second Form 4868 by August 15 to get the additional two months.

Reason to get extensions: Even though audit rates are low, filing at the last minute reduces a taxpayer's risk. *Why:* The IRS requisitions the returns it is going to audit in September and early October. Returns filed on October 15 might miss that particular selection process. The IRS denies this is true, but my experience shows otherwise.

Trap: Filing after the extended due date, especially year after year, will definitely increase the odds that you will be audited.

Loophole: Avoid penalties for underpayment of your estimated 2001 tax. You must pay 100% of last year's tax liability to avoid underpayment penalties (110% if your adjusted gross income in 2000 was over $150,000).

Alternative: Pay at least 90% of your current year's tax liability through a combination of withheld taxes and estimated tax payments.

Loophole: Pay the first quarter's estimate with your extension application. When you file for the extension, include the first quarter's estimated tax payment with the balance of tax due for 2000 in your application. This eliminates the need to file a first-quarter estimated tax statement. It also covers any shortfall in your extension estimate of tax due. Then, when you complete your 2000 return, indicate that overpayments should be applied to 2001 estimated tax.

Loophole: File a tax return even if you don't have the cash to pay the tax. The IRS allows monthly installment payments for taxes and interest owed. File Form 9465, *Installment Agreement Request.*

Reason: The IRS levies two separate penalties, one for failing to file a return and a second for failure to pay the tax owed. By filing the return or for an extension, you can avoid at least one of these penalties.

Opportunity: File Form 1127, *Application for Extension of Time for Payment of Tax.* You will be granted such an extension if you can show, among other things, that you will have a substantial financial loss if you pay your tax on the date that it is due.

Loophole: **Pay your taxes by credit card.** The IRS will let you charge your federal income taxes to your MasterCard, Discover or American Express credit cards. The fee for the service averages between 1.5% and 2.5%, depending on the amount you owe. To pay by credit card, call 888-272-9829.

Loophole: **Reconstruct missing W-2s.** If your employer hasn't yet given you a W-2 or the company you worked for went out of business, you can reconstruct your salary and withholding records on Form 4852, *Substitute for Form W-2, Wage and Tax Statement,* and send that with your return. Put down your best estimate of your salary and withholdings and how you arrived at it.

Loophole: **Report incorrect or missing 1099s on your return.** Banks, brokerages and other payers of income file directly with the IRS, which cross checks that information with the 1099s that individuals report on their returns. Discrepancies automatically trigger written inquiries from the IRS.

What to do: If you don't get a 1099, you must still report the amount received. Enter the information on the return in the usual place.

If you receive an incorrect 1099 and can't get it corrected by the time you file, report the incorrect figure on your tax return on a separate line, enter the same amount as a negative number on another line and explain why it is wrong.

Example: Your broker sent you a 1099 reporting a dividend on a stock you don't own. List the incorrect dividend on your return. Beneath that entry, subtract the dividend amount. Write the following explanation beside the figure: "The 1099 was issued in error by my broker. Stock was not owned by me during 2000. Corrected 1099 requested but not yet issued."

Loophole: **File your return separately from your spouse if you're not sure which** **filing status is best.** Married couples who file jointly save taxes. But filing jointly doesn't always makes sense.

Reasons: One spouse owes back taxes or doesn't want to share information with the other spouse or is taking a particularly aggressive position on the return.

Solution: If the event you worry about passes, you can file separately and then file a joint amended return before the statute of limitations expires. However, if you filed a joint return originally, you cannot later refile separate returns.

Loophole: **File your return electronically if you expect to get a refund.** When you file your return through the IRS's e-file program, you can receive a tax refund twice as quickly as you would with a paper tax return—usually within three weeks. You can shorten that even more by allowing the IRS to deposit your refund check directly into your checking account.

Important: Don't forget to send IRS Form 8453-OL, *US Individual Income Tax Declaration for Online Filing,* along with your Form W-2 and any other necessary documents.

Loophole: **File your return by certified mail.** This year, a return will be considered to be filed on time if it is mailed on or before April 16, 2001. The envelope should have a timely US Postal Service postmark.

Important: Get a post-office-stamped receipt when you send your return by certified mail. This will give you proof that you mailed your return on time.

Warning: When your return is filed late, the postmark date is not considered the date of filing. Your return is not considered filed until it is actually received by the IRS.

Loophole: **Use an IRS-approved private delivery service to file your return.** Great for when you can't get to the post office on time.

Examples: FedEx, UPS and Airborne Express. Don't forget to ask for written proof of the delivery date for your records.

Caution: Private delivery services cannot deliver tax returns to IRS post-office-box addresses.

Loophole: **Overcome your fear of filing.** As a matter of policy, the IRS won't file criminal charges against people who voluntarily come forward and file overdue returns. If you haven't filed, do so ASAP.

Loophole: File amended tax returns to get refunds from prior years. In my experience, filing an amended return on Form 1040X decreases the chances that you'll get audited when you include copies of all the backup and substantiation for the items that you're amending.

Edward Mendlowitz on...

Simple Tax Mistakes That Can Be Very, Very Costly

The mistakes with tax filings, paperwork and elections can cost you big tax dollars.

RETIREMENT SAVINGS ERRORS

Many families have *most* of their wealth saved in retirement accounts.

●**Keogh plan mistake.** Not filing a form in the 5500 series. The exact form depends on the number of participants and assets in the Keogh plan. These information returns must be filed for *all* plans that provide benefits to employees and for one-person plans with more than $100,000 of assets. The late-filing penalty is up to *$1,000 per day.*

Trap: With the booming stock market, owners of one-person Keoghs may not realize their accounts are now worth more than $100,000.

Self-defense: If you are behind on filing the 5500 form, consult a Keogh plan expert *immediately*. File the form, and have your adviser ask the IRS to abate penalties. You have a *much* better chance of reducing potentially huge penalties if you bring the problem to the IRS than if the IRS learns of the problem on its own.

Trap: The 5500 form is *not* filed with the IRS, but with the Department of Labor's Pension and Welfare Benefits Administration.

●**401(k) plan mistake.** Taking a distribution of employer stock from a 401(k) and rolling it over into an IRA.

Snag: When you finally cash in the stock and withdraw the proceeds from the IRA, they will be taxable as ordinary income. You will lose favorable capital gains treatment for the shares.

Better: If you intend to hold the shares, take a distribution so you own them. You'll owe a current tax on their appreciation since your 401(k) account acquired them. All further long-term gain will be taxed at a rate of up to 20%.

●**IRA mistake #1.** Not naming beneficiaries—either your estate will become your beneficiary or default provisions established by your IRA's trustee will go into effect. *Either case is bad...*

●If your estate becomes your beneficiary, you forfeit your ability to have your heirs stretch out the distribution.

●If default provisions go into effect, your IRA probably won't be distributed as you wished.

Warning: After age 70½, the ability to change IRA beneficiaries may be limited.

●**IRA mistake #2.** Using the "recalculation" method to compute the size of minimum annual required IRA distributions. This method recalculates life expectancy each year and is the default provision for most plans.

Trap: If either the IRA owner or the beneficiary dies, the IRA distribution is immediately accelerated.

Better: Use the "term certain" method to set distributions over a fixed term equal to the IRA owner's life expectancy. If either the IRA owner or the beneficiary dies, distributions can continue at the same rate as if the person lived.

●**IRA mistake #3.** Changing the name on the IRA to that of the beneficiary when the owner of an IRA dies. This accelerates IRA distributions.

Better: Keep the IRA in the name of the deceased owner to extend the IRA distribution period.

FILING ERRORS

●**The worst mistake anyone can make is not filing.**

●**If you are owed a refund, the statute of limitations expires after three years.** After that, you lose the ability to collect your refund.

●**If you owe tax, the statute of limitations never expires.** You will accumulate nonfiling penalties, plus late-payment penalties and interest. Even if you can't afford to pay the tax, file a return to avoid nonfiling penalties. Use the IRS's new installment payment option by filing IRS Form 9465, *Request for Installment Agreement.*

●**Filing a joint return when one spouse owes a bill for the past year and the other is due a refund.** The IRS may take the refund to pay back taxes.

Better: File separate returns to protect the refund. While this may increase the overall tax rate for the couple, if the back tax bill is paid within three years, you can file an *amended* return claiming joint filing status for that year. This lowers the tax rate, and you can file for a refund.

●**Not completing the tax return and filing all required supporting documents.** Such mistakes cost you deductions…or increase your risk of being audited. *Examples…*

●For charitable gifts of property valued at more than $500, you must file Form 8283, *Noncash Charitable Contributions.* You will need qualified appraisals for donated property worth more than $5,000.

●When claiming a home-office deduction, you must file Form 8829, *Expenses for Business Use of Your Home.*

●On Schedule B of Form 1040, check a "yes" or "no" box for the question asking if you have a foreign bank account.

●**Not filing the IRS's Form 8822,** *Change of Address,* when you move. If you don't, IRS notices sent to your old address may be deemed effective even if you never receive them…and you may lose a tax case by default.

FAMILY ERRORS

Errors in family finances that can boost the tax bill…

●**A grandparent puts money in a child's name** in a Uniform Gifts to Minors Act (UGMA) or Uniform Transfers to Minors Act (UTMA) account…then acts as custodian of the account.

Trap: Because the grandparent retains control over the funds, they remain taxable to the grandparent's estate despite of the gift.

Better: Name someone else as custodian of the UGMA/UTMA account.

●**A couple separates,** and one spouse voluntarily pays support to the other until they work out a formal separation or divorce agreement.

Trap: The payments are not deductible as alimony because they are not made under a written agreement.

Better: Have a written agreement covering such payments from the start.

●**A will doesn't specify the account** from which estate taxes are to be paid.

Trap: A conflict over who pays the tax may arise. The entire cost of estate tax may fall on beneficiaries paid from the "residual estate"—the amount left after bequests of specific items and amounts—with other beneficiaries paying nothing.

Better: Have your will explicitly state how estate tax will be paid.

A Very Powerful Tool to Beat The IRS

Ms. X, Esq., a former IRS agent still well connected.

The IRS's own text on standards and procedures known as the Internal Revenue Manual lays out the duties and responsibilities of IRS employees in thousands of situations. A failure on the part of an IRS employee to follow these rules gives a taxpayer the opportunity to request that a Taxpayer Assistance Order be issued to correct the situation.

Rather than failing to follow existing rules, IRS employees frequently make up their own rules or resolve factual issues using a strained interpretation of the existing rules.

Strategy: Most provisions of the Internal Revenue Manual are now available from a number of legal publishers on CD-ROM for a modest charge.

Cheaper: Review the Internal Revenue Manual free on the IRS's own Web site. It's listed in the Tax Professionals' Corner under Administrative Information & Resources at *www.irs.gov/prod/bus_info/tax_pro/irm-part/index.html.*

More from Ms. X...

Uncovering the IRS's Best-Kept Secret

Taxpayers can avoid the payment of all personal income tax they owe by filing for bankruptcy. The IRS is careful not to explain this to the public. As a matter of law, personal income taxes are dischargeable in bankruptcy after they are at least three years old. Also, newly assessed tax liabilities—caused by a tax audit, for example—are dischargeable 240 days after they have been assessed. IRS executive management is concerned that if too many people understood that they could walk away from old tax debts by filing for bankruptcy, the tax collection process would be severely undermined.

Best strategy for those in financial difficulty: Speak to a knowledgeable bankruptcy attorney to determine if unpaid tax debts are dischargeable. Also discuss the consequences, including the pitfalls, of going through the bankruptcy process.

Also from Ms. X...

Preparing for an Audit

First, anticipate the issues the revenue agent is likely to raise. Then, figure out how to answer difficult questions. The best way to answer tough questions is with an answer that is truthful but does not give the agent any real information he can use against you.

Best: Keep your answers short. Don't elaborate. If the question is repeated, repeat the answer you just gave.

Best answer when you don't want to answer a question: "I'll have to think about that. I'll get back to you."

Ms. X on...

Getting the IRS To Change Its Mind

After a revenue agent has completed his/her report and proposed the adjustments that will increase the amount of tax you owe,

you still have a chance to negotiate a favorable settlement.

Strategy: Tell the agent that you'll write a check on the spot if the amount of extra tax is reduced. Suggest a meeting to review each of the agent's proposed adjustments. Point out areas where you feel that extra consideration should be given to your position. If this approach fails because the revenue agent wants to close the case, make the same pitch to his group manager. The group manager will almost always accommodate a reasonable request to settle a case.

Finally from Ms. X...

A Small Price May Help You Win in Court

It's very important to gain access to the revenue agent's work papers, especially if you plan to take your case to the IRS Appeals Division. Generally, for less than $25 in search and copying charges, the local IRS district Disclosure Officer will provide you with copies of the work papers. When reviewing the papers, be aware of the tone of the revenue agent's writing. See if you can detect a bias in the tone.

Example: The revenue agent may have reached conclusions based on emotional reactions rather than facts.

The work papers may also contain references to documents the agent reviewed and found no problem with, while the deduction claimed on your tax return was nevertheless disallowed without adequate written explanation.

E-Commerce And Taxes: What You Need Now To Avoid Tax Troubles

James Piazza, tax partner, Arthur Andersen LLP, 101 Eisenhower Pkwy., Roseland, NJ 07068.

For companies of all kinds and all sizes, the hottest business tax issue in 2001 will be the question of taxation of electronic commerce.

Mistake: Many businesses are rushing into E-commerce without considering taxes at all. They risk incurring enormous unexpected tax bills—and losing the opportunity to reduce their overall tax liability with smart planning as well.

Soon almost every business in the US will have to come to grips with the new tax issues of E-commerce.

In 1996 only 200 small businesses—with total annual sales of less than $10 million—were selling on the Internet. By the year 2003, there will be 400,000. And the number of users of the Internet is projected to grow from 200 million today to one *billion* in 2005.

So—while many firms today look at E-commerce as an opportunity, soon it will be an absolute necessity.

Problem: E-commerce raises a whole new set of tax problems. If your business doesn't recognize and plan for them, you may unexpectedly incur sales taxes, income taxes, property taxes and even foreign taxes on international sales made through a Web site. Enormous back-tax bills with interest and penalties added may arrive a few years down the road—and give you a shock.

DON'T DELAY ANY LONGER

Opportunity: With careful planning, expansion into E-commerce can enable a business to lower its tax bill in many areas. *Examples...*

• **Sales and use taxes.** These present by far the biggest immediate danger for most firms engaged in E-commerce. Today, there are 7,600 different sales taxes imposed in the US at state and local levels—and a company engaged in E-commerce may unexpectedly become liable to collect many of them.

Key: E-commerce suddenly lets even a small business make sales *anywhere*. So it may become liable for taxes it never even thought about until now.

Why you need to take this seriously: Sales and use taxes are among the largest sources of tax revenue for states—and already are among the hottest state tax audit issues.

Many state governments are becoming alarmed by the loss of local sales tax revenue due to Internet sales made by out-of-state firms to state residents. So you can expect that the states will make those firms a special audit target.

Self-defense: The Supreme Court has held that a business cannot be required to collect taxes on sales for a state if it has no presence in the state.

Trap: Even a *slight* presence in a state may create liability to collect taxes on all sales made in that state.

This may be deemed the case if the company establishes a Web server in the state. Or, as a result of sales made in the state, it contracts with a service agent there...stores inventory there ...hosts a product display...or establishes any other presence in the state.

Example: A local company operating only in New Jersey hires a New York City firm to host its Web site on a server. The company may become liable for tax on all Internet sales made in New York State.

Risky: If a company assumes it does not owe tax to a state because its presence there is slight, it may not file tax returns there. In that case, it will never be protected by the statute of limitations. The state will be able to collect back taxes, penalties and interest going back any number of years.

And—more and more states are becoming very aggressive about identifying out-of-state sellers with any in-state presence. They examine motor vehicle records and similar data, monitor advertising and share information with other states.

PLAYING IT SAFE

To minimize sales tax liability...

• **Assume that any presence in a state may trigger tax collection liability.** Rules vary by state, so consult a local expert.

• **Consider forming a separate corporation to handle E-commerce sales.** If it doesn't have any presence in states where other members of the group operate, it may avoid tax on sales made in those states. Again, there may be other implications of separate incorporation, so you should consult a professional.

Important: Carefully manage the corporation—to segregate its operations from the rest of the group so that its tax liability isn't based on the other operations. If it simply makes Internet sales for the group, it may be deemed an "agent" of the group and owe tax in all the states where any member of the group has any presence.

Example: If the new Internet corporation makes E-sales for a retail store chain, retail stores should not handle service or returns on Internet sales...or promote Internet sales.

The rules of Internet commerce are changing so fast that there may be many unanswered questions that even the best tax professionals struggle with.

These include...

●**When a seller doesn't know the location of the buyer** of items delivered electronically, what is the tax result?

●**Do formerly taxable tangible items remain taxable** when newly delivered in an "intangible" mode—such as music?

Music formerly sold on a CD is now downloaded from Web sites. Computer service that was formerly performed by a visiting technician now is done by remote connections.

These activities will potentially erode a state's tax base—therefore, states need to look for other taxing opportunities.

●**A business customer orders and pays for electronic goods** from one location but has them transferred to another. Where is the tax incurred?

Self-defense: While answers to these questions get debated, your job should simply be to stay informed about the issues and get the best professional advice possible regarding local laws.

MORE TAX ISSUES FOR E-COMMERCE

●**Additional state taxes.** Many of the same traps exist for E-commerce firms with state income taxes as with sales taxes. By establishing even a slight presence in a state as a result of Internet sales, a company may unexpectedly become liable for state income taxes. And again, if the company isn't aware of its liability and doesn't file tax returns, the state may someday go back several years to collect back taxes, penalties and interest.

Opportunity: You can actually reduce state income taxes by selling over the Internet. By moving sales outside of states where it owes income tax, a company may lower its income tax bill overall.

Reason: When a company operates in more than one state, a formula is used to apportion its income among the states. Most states use a formula based on the percentage of total sales, payroll and property that are located in-state.

Key: When a company makes Internet sales outside of its home state for the first time, it reduces the "sales" factor in the formula—and thus its taxable income in its home state is reduced. If it doesn't owe income tax in other states where the sales are made because it has no presence there and the home state does not require that these sales be allocated back to it under a "throw-back" provision, its total tax *declines.*

Bonus: Because Internet shoppers don't care where the company is located, as your Internet sales grow, you can relocate inventory and fulfillment operations to a low-tax or no-tax state such as Nevada. That can further reduce state income tax.

●**International taxes.** The Internet creates the opportunity for many companies to generate international sales for the first time ever.

Trap: These sales can make the company subject to foreign taxes—such as European Value Added Tax at rates that range from 15% to 25%. Moreover, the company may also incur customs obligations and import duties. And—it may become subject to non-tax foreign commercial laws and regulations of all kinds.

Self-defense: Hold off selling to any foreign country without first discussing the implications with an expert.

LOOKING AHEAD

Major changes in the tax laws regarding E-commerce are a certainty.

For a view of the kinds of changes likely to come, visit the Web site of the Congressional Advisory Commission on Electronic Commerce at *www.ecommercecommission.org*.

The commission calls its task of reforming tax policy for E-commerce "arguably the most important policy initiative of the information age ...with global implications." To date, little has been done.

The Most Useful Tax Resources On the Internet

James Glass, a New York-based tax attorney and a contributing writer to *Tax Hotline*, Box 2614, Greenwich, CT 80328-2614.

The Internet presents a wealth of free tax resources that can help you reduce your tax bill. *Here are some of the best...*

YOUR QUESTIONS ANSWERED

•**Misc.taxes.moderated.** A continuing discussion of tax questions is hosted in this news group. A number of tax professionals are "regulars" and are happy to answer questions posed by laypersons. The discussion is moderated by a tax professor, so all comments are polite and relate to practical tax questions.

•**Misc.taxes** hosts more spirited discussions of taxes—it is unmoderated so "anything goes." Conversations range into politics and other areas that are likely to elicit more heated opinions. Professionals and amateurs alike exchange views.

STATE AND LOCAL TAXES

•*www.irs.gov,* the IRS Web site, provides federal tax forms and information—but where can you get the same information for the states (especially if you must file in more than one)? Here...

•*www.taxsites.com/state.html.* Dennis Schmidt's State and Local Taxes Web page provides the most comprehensive list of state tax resources for all 50 states. *Included:* Links to state tax agencies, downloadable tax forms, tax codes, courts and court decisions, property tax boards, and so on.

The site also links to state taxpayer organizations (of employers, home owners, etc.), state tax on-line publications, news bulletins, and research organizations.

DEALING WITH THE IRS

•*www.ustaxcourt.com.* The US Tax Court has a Web site where you can learn the rules for fighting the IRS in court, and get the full text of recent Tax Court decisions for free.

Key: Use the Tax Court's Small Case Division to contest tax disputes involving up to $50,000 of tax per tax year, without a lawyer and under simplified procedures.

•*www.nolo.com.* Nolo's Legal Encyclopedia: Tax Problems gives inside information on how the IRS actually operates (and is edited by frequent *Tax Hotline* contributor Frederick W. Daily, tax attorney).

Other sources tell you about the law. This one tells how the IRS *thinks and acts*—such as what concerns an IRS auditor *really* will have during an audit, and how to speed through the process as painlessly as possible.

Subjects covered include: How to deal with the IRS...audits and appeals...tax bills, cheating, fraud and other tax crimes...small business tax concerns...and more.

•*www.timevalue.com/irsindex.htm,* the comprehensive IRS Phone Directory, can help you find the right real person to talk to inside the IRS—and escape dealing with its faceless bureaucracy.

The directory is indexed by Tax Code section and subject, giving the names and phone numbers of the IRS specialists who are expert on each part of the Code. It also includes IRS officials at the district, regional and national offices, and at service centers, problem resolution centers, the chief counsel's office and state tax officials.

The directory is searchable by name, title, Code section and geographical area.

ROTH IRAs

•*www.fairmark.com* hosts Fairmark's *Guide to the Roth IRA,* a comprehensive explanation of Roth IRAs. It gives 150 pages of information ranging from simple rules to detailed financial analysis.

The guide is part of the 700-page *Fairmark Press Tax Guide for Investors,* which also includes tax news and discussion boards.

CONSUMER RESOURCES

•*www.unclefed.com,* Uncle Fed's Tax Board, provides a broad range of federal tax resources from the technical (IRS rulings, procedures and tax court rules) to the practical (how to find a tax adviser and survive an audit) to the educational (historical documents).

●*www.taxweb.com,* Taxweb, may provide the broadest collection of links at one place to tax information of all kinds throughout the Internet.

Included: FAQs, links to federal and state tax authorities, tax discussion groups, taxpayer organizations, tax news sources and other tax resources of all kinds.

HELP FROM THE BIG FIVE

Tax help from the Big Five accounting firms is available even if you can't afford the fees you'd pay to become a client. All provide tax analysis over the Web. *Examples...*

●**Arthur Andersen's State and Local Tax Guide and News,** *www.arthurandersen.com/tax/salt.*

●**Deloitte & Touche's Tax News and Views,** *www.dtonline.com/tnv/tnv.htm.*

●**Ernst & Young's 1040 Survival Kit,** *www.ey.com/tax/survival/default.asp.*

●**KPMG Peat Marwick's Strategies for Financial Planning,** *www.us.kpmg.com/pfp/strategies/.*

●**PricewaterhouseCoopers' Tax News Network,** *www.taxnews.com/tnn_public/.*

DISCUSSION GROUPS

If you have an interest in a specialized area, you can find others (including pros) with whom you can exchange news and views. *How...*

●**www.tax.org/Discuss/discussion.htm.** Tax Analysts hosts 22 moderated tax discussion groups on subjects such as insurance, real estate, pensions, individual, estate and international taxes. Archives of past discussions can also be reviewed.

●**www.lib.uchicago.edu/~llou/lawlists/info.html.** The Law Lists Information Site will search the Web for discussion groups on the subject of interest to you that may be hosted by universities, professional groups, or others.

Entering the word "tax" in the Law Lists search engine produces more than 30 discussion groups on all kinds of tax subjects.

More from James Glass...

Use Retired Parents As a Tax Shelter

If parents are in a lower tax bracket than you, make gifts to them of income-paying securities—such as dividend-paying stock—that have appreciated in value or are expected to. Income received by your parents will be taxed at a lower rate than it would be to you, reducing the family's tax bill. And when you inherit the securities back from your parents, the securities will receive stepped-up basis and all taxable gain on them will be eliminated.

Important: Make tax-free transfers to parents using the annual gift tax exclusion or your personal gift and estate tax exempt amount.

Caution: Non-income tax considerations may apply. Consult estate planning and social services experts.

Get Tax Refunds for Past Years Now...Using Amended Returns

Laurence I. Foster, CPA/PFS, tax partner, personal financial planning practice, KPMG LLP, 345 Park Ave., New York 10154. Mr. Foster is former chairman, estate planning committee, New York State Society of Certified Public Accountants.

It's possible to claim tax refunds going three years back by filing amended tax returns. And, you can sometimes claim refunds that go back even longer than that.

How much longer? Amendments for bad debts, for example, can go back seven years.

If, while preparing the return due this past April 15, you found a new tax strategy or deduction that you overlooked in the past, it is not too late to claim it for prior years.

Amended returns also can be used to correct mistakes made on past years' tax returns that may have left you owing tax. Promptly filing an amended return after discovering a mistake will minimize its cost and avert the worst IRS penalties—those imposed for willfully or intentionally underpaying taxes.

<h3>HOW TO USE THEM</h3>

You can obtain an amended tax return, IRS Form 1040X, by calling the IRS at 800-829-3676, or downloading it from the IRS Web site at *www.ustreas.irs.gov.*

You can file an amended return any time within three years after the due date of the original return that is being amended, or the date on which the original return was actually filed, whichever is later. *Reasons to file an amended return...*

●**Correct recent filing mistakes.** The most common reason for filing an amended tax return is simply to correct a straightforward mistake made on a recently filed original return.

Examples: You made a mathematical error, omitted income, took an improper deduction, or overlooked a deduction that you were entitled to take on the return filed this past April 15.

●**Provide documentation omitted from a tax return.** Perhaps a corrected Form W-2 was issued to you by your employer after you filed, or you forgot to attach a schedule to your return, or you forgot to include a necessary appraisal or statement. You can file the omitted documentation with a 1040X.

●**Claim overlooked deductions for past years.** When preparing one year's return you may discover new deductions or tax-saving strategies that you could have used, but didn't, in prior years.

This is especially likely to happen when you have your return prepared by a professional for the first time...or move from one professional to another...or use a tax return preparation computer program for the first time.

With an amended tax return you can use the newly discovered deduction or strategy to claim tax refunds going back up to three years.

●**Deduct worthless securities.** You can go back seven years to deduct these, instead of the normal three years.

Why: Worthless securities can be deducted only in the year in which they become worthless. But this often is uncertain at the time, especially if litigation is pending. So the statute of limitations is extended to seven years to allow a deduction even when the date of worthlessness is determined retroactively, several years after the fact.

Review investment records now. You may find you are entitled to surprising tax refunds as far back as seven years.

●**Utilize retroactive impact of tax law changes.** When Congress changes the Tax Code it may affect tax-saving strategies retroactively.

Talk to your tax adviser to see if several tax laws enacted in recent years have any other retroactive provisions that may affect you.

●**Get the most from a casualty loss.** Persons who live in a Presidentially declared disaster area and who suffer a related casualty loss can choose the year in which to deduct the loss.

Options: Deduct the loss in the year in which it occurs, or on the return filed for the prior year. *Considerations...*

●**Claiming the deduction on the prior year's return** can speed your refund.

●**The cash value of a casualty deduction** may vary in different years, because...

●Casualty losses are deductible only to the extent they exceed 10% of Adjusted Gross Income (AGI)—so a larger deduction will be available in the year in which your AGI is lower.

●The value of the deduction depends on your tax bracket—so it may be worth more in the year in which your tax bracket is higher.

Strategy: If you suffer a qualifying casualty loss in 2000, you can deduct it on an amended return filed for 1999 to get an immediate refund, rather than wait to deduct it on your 2000 return.

Strategy: If in 1998 or 1999 you suffered a qualifying loss, you may have deducted it on that year's return without realizing you had the option of deducting it in the prior year. If so, you can file an amended return to deduct it in the prior year now.

<h3>IMPACT</h3>

Filing an amended return does not give the IRS any extra time to audit your return for that year. So you don't have to worry that by claiming a legitimate overlooked deduction you will be giving the IRS extra time to examine other items on the return.

Last minute: Some tax advisers recommend that an amended return not be filed until the last moment, so the IRS won't have any chance to look at other items.

Downside: The IRS may reject a claim for a refund made on an amended return filed at the last minute. Then the statute of limitations will run out on you, or you will have to sue for the refund—an action that will keep the statute of limitations open for your whole return until the case is resolved.

Best: If you have a documented claim to a legitimate deduction that you overlooked in a prior year, claim the deduction in a straightforward manner on an amended return when you discover it.

What the IRS Won't Tell You About Audits... What They *Really* Want to Know...But You Don't Have to Tell

Frederick W. Daily, Esq., tax attorney, 302 Warren Dr., San Francisco 94131. He is author of *Stand Up to the IRS* and *Tax Savvy for Small Business*. Both from Nolo Press.

Most taxpayers who face an IRS auditor fear how much the IRS knows about them. Auditors use this fear to intimidate taxpayers into making concessions and revealing more.

With the right tactics, you can keep the IRS auditor from learning any more...and help move the audit to its best possible conclusion.

WHAT THE IRS KNOWS

When you appear for an IRS audit, the auditor will have a file on your case that typically contains only three sources of information about you...

● **Tax return being audited.**

● **Your tax-filing history for the past six years.** This tells whether you filed tax returns ...were audited...or had a tax bill adjusted for those years. It does *not* include copies of prior years' tax returns.

● **List of third-party payments made to you** that were reported to the IRS on W-2 and 1099 forms or other information returns.

In 90% of cases, that's all the information the auditor will have about you before the audit begins.

If information that could cause you audit problems is not contained among these three items, the overwhelming odds are that the auditor doesn't have it.

Then the only way the auditor can get it is from you or by issuing a summons on the record keeper.

The auditor will not have: Copies of bank statements, motor vehicle records, property deeds or police records.

Nor will the auditor have copies of 1099s or other information returns sent to the IRS under a Social Security or taxpayer ID number other than yours.

Key: Don't volunteer any information to the IRS auditor that you aren't legally obligated to give—even if he/she asks for it.

THE BIGGEST MISTAKE

By far the most common audit mistake is providing copies of your other years' tax returns just because the audit notice asks you to do so.

Doing so greatly expands audit risk by giving the auditor many things to look at that he otherwise would not see.

Patterns of income and deduction amounts reported over multiple years may raise questions that would not arise when looking at just a single year's return.

The fact that an auditor doesn't have information doesn't mean he won't ask for it. So it's important to know what you are legally required to provide to an auditor...and what you aren't.

Rule: You are required to provide an IRS auditor only the information relating to the specific tax year listed in the audit notice. You are *not* required to provide information relating to any other tax year, except as it might relate to the year under audit—as carryover items might.

SAYING NO

Most people never imagine saying *no* to an IRS auditor for fear the auditor might retaliate by expanding the audit.

This fear is greatly exaggerated—retaliation is unlikely. IRS auditors have no incentive to expand an audit. They are evaluated by how quickly they close cases and work through their caseloads. And those caseloads are very heavy.

Inside secret: An auditor who feels there is good reason to examine another year's tax return can obtain it from the IRS's own files, but it may take weeks or months for the IRS to retrieve that old return. One who doesn't take the trouble to do so probably is "just fishing" for the taxpayer to reveal something.

The way to say *no* safely to such an auditor is to respond politely, "I don't believe that this relates to the year or issues being examined." Almost always, that will end the matter.

THE RIGHT REPRESENTATION

If there is information you want to protect from the IRS, consider being represented at your audit by a tax professional—instead of attending the audit personally. They are experienced at dealing with auditors.

A professional representative will not have the answers to some of the auditor's questions —including any information that you might reveal unintentionally.

Your representative will ask the auditor to put the request in writing. Then, in responding to a written request, your representative can discuss things with you and draft as narrow an answer as possible.

The whole process will slow the audit, which the auditor doesn't want. So attempts by the auditor to "go fishing" will be frustrated.

The IRS cannot conduct a "lifestyle or economic reality audit," asking questions that are unrelated to the preparation of the return being examined, unless it already has a reasonable indication that income has been understated.

A professional representative will also prevent your emotions or personal factors from complicating an audit. No matter how difficult the audit may be, your representative should be able to deal with the auditor in a calm and professional manner.

The fee you pay may be a bargain for both the taxes it saves and the anxiety you avoid by not dealing with the auditor personally.

And, last but not least, fees paid to a tax professional for defending an audit are deductible.

More from Frederick W. Daily...

The Ten Deadly Sins For Which Agents Can Be Fired

1. Willfully seizing taxpayer assets without authorization.

2. Making false statements under oath about a taxpayer or taxpayer representative.

3. Violating the constitutional or civil rights of a taxpayer or taxpayer representative.

4. Falsifying or destroying documents to conceal mistakes.

5. Committing assault or battery on a taxpayer or taxpayer representative.

6. Retaliating against or harassing a taxpayer or taxpayer representative, in violation of the Tax Code or IRS rules.

7. Willfully misusing "confidentiality" rules to conceal information from a Congressional inquiry.

8. Willfully failing to file tax returns.

9. Willfully understating tax liabilities.

10. Threatening to audit a taxpayer for personal gain.

The IRS Is Using the Internet to Gather Audit Information

IRS officials say the Internet contains "amazing" amounts of information about companies. It warns executives to be familiar with what is on their own company Web sites, since its agents may use that information to develop an audit.

IRS auditors also use Internet search engines to collect news reports about audited taxpayers, and to learn of industry standard pricing, financial and business practices, to compare them with what a company reports.

Point: Right now, the IRS is using the Internet mainly for business audits. But as individuals make greater use of the Internet, expect the IRS auditors to begin using it for personal audits, too.

Randy Bruce Blaustein, Esq., senior tax partner, Blaustein, Greenberg & Co., 155 E. 31 St., New York 10016.

Keep Much More of Your Investment Gains...Give Much Less to Uncle Sam

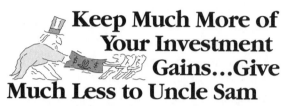

Janice Johnson, CPA, JD, D.S. Wolf Associates Inc., 330 Madison Ave., New York 10017. She is former chairman of the American Institute of Certified Public Accountants (AICPA) Tax Simplification Committee.

No matter how well your investments perform, it's the money you keep after taxes that counts. Here's how to avoid the most common investment mistakes that result in higher taxes—and how to keep more of your gains.

MOST COMMON MISTAKES

Mistake: Not identifying specific shares being sold. You probably own shares of a stock or a fund that you bought at different times and prices.

If so, you have the opportunity to sell specific shares that produce the least amount of taxes. If you don't identify specific shares being sold (at the time of the sale), the IRS will assume you're selling the first shares you purchased—which may not be best for you.

Example: You bought shares of the same stock at different times, paying first $10, then $20, then $30 per share. Today the stock trades at $25, and you intend to sell some of your shares. But the tax effect per share can be a $15 gain, $5 gain, or $5 loss, depending on which shares you sell.

By selecting the most expensive shares to sell—in this case, the ones that cost $30—you can take a $5 loss deduction per share.

Check whether you need long- or short-term gains or losses—look at the holding period of the various lots of stock you own. Holding more than one year gets you long-term treatment.

If you don't identify the specific shares being sold, the IRS will say you sold the $10 shares first and impose tax on the $15 gain per share.

Of course, if you have realized net losses so far for the year, you can sell the least expensive shares first to take the biggest gains tax-free, sheltering them from tax with the losses.

Mistake: Neglecting deductible fees. Many investors now have wrap fee accounts, which simplify broker fees by imposing a single fee that covers all investment advice and transactional costs.

Wrap fees and other investment expenses are deductible as miscellaneous expenses. But the total of these expenses is deductible only if it exceeds 2% of your Adjusted Gross Income (AGI). This limit may reduce or eliminate your deduction for the fees.

Better: Ask your broker for a statement saying how much of your total wrap fee is for transactions related to actual buying and selling of shares. These costs are added to the basis of the shares to reduce your gain or increase your loss.

Mistake: Not minimizing interest paid on borrowings. Investors often put more effort into maximizing the interest rates they receive than reducing the interest rates they pay.

Example: Many investors neglect to use low-cost margin loans against their investments. These loans are available from your broker. Instead, they run up high-rate consumer loan debt.

People often seem to avoid margin borrowing because they associate it with risky margin investing—which is borrowing to invest.

But it isn't reckless to use margin loans to pay off higher-rate debt. You wind up with the same amount of debt either way, but you'll pay less interest and the interest is deductible to the extent of investment income.

Mistake: Having too many accounts with different brokerages. Over the years, many people accumulate a growing number of investment accounts. Some of these accounts are likely to have small amounts in them. But there's a triple cost to owning so many accounts.

●**Investments are harder to monitor and manage** when they are dispersed over several accounts.

• **Duplicate fees are charged** for the services.

• **Tax paperwork is multiplied** when you receive numerous statements in different formats.

Better: Consolidate investments into a small number of easy-to-manage accounts at one broker.

Mistake: **Making charitable gifts with cash raised by selling stock.** This is one of the simplest but most costly and common mistakes that investors make.

Much better: Donate appreciated shares to a charity, and let the charity sell them. When you donate appreciated shares that you have owned for more than one year to charity, you get a deduction for their full market value—without ever paying any capital gains tax on their appreciation. The charity (a tax-exempt organization) then can sell the shares tax-free to raise cash. The IRS gets nothing.

But if you sell the shares yourself, the IRS takes capital gains tax first. Only what is left after taxes will be available to give to the charity.

Mistake: **Not matching gains against losses all year long.** Minimize taxes on investments by matching gains against losses.

Try to achieve net long-term capital gains in one tax year—taxed at no more than 20%. Use both long- and short-term capital losses in another year to offset short-term gains—taxed at your maximum ordinary income tax rate of up to 39.6%.

• **Use the 30-day rule.** When you have gains, you can sell securities that have lost money to offset them. Then, after 30 days, you can repurchase the same securities that you sold at a loss to restore your original investment position.

You also will have eliminated the tax on the gain. *Caution:* If you buy back the same securities within 30 days, the loss will be disallowed.

Or you can immediately repurchase similar securities, such as shares of another fund with the same investment objectives as the one you sold, without losing the loss write-off.

• **Or avoid the 30-day rule.** When you already have losses, you can sell other securities at a gain and then immediately repurchase the same securities. No 30-day rule applies.

You take your gain tax-free, restore your original investment position and increase your tax basis in the repurchased shares so any future gain on them will be correspondingly reduced.

Mistake: **Paying off the mortgage on a home too soon.** Many people start prepaying the mortgages on their homes without thinking of all the long-term consequences.

Key: Mortgage interest is generally fully tax-deductible. But this is true only of mortgage debt used to buy or remodel a home.

Once you finish paying off a mortgage, only $100,000 of home-equity loan borrowing produces deductible interest.

Beware: In the future, you may need a source of funds to pay children's college costs. But you won't be able to borrow on a tax-deductible basis against the full value of your home because you paid down your mortgage too soon.

Alternative: Consider using the funds that you would use to prepay your mortgage to start a new investment account. If you need cash in the future, you'll have the account and a larger amount of deductible borrowing in place.

With the use of a home-equity loan, you can borrow the full equity value of your home and deduct the interest payments up to $100,000 of the borrowing.

This strategy also is likely to be more profitable than prepaying a mortgage. Mortgage rates today are low, and mortgage interest is deductible.

Prepaying a mortgage may not save much after taxes, while the alternative investment account may produce substantial returns.

Offset Capital Gains and Losses...and Save Taxes In the Process

Larry Torella, CPA, tax partner, Richard A. Eisner & Company, LLP, 575 Madison Ave., New York 10022. He is author of his firm's annual year-end tax-planning guide.

The Tax Code now contains no less than six different tax rates for capital gains. *The most common rates are...*

●**Long-term gains,** on assets held more than a year, are taxed at a top rate of 20%.

●**Recaptured depreciation** on real estate is taxed at 25%.

●**Collectibles** (such as art works and stamp collections) are taxed at a top rate of 28%.

●**Short-term gains** are taxed at ordinary income rates up to 39.6%.

Problem: Having four different categories of gains can make it a complex task to offset different kinds of gains and losses. But taxpayers must offset them on their tax returns—and should know how to offset them to be able to realize the right amount of year-end tax-saving gains and losses.

The rules for offsets...

All gains and losses for a year are assigned to their appropriate categories, and then are netted against each other. *If the result is...*

●**Net gain in each category,** the appropriate tax rate is applied to each.

●**Net gain overall,** but net losses in some categories, then losses are applied against gains in this order...

●Net short-term losses apply first against 28% gains, then 25% gains, then 20% gains.

●Net losses on collectibles apply first against 25% gains, then 20% gains, then short-term gains.

●Net long-term losses apply first against 28% gains, then 25% gains, then short-term gains.

●**Net loss overall,** up to $3,000 of loss can be deducted against ordinary income. Remaining net loss can be carried over to future years and be deducted against future gains, in the following order...

●Long-term loss carryovers apply first against 28% gains, then 25% gains, then 20% gains, then short-term gains.

●Short-term loss carryovers apply first against short-term gains, then 28% gains, then 25% gains, then 20% gains.

Up to $3,000 of any remaining net loss can again be deducted against ordinary income, with excess net losses again carried forward.

Opportunity: Because losses generally offset the highest-rate gains first, it may be possible to generate low-rate losses that offset high-rate gains to preserve gains taxed at more favorable lower rates.

Example: A person has only unrealized gains and losses in the current year, but expects to take both 25% and 20% gain from the sale of real estate in the following year. *If he voluntarily realizes a long-term loss in the current year he can...*

●**Deduct up to $3,000 against current income** taxable at rates up to 39.6%.

●**Carry over the remainder of the loss** and deduct it first against 25% gain earned from the sale of the real estate.

Result: The loss will offset both ordinary income—taxed at up to 39.6%—and 25% income.

Contrast: If the same loss had been taken the following year, it would be applied against 20% income first, and perhaps none of it would offset higher-rate income.

When planning investment moves, be sure to consider the tax impact of capital gain and loss offsets.

How to Protect Huge Stock Market Gains

Richard J. Shapiro, Esq., tax partner, Ernst & Young LLP, 787 Seventh Ave., New York 10019. Mr. Shapiro is author of *Taxes and Investing: A Guide for the Individual Investor.* The Options Clearing Corporation.

A soaring stock market is good news for just about everyone, including the IRS. If you take your gains, you'll owe 20% of them to the federal government, assuming you held the stock for more than a year. You may also owe state or even local income tax on the gains.

The tax problem is even more pronounced if you hold an outstanding stock—say you bought Intel or Microsoft ten years ago—that has appreciated many times over.

True, you don't *have* to sell and take your gains. But what if you want to cash in some of your chips or feel it would be prudent to reduce your exposure to the single strongest holding in your portfolio?

The following savvy tax strategies can help you cash in, diversify or both...

OFFSETTING LOSSES

Track your portfolio carefully and take losses whenever a stock or mutual fund heads deeply south. Accumulate these losses during the year. Then, when you've built up a pile of losses, you can sell enough of your big winner to end up with no net capital gains for the year. By offsetting winners and losers, you'll avoid a capital gains tax bill.

The proceeds from these sales can be used for spending money or reinvested in diversified holdings.

USE MARGIN

Generally, you can borrow from your broker up to 50% of the value of stocks you hold.

Example: If you're holding $500,000 worth of Intel, you can borrow up to $250,000 (and pay interest at about 8%).

Tax break: The interest you pay on a margin loan is deductible, as long as the money is used to buy other securities—but not tax-exempt bonds—and you have enough qualifying investment income (e.g., interest, dividends, short-term gains) to offset the margin interest. Deductibility could cut your borrowing cost to as much as 4% to 5%, after tax.

Strategy: Use the borrowed money to invest in a more varied portfolio.

GO FOR OPTIONS

Listed options trade on hundreds of stocks. *If your big winner is one of these, consider...*

• **Buying a put.*** With a stock now selling at $100, you might buy a put at $100. If the stock price falls, you can exercise your put. This locks in your profit.

You can think of the money you pay for the put as insurance against a decline in the stock price.

• **Selling a call.**** If your stock is selling at $100, you might sell a listed call at $105 or $110 (an "out-of-the-money" call). The sales will generate cash (the premium) without triggering your gain on the underlying stock.

Trap: In the above example, if your stock goes over the exercise price, your shares probably will be called away, triggering the long-term gain on the stock.

Strategy: Buy back the call, incur a short-term capital loss, and keep your appreciated position intact.

Alternatively, you can buy stock on the market, at the higher price, to satisfy the call. Again, you'll incur a short-term capital loss while maintaining your original position.

Key: Buying an "in-the-money" put above the current price or selling an "in-the-money" call below the current price may cause your deferred gains to be taxed, so work closely with your tax professional.

PUT TOGETHER A COLLAR

A sophisticated options strategy, called a collar, consists of using both puts and calls. If you have a truly large gain, your broker may fix you a custom-made collar.

Example: You own $1 million worth of one highly appreciated stock, now selling at $100 per share.

Your broker might offer to sell you a two-year, $95 put option. Such a put option, though, might cost $50,000 or more. To offset this cost, the brokerage firm might pay you $50,000 for a two-year call option at a strike price of, say, $110.

Result: You pay $50,000 for one option and receive $50,000 for selling another, avoiding an out-of-pocket cost. You've limited your downside risk while retaining some upside potential.

And...the brokerage firm may lend you money against the shares you're holding,

---

*A "put" is the option to sell at a specified price a specific number of shares by a certain date.

**A "call" is the option to buy at a specified price a specific number of shares by a certain date.

depending on your creditworthiness and overall financial picture. Then, you can use the proceeds to spend or invest elsewhere.

Strategy: You don't have to use this type of customized collar. You can create your own collar with listed stock options, selling calls and buying puts.

Trap: In some situations you'll incur a "constructive sale," triggering all the deferred capital gains. Again, be sure you work with a savvy tax pro to help you put together a tax-sensitive collar.

DO AN EQUITY SWAP

These deals are offered by some banks and brokerage firms, generally for investors with appreciated stocks worth more than $1 million. They allow you to substantially shift your investment return from one stock to another stock or a diversified portfolio—say, the S&P 500 index—without having to pay capital gains tax on the appreciation you've already built up.

Example: You own 10,000 shares of XYZ Co. you bought at $20 per share but are now selling for $50. You enter into a contract in which you keep the legal title to your 10,000 shares. The other party assumes the risk of most of the losses on those shares as well as the rights to most of the gains for, say, five years. In addition, under the contract, you get the risks and rewards from another investment (such as the S&P 500 index).

When the period is up, gains or losses during the period of the contract are tallied and the loser pays the winner.

You may have to pay if the S&P 500 lags your stock. However, you still own your original 10,000 shares of XYZ Co. and have not paid capital gains tax on them.

When the contract expires, you can renew it, continuing to defer capital gains while maintaining your participation in S&P 500 gains.

Tax Consequences of Refinancing a Mortgage

Points paid are not deductible in the year you pay them. They must be amortized over the life of the mortgage. But if you refinance for a second or third time, any points paid on a previous refinancing and not yet written off are fully deductible for the year in which the new refinancing is completed.

R. Milton Howell, III, CPA, tax manager, Davenport, Marvin, Joyce & Co., LLP, certified public accountants, Greensboro, NC.

How to Lower Property Taxes

David Schechner, Esq., real estate attorney, Schechner & Targan, West Orange, NJ.

Don't just grumble and accept a property tax bill you feel is too high. You have the right to appeal an assessment. But before you do, make sure you have a fact-based case. *Steps to take...*

●**Find out where to file an appeal and when the deadline is.** The deadline is usually statutory and can't be extended.

●**Call the assessor's office**—or pay a visit —to find out exactly how your tax figure was determined.

●**Look for mathematical errors in the calculation of your tax.**

●**Look for factual errors in the description of property that overestimates its value**—a basement erroneously listed as finished...a one-car garage listed as a two-car... incorrect lot size, etc.

●**Compare your assessment with your neighbors'.** To see if there is "discrimination," check the assessments of your block and compare them to value to determine a ratio. If your figure is correct but theirs are underestimated, find out the practice in your area. The answer may be that they will raise your neighbors' taxes and not lower yours.

• **Compare the assigned market value with recent sales prices** of comparable houses in the neighborhood.

• **Make sure you have any tax breaks for which you qualify**—senior citizen...disabled ...veteran...low income.

If you feel you need professional advice, look for an attorney who specializes in this work or a licensed appraiser with the qualifications MAI (Member of the Appraisal Institute) or SRA (Senior Residential Appraiser). *Note:* In most cases their services are on a contingent-fee basis.

Once your research is done, file your appeal and attach copies of any relevant backup materials to support your case.

Most Valuable Tax-Cutting Tools for You

Sidney Kess, attorney and CPA, 10 Rockefeller Plaza, Suite 909, New York 10020. Over the years, he has taught tax law to more than 600,000 tax professionals. Mr. Kess is coauthor/consulting editor of *Financial and Estate Planning* and coauthor of *1040 Preparation, 2000 Edition.* CCH Inc.

Here are some of the best of the dozens of tax-saving strategies I pass on to the tax professionals who attend my seminars, held throughout the year in major US cities.

These ideas can help you save taxes right from the start of 2001 and all year through.

FAMILY TAX SAVINGS

Strategies involving your children...

• **Fund Roth IRAs now** for children who will have wages during the year, such as from a summer job. You can fund the account with money given to the child as a gift at the beginning of the year.

Roth IRA funds will compound to a tremendous amount over a child's life and be totally tax free. After age 59½, in fact, earnings can be withdrawn tax free and without penalty. Contributions can be withdrawn tax free at any time.

The benefit of a Roth IRA is tax-free appreciation. Funding the Roth at the start of each year instead of later will make a big difference over the long run due to the power of tax-free compounding.

If, for some reason, it turns out later the child isn't eligible for the Roth IRA—say he/ she doesn't get a job—contributions can be withdrawn penalty free until April 16, 2001.

• **Give appreciated stock to children over age 13** who need money to pay college costs or other expenses. Don't sell the stock and give the child cash.

Reason: When you give the child the stock and he sells it, he will pay tax on the appreciation at his own tax rate—probably 0% or 10%—instead of your own 20% capital gains tax rate.

You can make tax-free gifts of $10,000 annually—$20,000 when gifts are made with the consent of a spouse—to each child.

• **Defer investment income for children under age 14** to avoid the "kiddie tax." This tax imposes the parents' tax rate on a young child's investment income.

Example: Have the child invest in appreciating assets—index funds, growth stocks—rather than in income-generating assets, and sell them after reaching age 14.

• **Set up education IRAs for children under age 18.** Each child can receive up to $500 annually that has been deposited on his behalf in an education IRA. The funds will be tax free when spent on qualified education expenses. Again, fund the education IRAs early to maximize appreciation.

• **Take advantage of the child care credit.** This can reduce your tax bill if you pay for child care that frees you to be employed, rather than provide the care yourself.

Expenses you might not have thought of may qualify for the credit, including summer day camp and amounts paid to a relative such as an aunt or grandmother who looks after a child. *Strategies involving other family members...*

• **Make interest-free loans to adult children or other relatives.** This cuts the family tax bill when the money is taken from a taxable account and is used on expenditures that create deductions.

Example: A grown child uses the loan to fund a new business that produces start-up losses, or to buy a house that generates deductible property taxes, mortgage interest and loan fees.

Limits: Loans of up to $10,000 per recipient have no adverse tax consequences. And, loans of up to $100,000 have no adverse consequences so long as the borrower has no investment income.

●**Support retired family members with gifts of dividend-paying stock or fund shares.** This is better than making cash support payments.

Why: Much of the dividend income will be tax free because of the recipient's personal exemption, extra standard deduction for persons over age 65 and standard deduction.

Bonus: When these shares are later inherited by you or another relative (such as a child of yours), they will receive stepped-up basis—so all taxable gain on the share's appreciation is eliminated.

Caution: You'll only get the stepped-up basis when the inheritance is more than one year after the date of the gift.

Key: You can't legally require the gift recipient to bequeath gift shares as you wish but must trust him to do so.

●**Use a multiple support agreement** (IRS Form 2120) to obtain a dependency exemption when a group of individuals supports a dependent without any one person providing more than 50% of the support. The group can then assign the exemption to one of its members.

BUSINESS DEDUCTIONS

Business ideas to cut taxes...

●**Buy a sport-utility vehicle (SUV)** that weighs more than 6,000 pounds for business driving.

Why: Depreciation deductions for cars weighing less than 6,000 pounds are restricted by the Tax Code. But depreciation for vehicles weighing more is not—so you may obtain thousands of dollars more of up-front deductions for a heavy SUV that is used primarily for work.

●**Set up a home office.** This lets you deduct a portion of household expenses that normally wouldn't be deductible.

Examples: Utilities, insurance, repairs and depreciation. Also, when your home is a workplace you may be able to deduct commuting between it and other work locations.

Requirement: The office portion of your home must be used exclusively for work. It also must be the primary place where you conduct your business, or a place where you meet clients or customers on a regular basis, or be necessary to maintain business records or perform other managerial or administrative duties due to a lack of other office facilities.

●**Establish your own business, even if it is only a sideline.** This creates numerous potential tax breaks such as home-office deductions and a Keogh plan. You can hire your children and your spouse and set up a medical reimbursement plan that can turn all your family's medical expenses into a deductible business expense.

Requirement: You must have a genuine intention to make a profit from your sideline activity—but you are not required to actually make a profit.

INVESTMENTS

Strategies that enable you to keep the most from your investments after taxes...

●**Specifically identify shares of securities that you buy and sell.** That way, you can select for sale those in which you have the highest or lowest tax basis.

Snag: If you don't do so, the IRS requires shares of a single stock or fund that you bought at different times be sold on a first-bought, first-sold basis.

●**Invest in mutual funds that are tax efficient.** Funds generally make taxable distributions at year-end of taxable gains they realize internally. With low-turnover funds, such as index funds, this tax charge is usually much smaller than with actively traded funds.

Strategy: If your portfolio includes both income-producing and appreciating assets, consider holding the income-producing assets in a retirement plan to avoid current tax on the income, while holding gain-generating investments personally to obtain the benefit of the favorable 20% top gains tax rate.

●**Deduct bad debts and worthless securities.** The statute of limitations is six years on these, so you can file amended returns that far back to claim them.

●**Pay IRA and Keogh trustee fees by check,** rather than have them deducted from the account, to retain a tax deduction for them.

More from Sidney Kess...

New Opportunities To Deduct Medical Expenses

You might think that because medical expenses generally are deductible only to the extent they exceed 7.5% of Adjusted Gross Income (AGI) very few taxpayers ever get to deduct them.

Surprise! The latest tabulation based on IRS statistics shows that taxpayers are taking medical expense deductions at an impressive rate —despite the 7.5%-of-AGI floor.

AVERAGE MEDICAL DEDUCTION CLAIMED ON 1998 RETURNS

AGI	Medical Deduction
$Under $15,000	$7,048
$15,000–$29,999	$5,902
$30,000–$49,999	$4,530
$50,000–$99,999	$5,769
$100,000–$199,999	$12,815
$200,000 or more	$35,759

These figures may seem surprisingly high in view of the fact that only those expenses not covered by insurance are deductible. But costly premiums for medical insurance are included as a medical expense.

WHAT THE INSURANCE PLANS DON'T COVER

Even the best health insurance policies don't cover every medical cost. The more common medical expenses that may not be fully or even partially covered by medical insurance, but are nevertheless deductible as a medical expense on your tax return...

●**Insurance premiums** an individual taxpayer pays for a policy are considered to be deductible medical expenses. Premiums can be big out-of-pocket expenses. Individually purchased family coverage, for example, can cost as much as $10,000 a year!

●**Certain drugs** may not be covered by insurance.

Examples: Viagra and birth control pills.

Also not covered are any drugs still considered "experimental" by the insurance companies.

●**Psychiatry/therapy.** Most policies limit the number of visits the insurance company will pay for. Most also require the policy holder to make bigger copayments for psychological care than for other medical care.

●**New medical procedures.** Procedures that the insurance company determines haven't yet become widely accepted may be treated by the insurer as "experimental" and not covered by the policy. This experimental exclusion often affects cancer patients who receive breakthrough-type treatment.

STOP-SMOKING PROGRAMS

The IRS recently added the cost of doctor-prescribed stop-smoking programs to its list of deductible medical expenses.

Before this announcement the cost of a stop-smoking program was deductible only if it was prescribed for treatment of a *specific* medical condition, such as emphysema.

But now, apparently in recognition of the Surgeon General's position that nicotine is an addictive drug (and smoking cigarettes a killer), the IRS will allow a deduction for the cost of a stop-smoking program. The program must be prescribed by a doctor, but does not have to be for treatment of a specific disease.

The new IRS anti-smoking stance does not extend to over-the-counter stop-smoking aids such as nicotine gum and patches.

Refund opportunity: The new IRS ruling applies to all open tax years, therefore, individuals who paid out-of-pocket for such programs can amend their tax returns and take the deduction for any tax year not closed by the statute of limitations (generally three years from the tax return's due date).

BIGGER DEDUCTION FOR SELF-EMPLOYEDS

Self-employed individuals, including partners and more-than-2% S corporation shareholders, cannot deduct business-provided health insurance for themselves, spouses and dependents as a business expense.

Instead they deduct a portion of their medical insurance costs as an adjustment to gross income.

There is a limit on this deduction, though. For 2000 only 60% of a self-employed person's insurance premiums can be deducted as an adjustment to gross income.

The balance of the premiums must be treated as an itemized medical expense subject to the 7.5% floor.

The percentage limit on premium deductions is scheduled to increase to 70% in the year 2002, and to 100% by 2003.

Pending legislation now before Congress would accelerate the 100% deductibility to the year 2000.

FULL DEDUCTIBILITY FOR SELF-EMPLOYEDS

A self-employed individual may be able to obtain full deductibility for medical expenses (not just health insurance) if his/her spouse works for the business.

The IRS has endorsed an arrangement that permits an otherwise nondeductible expense to become fully deductible as long as the spouse does real work for the business.

How it works: The self-employed person deducts as a business expense the cost of a medical reimbursement plan. The plan provides medical benefits for a spouse-employee and that person's dependents and spouse— this being the self-employed person himself.

Caution: Taxpayers who use such an arrangement should be aware that the IRS will look closely at whether the spouse is, in fact, an employee. *Trap:* If the spouse is a joint owner, then the spouse is also a self-employed person and not an employee of the business.

Key: Document fully the employment status of the spouse (hours worked, tasks performed, etc.) and treat that person consistently as an employee—by paying Social Security tax on his wages, for instance.

Caution: If the company decides to adopt a medical reimbursement plan to cover the spouse-employee, it must also cover other employees on a nondiscriminatory basis.

The cost of covering other employees must be weighed against the benefit to be achieved for the self-employed person.

Sidney Kess on...

Great Tax Breaks For Helping Out Your Parents

There are a number of breaks in the tax law for children who provide their parents with care and financial support. The breaks aren't big and the rules are very tricky, but they're well worth looking into.

THE DEPENDENCY EXEMPTION

You may qualify for an extra dependency exemption for supporting your mother or father. You may qualify for two exemptions if you support both your mother and father.

In 2000, a single dependency exemption is worth $2,800.

Two key requirements for taking a dependency exemption for a parent you're supporting...

●**The parent cannot have gross income of more than $2,800.** In figuring gross income you do not have to include Social Security benefits...health and accident proceeds...deferred interest on federal EE bonds...tax-exempt interest...gifts and inheritances...life insurance proceeds...other tax-exempt income.

Catch: If the parent is receiving a pension or taking required minimum distributions from an IRA, it generally won't be possible for you to meet the "gross income test."

●**You must provide more than one half of the parent's support.** Included in the meaning of "support" are food...lodging...clothing...medical and dental care...transportation...recreation...and other similar expenses.

If the parent lives with you, you can include his/her portion of household expenses in calculating support.

Example: Say your rent is $1,500 a month, and your mother lives with you and your spouse. One-third of your rent—$500 a month—can be included in support.

If you're not sure if you provide more than half of your parent's support, take steps before year-end that will help you meet the 50% requirement. *Among the things you can do are...*

●**Designate payments as being for the support of the parent for whom you are**

most likely to get an exemption. This is especially important where you may be supporting two parents but can only qualify one for the exemption (because the other parent's gross income is over the limit).

What to do: Make all your checks out to the parent you intend to claim as a dependent.

•**Have your mother or father deposit Social Security checks in the bank** so they're not used for his/her part of support.

•**Increase your support payments if necessary by paying for additional items—** such as clothing, recreation and transportation.

MULTIPLE SUPPORT AGREEMENTS

If you're supporting a parent with your siblings, only one of you can claim the dependency exemption. To get the exemption at all, though, you must together provide more than half the parent's support.

Any one of you who provides at least 10% of the support can claim the exemption.

The group must agree on who will take the exemption. All of you must sign a *multiple support declaration,* IRS Form 2120, which is then attached to the return of the person claiming the exemption.

How to decide who should take the exemption...

•**As a general rule, the sibling in the highest tax bracket will get the greatest benefit** from claiming the exemption.

•**Where that person is subject to the cutback of exemptions for high income taxpayers,** then a sibling not subject to this cutback should claim the exemption for supporting the parent.

•**The person who takes the exemption** can be changed from year to year. *Strategy:* Run the numbers every year to see who will benefit the most from the exemption.

•**The person who claims the exemption** should be the one to pay the medical bills (to deduct these expenses as explained below).

DEDUCTIONS FOR MEDICAL BILLS

If you pay your parent's medical expenses —insurance premiums, prescription drugs, copayments on doctor's visits, etc.—you may be able to add these payments to your own medical expenses even if your parents did not qualify as dependents.

As long as you pay the expense, you can include it as one of your medical expenses if your parent would have been a dependent but for the amount of his gross income.

Example: You pay more than half of your father's support although his gross income exceeds $2,800. Of your support payments, $2,500 are medical expenses for your father. You can add these expenses to your own in figuring your medical deduction.

Also, if you are a party to a multiple support arrangement and you claim the exemption, you can deduct your parent's medical expenses on your return.

INCOME SHIFTING

If your parent is in a low income tax bracket, you should consider taking advantage of the process of income shifting to cut the family's overall tax bill.

Transfer income-producing property to your parent. Keep the gifts under the $10,000/ $20,000 annual gift tax exclusion so you don't have to worry about gift tax.

Your parent then reports the income from the property on his return and pays tax on it at his low rate. Little or no tax may be due on this income.

If, in 2000, your parent is over 65 and single, he can receive income up to $8,300 without any tax due (assuming your parent is not claimed as a dependent). If both parents are older than 65, you can give only up to $14,650.

Example: You (and your spouse) can give your parent $20,000 worth of corporate bonds that pay 7% annually. Your parent now reports the $1,400 interest on the bonds. If you are in the 40% tax bracket (federal and state), you'd have only $840 after tax available ($1,400–$560) from this income for your parent.

Your parent, who can shelter this income with his increased standard deduction for being 65 or older, pays no tax and can use the full $1,400 to pay expenses.

Even if your parent is subject to tax, being in a lower tax bracket than you means he will pay less tax on that income than you would.

If your parent sells the property for long-term capital gains, the tax on the gain may be only 10% for your parent, compared with 20% for you. The low 10% capital gains can be used by taxpayers in the 15% tax bracket on their other income (this bracket applies to singles in 2000 with taxable income up to $26,250).

Income boosting trap: Before you transfer property to your parent, keep in mind that boosting your parent's income may prevent you from taking the exemption for your parent. *Reason:* The gross income test will be exceeded.

Note: This may not be an issue if you are a high income taxpayer already subject to the phase out for exemptions.

LOOKING AHEAD

In 2001, a parent in the 15% tax bracket will pay only 8% on long-term capital gains from property you hold more than five years.

Giving appreciated property to your parent and having your parent leave it to you in his will can be a way to boost the tax cost of the property (and cut the tax you'll pay when you sell it).

As long as your parent outlives the transfer by more than one year, you'll get a stepped-up basis for the property when you inherit it back. The basis will be increased to the property's value on the date of your parent's death.

This means that if you then sell the property, you'll avoid capital gains on the prior appreciation.

Example: You own stock that cost you $5,000 but is now worth $20,000. You (and your spouse) give it to your father, who in turn leaves it to you when he dies two years later. The stock is now worth $25,000. Your basis is $25,000 (and no one has ever had to pay capital gains tax on the appreciation in the stock).

Tax Break for Smokers Trying to Quit

The IRS ruled smoking-cessation costs, including prescription drugs, doctors' bills and many programs, are deductible. *However:* Only total medical expenses exceeding 7.5% of

AGI are deductible. Nonprescription products, such as nicotine gum, certain patches and expenses reimbursed by employers or insurance are not deductible.

Internal Revenue Service, Washington, DC.

Skip Generations ...And Skip Taxes

Generation-skipping tax planning allows you to build up wealth for your children, grandchildren and descendants to come.

Benefit: A $1 million exemption (adjusted annually for inflation) from generation-skipping transfer tax.

Important: Making gifts during your lifetime can maximize that exemption. *To maximize:* Transfer assets with fairly low current value but significant expected future growth—such as stocks, real estate and life insurance. Rules on generation-skipping transfers are very complex—be sure to get solid financial advice.

David S. Rhine, partner and national director of family wealth planning, BDO Seidman, LLP, 330 Madison Ave., New York 10017.

Ways to Cut Taxes and Build Real Wealth with a Family Business

Steven J. Brown, CPA, tax partner, Rubin, Brown, Gornstein & Co. LLP, 230 S. Bemiston Ave., St. Louis 63105.

A family business, even if it is only a sideline, can provide valuable tax-favored ways to build family wealth...

SHIFT INCOME

Income taxes can be reduced by moving income to low-tax-bracket family members. *How to do it...*

•**Employ family members.** When children, grandchildren and other family members in low tax brackets are employed by the business, it can deduct their compensation at its high-tax-bracket rate while they report income at their low tax rates.

•The kiddie tax, which taxes the investment income of children under age 14 at their parents' tax rate, does not apply to earned income.

•No Social Security tax is due on the income of a child under age 18 who is employed by a parent's unincorporated business.

Even very young children can be paid a deductible wage by a family business if they do real work and are paid a reasonable wage rate.

Deductible salaries that reduce the family's overall tax bill also can be paid for full- or part-time work to retired parents and other family members not in the top tax bracket.

•**Organize the business as a pass-through entity.** These include limited liability companies (LLCs), partnerships, and S corporations, which have their income taxed directly on their owners' returns.

Using a pass-through entity makes it possible to shift business income to low-tax-bracket family members who don't work for the business by giving them shares in it. Each owner pays tax at his/her own tax rate on his share of the business's income.

At the same time, the principal owner of the business can keep control of it even after transferring a majority of the ownership to others. *How:* By acting as the general partner of an LLC or partnership, or keeping most of the voting shares of an S corporation while others receive nonvoting shares.

Strategy: Consider creating a new business as a pass-through entity.

If a business already exists as a regular C corporation, consider converting it to an S corporation, or organizing future expansion and acquisitions through new pass-through entities.

RETIREMENT PLANS

Retirement plans are the best tax shelter for most people, and a family business of any size can help provide them. *Examples…*

•**Roth IRAs for children.** An extra benefit of paying a wage to a child is that it enables the child to make a Roth IRA contribution of up to $2,000. The child doesn't have to use the earned income to make the contribution—he/she can spend or save all of his wages and make the contribution with funds received by gift from parents or other family members.

A Roth IRA contribution can provide huge benefits to a child. Decades of tax-free compounding can build up the amount tremendously…future distributions can be totally tax free…and contributions can be withdrawn tax free without penalty before age 59½.

•**Keoghs.** Even a modest sideline business can fund a Keogh plan for its owner. Deductible contributions can equal 20% of self-employment income—maybe more for age 50-plus owners who use a "defined benefit" Keogh. Consult your tax professional.

TAX-FAVORED BENEFITS

Valuable perks may flow from a family business. *Examples…*

•**Home office.** If the business is run from your home, you may qualify to deduct a home office and obtain deductions for a portion of previously nondeductible home ownership costs such as insurance, utilities and rent or depreciation.

You may also obtain larger deductions for business driving, because while commuting between home and work generally isn't deductible, driving between two work locations is deductible.

•**Company car.** Employees can deduct business driving only among their miscellaneous expenses, the total of which is deductible only to the extent that it exceeds 2% of AGI. So, driving deductions may be limited.

In contrast, a business can deduct the full leasing or depreciation cost of acquiring a car, as well as interest on a car loan.

If the business then provides the car to you, the portion of the car's value that is attributable to your personal use will be taxable income to you. But the tax on this will be less than the cost of acquiring the same car for yourself directly.

The result is that the business gets a larger deduction for the car than you would as an employee, and you get the car at reduced out-of-pocket cost.

●**Computers and other electronic equipment.** "Listed property" is subject to strict rules. Employees who wish to deduct such items are required to document business use and can deduct only a corresponding portion of their cost. Employees also must show that they use the equipment "for the convenience of the employer."

Again, larger total deductions may be obtained if the company buys the equipment, deducts or depreciates its full cost, and provides it to the individual, while including only the appropriate portion of the equipment's value in the employees' income. There will be less cash cost to the individual as well.

●**Health benefits.** Larger businesses can set up medical benefit plans and other more formal benefit programs as well.

OWNERSHIP OF ASSETS

If a business uses real estate or other tangible property, family members can own the property personally and lease it to the business. *Advantages...*

●**Income is received from the business with no employment tax being owed on it.**

●**Family members not employed by the business can receive income from it.**

●**Family members can utilize the property for their personal benefit**—by borrowing against it, selling it or even retaining it after they sell the business.

Tactic: If ownership of the property is placed in a pass-through entity, lease payments can be distributed among low-tax-bracket family members while the senior business managers retain control over the property.

TAX-FREE BORROWING

When a business has amassed significant funds, owners may obtain use of them through tax-free borrowing rather than taxable wages or dividend distributions. Be sure all loans from the company are fully documented and carry fair-market terms regarding interest and repayment—and that borrowers follow those terms.

REDUCE ESTATE TAXES

It's possible to save future family wealth from the IRS by transferring shares in a family business to the younger generation now. This removes both the transferred property's current value and also future appreciation from your estate.

Opportunity: Minority interests in a private business can receive substantial valuation discounts for gift and estate tax purposes. So the $10,000 per recipient annual gift tax exclusion ($20,000 when gifts are made jointly by a married couple) may be used to pass tax free more than that amount of assets with each gift.

Once more, pass-through entities are useful because they enable senior family members to pass ownership of the business to the younger generation while retaining control of it themselves.

Retirement Tax Strategy

Many people today have both taxable and tax-deferred investment accounts. Often their major stock holdings are in a tax-deferred plan such as a 401(k) or IRA rollover. When money is taken out of these plans, it's taxed at ordinary income tax rates, not at the more favorable long-term capital gains rate.

Strategy: Before you reach 70½, when you must start withdrawing funds, sell stocks or stock funds in your tax-deferred accounts and use the proceeds to buy bonds with taxable interest.

At the same time, sell any bonds that are held in taxable accounts and use the money to replace the sold stock positions. This keeps your asset allocation the same.

When you eventually sell these stocks (after holding them for at least a year), you will have a higher cost basis (thus fewer gains) and the proceeds will be taxed at the capital gains rate.

Victor Levinson, Esq., managing director, Balis, Lewittes & Coleman, Inc., an investment management firm for individuals and smaller institutional clients, 575 Lexington Ave., New York 10022.

Financial Fun...
It Pays to Turn Your
Hobby into a Business

Barbara Weltman, an attorney with offices in Mill-wood, NY. She is author of numerous books, including *The Complete Idiot's Guide to Making Money After You Retire.* Alpha Books.

Freedom is the greatest gift retirement gives...freedom...to follow your bliss... pursue your passion...develop your talent. You can make money, too, *by turning your hobby into a business...*

•**Craftspeople** *can sell their wares* at craft shows and church bazaars.

•**Collectors** *can buy and sell at flea markets* or on the Internet.

•**A person who loves to travel** *can become a tour guide.*

•**A passionate gardener** *might sell orchids* and other exotic plants to local garden centers.

Benefits of turning your talent and skill into a business...

•**When you are in business,** expenses that formerly were not tax deductible become deductible.

•**You get to pursue something you love to do.**

•**You can supplement your retirement income.**

•**You can build up additional retirement savings** by setting up a new retirement plan for this business.

There's no age limit on setting up a retirement plan for your business although you may have to start taking distributions from the plan if you are age 70½ or older.

THE RIGHT WAY TO SET UP A BUSINESS

Whether you plan to pursue your activity part-time or full-time, be sure that you are *working within the law...*

•**Register your business.** If you operate as a sole proprietor or partnership, you must register the name of your business with your city or county.

This registration is known as "doing business as" or DBA. You need a DBA paper to set up a business bank account.

If you decide to incorporate or form a limited liability company for your activity, you must also follow state law.

•**Get a tax identification number**—called an employer identification number—whether or not you have employees.

This is the number you use on your business bank account, any retirement plan you may set up for your business and on payroll forms if you have employees—or are yourself an employee of your corporation.

To get a tax identification number: File Form SS-4, *Application for Employer Identification Number,* with the IRS. Or, you can have a number assigned to you over the telephone by following the instructions on the SS-4 form.

•**Get a state sales tax number**—called a *resale number*—if you plan to buy goods that you will sell or if you offer services subject to this tax.

Your state tax authority can provide you with a sales tax kit explaining your obligations.

•**Set up your books.** While records for your personal tax return can be informal, you must keep accurate books and records for your business.

You may want to consult an accountant for this—or use the services of the Federal Government's SBA volunteers, such as SCORE (Service Corps of Retired Executives). Visit *www.irs.gov* for information.

•**Get licenses and permits.** If you need these to run your business, be sure to have them before you start in order to avoid penalties.

Not sure if you need them? Call your city, town, county or state government offices listed in your local phone book.

BUSINESS TAX WRITE-OFFS

Turning your hobby into a business generally entitles you to deduct your activity's expenses.

If these expenses are greater than the income from your business, you can use your losses to offset income from other sources (such as interest, dividends and taxable Social Security benefits).

139

Caution: If your business is unincorporated and the IRS finds that you do not have a profit motive—you're only pursuing your hobby—then you're subject to the "hobby loss rules," which may prevent you from deducting your losses.

●**If you have a profit, you must report it.** You can deduct your expenses in figuring your profit.

You must also pay self-employment tax on your net earnings—even if you are already collecting Social Security benefits.

●**If you have a loss, you cannot deduct expenses in excess of your income from the activity.** It's common for businesses to suffer losses in some years, especially in the start-up years. But if a business has losses year in and year out, the IRS may question your profit motive.

How do you prove you have a reasonable expectation of making a profit from your business? There's no single factor you can use, but here are the main considerations the IRS takes into account in determining whether you have a profit motive. *Questions they ask...*

●**Do you run your activity like a business?** Do you keep good books and records? Do you have a business bank account?

●**How much time and effort do you put into the activity?** If you spend only a few hours a month on your "business," it may be hard to show you have a profit motive.

●**Do you use methods of operating your business that are designed to make it profitable?** Be sure to take the trouble to adopt the best methods for your business.

Example: Advertise to stimulate sales. If one type of advertising doesn't work, try another. If you run out of ideas, consult experts.

●**Do you have expertise in the field you're pursuing?**

You may be great at your hobby, but you also have to know how to run a business. If you've never run a business before, take courses at adult education centers and community colleges.

AVOIDING TROUBLE WITH THE IRS

You can sidestep the hobby loss rules (which, to repeat, may prevent you from deducting your losses) by incorporating your business.

Losses of a *corporation* are not subject to these rules.

Alternatively, you can rely on a legal "presumption" that you have a profit motive. If you can show profits in three out of five years (two out of seven years in the case of horse-related activities), then you are presumed to be in business for profit and your losses are deductible.

To rely on this presumption, you must file IRS Form 5213, *Election to Postpone Determination as to Whether the Presumption Applies that an Activity is Engaged in for Profit,* for the *first year* you are in business. If you don't file this form with your return for your first year, you can always file an amended return for the first year and include Form 5213. You have up to three years to do this.

Caution: Filing Form 5213 is a red flag. The IRS is sure to look at your returns for the next five years to see that you have at least three profitable years.

If you don't have three profitable years, you can still try to show a profit motive in the way you run your business. *Examples...*

●**Operate in a businesslike way.**

●**Spend significant time at the business.**

●**Consult with experts on how to run the business.**

●**Have every intention of making a profit** —as soon as possible.

More from Barbara Weltman...

Home Owners' Tax Victories That Can Mean Big Money to You

Your home may be both your most substantial asset and your best tax shelter, too.

You probably know that after using a home as your primary residence for two out of five years, you can exclude from income up to

$250,000 of gain on its sale—$500,000 on a joint return.

But there are many more ways to use your home to save taxes. These home owners' victories over the IRS show how.

MORTGAGE INTEREST

You can take a mortgage interest deduction for the interest you pay on a loan of up to $1 million used to acquire, build, or substantially improve a home, plus subsequent home equity loans totaling up to $100,000 at any one time. *In addition...*

● **Bigger home equity interest deductions.** Interest on home equity loans exceeding $100,000 may be deductible as business or investment interest if the borrowed funds are used for a business or investment purpose. This may give a person who owns an appreciated home a low-cost way of financing a business or investment opportunity.

Letter Ruling 9335043.

● **Sometimes points on refinancing are deductible.** Points, or loan origination fees, incurred when refinancing a home mortgage generally are not deductible—but *were* deductible when a new home was acquired using a three-year balloon loan that had to be refinanced at the end of its term. The IRS disallowed the home owner's deduction for the points on the refinancing—but the Court of Appeals said the short-term nature of the original loan made the refinancing an "integrated step" in the acquisition of the home, so the points were deductible.

James R. Huntsman, CA-8, 905 F.2d 1182.

● **Deducting points paid by the seller.** Home buyers can deduct points on a home acquisition loan even if the seller pays them. The rationale is that the seller's payment of the points is reflected in the purchase price, so the buyer is the "real" payer. The amount of points paid by the seller is subtracted from the buyer's basis in the new home.

Revenue Procedure 94-27.

● **Benefit of spreading out points.** The deduction of points on a home mortgage can be deferred by deducting them over the life of the loan rather than in the first year. This was the decision in a case where a young couple buying their first home didn't have sufficient deductions to itemize in the year they bought the home—so they would have received no tax benefit from the points. By deducting the points over the life of the loan they may obtain a tax benefit from them in future years.

Letter Ruling 199905033.

HOME OFFICES

A home office deduction can provide a tax write-off for a portion of home ownership expenses such as insurance, utilities, maintenance, repairs and depreciation—the latter being a no-cash-cost deduction you can claim even if your home is appreciating in value.

New break: More people can deduct home offices. New law lets an office be deducted if it is needed for keeping records for a business primarily conducted elsewhere—an exception to the general requirement that a home office be the principal place where the taxpayer conducts a business.

Deduction opportunities...

● **Part of a room.** An office that is only part of a room is deductible, so long as that part of the room is used exclusively for business.

George H. Weightman, TC Memo 1981-301.

● **Sharing an office.** When two spouses use a home office exclusively for work, but only one spouse qualifies to take a home office deduction because the other spouse has a regular office elsewhere, the home office is deductible.

Max Frankel, 82 TC 318.

● **Freestanding home office.** When an office is in a separate structure apart from your residence—such as a converted gardener's shed or freestanding garage—the requirement that the office be your "principal place of business" does not apply. So a top executive could deduct a freestanding office that he built next to his beach house in spite of the fact that he had a regular business office elsewhere.

Ben W. Heineman, 82 TC 538.

Extra: A home office may also give you a deduction for commuting between home and other work locations. Normally, commuting between one's residence and work locations is not deductible—but travel between two work locations *is* deductible.

RENTING FOR PROFIT

● **Ownership costs deduction.** If you rent part of your home or another property out for income, you can deduct ownership costs such as insurance, maintenance and depreciation against rental income, to help shelter it from tax.

If your income doesn't exceed $100,000, you can deduct up to $25,000 of tax losses from the rental activity against ordinary income such as salary, even if the property is appreciating in value—turning it into your own personal tax shelter.

This is true even if you rent to family members and give them a discount rent.

Rule: To deduct tax losses from a rental, you must charge a "fair" rent—but this may be less than a "fair market" rent when you rent to relatives, because of the reduced risk involved. The Tax Court has suggested that a rent discounted 20% below the market rate may be "fair" when renting to relatives.

Lee A. Bindseil, TC Memo 1983-411.

IMPROVEMENTS

Home improvements may qualify as deductible medical expenses when made to alleviate a medical condition.

The amount of an improvement that qualifies as a medical cost is its total cost minus any increase in your home's value that results from the improvement. Operating expenses also are deductible in the case of items such as air conditioners. *Deductions have been allowed for...*

● **New siding** on a house when the taxpayer was allergic to the moldy old siding.

Letter Ruling 8112069.

● **Central air conditioning,** when a member of the family suffered from respiratory ailments.

Raymond Gerard, 37 TC 826, Acq.

● **An elevator** installed for a person with a heart condition.

John Riach v. Frank, CA-9, 302 F.2d 374.

● **An attached garage,** even though the house already had a freestanding garage, when a doctor advised that the taxpayer not walk through the open air in winter.

Karlis A. Pols, TC Memo 1965-222.

● **A health spa** built in a home on a doctor's recommendation to treat arthritis.

Sidney Keen, TC Memo 1981-313.

● **Swimming pools,** such as lap pools, designed for therapeutic purposes and with medical equipment, are deductible under the IRS's own rulings, such as *Revenue Ruling 83-33.*

But all or a part of the cost of normal recreational pools, with no medical equipment, has been ruled deductible when no other pool was conveniently located for the taxpayer.

Collins H. Ferris, CA-7, 582 F.2d 1112, *Herbert Cherry,* TC Memo 1983-470.

Note: Total medical expenses are deductible only to the extent they exceed 7.5% of Adjusted Gross Income (AGI). By getting you over this limit, a home improvement may enable you to deduct many other small, routine medical expenses that otherwise would be nondeductible.

Year-End Distribution Trap

Beware of year-end taxable distributions from mutual funds.

Many mutual funds make distributions to shareholders at year-end of gains on trades made inside the fund during the year. These distributions are taxable even if you reinvest the money to buy more shares of the fund and even if the gains arose before you became a shareholder and even if the fund has lost value since you bought it. *Self-defense...*

● **Don't buy shares in the fund until after its distribution date.**

● **Consider selling shares before the distribution date.** Buy them back after the date if you wish (but not within 30 days if you sold them at a loss).

● **Before year-end sell losing investments and use the losses to offset taxable mutual fund distributions.**

Martin Nissenbaum, Esq., CPA, national director of retirement and personal income tax planning for Ernst & Young LLP, 787 Seventh Ave., New York 10019.

What Tax Advisers Must Do to Protect Your Adviser-Client Privilege

Joyce Bauchner, Ernst & Young LLP, Washington, DC, quoted in *Tax Notes*.

A new tax practitioner-client privilege was created by the *IRS Restructuring and Reform Act of 1998*. This privilege is similar to, but more limited than, the attorney-client privilege clients have with their lawyers.

Although the privilege may be helpful to clients seeking federal tax advice from tax practitioners, there are many instances in which the privilege will not apply. Also, like the attorney-client privilege, the new privilege can be waived, i.e., lost by careless or uninformed actions.

Many tax professionals and clients who aren't accustomed to the rules that must be followed to protect privilege may waive it in a way that proves costly to a client.

THE LIMITS

•**The new tax adviser-client privilege does not apply to communications with all tax advisers.** It applies only to communications between federally authorized tax practitioners—CPAs, attorneys, enrolled agents, and enrolled actuaries—and their clients. The new privilege applies only if the attorney-client privilege would apply to the communication. Like the attorney privilege, it does not apply to communications with respect to tax return preparation.

Example: Papers related to preparing a tax return are not privileged. But if you anticipate that a particular item on a return may be challenged by the IRS, papers drawn up detailing strategies that may be used to defend that item may be privileged.

•**Privilege applies only to matters held in confidence between the client and the adviser.** If any third party is provided the information—perhaps by being told of a conversation, or receiving a "confidential" document—the privilege is lost for that information.

•**It applies only to communications related to the rendering of federal tax advice.** So it does not apply to state tax advice or business advice.

•**This new privilege applies only in noncriminal tax proceedings,** i.e., administrative proceedings before the IRS and civil federal court proceedings in which the IRS is a party.

•**It applies only versus the IRS,** not against state tax agencies, private parties, or other federal government agencies.

•**It does not apply to criminal matters.**

•**It does not apply to written communications to a corporation** about the promotion of a tax shelter.

TRAPS TO AVOID

These rules may sound simple, but they create traps. *Danger areas...*

•**Waiving privilege by disclosing documents.** Tax advisers routinely keep all of a single client's records in a single file—but this now means mixing privileged and unprivileged documents. *Traps...*

•If the file containing privileged communications is given to a third party, the privilege may be lost.

•If the IRS summons the file, privileged documents inadvertently may be handed over with the rest—again possibly waiving the privilege. *Safety...*

☐ If possible, separately store privileged and unprivileged documents.

☐ Stamp privileged documents as such so they can easily be identified.

☐ Apply the same safeguards to electronic documents and E-mail.

☐ Sort and stamp documents as they are created.

•**Dual-use documents.** If a privileged document is put to a non-privileged use, the privilege may be lost.

Example: The courts have ruled that privilege is lost for documents used to help prepare a tax return.

Safety: Again, apply privileged documents only to uses that preserve the privilege. Create separate documents containing only non-privileged information as support for tax return filings.

●**Billing.** Bills generally are not privileged. If clients demand itemized bills, take care to exclude references to privileged information. Create specific billing arrangements that will protect privilege.

●**Production for third parties.** Privilege applies only against the IRS. So you may be required to produce privileged documents for a state tax agency or in a private-party legal proceeding.

Trap: Giving the documents to a third party, too, violates confidentiality and waives the privilege versus the IRS.

Defense: Don't produce the documents until a court orders you to do so. Under the rules of attorney-client privilege, when documents are provided under court order to a third party, they retain their privilege. Although there are no guarantees, this rule may be extended to tax adviser privilege.

●**Criminal matters.** No privilege exists versus the IRS regarding criminal matters. But tax advisers know that the dividing line between "civil" and "criminal" in tax matters often is not at all clear.

Example: An IRS "special agent" may request files that are privileged for civil purposes. If these are provided, and the agent decides there was no criminal violation, do the files lose their civil privilege? Nobody yet knows what rules will apply in such cases.

Best: Be alert to new rulings issued by the IRS and the courts regarding such matters.

●**Promoting tax shelters.** Under present law, a tax shelter is defined as any arrangement a significant purpose of which is the avoidance or evasion of income tax. There are no regulations or cases clarifying this broad definition. Therefore, it is unclear exactly which arrangements will fall within this expansive definition and which will escape it.

Again, look for forthcoming IRS rulings and court decisions that may clarify the issue.

Tax Planning to Preserve Family Assets From the Cost of Long-Term Care

Michael Gilfix, Esq., Gilfix & La Poll Associates, a firm that specializes in tax, estate and active preservation planning in the context of long-term care and public benefits, 4151 Middlefield Rd., Suite 213, Palo Alto, CA 94303.

The financial risk of someday requiring long-term health care is something everyone should prepare for. And tax planning is essential.

Snag: Experts on the legal rules that apply to financing long-term care often don't understand the tax law. And tax experts often don't understand the long-term-care rules.

Here's what you need to know about both sets of rules to protect your family's financial security...

BASICS

Long-term care in a nursing home now costs an *average* of $50,000 annually nationwide—more than double that in some areas. At-home care is comparably expensive.

Risk: A future extended stay in a nursing home may cost hundreds of thousands of dollars —and consume your family's accumulated wealth.

If you can't afford to finance such costs out-of-pocket, there are two other ways to do so—with insurance or through Medicaid. *Rules...*

Insurance. Tax-favored status was extended to long-term-care insurance by federal law effective in 1997.

●**Benefits received under a long-term-care policy** are not taxable income so long as payments exceeding $190 per day do not exceed the actual cost of care in 2000. (Benefits exceeding both $190 per day and the cost of care are taxable.)

●**A portion of the premium payments for long-term-care insurance** qualifies as a deductible medical expense. *Qualified amounts for 2000...*

Age	Amount
Up to 40	$220
41 to 50	$410
51 to 60	$820
61 to 70	$2,200
71 and over	$2,750

These amounts are added to other medical expenses, and the total is deductible to the extent it exceeds 7.5% of Adjusted Gross Income.

•**Employers** can deduct long-term-care insurance premiums they pay on behalf of employees.

•**Self-employed persons** can treat long-term-care insurance as "health insurance" to obtain a 60% deduction for it (increasing to 100% in 2003).

•**State-approved, pre-1997 policies** are "grandfathered" under the law to be treated the same as policies purchased after the law became effective.

As a result of this law change, the popularity of long-term-care insurance is rapidly growing and many new policy offerings are becoming available…

•**Annual premium cost will be lower if you buy while still young.**

•**Insurance does not cover care required by "preexisting conditions."**

•**Long-term-care insurance is becoming a popular employee benefit** offered under "cafeteria" benefit plans. If offered to you, consider taking it.

No one policy is "best" for everyone. Discuss your entire situation, including both your health and family financial needs, with a long-term-care insurance expert.

WITHOUT INSURANCE

Medicaid. If you lack insurance, the government may pay all or a portion of the cost of nursing home care—if you qualify. Beware of the many common misconceptions about how the government pays for long-term care. Actions based on false beliefs can be very costly.

Mistake #1: Believing Medicare, the basic health-care program for seniors, pays for long-term care.

Mistake #2: Believing that to obtain long-term care through Medicaid, the government's medical program for low-wealth families, you must first voluntarily impoverish yourself by giving away your home and other assets.

Reality: You and your spouse can keep your home as long as you live, even if Medicaid pays for your care.

MEDICAID RULES

Each state has its own Medicaid program subject to general federal rules. Thus, specific rules and dollar limitations vary by state. *But most programs share these traits…*

•**To qualify to receive care through Medicaid,** you must reduce your "countable" assets to a small amount, typically $3,600 for an individual in New York.

However, substantial assets are exempt from this dollar limit. *These include…*

•Your home.

•Your car.

•A cash "allowance" for one spouse of no less than $84,120 in most states, and no less than $16,824 in others, when the other spouse is in a nursing home.

•Burial funds (with dollar limit).

You and your spouse can keep these assets while you live and receive an amount of income specified by state law.

•**Assets transferred by you to others** within the prior 36 months may limit your access to care provided by Medicaid. But a transfer does not make you ineligible to receive Medicaid for a full 36 months—another common false belief.

Rather, eligibility will be delayed by the number of months for which the value of the transferred assets could have financed benefits. Thus, if you transfer $10,000 of assets and care costs $5,000 per month, you will lose two months of eligibility.

•**The state retains the right to "reclaim" the cost** of Medicaid benefits from the recipient's estate.

Example: You receive $100,000 worth of care through Medicaid. On your death (or that of your surviving spouse) the state may make a claim for $100,000 against your (or your spouse's) estate.

Any "exempt" assets you continued to own—such as a home—will be reduced by that amount.

While you don't have to give away your home and other exempt assets to receive Medicaid, those assets may be placed at risk when you die, depending upon how much Medicaid pays on your behalf.

Planning: To avert this risk, some people may carefully consider giving away assets while still healthy to become eligible for Medicaid in the future. But this decision should not be made lightly.

Key: Giving away assets *after* a need for care arises does not leave you ineligible for Medicaid for a full 36 months. You're ineligible for a limited time only, say 18 months. You can "split the difference" while keeping enough assets to pay for your care until Medicaid kicks in.

Example: Care costs $5,000 per month and you have $180,000 of assets. After need for care arises, you can give away $90,000 and use the remaining $90,000, plus your income, to pay for care during the 18 months of ineligibility for Medicaid.

Strategy: Give away the assets that will have the most value to heirs in the *future*—such as appreciating stocks, real estate or business property. Their value to you may be slight. This way you'll avoid giving away too much too soon.

TAX PLANNING

Tax and Medicaid rules can interact in surprising and costly ways.

●**Transferring assets to protect them from potential Medicaid claims** can lead to tax traps.

Example: To save the value of a house from Medicaid, a parent may make a gift of it to adult children. But the children then take the house with the parent's basis in it. If they don't live in the house, they won't qualify for the home-sale exclusion—and may face a big capital gain tax on its sale.

The same capital gain tax trap may apply to other appreciated assets transferred to avoid Medicaid claims.

●**Standard tax planning** can lead to Medicaid traps.

Example: A couple uses a standard "by-pass trust" to utilize two estate tax exemptions

between them. Thus, the first spouse to die uses his/her $675,000 exemption (in 2000 and 2001) by bequeathing that amount to a trust that will pay income to the surviving spouse for life and then pay its principal to children.

Snag: If the trust contains typical language authorizing it to pay for the medical care of the surviving spouse, it may disqualify that spouse for Medicaid regardless of how he disposes of the assets he owns outright. Thus, trust assets may have to be used on long-term care and be lost to the children. This is very common.

Workable solutions to all the tax-and-Medicaid problems do exist. But to find the solutions you must first be aware that these problems exist—and too many people are not aware of them.

Details of solutions will depend on local state law—both Medicaid law and law relating to trusts, gifts, etc.

Beware: Medicaid law and tax law are different fields, and genuine experts in one field may know little about the other. Consult with experts in both fields when you make your plans or consult with those few experts who have knowledge of and experience in both.

Good Reasons to Put Money in an Offshore Tax Haven

Jerome Schneider, Premier Corporate Services, Ltd., 900-1285 W. Pender St., Vancouver, British Columbia, Canada V6E 4B1. He is author of The Complete Guide to Offshore Money Havens. *Prima Publishing.*

With an investment in an offshore tax haven you can make money and have fun in the sun at the same time. *Offshore havens offer...*

●**Profits.** Many offshore mutual funds offer higher growth rates than US funds, and offshore banks pay higher interest rates.

●**Privacy.** Offshore havens have ironclad secrecy laws that legally prevent unauthorized disclosure of your personal financial records.

●**Protection.** You can set up a trust known as an *asset protection* trust whose assets are immune from seizure if you're ever sued—even just a nuisance suit—and lose. Money in the trust will be beyond the reach of the US judicial system.

Keep in mind that experts predict that one in four adult Americans will be sued this year.

Going offshore can provide tax protection, too.

Strategy: Set up an offshore asset protection trust (or your own private bank in an offshore haven—details further on). As long as the trust has an offshore trustee, you're judgment-proof. And if the bank you set up does its business offshore, the IRS won't be able to tax its profit.

●**Fun.** Offshore havens such as the Cayman Islands and Costa Rica are travelers' paradises. If you have investments there, you could possibly take tax-deductible trips to monitor those investments.

Money haven locales may be desirable places to retire to, also, with low living costs and balmy climates.

THE BANKING BUSINESS

The best ways to enjoy all these benefits...

●**Open an offshore bank account.** Interest rates are generally higher than they are in the US. And you'll gain access to services such as brokerage and money management.

●**Buy a foreign annuity or insurance policy.** These arrangements offer tax deferral of investment growth and can be denominated in a foreign currency. These annuities or policies can provide a hedge in the event the dollar weakens.

The US dollar retains only a fraction of the value it had in the 1950s.

●**Buy an endowment policy,** which includes life insurance protection while enabling you to invest in offshore ventures.

●**Establish your own offshore bank.** This is the most complete and profitable move you can make offshore. You can run a small-scale banking business, set up your own checking account and issue yourself a credit card.

●All your transactions can be handled in your bank's name so privacy is assured.

●Your bank can manage your investment portfolio. Gains may be tax free until repatriated.

●You can provide yourself with a tax-free mortgage and pay interest to your own bank, establish your own line of credit, and borrow from other banks at wholesale rates.

Cost: In some havens, $40,000 will establish an offshore bank. Such an outlay can have a swift, sizable payoff.

Where to set up: Besides the Caymans and Costa Rica for retirement, consider establishing your own private bank in Barbados in the Caribbean or Cook Islands, Nauru, and Vanuatu in the Pacific. *In the USA:* Alaska recently passed laws authorizing asset protection trusts.

Getting started: Ask your banker, broker, or financial planner to connect you with an offshore network. If that's not possible, contact a specialist such as Premier Corporate Services, Ltd.

IRD Deduction

Little-known income tax break can save heirs hundreds of thousands of dollars in *income* taxes. Estate tax on *Income in Respect of a Decedent* (IRD) is an income tax deduction allowed heirs when they file an income tax form that reports inherited assets, such as IRAs, lottery winnings and interest on unredeemed US savings bonds. The deduction for estate tax on IRD was designed to prevent double taxation of inherited assets—through estate and income taxes. The larger the assets, the greater the importance of the tax on IRD.

Problem: Many accountants and attorneys are unfamiliar with this deduction. Calculations can be complex—consult a tax specialist.

Seymour Goldberg, Esq., CPA, tax attorney, Goldberg & Goldberg, PC, 666 Old Country Rd., Suite 600, Garden City, NY 11530. He is author of *J.K. Lasser's How to Protect Your Retirement Savings from the IRS.* John Wiley & Sons.

Economic Hardship Now Is Grounds for Compromising a Tax Bill with the IRS

Marvin Michelman, CPA, a director and specialist in IRS practice and procedure, Deloitte & Touche LLP, Two World Financial Center, New York 10281.

T he IRS will now consider the economic hardship that full payment of a tax bill may cause the taxpayer to be grounds for compromising the tax bill.

Until now, the IRS would compromise a tax bill only if it considered the full tax to be uncollectible.

The change in policy results from the *IRS Restructuring and Reform Act of 1998,* in which Congress indicated that factors such as equity and hardship should be considered by the IRS when evaluating compromise offers.

The IRS says it began processing offers under the new rules in mid-September, and it has printed a new compromise application form, Form 656-A, for taxpayers seeking relief under the new rules to use.

Under the new rules, taxpayers may submit an offer in compromise even when they can pay a tax bill, if full payment of the bill would result in serious hardship or prevent them from being able to meet basic living expenses.

Examples: A taxpayer has a savings account that holds just enough funds to pay a large tax bill. *But the taxpayer...*

●**Has a chronically ill dependent,** and using all the funds to pay the tax would make it impossible to pay for the dependent's medical care.

●**Has recently retired,** and using the funds to pay the tax bill would leave the taxpayer unable to meet basic living expenses during retirement.

In each case, the IRS says it will consider a compromise offer made by the taxpayer.

The IRS also says that all tentatively rejected compromise offers will receive independent review before rejection becomes final. And taxpayers may appeal rejections of offers to the IRS Office of Appeals.

Limits: IRS Commissioner Rossotti emphasizes that the new rules are intended to apply only to taxpayers facing severe circumstances, and are not an open door to compromise all kinds of overdue tax bills. To qualify to use the new rules, a taxpayer must have a record of properly paying taxes and filing returns. Offers in compromise will not be approved when their acceptance would undermine enforcement of the tax laws. *Details...*

●**IRS News Release 99-64,** describing the new rules, is on the IRS Web site at *www.irs. gov/prod/news/nandf.html.*

●**The full text of the new temporary regulations that enact the new rules for a period of three years, TD 8829,** is also on the IRS Web site at *www.irs.gov/tax_regs/ regslist.html.*

Late Filing Excuse That Works

E ven a valid excuse for filing late will be dismissed by most IRS personnel if they determine that a taxpayer has a chronic problem filing or paying on time. "Chronic" generally means more than one time within a five-year period. To have a penalty excused, the taxpayer must establish "reasonable cause" for the late payment or late filing. *Excuses that work:* Serious illness (physical or mental) which did not prevent you from working but did prevent you from being able to compile the information required to prepare your income tax return...being the caregiver of a child or elderly relative/friend who demands your attention virtually day and night is generally taken into consideration to abate a penalty...devoting your time to a business that has unusual problems and demands your attention 16-plus hours a day, seven days a week will also be considered favorably.

A former IRS agent.

9

Investment Wisdom

Inside the Hot Financial Services Sector

When interest rates are rising, conventional wisdom dictates staying away from financial stocks. But on November 20, 1999, Congress eliminated the *Glass-Steagall Act* that separated banking from investment banking, brokerage activities and insurance. Now the financial services industry is a whole new ball game.

For expert opinion on how the financial services sector will evolve and how individual investors should play it, we spoke with two experts—a financial adviser whose clients invest solely in mutual funds…and a broad-based financial industry fund manager about which individual stocks he likes.

FINANCIAL FUNDS
Robert Markman

Investors can make a lot of money in the financial services sector in the next few years.

Since I'm a tech-heavy investor, it is nice to counterbalance those holdings with a growth area in which the price-to-earnings multiples (P/Es) are not out of sight.

Financial stocks are now selling at a discount to the rest of the market, largely due to the perception that higher interest rates are bad for them. In fact, rates are not nearly as critical for banks as they were 10 or 15 years ago. Today's financial services industry is moving toward generating fee income that will hold up in any economic environment.

The removal of Glass-Steagall restrictions will have a huge effect on the delivery of financial services. No one can tell who the winners will be—banks…brokers…or a combination parallel to America Online and Time Warner that creates new synergies. To cover

Robert Markman, president of Markman Capital Management, 6600 France Ave. S., Edina, MN 55435. He is author of *Hazardous to Your Wealth: Extraordinary Popular Delusions and the Madness of Mutual Fund Experts.* Elton Wolf.

Thomas Goggins, co-manager of John Hancock Financial Industries Fund, 101 Huntington Ave., Boston 02199. The fund has more than $2 billion in assets.

all possible opportunities, investors should buy into a broad array of financial stocks. The new-world context in which these companies are operating has so much growth potential that the majority of your returns will come from simply participating in it—not from specific stock selection. *My favorite mutual funds in this area...*

●**Davis Financial Fund.** RPFGX. *Load:* 4.75%. 800-279-0279.

●**Invesco Financial Services Fund.** FSFSX. *Load:* None. 800-525-8085.

●**Selected American Shares,** a diversified growth-and-income portfolio that is about 50% invested in financial services stocks. SLASX. *Load:* None. 800-279-0279.

FINANCIAL STOCKS
Thomas Goggins

Our fund invests in financial services across the board, from banks to insurance companies, brokers, asset managers, technology providers and also Western European financial companies.

Since the US was the only place that had those Depression-induced barriers between financial services, we foresaw their eventual breakdown as business became global. The merger between Travelers Group (which owned Salomon Smith Barney) and Citicorp to form Citigroup created a new global financial services template. We're now seeing a blurring of distinctions among banks, brokers and insurance companies.

Examples: Charles Schwab is no longer just a discount broker. With its pending acquisition of US Trust Co., it is going into the high-net-worth-client trust business in a big way. Merrill Lynch is expanding its *banking* business.

Eventually we may see 20 mega financial services firms, plus other smaller companies in various niches.

The financial services sector is undervalued, particularly insurance companies. Since there's been a link between banks and insurers in Europe, we expect most US life insurance companies to merge with banks. At the same time, however, many former mutual insurance companies (policyholder-owned) are turning into stock companies, so they will be able to make acquisitions, too.

Our favorite insurance stocks...

●**AFLAC & Co.,** Columbus, Georgia–based marketer of supplemental health insurance to workers. This family-run company also has a strong position in Japan. NYSE:AFL.

●**AXA Financial, Inc.,** New York–based financial services company that encompasses the old Equitable Life, Alliance Capital Management and Donaldson, Lufkin & Jenrette brokerage—and all are doing very well. NYSE:AXF.

●**Protective Life Corp.,** Birmingham–based insurer whose CEO has been an astute acquirer of related businesses. NYSE:PL.

We prefer full-service brokers, which are now very cheap, over the electronic-trade group with its extremely high P/Es. *Brokers we like now include...*

●**Charles Schwab Corp.** NYSE: SCH.

●**Merrill Lynch & Co. Inc.** NYSE: MER.

●**Morgan Stanley Dean Witter.** NYSE:MWD.

Our picks among asset managers...

●**Franklin Resources, Inc.** NYSE:BEN.

●**T. Rowe Price and Associates Inc.** NASDAQ:TROW.

Lesser-known banking favorites...

●**City National Corp.,** Los Angeles leader in middle-market lending. A good percentage of the stock is held by insiders. NYSE:CYN.

●**First Tennessee National Corp.,** regional powerhouse that has a big operation in mortgages. NYSE:FTN.

●**State Street Corp.,** Boston giant that excels in back-office processing. NYSE:STT.

More from Robert Markman...

Do Not Buy International Funds

No one needs an international fund in his/her portfolio. Research into historical performance of different investments shows that putting part of a diversified portfolio into international mutual funds produces no higher return—but increases volatility and risk. That means buy-and-hold investors can stick to domestic investments without fear they are missing out on a valuable source of diversification.

IPOs for the Little Guy

Ross Levin, CFP, president of Accredited Investors, Inc., a financial and investment management firm, Edina, MN.

IPO mania. Stories of newly public companies—Initial Public Offerings (IPOs)—are reported daily. Many Internet-related IPOs generate triple-digit returns in their first weeks—or even days—of trading.

Until recently, buying IPOs *before* they hit the market was the exclusive domain of institutional investors and wealthy individuals. But in the last year, on-line discount brokers—including the leaders E-Trade.com, Garage.com, OffRoadCapital.com and WitCapital.com—have begun offering IPOs to average investors.

Beware: Before you get in on IPOs, consider the reality behind the hype.

•The IPO bubble could burst anytime. IPOs are hot because of euphoria over all things Internet. Speculative buying has grossly inflated share prices for dot-coms. But many investment professionals expect this will eventually lead to major corrections in most of these stocks. The newest, least-proven companies are likely to fall hardest.

•High-quality IPO offerings are unavailable to individuals. Established brokerage firms, such as Goldman Sachs and Merrill Lynch, still underwrite the top-quality new issues...and they still offer shares at the discounted preoffering prices only to institutions and favorite individual clients.

Exception: Top underwriter Morgan Stanley Dean Witter is offering the IPOs it underwrites to its on-line brokerage clients with accounts greater than $100,000.

SAFER IPO STRATEGY

Until high-quality IPOs are widely available, I recommend that clients...

...invest in IPO mutual funds. *Current no-load favorite:* Renaissance Capital Management's IPO Plus Aftermarket Fund. IPOSX. 888-476-3863.

...invest in small-cap mutual funds. These invest in newly public and established companies. They're less risky than funds that invest only in IPOs. *My current no-load favorite:* Fremont US Small Cap Fund. FUSSX. 800-548-4539.

...wait before investing in an IPO, until some of the offering hype has calmed down. Most IPO shares trade below their offering prices within nine months of coming to market.

All About I Bonds... The New US Savings Bonds Are Very Attractive Now

Richard J. Shapiro, Esq., tax partner, Ernst & Young LLP, 787 Seventh Ave., New York 10019. Mr. Shapiro is author of *Taxes and Investing—A Guide for the Individual Investor* (Options Clearing Corporation/available free from the various national stock and option exchanges).

US savings bonds, often given as gifts to newborns and for other life cycle events, may also be appropriate investments to consider for a broader range of purposes.

A relatively new type of savings bond—the *I bond*—is especially attractive for some investors.

WHAT ARE I BONDS?

I bonds are federal government savings bonds issued at "face," meaning a $50 bond costs you $50.

In contrast, EE savings bonds are discounted bonds. They're issued at one-half of face value (a $50 bond costs $25).

Unlike EE bonds, however, I bonds pay two types of interest—a fixed rate (3.74%), plus a rate adjusted every six months for inflation.

•The I bond inflation rate is adjusted semiannually based on the Consumer Price Index (CPI-U).

•The EE bond interest is 90% of the six-month averages of five-year Treasuries.

Note: If the country runs into a period of *deflation,* the value of the I bond does not decrease. This is so even if the rate of deflation exceeds the fixed rate portion of interest.

I bonds continue to earn interest until they are redeemed or reach their final maturity—30 years from issuance. They cannot be redeemed for the first six months and any redemption during the first five years results in a three-month interest penalty.

THE TAX ANGLES

Like EE bonds, I bonds offer a number of tax incentives to people who invest in them...

●**Interest is exempt from state and local income tax.**

●**Federal tax on interest can be deferred until the bond is redeemed or reaches final maturity.** Deferral applies to both the fixed rate and semiannual inflation rate earnings.

Caution: Unlike EE bonds, interest deferral cannot be continued by exchanging I bonds for HH bonds.

●**Interest on I bonds redeemed to pay higher education costs may be partially or fully excludable.**

Caution: Don't confuse I bonds with Treasury inflation-indexed bonds, which are issued in five-year, 10-year, and 30-year maturities. These inflation-indexed bonds pay an interest rate as well as adjust principal for inflation. Both the interest and principal adjustment are currently taxable.

ADVANTAGES

I bonds certainly won't produce the type of growth we've seen from the stock market in recent years. *But there are certain pluses of I bonds to consider, especially for those who routinely roll over bank Certificates of Deposit (CDs)...*

●**They're entirely safe.** Like other instruments issued by the US Treasury, they're backed by the full faith and credit of the federal government. In contrast, CDs are protected only to the limit of FDIC insurance.

●**They're easy to purchase.** They can be bought from banks or on-line at *www.savings bonds.gov.* On-line purchases are limited to $500 in a single transaction, but can be made 24 hours a day, seven days a week by charging the purchase to MasterCard or Visa. There's

also an "Easy-Saver Option" for automatic purchases on a pre-fixed schedule.

Limit: There's an annual purchase limit of $30,000 per Social Security number.

●**They don't require any monitoring or other action.** Unlike other investments, I bonds can be bought and virtually forgotten about. They'll continue to build up in value (interest added to the purchase price) until the final maturity date 30 years from issuance.

There's no annual reporting required. The holder doesn't have to present any passbook for interest crediting.

INVESTMENT STRATEGIES

I bonds aren't for everyone. But they can be good investments for...

●**Children younger than age 14.** Children in this age group with income otherwise subject to the kiddie tax may benefit from I bond investments. Since interest on the bonds need not be reported currently, there's no additional kiddie tax to worry about.

Idea: When a child reaches age 14 and is no longer subject to the kiddie tax, an election can be made to switch from the deferral method to reporting interest each year. Depending on the child's other income, it may be possible to avoid tax entirely on the accrued interest in the year of the change in accounting method.

Caution: Once the change in accounting method is made, all future interest must be reported currently.

●**Education purposes.** Like EE bonds, parents of young children may want to invest in I bonds with an eye to redeeming them to pay college expenses. If the parents' income is below a threshold amount in the year the bonds are redeemed, the interest may be fully excludable.

For purposes of qualifying for student aid, investments in a parent's name do not count as negatively against a family as investments in a child's name.

Caution: It's the income in the year of redemption, not the year of purchase, that controls the interest exclusion. Since no one has a crystal ball, it's impossible for parents to predict their income levels many years ahead. Thus, it's really a gamble that they'll qualify for the exclusion at all.

●**Alternative to CDs.** Individuals who typically buy bank CDs and continually roll them over may want to invest in I bonds as an alternative.

The I bonds are even safer than CDs and may pay a higher interest rate. When the state tax exemption is factored in, I bonds come out even further ahead.

Caution: I bonds are not as liquid as CDs since they can't be redeemed within the first six months and lose three months of interest if redeemed within the first five years.

More from Richard Shapiro...

An Investor's Guide to Listed Stock Options... Beware of Implications

Trading listed equity options can enhance your performance in the stock market.

However, to truly make the most of these vehicles, it's important to understand the tax implications.

BASICS

There are two main types of equity options...

●**Calls.** These are options to buy a stock or security at a certain price within a certain time period.

Example: An Intel/January/65 *call* is an option to buy Intel at $65 per share between now and a specified date in January.

Listed options cover 100 shares per option. Thus, if this option is priced at 12½ in the newspaper listing, investors would pay $1,250 for an option to buy 100 shares of Intel.

●**Puts.** These are options to sell a stock or security at a certain price, up to a certain date. As with calls, puts cover 100 shares per option.

Example: An Intel/January/75 *put* is an option to sell Intel at $75 per share between now and a specified date in January.

If the listing reads 8¼, investors would pay $825 for an option to sell 100 shares of Intel.

Exception: Some options are "cash settled" options, meaning that you don't buy or sell the underlying item, such as a stock market index, but you pay or receive an amount equal to your gain or loss on the trade.

THE FOUR KEY TRANSACTIONS

There are four fundamental transactions you can make with listed options on individual stocks...

●**Buy a call.** This allows you to participate in a market move at a relatively low price because an option costs less than the underlying stock.

If the stock goes up, you'll enjoy a greater percentage gain. However, you will lose all of your money if the stock does not reach the target price within the specified period.

Tax treatment: Buying a call on an individual stock is similar to buying the stock. You'll have a capital gain or loss, long- or short-term, depending on the holding period.

If you exercise a call and buy the underlying stock, all of your costs, including the option premium, are included in your cost basis in the stock. However, your holding period in the stock won't start until after you exercise the option.

●**Buy a put.** Buying a put locks in a selling price for a stock. Although you can buy a "naked" put (a put on stocks you don't own) just as you can buy a naked call, many investors buy puts on stocks they do own. In this manner, investors with appreciated positions can protect their gains without triggering capital gains tax under current law.

Example: You bought Intel many years ago and have enjoyed substantial appreciation. Now, with the stock selling for more than $70 per share, you are uneasy about future prospects. You buy an October/65 put, which locks in a selling price if the stock skids. Simply buying the put does not trigger a long-term capital gain.

Trap: An anticipated change in the tax law may mean that buying an "in-the-money" put (the exercise price is higher than the stock's trading price) when you own the stock will trigger a taxable gain. For instance, if Intel sells at $72, a $75 put is in-the-money. Check with your tax pro before proceeding.

Suppose the stock goes down... If you buy a $65 put and your long-held, highly appreciated stock falls below $65, you can sell your shares for $65. In this case, you'd recognize a long-term capital gain, which would be reduced by the amount you paid for the put.

If the stock goes up... If the stock continues to rise or just holds its own, your put may expire without being exercised (why would you sell Intel for $65 if it's trading for, say, $70?). You'd have a capital loss from your put purchase that can be used to offset taxable gains, although the use of that loss may have to be deferred under the tax rules.

●**Sell a call.** You can sell a call on shares you own ("covered call") or on shares you don't own ("naked call"), which means you're speculating the stock price will fall. Some investors regularly sell covered calls to squeeze income from the stock market, at the expense of potential capital gains.

Tax treatment: The cash you receive when selling a call is not considered taxable income when received. Instead, tax consequences aren't triggered until the option expires, is sold, or is exercised, which may be in the next taxable year. Thus, selling a call can provide tax deferral.

Trap: Selling a "deep-in-the-money" covered call (the exercise price is well below the stock's trading price) may trigger a gain if the tax law changes, as now expected. Again, check with your tax pro.

If the stock goes down... If the underlying stock stagnates or drops, the call option you sold may expire worthless. You'd have a short-term capital gain equal to the amount of the premium you received. If you wish, you can sell another call and receive another premium.

If the stock goes up... When the stock price exceeds the exercise price the underlying stock probably will be called away. You'll have a short-term or long-term capital gain on the disposition of the stock, with the option premium added to your selling price for tax purposes.

Strategy: If you sell a covered call and the underlying stock continues to rise, you can avoid an exercise (and the resulting tax obligation, if the stock has appreciated) by buying back the call. You'll lose money on the options trade—that capital loss may be required to be deferred under the tax rules.

●**Sell a put.** Again, you'll receive cash from the option sale.

In essence, you're promising to buy a stock in the future so you're hoping that (1) the stock will go up in price and the put will not be exercised or (2) the stock will go down so you will be able to buy stock tomorrow at a lower price.

Example: You sell an Intel/October/70 put. If the stock moves up to $75, the put won't be exercised and you'll keep the option premium.

If the stock goes down... If the option is exercised, you'll wind up buying the stock. The put premium you received will reduce your basis in the shares.

If the stock goes up... You'll recognize a short-term capital gain when the option expires.

Bottom line: This is a very simplified rundown of the options business. If you participate in sophisticated options strategies (spreads, straddles, collars, etc.), you may face tax complications, so look before you leap into any exotic transactions.

Investing in Technology

Michael Murphy, president, Murphy Investment Management, and founder and editor of the *California Technology Stock Letter,* Box 308, Half Moon Bay, California 94019. He is author of *Every Investor's Guide to High-Tech Stocks and Mutual Funds.* Broadway Books.

The "new economy" is clearly saying that tech is the way to go now if you want to make money in the stock market.

Other advisers might differ—many will tell you to be wary of investing in technology stock, because the "bubble" will burst sooner than you think. I disagree.

I'm convinced that the action in the market will continue to be centered on technology, biotech and e-commerce/e-business companies for a long time to come. *Here are the highlights of the talk I give my tech-resistant clients...*

●**The world is no more than halfway through a massive 30-to-40-year growth cycle in electronics and computer technology,** and we are just beginning an equally massive 30-to-40-year cycle in medical and biotechnology.

•**Historically, what has happened in great economic revolutions is that somewhere about 20 years along,** the "old" economy takes a terrible dive.

•**It is often riskier to stay too long with the old economy** than it is to get involved with the new.

•**What's happening is such a dramatic shift in the economy**—an economic revolution—that it's irrelevant whether you're age 20 or age 60. Every investor must change with the times. Everyone, no matter what his/her age, needs to be in technology stocks to some extent.

•**Rates of return will be much higher in the new economy.** This is already visible in the performance of new-economy stocks—Internet, biotech, e-business, for example—versus old-economy favorites.

•**Technology stocks are volatile**—it's true. But, virtually every year, the highs on most tech stocks are double the lows.

•**Sometimes the volatility is much more extreme than usual.** So, the big question for investors is, "How do you control the risk?"

RISK MANAGEMENT

Two good ways to control the risk of investing in the volatile technology sector are diversification and asset allocation. Here's how...

•**As you get closer to retirement and have less time to recover from a serious down market,** it's prudent to reduce your exposure to all equities, including technology stocks.

But most people are far too conservative in their asset allocation. How much should you target for technology investing?

My guideline for my clients: Invest 100% minus your age in new-economy stocks.

Examples: At age 50, you should be 50% in technology. At 75, you still need 25% of your assets in technology because you're going to live a long time.

•**Decide now to increase your participation in technology.** If you have holdings in an S&P 500 index fund, you already have a representation of 35% in technology. But, that's

really not enough and if you don't have even that much, you're hurting future growth.

•**Decide this year to gradually redeploy assets** out of underperforming old-economy stocks and funds and put them into technology.

A prudent way to get into the technology field is by dollar averaging into broad-based no-load technology funds, such as...

•Firsthand Technology Value Fund. 888-884-2675.

•T. Rowe Price Science & Technology Fund. 800-638-5660.

Another way to get into play is through diversified and specialized load funds. *These include...*

•Fidelity Select Software & Computer Services. 800-544-8888.

•Fidelity Select Telecommunications. 800-544-8888.

•Fidelity Select Technology. 800-544-8888.

•Seligman Communications & Information Fund. 800-221-2783.

The last four of the funds listed carry loads. But is this really a drawback today when many technology funds are turning in triple-digit gains?

ALTERNATIVES TO MUTUAL FUNDS

A growing number of trusts, closed-end funds and index shares are being offered on the American and New York Stock Exchanges that let investors diversify into different technology fields and also enjoy the benefits of trading like an individual stock. *Some of my favorites...*

•**B2B Internet HOLDRS (AMEX:BHH).** This fund, sponsored by Merrill Lynch, is based on the huge potential of business-to-business (B-to-B) Internet commerce, where traffic is doubling every 100 days. B-to-B is expected to be five times as large as the consumer Internet business.

•**H&Q Investors (NYSE: HQH).** This professionally managed closed-end fund currently sells at about a 12% discount to net asset value and distributes 2% of net asset value quarterly.

FOR INCOME SEEKERS

For investors who need income—which most tech stocks don't provide much of—our firm has put together *Murphy New World*

Technology Convertibles Fund (MNWCX, 800-998-2875), a no-load fund that buys convertible securities and preferred stocks of various types of technology companies.

Goal: To provide coupon income, plus the long-term growth potential of the common-stock "kicker" provided by the conversion feature. We believe that convertible bonds of technology companies are suitable investments for IRA, Keogh and pension plans.

The current income is sheltered from current taxes in the IRA and the potential of conversion to common stock can make a meaningful difference in your return by the time retirement rolls around.

According to Value Line statistics, convertibles in general offer about 85% of the upside potential of stocks, with only 50% of the downside risk.

As far as I know, there aren't any other pure tech convertible funds. *But the following have a percentage of their portfolios in technology...*

●**Fidelity Convertible Securities (FCVSX).** 800-544-8888.

●**Vanguard Convertible Securities (VCVSX).** 800-523-7731.

To get the money to invest in convertibles, consider switching some assets from other bond funds into a convertible bond fund that's focused on technology.

More from Michael Murphy...

All About the Technology-Stock Cycle

Summer is usually a down period. From Labor Day to mid-October, the sector tends to be very volatile.

●**Tech stocks tend to rally beginning at the end of October**—after third-quarter earnings are reported.

●**The rally tends to accelerate into the new year, especially for smaller stocks.**

●**Biotechnology stocks usually do well starting in early December.**

●**Technology stocks often falter in February and March** as their year-end rally runs out of steam.

Harold Evensky's Rational Investment System for Web-Crazed Times

Harold Evensky, CFP, whom *Worth* has named one of the country's top 100 financial advisers. He is president of Evensky, Brown & Katz, 241 Sevilla Ave., Coral Gables, FL 33134. He is author of *Y2K and Your Money.* Sitting Duck Press.

With the Dow now at record highs and Internet stocks continuing to rise despite occasional corrections, it's easy to assume the market will continue its march upward.

But—there are troublesome signs on the horizon. Many world economies have not yet stabilized, leading experts to worry that US corporate profits will slump. Other experts are concerned rising energy prices may reignite inflation.

Harold Evensky, one of the country's leading financial advisers, answers questions about the issues many investors are facing now.

How much of an investor's portfolio should be invested in technology stocks? Experts forecast that the technology sector will account for one-third of the US economy by the year 2004, up from about 15% today. This means that everyone should have part of his/her assets invested in technology companies.

Aggressive investors could allocate 85% to stocks and 15% to bonds, with as much as 20% of their portfolios in technology. Conservative investors could allocate 60% to stocks and 40% to bonds—but limit technology to 5% of investments.

Though tempting, don't buy individual technology stocks. Despite the sector's surge, technology stocks are extremely risky. The prices of the best companies are high, while stock prices of small- and mid-cap companies swing dramatically.

And many technology companies continually have to reinvent themselves to stay competitive.

Better: Invest in a technology sector fund that has a good risk-adjusted performance record, such as...

- **Fidelity Select Technology.** 800-544-8888.
- **T. Rowe Price Science and Technology.** 800-638-5660.

Important: You may not even have to invest in a sector fund to add technology stocks to your portfolio. Many diversified funds have significant technology investments. Call the funds you own, and ask what percentage is invested in technology.

My favorite diversified *no-load* fund with a good technology position…

- **Wilshire Target Large-Company Growth Portfolio.** About 30% is invested in technology. 888-200-6796.

How important are index funds to an investor's portfolio, given current market conditions? If you believe, as I do, that the US stock market will continue to rise dramatically over the next 10 years, index funds are ideal investments. Index funds' low turnover means they realize taxable gains less often, making them more tax-efficient investments.

I believe all investors should put the core allocation of their stock assets in a fund that mirrors the S&P 500 or Wilshire 5000.

In fact, there are many different types of index funds. You could use them to create an entire stock portfolio, if you don't have the time or expertise to find good stock-picking fund managers. *Here are my choices for a* no-load *index fund portfolio…*

- **60%/Vanguard 500 Index Fund.** 800-523-7731.
- **20%/Schwab International Index.** 800-435-4000.
- **20%/Vanguard Small-Cap Index Fund.** 800-523-7731.

Given that large-cap growth companies outperform the S&P 500 by wide margins, why bother investing in other sectors? Large-cap stocks have done well because big companies have developed a strong global presence…and their sheer size makes them more competitive in the increasingly global economy.

Large companies also have invested heavily in technological improvements over the past five years, which has improved their efficiency and profits.

But years of investing history show that diversification is still the best way to reduce risk without giving up long-term returns. And with the prices of many large-company stocks very expensive now, the sector's dominance could change if earnings forecasts are not met.

What are the best ways now to reduce portfolio risk? Put up to 15% of your equity allocation in convertible stocks. These are preferred stocks that can be exchanged for common stock when they reach a prestated price.

Convertible stock or stock funds reduce risk because they offer some of the growth potential of stocks and some of the stability of bonds. They are for investors who are sophisticated enough to understand and evaluate the strategies of the stocks or the funds.

Individual convertible stocks are difficult to understand, and finding convertible stocks worth investing in can be a tricky process. Most investors are better off buying funds that invest in a wide range of convertible stocks.

I look for funds that avoid high-yield convertible stocks. They are usually issued by companies with low credit quality.

I also prefer funds that invest in convertible stocks issued by companies with market capitalizations of at least $5 billion. *Two well-managed funds that fit my criteria…*

- **Calamos Growth & Income.** *Load:* 4.75. 800-823-7386.
- **Northern Income Equity.** *Load:* None. 800-595-9111.

Another way to reduce risk without completely giving up the stock market is to allocate up to 10% of your investment portfolio to a balanced fund. These funds invest in a mix of stocks and bonds.

During bull markets, balanced funds perform about as well as convertible stock funds. But balanced funds historically hold up better in tough times.

Between September 1 and October 31, 1987—during which time the stock market crashed—balanced funds fell 14.3%, compared with a loss of 19.3% for convertible funds and 23.3% for the S&P 500.

Leading no-load balanced funds…

- **T. Rowe Price Balanced.** 800-638-5660.
- **Vanguard Wellington Fund.** 800-523-7731.

Selling Mutual Funds Quickly

If you're trying to sell mutual fund shares in a hurry and the toll-free line is busy, try the fund's regular listed number. If that number is tied up and the fund has an office in your area, go there in person. If there is no office close by, keep calling outside of normal office hours or try calling other offices in small towns.

Also: Many funds have 24-hour lines, and some will accept orders via the Touch-Tone phone pad or through their Web sites. *Advance planning:* Call your fund today to find out if it will accept orders by fax. If so, get the fax number in case you need it later. *Important:* Confirm that your order was executed correctly by checking your next statement.

Paul A. Merriman, president, Paul A. Merriman & Associates, Inc., a money-management firm, Seattle.

Day-Trading Alert

Many day traders end up actually *losing* money. Most would do better with a buy-and-hold strategy and a more balanced portfolio.

Possible exception: Individuals who have extensive trading experience...*and* a thorough understanding of trading systems...*and* money they can afford to lose.

Charles Schwab, chairman of Charles Schwab & Co., Inc., San Francisco.

Internet Stock Games Sharpen Your Skills... Win Prizes, Too

Preston Gralla, computer and Internet journalist in Cambridge, MA, author of *The Complete Idiot's Guide to Online Shopping* and *How the Internet Works*. Both from Macmillan.

Stock games mimic real trading sites and offer a risk-free way to practice buying and selling stocks and sharpen trading skills. *Precautions...*

●**Never pay a fee to play a stock game.** There are plenty of free games.

●**If you don't want to be bombarded with junk E-mail,** indicate that on the registration form.

MOST REALISTIC

●**E*Trade Game** *(www.etrade.com)*. Mimics the popular site E*Trade by providing the feel of real stock trading. Log on to the real E*Trade site...click the "Game Icon" to register for $100,000 of virtual money. A new game starts each month, with the most successful trader winning $1,000.

BEST FOR TECH STOCKS

●**Inter@ctive Investor** *(www.zdii.com)*. Similar to the E*Trade game, but with technology stocks. Click on "Investment Challenge" icon...register for $100,000 of virtual money... buy and sell from 343 stocks in 18 computer and Internet-related categories. *Recent prizes:* Palm PCs...camcorders.

SPORTS FANS

●**Wall Street Sports** *(www.wallstreetsports. com)*. Trades the value of professional athletes, not stocks. Log on and register like other game sites, but instead learn the current trading value of different athletes and try to figure out whether, say, Patrick Ewing's shares will rise in value...or Derek Jeter's shares will fall. *Recent prizes:* Sega Dreamcast, gift certificates, T-shirts, hats.

SITE WITH BEST PRIZE

●**Yahoo! Finance—The Investment Challenge** *(http://finance.yahoo.com)*. Works like the other stock games. Each month, first prize gets $5,000... second prize, $3,000...third prize, $1,000.

The New Value Investing Rules from John Neff... *The* John Neff

John Neff, author of *John Neff on Investing*. John Wiley & Sons. He was the legendary manager of Vanguard's Windsor Fund from 1964 through 1995. Today, he is a private investor in Radnor, PA.

John Neff is a legendary value investor from his 31 years as manager of Vanguard's Windsor Fund. By finding bargain stocks that others had passed over, Windsor, under Neff, returned an average of 13.7% a year over three decades—averaging 30% more than the S&P 500.

Neff, now a private investor, sees plenty of undervalued stocks—even in today's highly valued and volatile market. And—he foresees market corrections that will create more opportunities for value investors.

VALUE OUTLOOK

With the average stock selling at 27 times earnings, people say there are no values left. That simply isn't true. Look past those companies that have high price-to-earnings ratios (P/Es), and you'll find plenty of great companies that are selling at 10 times earnings or less.

BASIC STRATEGY

Be a low-P/E investor. Instead of buying Internet stocks at multiples that can't be calculated because the companies have no earnings, buy solid companies at five times earnings. They will hold up better in a correction than Internet stocks.

The lower the market goes, the easier it will be to find undervalued gems. Don't be afraid to hold cash. You can invest when the correction turns up values.

Check your newspaper each day for the list of stocks hitting new lows for the year. Look for companies with familiar names that you wouldn't expect to be on the list. *Then look for stocks that...*

●**Trade at single-digit P/Es.** Windsor Fund always looked for stocks selling at a discount of about 50% from the market. That meant stocks with single-digit P/Es. The lower, the better.

●**Offer the right amount of growth.** Once a company's earnings growth gets up into double digits, it ceases to be a low-P/E stock. But if there is little or no growth in earnings, the stock may not have a future worth investing in. Low-P/E companies whose earnings per share are growing at least 7% often have signs of life that other investors haven't spotted. Earnings growth is reported in company annual and quarterly reports.

●**Have strong fundamentals.** That means a solid company in a growing field whose problems are likely to prove temporary. Read company reports...follow the company and its industry in the press...collect reports from analysts covering the industry, trade publications and industry statistics.

●**Have yields that enhance your investment.** Over my years with Windsor Fund, we beat the market by an average 3.2% a year after expenses. About 2% of that came from the dividends our stocks paid. I own home-building stocks that pay no dividends, but I also own Real Estate Investment Trusts (REITs) that pay 9%. Overall, aim for a value stock portfolio that yields two percentage points better than the S&P 500.

Sectors I think offer value now...

HOME BUILDING

Many home builders are selling at multiples 80% below that of the market.

SUPPLIERS TO HOME BUILDERS

Building-supply manufacturers will benefit from strong new home construction and home renovations.

REITs

REITs are selling for around six times funds from operations—the proper way to measure the multiple of a REIT. Also, REIT yields average 8.7%, versus 1.3% for the market. I favor REITs that invest in office buildings and apartment houses. Consumer spending on the Internet could hurt REITs that invest in brick-and-mortar retail stores.

AIRLINES

Business is good for airlines, and most face far less price competition than they did a few years ago.

FINANCIAL INSTITUTIONS

Banks and savings-and-loans were tremendous bargains until recently, when they rallied by around 20%. But even now, you can still find top-notch institutions that are selling at below-market P/Es.

On-Line Investment Analysis

Quantitative-analysis Web sites to help find undervalued companies...

●**Investor Home,** *www.investorhome.com,* includes links and information for each step in the investment process.

●**InvesterTech,** *www.easystock.com,* has volatility data going back one year.

●**MarketPlayer,** *www.marketplayer.com,* uses more than 100 variables to screen stocks and industry groups.

●**PanaGora Asset Management,** *www.panagora.com/qicindex.htm,* helps you understand quantitative strategies and analysis.

●**Yahoo! Finance,** *www.finance.yahoo.com,* has basic quantitative tools, market data, news, more.

James O'Shaughnessy, chairman, O'Shaughnessy Capital Management, Inc., investment advisory firm, Greenwich, CT, and author of *How to Retire Rich.* Broadway Books.

Bear Market Warning Self-Defense Steps

Margaret Miller Welch, CFP, president of Armstrong, Welch & MacIntyre, Inc., a financial planning firm, 1155 Connecticut Ave. NW, Washington, DC 20036. She was named by *Worth* as one of the top 250 financial planners in the US.

Even though I expect the Dow to rise to about 20,000 in the next 10 years, we are now in a tricky economic environment that could easily result in a correction or a bear market.

A prolonged period of falling stock prices could be triggered by any of a wide variety of economic factors. The key for investors is to spot signs early, when they are reported in the financial media, and take steps to protect gains.

BEAR MARKET TRIGGERS

Unlike a correction—a rapid decline of stock prices—a bear market lasts at least several months. *Key factors that could cause stock prices to decline steadily over an extended period...*

A string of major corporations fail to meet their earnings projections. This would be the most serious development—and the one most likely to trigger a bear market. Investors react strongly when companies fail to meet earnings expectations.

Example: Bank One recently missed Wall Street's earnings estimates by 8%, and its stock price fell 25%.

Earnings that fall short of expectations won't necessarily be a problem for the whole market if the problem is confined to a few stocks. But if 10 or so of the companies in the top 100 stocks in the S&P stumble, it could spook the market.

Data showing inflation is truly heating up. The annual rate of inflation now is between 2% and 2.5%—a comfortable rate. In recent months, each time the Federal Reserve has voiced concern about rising inflation, its fears have been eased by new favorable economic data. However, if inflation rises above 3%, investors will become fearful that rising prices may put a damper on consumer spending and limit corporate earnings. This will cause investors to stop investing in stocks and even to sell shares.

Sharp and sustained rise in interest rates. When inflation rises, the Fed raises short-term interest rates. Long-term rates, which aren't set by the Fed, frequently rise as well. Unlike the stock market, where demand for a company's shares can cause its price to skyrocket, demand for higher-rate bonds does not cause their rates to rise. Instead, their prices rise and rates decline.

Good news: If long-term rates rise, I don't think they will do so rapidly. Fed chairman Alan Greenspan prefers to delicately raise rates rather than vigorously boost them.

PORTFOLIO PROTECTION

Here's how to adjust your portfolio if you believe that a bear market is closing in on the stock market...

●**Set aside enough cash to pay for any major upcoming expenses.** In a bear market, you'll want enough cash on hand so that you can handle big expenditures that are coming due within the next year, such as college tuition, a new roof or a new car.

●**Sell shares of your big winners.** To shield yourself from a downturn, prune your holdings of large-cap growth stocks or stock fund shares that have risen by 50% or more in the last 12 months.

But don't sell more than 30% of your position ...and don't abandon these stocks altogether. Most of them still have plenty of room to appreciate over time.

●**Invest the proceeds in income-producing stocks that pay healthy dividends.** Even though income-producing stocks may not be stellar performers over the short term, their steady dividends are a good way to fatten your portfolio in tough times.

By reinvesting the dividends you receive each quarter instead of taking them in cash, you'll be purchasing additional shares at relatively modest prices.

There are four major sectors that offer top income-producing stocks. *My favorites...*

●Financial Services
●Oil
●Telephone Companies
●Utilities

●**Invest in stocks that make products people use in a bear market.** *Two leaders...*

●The Procter & Gamble Co. Largest US maker of household products. NYSE:PG.

●Sara Lee Corp. Underwear maker (Bali, Hanes and Playtex)—and a leading food producer. NYSE:SLE.

●**Invest in a growth-and-income or balanced fund**—if you prefer not to invest in individual stocks. Choose funds that invest in dividend-paying blue chip stocks...or funds that invest in a combination of stocks and bonds. *My choices...*

●Dodge & Cox Balanced Fund. *Load:* None. 800-621-3979.

●Washington Mutual Investor Fund. *Load:* 5.75%. 800-888-0055.

●**Shift part of your stock portfolio into short- and intermediate-term bonds or bond funds.** For aggressive investors who can ride out volatile markets, I suggest an allocation of 80% stocks and 20% bonds.

For conservative investors who want to be ready *before* a bear market materializes, I suggest an allocation of 60% stocks and 40% bonds.

The Right Time to Buy Stocks

Buy when corporate insiders do for a good chance to outperform the market. In general—especially for small-cap stocks—heavy insider buying often comes before a run-up in a stock's price.

Don't rush to buy: Two-thirds of a stock's "outperformance" over the next year—compared with the market as a whole—comes after the first month of insider buying. So any investor can wait for public reports of insider trading to take advantage of them.

Caution: Stock performance has nothing to do with insiders' selling since they have many reasons for raising cash.

Mark Hulbert, editor, *Hulbert Financial Digest,* 5051-B Backlick Rd., Annandale, VA 22003.

Better Index Fund

Enhanced index fund is designed to outperform the S&P 500 index. Instead of investing in the 500 stocks that comprise the S&P 500, "enhanced index funds" invest a small portion in options and futures with the objective of earning more than the index. The bulk of the portfolio is invested in money market instruments.

Favorite no-load examples now: Rydex Nova (800-820-0888)...ProFund Ultra Bull (888-776-3637).

Caution: When the S&P 500 declines, these funds decline more than traditional index funds.

William E. Donoghue, chairman, W. E. Donoghue & Co., Inc., 100 Medway Rd., Milford, MA 01757.

Opportunities in Energy Stocks

Continuing volatility in the stock market presents a real opportunity for investors to take advantage of a very sound up-cycle in energy stocks.

●**Underlying fundamentals remain sound.** For the first time in seven years, global oil demand reflects growth in all major regions including recovering Asian economies.

●**OPEC is presenting a united front.** As a result, inventories should reach "normal" levels in the fourth quarter.

●**Oils look inexpensive relative to the overall market.** At the same time, earnings power looks strong for 2001 and 2002. *Our favorite companies...*

Chevron (NYSE:CHV).

Royal Dutch Petroleum (NYSE:RD).

Valero Energy (NYSE: VLO).

James F. Clark, chief energy analyst for Credit Suisse First Boston Corp., 11 Madison Ave., New York 10010.

Stock for All Seasons

If you could buy only one stock, it should be Warren Buffett's Berkshire Hathaway, one of the cheapest and deepest "franchises" in the world, especially at recent prices. Besides holding global franchise stocks like Coca-Cola, Disney and Gillette, it purchased big reinsurer

General Re in 1997, becoming the dominant operating company in that inflation-proof business. It doesn't pay dividends, but has returned an incredible 25% a year from 1965 through 1998, with never a negative year. Brokers don't follow it because it's so pricey it rarely trades. *Choose either of two classes of stock:* NYSE: BRKA...or NYSE:BRKB.

Stephen Leeb, PhD, editor of the investment newsletter *Personal Finance,* 1750 Old Meadow Rd., Suite 301, McLean, VA 22102. Dr. Leeb is author of *Defying the Market.* McGraw-Hill.

Where Is Our Crazy Stock Market Headed Now? Where Is Our Lively Economy Headed Now?

Abraham Gulkowitz, chief global strategist for Deutsche Banc Alex. Brown, 130 Liberty St., New York 10006.

The heightened risk of inflation—and the widening chasm between the New Economy and Old Economy—will make this a very tricky year for investors.

Equity markets around the world have traded down in concert with the downdraft in the US technology sector, raising serious issues for global investing and risk management.

Strategy: Remain heavily committed to stocks. This is still very much a growth economy. The only way to benefit from growth is by investing in stocks in our economy, which still shows more vibrancy than any other major country's.

Technology remains the dominant investment theme. But don't limit your focus to companies that are clearly labeled technology or Internet. The biggest gains may go to investors who bargain-hunt among Old Economy stocks that are moving quickly to embrace technology.

IS IT REALLY BUBBLE.COM?

The greatest concern for investors today is whether the recent setback turns into a riot. The turbulence in the markets may actually serve a therapeutic purpose by eliminating some of the excess.

Throughout all this confusion, however, it is important to recognize that technology is more than just a sector that rose temporarily above traditional stock market valuations. It has become a catalyst for change across wide swathes of the economy.

There really is a technology-driven economic revolution that is significantly different from the Old Economy of the 1970s and 1980s...and the financial markets reflect that transformation.

Given the deep-seated structural changes currently underway in the world economy and a technology revolution that is still difficult to gauge, any shifts in investor sentiment are magnified both on the upside and the downside.

Look at history: Other sectors have dominated the economy in the past—oil and energy in the 1970s, for example. The global economy was dominated not only by the companies that produced and traded energy and other commodities, but also by the international banks that financed the trade in oil.

Today, technology is the dominant sector—but I would differentiate it from previous waves. It will last longer and have a more sweeping and constructive impact on the economy because it involves more than just technology companies.

The economic impact of the Internet, for example, is so profound that every business in every industry in every country must scramble to redefine itself.

Not all the dot-coms of the New Economy will succeed. Some will fail and cost investors a lot of money. But the New Economy won't fail.

Technology will spread into more and more businesses until the gap between the New Economy and the Old Economy closes and we have an economy remade by technology.

HOW TO INVEST NOW

Investor emphasis will continue to focus on the key areas of technology—information technology, the Internet, telecommunications and biotechnology.

But picking pure technology stocks is difficult. Most investors find it much harder to exercise due diligence on a leading-edge technology company than on a company such as General Motors or General Electric.

The more money you invest in companies that are based on technologies you don't really understand, the more you engage in a crap shoot. We all need to do more homework on the New Economy.

Important: You should search for the technology component in Old Economy companies. Value investing is being defined in 2000 as a search for Old Economy companies that are getting the hang of technology.

The automobile industry, retailing, finance—and even the utility sector—all must now redefine themselves and their business practices in terms of technology.

When the pendulum swings back from those companies that are exclusively technology-oriented, it will swing back to the "neglected" companies—even in the most staid of sectors—that are racing to leverage the new technology. That's the next stage of the revolution.

How #1 Fund's Manager Buys Technology Stocks

Kevin Landis, portfolio manager of Firsthand Technology Value Fund (*www.firsthandfunds.com*).

Technology stocks are expensive—still... and very, very volatile. So how has the top technology value fund outperformed all of its peers?

Fund manager Kevin Landis shares his secrets.

FINDING OPPORTUNITIES

I look for the lesser-known leaders of tomorrow. The core of the fund's success—investing in infrastructure that supports the Internet.

Important: What's happening now in tech stock prices due to recent Internet hacker attacks has no long-term effect on our strategy.

• **Traditional valuations are not meaningful.** Turnover of *leading companies* versus *lagging companies* is continuous. Traditional valuation methods will turn up many companies with real problems. I look at valuation but intentionally put that screen toward the end of the stock-picking process. I also look for good management—*and* strong vision.

Best indicator: Good products and happy customers. The best indication that management has vision is if the company is serving high-growth markets.

●**Trend spotting.** I start the process by asking myself what powerful trends will open up new markets. I then look for companies making these trends happen. I price them by estimating what I foresee for the company two or three years out...and then what I would be willing to pay for that growth. *Some of the trends that I believe will be the next wave...*

●Switch to flat-panel displays.

●Wireless—I think it will be hotter than the Internet boom.

Warning: Don't buy what's obvious. If you bought the biggest computer companies at the end of the 1970s, they wouldn't have been part of the PC boom in the 1980s. If you bought the strongest PC companies in the beginning of the 1990s, you wouldn't own the Internet.

●**Look for companies that are early to market.** I look for companies that will be recognized as the cream of the crop. If I'm early in the companies' development, I look for companies that are first to market with products people need.

Advantages for these companies: They develop relationships with customers...and, more important, they receive crucial feedback about what works and what doesn't.

●**Look for problem-solvers.** The easiest sale is a solution to a problem. So I look for companies with solutions—for current or anticipated problems.

●**Buy what you know.** It is very hard for individuals to track the kinds of technologies that professionals do. To be ahead of the crowd, invest in something you know—that's the philosophy of Fidelity's Peter Lynch. If you know about electronics, you have an advantage with those companies. If you're a chemist, you have a different advantage.

Bull-Market Loopholes for Short-Term Investors

Martin Nissenbaum, national director of personal income tax planning, Ernst & Young LLP, 787 Seventh Ave., New York 10019.

The growing popularity of day trading and on-line brokerages have boosted the amount of short-term trading by average investors.

But buying and selling shares within 12 months is expensive. Your short-term capital gains are taxed at the same rate as ordinary income.

Here's how to keep more of your short-term gains and minimize your tax shock next year...

●**Qualify as a *trader* to deduct expenses.** While there is no precise definition of the term *trader,* you are likely to qualify for trader deductions if you make 50 or more market trades per month and if you try to profit from daily market movements.

Advantage: Under normal tax rules, investment expenses, such as the cost of research, are deductible only among miscellaneous expenses. And these expenses are deductible only to the extent that they exceed 2% of your *Adjusted Gross Income* (AGI).

Also, investment interest is deductible only if you itemize and your deduction is limited to investment income.

Example: If your AGI is $75,000, you will receive no deduction on your first $1,500 of expenses.

But if you qualify as a trader, all of your investment expenses are deducted *as trade or business expenses* on Schedule C of your tax return. You'll also avoid the AGI-related deduction limit entirely. *Benefits of qualifying as a trader...*

●**Investment expenses are deductible** even if you don't itemize.

●**Investment interest is deductible** even if you don't itemize, and it is not subject to investment income limitations.

●**Your deduction of investment expenses is sheltered** from the *Alternative Minimum Tax (AMT)*. The AMT is a special tax that applies to people whose regular tax is low because of certain deductions and credits although their income is high.

The AMT can be triggered by state and local income taxes, including taxes on long-term capital gains. Such taxes are not deductible for AMT purposes. Similarly, miscellaneous deductions that include investment expenses can trigger AMT since they too are not deductible for this tax.

By contrast, Schedule C deductions are available in calculating the AMT.

Traders' long- and short-term gains and losses are taxed under the same rules that apply to other investors.

●**Use the wash sale rule to minimize gains.** Investors who trade frequently should pay special attention to the wash sale rule.

Rule: If you sell a security at a loss and then buy it back within 30 days before or after the sale, you won't be able to deduct the loss.

But the wash sale rule applies only to securities that are issued by the same company. You can deduct the loss if you repurchase a very similar security issued by a different company.

Example: After selling a sector fund, you can immediately purchase shares in a different fund that invests in the same sector.

Good news: The wash sale rule does not apply to gain sales. So—if you sold a stock at a loss, you could sell another security at a gain and immediately buy that security back. You can deduct the loss to offset the gain.

Example: Let's say you've realized a $40,000 net capital loss for the year and you also have large unrealized gains. Because only $3,000 of losses are deductible in a year, you won't receive a tax benefit from $37,000 of the losses in the current year.

Better: Sell selected securities to generate $37,000 of gains. *You then can...*

●Cash out the gains tax free since tax on them is offset by the loss, or...

●Repurchase the same securities, increasing your cost basis in them and reducing future taxes accordingly.

●**Avoid or defer realizing long-term gains.** Long-term gains are taxed at a top rate of 20%. *But you can take steps to pay no tax at all on these gains...*

●Make charitable gifts with appreciated securities rather than cash. You can deduct donations of long-term assets at full market value. You'll get the same deduction as from a cash contribution but avoid paying gains tax on donated property.

●To pay a child's college costs, instead of cashing in investments yourself, give appreciated securities to the child. Then have the child cash them in to pay his/her own expenses. The child will pay a capital gains tax at his rate— probably no tax or 10%, instead of your 20%.

You can make gifts of securities to a child using your annual gift tax exclusion of $10,000 per recipient—$20,000 when gifts are made jointly with a spouse. This exclusion applies to the value of the securities, not your cost.

●Turn long-term gains into retirement income by donating appreciated assets to a Charitable Remainder Trust (CRT). The CRT pays no tax when it cashes in the securities. So it can pay a larger annuity on proceeds than you would get if you cashed them in. And you can defer tax longer by delaying tax annuity payments through a Net Income Makeup Charitable Remainder Unitrust (NIMCRUT). The charity gets a gift, and you get a deduction. Major charities can arrange this for you. Consult an expert for details.

●**Beware of surprise tax bills from funds.** Funds generate internal taxable gains and losses as a result of trades their managers make. These are distributed to shareholders at year-end. If a fund generates a lot of high-tax, internal, short-term gains during the year, the resulting bill reduces real investment returns.

Invest in funds with *tax profiles* that meet your needs. The lowest tax liabilities usually are produced by index funds because they rarely trade internally. There also are funds now that are actively managed but also minimize their internal tax bite by generating mostly long-term gains.

What to Look for In Internet Companies Before You Invest

Dan Burstein, senior adviser, The Blackstone Group, an investment banking firm in New York City.

How do you decide whether an Internet stock is worth buying when many Internet companies have little history and no earnings? *Here are my rules...*

●**Buy Internet stocks whose prices are down roughly 50% from their 52-week highs.** As a group, Internet stocks can be extremely volatile. Prices shoot up and then fall just as quickly. The trick is to buy the *best* Internet stocks when their prices have been beaten down, which is the case with many of them currently. You can find a stock's 52-week high and low in the newspapers or on the Web.

Caution: Many Internet stocks have split over the past year. Take stock splits into account when you calculate price declines.

●**Don't buy Internet stocks whose *lock-up periods* are about to end.** After an initial public offering, a company's management, founders and venture investors are generally prohibited by SEC regulation from selling their stock for six months. This restriction gives new stocks a chance to find their true public value and helps ensure a fair marketplace.

Because there is so much money in the Internet sector, some company insiders cash out as soon as this six-month period has expired. If you are thinking of buying a stock, wait at least four weeks after the initial lockup period is over.

●**Consider Internet companies whose management is buying stock.** Because many Internet stocks have no earnings at all, conventional valuation methods, such as earnings growth rates, are not useful when assessing them.

More useful: Management confidence in the company. I buy stock in Internet companies in which a majority of top management is buying shares.

●**Look for takeover targets.** Internet companies that have strategic technology or marketing advantages are often acquisition candidates.

●**Look for companies that are either profitable now or will be soon.** The market is getting tired of the current "fashionableness" of having no profits or prospects of profits.

I look for revenue growth of at least 20% from one quarter to the next one. While there's no similar formula for profitability, I do want to see that some profit—however small—is within one year away.

10

The Smart Consumer

Bargain Hunting... How to Buy Almost Anything for Much Less

Real bargain hunting is an art, a quest and a game—and it can save you a small fortune. If you follow these strategies, you can sometimes find bargains you never even knew existed.

The greatest bargain hunters aren't shy. They know that the best deals aren't always the ones that are advertised and often it pays to haggle. Many retailers are surprisingly receptive to this approach.

Strategy: Bargain out of earshot of other customers. The store can't afford to give everyone the same great deal.

The first rule in bargaining: Explain why you deserve the bargain...

- **You're buying many items.**

- **The item is damaged.** (We look for appliances that have dents in the back where no one can see them.)

- **You're willing to buy a display item.**

- **You've noticed that the item has been on sale for a while** and it still isn't moving.

Tactic: You're in a powerful position if it's the last one of last year's models. That's when you know the store is dying to get rid of it.

Example: Wal-Mart marked down a single old-model VCR from $150 to $100. Our friend negotiated an even lower price. He had to go back twice, but eventually he took it home for $50.

- **You'll pay cash.** (This is most effective at small stores.)

SUCCESS SECRETS

Here's how to win the bargaining game...

- **Be prepared to walk away from a price you don't like.** Then come back a few days

---

Rob and Terry Adams, freelance writers and long-time bargain hunters. They are authors of *The Bargain Hunter's Handbook: How to Buy Just About Anything for Next to Nothing.* Career Press.

later and give the vendor another chance to meet your terms.

●**Talk to the department manager or, for a smaller store, the store manager,** instead of bargaining with the salesperson. In most cases, the salesperson doesn't have the authority to give you what you want. (If a salesperson has been helpful, let the manager know so he/she gets a commission.)

Note: Don't haggle during peak hours when the person you're negotiating with is likely to be distracted. Avoid the Saturday afternoon crush. With home-improvement stores, also avoid the 4 pm to 6 pm period when contractors mob the store.

●**Strike while the iron is hot.** If you see a great price on a TV that you hadn't planned on buying until next year, grab it.

●**Look for closeout items.** End-lot sales items are generally in the very back of the home-improvement stores. Other sales items may not even be displayed. Ask a manager what gems are hidden in a back room.

Example: We once bought a Whirlpool electric range this way. It had no box or instruction manual but it was brand new and a great deal.

●**Don't turn up your nose at items that have been returned.** That doesn't mean an item is defective, although the packaging may no longer look attractive.

●**Negotiate for services, too**—not just products. Even a fee from a dentist, doctor, air-conditioning technician or landscape artist can be negotiated.

●**Tell a doctor that Medicare will cover only so much** of the cost for a particular procedure. Take it or leave it.

●**Ask your doctor for free samples.** You may save on the cost of a prescription.

●**Tell your mechanic,** "I'm a good customer, but your prices are killing me." Do it nicely and you won't ruin the relationship whether he gives you a price break or not.

●**Fees that you may think are chiseled in stone are not.** When a hotel quotes you a price for a wedding, it probably allows wiggle room of 10%. You can negotiate with caterers as well.

●**Go to garage sales.** You can find real bargains, especially at moving sales (people would rather leave behind some good stuff than lug it to a new place) or multifamily sales.

Go early in the morning when the best items are there, then check back at the end of the sale. You can drive a very hard bargain in that final hour.

Learn about garage sales in the classified section of your local paper or in a *Penny Saver*.

●**Attend small auctions.** You seldom get great bargains at Sotheby's or Christie's, but you can often do well at a much smaller auction. *Reason:* You might be the only person who wants a certain item. Without competition, you can get a great deal.

During the auction preview, ask if the piece you like has a "reserve," or minimum, price. If that price is more than you want to pay, even a lack of competitive bidding won't help you.

Warning: Be sure you can take home whatever you buy. Auctions rarely deliver.

GET A CAR FOR THE RIGHT PRICE

You can get a better deal in person than via the Internet. Begin by knowing all the key numbers. Go to *www.edmunds.com* (use the public library or a cyber-cafe, if you don't have a computer of your own) to find out the manufacturer's suggested retail price, the dealer invoice, the holdback (which you subtract from the invoice price) and any dealer incentives (which you should also subtract from the invoice) to find out the dealer's true cost. Do the same for options you want. Now you have negotiating power.

Car buying strategy 1: Go when the weather is bad, so there are few customers. The salesperson will be more eager to agree to your terms. Go at the end of the month when the salesperson is eager to meet his quota.

Car buying strategy 2: Pull in a "higher authority." Just as a salesperson will often offer great terms only to be vetoed by his sales manager, you can turn the tables by repeatedly calling your spouse at home with the latest offer. After each time, come back and say, "He/she still says it's not low enough."

CRUISE FOR LESS

If you have the flexibility to leave with just a few days' notice, you can sometimes travel for half price, or even less, by asking cruise lines about last-minute vacancies.

Check the Web sites *www.expedia.msn.com, www.previewtravel.com, www.travelweb.com* and *www.priceline.com* for information.

Attention Shoppers: Buy Anything at Wholesale...Anytime

Gail Bradney, consumer bargains expert, Woodstock, NY, and author of *Wholesale By Mail and On-Line 2000.* HarperCollins.

There is no reason for shoppers today to wait for great sales on selected items at retail stores.

You can buy almost anything you need at wholesale prices right now if you know where to go.

The companies below offer products and services starting at 30% below suggested retail prices. *Ordering in large quantities can get you as much as 90% off...*

BED AND BATH TEXTILES

•**Bates Mill Store.** Sturdy cotton bedspreads and blankets sold direct from this 1850s Maine mill—no middleman to up the prices. *Bargain hunters take note:* Bedspread seconds are marked down here an additional 40%. 800-552-2837...or *www.batesbedspreads.com.*

•**J. Schachter Corp.** Down-filled luxury comforters and pillows. Buy a high-end comforter—$700 at top New York department stores—for at least 40% less. 800-468-6233.

CAMERAS/PHOTO SERVICES

•**Owl Photo Corp.** Photofinishing and video transfer are cheaper than at any other mail-order photo lab. 580-772-3353.

•**Porter's Camera Store.** Photographic and darkroom equipment and supplies. The prices on cameras, video equipment and optics are slashed by about 60%. 800-553-2001...or *www.porters.com.*

CHILDREN'S CLOTHING

•**Basic Brilliance.** 100% cotton everyday wear for infants, children and mothers—all at 30% to 50% off. 360-385-3835...or *www.basic brilliance.com.*

•**Gohn Bros. Manufacturing Co.** Low-cost, high-quality, name-brand children's clothing, underwear and outerwear. 219-825-2400.

FOOD AND BEVERAGES

•**Gibbsville Cheese Company.** Wisconsin cheeses, specializing in cheddars, Colbys and Monterey Jacks. Sausages, too. Ships October through April. 920-564-3242.

•**Jaffe Bros. Natural Foods.** Organic dried fruits—Fuyu persimmons, Black Mission figs, kiwi—and nut butters. 760-749-1133...or *www. organicfruitsandnuts.com.*

HOME APPLIANCES

•**ABC Vacuum Cleaner Warehouse.** Top brands and models up to 70% off. Free shipping on many items. 800-285-8145...or *www.abc-vacuum.com.*

•**EBA Wholesale.** Save hundreds of dollars on appliances and pluggables—from TVs and video equipment to refrigerators. Nationwide delivery. 800-380-2378.

LAWN AND GARDEN

•**Butterbrooke Farm Seed Co-Op.** Very low prices on vegetable seeds. For a free price list, send a self-addressed, stamped, business-sized envelope to 78 Barry Rd., Oxford, Connecticut 06478.

•**Le Jardin du Gourmet.** Offers 30-cent sample seed packets of lemon balm...German chamomile...spearmint...and hundreds of culinary herbs. Flat-rate shipping charge of $2. 802-748-1446.

•**Prentiss Court Ground Covers.** Save 50% on more than 50 varieties of live ground cover plants...ornamental grasses...and more. 800-577-9778.

●**Van Dyck's.** Exhibition-quality Dutch flower bulbs and perennials at 40% below retail prices. 800-248-2852...or *www.vandycks.com.*

HEALTH & BEAUTY PRODUCTS

●**AARP Pharmacy Service.** You don't have to be a member of AARP to make use of this full-service drugstore. Generic medications at half the cost of the brand-name items. And an on-duty pharmacist is available to answer questions via phone six days a week. Honors most prescription insurance plans. Flat-rate shipping charge of $1.50. 800-456-2277...or *www.rps pharmacy.com.*

●**American Health Food.** Vitamins and health supplements up to 33% off retail—60% if you buy the company's brand. Flat-rate shipping charge of $3.95. 800-858-2143...or *www. amerhealth.com.*

●**Perfumania.** Up to 50% off suggested retail prices on fragrances for both men and women. 800-927-1777...or *www.perfumania.com.*

KITCHEN EQUIPMENT

●**Cook's Wares.** Discounted gourmet ingredients, cookware and cookbooks. A Cuisinart Pro Classic listed at $240 costs $155. 800-915-9788...or *www.cookswares.com.*

●**Kitchen Etc.** Up to 50% off on tableware from Lenox, Mikasa, Pfaltzgraff and Wedgwood. 603-773-0020...or *www.kitchenetc.com.*

LUGGAGE AND LEATHER GOODS

●**Santa Maria Discount Luggage.** First-quality travel and business bags and cases. A Samsonite 29" Oyster hardside listed for $200 costs $69.97. Buy five pieces of luggage and get an additional 10% off. 888-832-1201...or *www.luggageman.com.*

LUXURY ITEMS

●**Bennett Brothers.** Corporate gift catalog with dress and casual watches at 40% off retail, including styles from Seiko, Geneve and Jules Jurgensen. 800-621-2626...or *www.bennettbros.com.*

●**Evergreen Farms.** Cut fresh flowers. 30 stems of snapdragons or 15 stems of Asiatic lilies cost just $29.95 plus $12 overnight shipping. *Phone hours:* 8 am to 5 pm CST, Monday through Friday. 877-868-6985...or *www.ever greenfarms.com.*

●**House of Onyx.** Investment-quality, imported gemstones and jewelry at wholesale prices—50% to 60% less than you would find elsewhere. 800-844-3100...or *www.houseof onyx.com.*

OFFICE SUPPLIES/EQUIPMENT

●**Affordable Photocopy.** Top brands of photocopiers, faxes and printers at 60% off suggested retail prices. Free shipping on business-grade machines. 888-293-8071...or *www.photocopiers.com.*

●**Factory Direct Furniture.** Office furniture and institutional equipment. Discounts of 50% off retail are common here. Additional discounts on orders over $1,000. 800-972-6570.

●**Recycled Software.** Used IBM-compatible software at 50% to 90% off retail. Thousands of titles available. Orders include all original manuals and discs—virus free. 800-851-2425...or *www.recycledsoftware.com.*

PET SUPPLIES

●**Omaha Vaccine Company.** Prescription and nonprescription medications, grooming supplies and accessories for all animals—at up to 50% off retail prices. Many veterinarians buy here. 800-367-4444...or *www.omahavac cine.com.*

●**That Pet Place.** Huge discount pet supplier for birds, fish, reptiles, dogs and cats. 717-299-5691...or *www.thatpetplace.com.*

PRINTING AND STATIONERY

●**Brown Print & Co.** Custom-designed business cards, stationery, invitations and more. Proprietor works one-on-one with every client. Prices are competitive with those of large chains. *Samples and price list:* $2. 626-286-2106.

TOOLS AND HARDWARE

●**Harbor Freight Tools.** Save up to 70% on tools, hardware, camping equipment and lawn and garden machinery. Free shipping for orders over $50. 800-423-2567...or *www.har borfreight.com.*

Amazing Deals at US Government Sales

Nancy Tyler, broadcast manager of the federal government's Consumer Information Center, which offers free and low-cost publications, Washington, DC.

***

Just about every day, a government office is selling valuable assets, from fine jewelry to office equipment—all at great prices.

●**Department of Defense.** The Defense Reutilization and Marketing Services (DRMS) gets rid of excess military property. Thousands of items are available each day, including tents and air conditioners. National sales are held in Battle Creek, Michigan—but local sales are held throughout the country.

Information: 888-352-9333. Ask for a DRMS kit that lists its offices. For detailed property information: *www.drms.com.*

●**Department of Justice.** The US Marshals' Service sells property that has been forfeited by law. Everything from commercial real estate to art and antiques is sold through auction as well as sealed bids.

Information: Check the Consumer Information Center's Web site, *www.pueblo.gsa.gov* and search for the National Sellers list by clicking on "Search CIC."

●**General Services Administration (GSA).** GSA's Federal Supply Service sells boats, cameras, communications equipment, hardware and office equipment that is no longer needed by the federal government.

Information: www.pueblo.gsa.gov. Click on "Federal Programs" and then "How You Can Buy Used Federal Personal Property" for a free list of GSA offices. Or order the list by phone for 50¢. 888-878-3256. Contact the office nearest you to find out about current sales.

●**US Postal Service.** The Postal Service sells items that have been unclaimed or lost in the mail. Merchandise includes clocks, televisions, radios, jewelry, tape recorders, VCRs and clothing.

Information: For personal property sales, look up the office closest to you in the GSA Guide to Federal Government Sales. It is available free at *www.pueblo.gsa.gov* or for $2 by phone. 888-878-3256.

Flea Market Shopping Secrets of Champion Collectors

Steven Sclaroff is an architect, interior designer and president of Steven Sclaroff Design, 414 W. 14 St., New York 10014.

Jennifer Streit and Christina Ecklund own Prize, an antique shop specializing in vintage furniture and lighting, 2361 San Pablo Ave., Berkeley, CA 94702.

Ellen Schroy is an avid collector in Quakertown, PA, who attends many flea markets each year. She is author of eight books on collecting, including *Warman's Flea Market Price Guide.* Krause Publications.

***

Internet auction sites may offer a wide variety of collectibles—but there's nothing like a flea market when you are hunting for bargains.

Here are the tricks the pros use when searching for vintage home furnishings at flea markets—and the hot collectibles they're looking for now…

INTERIOR DESIGNER
Steven Sclaroff

●**Shop late in the day.** Many people believe they must hit flea markets early in the day.

But they are often disappointed by what they find. That's because very serious collectors—and even professionals—get there even earlier, before dawn, and, using flashlights, comb the merchandise as the vendors stock their booths.

Opportunity: Attend flea markets in the late afternoon to get a good deal on the remaining items that sellers don't want to cart back to storage.

●**Look for items that don't fit the dealer's specialty.** If the dealer is selling an item that isn't in harmony with the rest of his/her collection, he might not know its value…or he might be selling it for a friend.

Either way, he is probably eager to part with the item, creating an opportunity for you.

●**Scout out electrical outlets.** Before purchasing any used appliance, make sure it works.

Find an outlet in a nearby community building or in a rest room, on a light pole or at a food stand.

Avoid vintage electric fans, which may look nice but generally sound like lawn mowers when you get them home.

Self-defense: Time the minute hand of vintage electric clocks for accuracy before buying.

● **Assume all upholstered furniture will have to be redone.** *Before you buy furniture…*

● Check the frame for sturdiness.

● Shake cushions, and watch for red dust—a sign that the foam inside is crumbling and the cushions need to be replaced.

● Bargain using the cost of recovering the piece as leverage. The big cost of antique furniture is reupholstering it—not the price you're charged at the flea market.

Example: A six-foot sofa will cost from $150 to $3,000 for 15 yards of fabric, depending on the quality you select. Then it will cost $750 to $2,500 for the labor. Total: $900 to $5,500.

Since a decent new sofa can be purchased for about $1,500, a vintage piece is rarely worthwhile—unless you truly love the piece.

● **Be a stickler about furniture's condition** —if you expect to resell it later at a profit. A chipped tabletop will greatly reduce an antique piece's value.

HOT NOW

● **Audio equipment from the 1950s and 1960s.** Top brand names are Braun and Brionvega. Items must be in good working order, although true collectors rarely use the pieces.

● **Geometric carpets from the 1930s through the 1960s,** including Art Deco pieces and Swedish Ryas.

● **Household hardware from the late 1800s through the 1940s,** including door handles, knockers and mail flaps and bathroom hardware.

ANTIQUE STORE OWNERS
Jennifer Streit and Christina Ecklund

● **Shop at the once-a-year flea markets rather than at the every-weekend events.** The vendors' wares are less picked-through at the annual events.

Helpful: Call the chambers of commerce of towns in your area to find out when events are scheduled.

● **Look for slightly worn items.** Conventional wisdom holds that collectibles must be in perfect condition. That's true only if you intend to resell what you buy.

If you're shopping to decorate your home, a weathered or worn look provides a warm or friendly feeling. Plus, you can use an item's imperfect condition for bargaining leverage.

Just make sure the structure of the item is sound and that the items only look worn— and are not falling apart.

Flea market tool kit…

● **Tape measure**—and important dimensions of your home.

● **Cardboard box with bubble wrap or Styrofoam,** for small, fragile items.

● **Wet wipes.** Digging through flea markets is messy business.

HOT NOW

● **Wrought-iron outdoor furniture.** There's plenty of it available at good prices. But— avoid cheaply made folding patio furniture.

● **Vintage books from the 1930s and 1940s.** Certain first editions and other high-end fare are pricey. There are plenty of cheaper old books available that are both interesting and nice looking.

● **Office furniture from the 1950s.** Solid metal cabinets and desks meant for the workplace are inexpensive and were built to last.

ANTIQUE BOOK AUTHOR
Ellen Schroy

● **Shop when there is a chance of rain.** Crowds stay away from flea markets when the forecast is for light rain. That can make for some great deals, especially toward the end of the weekend, when dealers start to worry about covering the cost of their booths.

But don't bother going if the weather is really bad. Many dealers will have packed up and left.

● **Be picky about the condition of modern collectibles.** If you expect any toy or collectible from recent decades to be worth top dollar when you sell it, the item needs to be in great shape and in its box.

● **Decide why you want to buy an item before you buy it.** *The answer will help you determine what to buy and how much to pay…*

● If it's an investment: Be extremely cautious about the condition, and drive a hard bargain.

● If it's for your home: Spend a few dollars more to find just the right item. Be sure it fits in with the other things at home.

•If the item is for reuse: Focus on its usefulness. *Price:* How does it compare with the cost of a new one?

•Consider attending setup day. Many of the best items at flea markets are sold a day before the general public is allowed in. That's when dealers are setting up booths.

Some flea markets allow individuals without booths to pay their way in on set-up day. *Note:* The fee could exceed $50.

Going on setup day is worthwhile if you're willing to spend big on items. If you're just hunting for cheap furnishings, it may not be worth the expense. Call the flea market to learn its policy before arriving.

•**Ask for a signed receipt.** Almost no one does this at flea markets, but it's a good way to avoid counterfeits. Get the dealer's name, signature and phone number, as well as the date, amount paid and a description of the item.

If it turns out later that you bought a fake, you might have some legal recourse, depending on your state's laws.

At the very least, asking for a signed receipt can weed out some of the disreputable dealers. If they know they're selling you a fake—or a stolen item—they might be less willing to sign the receipt.

HOT NOW

•**Automobilia.** Gas station signs and antique car memorabilia are on the rise.

•**Toys from the 1970s.** Watch for My Little Pony, Boyds Bears, Little Tikes and Liddle Kiddles.

•**Architectural hardware,** including doorknobs and hinges.

Guerrilla Shopper's Guide to Outlet Malls

Elysa Lazar, author of *Outlet Shopper's Guide.* Lazar Media. Her Web site, *www.lazarshopping.com,* includes a database of factory outlets nationwide and mail-order companies.

Hundreds of factory-outlet stores have popped up around the country—all claiming to offer great bargains.

Careful…many of those bargains can be buried under loads of inferior merchandise.

Here's how to avoid the big traps and how to find the best deals…

•**Order coupons to maximize savings.** With very little effort, you can cut your bill at outlet stores by an extra 25%…

•Visit *www.outletbound.com* before you shop, and request a free VIP Voucher. It is redeemable for coupons or special offers worth hundreds of dollars at more than 200 participating outlet centers nationwide. The site also lets you search outlets by location, store, brand or product category.

•Request a coupon book from the store manager. These books are presented to members of bus tours, not to individuals. But the store will usually let you have a coupon book as a gesture of goodwill. Another place to find these books is at an outlet center's information desk or management office.

•**Ask for "early markdowns."** Most stores will give you the sale prices on any items you're buying that will go on sale within the next two weeks. Ask the store what its policy is.

•**Sign up for the store's mailing list.** You will receive advance notices of special sales, as well as vouchers for 5% to 15% off.

My favorite outlet-store mailing lists: Donna Karan…Joan & David.

•**Ask for a "volume discount"** from store managers if you're buying a large amount of merchandise at once.

•**Beware of items that were never sold in retail stores.** Many popular stores create lower-priced lines, with the same brand name and style, and sell them through their outlet stores.

Examples: I've seen outlet coats and sweaters with plastic buttons instead of the leather ones on the retail versions. Other garments lack quality work, such as reinforced stitching around the sleeves.

How to spot the difference: Most inferior *made-for-outlet* merchandise has "factory store" stamped on its label or tag. Items from the designer's retail stores will have labels that are sliced in half or are marked with ink. When in doubt, ask a salesperson.

●**Give clothing the quality test before buying.** I perform a wrinkle test on every garment I buy. I grab a fistful of the fabric, squeeze it, then release. Except for linen, the item should retain its shape and wrinkle very little.

Many outlet stores post charts that decode the flaws in the merchandise. *But you can do your own quick check...*

●***Bath towels:*** Are the hems even? Are the stitches near the borders tight?

●***Belts:*** Does it say "full-grain" leather? Full-grain is almost twice as thick as "split-grain" leather, which is brittle and wears out quickly.

●***Dress shirts:*** Turn the shirts inside out to see if the lining at the collar and armholes is sewn well. Pay more for 100% *two-ply* cotton. It stands up much better to repeated washings than polyester blends.

●***T-shirts:*** Is there strong, close stitching around the neck, shoulder seams and armholes? If not, the shirt will lose its shape quickly.

●**Consider items that fail to meet manufacturers' standards.** These are marked off by up to 70%. The items that are worth buying are labeled "irregular." They have minute flaws, such as crooked waistband seams or missing buttons.

Usually not worthwhile: Clothes that are labeled "seconds." They typically have serious flaws, such as stains or seams that pull. Clothes made of 100% silk rarely hold their color or shape more than one season.

●**Ask about the store's refund and exchange policy.** They vary greatly, especially during the holidays.

Before you buy, find out if you can return outlet items through the mail...or to full-price retail stores. *Examples...*

●**AnnTaylor outlets** let you return items to their full-price branches.

●**Levi's outlets** will take back an irregular garment—even after you've washed it.

Self-defense: Save the tags. If you purchase an "all-sales-are-final" item and then discover you want to return it, look for a defect. If the garment wasn't specifically marked imperfect, you can bargain to get a refund.

Or find a substitute garment in the store that costs a bit more. Ask the manager if you can use your "final sale" purchase as partial payment for the new one you chose.

●**Don't assume outlet stores have the lowest prices.** Many stores mix in full-price items with discount merchandise. So—an item on sale at the company's retail store can be priced less than in the outlet. Research prices of merchandise at retail stores. Then look to pay at least 25% less for the same item at the outlet store.

Also, ignore the "suggested retail price" listed on the merchandise tag at outlets. It is usually inflated to make the saving look big.

Focus on quality rather than the discount. If you don't love a garment, you won't wear it, no matter how much you've saved.

Formula: Before I buy, I ask myself a simple question—*If the item was full price at the retail store, would I still buy it?* If I hesitate when answering, I put it back.

●**Shop from home or on-line before making the trip to the outlet.** Some stores allow you to make purchases over the phone with a credit card if you describe what you're looking for. Others offer a catalog of their outlet merchandise.

Resource: *OutletsOnline* has a complete listing of names, locations and phone numbers of outlet centers and their stores in the US by state. It indicates which ones will let you shop on-line. *www.outletsonline.com.*

Save on Vitamins

Nearly all vitamin supplement makers buy their raw vitamins from the same suppliers.. Just three major manufacturers—Roche, BASF and Rhone-Poulenc—produce 90% of the world's vitamins. So, no matter which brand you buy or how much you pay, and regardless of the appearance of the vitamin pill, you are getting the same basic vitamin product. You can save a lot of money if you buy the drugstore's house brand.

Caution: How the raw vitamin is formulated for use—tablets, gel caps, capsules, etc.—can affect how well it dissolves in your body. Look for "USP" on the label to be sure the product meets US Pharmacopeia standards for dissolvability.

V. Srini Srinivasan, PhD, director, dietary supplements division, US Pharmacopeia, 12601 Twinbrook Pkwy., Rockville, MD 20852.

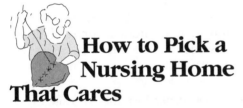

How to Pick a Nursing Home That Cares

Eileen Kraatz, who has 20 years of experience as a staff member and volunteer at nursing homes in the US and Canada. She is author of *A Spy in the Nursing Home: Inside Tips and Tactics for Choosing the Right One in Five Days.* Health Information Press.

Few nursing home residents are actually beaten or starved by their caregivers. Even in homes that enjoy good reputations, however, it's not uncommon for residents to be neglected or otherwise subjected to subtle forms of abuse that undermine their sense of dignity.

Here's how to find a nursing home that truly takes care of its residents.

GOING UNDERCOVER

Ask friends, family members, doctors, etc., to recommend nursing homes. Once you have three or four names, make plans to visit each one.

Trap: If nursing home employees know you're evaluating the facility, they may try to hide unpleasant truths about it.

To get a true picture: Don't reveal your mission. Tag along when a friend goes to visit a relative who lives at the home.

What if you don't know anyone with a relative there? Ask friends, colleagues, etc., if they know someone in a particular nursing home. Get them to "hook you up" with that person.

YOUR UNDERCOVER VISIT

On your initial visit, pay attention to the basics—the level of cleanliness and orderliness, the general attitude of the staff, the demeanor of the residents and the overall ambiance. *Here's what else you should do...*

•**Observe staff members.** Are they gentle with the residents? Do they use a pleasant tone of voice? An impatient or harsh tone strongly suggests that you should look elsewhere.

•**Check the general appearance of residents.** Cleanliness and good grooming suggest that residents are getting proper care. Do they look well-fed?

Notice, too, whether residents have any bruises. Bruises can suggest rough handling during bathing, getting into and out of bed, etc.

•**Check the level of privacy.** As you walk down the hall, are you able to peer into rooms and see the residents being bathed, changing clothes, etc.? Avoid homes that fail to safeguard this basic right to privacy.

•**Speak with residents.** Introduce yourself politely, then ask how they like the food, the activities, etc. In good homes, residents speak freely—even when complaining.

•**Look for the Residents' Bill of Rights.** This document, outlining rights to privacy, choice in treatment and freedom from abuse, should be posted in the lobby and in every room.

For a free copy, contact the National Citizens' Coalition for Nursing Home Reform, 1424 16 St. NW, Ste. 202, Washington, DC 20036. 202-332-2275.

DIGGING DEEPER

If a particular nursing home looks promising on your undercover visit, call to arrange a formal visit.

Use this visit to conduct a more thorough investigation of living conditions, rules, activities, etc.

Schedule meetings with the nursing home's social service director, activity director and dietitian. The activity director should oversee a full roster of recreational, cultural and physical activities for residents.

If no staff member devotes all of his/her time to this function—in some homes, for example, the social service director doubles as activity director—look for another nursing home.

In many homes, activity schedules are posted. If so, check to make sure these activities really are taking place as scheduled.

Residents should have access to lots of books—and books on tape. Make sure the tape players are in working order.

Each resident should have access to a telephone—ideally in his/her room. Visiting hours should be liberal. Close family members should be able to visit until late in the evening.

Few homes have physicians on the premises, but one or more should visit the facility several times per week. At least one physician should be on call at all times.

When you're reasonably sure a nursing home fits the bill, speak with the administrator. This is the person who is ultimately responsible for how the facility is run.

SATURDAY AFTERNOON INSPECTION

Make your last visit on Saturday afternoon. That's when the staff is leanest and problems are most apparent.

Everyday Opportunities For Free...or Almost Free...Medical Care

Matthew Lesko, a syndicated columnist based in Kensington, MD, who specializes in advice on receiving free services. He is author of *Free Health Care! Information USA.*

There are many ways to get free or low-cost checkups...vaccinations...drugs... even surgery and dental care.

To receive this care, it's not necessary to be unemployed, elderly or in a low-income bracket. Nor is it essential to have some rare disease. *In many cases, all that's required is the willingness to do a little detective work on the phone or on the Internet...*

●**Visit a government health clinic.** Free checkups, vaccinations and other kinds of care are offered at clinics operated by state and municipal governments. Some clinics provide free prenatal and well-child care, too.

More information: Call your state public health department. The number should be listed in your phone book's "blue pages." Or call your state medical association.

Hint: Bring along a book or magazine. Government health clinics are busy—and noisy—places and they don't make appointments. Expect to spend more time than usual in the waiting room.

●**Get free medications.** Most pharmaceutical manufacturers have programs that provide medicine for free. These are often called "indigent programs." In fact, however, the income requirements are often quite lenient. People with an annual household income of up to $45,000 are sometimes eligible.

The request for the medication must come from the patient's doctor.

More information: Visit the Web site of the Pharmaceutical Research and Manufacturers of America at *www.phrma.org/patients.* The site lists companies that provide free medication, types of medication available and information about applying.

●**Get care at a dental school.** There are 53 dental schools in the US. All operate clinics that provide basic services at great savings. That includes checkups, cleaning, X rays and fillings.

More advanced services such as fitting bridges, dentures and implants may also be available.

Student dentists do the work but are closely supervised by their professors.

Bonus: Care may be free for conditions the professors are studying.

More information: To locate a nearby dental school, visit the American Dental Association Web site at *www.ada.org.* Click on "Education" and follow the links. Or call local universities and ask if they have dental schools.

● **Join a clinical study.** The National Institutes of Health (NIH) spend billions of dollars annually to study cutting-edge treatments for every imaginable ailment. Physicians conducting these studies always need patients to participate.

The NIH conducts some studies at its Clinical Center in Bethesda, Maryland. But most are conducted at academic medical centers across the country.

Important: Some NIH studies compare the effectiveness of new treatments with placebos and/or standard treatment. Participants are assigned randomly to study groups and they cannot choose the treatment they will receive.

More information: Visit the NIH Web site at *www.clinicaltrials.gov*. It lists studies by condition, explains requirements for joining and identifies researchers to contact.

If you lack access to the Internet, call the NIH Clinical Center at 800-411-1222.

● **Get a free "second opinion."** The proliferation of Web sites devoted to health and medicine makes it easy to learn about virtually any condition. *Some reliable sites...*

● Mayo Clinic Health Oasis, maintained by the Mayo Clinic *(www.mayohealth.org)*.

● CBS Health Watch, the consumer health Web site maintained by Medscape, a comprehensive site for physicians *(www.cbshealth watch.com)*.

● Intelihealth, maintained by Johns Hopkins University School of Medicine *(www.intelihealth. com)*.

Another option: For nearly every condition, there's an organization and/or government agency that provides printed material for no more than the cost of a stamped, self-addressed envelope.

More information: Contact the National Health Information Center in Washington, DC. *www.nhic-nt.health.org.* 800-336-4797. It will direct you to the appropriate organization for your condition.

Especially Good Deals... But You Have to Be Over 50 to Get Them

Joan Rattner Heilman, author of *Unbelievably Good Deals & Great Adventures That You Absolutely Can't Get Unless You're Over 50*. Contemporary Books.

If you're willing to speak up and identify yourself as a "senior," you can save a lot of money.

Here are some of the best moneysavers available today for people over age 50.

BARGAIN LEGAL SERVICES

Members of AARP are entitled to a free 30-minute consultation with a lawyer participating with the AARP Legal Services Network.

In addition...for a fixed fee, you can get a simple will ($50 for singles, $75 for couples) or a power of attorney ($35 each).

For other legal services, the cost is 20% less than the attorney's usual fee.

AARP maintains a roster of community lawyers with experience in areas of legal practice that older people need.

The Legal Services Network is available in close to 300 locations in 31 states and the District of Columbia. AARP expects the services to be available in every state in a couple of years.

You can also find a list of lawyers' names and locations in your area on the Internet at *www.aarp.org/lsn* or by writing to LSN Fulfillment, Box 1000084, Pittsburgh 15233.

Or—look in your local Yellow Pages in the "Associations," "Attorneys" or "Lawyers" sections under the heading "AARP Legal Services Network."

CAMPING WITH GRANDKIDS

For a cheap, fun holiday with grandchildren next summer, check the Sierra Club's list of outings for a six-day stay just for kids and grandparents at a rustic lodge in California's Sierra Nevada Mountains. You get lodging, meals and your choice of activities from hiking and swimming to fishing and sightseeing.

HOTEL DISCOUNTS

You can get up to 50% off standard rates at all Novotel Hotels (800-668-6835) in the US and Canada simply by stating your age. You need only be 55—and ready to prove it—to get your discount.

Exceptions: At the Novotel New York, the age requirement is 60, and at the Novotel Montreal Center, the requirement is age 65.

SCANDINAVIAN BARGAINS

If you buy tickets in the US, you'll get special senior fares from SAS Airlines on flights within Norway.

Purchase your tickets in Norway and you'll get an even better deal—half fare—if you've hit 67.

In Denmark, SAS gives you 20% off some domestic fares at age 65.

In Sweden, inquire about the special senior fares.

Finland has the best deals. Finnair offers you tickets at 70% to 75% off the regular fares on domestic flights.

You must be at least 65 years old and buy your tickets in Finland three days in advance. Call Finnair at 800-950-5000.

NEW YORK CITY

You can eat cheaper in New York if you get a copy of the free *Fifty Plus Diner's Guide,* a directory published by New York City's Department of Consumer Affairs.

It lists scores of restaurants—in every neighborhood of the city—that offer special dining deals for the older crowd.

Some restaurants give discounts of 10% to 20% to diners over the age of 50, while others give special breaks on early bird or pretheater dinners.

For a free copy of the guide, call 212-487-4444 or download the guide from the Web at *www.ci.nyc.ny.us/consumers.*

CAR RENTAL

If you're renting a car, shop around, but be sure to check out Thrifty Car Rental (800-367-2277). Customers over age 55 get a straightforward deal—10% off Thrifty's lowest rates. *Bonus:*

This price break even applies to most of the company's promotional and already discounted rates. Most other car rental agencies give you a discount, but only on the regular rates.

When you make a reservation, first ask for the very best rate for the car you want, then ask for the 55-plus discount on top of that.

Cindy McIntyre's System To Save a Small Fortune Shopping On-Line

Cindy McIntyre, editor of *The Frugal Gazette,* Box 3395, Newtown, CT 06470.

The Internet is a bargain hunter's paradise—if you know where to find the best deals.

SAVING BIG ON-LINE

●**Take advantage of secret catalog sales.** Many companies hold clearance sales on their Web sites that are not otherwise advertised in their catalogs. *Examples...*

●**J. Crew** recently offered a V-neck merino-wool sweater for $12.99, reduced from its $60 catalog price. *www.jcrew.com.*

●**Lands' End** offered an overstocked wool tartan robe for $51.50, reduced from $175. *www.landsend.com.*

Each retail Web site asks for your E-mail address so you can receive notices of special deals and sales that don't go out to their customers who receive catalogs by mail.

Use your Internet service provider's search engine to see if your favorite store has a Web site. Or visit *www.catalogzone.com* for a list of retailer Web sites.

●**Compare prices at on-line stores.** I speed up the bargain-hunting process by visiting *http://shopping.yahoo.com.* It scans hundreds of merchant Web sites and provides side-by-side price comparisons of equipment, including videocassette recorders, computer software, compact discs, flowers, office supplies and much more.

Once armed with this price information, I visit *www.buy.com,* which offers to beat the lowest on-line competitor's price by 10%.

●**Visit sites with links to consumer-conscious sites.** Perhaps my all-time favorite Web site for saving money is *www.consumer world.org.*

Run by Consumer World, this noncommercial site was created by a former director of consumer education for the Massachusetts State Consumer Affairs division.

This site features links to more than 1,800 other consumer-related sites that offer discount prices and coupons on everything from luggage to wedding gowns to car rentals.

Example: Recently I found a link that allowed me to book a hotel room that normally cost $75 per night for just $44.95.

It also has valuable links to sites that provide rate-saving advice on credit cards and mortgages.

●**Link up with other bargain hunters.** The new Mercata Web site *(www.mercata.com)* pools buyers for deep discounts on products ranging from golf clubs to blenders.

Mercata is run by Vulcan Ventures, a venture capital group. It prenegotiates volume discounts with about 150 manufacturers, including Cuisinart, RCA and Top-Flite.

There is no fee, and the more people who sign up for a particular item at the Web site, the faster the price drops.

You can even use this collective concept to reduce costs in your own neighborhood.

Example: After using the Internet to research how to start a heating-oil cooperative, I gathered several neighbors together and began bargaining with local fuel companies.

One company offered a group rate of 79 cents per gallon, saving each of us more than $300 per year. *Contact:* Center for Cooperatives at the University of Wisconsin *(www.wiscedu/ uwcc).*

●**Use Web prices to get better deals at your local stores.** More store managers are ready and willing to cut deals to get your business rather than see it go to Web merchants.

What to do: Use an on-line search engine such as AltaVista *(www.altavista.com)* or Yahoo *(www.yahoo.com)* to find the items you want to buy and the names of on-line stores that are selling them.

Print out this information, and take it to retailers in your area that carry the items. Ask if they will meet or beat the prices.

Example: My local bookstore manager agreed to drop the price of a book from $14.95 to $9.95 to match a deal that was offered by Amazon.com.

●**Become an educated used-car buyer.** Cut the cost of a used car by visiting the Kelley Blue Book Web site *(www.kbb.com).* It's a free price guide that helps consumers determine the value of a used car they're considering buying.

Then access *www.edmunds.com,* which asks for the vehicle's ID number. It provides free information on whether that used car is a "lemon."

The motor vehicle departments of 12 states currently submit data to this service.

BEFORE YOU BUY

●**Determine if the Internet merchant has a clean record.** *Two new Web sites provide free information about the reliability of on-line retailers…*

●The Better Business Bureau posts official complaints about Web merchants *(www.bbb.org).*

●BizRate gives customer ratings of on-line merchants *(www.bizrate.com).*

●**Steer clear of merchants that don't list direct contact information.** Reliable merchants clearly list their phone numbers, addresses and refund/return policies on their Web sites.

●**Pay by credit card rather than by debit card** to limit your liability if a dispute comes up.

Important: Use a secure Web browser, such as Netscape and Microsoft's Internet Explorer. Such Web browsers scramble sensitive financial data so that they remain private as they travel through the Internet.

Also print a copy of the order, including the URL of the site, before it is sent.

How Not to Be Ripped Off When Shopping for TVs, Car Stereos, Cell Phones And Cameras

David Elrich, independent reviewer of consumer electronics and cofounder of etown *(www.etown.com),* the largest independent consumer electronics guide on the Internet. He has tested consumer electronics for more than 20 years.

Buying consumer electronics isn't easy. Prices on specific models vary widely from store to store, leaving dishonest salespeople plenty of room to manipulate your impressions and talk you into buying what they want you to buy. *Here are some of their dirty tricks...*

TVs ON THE BLINK

To convince consumers to buy more expensive TVs, some stores purposely alter the pictures of cheaper sets to make the expensive ones look better.

Some stores also leave the cheaper sets' remote control handsets broken or without batteries. This move further enhances the image of the more expensive TVs that are working perfectly nearby. *Self-defense...*

● **Know the exact model you want before you buy.** You can decide on the model that's right for you by visiting a few electronics stores and company Web sites. Fully examine the ones that are within your budget, and insist on a working remote.

● **Never compare the picture of a large set with that of a smaller one.** The pictures on larger screens are never as bright as smaller ones. And...the pictures produced from a VCR feed are rarely as sharp as the pictures from the new Digital Video Disc (DVD) players. Make sure you are comparing apples to apples.

● **Look head-on at big-screen pictures.** Rear-projection images look sharper when viewed at eye level. If a rear-projection screen is on the floor, squat down for a better angle when viewing these screens.

UNSOUND CAR STEREOS

In many stores, stereo-speaker customers are led into a sound room where a salesperson sits them down in a chair and plays a wide range of speakers for them. *Traps...*

● **The quality of the sound** that you hear from speakers is heavily dependent on the room in which they're played.

● **A disreputable salesperson** might not be playing the set of speakers he/she claims he's playing.

Self-defense: Purchase a set of speakers only if they come with a guarantee that they can be returned for a complete refund if you don't like the sound once you install them.

Many stores will try to charge a restocking fee for returns or will not allow returns unless the item is broken. Ask about this policy prior to purchase.

Important: Be sure the sound you hear is coming from the speakers the salesperson claims. Get close enough to tell.

● **Don't be drawn in by low-cost car-stereo stores or the promise of free installation.** With car-stereo products, especially speakers, the quality of installation is at least as important as the quality of the components.

An expert installer will have worked with many different cars and will take the time to get it right before cutting into your vehicle. It makes sense to buy from an expert and to pay a bit more for installation.

● **Beware of car-stereo subwoofers and graphic equalizers.** The former is only necessary if you're a teen who listens to music that requires super-enhanced bass. The latter adjusts the tone of the sound with up to 15 different buttons and is totally unnecessary if you buy a decent and well-installed stereo and speakers.

EXCESSIVE CAMERAS

There are three popular formats—35mm... Advanced Photo System (APS), which uses special film...and digital cameras. Most salespeople will push the digital technology—the latest—as the greatest.

Reality: Even though digital cameras are much more expensive, the quality of the printed picture isn't as good as those from 35mm or

APS. It's also more expensive to get digital and APS pictures developed.

Unless your intent is to view your photos primarily on a computer screen, wait for digital technology to improve further. *Other traps...*

•Don't buy more lens than you need. A lens range of 45mm to 135mm is all most amateur photographers need. More powerful lenses will be heavy, expensive and—unless you're interested in quite specific nature photos or other specialty photography—you won't be using them much.

•Beware of unfamiliar names or model numbers from well-known manufacturers. Stores sometimes sell name-brand models that were destined for foreign markets. There usually isn't anything wrong with these "gray market" goods—but they might not be covered by a manufacturer's warranty when sold in the US.

UNREAL PHONE DEALS

One of the most popular cell-phone sales pitches is "Sign up for a long-term plan, get the phone free." A free phone might have been a big deal a few years ago, but today many phones cost far less than $100—close to free.

Meanwhile, the cost of cell-phone service is dropping so rapidly that a long-term arrangement that sounds fine today could look pricey tomorrow. *Other traps...*

•Skip the cell-phone bells and whistles. Very few people use text messaging or other high-end options. *Options consumers find worthwhile:* Digital capability and compact size.

•Shop elsewhere for accessories. Some cell-phone store salespeople will try to sell you cigarette-lighter cell-phone battery chargers, leather carrying cases and dozens of other things. If you want these items, shop around at major electronics retailers...and check on-line deals, too. *Examples...*

- •Motorola, *www.mot.com*
- •Nokia, *www.nokia.com*

MORE MONEYSAVERS

•Don't buy an extended warranty. With modern consumer electronics, the vast majority of problems will be obvious right out of the box—at which point you're still covered by the manufacturer's warranty.

•Buy the floor model if you'll save at least 20% off the sale price. In my experience, virtually all retailers should be willing to go *at least* this low to sell a floor model. But before buying, test the unit to be sure it's working. Then lift and shake the item. If you hear any loose parts inside, don't buy it. Be sure the model comes with a full manufacturer's warranty and the right to return it for a full refund within at least a week.

Supermarket Savings
Secrets of Super Shoppers

Janet Paré, who lives in Nashua, NH, with her husband and two children. She teaches seminars and writes a newspaper column on couponing.

Susan Samtur, editor of *Refundle Bundle,* which lists manufacturer rebate offers, Box 140, Yonkers, NY 10710.

It is a myth that clipping coupons and filling out manufacturer rebate forms are too time-consuming for too little reward. Some shoppers have become so masterful at both that they save thousands of dollars a year on groceries. And—it takes them just one hour of work each week.

Two of the country's leading coupon and rebate experts share their secrets...

COUPONS
Janet Paré

I recently bought $469.07 worth of groceries and paid just three cents for them by using coupons. *Here are my best coupon strategies— for saving the most money at the supermarket...*

•Size up your local supermarkets. To attract business, many supermarkets will automatically double or triple the value of cents-off coupons.

Helpful: Call all your local supermarkets to see which ones offer the best deal on coupons. Or visit *www.fluffynet.com/doubles/* for a list of stores in your state that double and triple coupons.

•Use your coupons to buy the smallest sizes. Coupons that don't specifically require a certain size to be purchased are best for products that come in tiny, travel sizes.

Example: I use my 50-cents-off shaving cream coupons to buy the manufacturer's three-ounce canisters. They cost 59 cents each, compared with the 11-ounce canisters that cost $1.50 each. Because the coupon is doubled, I get "paid" 41 cents to take the three-ounce size...rather than paying 50 cents for the 11-ounce size.

●**Ask for a rain check when your store runs out of a product.** Your store's inventory problem can actually be a bonanza for you.

Example: My supermarket advertised that a deodorant was on sale for 99 cents each. But when I arrived, the store had run out of it. So the store manager offered me a rain check on as many sticks of deodorant as I wanted. I asked for 10. Then I asked a friend who clips coupons for 10 $1-off coupons for the brand—and got all of the deodorants for free when they came in one week later.

●**Find the coupons you need on-line.** You can sign up on Internet coupon-trading bulletin boards for free. You type in the coupons you need and swap with other shoppers around the country for the coupons they need. Coupons are exchanged by regular mail and arrive within five days.

Helpful: Clip the most sought-after coupons from your Sunday newspaper—even if you don't use the products featured. They'll come in handy to trade for the things you want.

Most desirable: Coupons with high value —75 cents or more—on everyday items. *Also:* Any coupon for juice, cheese, baby formula or diapers. *My favorite coupon-swapping sites...*

●*www.kachinaweb.com*

●*www.jlyne.com*

●**Visit manufacturer Web sites.** Many companies will send you free coupons for filling out brief customer surveys on their Web sites.

To find a site: Type the name of the product or manufacturer into a search engine such as *www.yahoo.com.*

●**Order the coupons you want.** When I want a certain coupon—or I need to stock up on coupons that I use frequently—I'm willing to pay a handling charge of five to 10 cents for a $1-off coupon.

Leading source: Mary's World. Mary Pohli clips hundreds of coupons. Then she posts them on her Web site. She charges five to 10 cents per coupon as a handling fee. The site's coupons are updated weekly. *www.marys world.com.*

REBATES
Susan Samtur

I haven't had to pay for spaghetti sauce, toilet paper or razor blades in years. I'm able to get them for free at the supermarket by sending in for manufacturer rebates.

How rebates work: Manufacturers reward you with cash—typically $1 to $5—coupons and merchandise in return for receipts and proof of purchase labels from product packages.

Rebate forms are available at supermarket courtesy counters and in popular women's magazines.

It takes six to eight weeks to receive your rebate from the manufacturer. The cash you receive is considered a discount by the IRS—not income—so it is tax free.

The bank account that I opened 27 years ago just for the cash rebates that I receive in the mail has grown to more than $35,000 now. *My best rebate strategies...*

●**Use the SOS method (Save/Organize/Send) to keep track of rebates.** Rebating requires a little more work than couponing, but it's worth it. *To streamline the process...*

●Save. When I buy many products involved in a rebate offer, I request a separate receipt for each one purchased. If the cashier is too busy, I'll ask for "duplicate" receipts from the manager. If this type of receipt is not available, I'll cut each item listed on my original receipt...tape it onto a letter-sized sheet of white paper...and write the date and store name on it. Manufacturers have accepted all of my receipts in this form.

●Organize. Peel off the UPC codes from all packages as soon as you get home. Jot down the product name and weight, and staple it to the cash register receipt. Then file your UPCs and receipts alphabetically by product name. File your rebate forms by expiration date so you know which offers are winding down each week.

●Send. I read each rebate offer form carefully to see what's required. Manufacturers will reject a form if it has expired—or if the instructions were not followed perfectly.

Common mistakes: Forgetting to circle the purchase price of an item on the cash register receipt…buying the wrong size product in order to qualify for the rebate…listing a post office box number instead of a street for your return address. (To prevent fraud, many companies will not honor rebates unless you use a street address.)

I also keep a notebook in which I write down the date that I send away for an offer …what the offer required me to send in…and the date that the offer expires.

●**Look for *no-size* rebate offers.** Some mail-in rebates require a UPC bar code from a product but allow you to buy any size to qualify. That lets you buy the most economical item in the brand line and still get the same amount of money or merchandise back.

●**Use premium offers as holiday gifts.** Premiums are rebate offers that reward you with merchandise such as CDs, clothing, free movie-rental certificates, etc. The best place to find them is on cereal and health and beauty aid packages and in Sunday newspaper inserts and magazines.

●**Combine couponing and rebating.** This is called a *triple play*. You buy an item on sale, use a coupon to reduce the cost and then get more money back in the mail through a rebate offer.

Example: At one of my supermarkets, an 11-ounce tube of my favorite toothpaste costs $2.49. I waited for a sale, when the price was $1.99. Then I used a coupon that appeared in my Sunday newspaper for $1 off any product made by the company. Then I mailed in a $2.49 rebate form that came inside the package. Even with the cost of a stamp, I still made $1.17 on the tube.

Buy Sister Brands

Major manufacturers often make several virtually identical lines of appliances—and charge more for the one with the manufacturer's name on it. *Alternatives to consider:* Frigidaire makes Gibson, Kelvinator and Tappan…Maytag makes Admiral, Magic Chef and Jenn-Air.

Tightwad Living, Box 629, Burgin, KY 40310.

Wonderful Ways To Slash Travel Costs Without Giving Up Service, Style, Fun…

Steve and Patty Tanenbaum, editors of *Steve and Pat's Cheap Travel Newsletter,* Box 1956, Lafayette, CA 94549. They are coauthors of *The Cheapskate's Guide to Cruises* and *The Cheapskate's Guide to Vacations,* both from Carol Publishing.

There are dozens of ways to cut the cost of travel. But too often those corner-cutters force you to take flights that are inconvenient or stay at hotels that don't meet your standards. *Most helpful…*

●**Pay a small commission…earn big savings.** Few travel agents charge to set up travel plans. That's because airlines and cruise lines pay their commissions. Travel agents that do charge small fees share their airline commissions with you—which can cut the cost of your trip by hundreds of dollars.

Example: You can pay a booking fee of about $35 to arrange a $3,000 Caribbean cruise. Discount agencies may give you a $210 discount. The incentive for the agency to share the commission up front is to bring in more money in the long run by attracting volume and repeat business.

Examples of travel agents who share commissions…

●**Travelers Advantage** provides members with a 5% rebate on all travel arrangements. *Membership:* $59.95/yr. Includes one-night-free hotel voucher…and four American Airlines vouchers for up to $700 in discounts. 800-548-1116.

●**Travel Avenue** offers a 7% rebate on vacation packages and cruises. *Fee:* $35/person/trip. 800-333-3335.

183

•**Book passage aboard *repositioning* ships.** Twice a year, certain cruise ships reposition from one area of the world to another. In September, ships sailing in Europe or Alaska reposition to the Caribbean…and in April, they reposition to Europe or Alaska. The courses that these ships take are often deeply discounted.

Example: The Dawn Princess of Princess Cruise Lines repositions in September and April between Vancouver, British Columbia, and San Juan, Puerto Rico. The ship makes 14 stops along the way. *Rates:* $1,000 for 21 days—which is about what it costs for a seven-day trip any other time of the year. 800-774-6237.

Travel agents can access lists of cruise ships that sail these relocation routes.

•**Send for free travel coupons.** Large food companies sometimes offer special little-known travel-savings coupons.

How it works: Look for coupon-offer forms in the glossy inserts in Sunday newspapers. Buy the products required to take advantage of the promotions. Then mail in your purchase receipts or bar codes along with the form to obtain the coupons.

Within four to six weeks, the company will send you travel coupons with the company logo. The coupons can be used as instant cash discounts when you book your trip through a large, national travel agency that the company has selected.

The chosen travel agencies usually accept $100 of your travel coupons for any three-day air-and-land vacation, excluding charter flights …$300 for a seven-day package…and $500 for a 14-day or longer package.

Example: Last year, we purchased $104 worth of Johnny Cat kitty litter and received $3,000 in travel coupons.

In all, I've received $11,000 in travel coupons to use as discounts on trips. In most cases, there is no limit on how many travel coupons you can accumulate. And what you don't use, you are allowed to give to family and friends.

•**Buy entertainment/dining discount books.** Entertainment Publications publishes editions for more than 100 foreign and domestic cities, filled with discount coupons. Two-thirds of each book usually is devoted to two-for-one dining discounts. The rest covers tourist activities. *Cost:* About $40. The books pay for themselves within the first few days of a vacation. *To find a local distributor who sells the books:* 800-374-4464.

Example: On a recent trip to Maui, Hawaii, we used the book's coupons to save $290. We received a free $45 parasailing ride…a free $50 luau…$65 off on a snorkeling cruise…and a free $130 interisland Aloha Airlines ticket.

For international cities, there are discounts in the *For Less* series of guidebooks, published by Metropolis and sold in bookstores and at *www.for-less.com.*

Example: *Paris for Less* comes with an eight-day discount card that gives about 25% off at hundreds of restaurants and sights. We have saved hundreds of dollars using this book.

Frugality Secrets from The World's Tightest Penny-Pincher

Amy Dacyczyn, author of *The Complete Tightwad Gazette: Promoting Thrift as a Viable Alternative Lifestyle.* Random House. She lives in Leeds, ME, with her husband and their six children.

Frugality is nothing to be ashamed of. Frugal people are just making choices—the trade-offs necessary to reach their financial goals.

Wealth is not how much you *earn*…it is how much you *accumulate.* Wealthy people tend to be those who work hard, save and thoughtfully invest money.

Golden rule of penny-pinching: Use materials you have before you spend money on new items. *Here are the best ways to do that, along with my favorite money-saving strategies…*

BEST BARGAINS EVER

•**Toothpaste and dental floss.** Next time you're at the dentist, think about how much toothpaste and floss you could buy for the cost of that filling.

•**Paper and crayons**—they are still the best gifts for any child.

•**Noncable television.** People like to bash TV, but there are plenty of worthwhile programs.

•**Postage stamps.** The sheer volume of material that can be included in a one-ounce letter is amazing—and the post office will carry it thousands of miles for only 33 cents.

And E-mail, of course, is a great bargain for computer owners.

•**Potatoes.** Pound for pound, potatoes offer more nutrients for lower cost than any other food.

My favorite cheap-and-easy meal: Baked potato (cooking in the microwave costs less than the oven) topped with chopped, steamed broccoli and cheese sauce. Sprinkle with bacon bits. I feed my entire family for about $1 because I buy economy-size bags of potatoes and make my own sauce.

Other tasty-but-tightwad topping combinations: Chili and cheese...sour cream and chives...cheese and mushrooms...meat sauce.

FREEBEES

•**Free attractions.** Look in your local paper for museums, gardens, historical buildings, etc. They are often listed in the calendar section. Check the library for *Guide to Free Attractions, USA* and *Guide to Free Campgrounds.*

•**Free information.** The federal government publishes hundreds of free consumer guides, from *College Handbook* to *Understanding Social Security.* For a free catalog of publications, call 888-878-3256...or go to *www.pueblo.gsa.gov.*

•**Free posters.** The US Postal Service sends promotional posters for new stamps to every post office in the country. If you see one you like, ask the postmaster if you can have it when the office is done with it.

Also ask at your video store for outdated movie posters.

•**"Free" health club membership.** See if you can work part-time in exchange for free membership. Many clubs have child-care rooms and are looking for moms to staff them.

•**"Free" baby-sitting.** Know a college student living in your area? Offer to let him/her use your washer and dryer in exchange for a night of baby-sitting at your house.

•**Freebees from your congressperson.** Elected officials occasionally offer free calendars and other items. If you're planning a trip to Washington, DC, ask your congressional representative for free passes to restricted Senate and House galleries.

IN YOUR CAR

•**Car repairs.** Inquire at a local vocational school—students may need cars to fix. Most schools charge only for paint and parts.

•**Obey the speed limit.** This saves on gasoline, of course, but it also reduces wear on tires, brakes and other car components. And it reduces your risk of costly (and dangerous) accidents and speeding tickets—and the increased insurance premiums that go along with them.

IN THE KITCHEN

•**Save energy when cooking.** When preparing rice or pasta, bring water to a boil... add noodles or rice...bring back to a boil *...and turn off the burner.* Leave covered for 10 to 20 minutes, stirring occasionally to prevent sticking.

Many other foods can be prepared using residual heat, rather than keeping the burner on the entire time.

•**Watch what you drink.** Tap water is the cheapest thirst quencher. Homemade iced tea costs five cents per eight-ounce glass...Kool-Aid, 13 cents...apple juice, 25 cents.

If you must have a soft drink, a serving from a one-liter bottle costs about 20 cents, versus 30 cents for the same amount from a can.

AROUND THE HOUSE

•**Carpeting.** When replacing wall-to-wall carpeting, cut out sections from under the beds and sofas where the carpet is not worn. Take them to your carpet dealer for binding and use them as area rugs.

Opportunity: Ask your carpet store for old samples, which are often thrown out. Use them in the car, bathroom, doorways or basement.

•**"Free" paint.** Don't throw out old, half-empty cans of paint. Instead mix them together, and use to repaint the basement, garage or toolshed—someplace where you're not picky about the color.

Caution: Don't use paint from before 1980 —it may contain lead. And never mix oil-based paint with latex paint. But you can mix interior paint with exterior...and flat with semigloss.

Better Home Computer Buying

Visit retail stores in the middle of the week —not on weekends—to avoid crowds and to get more attention from salespeople. Buy from salespeople who help you figure out the right machine for the work you do and the space you have available. Get all product recommendations and prices in writing. Contact at least three different retailers to comparison shop. When checking prices from telephone and Web sellers, don't forget to include shipping costs and sales tax if it applies.

Eric Grevstad, editor in chief, *Home Office Computing*, 156 W. 56 St., New York 10019.

Long-Distance Calling Alternative

If all the "discount" long-distance calling plans you try turn out to have unexpected charges, cancel all your long-distance services and use prepaid calling cards instead. *Example:* Co-branded AT&T/ Sam's Club calling cards cost 10 cents a minute, and that's it. *Option:* Go "partway" by using prepaid cards when traveling, instead of using credit cards or reversing charges. And give prepaid cards to grandchildren when they go away to college, summer camp, etc.

Neil Sachnoff, president, TeleCom Clinic, 4402 Stonehedge Rd., Edison, NJ 08820.

Not All Tickets Are Non-Refundable

Refunds on nonrefundable tickets may be available if you book through a travel agent—not directly from the airlines—and are a good customer. Some agents will allow refunds on any tickets if you ask the same week you buy them, before the agency closes its books for the week.

Reason: Airlines do not see the tickets some agencies have written until the agencies close their books.

Caution: Not all agents' systems allow this special service. Agents that do offer special treatment reserve it for good customers.

Randy Petersen, publisher, *InsideFlyer,* 4715-C Town Ctr. Dr., Colorado Springs, CO 80916.

New Privacy Danger

A federal court decision allows phone companies to sell data about customers to third parties—without customers' permission. Phone companies successfully argued their right of free commercial speech lets them use data they collect any way they wish.

Troubling trend: Many Web sites collect browsing preferences...banks sell account information...and even medical files are not fully protected. The court decision on phone data is being appealed. If it stands, contact your local and long-distance companies and opt out of all data-transfer arrangements.

John Featherman, president, Privacy Protectors, consumer consultants, Philadelphia.

Related Useful Sites

Finance

☐ CNNfn—The Financial Network
www.cnnfn.com

Comprehensive, up-to-the-minute coverage from CNN. Market reports, business features, instant stock quotes and more.

☐ CNBC.com
www.cnbc.com

More than the adjunct of a popular cable station, CNBC now offers the best stock charting software on-line. You can track stocks against one another going back 5 years, create your own "ticker" of stocks you own and get tons of stock tips from reputable investment bankers and mutual fund managers.

☐ The Street
www.thestreet.com

Unlike the typical dry prose of most popular financial and investment publications, this on-line e-zine/investment newsletter offers lively, somewhat irreverent, yet thoughtful comments on current investment issues. Also, discussion forums on mutual fund issues, stocks, individual companies and more. Well-written content rich and useful to individual investors seeking hard-hitting analysis.

☐ The Wall Street Journal
www.wsj.com

Not free, but well worth the money if you need good financial information. For $59 a year ($29 for those who subscribe to the print version), you get the full content of the newspaper on-line, plus stock and mutual fund quotes updated every 15 minutes and detailed financial reports on more than 9,000 publicly traded companies. Track your investments with your own on-line portfolio. Especially useful: Personalized "clipping" service reports news on only the topics you request.

☐ NASDAQ
www.nasdaq.com

There are lots of sites that offer stock quotes. This is Nasdaq's own, so you can check only your Nasdaq stocks and mutual funds. But it's straightforward and simple to use. Don't know the "ticker" symbol? Go to Symbol Look-Up. Quickly get full quotes (best bid, best ask, today's high, today's low, last sale, previous close, net change and share volume). Press button bar for Market

Activity, the Nasdaq Companies, Investor Resources and News. There is even a Portfolio Tracking feature that lists the performance of your picks at a glance. Site is very fast and efficient, with few bells or whistles to slow you down.

☐ Quotesmith
www.quotesmith.com

Get quotes for life insurance policies from a long list of different insurers by simply typing in your unique circumstances where prompted. It takes no more than 10 minutes to fill out the form and another 30 seconds for a list of quotes to pop up on your screen.

☐ Savvy Discounts
www.clis.com/savvynews

Check here for great tips on saving money. Simple, speedy site offers *special reports* from past issues: Pay less for gas, save on long-distance phone calls, 16 ways to save money on medicine, more. Order back issues or subscribe while on-line and get a free review of 50 great mail-order deals.

☐ The Dollar Stretcher
www.stretcher.com

Here's a great site for people who are trying to make their budgets work (aren't we all?). There are tons of tips on all different subjects. Learn the *10 most common mistakes people make when setting up an on-line business*, get the very latest on bank rate information and be sure to check out the *car care clinic*.

☐ Newslinx.com
www.newslinx.com

Want to know what's happening in electronic commerce? This simple page of links is updated each minute with new stories from newspapers, wire services, magazines and more. It's the first place top reporters in the field turn to each day to keep up with what's happening.

☐ Freetimejobs.com
www.freetimejobs.com

A great site for those looking to make a few extra dollars in their spare time, from manual labor to high-tech applications, or for people looking to hire freelance help.

Taxes

☐ TaxWeb

www.taxweb.com

Information on federal, state and local tax developments. Categories include tax forms, where to file, filing extensions, refunds, federal and state legislation and more.

☐ The Digital Daily

www.irs.gov

The IRS's user-friendly site, packed with easy-to-read information on tax issues for individuals as well as businesses. Also allows you to quickly download tax forms, which means no more visits to the post office.

☐ Tax and Accounting Sites Directory

www.taxsites.com

Handy guide to tax and accounting sites, including articles, forms, software and associations.

☐ Nolo.com

www.nolo.com/category/tax_home.html

From Nolo Press, publishers of consumer and small business legal and tax information, this site contains abundant information for individuals who need to know how to survive an audit, how to file late without penalties and much more. Also answers to frequently asked questions about small business taxes.

Consumer Information

☐ Better Business Bureau

www.bbb.org

Before making a purchase from a business you've never patronized before, make sure it hasn't received an unusual number of complaints from customers. Easy on-line searches through Better Business Bureau databases turn up useful consumer information. Or use the site to locate the BBB office nearest you.

☐ National Fraud Information Center

www.fraud.org

You'll want to check this site frequently to learn how to protect yourself from Internet scams and telemarketing schemes. Also includes excellent information on specific frauds perpetrated against the elderly, how to report fraudulent activity and which questions to ask.

Shopping

☐ BarnesandNoble.com

www.bn.com

Shop this world famous bookstore on-line. Browse all the current bestsellers as well as the classics. You can also purchase CDs, magazines, software and more. Be sure to check out the *New Yorker Magazine's Cartoon of the Day.*

☐ CNET Shopper.com

www.shopper.com

This easy-to-navigate site compares more than a million prices from computer cyberstores. There are links to more than 100,000 products, a Hot List, which lets you easily browse through various products and much, much more.

☐ 911gifts.com

www.911gifts.com

An excellent site if you need to send a gift in a hurry. Choose from a long list of categories to find something that will delight the person you're shopping for. You can even consult the gift expert for help with your selection and get a personalized E-Mail response within 24 hours.

☐ eToys

www.etoys.com

This site is billed as the "Internet's Biggest Toy Store." There's a searchable database, or you can select from a long list of categories and well-known brands. You can also choose from software, music, videos and video games.

11

Retirement Planning

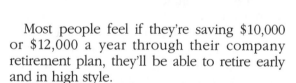

How to Save for Your Retirement...in 40s... In 50s...in 60s...Beyond

 s rewarding as large-cap growth stocks have been over the past year, concentrating most of your retirement savings in this hot category can imperil your financial future.

Example: In the early 1970s, investors who were nearing retirement and who put all of their assets in large-cap growth stocks saw the value of their holdings drop by at least one-third during the 1973–1974 bear market.

Diversification is the best approach for reducing risk and boosting returns over the long term. But the type of diversification you choose depends on how close you are to retirement.

20 YEARS UNTIL RETIREMENT

If you are in your 30s or 40s, your 401(k) plan is a major threat to your financial future. *Reason:* Complacency.

Most people feel if they're saving $10,000 or $12,000 a year through their company retirement plan, they'll be able to retire early and in high style.

Reality: You probably need to save a lot more than you have been saving—outside of your 401(k) and IRA—and for a longer period of time.

My savings rule is that the number of years you must save for retirement while you're still working must equal the number of years you expect to spend in retirement.

A sure way to create future wealth when you are in your 30s or 40s is to concentrate on growth stocks or stock funds. These are stocks whose earnings, sales and market shares are expanding faster than the market in general.

My allocation: 80% to 90% in stocks...and 10% to 20% in bonds. *My formula for dividing the stock portion...*

David Foster, president of Foster & Motley, Inc., an investment advisory firm, 9477 Kenwood Rd., Cincinnati 45242. He was named by *Worth* as one of the country's top financial planners for the past three years.

●**Large-cap stock funds/55%.** Large-cap stocks are still the most stable asset class around. *Consider investing half of this allocation in a fund that tracks a major stock market index...*

●Vanguard Tax-Managed Capital Appreciation Fund. This fund tracks the Russell 1000 Index. 800-523-7731.

Put the other half in a "concentrated fund"—a fund that holds relatively few stocks in important sectors of the market...

●White Oak Growth Stock. This fund holds fewer than 25 stocks with more than half of its assets in technology. 888-462-5386.

●**Mid-cap/15%...**

●Longleaf Partners. This conservative value fund recently reopened to new investors. 800-445-9469.

●**Small-cap/15%...**

●Royce Premier. This low-risk value fund is run by top manager Chuck Royce. 800-221-4268.

●**International/15%...**

●Acorn International. This diversified growth-oriented fund holds 172 stocks in 34 different countries. 800-922-6769.

For the bond portion of your holdings, consider investing in one of two Vanguard no-load bond funds, depending on your tax bracket...

If you're in the 28% tax bracket: Vanguard Total Bond Index Fund.

If you're in the 31% or higher tax bracket: Vanguard Intermediate-Term Fund.

10 YEARS UNTIL RETIREMENT

If you are in your 50s and have saved a sizable amount for retirement, you should be able to achieve your goals with a moderate-growth portfolio. Such a medium-risk portfolio should return about 8.5% a year over the long term. To create this portfolio, you'll need to shift some of your stock allocation to bonds.

My allocation: 70% stocks/30% bonds.

●**Large-cap/55%.** *Put half of these assets in...*

●Vanguard Tax-Managed Capital Appreciation Fund. 800-523-7731.

Divide the remainder between...

●T. Rowe Price Dividend Growth. This is a conservative value-oriented fund. 800-638-5660.

●White Oak Growth Stock. 888-462-5386.

●**Mid-cap/15%.** *Invest all of this portion in...*

●Longleaf Partners. 800-445-9469.

●**Small-cap/15%.** *Invest the total amount in...*

●Royce Premier. 800-221-4268.

●**International/15%.** *Divide assets between...*

●Acorn International.

●UMB Scout WorldWide. Invests mainly in foreign stocks listed on US exchanges. 800-996-2862.

To diversify your bond portion, invest half in one of the two tax-advantaged bond funds in the portfolio for 20 years until retirement. *Invest the other half in...*

●**Metropolitan West Low Duration Bond Fund.** 800-241-4671.

FIVE YEARS UNTIL RETIREMENT

When you are in your early 60s, it is time to invest your money more conservatively. But you will still need the money for at least 30 years. That's why you should keep a substantial amount in stocks to protect against inflation.

My allocation: 65% stocks/35% bonds.

●**Large-cap/55%.** *Invest half of this position in...*

●Vanguard Value Index Fund. This fund holds stocks with the lowest price-to-book ratios in the Standard & Poor's/BARRA Value Index. 800-523-7731.

At this point in life, you're more concerned with creating a predictable stream of dividend income than with taxes. *Divide the remainder between...*

●T. Rowe Price Dividend Growth. 800-638-5660.

●White Oak Growth Stock. 888-462-5386.

●**Mid-cap/15%.** *Consider investing in...*

●Longleaf Partners. 800-445-9469.

●**Small-cap/15%.** *Divide your assets between...*

●Royce Premier. 800-221-4268.

●Vanguard Small-Cap Index Fund. Its low expenses enable it to beat many of its actively managed competitors. 800-523-7731.

●**International/15%.** *Divide assets between...*
●UMB Scout Worldwide. 800-996-2862.

• Vanguard Total International Stock Index Fund. 800-523-7731.

Divide the 35% bond allocation between one of the two tax-favorable funds mentioned earlier and *Metropolitan West Low Duration Bond Fund* (800-241-4671).

Too Much of a Good Thing Can Be Risky

Owning too much of an employer's stock can be risky—especially near retirement. Many people hold large investments in employer stock through 401(k) plans or stock options. *Risks:* Stocks can always fall sharply in value—and having too much invested in one company's stock increases the risk. When young, there may be plenty of time for the stock price to recover. But as retirement nears, there will be less time for an investment to recover from a sharp drop before you need money. *Safety:* As you approach retirement, diversify so as not to have all your eggs in one risky basket.

David Strege, CFP, CFA, Financial Planning Association, Denver.

The IRA Mistake Nearly Everyone Makes...and How to Keep It from Costing You Dearly

Melvin L. Maisel, president and CEO, Stabilization Plans for Business, Inc., 1025 Westchester Ave., White Plains, NY 10604, and chairman of the board, Cornerstone Bank, Stamford, CT.

There's a basic mistake that nearly everyone makes with their qualified retirement plans and IRAs, and it could cost your family hundreds of thousands—or even millions—of dollars.

THE BASIC PROBLEM

When you drew up your will you probably consulted with an estate planner, spent several hours working with him/her on it, and reviewed and revised it before it was finally satisfactory.

Moreover, you still revise your will periodically in light of changing family circumstances and changes in the law.

Contrast: When you first set up your qualified retirement plan accounts and IRAs, you probably did little more than sign on the line that was pointed out to you...plus made beneficiary designations without much thought. And you probably haven't reviewed the plans since.

Trap: Each of your retirement plans is in effect a will—controlling the disposition of assets that will pass outside your will.

These plans may be more important than your will to your family. That's not just because of the amount they contain now—often most of a family's wealth—but also because of the decades of tax-favored accumulations they may earn if they are set up correctly.

The big mistake—and nearly everyone makes it—is not realizing that planning for IRAs and other retirement plans requires at least as much thought and planning as drafting a will. This is both because of their importance, and because of the complex, technical rules that apply.

Real danger: An IRA that might have earned tax-favored income through three generations, down to your grandchildren—literally millions of dollars—could be taxed away almost entirely at your death. If not planned for, combined estate and income taxes can reach as high as 80% on the death of the IRA owner and in certain situations can even exceed 100%.

TRAPS TO AVOID

The tax traps waiting for people who fail to plan for IRA distributions are far too numerous to all be listed here.

But the following examples illustrate how much can be at stake—and the importance of getting expert help—in your IRA planning...

Trap: Not moving employer plan funds to an IRA. Upon leaving an employer you can obtain much more control over your retirement plan funds if you roll them over from the employer's retirement plan into your own IRA.

Funds that remain in the employer plan will remain subject to the plan's rules concerning distribution and investment options. And if the plan is terminated—something you can't predict or control—balances may be distributed prematurely relative to your intentions, at potentially great cost.

Trap: Not using the intergenerational power of IRAs. Even a small IRA can become worth millions when left to a young child.

Key: If a beneficiary inherits an IRA before the owner's required beginning date for distributions at age 70½, the beneficiary can take distributions over his own full life expectancy. This can provide tremendous tax-deferred investment returns over many decades.

Example: A 10-year-old child/grandchild inherits an IRA worth $100,000 that earns 10% annually. The child will be able to withdraw $16.4 million from the IRA over his 72-year life expectancy. If the IRA contained only $10,000, then he could receive $1.64 million!

The IRA beneficiary should not be the child and/or grandchild personally, but a trust benefiting the child. That way, the child won't be able to spend all the IRA money at age 18—exhausting it before it has a chance to accumulate.

This is another detail of the kind that requires expert planning.

Trap: Not reducing the minimum annual IRA distribution. As long as money stays within an IRA, funds that would have to be used to pay taxes on a distribution can instead earn tax-deferred investment returns. So you want to reduce your minimum required annual distribution to as little as possible.

Key: If your beneficiary is 10 or more years younger than you, you calculate your required distributions using a joint life expectancy as if the other person were 10 years younger (or the actual age in the case of a spouse). This sharply reduces distributions and the taxes on them.

Example 1: You and your spouse are both age 70, so you have a joint life expectancy of just over 20 years. If you name your spouse as your IRA beneficiary, you will pay 49% more

income tax on minimum IRA distributions over the 20 years than you would if you named your child as the beneficiary.

Example 2: It's even worse if you are single. If you take minimum distributions over a single life expectancy of 16 years, you will pay 90% more tax than if you had a beneficiary 10 years younger than you. This is a second reason to have a young person as an IRA beneficiary.

Planning: As a by-product of the dramatic income tax savings in these examples, family estate tax savings can also occur.

By leaving IRA funds to a child and/or grandchild rather than to the surviving spouse, the family can obtain estate tax savings as high as $359,700.

How: When funds are left to a child and/or grandchild, they get the benefit of the lowest estate tax brackets, so a couple can get the benefit of the lowest brackets twice.

Trap: Using the "recalculation" method to compute minimum required distributions. When you start taking minimum required distributions, *you can elect to receive them using one of two basic methods...*

●**Term certain method.** Annual amounts over your life expectancy determine when you start taking distributions.

If you outlive the distributions or die before they are completed, they will be paid to your beneficiary.

●**Recalculation method.** Your life expectancy and that of you and your spouse is recalculated each year. This allows you to take slightly smaller minimum distributions, which is a small benefit. *But it also contains big tax traps...*

●If your beneficiary dies before you, further distributions are recalculated using a "single" life expectancy, which greatly increases the amount of minimum distributions and taxes on them.

●When you die, your life expectancy becomes zero, so the entire account must be distributed in the next year—taxing everything and eliminating any hope of intergenerational planning.

Caution: The Tax Code makes the recalculation method the "default" method. It is elected automatically unless the term certain method is affirmatively chosen by the taxpayer. And the election, even if made by default, is *irrevocable*.

Best: Overall, the term certain method is best for almost everyone.

Escape: If you've elected the recalculation method but now wish to escape it, you can by converting your IRA to a Roth IRA, if eligible to do so.

Trap: Not using multiple IRAs. You can have as many IRAs as you want, with as many different beneficiaries as you want. You have complete flexibility to change beneficiaries until you begin taking required annual distributions. And you have limited flexibility thereafter. You can, of course, withdraw all the money from any of them as long as you live, under normal rules (subject to the 10% early withdrawal penalty if you're under age 59½).

Best: Set up several IRAs naming your spouse, children and/or grandchildren as separate beneficiaries. Discuss with your estate planner the best assets to put in the various IRAs.

SELF-DEFENSE

The above traps are only the first hurdles in IRA planning. Consult with an IRA specialist to make sure your IRA planning is in accord with your overall estate plan.

Early Withdrawal Trick

You can take funds out of an IRA before age 59½ without penalty through annuity payments of a size calculated to last over your life expectancy.

Catch: Payments must last until you reach age 59½ and at least five years. If you violate the payment schedule, the 10% early withdrawal penalty will apply not just to any improper withdrawal but to all amounts received through the annuity. So you are committed to the annuity schedule.

Example: After an individual started to take early payments, his IRA earned big investment gains. So he asked if he could increase his annuity by an inflation adjustment. *IRS ruling:* No. Any change will result in the penalty.

Letter Ruling 199943050.

Having Several IRAs Can Provide Great Tax Savings...Estate-Planning Benefits, Too

Ed Slott, CPA, E. Slott & Co., CPAs, 100 Merrick Rd., Rockville Centre, NY 11570. *www.irahelp.com.* Mr. Slott is editor and publisher of *Ed Slott's IRA Advisor.* 800-663-1340.

You can own as many IRA accounts as you want. And for most people, it is a good idea to have more than one—probably several.

Having multiple IRAs can help you keep funds in them longer...to earn more tax-deferred investment returns...meet family financial planning goals...reduce estate taxes...and attain other valuable objectives.

IRA FLEXIBILITY

Multiple IRAs can greatly increase your flexibility in managing your IRA wealth. *Keys...*

●**Each IRA can have different beneficiaries.**

●**After reaching age 70½,** your total minimum required annual distribution from all your IRAs can be taken from any one of them—leaving the other IRAs intact.

●**You can transfer funds between IRAs** without any negative consequences until you begin taking required distributions at age 70½.

You can use these rules to get the most from your IRA savings and maximize family wealth. *How to do it...*

●**Preserve funds for children.** When one spouse inherits an IRA from the other, the surviving spouse can place the inherited funds in a *new* IRA set up for this purpose instead of rolling them over into his/her existing IRA. By doing so—and by naming children or grandchildren as beneficiaries of the new IRA—current minimum required distributions may be reduced...and decades worth of tax-deferred IRA earnings may be saved for the children.

Example: Two spouses are both over age 70½, and each owns an IRA. Each has named the other as his IRA beneficiary and is taking minimum annual distributions under the "recalculation" method.

If one spouse dies, the survivor can place inherited IRA funds into either his existing IRA or into a newly created IRA. *If the funds go into...*

The surviving spouse's existing IRA, they must be distributed at a rate based on the spouse's remaining life expectancy—for instance, about 10 years for a 79-year-old. When that spouse dies, all the funds in the IRA must be distributed and taxed within one year.

A new IRA created by the surviving spouse with children named as beneficiaries, the funds may be distributed over the joint life expectancy of the spouse and beneficiaries. (Nonspouse beneficiaries are treated as no more than 10 years younger than the IRA owner regardless of actual age.)

Result: The payout period over which minimum annual distributions must be made is increased to 19 years from 10 years for a 79-year-old IRA owner. This reduces required annual distributions almost by half, leaving more funds in the IRA for the children to inherit.

When the children do inherit the new IRA, they can take distributions from it based on their own life expectancies, which may cover decades. They may receive 30 or 40 years (or more) of tax-deferred IRA earnings and distributions that would have been lost entirely had the second IRA not been created.

That's one benefit of establishing a new, separate IRA to hold the inherited funds—and there's also another.

After the surviving spouse establishes the new IRA, he will own two IRAs—his own old IRA, plus the new IRA with the children as beneficiaries.

The surviving spouse's minimum required annual distribution will be based on the combined balance in both IRAs. But he does not have to take distributions from both IRAs each year. In fact, doing so will deplete funds in the new IRA that benefits the children, while helping preserve the funds in the old IRA—which must be liquidated and taxed on the surviving spouse's death.

Better: The surviving spouse's full minimum required annual distribution can be taken from his own old IRA, leaving the new IRA untouched.

That way, only the old IRA that must be liquidated anyway on the surviving spouse's death is depleted—and the new IRA that benefits the children is left totally intact to grow for their benefit.

●**Flexibly provide for spouse and children.** Before reaching age 70½ you can divide your IRA assets into two IRAs, one with your spouse as beneficiary and the other one with a child as beneficiary.

Later, if your spouse seems adequately provided for (by insurance or otherwise), you can take all your IRA distributions from the IRA with your spouse as beneficiary to leave more for the children—who again may receive decades of benefits.

But if it seems your spouse may need extra funds, you can take all distributions from the IRA with the children as beneficiaries to leave more for your spouse.

Point: You can use the same strategy with several IRAs set up for children, grandchildren or other beneficiaries.

But if you don't create the separate IRAs, and it turns out your spouse won't need the IRA funds, you won't be able to flexibly shift IRA funds to the children or others in this manner—and a big opportunity may be lost.

●**Manage broad family bequests.** By setting up separate IRAs that each have a different child, grandchild or other person as beneficiary, you can fund each IRA with an appropriate amount for the beneficiary's particular needs.

Example: You may place a smaller amount in an IRA with a grandchild as a beneficiary than in one with a child as a beneficiary, because of the extra years of IRA earnings that the younger grandchild will expect to receive.

Tax advantage: By having a separate IRA for each beneficiary, each will be able to take future distributions from the IRA using his own life expectancy. In contrast, if you name several beneficiaries to a single IRA, all may be required to take distributions using the life expectancy of the oldest beneficiary—or else go through the potentially difficult process of breaking up the IRA into separate IRAs.

If the needs of your beneficiaries change over time, you can transfer funds among IRAs. After you begin taking IRA distributions, you can adjust the amount in each IRA by choosing which IRA you will take distributions from.

●**Take penalty-free early distributions.** If you have two or more IRAs, one of which was inherited, you have a special opportunity to take penalty-free early distributions.

Key: The 10% penalty on distributions taken before age 59½ does not apply to funds in an IRA that you inherit as a beneficiary.

That's good enough—but with planning, you will be able to take funds from both IRAs before age 59½ without penalty.

How: Even if you are under age 59½, you will be required to take minimum IRA distributions due to your ownership of the inherited IRA funds. But you do not have to take them from the inherited IRA—you can take them from either IRA.

Strategy: Take the required distributions on the inherited IRA from your own IRA. Because distributions from an inherited IRA are required, they will be penalty free, even if taken from your own IRA. That will leave the funds in the inherited IRA untouched—and you can take all of them penalty free any time you wish.

Payoff: Each year you will find yourself with a larger amount accumulated in the inherited IRA—all of which you can withdraw at any time, penalty free.

●**Manage investments.** You may find it easier to fund different IRAs with different kinds of investments, depending on the particular investment expertise of different IRA trustees—such as banks, brokers, mutual fund companies, etc.

Before you begin taking required distributions, you can rebalance your portfolio periodically with IRA-to-IRA transfers.

After you start taking distributions, you can take all of them from one IRA with investments you want to liquidate...while leaving more promising investments in other IRAs intact.

When Designating IRA Beneficiaries... Biggest Mistakes To Avoid

Seymour Goldberg, Esq., CPA, and Jason S. Goldberg, Esq., partners, Goldberg & Goldberg, PC, 666 Old Country Rd., Suite 600, Garden City, NY 11530. One of the nation's leading authorities on IRA distributions, Seymour Goldberg is author of *Pension Distributions: Planning Strategies, Cases and Rulings.* CPA Journal.

The beneficiary designations you make to your IRA can be vital for protecting your family's financial well-being.

Danger: Beneficiary rules are much more complicated than most people realize—and a mistaken choice can prove tremendously costly to your family.

ERRORS TO AVOID

●*Error.* **Accidentally disinheriting a child's family.** Many people choose to name more than one beneficiary of an IRA. For instance, if you have several children, you may name each a beneficiary, intending to divide the account evenly among them.

Trap: Most IRA beneficiary designation forms provide that if one beneficiary dies before the IRA owner does, all the IRA funds will pass to the surviving beneficiaries on the IRA owner's death. So if you don't—or can't—make out a new beneficiary form, nothing will pass to the family and heirs of the deceased beneficiary.

Example: You have three children, and your oldest child has two children. You name all three of your children as beneficiaries of your IRA, intending each to inherit one-third of it. If your oldest child predeceases you, then when you die your other two children will each receive 50% of the IRA, instead of the 33⅓% you intended—while your grandchildren by the oldest child will receive nothing.

Key: Review your IRA beneficiary designation forms to see how funds will be distributed if a beneficiary dies. Make sure the forms comply with your wishes. *Distributions will be described as being made...*

• **"Per capita"** if they will be made only to surviving beneficiaries.

• **"Per stirpes"** if they will be made to heirs of beneficiaries who die before you.

Problem: Many IRA trustees are reluctant to allow "per stirpes" distributions because they are more complex and increase risk of liability if improper distributions are made.

Example: One of the country's largest mutual fund groups allows "per stirpes" elections to be made only by "premium" customers who have account balances over a specified amount.

If you wish to make "per stirpes" beneficiary elections, you may have to make a special request. If the trustee doesn't allow it, consider moving your IRA to another trustee.

• *Error.* **Naming a minor child as an IRA beneficiary.** *Trap:* When a minor child inherits an IRA directly, a court-appointed legal guardian must be named to administer the IRA funds on the child's behalf.

As a result, your family will get tied up in the court system with all the cost and aggravation that it involves—and with outsiders making decisions that affect your family's welfare.

What to do: Leave the IRA funds to a custodian who will act on behalf of the minor child under the Uniform Transfers to Minors Act (UTMA)—if recognized in your state—or to a trust that you set up on the child's behalf...

• **Under the UTMA,** the child will receive direct control over the IRA upon reaching the age of legal majority, 18 in most states, or until reaching the maximum age permitted by state law.

• **A trust can control the IRA funds** for a longer period of time and under a wider range of conditions.

The UTMA custodian or trustee of the trust can be a person you name, such as a spouse, relative or trusted friend.

• *Error.* **Not naming sufficient beneficiaries.** Many old IRA beneficiary forms provided room to name only two beneficiaries... or even only one.

But for an IRA holding significant funds, and/or in a complex family situation, it is very unlikely that such a form will meet your family and tax objectives.

Best: Review your IRA beneficiary designations in light of your entire estate plan. You may wish to name more beneficiaries to your IRA.

If the form provided by the IRA trustee doesn't have room to name all the beneficiaries you desire, add an attachment that names them and explains your intentions.

• *Error.* **Not naming contingent beneficiaries.** It's important to name a person to take the place of a primary beneficiary who may die before you, or with you.

Example: You name your spouse as your sole beneficiary, and then you and your spouse die simultaneously in a travel accident. Your IRA then will have no beneficiary, so it must be liquidated, taxed and paid to your estate.

Contrast: If you name a contingent beneficiary to take the place of your spouse, the IRA may remain intact and earn tax-deferred investment returns for many years longer.

Even if you have multiple primary beneficiaries, you will want to put thought into naming contingent beneficiaries for each to assure that funds will be passed along as you desire.

• *Error.* **You are a non-spouse who inherits an IRA and you fail to name a successor beneficiary.** It's possible that you will inherit an IRA as a beneficiary. In that case, you should name beneficiaries to the inherited IRA to keep it intact should you die during the payout.

Opportunity: In a new private ruling not yet published, the IRS told a man he could name his own beneficiary to an IRA inherited from his mother. This enables the IRA to remain intact after the death of the person who inherited it, and continue into a third generation.

Contrast: If you die without naming a beneficiary of your inherited IRA, it may then be liquidated and taxed depending on the IRA custodian's internal rules...

• **A person other than a spouse who inherits an IRA** generally is required to take minimum distributions from it over a "term certain" equal to his life expectancy.

• **If that person names a beneficiary to the IRA and then dies,** the beneficiary can take distributions for the rest of the original heir's remaining "term certain." But if there is no beneficiary, the opportunity to preserve the IRA may be lost.

Key: Again, the practical problem is that not all IRA trustees allow such beneficiary designations. The IRS has ruled that designations of successor beneficiaries are legal—but it does not require IRA trustees to accept them.

What to do: Explicitly ask to make such a designation. If the IRA trustee does not permit it, consider moving the IRA to another trustee.

•*Error.* Not naming the right beneficiaries. Making the right beneficiary selection is vital to getting the most out of your IRA. It sounds simple, but it's not—as much thought and planning should go into making IRA beneficiary elections as go into drafting your will.

Indeed, your will and IRA beneficiary selection should be crafted to fit together as part of a unified estate plan. This takes special effort because your will and estate plan are subject to different legal rules.

Important: Review the IRA beneficiary selections you have made to date to assure that...

•They are up to date. You may want to change beneficiary selections if there have been changes in your family situation—marriage, the arrival of children, divorce, changing financial circumstances, or deaths.

•You fully understand them. Do you really understand what will happen to your IRA funds under every different possible set of circumstances?

•The forms do what you want them to do. Do the forms provided by your IRA trustee allow you to do such things as make "per stirpes" beneficiary designations, or successor beneficiary designations? If not, you may want to move your IRA to another trustee.

Critical: All the care you put into beneficiary designations will be for nothing if the forms you file are lost by the IRA trustee—which may happen, since they may not be called upon for years or even decades.

Safety: Obtain an acknowledged copy of your beneficiary forms from the IRA trustee and keep it with your will and other important legal documents.

The Best Place to Retire

Alaska is a tax haven for retirees who don't mind the cold. There's no state income tax or sales tax. Residents also share profits of the state's oil industry, receiving annual disbursements that generally exceed $1,000. Residents age 65 and over receive generous exemptions from property taxes and are exempt from car registration fees. Most cities, including Anchorage and Juneau, have no local sales tax.

R. Alan Fox, editor, *Where to Retire*, 1502 Augusta Dr., Houston 77057.

Social Security Lessons... What Everyone Should Know but Too Few Do

Andy Landis, Seattle-based author of *Social Security: The Inside Story*. Crisp Publications. He was with the Social Security Administration and served as an economic security representative for AARP. He now consults and conducts "Thinking Retirement" seminars on Social Security and retirement lifestyles.

Nearly one in six Americans—some 44 million individuals—receive a Social Security check each month.

But more people could qualify for benefits if they knew the ins and outs of Social Security regulations. This is important if you or someone in your family is disabled or you are a surviving spouse and are caring for children generally until age 18 or 19 who are still in high school. Misconceptions about benefits also keep people working who would prefer to retire early.

Here's what you need to know in order to receive all the Social Security benefits to which you are entitled.

QUALIFYING FOR DISABILITY

If you meet the tests for disability, you, your spouse and your children can qualify for benefits regardless of your age. This has major implications for younger people, who stand a greater chance of becoming disabled than they do of dying. Social Security pays disability benefits to 4.7 million workers and to 1.6 million of their spouses and children.

Social Security has a strict definition of disability. To qualify, you must be unable—or expected to be unable—to do almost any sort of work for at least one year, starting with your "disability onset." This is usually the date you are no longer able to work. Actual payments begin about six months after onset.

This is different from corporate disability policies, which normally pay benefits after a much shorter period…and from private insurance, which generally will cover you if you can't perform your normal and customary job. Because of its tough definition of disability, Social Security approves only about 50% of the claims filed. But those who qualify receive an average monthly benefit of $754. And they receive an additional 50% for a spouse who cares for their minor children, for a total average monthly benefit of $1,131.

To coordinate Social Security with any coverage you get through work and any private insurance you may have, assume that you'll receive about $750 a month (or $1,255 if you have a spouse who is caring for your minor children) after six months of disability.

Use your group coverage at work *and* a private policy to fill in the gap before Social Security kicks in.

Those who have received Social Security disability payments for at least two years qualify for *government-subsidized health insurance*. That's when they automatically qualify for Medicare.

DISABLED CHILD

Your disabled child may qualify for lifetime Social Security benefits on the basis of *your* earnings record.

This can be enormously helpful to parents caring for physically or developmentally disabled children and facing continuing child-care costs, even after the parents are retired.

To qualify, the child must meet the same definition of disability as an ordinary worker and the disability must have started before the child reaches age 22. Once a parent retires, the disabled child receives 50% of his/her parent's full retirement benefit and 75% of that benefit after the parent dies.

DIVORCED

You may be entitled to receive benefits even if your former spouse has remarried and is still working.

It used to be that divorced spouses were subject to the same rule as current spouses— the "ex" could not draw benefits until the former spouse retired. But some former spouses held grudges and vowed they would never retire, thus preventing their ex-partners from ever receiving benefits.

The law was changed, but you must meet three important tests to qualify…

●**You must have been married to the person for at least 10 years.**

●**You must be at least age 62.**

●**You must be unmarried.**

If you have worked yourself (either before or during the marriage or after the divorce), Social Security will automatically check to see if you can draw more on your own earnings record than your former spouse's and will pay you the higher of the two amounts.

FRAUD AND ERRORS

Contact Social Security immediately if you suspect someone is fraudulently using your Social Security number. While it's very rare for someone to deliberately appropriate and misuse your Social Security number, it does happen occasionally. Usually such fraud occurs with nonexistent numbers or with the numbers of deceased individuals.

Trouble more often arises when there is a mistake in the payroll process and a Social Security number is entered incorrectly. But the Social Security Administration says it has a 99.1% accuracy rate for individual earnings' records.

If an error does occur, the best way to catch it is to take the time to carefully read your Social Security earnings history. The government now automatically mails these records annually to every worker over age 25 (about three months before your birthday). Eyeball the numbers to make sure they agree with your recent annual earnings. If they don't, call the toll-free number on the statement to make corrections.

A more common problem is when you are confused with someone who has a similar name. Often, you first learn of this when that person applies for a loan or mortgage...and you are notified by a bank or credit union that you are being denied credit because of the other person's credit problems.

Immediately notify the major credit-reporting services in writing that you are not the person in question and demand that your credit history be corrected.

STARTING BENEFITS

Don't force yourself to continue working because you're afraid that by retiring early you will reduce your final benefits. Many people think their Social Security check is based on their last five or 10 years on the job.

It is actually based on their average lifetime earnings. So whether or not you work in your last two or three years before starting to draw benefits usually doesn't make a large difference in what you'll receive...but retiring a decade early might.

It usually pays to start Social Security benefits as early as you can. The Social Security Administration would like most people to wait until the "normal" retirement age—now about 65 but gradually rising to 70. But "present value" financial calculations show that it's usually better to start receiving benefits earlier.

The bad news is that if you opt to draw benefits at 62, which is the earliest possible age to get a Social Security retirement check, you'll get less than what you would have received if you waited. The good news is that most people come out ahead if they start early.

Reason: It takes about 15 years to break even with people who wait until age 65. Until then, you'll be getting a stream of monthly income that is totally tax free for most individuals—only one-quarter of beneficiaries wind up paying some tax on their benefits.

Social Security benefits are automatically indexed each year to keep pace with inflation, unlike corporate pensions, which are usually fixed for life. The only reason you might want to delay drawing benefits is if you come from a long-lived family and are worried that you won't have enough total income to last your lifetime.

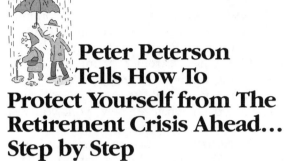

Peter Peterson Tells How To Protect Yourself from The Retirement Crisis Ahead... Step by Step

Peter G. Peterson, one of today's foremost thinkers on the aging of the world's population. He is chairman of The Blackstone Group, a New York investment banking firm. A former Secretary of Commerce, he also chairs the Council on Foreign Relations. He is author of *Gray Dawn: How the Coming Age Wave Will Transform America—and the World.* Times Books.

Coping with an aging population will be the great global challenge for societies and families in the 21st century.

As life expectancy grows and baby boomers age in the US, it will become increasingly difficult for government to provide for the growing army of elderly who will no longer earn enough to provide for themselves.

The best way to prepare for this crisis is to recognize in advance that more of your retirement financial burden will fall on you. *Here is what you can do...*

●**Plan ahead for a longer work life.** I am amazed at how many middle-aged Americans have convinced themselves that their retirement will be a breeze. Most baby boomers expect to retire by age 60...haven't saved very much...doubt they will get all their Social Security benefits...and yet still expect to live as well in retirement as they do now.

They're bound to be disappointed.

One sure way to live well in retirement is not to begin it earlier than you can afford it. Another is to find ways of mixing retired leisure with some form of continued employment.

At the very least, we need to face up to the actuarial reality. In the early years of Social Security, when the average age of retirement was 69, US life expectancy at that age was 10 years. Today, when the typical American worker retires at age 62, life expectancy at that age is 20 years.

Planning pays: Prepare now to continue earning an income in your 60s and 70s. Will you continue in the job you're in now? Would you like a new career that might be less demanding or more interesting? What steps will you have to take to become educated and trained for whatever new work you will be doing?

Just *wanting* to work in retirement isn't enough. You must take responsibility for making yourself economically *relevant* in your older years.

●**Make plans to care for your parents—** and for your kids to care for you. In many other countries, caring for an aging population is considered a family responsibility.

In Japan, well over half the elderly still live with their children. Singapore officials are now considering requiring children to care for their aging parents.

In America, we have created a culture of independence of parents from their children. Both parents and children are happy—or at least say they are happy—with the arrangement. But we must recognize that this approach may not be affordable when a quarter or more of the population is elderly.

What to do: Discuss the issue with your family now. A typical session might run like this…"Mom and Dad, let's talk about what it costs you to live. And—let's talk about how much you are saving, too. Let's assume you don't get all your Social Security. Let's talk about what you need and what plans the whole family can make together so you never have to do without."

You should have a similar conversation with your adult children.

Very little parent–child dialogue now takes place—not because families don't care, but because we are all still in a state of denial about the coming retirement crisis.

●**Expect smaller public benefits.** Aging baby boomers say they don't expect to get all their promised Social Security benefits, but they don't act as if they believe it. Many will receive smaller benefits because the system, I am convinced, will have to be redesigned so that the bulk of its resources go to those who need them the most.

Reality: About $200 billion a year in benefits goes to the 25% of the elderly population with the highest incomes. At the same time, half the people on Social Security have incomes of less than $20,000 a year—with the vast majority of that income coming from Social Security.

What to do: Base your plans on the assumption that eventually the government will establish a means test so that the public pension and health-care systems care first for the elderly who really need it.

We can't say precisely how much the Social Security benefit will be reduced for those older people who are better off. To play it safe, assume you will be collecting 25% less than what the system now provides you.

●**Save more for your retirement.** That may sound obvious—yet the savings rate among middle-aged Americans is unbelievably low. Half have net financial assets of less than $10,000—despite warnings about how much it will cost to live in retirement. More countries are *requiring* people to save for retirement.

What to do: Decide on when you want to retire and whether you plan to work in retirement. Determine the minimum annual income that is acceptable as a standard of living in retirement—and how much more you must save to achieve it—assuming a reasonable rate of return.

If you must start saving $10,000 a year more than you are saving now, make saving your top priority instead of your last priority.

12

Estate Planning

Zero Estate Tax Opportunities—Zero Estate Tax Traps, Too

 ou may hear about the "zero estate tax" strategies adopted by some superwealthy people. You certainly have seen ads for books that promise to show you how it's possible. But before you decide to zero out your own estate, you should know how these methods work.

GROUND RULES

As a matter of fact, you may not need to consider drastic zeroing tactics. This year, you can leave any amount of property to your spouse and up to $675,000 to other heirs—and pay zero federal estate tax.

With modest planning, a married couple can pass up to $1.35 million in 2000 to their beneficiaries, estate and gift tax free. These tax-free amounts are scheduled to increase gradually to $1 million per person ($2 million per couple) by 2006.

Therefore, zero estate tax strategies are only for those who expect to have larger estates. If you're in that position, you should know that estates larger than $1 million are taxed at rates that run from 41% to 55%.

Cruel math: If you're married and have a $4 million estate, you and your spouse can shelter $2 million from tax (assuming both deaths occur after 2005) yet still owe nearly $1 million in federal estate tax.

THE ZERO-SUM GAME

To avoid making a huge "bequest" to the IRS, here's how to go about whittling down estate taxes…

●**The first spouse to die** can leave up to $1 million to a credit shelter trust for the survivor. If the death occurs after 2005, this bequest (outright or in trust) would escape estate tax in both estates.

David S. Rhine, CPA, partner and national director of family wealth planning, BDO Seidman, LLP, 330 Madison Ave., New York 10017.

●**Another $1 million** would be passed on by the surviving spouse to the children at his/her death. Again, no estate tax will be due on this amount, starting in 2006.

●**Then, if the remaining $2 million** (assuming a $4 million estate) were to be left to charity no later than the death of the surviving spouse, the whole taxable estate would have been given away and no estate tax would be due.

For a $5 million estate, such a plan would require a $3 million charitable donation, and so on.

BUT WHAT ABOUT THE KIDS?

Under a zeroing plan like the one above, your children will wind up losers. They get only $2 million of your $4 million estate.

With larger estates, where more of the estate would have to be given to charity, the children stand to lose even more.

How much do they really need? You may think that $2 million is enough for your children and you'd like the rest of your assets to go to a favored cause. Many people, though, prefer to see their children get more than half of their estate.

How: Zero estate tax strategies usually call for a life insurance policy to be purchased covering the life of one or both spouses. The children are the beneficiaries. The policy proceeds will replace the inheritance the children lost to charity.

Example: A $1 million policy could bring the children's share up to $3 million, the amount they would have wound up with after tax on a $4 million estate. A $2 million policy would bring their inheritance up to the full $4 million size of the estate before taxes.

Trap: If you or your spouse owns the policy or has any "incidents of ownership," such as the right to change beneficiaries, the policy proceeds will be included in your taxable estate.

Avoidance: Have some other "party" or entity own the policy. Most people either have the children own the policy or establish a trust to own it—a life insurance trust.

Loophole: Life insurance proceeds typically escape income tax, so a strategy that also avoids estate tax can deliver the policy proceeds tax free.

WEIGHING THE COSTS

If you decide to create a trust to hold the life insurance policy, you'll incur legal costs—these could run several thousand dollars, depending how complex the trust.

You'll pay much more, over the years, for the policy itself, but still much less than the payoff. You'll also pay premiums for the life insurance, but those premiums should be much less than the value of the policy at your death. But remember that the payment of the premiums may be a taxable gift.

Example: A couple in good health, ages 60 and 58, might be able to buy a $1 million policy that pays off after the second death for about $165,000 in premiums, payable $16,500 per year for 10 years.

Such projections are estimates, subject to change due to interest rate movements, age and health.

Bottom line: You need to decide if you want to spend money on life insurance so that your wealth can be directed to favored causes and to your heirs rather than to the IRS.

PLANS CAN CAUSE PROBLEMS

When one spouse is much wealthier than the other, if the spouse who's short on assets dies first, most of that spouse's estate tax shelter may be lost.

Equalizing the assets is one solution, but if most of your wealth is concentrated in a retirement plan, it may be difficult to equalize estates so that each spouse has $1 million worth of assets. *Strategies…*

●**Hold other assets in your spouse's name.** You can transfer these assets—such as the family residence and a vacation home—into your spouse's name free of gift tax.

Assuming your marriage is sound, you may like the idea of holding some assets in your spouse's name, for creditor protection.

Trap: You can't just move money from your retirement plan to your spouse's name. You'll have to make withdrawals and trigger an income tax.

●**Make charitable bequests from your tax-deferred retirement plan.** That will permit your family to avoid paying income tax as well as estate tax on plan assets. The beneficiaries can get life insurance proceeds tax free, to replace the amount passing from the plan to charity.

CHARITABLE CHOICES

You need to decide exactly which type of charitable donation you are going to make…

●**Outright bequest.** This method is simple and straightforward.

●**Charitable remainder trust (CRT).** Setting up a CRT gives you an immediate income tax deduction and lifetime income for you and your spouse. The income distributed and the tax savings can help you pay the life insurance premiums on a policy purchased to replace the children's inheritance.

●**Private foundation.** Instead of bequeathing $2 million to a public charity, you can leave that money to the "What's Your Name" Foundation. Again, the assets will avoid estate tax.

After your death, the foundation will be led by a board of directors you choose, possibly including your children. They'll be responsible for making charitable grants each year.

Thus, your children and perhaps other descendants can continue to do meaningful work and build relationships with community leaders. Go over each strategy with a knowledgeable professional.

THE PRIVATE ANNUITY

If you're in poor health and unable to buy life insurance at a good price, consider a private annuity instead.

You transfer assets to a younger family member and receive a series of payments. Assuming the assets are fairly valued, no gift tax consequences are incurred and the assets are out of your taxable estate.

Key: With a private annuity, smaller is better. Smaller payments are easier for your children to manage and there is less cash flowing back into your taxable estate.

Loophole: New IRS mortality tables, which indicate longer lives in most cases, allow private annuity payments to be smaller.

Example: Mary Smith, age 80, transfers real estate worth $200,000 to her daughter Nancy. At current levels of interest rates, Nancy would have to pay about $33,000 per year. Under the old tables, her annual obligation would have been about $35,000.

If Mary dies after two years (and $66,000 worth of payments), that real estate worth $200,000 would be out of her estate with no gift or estate tax consequences.

More from David Rhine…

Gifts Cost Lots Less Than Bequests

Rather than making a bequest to a relative or other favored individual through your will, consider instead making a gift to that person *before* you die. A lot of tax can be saved that way.

Background: When you die, estate tax will be due on your entire estate, including the money used to pay estate taxes, so you wind up paying tax on your tax payment.

In contrast, gift tax is due only on the gift property itself—not on the money used to pay the tax.

Example: You are in the 50% gift and estate tax bracket, you've already used up your estate and gift tax exemption ($675,000 in 2000), and plan to transfer $100,000 to a favored relative.

If you make the transfer…

●**By bequest,** you will need $200,000 in your estate to fund the $100,000 bequest. Since you're in the 50% bracket, a full $100,000 will go to taxes.

●**By gift,** you will need only $150,000 to finance a $100,000 gift. The 50% gift tax rate applies only to the gift itself, so the tax is only $50,000.

Thus, simply by making the transfer by gift instead of bequest, you cut the taxes paid to the IRS by 50%!

New Way to Cut Estate Taxes

Owners of stock options can give the options to their heirs. Through the "gifting" of options, enormous wealth (taxable at rates as high as 55%) can be moved out of the owner's estate in a tax efficient way. *Rules:* The options must be fully vested. Favorable IRS rulings have applied only to *non-qualified* options. The market value of the options is subject to gift tax, but may be sheltered by the owner's annual gift tax exclusion. The original owner recognizes gain—subject to income tax—when the new owner exercises the options. This income tax, though, is a small price to pay for vast estate tax savings later on.

Ralph Anderson, CPA, co-chairman of the tax department, Richard A. Eisner & Company, LLP, 575 Madison Ave., New York 10022.

How to Put Your Critical Papers in Order

Peter J. Strauss, Esq., partner in the law firm Epstein Becker & Green, PC, 250 Park Ave., New York 10017. He is a fellow of the National Academy of Elder Law Attorneys and coauthor of *The Elder Law Handbook—A Legal and Financial Survival Guide for Caregivers and Seniors.* Facts on File.

What if you're run over by a bus, or incapacitated by a stroke? Will your family be able to find the information they need to handle your affairs? Probably not.

Most people put off organizing documents that will be needed should they die suddenly or become incapacitated—*until it's too late.* This leaves their survivors, who are then in no condition to do much of anything, to bumble their way through.

Don't leave a mess for your family. Pull together the papers they'll need *now*—even if it means getting a new will and other legal documents—and tell at least one family member where they can be found.

LEGAL DOCUMENTS

•**Your will.** Keep it in a safe place. Leave the original with the attorney who drafted it— but be sure he/she has a fireproof vault or bank vault and a good index of wills—and keep a copy at home. Write the attorney's address and phone number on the cover of the copy.

Caution: Don't put your will in your own safe-deposit box. In many states, the family can't get immediate access to the contents of a safe-deposit box. Delay in obtaining your will causes probate to be delayed, and this means additional probate costs.

•**Letters of instruction.** Letters expressing wishes about funeral arrangements or listing items of jewelry each grandchild is to receive, etc., should be easily accessible.

•**Durable power of attorney.** Give signed copies of this legal document to the person named to act on your behalf in financial matters should you become unable to do so…or keep the form at home or with your attorney. But tell the person of his appointment and where the document can be found.

•**Trusts.** If you've set up a living trust to hold your assets and simplify the settlement of your estate, keep the trust document in a safe place. Leave the original with your attorney and keep a copy at home. Give a copy to any cotrustees and a copy to the successor trustee.

•**Health care proxy and living will.** If there are written expressions indicating the kind of treatment you want if your condition prevents you from writing and speaking, make sure such "advance medical directives" can be found quickly.

Give a copy of your "advance directives" to the person you've named to speak on your behalf.

Precaution: Give your doctors copies of the proxy and living will.

•**Other papers.** *Be sure your family knows where to find…*

•**Your old tax returns.**

•**Copies of leases you've signed.**

•**Mortgages.**

•**Insurance policies.**

•**Bank account records,** including canceled checks and other documents relating to your finances.

If you've given someone power of attorney over your checking account, make sure the person knows where you keep your blank checks.

ASSETS

Make a detailed list of assets and state where they can be found.

Example: If you have a safe-deposit box, note where it's located and where you keep the key. Make sure your agent has access to the box.

Include in your list of assets...

●**Retirement accounts:** Account numbers, beneficiary designations.

●**Bank accounts:** Account numbers and branch locations.

●**Brokerage accounts:** Account numbers and branch locations.

●**Mutual funds:** Account numbers and names of each mutual fund and fund family.

Important: Put bank books, insurance contracts, deeds to property and other evidence of ownership together and tell someone where these items can be found.

Also, keep year-end statements from banks, brokerage firms and mutual funds.

If you've hidden cash or jewelry, let someone know where.

Also include with your list...

●**Outstanding loans** you may have that need to be repaid.

●**Information about your other debts.**

●**Life insurance information.**

●**A family tree.**

●**Vital records,** birth and death certificates, etc., of family members.

MEDICAL INFORMATION

In addition to a health care proxy and/or living will, your family needs to know about any special medical conditions you have.

They also need to know about your medical insurance—including your Medicare card number and any Medigap or long-term-care coverage you carry.

YOUR ADVISERS

Make a list of the professionals you use. Your family may want to retain them to handle your affairs. *Include the name and telephone number of the following people...*

●**Attorney.** He is the person who drew up your will and may be holding the original.

●**Accountant.** This person may have copies of your old tax returns.

●**Stock broker.**

●**Insurance agent.**

●**Financial planner.**

●**Employee benefits person or department if you are, or were, employed.**

●**Doctors.**

●**Spiritual adviser,** such as your priest... minister...rabbi.

ACT NOW

If you haven't put this information together, do it now.

●**Make sure papers are in order** before taking a trip or undergoing surgery.

●**Update information as needed** at year-end.

Overlooked Traps in Jointly Owned Property

Irving L. Blackman, CPA, founding partner, Blackman Kallick Bartelstein, LLP, 300 S. Riverside Plaza, Chicago 60606.

Placing property in joint ownership with a spouse or other close relative can be a mistake in three ways. *It may...*

●**Disrupt estate planning.** On the death of one joint owner, a property passes automatically to the other owner *outside* the deceased owner's will. Any contrary provision made for the property in a will will be *ineffective.*

Trap: When joint property—such as a home—is a major part of an estate, people often provide for it in a will without realizing that joint ownership overrides the will.

●**Increase estate taxes.** When one spouse leaves joint property to the other, the deceased spouse cannot apply his/her personal estate tax-exempt amount of $675,000 in 2000 (gradually rising to $1 million in 2006) against it.

Trap: If property then piles up in the estate of the surviving spouse, only one exempt amount instead of two will be available to protect it. Tax on the extra $675,000 (up to 55%) may be needlessly incurred.

●**Increase income taxes.** When property is inherited, normally all taxable gain on it to date is eliminated since it receives stepped-up basis to market value.

Trap: When joint property is inherited, only the deceased spouse's half interest in it receives stepped-up basis—so a survivor who sells the property will pay more gain tax.

Example: A husband put $2,000 into a hot Internet stock five years ago. When he dies, it's worth $100,000 and he leaves that to his wife. *If he owned the property...*

●**Separately,** his wife, who inherits it, obtains a basis of $100,000 in it, and can sell it for $100,000 *tax free.*

●**Jointly with his wife,** her basis in the property becomes only $51,000—stepped-up basis of $50,000 for his share plus half of the original $2,000 cost. So if she sells the property for $100,000, she will have a $49,000 taxable gain.

Grandchild Loopholes

Edward Mendlowitz, CPA, partner, Mendlowitz Weitsen, LLP, CPAs, Two Pennsylvania Plaza, Suite 1500, New York 10121. He is author of eight books on taxes, including *IRA Distributions: What You Should Know.* Practical Programs, Inc.

Gifts to grandchildren—or great-grandchildren for that matter—help them and cut the family's overall tax bill. *Here are the best tax-saving gift strategies...*

Loophole: **Pay a grandchild's tuition and medical expenses.** Generally, you owe gift tax when you give a particular grandchild (or anyone) more than $10,000 in one year. The tax-free limit is $20,000 per grandchild per year for a married couple who join in making the gift.

In addition to an annual $10,000/$20,000 gift-tax-free gift, you can give an unlimited amount to help with education expenses as long as payments are made directly to a school, college or other educational institution. On top of that, payments you make directly to hospitals or other medical providers to cover a grandchild's *medical* expenses are gift tax free.

Caution: You must make out the gift check directly to the institution (education or medical), not to your grandchildren.

New form of giving: A married couple can contribute up to $100,000 *in one year* to a qualified state tuition program (QSTP) with the money to be used for a grandchild's education.

The $100,000 can be offset with five years' worth of $20,000 joint annual gift-tax exclusions, making the contribution absolutely gift tax free. The election to apply the five years' worth of $20,000 exclusions is made on IRS Form 709.

Earnings on the money in QSTPs grow tax-deferred, but distributions of earnings that are used to pay tuition, fees, books and supplies are taxable to the grandchild.

Caution: A steep penalty applies to earnings that are distributed but not used to pay for higher education expenses.

Loophole: **Make your grandchildren partners in a family partnership.** The limited partnership interests that you transfer to your grandchildren are valued for gift tax purposes at less than the fair market value of the entire assets. A discount is applied because the partners/grandchildren have no control over the invested assets.

How to do it: Make yourself the general, or controlling, partner and your grandchildren limited partners. You will have complete control over the assets owned by the partnership. Income generated by the partnership assets will be paid to the grandchildren or accumulated for them.

Loophole: **Name your grandchild the beneficiary of your retirement plan.** You must start taking money out of your IRAs and other retirement plans by April 1 of the year after the year in which you turn age 70½. When you withdraw less than the IRS-required minimum amount each year, you owe a penalty.

Strategy: The minimum annual withdrawal is based on the joint life expectancy of you and the beneficiary you've named to your retirement account. You can minimize the annual payout—maximizing the tax-free buildup in the account—by naming a young grandchild as beneficiary of the account.

Reason: Your grandchild has a longer life expectancy than you do, and your combined expectancies would stretch the payout period longer than it would be had you named your spouse or another adult as beneficiary. Also, when you die, the balance in the account would be distributed over the beneficiary's life expectancy.

Loophole: Set up a custodial account for the grandchild—a Uniform Transfers (or Gifts) to Minors Act account with a bank or brokerage firm. The account will be owned by the grandchild and generally taxed at his/her lower tax rate. Transfer enough cash or assets to each grandchild so that they have $1,400 of investment income per year.

Reason: Because of the kiddie tax, children under age 14 can earn only $700 of investment income free of tax in 2000. The next $700 of investment income will be taxed at their low 15% rate. Investment earnings above $1,400 will be taxed at the parent's tax rate.

Best assets to give grandchildren under 14...

• **Index funds or growth stocks** that produce little or no current income. The shares can be sold after the children turn age 14, and the gains taxed at their low rate.

• **Series EE US savings bonds** that mature after your grandchild's 14th birthday. The taxes are deferred on these bonds until they are cashed in or mature.

• **Zero-coupon municipal bonds,** which don't generate any current income.

Best assets for grandchildren older than 14...

Take advantage of the children's low tax rate by giving them income-producing assets like high-dividend-paying stocks or bonds.

Alternative: Give appreciated assets and have your grandchildren sell them.

Trap: Grandparents who make gifts to custodial accounts should not act as custodians. If they do, any money left in the account when they die will be included in their taxable estates. Avoid this by having one grandparent make a gift to the other grandparent, who then gives the money to the grandchild. That way, the first grandparent can act as custodian without adverse tax consequences.

Loophole: Put your grandchild to work as a model or "actor" in advertisements for your business or its products. Children can earn income of up to $4,400 before owing any tax in 2000. Above that, earnings of up to $26,250 are taxed at their low 15% rate.

Strategy: Up to $2,000 of earned income a year can be contributed to a Roth IRA and never taxed there.

Caution: The business will owe Social Security and payroll taxes on salaries paid to your grandchildren.

Loophole: Set up a life insurance trust to hold policies on your life for the benefit of your grandchildren. When the trust is properly set up, the proceeds paid on your death will not be subject to estate tax.

Trap: Gifts to grandchildren that exceed $1 million (indexed for inflation) in total are subject to a 55% generation-skipping transfer tax. Avoid this tax by paying the gift tax owed on the $1 million you transfer into a life insurance trust. Then direct the trust to buy a single-premium life insurance policy on your life. This should pay a benefit of $2 million to $5 million, depending on your age.

When you die, the policy proceeds will be paid to your grandchildren free of estate tax. *Result:* You have passed on $2 million to $5 million for the price of gift tax on $1 million.

Caution: If the trust is set up incorrectly, the full insurance proceeds could be subject to the 55% generation-skipping transfer tax.

All About Defective Grantor Trusts... Very Helpful for Estate Tax Savings

T. Randolph Harris, Esq., partner, Davidson, Dawson & Clark LLP, 330 Madison Ave., New York 10017, a law firm primarily practicing in estate planning and related areas.

The tax law exempts most people from gift and estate tax. Still, for many taxpayers, the relief built into the law is not enough. They find themselves sitting on a potentially taxable estate.

Every break the law allows: In 2000, you can give or bequeath up to $675,000 worth of assets, tax free. Married couples can give away up to $1.35 million.

These limits will gradually increase until they peak—under current law—in 2006 at $1 million per person, $2 million per couple.

If your estate will be larger than that, taxes will be punishing. Federal estate tax rates for million dollar estates start at 41% and escalate to 55%.

Imperative: You must do everything you can to pare down the size of your eventual estate.

PAYING TAX TO CUT TAX

One technique for reducing your estate is to use what is called a *defective grantor trust.*

With proper planning, the transfer of assets to a defective grantor trust can be sheltered by the lifetime credit and will lead to a reduction in your taxable estate.

Bonus: Any future growth of those assets will escape gift and estate tax altogether.

Loophole: Even though the assets are out of your estate for estate planning purposes, they are still considered to be your property, for *income tax* purposes. This permits you to pay the tax on income that goes to someone else (i.e., remove more from your estate), yet not be treated as making a taxable gift to that person. Obviously, there is nothing to stop Jane (see below) from paying income tax for her children, or for anyone else. In other circumstances, though, paying income tax for someone else would be a taxable gift.

Classic example: Jane Smith, a widow, transfers a stock market portfolio worth $675,000 to a trust established for the benefit of her children. This transfer is covered by her federal $657,000 estate and gift tax credit, so no gift tax is due.

In subsequent years Jane can make additional gifts to the trust as the estate and gift tax credit increases.

Continued: Now, suppose that in 2000, the trust assets generate $50,000 worth of taxable income. This income is retained in the trust to compound, to the ultimate benefit of Jane's children.

However, with a defective grantor trust the tax on that $50,000 is owed not by the trust

or by the beneficiaries but by Jane, the person who set up the trust—otherwise known as the *grantor.*

Jane can—in fact, must—pay the income tax from her own funds, but she is not treated as though she is making a gift to her children.

ADDING UP THE ADVANTAGES

This strategy will produce the following advantages…

●**The trust fund builds to a greater amount** if no income tax needs to be paid out.

●**Jane's payment of income tax reduces her taxable estate** each year yet is not considered a taxable gift.

●**No gift tax returns need to be filed** on these income tax payments, no matter how much Jane pays in tax on trust income. (The original transfer to the trust requires a gift tax return.)

●**Jane can, if she wishes, make additional gifts to her children** or to the trust, sheltered by the $10,000 annual gift tax exclusion. Gifts to the trust, though, require extra planning in order to qualify for the exclusion.

Bottom line: The estate tax savings from Jane's annual tax payments are in addition to the general estate planning savings from making lifetime gifts.

MAKING IT DEFECTIVE

How is this favorable result accomplished? Ironically, it's the result of the government's attempt to restrain abusive tax tactics.

Formerly, some people tried to shift income tax to trusts, where rates were lower. So the Tax Code contains provisions to force trust grantors to pay tax on trust income, in some circumstances.

Today, trust income tax rates are so high there's little income tax benefit from doing this. There may be gift and estate tax benefits, though, in retaining the income tax obligation.

Key: You need to set up a trust that's intentionally defective, under income tax rules, so you'll be liable for the income tax.

How can you do so? *Here are a few strategies favored by tax pros…*

●**A close relative,** such as a spouse or a sibling, can be named as trustee with the power to allocate trust income among the beneficiaries.

●**Your spouse** can be named as trust beneficiary with the trustee having the discretion to distribute trust funds to your spouse.

Caution: Although these techniques are easy ways to make a trust income-tax defective, care must be taken to keep the trust assets out of your estate and your spouse's estate as well. In general, that means placing barriers in your access to trust assets.

Other approaches…

●**You, as grantor, can retain the power to reacquire trust assets** by substituting other assets of equal value.

●**You can add a "redisposition" power,** giving the trustee the ability to add another party (i.e., a charity) as a trust beneficiary. Because the trustee is named by the grantor, such a power is considered another indication of control by the grantor.

BUYBACK BONUS

Defective grantor trusts offer another tax advantage as well—transactions between the trust and the grantor aren't taxed. To the IRS, it's as if you were shifting assets from one pocket to another.

Tactic: Buy appreciated assets from the trust, hold them until death and avoid capital gains tax.

Example: Jane Smith transfers $1 million worth of stocks to a defective grantor trust between now and 2006, taking full advantage of her unified credit. Over time, those stocks appreciate in value to $2 million. If the trust were to sell those stocks to raise cash, it would incur a $1 million capital gain and owe at least $200,000 in tax.

Instead, Jane buys back the stocks for $2 million. There is no tax on this fair market value transaction between her and her own grantor trust. If she eventually dies when the stocks are worth, say, $2.2 million, her children can inherit with a full basis step-up to $2.2 million. All of the appreciation during Jane's lifetime will avoid capital gains tax.

What if Jane doesn't have $2 million in cash to buy back the appreciated stocks? She can borrow money and use the loan proceeds for the buyback. The tax savings likely will be greater than the cost to borrow the money.

Caution: Although the use of a defective grantor trust is supported by the Tax Code, the IRS doesn't like them and may take a closer look. Work with an experienced attorney who'll structure the trust meticulously.

How to Transfer $136 Trillion to the Future Generation Tax Efficiently

Sanford J. Schlesinger, Esq., partner and head of the wills and estates department of the law firm Kaye, Scholer, Fierman, Hays & Handler, LLP, 425 Park Ave., New York 10022.

Americans will be transferring *trillions* of dollars worth of assets to family members and other beneficiaries and heirs over the next 50 years. Possibly as much as $136 trillion will be given away or bequeathed.

No doubt your wealth, like that of so many others, is rapidly building up. *Impact:* Planning has never been so important.

This is the right time to review plans for gifts and estates, making sure your planning takes full advantage of what the tax laws allow.

Do not fall prey to two widely held misconceptions…

Misconception 1: **Congress will eliminate transfer taxes, so there is no need to act now.**

Eliminating transfer taxes would cost the government so much money that such a move is *highly unlikely.* And—no one knows what Congress will do in the coming year.

Bottom line: The only prudent way to plan is under the law as it stands now. If there are changes in the law, plans can always be revised accordingly.

Misconception 2: **My finances are fairly straightforward, so I don't need to worry about a lot of sophisticated planning.**

Even married schoolteachers in their 50s can have more than $1 million in assets today if they bought a home years ago and have contributed regularly to their retirement plans.

They need a lesson in estate planning if they want those assets to go to their children without the IRS taking a big cut. *How to get started...*

LIST YOUR ASSETS

First: **Make a list of your assets.** *Include...*

● **The equity in your home.**

● **Your investment portfolio.**

● **All retirement plans and IRAs.**

● **Investment real estate.**

● **Value of business interests.**

● **Other significant assets** such as artworks and collectibles.

Then: **Update your estate plan.** If total assets exceed $675,000 in 2000, you should proceed to update your trust and estate plans.

BEST WAYS TO CUT ESTATE TAXES

● **Divide assets with your spouse.** A couple can double the $675,000 that is exempt from gift and estate taxes simply by dividing ownership of assets into his and hers, rather than owning them jointly. A his/hers division creates two estates instead of one, fully utilizes each spouse's exempt amount and drastically cuts taxes.

● **Get insurance out of your estate.** Generally, insurance should be owned by an irrevocable life insurance trust or ownership rights should be relinquished. Many people mistakenly think of insurance as tax free.

It is true that beneficiaries do not owe income taxes on life insurance proceeds, but if you—or a business of which you own more than 50%—own the policy, it will be subject to estate taxes, which can far exceed income taxes.

● **Make annual gifts.** Remember, the law allows you to make gifts of $10,000 per recipient per year to as many recipients as you wish with no gift or estate tax consequences. A gifting program can reduce taxable estates for people whose assets clearly exceed their needs. The best time to make the gifts is early in the year, to get a full year's benefit of unloading the money and its appreciation.

● **Make tuition gifts.** The law allows you to make gift-tax-free gifts—in addition to the $10,000 a year gift—for tuition costs.

Say you want to pay your granddaughter's college expenses. You can pay an unlimited amount of tuition gift tax free as long as you make the payment directly to the university. In limited circumstances, you may even be able to take advantage of this tax break by *prepaying* your granddaughter's tuition.

UPDATE YOUR WILL

If your will was written before the *Taxpayer Relief Act of 1997,* it may use numbers pegged to the former law. That exempted $600,000 from gift and estate taxes and $1 million from the generation-skipping transfer tax. *New amounts...*

● **The exemption amount,** $675,000 for gift and estate taxes in 2000, will rise to $1 million in 2006.

● **The generation-skipping tax** exemption is indexed to inflation. This year the exempt amount is $1,030,000.

As a result of these changes, wills and trusts may need to be revised, using *formulas* rather than absolute numbers.

● **For the charitably inclined,** consider naming a charity as the beneficiary of an IRA, instead of bequeathing it to an individual via your will.

If the IRA goes to your child, say, up to 80% could be gobbled up in income and estate taxes. *Better:* Leave the child assets that are not subject to income taxes and give a charity the asset—the IRA—that would otherwise be subject to income taxes.

FAMILY-OWNED BUSINESSES

Despite politicians' claims that the 1997 law would protect family-owned businesses—up to $1.3 million may be excluded from gift and estate taxes—very few such businesses actually meet the stringent qualifications.

Still, for very closely held businesses, there may be some benefit. So, if you own your business outright, or with only one or two other families, this is worth discussing with your attorney.

INDIVIDUAL STATE CHANGES

Because many states have passed new laws concerning gift and estate taxes, it is advisable to check with your attorney as to whether your will or trust documents need to be updated because of state law.

●**Gift taxes.** Many states are repealing gift taxes. New York, for example, repealed its gift tax, effective January 1, 2000, and adopted a "soft" estate tax, effective February 1, 2000. A "soft" estate tax is one that is based on the federal return. The switch removes a tax incentive for moving to Florida, as many New York retirees now do. (North Carolina, Connecticut, Tennessee, Georgia and Puerto Rico still levy gift taxes.)

●**Dynasty trusts.** Many states have repealed what is known as "the rule against perpetuities," which prevented assets from being held in trust indefinitely. Now, if you want to put assets, or even a family business, into a long-term trust, you may be able to do so under the laws of your own state instead of setting up an Alaska or South Dakota trust. In practice, many people prefer to set a limit on how long trusts last.

●**Investing trust assets.** States are beginning to look at trusts' overall rate of return, recognizing capital gains as income, not just interest and dividends. Trusts are often set up to pay out income to beneficiaries with what's left over (the "remainder") going to someone else after a set period or upon the deaths of the beneficiaries. This state monitoring of a trust's return has profound implications on how assets are invested. Check with your attorney or trustee concerning the law in your state.

the third copy to a close family member. Have your family attorney hold onto the original. Execute documents in separate states if you spend significant time in more than one state.

Emily Card, attorney and personal-finance specialist, Los Angeles, and coauthor of *New Families, New Finances: Money Skills for Today's Nontraditional Families.* John Wiley & Sons.

Tax Deferral Tactic for Estates and Heirs

An estate can elect to have a noncalendar tax year.

Benefit: Having a year that ends on a date other than December 31 lets the estate postpone paying income taxes until the following year.

The estate's year-end also determines the year in which income distributions from the estate are reported by beneficiaries—so it may enable them to defer paying income taxes on income received from the estate until the following year as well.

Example: Heirs receive income from an estate in December of 2000. If the estate uses a calendar year, they owe tax on the distribution in 2000 and must pay the tax by April 16, 2001.

But if the estate's year ends on January 31, the income received from it in December 2000 will be taxed to those who receive it in the year 2001—and will be reported on the tax return filed April 15, 2000.

R. Eugene Marion, editor, *The Review,* Deloitte & Touche LLP, Box 820, Wilton, CT 06897.

Where to Keep a Living Will

Keep a copy of a living will in *each* of four different places. Have your primary-care physician keep one on file. Put another in a key-document envelope at home, together with other important papers. Give

Six Steps to Writing a Good Will

To draw up a will to accomplish all you desire...

●**Write down in your own words** what you want your will to do. Give this statement of your intentions to your lawyer so he/she understands.

●**Work with your lawyer.** As an expert, he should think of things that you haven't and ask you about them. Beware of any lawyer who doesn't ask questions.

●**Name the right executor.** Don't automatically name your oldest child as executor if he/she isn't fully capable, or if the decision will lead to family disputes. Consider naming someone outside the family who is impartial and has valuable professional expertise, but keep executor's fees in mind.

●**Head off family disputes.** When you divide an estate in equal shares among heirs, leave a letter of instruction advising the executor who should get what.

●**Provide for taxes.** If your estate owes taxes, remember to specifically provide for them in your will so they don't reduce bequests.

●**Update your will frequently,** adapting it to changes in law and family circumstances.

Barbara Weltman, Esq., an attorney practicing in Millwood, NY. She is author of *The Complete Idiot's Guide to Making Money After You Retire.* Alpha Books.

How You Can Win Big By Giving Up

Martin Shenkman, estate attorney and financial planner, Teaneck, NJ. Mr. Shenkman is author of *The Beneficiary Workbook.* John Wiley.

It seems improbable for most people, but some have more than enough money for their purposes. If you happen to be one of the lucky few and an additional inheritance would only complicate your already complicated estate plan, *you may want to...*

●**Consider "disclaiming" (giving up) your inheritance.** A disclaimer is a written refusal to accept an inheritance of property passing from someone who dies. It must be made within nine months of the date of death.

However, you cannot have accepted any benefits from the property (for example, received any dividend checks) and you cannot direct who gets the property instead (it passes automatically to the next in line). You must comply with strict IRS and court requirements.

●**Think about giving your inheritance to charity.** Extra money is an opportunity to benefit your favorite causes. Depending upon the amount involved, you might consider direct gifts to charity. For larger amounts, you could set up a private foundation to direct the disbursement of funds to various charities.

Additional benefit: You not only put this money to good use but you also enjoy tax deductions for your donations.

Estate-Planning Reminder

Any plan is better than none. People too often put off state planning because they simply don't want to think about it...or because they think it will take a lot of time to devise the perfect plan.

Don't make extra—and costly—trouble for your heirs: Get something on the records. You can always hone it later.

John Tuozzolo, JD, member of the law firm of Collins, Hannafin, Garamella, Jaber and Tuozzolo, PC, Danbury, CT.

Related Useful Sites

Financial Planning

☐ Fidelity Investments Workplace Savings

www.fidelityatwork.com

Helpful information from Fidelity about planning for retirement and IRAs. Also use the tools and calculators to assess your savings and investment situation and determine how much you need to save to reach long-term goals, such as retirement, funding a college education, etc.

☐ Find a Fund

www.findafund.com

One of several sites that claim to aid investors in navigating the tricky waters of mutual fund investing. But this one is among the few that really delivers. Search for a fund by name, category or ticker symbol. You instantly get all of the essential data: Manager's name, performance numbers, portfolio breakdown, etc. Also offers *useful information* on picking funds, *top-performing funds* and more.

☐ Mutual Fund Investor's Center

www.mfea.com

This comprehensive site offers informative sketches of major mutual fund companies, daily listing of fund prices and much more.

☐ Mutual Funds Interactive

www.fundsinteractive.com

User-friendly site rich in basic information about mutual fund investing. Also offers links to Web sites of major *fund families* as well as a very active, moderated *newsgroup* for sharing questions, answers and ideas about mutual fund investing.

☐ Armchair Millionaire

www.armchairmillionaire.com

A partnership between the women's site iVillage.com and Quicken.com, this site features very readable articles about investing, a clearly explained *model portfolio* and the most interesting feature, a *five-step plan to financial freedom.*

Seniors

☐ Administration on Aging

www.aoa.gov

This government site includes a directory of *state agencies* on aging, a directory of state long-term-care ombudsmen and an Eldercare Locator, which provides information on contacting local agencies that can help you obtain services. Also available: *Resource directory.*

☐ ElderWeb

www.elderweb.com

An extremely comprehensive and well-organized site for seniors, ElderWeb contains more than 5,000 articles on eldercare. There is abundant information on physical and mental health issues of the elderly, legal advice, financial help and much more. Click on your state in *Regional Information* and link to region-specific information.

☐ SCORE Association

www.score.org

The Service Corps of Retired Executives (SCORE) is increasingly active as a source of valuable yet affordable advice to small business. The association's new Web site offers a searchable database of SCORE members who can provide free *E-Mail counseling* to businesses in need. Also, check out SCORE's *Guest Feature* and *Success Stories.*

Genealogy

☐ DistantCousin.com

www.distantcousin.com

Here's a good place to start if you're trying to trace your roots. The site offers many different ways to locate your ancestors. You can search by *ethnic group.* There are links to lists of the *passengers* aboard thousands of immigrant ships. You'll find an index to some of the best genealogy sites on the Web and lots of secrets on how to start your search.

☐ Genealogy Toolbox

www.genealogytoolbox.com

Vast electronic resources for locating family members and help for adoptees, adoptive parents and birth parents. Genealogies of prominent families.

Etc.

☐ FreeAdvice.com

www.freeadvice.com

This site has tons of legal information for free! Click on one of the many topics, such as bankruptcy, immigration, child custody, business and real estate. Get your questions answered in a straightforward (nonlegalese) way.

☐ Legaldocs.com

www.legaldocs.com

Get any legal form you need for business or personal purposes without having to go through a lawyer. Many free. Others are moderately priced.

☐ Parent Soup

www.parentsoup.com

Great discussion and chat groups. The home page displays selected, timely articles for parents. On-line library has articles on various topics. Browse through the categories for past articles. Best features: Several ongoing and well-tended chat groups (pick your topic and join right in) or search one of the information-packed communities, divided by age of children, prepregnancy through teen. Also explore the tools: health calculator, first-year pregnancy calendar, and more. Partners' lists and links to other useful Web sites and organizations.

☐ ParentsPlace.com

www.parentsplace.com

Chat with other parents. Check out this site's range of well-maintained bulletin boards on almost every aspect of parenting, including daycare.

☐ PBS Adult Learning Service Online

www.pbs.org/als

Sponsored by the Public Broadcasting System, this site contains information on how to sign up for telecourses, college-level courses offered by local colleges and universities for adults and taught over public television stations. Learn which colleges in your area offer which courses and how a study program can fit into a tight schedule of work and family activity.

☐ PatentCafe

www.patentcafe.com

Patent Information. If you've got a new invention, or even an idea about one, this is an excellent place to learn how to protect it. Just click on *Inventor's Starting Point* and you'll get a simple, step by step guide to how to transform your ideas into patents. This site is absolutely packed with information including how to market your ideas and inventions, fraud scams to watch out for and more. There's even a special section for kids.

13

Travel Confidential

The Secrets of Much Safer Air Travel

Air travel is by far the safest form of transportation. In fact, you would need to spend 2,500 years flying every day before it became statistically likely that you would be in a crash. Yet some crashes do happen.

Travelers can make this already safe form of travel even safer.

FLYING SMARTER

When a plane crashes, the intense media coverage often scares the flying public. Statistically, plane crashes are so rare and their causes so unique that there is little one can do to avoid them.

To lessen passenger fear and "white-knuckle flying," travelers can check the safety records of each airline through the Federal Aviation Administration (FAA) Web site, *www.faa.gov/ agc/enforcement/ index.htm.*

A history of repeated fines suggests systemic problems with a particular airline.

Example: AirTran—formerly ValueJet—is notorious for its 1996 Everglades crash. This carrier has a record of maintenance problems…and while it is improving, it has a long way to go.

THE RIGHT PLANE

Boarding a plane that was manufactured between 30 and 40 years ago concerns some fliers. Many planes from the 1960s are still in the air, but these "old" planes aren't really old.

Following the Aloha Airlines incident in 1988, in which part of a plane's metal "skin" peeled away from the fuselage, the FAA implemented a mandatory retirement age for certain plane parts. So even a 40-year-old plane will have components that are much younger than the manufacture date suggests.

Example: Until recently, TWA had the oldest fleet in the country. But its aircraft maintenance

---

Michael Goldfarb, FAA Chief of Staff from 1987 to 1989. He currently runs MGA, a management-consulting business specializing in transportation and information technology, based in Washington, DC.

records have always been among the best. There are few problems with this airline.

Safety concerns: Problems arise when older aircraft are not aggressively maintained under an airline's aging-aircraft maintenance program. Problems also arise when older aircraft, such as DC-9s, are not properly cared for or are not continuously upgraded by the airline to carry the latest safety equipment in the cockpit.

FLIGHT LENGTH

Airline passengers tend to be more concerned about long flights. But, in fact, shorter flights pose the greater risk per mile.

If I have a choice between a nonstop flight and a flight involving a transfer, I will take the nonstop—and not only because it saves time.

Of the few accidents that occur, most are the result of pilot error. And pilot error is most common on takeoffs and landings—so more takeoffs and landings mean greater risk.

AIRLINE SIZE

Looking at aviation safety statistics, it *appears* that small commuter planes are riskier than large commercial planes.

But these statistics are deceptive. Recently, the FAA adopted the same set of safety rules for small planes—fewer than 30 seats—that are in place for larger ones. You're just as safe on a commuter plane in the US as you are on a wide-body jet.

Exception: Alaska. The state is so big that commuter-type planes are among the most common forms of transportation, despite the fact that flying a small plane in Alaska's difficult climate is inherently dangerous.

FOREIGN CARRIERS

Airline passengers often hesitate to book a flight on a foreign-based carrier, assuming that safety regulations are less strict in foreign countries. These fears are unwarranted—unless your flight includes a foreign stopover.

All planes flying into and out of the US must comply with US safety guidelines, whether the airline is based here or abroad.

However, flying internationally does raise some fears. Safety regulations in *some* countries are not always as tough as in the US.

Additionally, some areas of the world do not have the radar and ground navigational aids that are needed for safe navigation. Most modern aircraft have avionics that allow pilots to compensate for the lack of ground radar.

Danger: If your flight includes a transfer once you're overseas, you may end up on a plane that is not up to US safety standards. Since most major US carriers have alliances with foreign carriers, this might be true even if you book your flight with a well-known US airline.

Problems with airlines and airports are most common in Africa...South America...and some parts of the former Soviet Union.

Self-defense: Check the International Aviation Safety Assessment's Web page for concerns about particular countries (*www.faa.gov/avr/iasa/index.htm*). When you book a flight with a US carrier that involves a transfer, ask if other carriers will be involved.

Foreign Airport Danger

Airport thieves target tourists *traveling* to their destinations, not returning from them. That's because tourists carry more money early in a trip.

This means that if you travel abroad, you will be more at risk when you arrive in a foreign airport than later when you depart from it.

Also, when you first arrive in a foreign land, you are least familiar with your surroundings—which increases your vulnerability to thieves.

More risk: Travelers are at special risk after changing money at an airport bank or ATM. Thieves watch these areas to see how much money travelers are carrying and where they are keeping it.

Jens Jurgen, president of Travel Companion Exchange and editor of *Travel Companions,* Box 833, Amityville, NY 11701.

Getting Through Security

Reminder: Heavy belt buckles, jewelry and too much loose change create problems getting through airport security. Besides wasting time, they make thefts easier. If you set off metal detectors, thieves can steal carry-on belongings while you are focused on getting through security. *Also:* Beware of people who try to distract you at security or during check-in—they may be trying to steal your baggage.

Jeanne Salvatore, vice president, Insurance Information Institute, 110 William St., New York 10038.

Airline Water Can Be Dangerous

Water systems used to fill airplane tanks occasionally become contaminated. Most water used on US flights is safe, but there is no US oversight of water on international flights—and no guarantee of water quality. *Self-defense:* When flying internationally, drink bottled water or soft drinks. Never drink water from an airplane lavatory.

David Hajduk, MS, senior environmental health officer, Food and Drug Administration, Washington, DC.

How to Stay Healthy While Traveling by Air

Thomas N. Bettes, MD, MPH, southwest area medical director for American Airlines in Fort Worth, TX. He wrote about medical advice for commercial air travelers in a recent issue of *American Family Physician,* 11400 Tomahawk Creek Pkwy., Leawood, KS 66211.

Recent air disasters notwithstanding, your risk of being killed in a plane crash is remarkably small. But the time spent on board can leave you tired, stiff and dehydrated...and, if you have a chronic health condition, raise your risk of serious complications. *Here are the leading threats to airline passengers' health—and how to counter each...*

●**Dehydration.** During flight, cold, dry air inside the cabin can dry the skin, throat, eyes and nostrils.

To protect yourself, drink noncaffeinated beverages—six to eight ounces per hour while aloft. Pass up caffeine and alcohol. They're diuretics. Use moisturizer to keep your skin from drying out. Over-the-counter saline eye drops can help prevent dry eyes.

If you're flying overseas: Ask to be booked on a nonsmoking flight. If no such flights are available, ask to be seated well away from the smoking section.

All domestic airlines are now smoke-free.

●**Altitude sickness.** Airliner cabins are typically kept at a pressure equivalent to that found at 8,000 feet above sea level. This reduced pressure can cause mild *altitude sickness*—headache, fatigue and trouble concentrating.

There's no way to prevent altitude sickness, but being aware of it can ease any anxiety you might feel as a result of the symptoms.

If altitude sickness doesn't cause you to have headaches, engine noise might.

Self-defense: Ask for a seat far away from the engines. Bring along earplugs and *acetaminophen* (Tylenol) or another nonprescription pain medication.

●**Blood clots.** Stiffness isn't the only problem that can result from spending long hours in a cramped airplane seat. If blood pools in the legs, dangerous blood clots can form.

If your flight is longer than three hours, try to get up once an hour to stretch and walk around. While seated, periodically extend and flex your feet.

Caution: If you're already at risk for blood clots—because of smoking, obesity, oral contraceptive use or a history of deep venous thrombosis—ask your doctor about taking aspirin and wearing support stockings during the flight.

If possible, get a bulkhead seat. It will provide more legroom. Prolonged sitting can also cause swelling of the feet and ankles, especially in pregnant women and people with kidney trouble or heart failure.

To minimize swelling: Elevate your legs… walk around the cabin…and avoid nuts, pretzels and other salty foods.

AVOIDING COMPLICATIONS

If you've had recent surgery or have a chronic health problem, ask your doctor if you're stable enough to fly…

•**Recent surgery.** Postpone flying at least one week after major surgery—two weeks after coronary bypass surgery.

The danger is that air that might have been trapped inside the body during surgery could expand under reduced air pressure. This could cause torn sutures and other problems.

•**Special oxygen needs.** If your doctor recommends that you have supplemental oxygen during the flight, you'll need to call the airline to order it at least 48 hours in advance.

You'll also need to provide the airline with a medical certificate that spells out the proper flow rate and other important points.

•**Heart disease.** Anyone who has had a heart attack should wait at least two weeks before flying. Wait at least six weeks if there were complicating factors, such as arrhythmia or left ventricle dysfunction.

If there's any doubt as to your ability to fly safely following a heart attack, your doctor should give you a treadmill stress test.

If you take an antihypertensive drug or another heart medication, be sure to bring enough to last the entire trip. Keep it in your carry-on luggage.

It's also a good idea to bring along a copy of your most recent electrocardiogram.

Caution: Flying is off limits to individuals with unstable angina, severe heart failure, uncontrolled hypertension and certain heart arrhythmias.

•**Diabetes.** Be vigilant about monitoring your blood glucose levels while flying…and about scheduling meals and medication dosing—especially if you'll be traveling across time zones.

Pack *twice* as much medication and supplies as you think you'll need. Bring half the supply on board with you in your carry-on luggage. Bring *all* of your insulin on board

with you to avoid exposure to freezing temperatures in the cargo hold.

Important: Bring a "diabetes alert card" and a doctor's note specifying your dosages and explaining why you're carrying syringes. To obtain a free card, contact the American Diabetes Association at 800-342-2383.

•**Pregnancy.** To avoid premature delivery, pregnant women should avoid flying for at least a week before their due date (four weeks for overseas travel).

Women at risk for premature delivery should avoid flying entirely in the third trimester.

IN-FLIGHT EMERGENCIES

Domestic airlines are required to carry basic medical equipment, and crew members are trained in basic first aid.

Unfortunately, the first-aid kit can be used only by a physician or another trained medical professional, such as a nurse or paramedic. Whether there'll be one on your flight is a matter of luck.

Good news: Many airlines recently upgraded their medical kits. A wider range of medical problems can now be treated on board, including heart attacks, asthma attacks and seizures.

These days some airliners are equipped with automatic defibrillators, which can shock an erratically beating heart back into a normal rhythm. These devices can be operated by flight attendants.

AVOIDING JET LAG

Many travelers rely on over-the-counter supplements, such as melatonin. But recent studies have had conflicting results. And since melatonin is not regulated by the FDA, its purity and long-term safety are uncertain.

To minimize fatigue and disorientation after your arrival, remain active during daylight hours…adopt local mealtimes and bedtimes… eat small, well-balanced meals…avoid alcohol…and get moderate exercise.

Travel Savings Up to 70%!!

Tom Parsons, editor of *Bestfares.com,* a clearinghouse of hidden travel deals, 1301 S. Bowen Rd., Suite 490, Arlington, TX 76013. He travels about 100 days a year and currently has about 600,000 frequent-flier miles.

Finding a good deal on an airline ticket, a hotel room or a rental car can be frustrating. The travel industry has set up complex pricing schemes with conditions and exceptions that usually overwhelm travelers—and cause them to pay far more than necessary.

Here's how you can save up to 70% on air, hotel and rental car expenses…

AIRLINES

●**Visit the Web sites of airlines that fly to your destination.** Airlines are so eager to attract people to their Internet sites that they are posting special deals only available on-line.

Example: Recently, if you used the Web sites of American, Delta or Northwest, each offered to fly your companion for $99 or less if you bought round-trip tickets to anywhere in North America.

Airline Web site promotions are updated weekly. Also, many discount ticket promotions are offered only through Internet booking sites. *Examples…*

●Microsoft Expedia Travel, *www.expedia. com.*

●Preview Travel, *www.previewtravel.com.*

●Travelocity, *www.travelocity.com.*

●**Book a fly/drive package through the airline.** Airlines' fly/drive packages combine airfare and a rental car at a discounted price.

Example: I recently saved nearly $600 on a round-trip flight from Dallas to San Francisco. If I had purchased the ticket and rented the car separately, the flight would have cost $1,052…and the rental car would have cost $80/day, instead of the $40/day I paid. I ended up paying only about $480 for my package.

Don't call an airline's standard 800 number for fly/drive information. The airline may try to book the flight through its regular, more expensive reservation service.

Instead: Call the Vacation Division of each airline. *Examples…*

●American Airlines, 800-321-2121.

●Continental, 800-634-5555.

●United, 800-328-6877.

To qualify for a low-cost fly/drive package, you must plan to spend at least two to four days at your destination before flying home. Some packages also require at least two passengers to travel together, but you can ask for a single supplement and you will pay a little more.

●**Cut fares with discount coupons.** Airlines sometimes issue coupons that entitle you to dollars off your airfare. The coupons can even be used when fares are already discounted. You'll often find these coupons included with your credit card bill or other purchases.

Example: Continental recently issued a coupon worth up to $200 if you bought a $14 Warner Brothers video.

Call the airlines you fly regularly to inquire about their coupon offers. Or you can access this information at my Web site *(www.best fares.com).* Click on "News Desk" for a complete coupon listing that is updated three times a day.

●**Look into rates to alternative airports.** Airlines often charge their highest rates for flights into the biggest cities. But you can save big on your fare by flying into a nearby city. Take a taxi or rent a car, and drive the remaining distance.

Example: The lowest published nonstop fare from Los Angeles to Boston's Logan Airport was about $700. But tickets from Los Angeles to Providence, Rhode Island…or Manchester, New Hampshire—both one hour's drive from Boston—were $198.

Just be aware that most flights to alternative airports are not nonstop direct flights and could add a few hours to your trip. The best way to find out which alternative airports are near your destination is to check with a travel agent.

●**Bid for airline tickets on-line.** A number of Internet sites now auction off airline tickets held by travel agents and passengers. *Examples…*

●eBay, *www.ebay.com.* Ticketholders sell their seats to people hoping to travel.

●TravelBids, *www.travelbids.com.* Type in the amount you want to spend, and travel agents try to come as close as possible.

●**Check in with ticket consolidators.** These firms buy blocks of tickets from airlines and sell them at huge discounts, sometimes 50% or more. My favorite consolidators…

●Domestic flights. Discount Airline Ticket Service, 800-576-1600.

●International flights. World Travel Network, 800-409-6753.

HOTELS

●**Book your reservation after joining a discount club.** Many hotels list as many as 10 to 12 different rates *per room*. Calling the hotel directly gives you a better chance to get a lower rate than the one offered through the hotel's 800 number.

And even better than calling the hotel is joining a discount club. These clubs are run by national hotel chains and offer members hotel-room discounts of up to *50% below most other rates*. Call several national hotel chains to determine their club fees, benefits and restrictions.

●**Save up to 50% by going through a hotel broker.** Hotel brokers book rooms in hundreds of hotels around the country. Because of the volume they handle, hotels give them steep discounts on rooms. *Examples…*

●Accommodations Express, 800-444-7666.

●Central Reservations Service, 800-950-0232.

●Hotel Reservation Network, 800-964-6835.

●Quickbook, 800-789-9887.

RENTAL CARS

●**Check the rates offered by all of your frequent-flier accounts.** Not all airline frequent-flier plans offer the same car discounts at the same time.

Example: One company's daily rate at Washington's National Airport recently was $36/day if you belonged to one airline's frequent-flier plan. The same car was $20/day for another airline's frequent-flier plan members.

Make a list of your frequent-flier programs. Then call the car rental firm's main number, and make a list of the different plans' discounts.

●**Use the Internet to reserve rental cars.** Like airlines, rental car companies are eager to promote their Web sites. Many rental car sites offer great discounts or free upgrades if you book over the Internet.

Example: One aggressive rental car agency on the Web recently offered discounts of up to 40% off list rates. And Budget is now offering a make-your-own-bid for a car on the Internet (*www.drive budget.com*).

Luxury Travel On a Shoestring

Joel L. Widzer, a travel expert who has traveled more than 1.5 million miles around the world. Mr. Widzer lectures on travel and assists travelers in arranging luxury travel experiences, and is author of *The Penny Pincher's Passport to Luxury Travel*. Travelers' Tales Guides.

I fly only first class and stay at the best hotels, but I don't pay a premium to do so. Last year, I took 35 round-trip first-class flights and paid—on average—only $243 per flight. I stayed in top hotels that cost—on average—only $122 per night. *You can get the same results…*

●**Loyalty pays.** You'll get the best deals by traveling on the same airline and staying at the same hotel chain as often as possible. This is how you get the most bang for your frequent-flier miles and the best deals on upgrades.

To enjoy luxury travel at the best possible price, choose your travel partnership wisely, based on where you live and where you're most likely to travel.

Your choice should be determined, in part, by your wish list of destinations during the next *decade*.

For people who do a lot of international traveling, the *Star Alliance*—which links the frequent-flier programs of United, Lufthansa, Thai, Air Canada, SAS, Varig, Air New Zealand and Ansett Australia—can be an excellent choice.

A similar appealing combination, called *Oneworld Alliance,* has been formed by American Airlines, British Airways, Canadian Airlines, Cathay Pacific and Qantas.

●**Get "elite status" with airlines.** Most large airlines have three elite tiers to reward their frequent fliers. If you travel 20,000 or 25,000 miles per year on one carrier, you qualify for elite status at major airlines. These must be real in-flight miles, not frequent-flier points accumulated with a credit card.

Benefits: Special check-in lines, special telephone lines, free upgrades and priority wait listing, preferred seating and free access to airport lounges.

Note: If you ever decide that you've chosen the wrong airline to have elite status with, you can usually switch your elite status to a competitor. Since, by definition, you are a frequent traveler, a competitor will be thrilled to get your business. Just tell them that you plan to remain loyal to them for the rest of your traveling days and you should get what you want.

●**Join frequent-guest programs.** Many of the best hotel chains offer discounts and free nights to guests who stay with them often. Unfortunately, you'll probably need to establish a relationship with several chains because no chain will be everywhere you want to go.

Even chains that don't issue frequent guest points, such as the Four Seasons and Ritz-Carlton, keep track of your stays. So if you're a good customer, don't hesitate to ask for an upgrade. The Ritz-Carlton gives me one every time I stay. Always call the front desk directly to get the best deal.

New: Starwood now has a new deal that links the reward programs of all its brands—Sheraton, Westin, ITT Luxury Collection, Four Points and Sheraton Inns.

●**Save by paying more.** I'm not kidding. Sometimes you can save money by paying more upfront.

Example: If you pay a bit more to stay on the Club or Concierge floor of fine hotels such as the Ritz-Carlton, you can more than recoup the extra outlay. With access to the club floor, you get free breakfast, free lunch, unlimited snacks and cocktails, soda, bottled water and newspapers.

●**Use loyalty to your advantage.** When you're a loyal customer, you have every right to ask for benefits that other travelers won't get. Don't be bashful.

A friend of mine wanted to take his family of five to Hawaii for the Christmas holidays using his frequent-flier miles, but was turned down because he was told no seats were available. So he called the airline's vice president of marketing, explained that he was a very loyal customer and—like magic—received five free first-class tickets to Hawaii in exchange for his miles.

Granted, you won't always get to talk to the VP of marketing. I usually start by calling the executive customer relations department. It's great if you can speak to a VP, but the executive assistant to a VP can also be quite helpful. These people have the power to turn your wishes into reality.

Always mention that you are a loyal customer…and have several possible travel dates in mind before you call. The more flexible you are, the more likely you'll get the deal you want.

●**Ask the gate agent for upgrades.** If there are vacant seats in first class (or in business class on international flights), the gate agent will almost always seek to fill them.

Reason: This generates goodwill for the airline at no extra cost.

Strategy: Dress as if you belong in first class. Then, realizing that the gate agent is busy and stressed, request an upgrade very politely.

Alternative: Try to get an upgrade while waiting in the airport lounge.

●**Travel when people need your business the most.** Traveling off-season is the easiest way to enjoy luxury at the right price.

Thanksgiving week is a great time to travel to Europe because airlines are desperate for business then.

Getting a bargain isn't your only benefit. You usually receive better service at a hotel when it isn't full.

●**Be opportunistic.** Always consider the relative value of the dollar when you travel. Right now, for example, is an ideal time to travel to Bali, where you can get a 3,200-square-foot villa with a private beach, plunge pool and 24-hour butler for just $335 a night.

Strategy: You can also save by using split airline tickets—paying dollars to travel to a foreign destination but using local currency for your return trip. You can also save sometimes by paying for your foreign hotel room in local currency. Consult a good travel agent for details.

●**Don't let travel agents cost you extra.** As just indicated, travel agents can be helpful, but they can occasionally undermine a bargain hunter's luxury strategy. Why? Because, by seeking to get the best deal on each particular trip, they focus on the "trees while ignoring the forest." In the long run, it's cheaper for a penny-pincher to fly on the same airline every time and stay at a partner hotel.

Over time, most major airlines charge about the same. The way you really save is by accumulating benefits and taking advantage of them.

Much More for Much Less...Almost Off-Peak Travel

Louise Weiss, author of *Access to the World: A Travel Guide for the Handicapped*. Henry Holt.

World tourism has grown so rapidly—*tenfold* since the 1960s—that today the world's great tourist attractions often are swamped with visitors during their peak seasons.

Result: The pleasure of travel is lost as you get stuck in a crowd. And hotels, airlines and restaurants charge top rates.

Off-season travel is an option. But "off season" usually is called that for a good reason—such as "off" weather.

Best: Travel in the "smart season." Usually this is adjacent to the peak season, when the crowds have left (or haven't yet arrived), but the weather hasn't greatly changed yet. *Visit...*

●*Egyptian pyramids* in March, when most tourists have left because the temperature is rising—but it hasn't yet risen much.

●**Taj Mahal** in September, before tourists arrive in droves in October.

●**New Zealand** in March, just after the Southern Hemisphere's summer.

●**Miami** in December—escaping the northern winter but beating the January tourist rush.

Also: Select "off the beaten path" destinations to escape the masses...

●**Egyptian pyramids at Saqqâra** instead of Luxor.

●**Chartres** instead of Versailles.

●**The Japanese island of Hokkaido** instead of Kyoto.

Both these strategies require you to research your destination. But combining them will let you have a "best" vacation—beating the crowd and saving substantial money as well.

More from Louise Weiss...

Safer Cruising

Pick a ship that sails from the US. Those ships get inspections twice a year from the US Coast Guard and Centers for Disease Control and Prevention (CDC). Check a ship's fire safety by calling the Coast Guard Information Line, 800-368-5647. Find out how the CDC ranked it for hygiene at the Summary of Sanitation Inspections of International Cruise Ships section of the CDC's Web site at *www.cdc.gov* (click on "Travelers' Health"). Plan for your own medical care—onboard medicine is not regulated. If you have special needs, consult your doctor before booking a cruise.

Fresh Thinking About Handling Money when You Travel

Bob Howells, correspondent for *Outside Magazine* and writer for *National Geographic Adventure*. He is author of *The RVer's Money Book*. Trailer Life Books.

Before you leave on a trip this winter, accommodations must be made to cover financial matters while you're away from home, especially if you plan to be gone for an extended period of time. *Here are a few areas to consider...*

●**Consolidate and simplify.** Arrange to have as few bills coming in as possible while you're away. *Helpful:* Limit the number of credit cards you carry.

Example: Instead of carrying five gasoline credit cards in your wallet, pay for fuel using a single Visa or MasterCard.

Contact creditors about setting up automatic payment plans to pay regular monthly bills directly from your checking account. *Including:* Mortgage payments...utility bills...insurance premiums.

Arrange for direct deposit of regularly arriving checks. *Including:* Social Security...dividends...pension payments.

● **Have a trusted friend or family member pick up your mail.** Leave a supply of pre-signed checks so they can pay any unexpected bills that arrive. *Also:* Have them review your mail to make sure nothing important—such as a notice from the IRS—goes unanswered.

Alternative: If you're going to be traveling on a schedule or will be in only one location, have your mail forwarded directly to you.

How: If you will be in only one location, have your local post office forward your mail. If you'll be moving around, contact a mail forwarding service—listed in the Yellow Pages (look under "Mail Receiving Services"). These services will receive your mail from the post office, bundle it up and forward it to you anywhere in the world. *Including:* To a private mailing address... a hotel...RV campsite office...post office general delivery.

● **Get an Automated Teller Machine (ATM) directory.** Contact your bank or ATM card network for a directory of locations. In the US, machines are easy to find, but in some countries, machines are tied into only one network.

ON THE ROAD

Gaining access to your money when you're on the road can be a problem. *There are several useful options...*

● **Traveler's checks.** The old standby for travelers, traveler's checks are readily negotiable in an emergency—or when you are temporarily unable to find an ATM for some reason.

Carry—at most—only several hundred dollars in traveler's checks. *Reason:* You usually have to pay a 1% service charge, plus you'll tie up money that could otherwise be earning interest.

● **ATMs.** ATMs give you instant access to your money, and with so many available in the US and Canada, one is always nearby. Plus, more and more businesses are accepting ATM cards for purchases.

Strategy: Keep most of your funds in an interest-bearing checking or savings account linked to your ATM card so you'll continue to earn interest on your money until the day you withdraw it.

Important: ATMs often charge transaction fees of $1 to $2 for network withdrawals, so compare charges when selecting a bank.

● **Credit cards.** A great convenience for travelers, credit cards eliminate the need to carry a lot of cash and allow you to "float" your money for as long as 60 days—the time from when you make a purchase to when you have to pay for it.

You may need to carry two credit cards. One for making purchases and the second for checking into hotels or renting cars.

Background: When a hotel or car rental company makes an imprint of your card, a portion of your credit line is tied up as a security measure to cover damage to the room or car. It may be two to three weeks before that amount is released—usually only when payment is received from the card company.

Problem: If you rent a few cars or stay in several hotel rooms, your credit limit can easily be exhausted, making the credit card worthless.

Self-defense: Carry another emergency card or a charge card—such as American Express or Diner's Club—which has no credit limit. In an emergency, most credit cards can be used to withdraw cash from ATMs.

Note: These withdrawals—via credit card —are considered cash advances and begin accruing interest from the moment the money is withdrawn.

Cash-advance fees: Most cards charge cash-advance withdrawal fees of up to 3% of the total amount withdrawn, not to exceed a maximum of $10 to $25.

● **Carry a telephone calling card.** Available from AT&T, MCI, Sprint and other long-distance providers, they let you bill telephone calls to a personal account, use the provider of your choice and avoid the exorbitant rates charged by no-name long-distance companies.

Little-Known E-Ticket Problems

To prevent fraud, airlines may require you to present the actual credit card with which an E-ticket was bought. If you don't have it with you, you may be denied boarding. If you buy an E-ticket for a family member, he/she will not have the credit card and may not be allowed to fly. *Bottom line:* Until E-tickets are made more consumer-friendly, insist on standard paper tickets.

Marty J. Fegley, Fegley Consulting, management consulting firm, Redondo Beach, CA.

Best Time to Book Airline Tickets

Randy Petersen, publisher, *InsideFlyer*, 4715-C Town Center Dr., Colorado Springs 80916.

The best time to book airline tickets is between midnight and 1 am. Airlines load low-priced fares into their computers...and restore bargain seats that were booked but never ticketed. Ask the airline you prefer when it updates its computers—many do it at mid-night Eastern time, but some use midnight in other time zones as their base.

More from Randy Peterson...

Flight Delays

Flights at the end of the month are more likely to be delayed or cancelled. *Reason:* By late in the month, many flight crew members may have reached the number of hours they can legally work per month because of overtime and work on delayed flights earlier in the month. When enough crew members have worked the maximum hours allowable, there can be crew shortages that cause flight delays or cancellations.

Beware: Airline Check-In Times

The check-in times refer to a flight's scheduled departure time, not its delayed time. Even if you call the airline and are told the flight will be delayed several hours, you must check in at least 20 minutes before the original scheduled departure time—or the airline can give away your seat. Airlines say they have this policy because delays change unpredictably. *Bottom line:* If you know a flight will be delayed, bring activities to keep you busy during a long wait at the airport.

William J. McGeer, editor, Consumer Reports *Travel Letter,* 101 Truman Ave., Yonkers, NY 10703.

14

Making the Most of Your Leisure Time

How to Outsmart Casinos at Their Very, Very Dirty Tricks

No matter how much we hope for big wins, casino odds are stacked against gamblers, to the benefit of the casinos.

You can still have fun gambling—and dramatically improve your odds and limit your losses—by knowing the strategies that casinos use to get gamblers to lose...and lose...

•**Casinos want you to forget you're gambling.** The carefree, party atmosphere in a casino helps soften the blow when a player loses. The last thing a casino wants a player to do is dwell on how much he/she has lost.

•**Greed is good**—for the casino. It's hard for gamblers to stop while they're winning. That's why casinos have pictures of big winners displayed when you enter. They want you to think, "Hey, I could win a pile, too."

That way, if you win a few hundred dollars—even $1,000—you'll feel unsatisfied and try to parlay it into a huge win.

•**Casinos hate players with a plan.** A casino's nightmare is a bettor who refuses to lose more than a certain amount, no matter what. Luckily for the casino, few players have such discipline. The majority of players violate the mental limits they set. After losing the allotted bundle, a player thinks he can break even by risking just a little more. So the losses add up. The more the player loses, the more desperate—and foolish—his bets become.

•**Cashing out is purposely difficult.** By design, gamblers who want to cash out have to get past a gauntlet of table games and slot machines before they get to the cashier's window. *Don't be tempted to bet more.*

You'll also often find a line of customers at the cashing-out windows. The casino wants

John Alcamo, a gaming expert who spent several years interviewing Atlantic City card counters. He is author of *Casino Gambling Behind the Tables.* Gollehon Books.

you to become impatient and resume play. Don't give in.

●**Every comp is strategic.** Casinos give out complimentary tickets—freebees—to customers because they want them to keep playing and eventually visit again.

Casinos roll out the red carpet for big winners because they don't want them to leave. The longer a player stays in a casino, the more likely he is to lose money.

Strategy: Accept comps...but don't be swayed by them.

GAME TRICKS

●**Blackjack.** Card counting doesn't work. Skilled counters can *theoretically* get a mathematical edge in blackjack. But casino employees are adept at spotting card counters. When they do, the pit boss can order the cards to be shuffled, negating the counter's hard work.

●**Keno.** Worse than a lottery—because there is no guaranteed winner.

●**Roulette.** Tracking numbers is a sucker's game. It gives you no mathematical edge. But casinos will gladly give you a scorecard because they know that people who keep "score" play longer—and lose more money.

●**Slot machines.** Credits are diabolical. Years ago, slot machines dispensed actual coins if you won. Today's slot machines register "credits." Casinos changed their methods because gamblers are more likely to fritter away credits since "they're not real money."

Remember: Credits *are* real money—with or without a dollar sign.

●**Video poker.** Misleading. If you're playing Jacks-or-Better and you end up with a pair of jacks, the machine will tell you that you won. If you bet five coins, five coins will be returned to you.

But you didn't win. You tied and got back only what you wagered. In blackjack, this would be called by its right name—*a push.* Video poker machines call it a win so you'll feel better and keep playing...and lose more money.

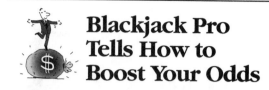

Blackjack Pro Tells How to Boost Your Odds

Ian Andersen, professional blackjack player and author of *Burning the Tables in Las Vegas: Keys to Success in Blackjack and in Life.* Huntington Press.

Even if you don't play blackjack more than 200 days a year as I do, you can still improve your odds of winning in casinos...

●**Memorize the game's basic strategies.** In blackjack, as in other card games, you can improve your odds of winning hands by doing the statistically right thing at the right time.

How you play in blackjack depends on your hand and the dealer's face-up cards.

Many casino gift shops sell wallet-sized plastic cards outlining these strategies to encourage people to play the game. The strategies people most often forget...

●**When you have two 9s...**

●Split the *9s* when the dealer has a *2, 3, 4, 5, 6, 8* or *9* card showing. You split by separating your two *9s* on the table and asking for two additional cards.

●Hold when the dealer has a *7, 10* or an *Ace.*

●**When you have an Ace and a 7...**

●Hold when the dealer has *2, 7* or *8* showing.

●Double your bet when the dealer has *3, 4, 5* or *6* showing.

●Ask for a card when the dealer has *9, 10* or *Ace* showing. If you don't catch an *Ace, 2* or *3,* continue to take additional cards until you get to 17 or break.

●**Don't give in to your hunches.** It's human nature to remember the hunches that proved to be correct—and to forget the ones that weren't.

All hunches diminish your chances of winning because they're based on little more than guesses. Hands that distract players and cause them to base decisions on hunches...

●**When your cards total 12 and the dealer has a 2 or 3 showing.** This combination causes many people to hold, thinking they're going to exceed 21 if they draw a card.

The right play in this situation is to take a card. The odds of drawing a card that is lower than *10* are higher than actually drawing a *10*—and even if you draw a low card, the dealer might exceed 21.

•When you have an Ace and a 6...

Never stand pat with this hand. Yes, a 17 could be the winner, but the odds are against you. When you have an *Ace* and a *6* and the dealer has a *3, 4, 5* or *6* showing, double your bet. Otherwise, take another card.

•Manage fear and greed.

Many players abandon strategy when they become emotionally involved in the game. Most people who are winning tend to get greedy. Unless you manage your greed, big wins almost always turn into losses. Set a target to avoid giving back all your winnings.

Let's say your goal for a particular evening is to double your stake. If you start with $200 and turn it into $500, set aside $400 and continue to play with the remaining $100.

If you lose the $100, stop playing immediately. If you dip into the rest of your chips, odds are that you'll lose it all eventually.

Alternative: When you're up, decide that you're willing to lose a certain percentage of your winnings—say 25%—but not a penny more.

Traps when you're losing: While most people set a loss limit before entering a casino, too many violate the promises they make to themselves.

When that happens and the cards continue to go against them, most players get frightened. They don't want to acknowledge to themselves or to a spouse how much they've lost.

So they start playing recklessly, taking bigger and bigger chances in a desperate attempt to break even. This is a sure recipe for disaster.

Set an absolute limit for your losses. And if you reach that limit in the first 15 minutes, stop playing.

Also limit the likelihood of making mistakes by taking a five-minute break every hour. Walk around the casino, or step outside for some fresh air.

Blackjack requires intense concentration, and most people can't stay at the top of their game for longer than 60 minutes at a time. Even a five-minute break can prove remarkably refreshing.

•Take advantage of the casino's generosity.

No institution gives out as many valuable freebees as a casino. If you're playing blackjack, you may as well take advantage of the comps that you're due.

Examples: Rooms, meals and show tickets.

Strategy: Ask the casino to "rate" you. This means casino personnel will watch your play to determine your average bet and how long you play.

In general, the casino expects to win 2% of what you bet and will give back 40% of those winnings in the form of comps.

•Count cards—

without being a counter. Counting cards is too much mental work for most players.

When playing one- or two-deck games, watch from the beginning of the deck and bet more if a bunch of small cards show relative to *Aces* and *10s.*

Better still: Walk around the casino looking for dealers who are doing fresh shuffles. If one looks good, jump in. If not, move on.

Reason: With many high cards available, players have a better chance of getting blackjack, which pays three-to-two odds. The odds are greater that the dealer will exceed 21 when he takes a card.

Warning: To make this approach work, you must pay attention to the cards from the first time they are dealt after a shuffle.

If you enter the game in the middle of a deal, you won't know what cards were dealt before you started to pay attention.

If you want to become a big winner, learn to count cards.

Poker Lessons from Four-Time Winner of the World Series of Poker

Tom McEvoy, one of the world's top professional poker players. He has won four World Series of Poker titles and writes a column for *Card Player Magazine.* He is author of five books, including *Tournament Poker.* Cardsmith Publishing.

After 20 years as a professional poker player, I've found that consistent winners follow just a handful of basic strategies.

These guidelines can work for anyone in any poker environment—as long as you have the discipline to stick with them…

●**Play in a game you can win.** The best players in the world don't necessarily make the most money playing at poker tables with the highest stakes.

More important than raw skill—finding a game in which you're up against relatively weak opposition.

In a friendly game at home, you can get a good feel for how you are doing by recording your wins and losses each month. Without such a log, many losing players deceive themselves into thinking they're better players than they really are.

If you've lost money in seven of 10 sessions, it's time to reevaluate your play. If you're playing in a casino for the first time, test the waters before plunging in.

Safe zone: A low-limit game—$1/$2 or $2/$4.*

Once you've had some experience and success, move up the ladder, to $5/$10 or even $10/$20 games. Amateur players are ill-advised to move any higher.

Trap: At the $15/$30 or $20/$40 level, you will run into a fair number of professionals.

As a rule, the higher the limit, the tougher the game. You are in over your head if you're consistently unable to *read* your opponents— you can't tell whether their hands are strong

---

*In $2/$4 Texas hold'em or seven-card stud, you can bet or raise $2 in the first two betting rounds, and $4 in subsequent rounds.

or weak. But when you have a good hand, they're reading you and folding before you can take much of their money.

If you find yourself in this situation at a casino, don't throw good money after bad. Ask to be transferred to a lower-limit game. The casino will be happy to accommodate you.

●**Play only at stakes you can afford.** When the limit is too high for your bankroll, you stop playing to win. Instead, you play *not to lose.*

Problem: You tend to protect your chips, especially if you win a pot early. You wait until you have nearly unbeatable hands. When you become that predictable, you don't get action on those hands…or you get timid and easily bluffed out.

My rule: Before sitting down at a table in *seven-card stud* or *hold'em,* be prepared to risk at least 15 times the maximum bet.

Example: In a $10/$20 game, you need a minimum bankroll of $300.

●**Protect your good starting hands by betting them aggressively.** When you start off strong, you want to drive opponents out …or make them pay to play. In "limit" poker, in which each betting round has a maximum bet, the game is designed to produce *showdowns*—two or more players showing hands at the end to determine the winner.

Example: Let's say you have a high pair as your first two cards in hold'em.** The more people remaining in the hand until the end, the less likely it is that your hand will hold up.

Reason: The remaining players will then be hoping to get common cards to complete flushes, straights or potential full houses, which your starting high pair is unlikely to beat.

Example: Against one other player in hold'em, your starting pair of aces will win more than 80% of the time. But if four or more people stay in through the first two betting rounds, your win rate drops to around 50%.

●**Fold early and often.** Most amateur players stay in too long with hands that simply aren't worth playing. They're in Las Vegas or

---

**In Texas hold'em, each player begins with two down cards. After a betting round, the dealer flips three cards faceup, to be used by all players. In succeeding rounds, two more common cards are also dealt faceup, one per round.

Atlantic City for just a few days, and they're there to play, not to sit patiently and fold one hand after another.

Some people actually play every hand. Those players may win the most pots, but they'll probably lose the most money.

To win consistently in a casino hold'em game, fold at least 75% of your hands on the first betting round.

In seven-card stud, fold 80% on the first betting round. If you find seven or eight people staying in for the second betting rounds in a nine-handed hold'em game, you'll know that you are in with weak players. You'll be tempted to loosen up and start playing some marginal hands yourself.

Danger: It's too easy to get caught up in a loose game and play down to the level of your opponents.

My rule: The surest way to make money is to play tighter—more selectively—than the players around you.

●**Be ready to fold a good starting hand that fails to develop.** The best starting hand in hold'em is two face-down aces. But if the dealer then turns over an *8-9-10* of diamonds and there's a bet and a raise to you, what do you think you've got?

The short answer: You've got nothing because at least one of your opponents almost surely has drawn a straight or flush.

Most players stay married to their aces at this point, even when it's obvious they are beaten. But they're pouring money into a lost cause. That hand should be folded...and quickly.

●**Choose your spots to bluff**—and bluff rarely. People overrate the power of bluffing in "limit" games. Remember, most hands in limit games end in a showdown. A worthless hand will generally lose. There are exceptions, however.

Example: You've been trying for a flush in seven-card stud, but you fail to complete it on your last card. You have only one opponent, who looks weak.

Unfortunately, he/she has an ace showing, while your highest card is a king.

If you simply check to him—don't bet and give your opponent a chance to bet first—you'll be conceding a large pot. But if you bet, and you've read him correctly, he just might fold.

If You Spend More Than An Hour in a Casino ...Collect Freebees

Gayle Mitchell, president, Casino Players Workshop & Seminars, 4001 E. Bell Rd., #114-270, Phoenix 85032. She is author of *All Slots Made Easier.* Casino Players Workshop & Seminars.

If you gamble at a casino, you're probably eligible for free or discounted meals, rooms, show tickets and, in some cases, cash or merchandise.

BEFORE YOU GO

Several Web sites offer free information about casino "comps" that are available. *My favorites...*

●**Casino Central.** Room, meal, beverage and other US casino promotions...coupons that can be downloaded and printed...and comps sent to your E-mail address. *www.casinocentral.com*

●**Las Vegas Online Entertainment Guide.** Internet links to individual hotels that list comps and other promotions. *www.lvol.com*

●**About.com.** The Casino Gambling portion of its Web site has loads of information about comps as well as gambling articles. Click on *Comps* and then choose the *Funbook Coupons* link. *www.about.com*

ONCE YOU ARRIVE

●**Join your hotel/casino's slot club.** Membership is free or for a low fee. Once you join, you receive a plastic card that earns points each time you play a slot or video poker machine. Points can then be used toward discounts on food, drinks and merchandise.

Smart play: Earn points twice as fast by requesting two member cards for the same account. On your first visit, request one for yourself...on a later visit, ask for one for your spouse. *Benefits...*

•**You earn points on the same account.**

•**You will receive twice as many offers in the mail** for free rooms.

•**You'll be able to book back-to-back reservations** for longer discounted stays.

•**Ask the pit boss to rate or monitor your play for comps.** When you join a table game such as blackjack, the pit boss will track your play to determine the value of comps you're due. The quality of your comps depends on the table's minimum bet...how many hands you play...and for how long.

Examples: Four hours spent playing at the $25 blackjack table usually entitles you to a free meal at the casino's buffet restaurant. Eight hours of play often results in a free room or a complimentary round of golf.

TOP LAS VEGAS COMPS

•**Tickets to shows.** Play the $75/hand blackjack table for three hours and receive a free $100 ticket. Most hotels also "bill-back" free show tickets. This means if you play for three hours at one hotel/casino, you can request a ticket to a show at another hotel/casino.

Important: Let the pit boss know which show you would like to see as soon as you sit down at the table.

•**Pick up a Boarding Pass club card.** This free, frequent-player program is offered at the four Station casinos in Las Vegas—Boulder Station, Palace Station, Sunset Station and Texas Station. Each time you play the slot machines or gaming tables, you earn points for free rooms, food and movie tickets.

TOP ATLANTIC CITY COMPS

The following casinos are the most generous with all comps—cash-back, rooms, food, show tickets and special promotional items. *They each return at least 25% of revenue in comps...*

•**Caesars**—voted "best" blackjack tables in Atlantic City.

•**Hilton** offers great funbooks filled with discount coupons. Room and package discounts are often available.

•**Trump Plaza/Trump's World's Fair.** Two-for-one cards can be used in both.

Other favorites...

•**Harrah's.** Total Gold Card is good at all 19 of Harrah's US properties. Comps include preferred restaurant seating...airline and other travel benefits...show tickets.

•**Showboat.** Voted best casino for quarter players. Cash-back incentives for all...room discounts for higher-level players.

Home-Video Directions From the Director of *The Godfather*

Francis Ford Coppola, a five-time Oscar-winning director. His films include *The Godfather, Apocalypse Now* and *Bram Stoker's Dracula.*

What advice does an Oscar-winning movie director have for people who want to improve their home videos?

•**Before your tape rolls, know what you want to say.** Think of yourself as an artist, not just an extension of the video camera.

Take a minute before you shoot to think about the images that will best convey the simple theme you have in mind.

Example: If you're trying to show how loving your family is at the dinner table, focus on images that drive home that point.

•**Plug in an additional microphone.** When taping, most people forget that their video cameras are not equipped to capture clearly what's being said.

Plug a microphone into your camera. Tape the mike to a stick.

Hold the stick close to the person you're shooting but out of the camera's frame. Or have someone else hold the stick. This will result in a clear soundtrack.

•**Don't use the camera to hunt for images.** When you are taping scenes, let your subject walk in and out of the frame.

Panning the camera to keep the subject in the frame only makes the recorded images look restless and jerky.

If you let your subjects walk out of the frame, you can stop the camera and start it again when they walk back into view.

This also will give you natural cuts in the tape, making it easier to edit segments later, and results in a more organized finish.

●**Capture close-ups of people and objects other than your subject.** In the film business, we call these images "cutaways." They are for suggestive purposes and are used to emphasize an image or mood on the tape. Such images can be close-ups of food, a clock or other people.

These cutaways also will provide you with material that can be intercut with the principal action if you edit the tape later.

●**Record clean tracks of music, from beginning to end...**or record other sounds and dialogue, separately.

When mixed into the tape during the editing process, those sounds create audio transitions between rough images that result when the camera starts and stops unevenly.

Use your camera or a tape recorder to capture these sounds. Don't worry about the images being recorded at the time. Instead, concentrate on the sound quality.

Learning to Play

It's never too late to learn a musical instrument—or to pick up again one that you used to enjoy playing. Music teachers often find that seniors show a greater love of music and musical expressiveness than their younger students.

Before taking lessons, decide what kind of music you like to listen to and what kind of sounds you'd like to make—brass, string, percussion, etc. Check music stores, local universities, schools, churches and synagogues for teachers. They can often lead you to groups you might want to join and teachers who can improve your skill.

Don Campbell, classical musician, composer and lecturer in Boulder, Colorado, and founder of the Institute for Music, Health and Education.

Adventures in Collecting

Ralph and Terry Kovel, collecting experts based in Cleveland. They are authors of many books on collecting, including Kovels' Antiques & Collectibles Price List 2000. *Three Rivers Press.*

Take a look around your house. Almost any object could be the inspiration for a collecting adventure.

Whether you're an executive who wants a challenging pastime or a parent whose child wants to have some fun with allowance money, there are endless examples of entertaining and affordable objects to collect.

When we got married almost 50 years ago, we started collecting the labels from canned food. Some were fished right out of the garbage. These days, an antique Shaker label can fetch $100, although most vintage labels still go for $1 to $5.

Key: Collect what you like, but have some focus. If you collect old postcards, for example, pursue a theme—postcards of Paris or landmarks...or even a single landmark like the Empire State Building.

More ideas for getting started...

POLITICAL MEMORABILIA

●**Campaign buttons.** As with all collectibles, older and rarer is better. But a presidential election year is a great time to start collecting political baubles. You'll be surprised at how soon the next election rolls around and your memorabilia suddenly become hard to find.

Aim for official campaign buttons, not the shoddy souvenirs hawked outside conventions.

To start: Visit party headquarters and ask to buy some material. Rare political buttons can sell for thousands of dollars, but you should be able to pick up some for as little as $1 each. Bigger buttons are better...so are those with pictures. Presidential buttons are especially valuable if the vice presidential candidate is included.

Search out minor party candidates or specific slogans. Hungarian-Americans for Ronald Reagan has greater potential value than the generic Ronald Reagan for President.

231

• **Offbeat stuff.** We collect campaign scarves. In the early 1900s, Teddy Roosevelt's campaign gave away kerchiefs that sell for $200 now.

Our son started collecting political knick-knacks, such as a Nixon for President lettuce crate. Posters are also fun...and sometimes you can get them free.

Collector's edge: Materials from early races by famous politicians are highly sought. So you might bet some pocket change on buttons for candidates running for lower offices. Who knew that young guy running for governor of Arkansas would become a two-term president?

SHAKER SETS

Salt and pepper shakers made into figurines were big collectors' items in the 1950s and 1960s—and they have recently come back into vogue. Most sets cost as little as $10, although limited editions can exceed $100.

Vintage salt and pepper sets included shakers shaped like the continental US. Fruit and animal combinations are popular. Disney and Warner Brothers make a lot of cartoon character sets.

Keep an eye out for "crossovers"—collectibles for two groups of collectors—such as a shaker set that says *Made in occupied Japan.*

Especially valuable: Shakers with moving parts, such as nodding heads...or mated pairs, called *huggers,* which feature embracing characters...or anything bearing the name Van Tellingen, an artist who is well-known for her hugger sets.

Buy only sets. Single shakers are not very valuable.

POT HOLDERS

Vintage pot holders can be beautiful—anything hand-stitched increases in value. You should be able to pick them up for $5 or less. Check out rummage sales. Look for pot holders in good condition, but even stained ones can often be cleaned. A friend collects pot holders from the 1920s and 1930s.

YESTERDAY'S TECHNOLOGY

Old manual typewriters, adding machines, radios, cameras and other outmoded office equipment or low-tech gear might not get much use, but they can be fun to collect. It's nice if the item works, but it's more important for it to look unusual or different from what is in use today.

Example: We recently saw a toaster from the 1950s selling for about $150. It took up the space of four contemporary toasters, but it was a real beauty—all chrome and "space age."

Don't collect old computers. They take up a lot of space and aren't very pretty. And, unlike mechanical office equipment, which is easy to repair, you have to be a real technophile to get an old computer to work.

TOYS

Action figures and toys from 1950 or earlier are always popular, especially items with an outer-space theme. Don't buy anything that is not in good condition. In the original box is good...still unopened and wrapped in plastic is best.

If you're looking at battery-powered toys, they should work. You might have to scrape the rust off the contacts. So when you're shopping, bring along batteries and sandpaper to clean contacts.

COLLECTING ON A TIGHT BUDGET

Individual dishes are cheap. If you have only a few dollars to spare, consider mixing and matching your own sets of items. Or buy a dinner set one piece at a time. You can start with plates for a few bucks. Pick a pattern to collect—or even just a style and color. We've seen people pick over piles of unmatched silverware looking for pieces with flowers.

Indulge your whims. We know of a movie star who collects metal lawn chairs in different colors—each costing less than $50—for her dining room.

Wooden country chairs from the 1890s are easy to find. Many look similar enough to match, but each still retains a distinctive touch. Originals are even cheaper than modern reproductions.

Visit an antique show, and ask a dealer how to judge the quality of the items that interest you. Most will be eager to give a lesson on what to look for.

15

Your Car

Car Dealers' Very Tricky Tricks...Now You Can Beat Them at Their Own Games

In today's supercompetitive marketplace, there's no reason to pay more than $500 over what a new domestic car costs a dealer—and no more than $1,500 over what the dealer paid for an import. Yet most people pay far more for a new car because they don't know the car dealers' inside tricks.

As a car salesperson for the past four years, I know all the tricks. *Here's what you need to know to get the best deal on a new car...*

•**Take advantage of unadvertised customer rebates and incentives.** Once you narrow down the models you are interested in, call each manufacturer directly and ask about its cash-back programs. Many dealers are unaware of them. *Examples...*

•College graduate rebate. *Value:* $400 to $500. Requires the buyer be one year away from graduation—or have graduated within the past two years.

•Customer loyalty rebate. *Value:* Several hundred dollars. Available if you already own or lease a car of the same make.

•Factory-to-consumer direct incentive. Offers you the choice of a cash rebate or low financing. But savvy customers who convince a credit union or bank to offer a low rate can get both.

Here's how it works: An auto-maker offered customers either a $1,000 rebate—or 2.9% financing on one of its models. A customer whose credit union matched the low financing offer secured the 2.9% rate and then opted for the carmaker's cash rebate.

•**If it is the same make, get your old car serviced through the dealer before you buy a new car.** Since dealerships make most

---

A senior salesperson at a major auto dealership in the Southwest. He has sold well over $10 million in new cars during the past four years.

of their profits on parts and service, most dealers will take hundreds of dollars off the selling price of a new car if they are convinced you will return for repairs.

● **Understand the dealership's secret code.** Some salespeople communicate with each other in code when they want to hide from you the real value of the car you are trading in—or the profit they are making on the deal.

Example: Letters may be substituted for numbers—*1* may be represented by *A...2* is *B...*and so on. Look for handwritten notes at the top of paperwork you're asked to fill out. If you see *FJJJ* scribbled on your old car's appraisal, it means that the dealer thinks your trade-in is worth $6,000 to them.

Not all codes are the same—so if you spot a secret code on a document, you can assume the dealer has a different number in mind than the one you've been given. Use the information subtly in your negotiations by fighting harder to get more for your trade-in.

● **Order directly from the factory**—rather than choosing from the dealer's lot. Though factory orders take six to 12 weeks for delivery, you will avoid having to accept costly options that you don't want. You'll also get a better deal on a factory-ordered car.

Reason: As a dealer, I'll accept a small profit from a factory order because it is a quick, easy sale for me. And—I don't have to pay the manufacturer interest for storing the vehicle on my lot.

Flip side: I also might be willing to cut the price of cars now on my lot if you're going to order from the factory.

Make sure that any rebates and incentives deducted from the price of the car don't expire before you take delivery. Also—get an appraisal value for your trade-in in writing to prevent a dealer from suddenly offering much less for your old car when your new one arrives.

● **Negotiate upward from the *dead cost* —not the invoice price**. The *dead cost* is the amount the dealer paid for the car after factoring in the rebates and incentives the dealer received from the manufacturer.

Dealers and manufacturers try to keep manufacturer deals secret. But you can dig them up before you start to negotiate.

To calculate the dead cost, you'll need to determine the dealer invoice, price incentives...and *holdbacks,* the dealer rebates for selling cars. *Sources of this information...*

● *www.edmunds.com.* This Web site offers on-line information about dealer incentives and holdbacks. *Free.*

● *Automotive News.* Weekly trade magazine for the auto industry. Publishes current incentives that are passed along to dealers on new models. $109/yr. 888-446-1422.

● **The Fighting Chance.** Consulting service that offers extensive reports on dead costs. Updated every two weeks. $24.95/report on one vehicle...$8/each additional vehicle. *www.fightingchance.com...*or 800-288-1134.

Once you have the dead cost—what the car really costs the dealer—use it as a starting point for negotiations.

● **Push to get dealers to reduce or drop add-on fees and the costs of options.** The most popular fees that dealers hit you with when they write your order now include...

● Dealer advertising fund fee. Also listed on invoices as *Sales Promotion Fund.* The charge is $200 to $1,000 for what the dealer paid to participate in the local or regional group advertising association.

● Floor plan assistance fees. Also listed on invoices as *Wholesale Financial Reserves.* You're asked to pay $150—or more—to cover the interest dealers pay on the factory invoice per month to the manufacturer for each car until they sell it. If a car has been on the lot three months, a dealer may try to charge you an additional $450.

● Window etching fee. This is a $300 fee to carve your Vehicle Identification Number (VIN) onto one or more windows so the car can be identified if it is stolen. Dealers contend this will reduce your annual insurance rates by 5% or more. This is often true, but any mechanic can perform the same service for much less.

● **Buy a quota car.** That's the car on the lot that a dealer needs to sell to make its quota for the month—or to reach a bonus or incentive level provided by the manufacturer. If your timing is right, most dealers will happily sell a quota car at a loss—or for no profit. Manufacturer incentives can change from month to month, and you never can be sure how close a dealership is to its incentive levels. But there are strategies to increase your chances for a quota car...

•Visit several car dealerships in the middle of the month. Tell the sales managers you're looking for a quota car. Then leave your phone number with them. Also send a fax or an E-mail with the same information to dealerships in your region.

Be specific about what you are looking for, and request a drive-away price. This is the final cost to you, including options, fees and taxes. If dealerships are in possession of quota cars, you'll likely receive calls on the 30th or 31st of that month.

If you like the price of a car, move quickly. The dealership is likely calling everyone else who expressed interest in that car in the past month.

•Talk to the general manager or fleet manager. Salespeople may not be aware of the larger dealership quotas. Be subtle. Asking how many more cars dealers will need to sell to get a bonus only puts them on the defensive.

Better: Say, "I'd like to know if you have anything special going on at the end of this month that would convince me to buy this car now versus later on, when it is more convenient for me."

Buying a Used Car? Lemon Self-Defense

Phil Edmonston, Fort Lauderdale-based author of *Lemon Aid Used Cars 2000*. Stoddart. He is a former member of the board of Consumers Union.

Thinking about buying a used car? About 10% of new vehicles sold in the US are lemons. The percentage of used-car lemons is much worse, since car owners are more likely to dump problem vehicles back on the market—and some used cars have been in accidents or caught in floods.

Fortunately, there are ways used-car buyers can avoid problems...

One of the best ways to avoid being stuck with a lemon is to avoid vehicles with the worst histories. *Among the biggest problem cars of the past decade...*

•**1995 Ford Windstar.** Automatic transmission failures and head gasket failures on the 3.8 liter engine.

•**Ford Taurus and Sable.** Very poor construction all around...body, electrical, brake, suspension, transmission and engine problems.

•**Chrysler Caravan, Concorde, Intrepid, New Yorker 5th Avenue, Vision.** Paint delamination, problems with air-conditioning and antilock brakes.

•**1994–1996 Saturn.** Head gasket failures.

•**1995–1998 Dodge Neon.** Poor quality components...premature failure of engine head gaskets.

•**Saab 900 and 9000.** Electrical problems ...and servicing is not widely available.

•**Jaguar.** The electrical system's maker has been tabbed "The Prince of Darkness" by the British press.

•**Front-wheel-drive Lincoln and Cadillac.** Problems with transmission electronics.

•**Kia, Daewoo and pre-1996 Hyundai.** Generally poor construction and durability, plus weak dealer networks for Kia and Daewoo.

OPPORTUNITIES

Bargains often can be found by shopping for Japanese-made vehicles with American nameplates stamped on them.

Good bets: Chrysler Colt (Mitsubishi), Ford Probe (Mazda), GM Tracker (Suzuki) and post-1992 Ford Rangers (Mazda).

MAKE THE RIGHT MOVES

•**Ask the right questions.** If you're buying from a car lot, start by asking who owned the vehicle previously. If the dealer says he/she can't share such information, just walk away.

If he swears it was purchased from "a little old lady who used it only to drive to church," ask to see the bill of sale. If he won't produce it, head elsewhere.

If you are buying from an individual, it still pays to ask to see the original bill of sale, so you can confirm he was the original owner.

Important: Ask if the seller has had any troubles with the vehicle. If it is a dealership, ask the salesperson if he or she knows of any mechanical problems. Some people don't ask these questions, assuming that they won't get straight answers. You might not—but if you are sold a lemon, the fact that you were lied to can help you in court.

●**Watch for lemon tip-offs when you inspect the car.** *There are a number of red flags that you or your mechanic can spot...*

●Check the trunk for water damage. If the trunk doesn't seal properly, it might mean the car has been in an accident or simply is poorly constructed.

●Check the floor for water damage. This might be a sign that the vehicle has been in a flood.

●Remove the wheels, and check for warped rotors. Also make sure the Antilock Brake System (ABS) is connected. When ABS goes bad, it can be extremely expensive to fix, so some unscrupulous sellers simply disconnect the ABS and hope the buyer won't notice. If this is beyond your mechanical abilities, be sure your mechanic takes a look.

●**Consult the right experts.** *It pays to go to the pros...*

●An independent garage inspection. For about $50, the car's basic components can be checked for signs of major problems.

●Government vehicle history records. For around $20, companies such as CarFax *(www. carfax.com)* will run any vehicle made since 1981 through state and federal databases to make sure it has never been labeled a lemon, a salvage vehicle or an obvious odometer-rollback vehicle in another state.

Since state laws regarding lemons vary, unscrupulous sellers can buy lemons cheaply in one state, then ship them to another state where they don't have to tag them as problem cars. This is known as *title laundering.*

You'll need the Vehicle Identification Number (VIN), which can be found on the dashboard. This search is important everywhere, but particularly in states with notably lax lemon laws, such as Texas and many states in the Southeast, where title laundering is particularly prevalent.

You can get a good idea of a vehicle's history by accessing the federal government's service bulletins, recalls and consumer-complaint database at the National Highway Traffic and Safety Administration (NHTSA) Web site, *www.nhtsa.org.*

●**Dealership search.** Take the VIN to the dealership in your area that sells cars of this make, and ask if they would be willing to run it through their system for a record of complaints, service history, recalls or warranty items. All dealerships can do this, but you might have to wait for a slow moment at the dealership and offer $10 or $20 to get it done.

IF YOU ARE STUCK WITH A LEMON

Believe it or not, you do have some recourse if you get stuck with a lemon—even if your sales contract says you bought the car in "As Is" condition. If the seller lied or intentionally concealed major problems when making the sale, you have recourse.

Precise definitions vary from state to state, but generally if your vehicle has a problem that *can't* be corrected with three trips to the garage, you have a lemon. *Here's what to do...*

●**Document the problem.** Keep all receipts...ask for mechanics' reports in writing...and get the opinion of an independent garage if you've been using the dealer that sold you the car to correct problems.

●**Send a registered letter to the seller** detailing the problem and requesting compensation. Include a copy of the independent garage's assessment.

●**Take the seller to small-claims court.** In my experience, lemon buyers have at least a 50/50 chance at satisfaction if it comes to this.

Leverage: Most dealerships, especially large, established ones, are anxious to avoid court since the publicity could be bad for business. They also know that they might face double or triple damages in open court.

Internetting for Car Bargains

Drew Long, a materials manager for a gas-equipment manufacturer in North Wales, PA.

Steve LaSala, a librarian in Manahawkin, NJ. He teaches workshops at the Ocean County Library, Barnegat, NJ, on how to buy cars over the Internet.

Jeff Ostroff, an engineer at Motorola Inc. He lives in Margate, FL, and runs *Carbuyingtips.com,* which educates consumers on purchasing and selling autos.

The Internet has made it easier to save money when buying a new or used car...and it can help you get the best price when selling your old car. Using the Web also can eliminate that awful haggling with dealers—and save you weeks of shopping time.

Practical step-by-step how-to advice from real buyers and sellers...

BUYING A NEW CAR
Drew Long

I bought my 1999 two-door Jeep Cherokee Sport without ever negotiating at a dealership. I financed it through an on-line bank...and negotiated the price by E-mail. *Total cost:* $20,209—just $200, or 1%, over the price the dealer paid for it.

The dealer even delivered the car to me. *My advice...*

●**Find your favorite make and model.** My first move was to visit *www.personalogic. com,* a consumer buying service that is run by America Online. After you type in answers to a series of questions, you are given a list of cars that meet your criteria. Next, read free reviews of the cars that were suggested.

My two favorite sites: www.auto.com and *www.caranddriver.com.*

Once I narrowed down my list to the Jeep, I visited the carmaker's Web site for details on colors, options and a 360° view of the exterior and interior.

Important: Test-drive the car you're interested in at the closest dealership. Wait until the end of the buying process—when you have found the lowest offer.

●**Get dealers to bid for your business.** After you decide on a specific vehicle and options, submit a price request to on-line car-buying services. It's free to submit price requests, and you are not obligated to buy.

How they work: Type in the vehicle, options and price you want to pay. Dealers will then contact you by phone—usually within 48 hours. They will present no-haggle prices—usually 3% to 5% higher than invoice price, including all fine-print charges, such as taxes and destination fees.

Important: Use several car-buying services at once. *My favorites...*

●*www.autobytel.com*
●*www.autovantage.com*
●*www.carpoint.msn.com*

●**Use on-line offers to reduce prices further.** Go to *www.edmunds.com* to find out what the dealer paid for the car. Negotiate with dealers by E-mail or phone. It's easier to resist the hard sell when you're not on their turf.

●**Shop for financing on-line.** On-line bank-loan rates are usually 0.5% to 2% below traditional banks' that are chosen by dealers for loans on new cars.

After you apply on-line, the bank E-mails you an answer, usually within 24 hours. *Popular on-line auto financing...*

●*www.carfinance.com*
●*www.giggo.com*
●*www.peoplefirst.com*

If you don't get approved by an auto-financing service: Try *www.lendingtree. com.* The site takes your original loan application information and finds four banks that are more likely to lend to people with your financial profile.

BUYING A USED CAR
Steve LaSala

I used the Web to purchase a used 1998 Chrysler Sebring Convertible JXI with 25,522 miles—and under warranty for two more years. *Cost:* $18,495. Although I bought my car through a local dealer, going on-line saved me about $3,000 and days of searching newspaper classified ads or visiting car lots. *My advice...*

●**Research what's available in your price range.** I started by visiting four popular classified ad sites...

● *www.edmunds.com,* which provides pricing and buying information.

● *www.cars.com.* Posts on-line auto classifieds from 130 major newspapers across the country.

● *www.autotrader.com.* More than 1.25 million listings, updated daily.

● *www.autobytel.com.* A 72-hour, money-back return policy and a free, 3,000-mile, three-month limited warranty.

Most Web sites have a free notification service. When the car you want enters one of their databases, you'll receive an E-mail.

● **Identify the most reliable cars.** For crash-test data, visit the National Highway Traffic Safety Administration's site—*www.nhtsa.dot.gov.*

To find out whether the car you want has been in an accident or had its odometer rolled back, visit *www.carfax.com* and *www.vehiclehistory.com.* A vehicle history report costs $19.95.

● **Establish the car's market value.** After you select the car you want, check *www.kbb.com* to find the going price for the car. Print your research, and bring it with you when you look at used cars. Negotiate downward from your printout market value, *not* from the seller's asking price.

Always visit a dealership's Web site before you go to the dealership to view used cars. To encourage on-line shopping, some dealers offer $100-off vouchers and other incentives that you can print from your computer.

SELLING A CAR
Jeff Ostroff

Instead of trading in my old 1988 Trans Am with 135,000 miles, I advertised it on the Internet and in print media. I spent less than $200 in advertising and received $5,600 for the car—about three times what any dealer would have given me. *My advice...*

● **Use on-line classified ads.** They're much cheaper than newspaper ads and run for much longer periods of time. You also can reach buyers who are hundreds of miles away.

Example: I received many E-mails from out-of-state people who were going to be in my area and were thinking of buying the car and driving it back home. My ads brought in about 20 inquiries.

● **Budget at least $100 to sell your car.** That should get you two ads on popular Internet classified Web sites for two 30-day runs and a few runs in local print media. *My favorite sites...*

● *www.autoweb.com.* No word limit. Space for a photo. If you get no leads, you receive a full refund or a one-month extension. Your ad also appears in the on-line versions of *Car & Driver* and *USA Today* at no extra charge. *Cost:* $19.95 for 30 days.

● *www.stoneage.com.* Your unlimited-word ad runs until the car sells. *Cost:* A one-time $19.95 fee.

● **Create a Web site for your car.** Most Internet service providers give you a free home page on the Web with your regular E-mail service.

● **Advertise in *Auto Trader* magazine,** available in convenience stores. Photo and ad runs for two weeks for $20.

● **List your site in your ad.** Scan in photos as well as a lemon-check report, available at *www.carfax.com,* to prove the car was never recalled or in a wreck.

● **Select a *nonnegotiable—firm—*price.** Never use the words "or best offer" in your ad or E-mail. It makes you seem desperate, and people will expect to get a huge bargain.

Visit *www.edmunds.com* or *www.kelleybluebook.com* to get market value—not trade-in value. After typing in the make, model and year, adjust the price for mileage...condition...and options.

● **Print out your Internet research.** If prospective buyers show up and claim your car isn't worth what you're asking, show them the printouts. Explain that any problems have been factored into the price. If they disagree, politely ask to see their research. Most people have none, and you can gain the upper hand.

Frank Billington's Car Still Runs Smoothly After 306,000 Miles!!!

Frank Billington, who drives a 1979 Dodge Diplomat.

One of the best ways to save money on a new or used car is to make the car you own now last as long as possible.

With proper care, a car can last hundreds of thousands of miles. I still drive my 1979 four-door Dodge Diplomat—even in the Wisconsin winters—and it now has 306,000 miles on the odometer.

While I'm not an auto mechanic, my father was, and I have worked on cars since I was a teenager.

Here are my secrets for keeping a car running for 20 years or longer—many of them I learned from my father...

•**Fix small problems right away.** Little problems become expensive repairs in the future.

Helpful: I budget $500 to $1,000 a year for maintenance and repairs. Having the money already set aside keeps me from dismissing what needs to be done immediately.

Example: I fill in the nicks in my windshield before every winter and summer. Temperature changes can cause a chip to spread into a crack as the glass expands and contracts. A new windshield can cost as much as $1,500. But a windshield repair kit, available at auto-parts stores for about $10, will do the job.

My favorite: Permatex Bullseye Windshield repair kit. 877-376-2839. Under $10.

•**Install a screen behind the car's front grille.** It prevents gravel, road debris and bugs from plugging up your condenser and cooling system. Replace the screen once a year.

•**Install a mud flap behind each wheel** —to prevent debris from flying up and scratching the car's body.

•**Check belts and hoses.** Belts snap and hoses leak at the most inconvenient times. Reduce the odds of either problem occurring by examining their condition once each season.

To check your hoses: Wait until the engine is cool. Then use your owner's manual to identify the cooling-system, vacuum and power-steering hoses. Grab each hose near the hose clamp, and make sure it is tight and doesn't turn. Then look for bulges and swelling in the rubber. Squeeze it slightly. If the hose feels soft and mushy, it probably needs to be replaced.

To check your belts: Look for shiny or frayed rubber. Twist the belts a bit to reveal any cracks. Make sure each belt has the right amount of slack. Push the belt gently. If it can be depressed more than one-half inch between the two pulleys that hold it in place, the belt needs to be tightened or replaced.

•**Keep a record of how many miles per gallon your car gets.** A 10% dip in mileage is an indicator of potential problems, such as a clogged fuel filter, a failing oxygen sensor or more serious problems. The earlier you troubleshoot a problem, the less damage it will cause to your car.

•**Keep the exterior and interior looking sharp.** Most people get rid of cars because they look terrible—not because the engine has become unsound. *Steps to take...*

•Fix exterior scratches yourself with touch-up paint. A three-ounce bottle of your car's exact color can be purchased at a local auto-paint dealer for about $20. It comes with an applicator brush.

Trick: Before you start painting, cut the bristles of the paintbrush with a razor blade at a diagonal angle. This will allow you to be precise when painting. After the paint dries thoroughly, gently sand any high spots or ridges with 400- to 600-grit sandpaper. This gentle grit won't scratch older cars. For newer cars, use rubbing compound. If in doubt, contact your dealer.

•**Consider replacing the interior of the car.** A new interior can make you feel as if you have a new car. The best place to look for interiors—seats, dashboard, etc.—is at a local wrecking yard. Many nearly new cars are totaled in collisions that do almost no damage to the inside. Items usually cost 75% less than retail prices.

- **Stick to your long-term maintenance schedule.** Here's when and what your mechanic needs to do…

  - *Every 3,000 miles:* Change the oil, and check your tire pressure.

  - *Every 10,000 miles:* Check the brake system, not just the disks and drums.

  - *Every 15,000 miles:* Check the air filter, fuel filter and PCV valve. Check boots for cracks and repack CV joints with grease.

  - *Every 30,000 miles…*

  Check the spark plugs and the condition of the wires leading to the plugs.

  …change the coolant after flushing the system.

  …get a wheel alignment. Do it sooner if you've had even a small accident.

  …change the transmission fluid and transmission filter.

  - *Every 60,000 to 90,000 miles:* Replace the timing belt and water pump.

  Helpful: AC Delco's Web site *(www.acdelco.com)* offers a free on-line Driver's Log. It allows you to create a personalized car-maintenance schedule and track the procedures for up to seven vehicles.

- **Drive defensively to extend longevity.** *There are several little things that can extend your car's life…*

  - Take your foot off the brake if you are headed for a pothole that you can't avoid. Keeping the brakes applied could lock up the wheel as it hits the hole, making the impact more damaging.

  - Treat the driver's side door carefully. Don't open it so hard that it bounces off the hinges, particularly when you're parked on a downhill slope.

  Squirt liquid-graphite oil into each lock at least twice a year to lubricate the minor parts. Squirt in WD-40 or silicon-lube spray. Work the key in and out. Lube each door hinge at the hinge pins as well as the door-stop device. Spray WD-40 in the recesses of the door mechanism.

- **Keep the radio off during the first five minutes of driving**—so you can listen for abnormal sounds.

Examples: Clatter under my right front wheel once alerted me to a loose tie rod and worn ball joints. A squealing sound when I applied the brakes, accompanied by a slight shiver in the steering column, told me it was time to have the brake pads replaced.

- **Avoid heavy key chains.** The weight, hanging from the ignition switch, can wear away at the switch and cause the key to get stuck or malfunction.

How to Cut the Cost Of Car Insurance

Jack Gillis, director of public affairs at Consumer Federation of America, 1424 16 St. NW, Washington, DC 20036. He is author of *The Car Book*. HarperCollins.

Despite declining auto insurance rates, 75% of car owners haven't changed their insurance policies—or even inquired about doing so—within the last five years.

How to pay less for your insurance coverage…

- **Compare policy rates on the Web.** This process takes about a half hour. First look at the sample rates charged by all insurers that do business in your state.

- *www.insure.com* provides a link to every state insurance department. At the home page, enter your state in the box labeled "insurance in your state."

Once you have a benchmark rate, visit a site that can locate policies with the lowest rates.

- *Insweb* *(www.insweb.com)* and *Quicken Insurance* *(www.insuremarket.com)*. You type in the information about your driving history. Then these Web sites sift through the insurance companies in their databases to find the ones that have the lowest prices. These services are free.

- **Shop aggressively every two years.** Different insurers target certain types of drivers at different times and then offer lower rates based on how closely you fit their preferred "top tier" profiles.

You're a candidate for a lower rate whenever…

- **Points are removed from your license.**
- **One of your cars is removed from your policy.**
- **Your kids no longer drive your car.**
- **Your car is no longer used for commuting.**
- **Maximize your policy's discounts.** Discounts can cut your premium in half. Most insurers offer as many as 20 different discounts. Most don't tell you about all of them unless you specifically ask. *Helpful...*
  - Air bags
  - Antitheft devices
  - Antilock brakes
  - Car-pool drivers
  - Graduates of driver-training courses
  - Low mileage
  - Multiple policies
  - No accident in three years
  - Nonsmokers
  - Older drivers who don't drive at night
- **Ask groups if they offer low-rate policies.** More insurers now offer organizations group policies that have discounted rates for members.

    Examples: Retirement organizations, alumni associations, credit unions...and some credit card issuers, too.

- **Eliminate unnecessary coverage.** Increasing your monthly deductible from $200 to $500 could reduce your collision and comprehensive premiums by as much as 30%.

    Consider eliminating collision and comprehensive coverage if your car is paid off... more than four years old...or worth less than $4,000.

    To research car values: National Automobile Dealers Association *(www.NADA.com)* ...or Kelley Blue Book *(www.kbb.com)*.

- **Buy a less desirable—or safer—car.** Buying a model that is a favorite with thieves or statistically in frequent accidents can send your premiums sky-high.

    For cars with low theft rates: The National Insurance Crime Bureau *(www.NICB.com)*.

    For cars with the highest safety ratings: Insurance Institute for Highway Safety *(www. highwaysafety.org)*.

Better Car-Phone Emergency Calls

For breakdowns and accidents, some wireless phone companies now offer *Wireless E911*, which automatically provides emergency personnel with your location. Another service, *Automatic Collision Notification,* makes a call automatically and sends information on the severity of a crash and type of vehicle, so rescue workers can estimate injuries.

Ask your local cell phone company if it offers these services. Either one is better than simply calling 911—which will not work in all areas because of system gaps and because 911 is not the correct emergency number everywhere.

Consumers' Research Magazine, 800 Maryland Ave. NE, Washington, DC 20002.

Car Insurance Smarts

Slash car-insurance premiums on unusual sports or specialty cars by buying a *collector-car policy.* Premiums on these little-known policies are two-thirds lower than traditional ones.

They cover liability and comprehensive/collision damage on such cars as Porsches and Dodge Vipers that are used purely for pleasure. Some policies will insure several specialty cars for the price of one, since only one car at a time can be driven. *Insurers with such policies...*

- **Condon & Skelly**/800-257-9496.
- **Hagerty Classic Insurance**/800-922-4050.
- **J.C. Taylor**/800-345-8290.

Stephan Wilkinson, automotive editor who has test-driven and reviewed cars independently for more than 20 years...and who also collects cars.

Don't Leave Home Without It...

David Solomon, president, Nutz & Boltz, automotive information membership organization, Box 123, Butler, Maryland 21023.

A fire extinguisher in the trunk is a valuable piece of car-safety equipment. Install the extinguisher with a mounting bracket so it cannot come loose in an accident. Practice releasing it from the bracket in case of a car fire. Consider mounting a flashlight next to the extinguisher—if there is a fire, the car lights may go out. Buy an extinguisher marked FM- or UL-approved and specified for class A, B and C fires. *For pickup trucks*: Mount it behind the seat.

More From David Solomon

New Trunk Safety Latch

Internal trunk-latch release can make it possible for young children who crawl into car trunks to get out safely. General Motors developed it after 11 children died when they became trapped in the trunks of three different GM vehicles. The latches are easy for even small children to use and can be seen in the dark. GM dealers can retrofit them in all GM cars made during the 1990s. *Cost:* About $50. Watch for other manufacturers to offer this feature in the future.

Airbag Danger

Automobile airbags can cause severe eye injuries when they deploy. Motorists have reported airbag-related injuries ranging from bleeding within the eyes to corneal burns to detached retinas.

Self-defense: Position yourself at least 18 inches away from the airbag. Always wear your seat belt. Never hold pens, cups, cellular phones or other objects in your hands while driving—they can be slammed into your face by a deploying airbag. If you are five feet, one inch or shorter, ask your car dealer about getting pedal extenders...or turning off the airbag. Children under age 12 should sit in the rear seat.

David C. Ball, MD, senior ophthalmology resident, Loyola University, Chicago.

16

Your Family and Your Home

The Busy Couple's Guide To a Very Good Marriage

Marriages start out tender and loving…but demanding careers and the daily job of running a home and raising children turns too many relationships into cold, methodical business arrangements.

As a marital therapist for more than 20 years, I've found that most couples have little time or energy for the complicated "relationship exercises" that are frequently suggested by some therapists.

So I've developed very simple strategies built on basic truths about what makes love last. These strategies can be integrated easily into everyday life to reverse negative relationship patterns and build on positive ones. They are effective even if just one spouse starts practicing them.

●**Make your spouse feel good about himself/herself**—and then your spouse will

feel good about you. In strong, loving relationships, couples make ego-boosting comments to each other every day. *Helpful…*

●Look for admirable qualities in your partner. It becomes too easy to focus on behavior or habits that you don't like in your spouse. But with practice, you can teach yourself to find and praise those characteristics that make you feel good.

●Be specific when you compliment. Details add meaning to your words. "I liked the way you handled the kids' crankiness by joking about it" resonates more than just remarking on your spouse's sense of humor.

●Be emotionally generous. Encouraging your spouse to take part in a favorite activity—even if it means he will spend time away from you—will make him feel loved instead of guilty.

●**Warm your partner's heart.** In many busy marriages, expressions of caring stop. We get lazy or think these expressions won't have much significance. But loving gestures

Ellen Wachtel, PhD, psychologist and marital therapist in private practice in New York. She is author of *We Love Each Other, But…* Golden Books.

243

don't have to be extravagant. Small but steady displays are more realistic—and often more meaningful. *Helpful...*

●Treat vulnerabilities as opportunities to be loving. You and your spouse have weak points. Use them as opportunities to be kind and understanding.

Example: Your spouse assumes too much responsibility at work, which cuts into family time. Instead of becoming angry and voicing resentment, recognize all that your spouse accomplishes. Then sympathetically encourage your spouse to look for ways to reduce the workload or delegate more to coworkers.

●Accommodate your spouse's sensitivities. Adapting to emotional sore spots need not be complicated.

Example: One couple—an outgoing husband and a quieter wife who felt ignored in social situations—used secret signals. When talking to others, the man would touch his wife's arm to show that he hadn't forgotten her. If she was feeling left out, she would squeeze his hand so he would bring her into the conversation.

●**Share tender, caring gestures.** These could include a quick "Hi, how are you doing?" through E-mail or a call at work...preparing a favorite dish...or helping to search for a missing item. All are nurturing and supportive.

And what was once considered exclusively gentlemanly behavior—helping with packages or a coat—can be done for men and will be appreciated.

●**Offer praise rather than criticism.** Criticism not only erodes love but rarely results in the kind of change that you're hoping to achieve. By contrast, praise always encourages cooperation. *Helpful...*

●Notice small steps in the right direction. When you want your spouse to behave in a specific way or to remember to take care of a chore, express your appreciation when he tries.

While it's tempting to say, "I wish you would do more around the house," tagging on a criticism overshadows your praise. If your spouse doesn't try at all, ask yourself whether it's worth fighting over or it's just easier for you to do it.

If that's unacceptable or impossible, wait until a time when you can express your complaint without becoming angry or condescending.

●Think before you carp. When you feel the urge to criticize, ask yourself, "Is what I'm about to say really going to have a positive impact?" Then speak carefully, not hurtfully.

A spouse's hurtful intent can cut every bit as deeply as harsh words. Try not to revisit old mistakes. Digging up the past is often the basis for even bigger and more painful arguments.

●**Being attractive counts.** "Attractiveness" is more than sexy underwear or strong muscles. Attractiveness is remaining thoughtful, engaging and interested in your spouse. *Helpful...*

●Be considerate. Feeling comfortable with your spouse is great. But that comfort level can also cause couples to intrude on each other's space or to take each other for granted.

Show your spouse the same courtesy you would extend to a friend. Give warm greetings after an absence...refrain from routinely *unloading* anger or frustration...pay attention when your spouse talks or explain why you're unable to give your spouse your full attention at that time.

●Continue to surprise. Romantic gestures, love notes or gifts remind your spouse you're still a couple.

●Recognize and support change. Holding on to an outdated view of your spouse can be alienating. It's far more loving for couples to acknowledge each other's new strengths, such as dealing with difficult relatives or controlling anger.

●**Don't give up being lovers.** The idea is to balance the needs of the relationship with other obligations. *Helpful...*

●Set aside "two-of-you" moments. Block out 15 to 20 minutes each day to connect as a couple. If you have children, plan your togetherness for when the children are doing homework before dinner...or while they watch TV afterward. Stick to the routine so your kids learn to respect "grown-up time."

●Have couple conversations. Put kids and chores off-limits during your moments together. If you sometimes feel at a loss for topics to discuss, keep a running list during the day as things occur to you, from a joke to a pleasant reminiscence.

Writing everything down also strengthens your own connection with personal thoughts and feelings.

•Keep on dating. Time together outside the house relieves family and job pressures and gets you to connect like yourselves before the marriage.

Also, arrange romantic dates at home, shifting the atmosphere away from the ordinary with a special late-evening meal. And as with your daily 20 minutes together, maintain "couple conversation."

•Play hooky. Ask the sitter to stay into the evening so you can meet after work for an early dinner. Or arrange child care for a few daytime hours on the weekend for a walk together. These small breaks in routine will seem like adventures.

•Steal a sexy moment. Even a few minutes of touching and hugging reminds couples that they are more than parenting partners.

Important: Remembering the experiences that brought you together.

How Parents Can Get the Very Best Medical Care for Their Children

Robert G. LaCamera, MD, clinical professor of pediatrics at Yale University School of Medicine in New Haven, CT.

To get first-rate medical care for their children, parents must be careful to avoid these all-too-common mistakes…

Mistake: **Not making the pediatrician a partner in child rearing.** After a child's infancy, most parents consult the pediatrician only about health concerns. Yet a doctor who has known your child for years can be a valuable sounding board. He/she can help guide your child's psychological and social development well into adolescence. In fact, your child shouldn't need an "adult" doctor until age 21.

The doctor's involvement can be useful in getting extra help from your child's school, if it's needed…or in taking advantage of useful community services—counseling, camps, etc.

Mistake: **Withholding vital information.** A pediatrician cannot fully understand your child without knowing all about him and the rest of your family.

It's essential that you share pertinent information with the doctor, even if you find doing so embarrassing. That goes for alcoholism in the family, marital strife, children's behavioral problems, etc.

In many cases, behavioral problems stem from medical problems. A child who is inattentive in school, for example, may have a hearing loss. A child who sits out physical activities may be bothered by chronic pain—of which parents are unaware.

Mistake: **Being unprepared for appointments.** The average pediatrician visit lasts 13 minutes. To make the most of this brief span of time, bring a written list of your concerns. Tell the doctor at the outset how many things you'd like to discuss.

If you don't get through the list—or if additional questions arise during the course of the visit—ask the doctor when you can consult him by phone…or arrange another appointment.

Mistake: **Not preparing your child for appointments.** Let the child know what to expect well before each appointment. Enact a physical exam with dolls…or use a toy doctor's kit to perform your own "examination" of your child…or read a book with your child about going to the doctor's office.

Young children: Lisa McCue's *Corduroy Goes to the Doctor* (Viking).

Older children: Fred Rogers's *Going to the Doctor* (Putnam).

If your child is unfamiliar with the doctor's office, take him to the office for a get-acquainted visit a few days before the initial appointment. If your child is unusually anxious, let the doctor know privately via a phone call or note.

Remember—if you're visibly anxious about the visit, your child will be, too.

Present the experience in a positive light—try to focus the child's attention on something upbeat—the fun toys in the office, the colorful stickers given out by the nurses, etc.

But be honest with him. Do not promise that an injection won't hurt.

***Mistake:* Coming between doctor and child.** It's important that your child establish a relationship of his own with the pediatrician.

By age 10, many kids prefer to see the pediatrician on their own. Even before then, it's smart to encourage your child to speak for himself in answering the doctor's questions. For young children, of course, you may have to correct or supplement the information.

***Mistake:* Being reluctant to call or visit the doctor.** If your child's symptoms do not seem to require urgent care, consult Dr. Spock's *Baby and Child Care* (Pocket Books) or another good book on children's health.

If the book seems to indicate that medical care is warranted, phone the doctor. Ask if you should bring the child in, even if the office is officially closed. Use your best judgment. Do not worry about seeming alarmist.

In an emergency, of course, call an ambulance.

***Mistake:* Failing to ask for help in getting** more information about children's health. No pediatrician should be relied upon as the sole source of information concerning your child's health.

Ask where you can get additional or more specialized information. The doctor may suggest helpful books, Web sites, support groups, subspecialists, etc.

Children's Vaccines

Don't get spooked by negative publicity concerning children's vaccines. The very slight risk of side effects from childhood immunizations should be viewed against the far greater risk of harm from the actual diseases. *Rarely*—whooping cough can kill... measles complications include encephalitis (brain inflammation) and pneumonia... and even "mild" illnesses can have dire consequences. *Example:* Flesh-eating bacteria can enter the body through chicken pox lesions.

Regina Rabinovich, MD, pediatrician and chief of the clinical and regulatory affairs branch, National Institute of Allergy and Infectious Diseases, Bethesda, MD.

How to Get Kids to Take No for an Answer

Lawrence Kutner, PhD, clinical psychologist in Basel, Switzerland. He is author of five parenting books, including Making Sense of Your Teenager. Avon.

As children grow and seek independence, they become masters at wearing down parents in an attempt to turn every no into a yes.

Here's how to stand your ground without making enemies of your kids...

●**Don't be pressured into giving an instant answer.** Take as much time as you need to arrive at decisions. If you're not sure of your response, stall. "That's an interesting question (or point). I need some time to think about it."

Once children realize that you are likely to delay your responses, they often try putting tight deadlines on requests.

Example: "Can I go to the concert tonight? I need to know right now, or I won't be able to get a ticket."

Appropriate answer: "Well, then I'll have to stay on the safe side and say no. I need more time to think. Next time, ask me earlier."

●**Acknowledge their feelings.** Rather than getting upset when children fight your response, let them know you recognize their frustration.

Example: "I know you're mad at me. You may want to go to the concert more than anything in the world, and I know what that feels like. But I've made up my mind, and the answer is no."

Children need to know that you are not making a random decision. They also need to hear you exercise reason and good judgment.

Don't berate children for wanting the wrong thing.

Example: "How could you be so stupid as to even ask me about going to the concert?"

If you can, praise their argument.

Example: "I'm impressed you are willing to work around the house to pay for the tickets. I can see why you asked."

●**Present a united front.** Children are quick to spot where you and your partner disagree, and they learn early how to divide and conquer.

To head off this maneuver, identify the issues about which you and your partner disagree and resolve them before your child brings them up.

●**Say yes at least occasionally.** When children hear you say *yes* from time to time, they are more willing to accept *no*. It's fine to back down after you've said no without thinking through your child's question...or if your child presents a good argument. By overturning your decision, you are rewarding logical thinking and good judgment.

Troublesome Teen Problems...and Practical Solutions

Lawrence Bauman, PhD, clinical psychologist in private practice in New York and a director of in-patient services at South Beach Psychiatric Center in Staten Island, NY. He is author of *Ten Most Troublesome Teenage Problems and How to Solve Them.* Citadel Press.

As kids turn into teenagers, they start to look big and talk big—and parents begin to feel less needed.

But despite their lust for independence, teenagers need and want parents to help them navigate this confusing stage in their lives.

How can parents stay close without being intrusive? How do you separate "normal" teenage moodiness and rebellion from problems that need to be addressed directly?

SIGNS OF TROUBLE

Before you step in and take action to correct teen behavior, know the difference between a harmless "phase" and signs of deeper trouble. *Red-flag behavior that requires action...*

●**Serious negativity about school.** Disrupting the whole class...grades that take a consistent change for the worse...poor class attendance...or talking about dropping out of school.

●**Being highly secretive.** Beware of teens who are secretive and keep you from knowing even the most basic facts about their lives, such as what group of friends they hang out with or the events and activities they participate in.

●**Telling lies.** Though most teenage lies are innocent, they should always be investigated. A lie may point to a more serious pattern, particularly cheating or stealing. Repeated lying also reflects a larger breakdown of trust.

●**Obsessing about weight and self-image.** Teenage girls tend to be highly conscious of their appearance. That's a natural part of growing up.

But girls who become angry when you bring desserts into the house...constantly complain about "looking fat"—even though their weight is perfectly normal...or are secretive about what they're eating may be headed toward anorexia or bulimia.

●**Having tantrums.** Teens are moody by nature. But there's a hidden problem when teen personality changes are sudden and long-lasting—or if your teen has trouble concentrating or regularly erupts in rage.

HOW TO TALK TO TEENS

While you may need to seek outside advice or counseling if your teen's negative behavior is irreversible, the first step is to attempt to engage him/her in discussion. *The key is to use an approach that encourages your teen to open up...*

●**Don't panic or punish immediately.** The older children get, the more parents worry about the kinds of adults they'll become.

This causes many parents to exaggerate the significance of their children's misbehavior. The result usually is panic at the first sign of a teen's negative attitude.

What to do: Stay objective by reminding yourself that the problem you're facing is not the end of the world and that it eventually will be solved. Don't take the problem personally. If your child gives you back talk or blames you for his problems, it's natural to feel hurt. In truth, you are more likely just a convenient target. Try not to respond in anger.

If your child is disrespectful to you repeatedly, punish him by treating him coolly. If he wants to know why you're behaving that way, remind him, "This is a two-way street. I don't like the way you're treating me."

●Be a partner—not an adversary. A teenager needs to know that you are on his side and you're willing to listen without judging or lecturing him.

Even if you disagree with your teen, keep an open mind and try to see his point of view. When he sees you are open to reason, he will be more likely to consider your point of view in return.

Keeping your mind open requires you to talk less and listen more.

Example: You find your teen playing a video game of which you disapprove. Instead of blowing up or punishing him, find out what he thinks about the images in the game and why he feels good when playing the game.

By discussing the subject openly, you are not showing that you are open to letting him play it. You are discussing the subject so that your teen can think through his actions.

If your child is playing these games to excess, it's often a sign of social trouble. Let your teenager know you think something is troubling him and you're available to talk when he is ready.

●Be indirect rather than confrontational. Teens quickly recognize exaggeration and theatrics. If you cast yourself as the voice of doom —"Keep that up and you'll go to jail or wind up a worthless bum"—you'll lose credibility.

They also reject unsolicited advice and clam up when you pry for details. Your teenager wants to solve things for himself. Prying can drive him farther away.

Instead, calmly convey your concerns. Express how you feel and why you're raising the issue. Explain why the behavior is so troubling and why it is unacceptable to you.

Punishment should be short-term and specific in response to repeatedly breaking a specific rule. If a child breaks curfew without a good reason, tell him he has to come home earlier the next time.

Important: Choose your time wisely when discussing behavior problems with teens. The surest way to shut down communication is to say, "I want to talk about this problem now."

When teens sense you're getting serious, they usually tune out.

It's more productive to initiate conversations casually—when the two of you are riding in the car…during a commercial break on TV…or as you both work on a project or chore.

●Consider compromising. Teenagers need you to acknowledge their growing independence, so it's important to give them more control in decision making.

This means allowing them some latitude— as long as their safety is not being threatened.

Example: Your 15-year-old wants a later curfew because all the other parents let their children stay out later.

Instead of being rigid about curfew, pick a time when the two of you are calm and can sit down to talk it through. Explain that although there have to be rules, perhaps some old rules should be reexamined.

Example: "I'm willing to consider a later curfew, as long as you stay where you say you're going to go—and only travel locally. If you break these rules, we'll have to reconsider."

But put your foot down when it's absolutely essential—"11 pm is too late for a school night. You need to get enough sleep."

When your teenager tells you that all the other parents are allowing their kids to stay out late, call and ask some of the other parents. It's a useful reality check.

●Preserve family rituals. Teenagers may object to going to family events or eating dinner together. But these kinds of rituals are important because they provide routine and safety, as well as a sense of connection.

Don't force a teenager to sit down to dinner with you. If he feels cornered, he's likely to resist. Even if he distances himself at dinnertime, he may join you later. If you are reasonable and don't insist on a command performance, his decision will likely be in line with your values.

Shy Kids Can Become Much Less Shy

Nancy Samalin, founder and director of Parent Guidance Workshops, 180 Riverside Dr., New York 10024. She is author of several books on parenting, including *Loving Your Child Is Not Enough.* Penguin.

When children refuse to try something unfamiliar, we often push them to participate. But that pushing makes most of them even more withdrawn or resistant.

●**Give children time to become comfortable**—if they react hesitantly or fearfully to new situations.

Example: If he/she signs up for karate but wants to quit after the first class, suggest he go once more as an observer.

●**Tell your children that *their* participation has to be partly *their* decision.** By giving children a choice in the matter, you support their autonomy and help them to feel that they have some control. It will also give them a little more confidence about venturing into uncharted waters in the future.

Criticizing children's character traits undermines self-confidence and does little to encourage them to try new things, take reasonable risks and be more outgoing.

●**Don't label your child shy.** When a child repeatedly hears his parents say about him, "He's so shy" or "He's the shy one in the family," his hesitancy about trying new things is only reinforced.

Instead, try a more supportive statement, such as, "It's OK to take a little extra time to get used to new things." This shows anxious children that you understand and accept their feelings.

●**Practice being outgoing at home.** Children who are naturally bashful can be taught certain skills to become more at ease. Let your child know in advance exactly what to expect in certain settings. Role-playing is also very effective.

Example: Teach your shy child how to answer the telephone in a clear voice and to take messages. This skill-building requires time and repetition, but it can build a child's confidence without his having to look a stranger in the eye.

Real-Life Lessons For Your Grandchildren

Carol Orsag Madigan and Ann Elwood. Their books include *When Kids Were Kids: Over 400 Sketches of Famous Childhoods.* Random House.

Instructive, amusing and inspiring true tales from the childhoods of youngsters who grew up to be rich and famous...

●**Britain's Princess Margaret,** sister of Queen Elizabeth II, had two imaginary friends when she was little—"Cousin Halifax" and "Inderbombanks." The princess blamed *them* whenever she did something wrong.

●**The only doll Barbra Streisand had was a hot water bottle,** which she dressed in a tiny pink hat and sweater knitted by a neighbor who baby-sat for her.

●**Film director Steven Spielberg was so frightened by the scary scenes in movies** like *Snow White and the Seven Dwarfs* that his parents often had to turn off the TV. He grew up to make terrifying movies such as *Jaws* and *Jurassic Park.*

●**Actor Burt Reynolds was snubbed by the popular members of his high school class** until the age of 14, when he became a hero after winning a race against the school's star athlete—while running barefoot.

●**President Harry Truman read every book in the Independence, MO, public library** before he graduated from high school.

●**Microsoft cofounder Bill Gates,** now the richest man in the world, read the entire *World Book Encyclopedia* by the time he was nine, and scored a perfect 800 on his math SATs.

How to Win a Bidding War For Your Dream House

If you've found your dream house, chances are other people will also be after it. *To help ensure you get what you want...*

●**Put down $5,000 to $10,000 as a binder** —instead of $1,000. That shows you are really serious.

●**Consider shortening or removing mortgage contingencies.**

Example: Agree to make the home inspection within five days. Be sure you have a pre-approval letter from a reliable lending institution.

●**Agree to close at the seller's convenience.** Be flexible within a time frame. But be sure you allow yourself enough time—usually at least 40 days—to obtain your mortgage.

●**Allow the sellers to rent the house back** for a week or two after the closing— longer if you're not pressed for time—if they need the money to close on another house.

●**Choose a pleasant attorney**—one who should get along well with the sellers, their attorney and their broker.

●**Offer to beat any competing offer** by $1,000, up to the maximum you can afford to pay. This is a tough move—so be absolutely sure you want the house before making this offer.

Karen Eastman Bigos, one of the country's top real estate agents, with Burgdorff ERA Realtors, Short Hills, NJ.

Ask the Neighbors

Talk to prospective neighbors when considering whether to buy a home. Ask if they would buy again in the area...whether the area is quiet...how much crime they have seen in the neighborhood...how quickly police and emergency vehicles respond...if there are water system problems...how good the schools are...where people shop... whether homeowners learned anything after moving in that they wish they had known before buying.

Julie Garton-Good, real estate columnist and educator, Miami, and author of The Frugal Homeowner's Guide to Buying, Selling & Improving Your Home. *Dearborn.*

The Best Mortgage for A Short Stay

Avoid a 30-year mortgage if you do not expect to be in the house for anything close to 30 years. The shorter the time period for which you borrow, the lower the interest rate. So if you plan to stay in a house for only five or so years, you are overspending by taking out a 30-year mortgage. *Alternatives:* Balloon mortgages, which have a fixed rate for five or seven years and then jump to a higher rate...or adjustable-rate mortgages if you plan to stay just a few years.

Robert Van Order, chief economist, Freddie Mac, McLean, VA.

Fast Home Fix-Ups Attract the Right Buyers

Patricia MacDonald, owner of Innovative Interior Design, a consultation firm in Orange County, CA, that specializes in helping homeowners prepare their property for sale.

First impressions are critical when it comes to winning over undecided home buyers. *Before putting your house on the market...*

●**Give the front of your home a "haircut."** Look at your home from the street. Trim hedges and overgrown landscaping. Add a coat of semigloss paint to the front door. Buy a new doormat.

●**Make the entryway look big.** When I enter a house, the first thing I like to see is a table with a mirror above it. That makes the entryway feel spacious. Setting a lamp on the table—perhaps with a vase of flowers—also helps.

Remove coat stands, keys and mail from the entryway.

●**Open up first-floor traffic patterns**. Rearrange furniture to create more spacious walkways. *Examples...*

●If you have a sofa dividing your living room from the dining area, move it against a wall.

• Take a piece of furniture out of the room if you have to make more space. Store the furniture in the garage or attic, where clutter won't come as a surprise.

• Remove the leaves from your dining room table.

• **Shine up the kitchen.** Put away large countertop appliances. Take down the magnets and kids' drawings from the refrigerator.

Place a big wooden bowl on the counter, and fill it with lemons or oranges.

No plants should be hanging from the ceiling. They clutter kitchens and block window views. The windows should be clean and offer a clear view. Get rid of any leftover hooks on the walls or ceiling.

• **Clean up the patio.** If your furniture is missing some parts, either repair the items or throw them out.

Put bikes and toys in the garage, and move your grill against the exterior wall of your home.

Moving Does Not Have to Be Traumatic...Around

The Corner Or Across The Country

Cathy Goodwin, PhD, author of *Making the Big Move: How to Transform Relocation into a Creative Life Transition.* New Harbinger Publications. She has moved more than 12 times in her life. Dr. Goodwin is currently professor of marketing at Nova Southeastern University in Fort Lauderdale, FL.

Whether you are moving to a smaller space in the same city...to a retirement community in another state... or to an apartment across the country, there are steps you can take to minimize the disruption that relocation invariably causes.

First, make sure moving is something you want to do. People who feel forced to move often experience anger and resentment on top of all the normal relocation-induced feelings of loneliness, anxiety, excitement and expectation.

PSYCHOLOGICAL ISSUES

If moving is something you've decided is right for you, make it easier on yourself by working through some of the psychological issues ahead of time.

• **List the activities you most enjoy doing.** Think of the roles you play in life that define you. Ask yourself what it is about your home environment that energizes you.

It's often the seemingly trivial routines and comforts—like a morning cup of cappuccino at the local coffee shop—that we miss most in a new location. If you make careful note of these comforts, you'll be able to duplicate them in your new home.

• **Prepare for moving by deciding who you are.** Decide what you need around you in order to fully express your identity.

Exercise 1: **Who are you?** As quickly as you can, complete the sentence, "I am a _____" 10 times.

Examples: I am a mother, I am an artist, I am a gardener, etc.

Review what you've written and think about what it reveals about you. What, if anything, will change if you move to a new location?

Exercise 2: **Which routines are important to you?** You will gain an understanding of the importance of your daily routines by writing them down. *As thoroughly as possible, write down...*

1. What you do on weekday mornings.

Example: Wake up without an alarm clock ...walk the dogs...drive to the local newsstand for the paper...stop at the corner coffee shop.

2. What you do to relax in the evening.

3. How you spend Saturday mornings.

When you've completed this exercise, ask yourself how you'd feel about interrupting these routines.

Though the details you record may seem trivial, it's often these little changes and losses that increase the psychological trauma of moving.

PRESERVING COMFORTS AND ROUTINES

By understanding which routines and comforts are important to you, you'll more easily develop replacements in your new community. *Do some homework before the move...*

●**Learn all you can about your prospective community.** Use the Internet to research the community and learn about its character/ culture.

By typing in the city and state you're considering, you can learn about museums and theater programs…local businesses and restaurants…opportunities for continuing education…medical services…transportation, etc.

Use the library to research the archives of the local newspaper.

Better: Make a premove visit to the area you're considering and talk to people of all ages about what it's like to live in the area.

●**Visualize how you'll spend a day in the new location.** Begin by visualizing your new home for 15 to 20 minutes. Relax, close your eyes and get comfortable.

Ask yourself: What is my ideal home? Where does the sun rise and set? Are there skylight windows? Lamps? Overhead lighting? What is the shape of each room, and what kind of furniture do I see in each? Who or what do I see in the home with me (spouse, dog, cat)?

After you've pictured your new home in your mind, visualize a day in your new community. See yourself waking up. What will you do next? What familiar roles might be useful in your new location? What new roles or activities might you engage in? What problems might you encounter (e.g., no coffee shop!) and how will you deal with these problems?

When you've completed this exercise, write down any insights you've gained, then compare your notes with your real life in the new location after you've moved.

FOR RENTERS

If you choose to rent, place a "Rental Wanted" classified ad in the local paper. I've done this twice. As a result, I've learned about really fine properties that are typically only rented by word-of-mouth.

And, contrary to what many people think, I didn't get any crank phone calls.

Sample ad: Model tenant with steady income seeks single-level, three-bedroom apartment. References provided.

PLANNING A NO-TEARS MOVE

●**Use checklists provided by moving companies as well as lists found in books,** such as…

●*Moving: A Complete Checklist and Guide for Relocation* by Karen G. Adams (Silvercat Publications).

●*Steiner's Complete How to Move Handbook* by Clyde Steiner (Dell).

●**Put together an emotional first-aid kit.** Your kit can include coping statements such as, "I will just let go and relax"…"I can deal with this"…or "I've survived this before—I can do it again."

Add to the kit meditation and visualization books and tapes. Also include the phone numbers of old friends—at least one to laugh with, one to listen to you and one who moved recently and can give good advice. Pick up a journal in which you can record your thoughts, concerns and feelings.

Preparing for A Major Renovation

Before kitchen renovations begin, ask your contractor about setting up a temporary kitchen. It should include a sink, a refrigerator and perhaps a stove. Your contractor can rough out the necessary piping and set things up for about $300. You will save that much on dining out alone. Also, have as many appliances and nonstock materials in your garage as possible *before* the renovation begins. Many suppliers are backed up with orders. Expect to wait at least six to eight weeks for cabinets and appliances on back order.

Tim Carter, award-winning contractor, Cincinnati, and author of *The Home Ranger: Helps You Figure It Out!* Prometheus Books.

Garage Sale Before Home Sale

Get rid of as much clutter as possible before putting your house on the market. An uncluttered house looks larger and is more attractive to buyers. Clear out everything you no longer use or do not expect to need when you move. The cleaning-out process may reveal things you should fix or clean before selling your home. After the garage sale and a sprucing-up, list your home for sale.

Robert Irwin, real estate investor and broker, Los Angeles, and author of the *Tips & Traps* home book series. McGraw-Hill.

How to Hire a Really Good House Painter

Andrew D'Amato, co-owner of Andrews Painting in Milton/Boston, MA, which specializes in older, historic homes. He has painted more than 1,000 homes over the past 20 years.

Painting the exterior of a two-story house costs between $10,000 and $20,000. But when the job is done right, it should last a decade or more.

Here are questions I would ask prospective house painters if I were hiring one to paint my own home—and the answers I would like to hear...

What is the right time of year to paint my house?

Late summer or fall are clearly best. Other times of the year are fine if the moisture levels of the wood are not too high. Otherwise the paint won't adhere properly.

I use a double-pronged moisture meter on several spots around the house. I won't paint unless the moisture content is below 12%.

The north side of a house gets the least amount of sun and is usually dampest.

Important: If it rains after painters have begun prepping your house, insist that they delay painting for at least a day or two to let the wood dry out.

What is my peeling paint really telling me?

Moisture has gotten beneath the paint and penetrated the wood. The culprit is often high on an exterior wall—a clogged gutter or cracked trim board behind the gutter that is collecting water.

If the problem is in one area, you may be able to repair it and not repaint the entire house for a year or two. If the paint is heavily "alligatored," it may be necessary to remove the paint to bare wood and repaint immediately.

How long does it take to prep the house?

Your house painter should spend most of his time prepping—twice as long as the actual painting.

Reason: The cleaner and drier the wood, the longer the paint job lasts. *I use a three-step prep process...*

• **Washing:** I gently spray with water to remove surface dirt and mildew, which turns up as black spots. I spray the wood with a solution of one cup bleach and one cup trisodium phosphate per two gallons of water. Then I scrub with a stiff-bristled brush. I let it sit for 30 minutes, then rinse.

Important: Do not let a house painter use a power washer—2,000 pounds-per-square-inch of water pressure—on your home. It oversaturates the wood and takes too long to dry.

To catch the debris, I create a drop-cloth basin around the perimeter of the house with six-millimeter plastic that extends at least six feet away from the exterior walls.

• **Scraping:** I hand scrape, using carbide blades.

• **Feathering:** I go over the edges around the bare wood spots with a palm sander and 80-grit sandpaper.

What should I do about all the little pits and cracks on my house?

On the cracks, I use a latex-acrylic caulk with a 25-year life span that dries hard in one hour. I use an exterior spackle on the dings and surface imperfections. Then I go over every square foot of the exterior.

I avoid caulking the cracks in between the clapboards in order to allow moisture to escape from inside the home. Ask your painter to check the window sash and reapply glazing putty as needed. The putty holds the glass pane in on the outside and prevents moisture from seeping in and rotting your window frames.

Does my house really need more than one coat of paint?

If you want a paint job to last a decade or more, you must treat the clean, bare wood with...

● **Clear water repellent.** It should contain an iodine-based preservative that contains 3-iodo-2-propynyl butylcarbamate, also known as IPBC.

● **Oil-based primer.** I work it in well to penetrate wood fibers. After it has dried for at least 24 hours, I go over the wood with 100-grit sandpaper.

Some painters look to save money by using leftover, top-coat paint from a previous job as primer. This can cause your paint to start peeling within two to three years.

● **Two thin coats of paint.** It costs about the same as one heavy coat but is more durable. The first coat of paint can be applied by brush. On detailed areas of the house, such as the front entryway, I lightly sand with very fine 220-grit sandpaper. It removes nearly all surface textures and gives the highest quality finish to the most visible areas.

Important: House painters always have leftover paint. For touch-ups, ask for at least one gallon of each color used, sealed and dated, with the manufacturer's name on it. It will be very helpful the next time you need a painter to work on your house.

Is it worth buying more expensive brands of paint?

Yes. The top, nationally known brands not only look better, they can last twice as long.

Personal favorites: Pratt & Lambert and Benjamin Moore. Do not use the "professional" grade of these brands because they're meant for commercial buildings.

There are two vital decisions you need to make about exterior house paint...

● **Oil versus latex** (water-based): Your painter should use oil-based primers on any bare wood. He/she should use latex for the body of the house, especially if moisture is a problem.

● **Flat versus gloss:** Regardless of what base paint you use, select a flat-finish paint for the siding of the house. It looks better because it minimizes imperfections from a distance.

Use a gloss or high-gloss finish for the trim, windows and doors. It's easier to clean and provides a sheen that makes details stand out.

How to Check Out A Contractor

Be sure a contractor is licensed before hiring him/her for home improvement work. Licensing adds protection for the consumer because the licensing authority often intercedes in a dispute with a contractor and home owner. Many areas have some licensing requirement for home improvement contractors—either at the state, county or local level. Most municipalities keep lists of licensed contractors.

Brett Martin, director of marketing, National Association of the Remodeling Industry, Alexandria, VA.

Simple Stress-Free System To Unclutter Your Home... And Keep It That Way

Donna Smallin, Troy, NY-based author of Unclutter Your Home: 7 Simple Steps, 700 Tips and Ideas. Storey Books. She writes for several major manufacturers and retailers and has contributed articles to Bridal Guide and Running Times magazines.

Too much stuff in your house? Many of us are troubled by the clutter...and overwhelmed by the imposing task of doing something about it. Here is a no-stress system to unclutter your home. *Key questions...*

If I had 20 minutes to evacuate my home, what would I take? That's when you realize that most things aren't very important.

How much is enough? On a scale of zero to 10—with 10 being everything you now own and zero being nothing—what amount of stuff would you prefer to own? Nine? Eight? Five? If five seems about right, your goal should be to eliminate half of your belongings.

If that seems like a lot, remember—you'll be getting rid of things you don't want, use or need.

TOSS OBVIOUS JUNK

Walk around your house with a plastic garbage bag. Toss out expired coupons or packages of food no one will eat...single or worn socks...old travel brochures...expired medicines...makeup that is more than one year old...extra grocery bags (10 are enough)...things that are broken...old, rusted tools and utensils. Do this the night before garbage pickup so you aren't tempted to retrieve anything.

SORT YOUR THINGS

Now comes the hard part—deciding what to keep. Bring a laundry basket or large box into a room, and gather everything that doesn't belong there. Carry these items into the rooms where they do belong, and put them away properly.

When you're done with the last item, look around the room you're in. Repeat the process, gathering all the things that don't belong and taking them where they do belong. Keep going until all your rooms are clutter-free.

For items that belong in a room, you need to make some decisions.

If you haven't used an item for a year or you don't like it anymore—*get rid of it.* If you really want it—*put it back.*

If it's hard for you to toss things, organize a cleaning party. Find a few people willing to help—in exchange for you helping them another time.

Touching an item increases your attachment. So ask a friend to hold each item while you decide whether to keep it.

Place items you're unsure of in a box. Seal the box and date it. After six months, if you haven't gone back to retrieve anything from the box, get rid of it or have a tag sale. Bring items to a church sale or donate them to the Salvation Army or another charity.

STAYING AHEAD OF CLUTTER

Organizing is a process, not a one-time event. If you spend 15 minutes a day on the task—while watching TV or waiting for dinner to cook—you'll stay ahead of the clutter. *Other strategies...*

●**Watch what you bring home.** When you buy something, get rid of something else. If you get two new sweaters for your birthday, get rid of two old sweaters.

●**Stay current.** Open, sort and file your mail every day. After you read a newspaper or a magazine, get rid of it. If you want to save an article, tear it out and file it. Clean up the kitchen every night. Hang up your clothes or put them in the hamper when you take them off.

●**Decide what you want to keep.** I know one person who saved every greeting card he ever received. If that's what you really want, go ahead. But if you're saving and saving just to toss later, purge the clutter now.

●**Save photos—not objects.** Take a picture of your daughter in her Brownie uniform. Keep the photo, and get rid of the uniform. It's the memory you're trying to hold onto, not the uniform.

STORING YOUR STUFF

Decide how much space to allocate for storage. When it is time to add storage, it's probably time to eliminate items instead. *Storage secrets...*

●**Buy different-colored bins.** Use green tops for Christmas materials, blue for summer clothes, etc.

●**Label everything with a wide-tip marker.** Store boxes with the labels facing out.

●**Buy furniture with built-in storage—** trunk-style coffee tables, beds with drawers underneath, covered benches with room for hats, mittens and bags underneath.

●**Think vertical.** Hanging shoe bags take up less room than standing shoe racks. They can also be used for sewing supplies, crafts, tools and toys. Floor-to-ceiling shelving uses space efficiently. Also, hang wire shelving or shoe bags on the backs of closet doors.

KIDS' STUFF

Go to your local pizza place and ask for a few clean boxes—one for each child. Store artwork and school papers in them. The boxes can slip easily under the bed.

●**Dressers.** For young children, tape pictures of what goes into each drawer. After they learn to read, replace pictures with written labels.

●**Bookshelves.** Store thin books in magazine holders. Make your own using cereal boxes, sliced on the diagonal.

●**Garage.** Designate a clean trash can for storing outdoor toys. Save only the sports equipment that you still use. Create "parking spots" along one wall for bikes and riding toys.

●**Artwork.** Keep tubes from paper towels or wrapping paper for rolling up artwork. When you get too much art at home, make a calendar…or create a collage that you can hang on the wall.

●**Follow the anticlutter ground rule**— whoever makes a mess is responsible for cleaning it up. Every family member has to clean his/her bedroom and leave the bathroom and kitchen the way he found them.

If family members leave things where they don't belong, put the items in a plastic bag in the garage. When the kids ask for their stuff, they can do an extra chore to earn it back. If they don't care enough to work, give the stuff away.

●**Recognize and reward good efforts.** Praise children for their cleaning accomplishments. Rotate jobs that everyone hates. And finally, if one approach doesn't work, try a different one.

Better Home Organizing

Start with what you can see. It is tempting to start organizing drawers, cupboards and cabinets to make room to store things now cluttering your rooms. But organizing less-visible areas creates *more* clutter—you have to put those things somewhere. That can quickly undermine your enthusiasm. So start by organizing things that have the most meaning and impact on your everyday life. Leave less-visible clutter until you have made good headway with what you can see.

Julie Morgenstern, founder, Task Masters, professional organizing company, New York, and author of Organizing from the Inside Out. *Owl Books.*

Drought Rarely Kills Lawns

Grass simply goes dormant when it does not get enough moisture. If your community is under water restrictions, focus on watering plants that cannot survive a prolonged dry spell. Leave the lawn alone to come back by itself when rain returns.

Joan Lee Faust, gardening columnist, The New York Times.

How to Cut Heating and Electric Costs

First, call your utility company. Many will do a free (or inexpensive) on-site check and make specific recommendations regarding insulation, the types of windows and doors to use, etc.

While waiting, go to the Web site of the Alliance to Save Energy at *www.ase.org* and click on "Consumers." The "Interactive Home Energy Checkup" will outline steps you can take using your current (or more efficient) furnace, water heater and other equipment.

Also, the US Department of Energy answers questions at *www.eren.doe.gov.*

Nancy Dunnan, a financial adviser and author of Never Balance Your Checkbook on Tuesday and 300 More Financial Lessons You Can't Afford Not to Know. *Harper Resource.*

17

The Winning Edge

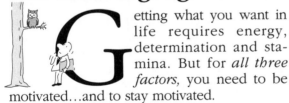

Lessons in Life… How to Get What You Want Teacher: The Great Zig Ziglar

Getting what you want in life requires energy, determination and stamina. But for *all three factors,* you need to be motivated…and to stay motivated.

To find out how successful people find their purpose and sustain their tenacity, we spoke to Zig Ziglar, one of the country's top motivational speakers.

Most of us can be motivated for *short* periods of time. What can we do to remain motivated for the long term?

Set long-range goals. Goals provide us with destinations. The more vivid our images of reaching those destinations, the stronger our desire and drive…and the less likely we are to be discouraged along the way.

Example: Legal immigrants are four times more likely to become millionaires than people who are born here. *Key:* They come to this country with their visions, and they work incredibly hard to achieve them.

Long-term goals also keep us focused on what is truly important in our lives. Without such goals, every challenge that emerges is viewed as a setback rather than a temporary distraction.

One-two punch: The way you end each day and start the next plays a major role in how productive and inspiring your days will be.

Examples: I start my day by doing something nice for someone. And before I go to bed each night, I love to listen to gospel music. It makes me feel good about myself and about all I'm going to do the next day.

What can we do to work more productively so we can reach our goals?

Zig Ziglar, one of the country's leading motivational speakers and president of The Zig Ziglar Corporation, consultants, 2009 Chenault, Carrollton, TX 75006. He is author of 15 books, including *Something Else to Smile About* (Thomas Nelson) and *Success for Dummies* (IDG Books).

Take the "day before vacation" approach. List all of your *must-dos* the night before in the order of their importance.

Get an early start the next day, and complete one task before turning to the next one on the list.

How can we become reenergized if we become bored or burned out?

Admit it to yourself. Say, "I'm down. I'm really down." Then ask yourself how long you want to stay that way. Set a time limit. Tell yourself that by 2 pm, you'll be fine. Why not 1 pm? Because you worked hard to be miserable and you want to "enjoy" it until 2 pm, and you won't give up your misery a minute sooner. By this point, you will probably be laughing.

To keep my mind fresh when I'm writing, I get a drink of water every hour or so or take a few deep breaths to relax.

When I hit a snag and don't know how to write what I want to say, I walk for 15 minutes to an hour. I always come back with an idea.

How can people avoid becoming distracted or discouraged by things that don't matter?

Have you ever noticed how often people who have nothing to do want to do it with you?

Staying focused requires that you have your objectives clearly defined. *To define your objectives, ask yourself these questions once a week...*

●**What is my objective in life?**

●**Will what I am working on bring me closer to or further from my goal?**

●**Is what I am now doing fair to everyone concerned?**

●**Will other people be helped by my reaching my goal?**

●**Do I have a legitimate chance to reach this goal?**

Are there great external sources to help us stay motivated?

Some people say all motivation is self-motivation. I have a problem with that view.

Early in my career, I struggled unsuccessfully for two years as a salesperson. It wasn't until I attended a sales meeting that a trainer persuaded me I had the ability to be great.

That external force aroused in me the belief and self-confidence to do it well.

A lot of people don't realize that they have far more ability than they think they do. One of the easiest ways to get external motivation is from audiotapes.

Example: One of my favorite motivational speakers is John Maxwell.

Audiotapes are infinitely more effective if they've been recorded in front of a live audience, not just dictated into a microphone.

Some of the best motivators are the people who make you feel good and who mean a great deal to you. The people who become your greatest mentors aren't always the most knowledgeable. Instead, they are people who believe in you and show it in loving, caring ways.

In my office, I have 21 pictures of men and women who have had huge influences on my thinking and behavior. The only one who is famous is Norman Vincent Peale. Looking at their pictures every day makes me feel loved, grateful and motivated.

Is it possible to become *too* motivated?

If you don't have a game plan that you've carefully thought out, you are more likely to make foolish moves and foolish decisions.

You also need to be careful not to confuse motivation with overconfidence. Becoming too excited or too sure of yourself leads to lapses in good judgment, which can result in self-doubt and emotional setbacks.

That's where realistic goal-setting comes in. I don't agree with the notion that positive thinking allows you to do anything.

Example: I am a very positive person— but I know I'll never be a good enough athlete to become a professional golfer.

On the other hand, positive thinking will allow you to perform whatever you choose at a much higher level than will negative thinking. Run your *life* with a vision...and run your *day* by the clock.

How to Plan the Best of All Possible Futures For Yourself

Margery Hutter Silver, EdD, associate director of the New England Centenarian Study at the Harvard Medical School Division on Aging/Beth Israel Deaconess Medical Center and coeditor of the *Journal of Geriatric Psychiatry*. She is coauthor of *Living to 100: Lessons in Living to Your Maximum Potential at Any Age*. Basic Books.

Today we all have a terrific opportunity that our parents and grandparents did not have—a tremendously expanded life span.

Three million baby boomers may live to be centenarians, and people in their 50s and 60s can expect to live into their 80s and beyond.

One key to getting the most out of these bonus years is to stay active. Activity and involvement keep you healthy and growing, even to age 100 and beyond. Inactivity and loneliness breed depression and physical illnesses.

YOUR LIFE PORTFOLIO

Middle age is a good time to take stock, to develop what Dr. James E. Birren (who founded the gerontology program at the University of Southern California and is now associate director for the Center on Aging at UCLA) calls a "life portfolio." *Steps to take...*

•**Develop your life portfolio** by writing down how you spend your time each week, what percentage of your waking hours is devoted to your work, your spouse, family, friends, arts, sports and exercise, leisure, volunteering and anything else that regularly takes a significant amount of time.

•**Then adjust the life portfolio,** just as you would a financial portfolio. Identify what is most meaningful and enjoyable to you in every phase of life—professionally, socially, culturally and physically.

•**See where you would like to spend more time** and where you want to cut back. Or, if you want to go in a different direction

altogether, start making the personal and financial plans needed to do so.

Some hypothetical examples of people moving toward or into the next phase of fulfilling lives...

•**A 60-year-old married pediatrician** spends about half her time working, which is down from three-quarters of her time when she was 35. She has doubled the time she spends with her husband, family and friends. Sports and exercise have held even, while leisure and arts have gone up a bit. Volunteer work has been added, taking 6% of her time.

While she loves medicine, her practice is demanding. By now she has a good investment portfolio...so looking toward the next decade, she can afford to cut back her working hours to 25% of her time. That will allow her to spend an equal amount of time on her volunteer work—which is quite meaningful to her—as well as to increase the time she devotes to the arts. Her other time allocations will remain about as they are.

•**A 50-year-old executive** makes a good salary, but is beginning to feel burned out. He and his wife are religious and see in their faith the answers to many of the problems troubling not only their family and friends, but society at large. He would like to become a clergyman.

He will be eligible to retire at age 60. By that time, his children, now both teenagers, will be through college, and his mortgage will be paid off. If he can also save a good chunk of money over the next decade—enough for three years' tuition and part of the couple's living expenses—he will be able to enroll in theology school. Fortunately, he will have a pension. And his wife, who is five years younger than he, will carry on working until he has finished his training and is ordained.

•**A widowed 45-year-old computer engineer** is chafing at balancing the demands of commuting to a job that involves long hours and travel with the need to provide a home life for his two children. His solution is to start his own home-based business as a computer consultant. By avoiding commuting and being flexible in his working hours, he will free up time for his family.

He cannot afford to make the change until he has at least one very solid consulting contract lined up, or has saved a substantial amount for the start-up phase of his business. Given his independent nature, the plan has long-term appeal as well. He can work as much and as long as he likes with no pressure to retire.

●**A 75-year-old who retired 10 years ago from a real estate firm** spent the next decade as an independent consultant. He is now a $1-a-year state legislator and works harder than ever. He is financially secure and feels he is making an important contribution to society.

●**A volunteer in her 60s** is also financially secure. She sold a successful dress shop she had owned for many years. That and the income from the Keogh plan to which she had long contributed enable her to devote herself to fund-raising for a school for disturbed children, as well as to work with the children, taking them to museums, to the aquarium and on other outings.

●**A 100-year-old artist** is not only doing the paintings he had dreamed of doing all his life, but also writing a novel and learning to play the violin. He married at an early age and soon had a family to support, so he went to work as a commercial artist for a catalog company. After he retired at 65 with a decent pension and savings, he seized the opportunity for artistic expression and has never stopped.

THE CENTENARIANS

However divergent the directions taken as we grow older, the underpinning for productive longevity is physical and emotional health. In the New England Centenarian Study (reported in the book I coauthored with Thomas T. Perls, MD, *Living to 100: Lessons in Living to Your Maximum Potential at Any Age*), we've identified these common factors, which spell out "ageing."

●**Attitude.** Centenarians rarely see age as a limitation. Rather, they take advantage of opportunities not available to them previously.

●**Genes.** The vast majority of people have the genetic potential to allow them to live to

at least age 85. With good health practices to minimize disease, an 85-year-old person has a good shot at living to 100.

●**Exercise.** Resistance training becomes increasingly important for maintaining strength and muscle. Increased muscle reduces risk of heart and other diseases and enhances your sense of well-being.

●**Investigate new challenges.** Keep your mind active with new activities, such as a second career, volunteer work, making art or travel.

●**Nutrition.** Emphasize fruits and vegetables in your diet and minimize meats, fats and sweets. Take vitamin E (400 to 800 IU) and selenium (100 to 200 mcg) daily.

●**Get rid of stress.** Humor, meditation, tai chi, exercise and optimism all help in managing stress.

Power Lessons for All: From Louis XIV... Napoleon...JP Morgan... George Washington

Robert Greene, author of the best-selling book *The 48 Laws of Power*. Viking. He is a writer and former editor at *Esquire*.

Great strategists as different as Queen Elizabeth I, Machiavelli, Sun Tzu and Henry Kissinger have all operated according to similar underlying principles—the rules of power. Knowing how to use power effectively—whether in the boardroom or the rec room—is the key to getting what you want.

I have studied thousands of years of history, looking for the universal laws behind the achievements of those who have successfully transformed their will into action. *Here is what I learned...*

●**Say less than necessary.** The less you say, the more profound, mysterious—and powerful—you appear.

Short answers and silences put others on the defensive, forcing them to jump in and fill the silence, thereby revealing information about themselves—and their weaknesses.

The more you say, the more likely you'll say something foolish.

French king Louis XIV always had two advisers argue different sides of an issue and always ended the discussion by saying, "I shall see." Louis never let anyone know what he was thinking. Therefore no one could ever tell him what they thought he wanted to hear. *Result:* He terrified his underlings and kept them under his thumb.

Henry Kissinger once returned a report to a subordinate with these curt seven words, *Is this the best you can do?* The writer reworked and polished the report, resubmitted it and got back the same note. Again he rewrote and improved the report, only to get the same response. *Damn it,* the official finally wrote, *this is the best I can do.* Kissinger replied, *I'll read it this time.*

•Guard your reputation.

Nothing is more powerful than your reputation. Creating and controlling a reputation exaggerates your strengths. If you're known for achievement, people expect those things from you and will go out of their way to make it happen.

Build a reputation by focusing on a single quality, such as honesty, diplomacy or awe-inspiring efficiency.

If you've already soiled your reputation, it's hard to regain it—but not impossible. Associate with those who have the reputation you want.

Another way to improve your reputation is to subtly destroy someone else's views. A bold attack will give you a reputation for being vengeful. But poke a few holes in someone else's opinion, and *public* opinion will do the rest.

Remember—a reputation is something you give yourself. If you don't like it, change it.

Example: JP Morgan and Henry Frick were symbols of greed and ruthlessness in the 19th century. But once they began collecting art, they permanently linked their names to the reputations of Da Vinci and Rembrandt. Today they're remembered as much for being great art collectors as robber barons.

•Avoid the unhappy and unlucky.

Some people bring misfortune to themselves through their own destructive behavior. If you try to change them, it's more likely you'll be changed—infected by their damaging emotions and ways of thinking...or at least frustrated.

Positive qualities are infectious. Some people draw prosperity upon themselves by good cheer and natural buoyancy.

Never associate with those who share your defects. They will reinforce everything that holds you back. If you are sullen, seek out the happy. If you are shy, force yourself to befriend the outgoing. You're judged by your peers—make sure they have the qualities you want to develop.

Example: Napoleon was a rough peasant with a bad temper, but his minister Talleyrand was a gracious aristocrat with courtly manners. Napoleon kept Talleyrand around to smooth out his rough edges.

•Transform weakness into power.

Don't fight for honor's sake. Deprive your foe of the satisfaction of defeating you. Giving in conceals power. It makes your foe complacent and gives you time to recoup and work on ways to undermine him/her.

People who care about showing their authority are easily undermined by the giving-in tactic. Outward submission makes them feel important, making them easier targets later for counterattack.

Don't sacrifice long-term maneuverability for short-lived martyrdom. If you stay firm inside but bend on the outside, you will confuse your adversary.

Example: In ancient China, King Gou Jian lost a major battle to the ruler of Wu. Instead of fleeing, he surrendered, gave his conqueror his riches and went to work for him as a stable hand for three years. Finally, Gou Jian was freed. He raised an army and, using the knowledge he had gained about his opponent, attacked and defeated him.

•Disarm and infuriate with the mirror effect.

Acting like someone else—whether it is a boss, peer or opponent—is what I call the *mirror effect.* Like a chameleon, assume the colors of your environment so no one can touch you.

Mirroring others will give them the feeling that you share their thoughts and goals. Everyone is consumed by his own ego. Try to impose your own ego and you meet resistance. But holding up a mirror makes others see what they want to see.

Feed the fantasies of others by finding out what they like and making those tastes your own. Put books by some of your boss's favorite writers on your bookshelf. Don't lecture people about their failings—they won't listen. If you mirror their behavior, they will either ignore you or think about their own actions.

Example: In ancient Greece, the general Alcibiades was indulgent and unprincipled. But whenever he met Socrates he mirrored the philosopher's behavior—eating simply and taking long walks to discuss the meaning of life and virtue. Socrates wasn't totally fooled, but he was won over by Alcibiades. Socrates became an ardent supporter and even risked his life in battle to save Alcibiades.

●**Never appear perfect.** Looking better than others is dangerous. People will become envious and look for ways to trip you up. When others envy you, they will work against you.

Weed out envy before it takes root. Appear unambitious to your colleagues. Make power seem like at least something of a burden and sacrifice—something imposed upon you. The appearance of self-sacrifice turns envy to pity. People will feel bad for imposing on you instead of resenting you for what you have.

Display some defects—admitting to harmless vices will let you disarm people. Self-deprecating humor is a good way to disarm others.

Example: George Washington refused to keep the position of commander in chief of the American army. He also resisted the presidency. People who would normally resent someone with so much power urged him to take more.

Machiavelli...The New Rules... "Softer" Ways To Achieve *Your* Goals

Harriet Rubin, a management consultant in New York and author of *The Princessa: Machiavelli for Women* (Dell) and *Soloing: Realizing Your Life's Ambition* (HarperCollins). She is founder of the Doubleday Books Currency imprint, where she has published the books of leading executives, management gurus and CEOs.

Machiavelli was the most famous political strategist of all time. A 16th-century diplomat in Florence, Italy, he was author of *The Prince,* the long-famous manual on how to wield power.

While most people think of Machiavelli's lessons as too tricky, many of them can be modified and constructively adapted to be used in today's workplace.

Modern-day strategies for gaining power— and using it well—short-run and long-run...

●**Make *big* requests.** Most people are afraid to ask for too much. They don't want to be perceived as selfish or inconsiderate. But when you ask for too little, both you and the person you are asking are diminished.

When you ask someone for a lot, you make the person feel capable of delivering a lot. You also find yourself growing to meet your own higher expectations.

Example: A vice president at a high-tech company wanted to work at home on Fridays so that she could be with her child. She asked me how to frame the request to her boss. I suggested that she not only ask for Fridays at home but also to be considered for election to the company's board of directors. Both requests were granted!

Action: For the next two weeks, make a point of not just asking for some of the things you want—*but for everything*. You'll start to make big thinking a habit...and your life will change quickly and dramatically for the better.

●**Be skillfully disruptive.** You don't get ahead by blending in, but by standing out. Machiavelli knew this better than anyone. A poet and playwright as well as a politician,

Machiavelli recognized that all human interaction is really theater.

To assert power, look for ways to stand out—visually or verbally…

●**Dress in a distinctive color at important meetings.** I always wear all white at key gatherings.

●**Coin a vivid phrase…**and use it often so that it becomes identified with you.

Example: I use the word "bull's-eye" a lot. In meetings where I've advanced an idea only to have someone else claim credit for it, I'll grab the credit back by saying, "That's another bull's-eye idea." That's how you keep your ideas identified as yours.

●**In conversation, don't use the same tone as the other person speaking.** If the other person is talking loudly and quickly, speak softly and slowly. This gets the other person to play to your tempo, giving you subtle authority.

●**Look below the surface.** People are motivated by many forces, and most of those forces aren't obvious. When you can identify and understand what motivates people, you gain power. *Helpful…*

●**Ask "Five Whys."** Start by asking the other person a why question, such as "Why is that beneficial to us?" Ask another why about the answer—and about the next answer. You can also draw on your intuition and ask yourself what the other person's agenda might be.

By the fifth *why,* you will have gotten right to the heart of your opponent's strategy…and you can use that information to create your own strategy.

●**Ask someone a probing question—twice.** Usually, the first answer will be what he/she thinks makes him look good. The second answer will be the truth.

Example: When the CEO of a Fortune 500 company hired me as a consultant, I asked him what he most wanted to accomplish. He said he wanted to make his company so strong it would be an example to every other company in the Fortune 500.

Asked that question again, he replied that he wanted to build the company's name so that his young granddaughter would think he

had made a difference in his career when she grew up.

I was able to advise him effectively because I had learned that his main concern wasn't management—but leaving a legacy.

●**Take your time.** Most people are in a hurry. Electronic communications are magnifying this trend. But when someone pressures you for an answer now, you are forced into a *reactive* mode.

Your judgment is impaired. You wind up getting caught in the other person's struggle at the expense of your own. To retain power, refuse to let yourself be rushed or bullied.

Example: I used this principle while attempting to close a deal to help build a Web site for a client. Negotiations had been proceeding fast and furious over a three-day weekend, with E-mails flying back and forth.

I decided that for one day, I wouldn't respond to anyone participating in the negotiations. Suddenly the messages I received changed from aggressive to concerned—*Was the deal still on track?…Was everything all right?*

By stepping back, I was no longer at the mercy of the people making the offers—and when I returned to the negotiations the next day, it was with greater authority.

Could this strategy have backfired? The negotiations were far enough along that it was highly unlikely. If the deal had fallen through, it would have told me that the negotiators were looking for an out—and I would have been better off knowing that.

●**Focus on *besting*—not winning.** You don't have to cripple or destroy your opponent to get what you want. Besting means achieving the most you are capable of while allowing the other participants to keep their confidence and dignity.

Focusing solely on winning can lead you to hurt your opponents unnecessarily. That results in ongoing battles and even attempts at revenge. You're much better off leaving room for antagonists to become your allies. *To accomplish besting…*

●**Let your behavior be a model for your opponent.** Act as if your enemy is already your ally.

●**Appeal to your rival's better self.** Remind the other person that he has a higher mission than just this. Talk about the great work he has done—and the kind gestures he has made in the past.

●**Be open about your expectations.** An executive once said that he and his rivals at work used to play golf in order to find out each other's bargaining position. Now when they meet in business settings, they tell each other what they hope to gain rather than waste time. Together they dream up collaborative opportunities that none of them would have thought of if they were trying to annihilate each other.

●**Never respond directly** if your opponent resists collaboration and attacks you. Acting wounded or copying his bullying tone lets him set the agenda—and gives him more power. Instead of trying to establish superiority, play your own game.

Simplify Your Life... It Pays

Richard Carlson, PhD, authority on happiness and stress management and author of 15 books, including the best-seller *Don't Sweat the Small Stuff...and it's all small stuff.* Hyperion.

Lightening your physical load by throwing garage sales, giving away your old clothes and moving to a smaller house won't automatically give you peace of mind.

To achieve calmness you need to break free of the mind-cluttering habits, worries and distractions that tie you in knots. Your life will be simpler only if you work on freeing your mind. *Here are some practical steps you can take now...*

ESSENTIALS OF SIMPLIFYING

●**Give yourself periods of "no phone calls" time.** The telephone is one of the most regularly stressful distractions of life. It can be helpful to set aside a certain time of the day when you turn off the ringer or don't answer the phone at all except in the midst of real emergencies.

Get an answering machine to take your calls so you can return them later.

●**Make a list of personal priorities.** Write them down on a sheet of paper and put the list away for a week or two. After some time has gone by, take out the list and reread it.

Ask yourself how you have spent your time and whether your actions were consistent with your list. If so, congratulations! If not, begin taking steps to line up your behavior with your priorities.

●**Learn to love voice mail.** It can be a huge time-saver and an excellent way to pass along information without being interrupted.

Example: Return telephone calls in the evening if you can answer specific questions on voice mail. This takes only a minute or two versus engaging in a 10- to 15-minute conversation.

●**Learn to say no without guilt.** The problem with always saying yes is twofold. It makes you feel overwhelmed, stressed and tired. And you end up doing things you don't want to or shouldn't be doing—all the while acting, on the surface, as if everything is just fine.

Helpful: When the request is made, ask yourself, "All things considered, is it in my best interest to say yes, or is it OK to refuse?" Put in this perspective, there are probably many instances when it's perfectly fine to say no.

●**Give yourself an extra 10 minutes.** Instead of always rushing, start out 10 minutes early instead of waiting until the last possible moment. You will find yourself with plenty of time to spare and feeling less stressed out in the process.

●**Create a "selfish" ritual.** When you have what you need in an emotional sense, you have plenty left over for others. Rituals can be as simple as squeezing exercise into your daily routine, browsing bookstores or having a quiet cup of coffee before work. The point is, it's your time—a special part of the day reserved just for you.

●**Let yourself off the hook.** We often try to do everything. We work hard, stay organized, try our best to be good parents, spouses, friends and concerned citizens. Sometimes it's too much.

Remind yourself that it's impossible to be all things to all people all the time.

Example: If you forget an appointment, don't berate yourself for being stupid. Instead, view the mistake as a signal that you probably have too much on your plate.

●**Speak softly.** When you speak too quickly and with a loud voice, the energy you send out into the world is frantic and nervous. People around you will feel pressured and slightly agitated. Speak more softly and you may discover that you begin to feel calmer and less stressed. Next, you'll discover that everyone around you will quickly start to quiet down, too.

●**Embrace change.** Truth is, everything is in a constant state of change—our bodies, homes, children. We can fight and resist change or surrender and embrace it.

The problem with resistance is it's a losing battle—100% of the time. When we try to resist the inevitable, we cause ourselves great pain and sorrow and miss out on a great deal of potential joy.

When we embrace change, we open the door to a far more peaceful existence. Then life becomes more of an adventure and each step seems more special and important.

●**Eliminate the "rat race" mentality.** One of the problems of thinking about and discussing your job/life as being stuck in the rat race is that it sets you up to be frightened, impatient and annoyed. Decide to stop talking about your situation that way. Instead, recharacterize it in healthful ways.

Example: Instead of saying, "I spent my day in boring meetings listening to arguments and dealing with constant conflict," try "The art of my work is bringing people together who, on the surface, don't seem to get along very well. It's a good thing I'm there to help." Can you feel the difference?

●**Don't dramatize deadlines.** A lot of deadline stress comes not from the deadlines themselves, but instead from the energy wasted thinking about them, wondering whether we'll meet them, feeling sorry for ourselves and, perhaps most of all, commiserating with others about them. Working toward your goal without the interference of negative mental energy makes any job more manageable.

●**Create a bridge between your spirituality and your life's work.** This means taking the essence of who you are and what you believe into your work space. If kindness, patience, honesty and generosity are spiritual qualities that you believe in, make every effort to practice them at work.

Example: If it's your job to reprimand someone, do so from a place of love and respect. Creating this spiritual bridge will remind you of a higher purpose and put your problems and concerns into a broader context.

●**Take breaks.** Failure to take regular breaks not only wears you down, but also makes you less productive. While you may not feel it at the time, slowly but surely, frustration will sneak up on you. You'll become less patient and less attentive.

Over time, you'll burn out more quickly and your creativity and insights will slowly fade away. Breaks don't have to be disruptive or last very long. Usually all we need is a few minutes every hour or so to clear our heads, stretch our arms—and get some air.

It's like pressing the reset button and providing ourselves with a fresh start.

Peter Drucker's Personal Management Program Works Well for All of Us: The Details...

Peter Drucker, eminent consultant to business and not-for-profit organizations around the world. He is professor of social science and management at Claremont Graduate University in Claremont, CA. His most recent book is *Management Challenges for the 21st Century.* HarperBusiness.

Peter Drucker, the eminent management consultant now in his 80s, continues to come up with bold, innovative advice. He discussed his book, *Management Chal-*

lenges for the 21st Century, and the personal management program that has served him well for more than 20 years.

BEING YOUR BEST

For years, I have urged managers to concentrate their efforts in areas in which they are strong and to waste as little effort as possible trying to improve the areas in which they don't have much competence.

I have also encouraged them to think hard about the skills they use to perform at a high level.

The goal is to find a way to identify what you do best and how you go about excelling at a high level. It is important to track your actions in some simple way so that you can measure results and improve your own performance.

This awareness enables you to...

●**Match your strengths to new tasks.** You can be flexible about shifting to a new career or new activities as you grow older and the world changes around you.

●**Put yourself into situations** in which your strengths are most likely to produce superior performance and results.

●**Develop the ability to recognize specific strengths** in people at work or in your personal life. That understanding can help you keep those relationships rich, evolving and satisfying.

TRACKING YOUR DECISIONS

For about 20 years, I have been writing down what I expect to happen whenever I make an important decision or take some major action.

Nine months or a year later, I go back and compare the results of that decision or action with my expectations. Even now, every time I look back, I'm surprised...and I learn something.

Routine quick and simple reviews of what happened versus what you expected to happen often reveal where you are out of date or incompetent. Be especially alert to signs that your performance is weakened because you resist skills and information that are outside your own specialty.

Bad habits that you need to remedy also show up.

Examples: You may notice that carefully drawn-up plans die because you don't follow through and take actions. Perhaps you fail to link up with the people necessary to move from plan to results.

Or you may see that brilliant, hard-driving work fails again and again as soon as the cooperation of others becomes essential.

Bright young people who see this pattern emerge might check their manners. Simple things, such as saying "please" and "thank you" and asking coworkers how members of their families are doing, are the lubricating oil of organizational and social life.

You may be shocked when you identify your weakness in certain skills or your lack of talent for certain activities. Use the information to avoid jobs that depend on those skills rather than waste time challenging yourself.

It takes far more energy and work to move from incompetence to low-level mediocrity than it takes to move from good performance to excellence.

Questions to ask yourself as you see what went well and what didn't...

●**Do I absorb key information more easily as a reader or as a listener?** Few people are adept at both. And most people never take the time to assess realistically how they deal best with data or conflicting ideas.

You may discover that you make bad decisions because you read carelessly or you put off reading essential materials. But you may realize that you absorb information well by listening carefully to people one-on-one or in meetings.

Change the way you acquire information, but don't try to change yourself. Few listeners can turn themselves into competent readers.

●**Does writing notes immediately following a meeting fix ideas in my mind?** Does it help to write a memo immediately afterward to summarize the issues and problems raised and the decisions made?

Do you find yourself arguing aloud with yourself before a small audience of coworkers about possible actions or decisions—taking one side and then another?

Most people already know how they learn best. But too few concentrate their efforts on acquiring and dealing with data in the most productive way.

●**Am I a loner?** Or do you work best as part of a team—or as an adviser? Some people are great advisers but fail under the pressure of making a decision. Others need an adviser to focus their own thinking before they can make a decision.

●**Am I best in a structured, predictable environment?** Or do you thrive under stressful conditions and have the discipline to work at several different tasks?

Strengths and weaknesses will be apparent as you review the answers to your questions. Looking for clues as to how you work best is a subtle task.

Difficult Conversations: How to Make Your Points Without Being Offensive

Douglas Stone and Sheila Heen, members of the Harvard Negotiation Project, lecturers at Harvard Law School who specialize in negotiation and founders of the consulting firm Difficult Conversations, Inc., 9 Waterhouse St., Cambridge, MA 02138. They have worked as mediators internationally and are coauthors of *Difficult Conversations: How to Discuss What Matters Most*. Viking.

Difficult conversations are part of life. You can't avoid all of them—but you can increase the odds that they will turn out well.

Over the past 20 years, members of the Harvard Negotiation Project have identified several techniques for handling a challenging conversation so that it results in a satisfactory outcome...

●**Look beneath the surface.** The typical conversation is not one but three conversations operating at the same time...

●**The "What happened?"** conversation. This involves each person's version of what took place...what should have happened... who said what...who is responsible, etc.

●**The Feelings conversation.** This involves how both people felt about what happened.

●**The Identity conversation.** Both parties are asking themselves, "What does this situation say about me—about my competence and my self-worth?"

Example: Let's say that whenever you take your children to visit your mother-in-law, she criticizes them and says they're undisciplined. You've asked her to respect your approach to child-rearing, but your attempts to talk about it always end in a fight.

The two of you aren't just arguing about how kids should behave. You're also experiencing conflicting feelings—hurt, anger, insecurity. And you're both confused about your individual roles...

"Maybe I really am a bad parent," you tell yourself.

"Maybe I'm turning into a nagging mother-in-law," she tells herself.

Often, simply being aware that the surface issue isn't the only issue can keep you from getting sucked into an angry dispute.

●**Begin conversations effectively.** Most people start by describing the conflict from their own point of view.

Example: Saying, "We'll never finish this project if you don't get your part of it done on time" is likely to put the other person on the defensive.

It's better to look at any situation as though you were a neutral observer. Then describe the differences in perspective between the two of you.

Better: Try saying, "We're behind schedule. My impression was that we each had made a commitment to finish our piece of the project by the end of last week. Our expectations may have been different. I'd like to find out what your understanding was and see if we can find a way to work together so this gets done on time."

●**Look for contribution—not blame.** When something goes wrong, assigning blame is an instinctive reaction. But it's not very productive.

Reason: Blame is focused on judgment and punishment. It doesn't help you understand how the problem happened...or how to keep it from happening in the future.

Contribution is focused on understanding— not punishment.

Problem-solving works best when both people examine their contributions to the problem. You can help pull the focus off blame by acknowledging your own contribution early in the conversation.

Example: "I was in a hurry that morning. I realize that I didn't take time to make sure you understood all of the instructions."

If you're having trouble identifying your part in the problem, ask yourself: "What would he/she say my contribution had been?" Then work together to figure out what both of you can do differently in the future.

●**Don't hide your feelings.** You may think you should check your feelings at the door before getting into a tough conversation.

But feelings will leak into the discussion, no matter how hard you try to hide them. They come out in your tone of voice and body language even if you don't put them into words. So you might as well state them clearly.

Sharing your emotions isn't the same as *getting emotional.* Yelling or bursting into tears in the middle of a business meeting would be unprofessional.

By expressing your feelings calmly and reasonably, you can usually inspire cooperation.

●**Try harder to listen more carefully.** The best way to become more persuasive is to listen before you talk.

When people don't feel understood, they stay focused on their own thoughts and feelings. That makes it hard for them to concentrate on what you're saying.

The other person's concerns may not be obvious. By listening carefully, you find out what those concerns are—so that you can address them.

Example: You're worried about a friend's health. You offer to drive her to the doctor. She chooses to drive herself, and you wind up arguing. If she's afraid to hear her diagnosis, then that's the issue on which you need to focus—not the logistics of getting her to the doctor's office.

One of the best listening tools is *paraphrasing.* Repeat back what you hear the other person saying. Pay special attention to the feelings behind the words.

Paraphrasing makes people feel understood very quickly. It also helps avoid misunderstandings—by allowing both of you to clarify what you mean.

Important: Don't use this technique in order to manipulate the other person. You'll sound phony. Paraphrasing works best if you are sincerely interested in how the other person sees things.

Also learn to say, "Tell me more."

●**Reframe the other person's statement.** Sometimes the other person stays on the attack even though you're using all the "right" techniques. When that happens, take the person's nonproductive statement and find the constructive piece buried in it. This is called *reframing.*

Example: If the other person says, "This is all your fault," you might respond with, "I believe I've made some contributions to solving the problem. Let's explore them. Also, I'd like to explore your contributions."

●**Be persistent.** You may have to use this technique repeatedly. Eventually, the other person will realize that you can't be dragged into a fight...and then a constructive discussion can begin.

Making a Great Impression Made Especially Easy

Dorothea Johnson, director of The Protocol School of Washington, 1401 Chain Bridge Rd., McLean, VA 22101. She is author of *The Little Book of Etiquette.* Running Press.

Knowing the basics of etiquette can make a tremendous difference in how others actually see us.

PROPER INTRODUCTIONS

●**When introducing yourself for the first time,** include your first and last names and something about yourself. Taking the extra moment to add that information leaves an impression of thoughtfulness and grace.

Examples: "I'm so glad to meet you, Mr. Doe. I'm John Smith from the XYZ Company," or, "I'm John Smith, Jodie's dad."

●**When introducing one person to another,** introduce the "less important" person to the "more important" person. Of course importance in this sense has nothing to do with personal worth but with seniority, status or age.

SHAKING HANDS

•**Shake hands with everyone in a group.** A casual wave won't do. Women should shake hands firmly with each other and with men. A woman or a man may initiate the handshake. Also—it is a sign of weakness and is rude for a woman to offer bent fingers instead of her full hand.

•**Wear name tags on your right shoulder area**...so when you extend your right hand, the other person's gaze naturally falls on the tag.

•**Hold your glass in your left hand** so your right hand will be free for shaking—and won't be wet and chilled from holding the glass.

THE DINNER TABLE

•**Think before you dig in.** Look at the place setting. It is a map of courses to come. *How to read a place setting...*

   •Utensils placed above the plate are for dessert.

   •A salad fork on the outside left indicates salad will be served before the entrée...if it's on the inside, the salad will follow the entrée.

   •Your bread and salad plates are always on the left...your beverage glasses on the right.

   •When the meal is over, visualize a clock face on your plate and place the knife and fork together in the 4:00 position. The fork should be on the inside...the knife above the fork with the cutting edge of the blade facing you.

•**Put your napkin on your chair** if you leave the table for a brief period. The napkin is placed on the table only when the meal is over.

BREAKING FREE FROM BORES

•**Be sincere, but don't stay long.** I learned this trick from Henry Kissinger, the master of the brief encounter. He would say, "Hello, my dear, it's so good to see you. You're looking lovely this evening. Excuse me, please, I have to go across the room and say hello to...." Henry would talk to you for 30 seconds—but during that time, you were the center of his focus.

Game Show Winner Tells Us All How to...Be a Contestant...Play to Win

Penny Hicks, a successful contestant on *Card Sharks, Now You See It, The Match Game* and *Hollywood Squares*. Her book is available through GameShowBook.com.

I am a game show fan...and I'm not alone. There is a growing number of prime time and cable game shows—including the new sensation *Who Wants to Be a Millionaire*. And there are reruns on the Game Show Network.

I first appeared on Card Sharks in 1988. Since then I've played on three other shows —and won more than $30,000 in cash, prizes and trips.

AUDITION SECRETS

For information on auditions, contact the show directly—an address or phone number is usually given at the end of the program.*

Many shows are based in New York or Los Angeles, but some hold auditions in other cities. Game show producers interview thousands of would-be contestants every year— and choose just a few. *Here's how to make yourself stand out...*

•**Be honest with yourself** about your abilities. Target a show that suits your talents.

   Examples: Contestants on *Jeopardy!* must know about geography, world affairs and many other topics. On *Wheel of Fortune,* you need a good vocabulary and the ability to recognize word patterns.

   Self-test: When you watch the program at home, if you get most of the answers right before the contestants do, you may have what it takes.

•**Study the prize distribution.** On some shows, winner takes all. You might do better on one that lets you keep whatever you've won, even if you lose later.

•**Practice, practice.** Producers want contestants who look relaxed...laugh easily...and are good sports. Before the audition, study the show carefully. Then pretend you're a contestant. Actually do the same things the

*You can also log on to the show's Web site...or *www.gameshowbook.com,* where you will find links to the major game shows that are currently being played.

contestants are doing—stand up the whole time…press a make-believe buzzer before giving your answer…phrase answers as questions, etc. The more familiar you are with the program, the smoother the audition.

Watch how the contestants behave. Jumping up and down and looking excited are part of the "look" of *Wheel of Fortune*—but not of *Jeopardy!*

●**Dress for success.** Don't go to the audition wearing lots of makeup or accessories. Dress as if you were going to a neighbor's for dinner. Some colors and fabric patterns show up better on TV than others. Ask the producers for advice when you make your appointment.

●**Reveal the "real" you.** Auditions often have up to 50 people in the same room. To make yourself stand out, be expansive when it's your turn to introduce yourself. Producers want contestants with a variety of interests. Talk about your hobbies…what you do for a living…volunteer work, etc. Above all, be enthusiastic and energetic.

PLAY TO WIN

If you make the final cut at the audition, the producers will invite you back to the studio at a later date to tape the show.

Important: Game shows do not pay contestants' expenses. Unless you live in the area or have family or friends with whom you can stay, budget for transportation, lodging and expenses.

A small fraction of the contestants actually walk away with prizes. *Here are my secrets of winning when I play…*

●**Stay alert.** A contestant spends hours at the studio before competing. The producers may cancel your appearance if you look bored or nervous. Act as though you're "on" all the time.

●**Focus only on the questions.** Don't let yourself get distracted once the taping starts. I try not to look at the other contestants or the audience. If your attention wanders even briefly, you might lose the edge you need to win.

●**Have fun.** Winning is great, but don't focus on it. That will make you more nervous and *decrease* your chances of doing well. The main thing is to have fun. I always have a great time. I've even made a few friends along the way.

You and Your Brain: Memory Secrets

It takes six hours for your brain to permanently store a new skill it learns. If you interrupt the storage process, what was learned may be forgotten.

Researchers have found that newly learned skills first go into temporary storage in the front portion of the brain for up to six hours, then are moved to permanent storage in the back.

During those six hours the newly learned skills are vulnerable to being lost if learning another skill is attempted.

Example: If after learning a new piano piece you try to learn another one within six hours, the memory of the first may be lost.

Researchers don't know if attempting to learn *any* new skill interferes with remembering the first (taking a tennis lesson after a piano lesson) or if only a new skill related to the first will interfere (trying to learn two piano pieces).

But they suggest, when at all possible, giving your brain a six-hour break between learning sessions.

Henry H. Holcomb, MD, psychiatrist, professor of psychiatry, University of Maryland, Baltimore, and researcher at Johns Hopkins University, Baltimore.

Forgiveness and Your Health

Robert Enright, PhD, professor of educational psychology at University of Wisconsin at Madison and founder and president of International Forgiveness Institute, Box 6153, Madison, WI 53716. He is a pioneer in the scientific study of forgiveness and is coeditor of Exploring Forgiveness. University of Wisconsin Press.

When we are hurt emotionally, our first reactions are anger and a desire to get even with the person who inflicted the pain. We want the people who hurt us to suffer…while a willingness to forgive them is viewed as weakness. But forgiveness is a powerful, courageous act that can ultimately be of great benefit to you and to those who are close to you.

BENEFITS OF FORGIVING

People who forgive those who inflict psychological pain on them reap huge emotional rewards. They have less hostility and anxiety and have a better chance of suffering fewer stress-related health problems.

When you forgive, you also become more hopeful about the future and your self-esteem rises.

By contrast, nursing a grudge takes an emotional toll. People who fail to forgive are prone to depression, and the more resentment they harbor, the more depressed they are likely to become.

The stress of resentment also takes a physical toll. Forgiveness is a release of the anxieties that put unhealthy strains on one's body.

Example: In one recent study, volunteers were instructed to think about an emotional injury that was done to them. Then they were asked to imagine getting even with the perpetrator. Their pulses accelerated and their blood pressures rose. When they were told to imagine empathizing with the offender, their signs of stress softened significantly.

INSULT AND INJURY

Virtually everyone has difficulty releasing themselves from feelings of resentment and anger. *Questions to ask yourself to determine your willingness to forgive...*

●**How angry do you become** when you are mistreated?

●**Are you still angry now** about being hurt recently?

●**How much time and energy** do you think you spend every day thinking about it?

●**Are you preoccupied with seeking revenge** for emotional mistreatment?

When the hurt we feel is substantial, the act of forgiving is a lengthy process.

To initiate the healing process, you must admit that you feel hurt...and that you understand what it means to forgive.

PREPARING TO FORGIVE

Many people find it hard to accept the reality of the injury they have suffered. It takes humility—and real courage—to acknowledge that someone had power over you that enabled him/her to hurt you deeply.

We resist forgiving because we misunderstand what forgiveness involves. Many of us think it means being a wimp—letting the other person "off the hook"—and inviting more mistreatment.

Forgiveness is purely an internal action—giving up feelings of resentment to which you're entitled and offering compassionate understanding to someone who may not deserve it.

Letting go of a grudge is an exercise in personal power, not weakness. It puts you in control, not at the mercy of others. Forgiving someone doesn't condone or excuse what he has done. By forgiving, you're not sheepishly accepting the action inflicted on you.

You don't need to forget about the mistreatment or pretend that the offense never happened. You don't have to allow the person who hurt you back into your confidence, your circle of friends or your home. You can forgive and still make the wise decision not to trust the offender or even to see him again.

TAKING ACTION

Once you have decided that you really want to forgive, *these exercises will help further the process...*

●**Imagine what it was like for the offender when he was growing up.** What mistreatment, deprivation and pain might have created the inner turmoil that led to his malicious action? Thinking about the person's past will plant the seed of empathy in your mind.

●**Put the offense in perspective.** Ask yourself what was happening in the person's life at the time of his offense. Acts that cause pain to others are often committed when the perpetrator is under temporary stress or pressure.

●**Accept the person as a human being.** You don't need to think of him as virtuous but as someone who, despite mistakes, has intrinsic worth because he is a human being.

●**Accept your pain, and let go.** In addition to accepting the offending person as truly human, you must feel free of negative energy rather than turning it into rage and fury. If you remain angry, the hostility will reverberate through all your relationships. When we're angry, we can't help but inflict pain on children, spouses, close friends and coworkers.

You Can Turn A Bad Mood into A Good Mood

Martin Groder, MD, a Chapel Hill, NC, psychiatrist and business consultant. He is author of *Business Games: How to Recognize the Players and Deal with Them*. Boardroom Classics.

We are living in a time of great expectations and big disappointments. When things don't go our way or stress at work or at home gets us feeling down, we become uncooperative, grouchy and even angry.

Though feeling blue or cranky is perfectly normal and healthy, there are times when we would like a bad mood to lift more quickly than nature will allow it to do.

WHAT ARE MOODS?

Moods result from a complex interaction between the internal brain chemistry and the external events that you experience.

In the brain, three major neurotransmitters affect the way we feel…

●**Serotonin,** which acts as a mood stabilizer.

●**Dopamine and norepinephrine,** which act as stimulants.

While the full extent of how these three neurotransmitters work is not very well understood, we do know that they are being generated all the time, and that they naturally move in their own cycles.

The chemicals are also affected by external stimuli—such as food, drugs, smells and interactions with others—which can cause rapid changes in the production and balance of neurotransmitters. This helps explain why people can plunge into bad moods after hearing bad news. Likewise, a person in a bad mood can snap out of it instantly after getting a phone call from a beloved or humorous friend.

SHAKING A BAD MOOD

While feeling sullen is important to the development of a sense of critical self-analysis, there are steps you can take to trick your mind into letting go.

Important: If none of the strategies I'm about to recommend brings relief and your bad mood persists for more than two weeks, see your doctor. The problem may be depression, which must be addressed and treated more aggressively.

Strategies for pulling yourself out of a bad mood…

●**Trace the source of your bad mood.** Common sources of bad moods include recent illness…loneliness…boredom…unrealistic expectations…failure to accomplish a goal…catastrophizing by making mountains out of molehills…and unacknowledged disappointment, guilt or anger.

In these cases, taking the time to analyze what was happening in your life before the bad mood occurred is useful. Knowing where the negative feelings come from gives you some sense of control, and uncovering the cause of your bad mood may actually give you clues to how to remedy it.

Example: One of my patients felt anxious and irritable but didn't know why. We talked about what had been happening during the past few days and discovered the patient's spouse was the target of unexpressed anger. The spouse had been spending money with little regard to the fact that the couple was trying to get out of debt. Once the source of the bad mood was identified, the patient was able to talk directly about it and felt better immediately.

Another often overlooked source of bad moods is having been in a good mood for a long time. People who are involved in highly intense projects at work find themselves disappointed when the projects end. In these cases, what feels like a bad mood is simply lack of rest or a neutral mood, neither good nor bad.

●**Make a list of all the positives in your life.** When you're in a bad mood, you view everything in a negative light. Setbacks and letdowns become magnified, while positive things aren't recognized at all.

Helpful: If you make a quick list of all the positive factors in your life, your negative perception will likely shift.

•**Exercise.** Physical exertion produces endorphins—natural chemicals in the brain that are responsible for creating good moods. Depending on the individual, the physical activity doesn't have to be strenuous—even a brisk 20-minute walk is sufficient to combat a bad mood. Just being outdoors will expose you to sunlight—another natural antidepressant.

Over time, exercise will make you look better and improve your overall health. And by providing a steady stream of endorphins, regular exercise will actually help protect you from future bad moods.

•**Socialize.** One of the biggest mistakes we make when feeling blue is to isolate ourselves, which can make a bad mood even worse.

Helpful: Force yourself to call someone... or even throw a simple party—take-out pizza will do—and invite some people you haven't seen in a while.

•**Seek humor.** Nothing dissolves a bad mood faster than laughter. Go to a comedy club, rent a funny video or call a friend who has a great sense of humor.

Helpful: Make a recording of your complaining, and listen to it. Even the most seemingly tragic woe-is-me complaint eventually sounds ridiculous.

•**Do something nice for someone else.** Forget yourself by concentrating on someone else. Buy a present for a friend. Call someone you haven't talked to in years. Volunteer at a hospital or a nursing home, where you'll likely see others who have much more serious problems than yours.

•**Change your immediate environment.** The simple act of moving furniture around will help freshen your attitude. Hanging new curtains, switching lamp shades, changing your bedspread or rearranging pictures will also give you an immediate lift.

•**Enjoy the arts.** For centuries, the arts have been civilization's tonic. It's hard to stay in a bad mood when gazing at a magnificent painting or listening to music you love. Even fooling around with paints or a piano will divert you from your woes and give you another way to express yourself.

•**Spend time in a natural setting.** Being close to nature makes us realize that no matter how we feel, the sun still rises and sets each day. Sitting on a bench in a garden, strolling on a beach or lying on a hillside and gazing at the sky will remind you that there is a larger world out there than your own.

MIT's Lester Thurow Welcomes You to the Brainpower Era

Lester C. Thurow, PhD, one of the world's leading authorities on the global economy. He is professor of management and economics at The Sloan School of Management at Massachusetts Institute of Technology. He is author of four best-selling books, including *Building Wealth: The New Rules for Individuals, Companies and Nations* (HarperCollins) and *The Zero Sum Society* (Viking).

All that we've learned in school and in life will no longer be enough to master the coming new economy.

This new period—which I call the *brainpower era*—will place more intense demands on our skills and knowledge. And these demands will change almost constantly.

New technologies—microelectronics...telecommunications...robotics...biotechnology...etc.—are the forces behind this new era, and knowledge has already become the new currency.

Example: Bill Gates doesn't own land or minerals or productive capital equipment. For the first time in history, one of the wealthiest men in the world owns nothing but knowledge.

Here's how to be a leader in the new brainpower era...

•**Prepare for a career in an economy in which there are no careers.** Fewer people will spend their entire careers at any one company.

Between 600,000 and 800,000 people a year are laid off from profitable companies. Layoffs to maintain profitability—commonplace in some industries—will spread until they become pervasive across the entire economy.

The growing threat of termination for reasons that transcend your abilities means individuals must take greater responsibility for their own careers. It is up to you to gain whatever new knowledge and skills are necessary to move up in an organization—or to become attractive to other employers.

●**Learn to love the technology that affects your field.** Employees have always had to sharpen their skills to advance on the job. What will make the brainpower era so different is the extent to which it will be dominated by *newly acquired* knowledge and skills.

What to do: Think hard about your present job and how existing technology specific to your field might develop. Ask yourself how that technology will make employees more efficient and your company more profitable. Then set out to learn as much as possible about the technology and how it can be applied to improve your company's business.

Your goal is to be viewed by your employer as someone who is vital to the company's future.

Key question: What training will I need to take advantage of these new technologies when they become more dominant in my industry? Most employers will gladly pay to have you tutored or trained in the technology that will allow you to help the company become more profitable.

Example: Cemex, a cement company in Mexico, uses satellite technology to guide its trucks as they make deliveries in Mexico City. Every truck driver had to be retrained to make effective use of that technology.

Expect that you will need to continue acquiring newer technology skills throughout your working life.

●**Force yourself to be more creative.** In the brainpower era, employers will increasingly value the level of creativity that employees bring to their jobs.

In most businesses, there is one highly creative worker for every 100 employees. Success in the future will go to that 1-in-100 highly creative employee. Steps to take now…

●**Seek creative challenges** by taking on assignments that will expose you to extremely bright people inside and outside your company.

●**Develop your entrepreneurial and organizational skills**…your curiosity…and your drive to improve your abilities.

●**Take courses** that are designed to enhance creativity.

Example: My son just graduated with a degree in engineering. To force himself to think more creatively, he took a course called *Left-handed Thinking*. Students were presented with different problems that could be solved using only *creative* approaches rather than obvious ones.

●**View risk as an opportunity**—not as a warning to stay away. Leaders in the brainpower era will give others the courage to take wise chances. They will recognize that risk includes reward. Risk must be evaluated for its opportunities, not just feared.

Already, more and more of the graduates from elite business schools are joining small start-up companies rather than large banking or consulting firms. While the prospect of earning great wealth is among the chief factors motivating them, these people are still aware of the tremendous risks. Nine out of 10 small companies eventually go out of business.

If you set up your own business and fail, you are still considered a desirable employee. You are thought of as hard-working and creative, a risk-taker and familiar with how the world of business works.

In general, look at the risks that the most promising people around you are taking and follow their lead. If you are smart in taking risks, eventually you will thrive in the new economy. At the very least, you will be prepared for change and be ready to take advantage of it.

Related Useful Sites

Food

☐ FoodWeb
www.foodweb.com

Food Web is the central link to hundreds of food-related sites. Order fresh seafood or aged prime steaks via E-Mail, shop for exotic ingredients by linking to any of a long list of gourmet shops. Cruise for exciting recipes or submit one of your own. Also includes information on planting and maintaining gardens.

☐ Global Gourmet
www.globalgourmet.com

The best e-zine devoted to food and cooking. Recipes from around the world, plus cooking tips and links to other food sites on the Web. Be sure to try the Orange Walnut Pancakes.

☐ Joy of Cooking.com
www.simonsays.com/joy

The classic cookbook is now on the net. It's a new, updated version, with tons of menus and recipes, links to other great culinary sites and more.

Home

☐ Hometime
www.hometime.com

The popular how-to TV show "Hometime" is now on-line. Site features how-to project information and summaries of past shows. Categories covered include kitchens and baths, landscape and garden, decks and patios, flooring, home maintenance and more. There's also a *User's Forum,* where you can share home-improvement questions, answers and ideas.

☐ WackyUses
www.wackyuses.com

Did you know that you could polish silver with a certain brand of toothpaste; clean your toilets with Alka-Seltzer; clean windows and mirrors with coffee filters? This site is filled with fascinating tips about how you can use everyday products in ways you've never thought possible. Be sure to check out the *Wacky Use of the Week.*

☐ Owners.com
www.owners.com

For Sale by Owner. Here's a good place to start if you plan to buy or sell your home yourself. If you're not sure whether using a real estate agent would be more prudent, you can get help with the answer to that question as well.

☐ DoItYourself.com
www.doityourself.com

If you're a do-it-yourselfer who sometimes has questions or is looking for a better way to do a job, check out this site. The frequently asked questions cover a wide range of subjects, from antenna and TV wiring to house painting to fire safety, even credit cards and credit repair.

☐ Garden.com
www.garden.com

Site offers garden products for sale, as well as advice and information on plants and gardens. Use the *garden planner software* to design your own garden.

☐ GardenWeb
www.gardenweb.com

Site features gardening tips for new gardeners and pros, a magazine for serious gardeners who like to have fun, a bookstore and discussion forums. In the *Garden Exchange,* gardeners can post requests for seeds and plants as well as offers of items for trade.

Travel

☐ Priceline.com
www.priceline.com

This site helps you to get the absolute lowest air-fares available. Priceline works to get you advance or economy fares when you can't get them yourself. Shop around for the cheapest tickets, decide what price you want to pay, and then let priceline find you seats.

☐ WebFlyer
www.webflyer.com

If you have frequent-flier miles, or if you think you should, check out this site. The publisher of *Inside Flyer* can answer all your questions about all the airlines' deals, how to earn miles, how to use them, which are the best programs and which to avoid. The site also offers direct links to your accounts on-line and more.

☐ Zagat Restaurant Survey
www.zagat.com

The world renowned Zagat's Restaurant Guide is also on-line. It's easy to find the top eateries in your area. Just click on the name of a city and learn the best places to eat in that area. There's a handy key that explains the rating system, and you can customize your search to meet your specific dining-out needs.

☐ All-Hotels.com
www.allhotels.com

This site has the all of the information on bed and breakfasts and inns that you'll ever need. Click on *Quick Search,* enter the country or city to which you'll be traveling and get a list of the best accommodations. You can also check out the latest *special deals* offered by the some of the world's nicest inns.

☐ Hotel Discounts
www.hoteldiscount.com

Planning a business trip? Here's detailed information on airports (including details on ground transportation, airlines and a map of the terminal) and hotels around the world, plus flight information.

☐ The Universal Currency Converter
www.xe.net/currency

Traveling to Saudi Arabia, Colombia or the Czech Republic? Find out how much your US dollars are worth in local currency with a single click. Site allows you to convert from virtually any currency to any other.

☐ Fodor's
www.fodors.com

Adult camps and recreational experiences you never knew existed. Search category listings, including academics, fitness/wellness, sports, arts, special interests, family camps, special needs, wilderness/adventure, even traditional. Home page hot button links to Kids' Camps.

☐ Travelocity
www.travelocity.com

This is one of the very best sites for planning a trip. Select a location from the handy Destination Guide and get all the information you need before traveling. Click on Last-Minute Deals for the latest in low-cost flights and hotels. Also great tips on vacations and cruises.

☐ National Park Service
www.nps.gov

This site offers a wealth of information about every national park in the United States. You can search by park name, region or state. Find directions, park maps, park fees, accommodation information and park hours. You can also find out about things to do at the park, the weather at various times of the year, activities that are available and much more.

Cars

☐ Autobytel.com
www.autobytel.com

Just specify the vehicle and options you want. You'll be contacted in a few days by a dealer in your area. Also features the latest news from the auto industry. You can even request a free auto insurance quote.

☐ Edmund's
www.edmunds.com

There are several very good and very useful auto sites on the Web. And this one deserves mentioning along with the rest. With its excellent *new-car pricing service,* this site provides more *helpful car-buying advice* than most auto sites.

☐ Kelley Blue Book
www.kbb.com

The 70-year-old Kelley Blue Book is now on-line. Go to New Car Pricing, and select a make and model. Go to *Used Car Values,* and get suggested retail prices and sale price or trade-in value for the vehicle you currently own. Site also provides links to other Web sites for buying or selling cars, getting more info, etc.

18

Business and Career Smarts

Entrepreneuring Lessons For People of All Ages From the Teddy Bear King

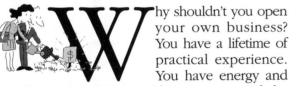

Why shouldn't you open your own business? You have a lifetime of practical experience. You have energy and a financial cushion to tide you over until the business catches on. And—you've always wanted to be your own boss. But...do you have what it takes to succeed as an entrepreneur?

ATTITUDE IS EVERYTHING

Your attitude will determine whether or not you'll be a success as an entrepreneur. *Key qualities...*

●**Persistence.** You have to be able to stay motivated through ups and downs in whichever business venture you embark upon.

●**Confidence.** You have to trust in your decisions and think positively. Your attitude will also rub off on those around you.

●**Trust in others.** You have to be able to place confidence in those you work with. You can't do it all yourself. And you won't be able to delegate to others if you don't believe they are capable of handling their jobs.

●**Courage.** You don't need the type of bravery it takes to run into a burning building to save a child, but you do need the ability to take on a certain amount of risk.

Helpful attitude: The worst that can happen is that the business will fail. So what! At least you'll have learned a lot.

There are no debtors' prisons in America today. You won't be shot at dawn if you have to file for bankruptcy. What you'll learn in this venture, you'll be able to apply to new business opportunities.

EYES WIDE OPEN

Be realistic about the life of an entrepreneur. Is this really how you want to live? *Take into account...*

John Sortino, founder of The Vermont Teddy Bear Company and coauthor of *The Complete Idiot's Guide to Being a Successful Entrepreneur.* Macmillan.

●**Long hours.** Be prepared to work until the job—no matter what it is—is finished. You can't always leave at 5 pm or start work at 9 am.

●**No guaranteed salary.** You can't expect to receive a regular paycheck for a while. Can you stay sane when you don't have a guaranteed flow of income?

In time, you'll be able to take money out of the company and have a generous expense account. But not in the beginning. Money may be very tight in your start-up years.

If you're looking merely to supplement your retirement income, consider taking a part-time job, rather than setting up your own business.

Key: If you decide to start a business, be sure you've put away enough money to live on during the times when business is slow.

●**Hard work.** A strong work ethic is essential for an entrepreneur. Many things won't get done unless you do them yourself. The true entrepreneur finds hard work satisfying.

●**Responsibility.** When you're on your own, the buck stops with *you*. Make sure you're prepared to follow through on every aspect of the business, from complying with government regulations to smoothing a customer's ruffled feathers.

BALANCING ACT

As an entrepreneur, you'll find it almost impossible to separate your business from your personal life. *How to do it...*

●**Keep balanced.** Starting and running a business takes up a lot of time. It will cut into your family time.

Self-defense: Make sure you find the time for the things that are important in your life, such as spending time with family, traveling, hiking or just spending an afternoon with a good book.

Be sure to talk to your family about your feelings toward your business *and them* so they don't feel overlooked.

●**Stay healthy.** Being your own boss can put a strain on your health. Make sure you find ways to alleviate stress, like regular exercise, taking time off for family and friends or just letting loose once in a while by doing something wild and enjoyable.

●**Set priorities.** To make all aspects of your life work together, make firm plans and stick to them.

Example: If you need to jog each morning as a stressbuster, don't make appointments that will interfere with your early run.

GETTING IT TOGETHER

Suppose you've got what it takes to be an entrepreneur and you're sure you can handle any challenge that comes your way. What else can you do to make the venture a success?

●**Find the right business.** Shop around carefully. *Make sure the business you choose suits you personally...*

●It should be a good match with your talents and experience.

●It should fit into your lifestyle.

Caution: Don't be afraid to make a lot of money. That said, make sure your choice of business has the possibility to lead to big things.

Example: If you want to open a restaurant, do you think there may be franchising opportunities down the road?

●**Find out if you'll need help.** It is important to decide whether to work utterly alone or start your venture with others.

Decide if you need someone else's talents or money to get started.

Caution: If you need only money, don't give away too much of the business too soon.

There are always people looking for good investments. You don't have to give up control or even a significant portion of ownership in return for a capital infusion.

●**Write a detailed business plan.** Everyone, including the teen with a paper route, should have a business plan. Don't push blindly ahead until you've drawn your roadmap to success. You need the plan as your guide.

You also need the plan if you want to raise seed money.

Worth repeating: Perhaps the most important thing an entrepreneur can do is to draw up a business plan. It can make the difference between success and failure.

Get Your Business Plan Funded

Start by giving possible investors a sense of excitement. Save the technical analysis for later. Make the executive summary interesting, clear and concise—and no more than four pages long. Within the business plan, get to the heart of the matter—profits—as quickly as possible. Show clearly where the earnings will come from. Explain in one sentence how the business will stand out from its competitors. Proofread the document carefully to make sure that all numbers in the executive summary match the ones that appear later.

Brian Hill, president, Profit Dynamics Inc., business consultants, Scottsdale, AZ, quoted in Investor's Business Daily, *12655 Beatrice St., Los Angeles 90066.*

How to Brand Yourself and Thrive in the New Economy

Tom Peters, management consultant with offices in Boston and Palo Alto, CA. His most recent book is *The Brand You 50: Fifty Ways to Transform Yourself from an "Employee" into a Brand That Shouts Distinction, Commitment and Passion!* Knopf. His Web site is *www.tompeters.com.*

Oprah is a brand. So is Martha. They don't need last names because virtually everyone knows what they represent. People watch their television shows or buy products associated with them because they trust Oprah Winfrey and Martha Stewart. People implicitly believe that whatever they peddle is worth purchasing.

You, too, can become a brand. In fact, to prosper in the new economy, you might not have a choice.

I believe that 90% of white-collar jobs are threatened by the explosion of the information economy. To survive in this new world, it is essential to distinguish yourself as a brand.

WHAT IS YOUR BRAND EQUITY?

The first step in branding yourself is to determine how you stand out. Evaluate yourself. *Steps...*

- **Name two to four things you are known for and one or two things you plan to be known for one year from now.**
- **List three ways your current projects challenge you.**
- **List one to three things you've learned in the last 90 days.**
- **Who are two to four important new contacts?**
- **What is your principal résumé-enhancement activity for the next three months?**

Then create a Yellow Pages ad for yourself. Imagine people are shopping for your service. What can you offer that no one else is offering?

Example: My Yellow Pages consulting ad would read, *Tom's Tantrums: He rants. He raves. He spits statistic after hard statistic...story after story. Then he demands radical action. Tom Peters is on a mission.*

TURN LITTLE TASKS INTO GOLD

Yucky assignment or great opportunity? It's all attitude. The path to excellence is to stop all *unexcellent* stuff. My motto is *100% braggable work.*

The low person on the totem pole gets the "small" stuff that no one wants to do. But if you rise to the challenge of such a project, you can turn it into something big. A church project for preschoolers can become the next national model for child care endorsed by the White House.

Seek out assignments no one wants or expects much from, and make them the next big things.

YOU ARE YOUR CLIENTS

You are professionally defined by those with whom you do business—so choose your clients carefully. List each one's strengths and weaknesses, what you can learn from him/her and how he will challenge you.

Become a client-satisfaction fanatic—for clients outside *and inside* your company. Empathy, helping and listening are what it's all about.

You want to be a leader, but you must also be a listener who can really help your client achieve his goals...and he in turn will help you. Emotional connection is the heart and soul of branding.

Example: Regularly sit down with each of your clients...and talk. It builds trust—and the brands we love are the ones we trust. If you can't build trust with a client, you have the wrong client ...or your client sees the wrong brand in you.

BUILD A WEB SITE

The Web is the future. Either you are there or you aren't. If you don't know the Web, get to know it...*fast*. Spend time on it every day. The Web is the great equalizer. Where else can a small start-up company go head to head with the big guys?

The Internet lets everyone go global, which means submitting résumés, recruiting, negotiating via E-mail, hiring, training. You can join communities that share your interests, create your own identity, attract clients.

Even if you're still working for someone else, start a bare-bones Web site. If nothing else, your site can be a professional place marker, getting the relevant information about you out there. This is your chance to create a distinct persona for yourself.

ME, INC., NEEDS A BOARD OF ADVISERS

Find two to five people you respect. Sit down with them on a quarterly basis and formally review your progress, plans and mistakes.

The more you have the support and advice of members of the establishment, the more you can push the bounds of the establishment.

Contact and cultivate people who think like you but are higher up on the "food chain." Appeal to their altruism and self-interest to get them to join your informal board of advisers.

In my experience, every establishment has a few closet renegades. Seek them out. Schedule a coffee or lunch with someone who seems in sync with you—maybe a former boss who admired your aggressive approach.

They'll admire your spunk, relive their own green-behind-the-ears days through you and get a kick out of being a mentor.

Remember: They get as much out of mentoring as you do.

How to Set Up and Run Your Own Web Page

Bud Smith, product manager in the technology department at AltaVista, a free Internet search engine. He is coauthor—with Arthur Bebak, editor of *Netsurfer Digest*, a weekly on-line magazine—of *Creating Web Pages for Dummies: Fourth Edition*. IDG Books.

You don't have to be a high-tech wizard to design a Web page these days. A number of Web publishing services provide free space and tools to make it easy to create your own site.

In less than one hour, you can design a page that announces a recent birth...tells about your favorite pastime...posts your résumé or vacation photos...or describes your business.

GETTING STARTED

Technology needed to get started...

- **Computer** that has at least a 566-megahertz processor and 64 megabytes of RAM.

- **56 Kbs modem,** which comes with most new computers and dials your connection to the Internet. If you have to buy it separately, a modem costs about $140.

- **Internet Service Provider (ISP),** which allows you to connect to the Internet. Cost: Around $20 per month for unlimited service.

Examples: America Online (*www. aol.com*, 800-827-6364) and AT&T Worldnet (*www.att.com*, 800-309-3349).

- **Web browser.** A browser is software that allows your computer to read Web pages.

Examples: Microsoft Internet Explorer (*www.microsoft.com*) and Netscape Communicator (*www.netscape.com*) are the most widely used browsers. Both can be downloaded free at their Web sites.

PLANNING YOUR SITE

Before creating your Web page, visit other Web sites for design ideas. *Steps to take...*

- **Visit a search engine's Web site,** such as AltaVista (*www.altavista.com*) or Yahoo! (*www.yahoo.com*). Enter the name of the subject that your Web site will cover.

The search engine will list all of the Web pages it can find on the subject. Then click on each title that appears in blue. The Web pages will come up on your screen.

●**Make notes on what you like and dislike** about each site. *While you're "surfing" the Web, notice that most pages are made up of the following elements…*

●*Background*—the color or pattern of the page.

●*Headline* appears at the top and tells visitors where they are in a site.

●*Text* is the body of the page on your screen.

●*Graphics* include pictures, company logos or other artwork. They add color and life to a site.

●*Links* are connections between two documents or sites. *Examples…*

☐ External link is text or a graphic that, when clicked, connects you to a page outside the Web site on your screen.

☐ Internal link connects you to other pages within the Web site on your screen.

☐ E-mail link is text or a graphic that, when clicked, sends mail to an E-mail address.

As you look at other sites, write down the features you would like to include on your site. Your site may consist of one page or a number of pages linked together.

Also write down the Web addresses of the sites to which you would like your site to be linked. You'll be asked to enter them when you design your site.

DESIGNING YOUR SITE

A number of Web publishing services offer free space and Web page design tools. *Leading services that allow you to create a Web site at no cost…*

●**Homestead** (*www.homestead.com*).

●**Tripod** (*www.tripod.com*).

●**Yahoo! GeoCities** (*http://geocities.yahoo.com*).

All share a similar sign-in process and are easy to use.

Yahoo! GeoCities and Tripod offer 11 megabytes of free space, which is about 11,000 pages of text or 80 to 100 large, quarter-screen graphics. Homestead offers 12 megabytes.

Each of the services walks you through the entire design process, which consists of about 15 to 20 steps. *Each service will also prompt you to do the following…*

●**Register your site.** You'll be asked to enter personal information—your name and E-mail address. You may also be asked to choose a category for your site.

●**Name your site.** In most cases, the name you enter for your site cannot exceed 26 letters and cannot include punctuation marks. The actual Web address of your site will contain the name of the on-line service with which you are registered.

Example: If you name your site "My Home Page" on Tripod, the address that visitors will type to open your page will be *www.tripod.com/myhomepage*.

Most Web publishing services that charge a fee will provide you with a more official address that includes your Web site's name plus *.com—www.myhomepage.com*.

Cost: About $70 to register your own address for two years, if you choose to do so, plus the cost of server space—usually $10 to $30 monthly.

●**Choose a template.** Templates are preformatted pages that allow you to insert text or graphics. Most templates have a theme, such as a photo album, a personal page or a business page.

You'll also be asked to select a background color or pattern as well as the color of the text.

●**Add text.** Since most people don't like to read long paragraphs on a computer screen, use short sentences to convey messages easily and clearly.

●**Add graphics.** Most services allow you to download images from their clip art galleries, free of charge.

Alternatively, you may download images—and text—from your computer's hard drive onto your site.

When adding images to your page, always provide a text description of each image. Some users with slow Internet connections disable their computer graphics displays in order to speed up download time. Such users won't be able to view your images, but they will be able to read your descriptions of those images.

●**Add links to other pages** within your site or to your favorite Web sites. You may also add a link that allows visitors to send you E-mail.

●**Add other elements.** Some services allow you to add special elements to your sites.

Examples: Homestead, Tripod and Yahoo! GeoCities all let you add "hit counters" that show the number of people who have visited your Web site. They also provide "guest books," which list the E-mail addresses of visitors to your site.

●**Publish your site.** In most cases, you officially post your site on the Web by clicking a box on the screen labeled "publish" or "upload." After this process is complete, anyone can access your site.

EDITING YOUR SITE

Don't let your site go stale. Making timely changes and adding pages often will keep visitors coming back.

Web publishing services may remove your site from their servers if you don't edit it or if no one visits.

Good Computer-Based Businesses to Start At Home

Paul and Sarah Edwards, authors of 10 books on self-employment, Pine Mountain Club, CA, including *Making Money with Your Computer at Home*. Putnam.

The rise of the Internet and faster computer modems have created new types of home businesses...

BACKGROUND CHECKER

Research the background and references of job applicants for employers. Requires understanding of how to use publicly accessible databases to track criminal records, credit histories, etc.

You can earn: $20 to $100/hour.

Information: *The Complete Reference Checking Handbook* by Edward Andler (Amacom).

DISK COPYING

Make copies of master CD-ROM disks for software publishers and corporations that use them for marketing and employee training. Ordinary computers can be outfitted with multiple disk drives.

You can earn: $1.10 to $1.75/disk.

Information: Copying software, such as *WinDisKlone* and *EZ-DiskCopy Pro* from EZX Corp. (*www.ezx.com*).

HOME-REMODELING ESTIMATOR

Develop cost estimates for home owners. Requires assembling a database of local costs of labor, materials, etc.

You can earn: $35 to $50/hour.

Information: National Association of the Remodeling Industry (*www.nari.org*)...and software such as BidMagic from Turtle Creek Software (*www.turtlesoft.com*).

SPECIALTY RETAILER

On-line retailing is one of the hottest areas of the Internet. To be successful, you have to sell products that fill a small but lucrative niche. *Examples:* Peacock products (feathers, novelties, etc.) and clothing for the handicapped.

You can earn: Up to $30,000/month.

Information: The Direct Marketing Association (212-768-7277/*www.the dma.org*).

WEBMASTER

Manage Internet sites for companies and individuals. Includes converting copy to HTML (Hypertext Markup Language)...fixing technical glitches...making sure all links work.

You can earn: $25 to $75/hour.

Information: World Organization of Webmasters (888-564-6279/*www.world-web masters.org*)...or The Web Career Research Center (*www.cio.com/forums/careers/*).

WEB-SITE PROGRAMMER

Create Internet sites for companies, associations and individuals. Requires knowledge of one or more Web programming languages such as CGI, HTML and Java.

You can earn: $30 to $150/hour.

Information: The Association of Internet Professionals (800-564 6247/*www.association.org*).

Start-Up Secrets from Weekend Entrepreneurs... How to Create A Prototype... Raise Money... Market...Etc.!!!

Corinne McCormack, founder of Corinne McCormack Inc., whose eyewear products are sold in 2,000 stores nationwide, 7 W. 36 St., New York 10018.

Mark Beckloff, cofounder of Three Dog Bakery, which makes 120 all-natural varieties of dog treats, 1627 Main St., Suite 700, Kansas City, MO 64108.

Sharon Zumm-Campbell, founder of Smile Time Inc., whose baby products and toys are sold in more than 100 stores, HCR 3, Box 310, Rochelle, VA 22738.

Thanks to the Internet and the availability of free and inexpensive resources, more and more people are starting businesses during their spare time.

To find out how to improve your odds of turning a great idea into a profitable enterprise, we spoke to three successful entrepreneurs who started businesses in their spare time. *Here's their advice...*

CREATE A PROTOTYPE
Corinne McCormack

You can improve the odds of success by taking the time to create a detailed example of your idea before you contract with a manufacturer to produce it.

When I started my company in 1993, I wanted to make moderately priced fashionable necklace chains that attach to eyeglasses. I could have told a manufacturer what I wanted. But I knew I'd be more likely to get a product that met my standards if I created a sample that the plant could copy.

How to create the right prototype...

●**Buy your rivals' products.** Before I designed my eyeglass chains, I wanted to find an untapped niche in the market. I also wanted to see what kind of quality and materials customers expect in my target price range. So I bought and studied chains being sold in the price ranges above and below my price target. I also looked at eyewear accessories advertised in magazines.

●**Find a fabulous factory.** The best way to find one is to join a trade group, attend trade shows and network with others in your field. Ask your contacts if they've found a plant that offers on-time deliveries and rigid quality control.

Also ask if their factories employ product designers who will help you create your prototype if you bring them rough sketches—and will help you select the right materials. This will save you time looking for your own sketch artist and product designer. My prototype cost only about $500 to make.

●**Put the prototype through the paces.** It can take a month or more to create and test a prototype.

Once I created my first sample, I wore it while jogging, to make sure my sunglasses didn't slip off the chain. They did. It turned out the rubber tips I used to attach the glasses to the chain weren't strong enough. It took me four more tries before they were perfect.

If you're planning to sell your product to stores by a certain date, make sure you leave enough time to get it right.

RAISE ENOUGH CASH
Mark Beckloff

When my partner and I started our dog-treats company in 1990, we turned to our charge cards for cash.

We had to. Banks don't lend to fledgling entrepreneurs. It's too risky. And most venture capitalists don't want to take a chance on someone who doesn't have a successful track record.

How to finance your business with a charge card...

●**Borrow only what you can pay back at month's end.** Instead of taking out a lump-sum loan, we borrowed what we needed each month from my Visa card to build up credit. Then we applied for an American Express card.

Relying on our American Express card rather than a credit card kept us disciplined. An American Express card requires you to pay your bill in full at the end of the month and doesn't charge interest. Over a period of nine years, we borrowed and paid back a total of $70,000. Last year, we used our prompt payment record to attract $6 million in venture capital.

●**Don't borrow big until you establish credit.** Early on, there were several times when we had to take out large cash advances on our charge cards—about twice the usual amount—to make payroll. American Express did not become alarmed because, by then, we had already built up a record of paying smaller amounts on time thanks to our sales.

●**Don't quit your day job.** My partner kept his job for the first three years, and I kept my job for one year after starting the business.

We wanted to have a steady source of cash to pay our bills and didn't want to have to borrow much. We also used a variety of small-business services offered by American Express, including an equipment-leasing plan and travel discounts.

GETTING THE WORD OUT
Sharon Zumm-Campbell

I used the Web to sell my huggable baby-bottle holder, which is shaped like a stuffed bunny. It's designed to hold kids' attention so they don't throw their bottles on the floor. I started my company in 1998, and by the end of this year, I'm projecting $1 million in sales. *Here's how I used the Web to sell my product…*

●**Protect your idea worldwide.** Once you launch a Web site, people around the world will be able to see your product. So before I put up my Web site, I filed for a trademark and patent for my bottle.

To apply for a trademark: Contact the US Patent and Trademark Office, 800-786-9199 …or *www.uspto.gov.* Ask for an application. There are issuing and filing fees.

To apply for a patent: You need to hire an attorney. It took me two years to get a patent…and it cost $6,000.

●**Build your own Web site.** Most Web site designers charge $1,000 to create a site where you can sell products. Expect to pay additional fees every time you make a change to the site.

I was on a tight budget, so I taught myself to build my own Web site. *The books I used were…*

●*HTML 4 for Dummies* (IDG Books).

●*Photoshop for Dummies* (IDG Books).

It took me five days to read these books. Then there were three long days of trial and error to create a rough Web site.

●**Create a customer-friendly Web page.** Your goal is to make life easy for customers and to make them feel that you're not going to scam them.

I included an icon at the top of my opening page on which customers can click to find out how to get in touch with me. I also included a picture of me and relevant newspaper articles about the business. I'm always surprised by how many sites risk losing sales by forcing customers to click their way through several layers to find this information.

●**Link up to popular search engines.** It's essential that potential customers be able to reach your site through major search engines such as Excite, InfoSeek and Yahoo!

Once a week, I use a software program called WebPosition Gold (888-275-1231…or *www.promotionsoftware.com*). It tells me whether my Bunny Bottle appears in the major search engines.

The Seven Big Negotiation Mistakes and How to Avoid Them

1. Preparing inadequately. Bring notes to use during the meeting.

2. Ignoring the give/get principle. Make sure that whenever you give up anything, you get something in return.

3. Displaying intimidating behavior. Never try to bully the other side…or let yourself be bullied.

4. Showing no patience. Hold all of your phone calls—and other interruptions—while you are negotiating.

5. Losing your temper. Stay cool—in voice and actions.

6. Talking too much. Spend more time listening.

7. Asking too few questions. Ask—then listen carefully to the answers.

Joan Mather, editor, *Meeting & Conference Executives Alert*, 554 Strawberry Hill Rd., Centerville, MA 02632.

How to Deal with Tough Customers

Jeffrey Gitomer, president, BuyGitomer, Inc., 705 Royal Ct., Suite 100, Charlotte, NC 28202. He conducts corporate training programs on sales and customer service and is author of many books, including *Knock Your Socks Off Selling*. Amacom.

In today's fast-paced business world, customers are increasingly demanding and less tolerant of delays, poor service or even honest mistakes.

That means that while all businesses have had their share of tough customers in the past, now they have to deal with complaints and demands from customers who would earlier have been normal, satisfied patrons.

For business owners, the message is clear: If you can't quickly turn a complaining customer into a smiling customer, you're likely to lose that account to your competition.

DIAGNOSE THE PROBLEM

Critical: Constantly remind yourself and your employees to take all customer concerns *very* seriously. No customer complaint is too small to shrug off. *Helpful steps…*

●**Reverse the situation**—and recall when you have been a tough customer…at the dry cleaners, the bank or the auto repair shop. Think about what would have made you feel better at the time. Often, that will give you ideas about how to quickly solve a customer's problem.

●**Remain friendly.** Always start by empathizing with the customer.

Three words that calm a tense situation: "Oh, that's terrible!" Use language that convinces the customer that your company cares about him/her and wants to fix the problem.

●**Ask questions.** Often there is an unstated skepticism or anxiety about making proper use of your product that has prevented the customer from getting the results he was expecting.

If the complaint is not a technical or mechanical one, ask questions such as, "Is there anyone in your company who could help you operate the product?" If you read anxiety in the customer's response, you may be able to provide a wonderful solution by simply giving him a special phone number to call for assistance.

HARD-CORE COMPLAINERS

In every industry there are a few customers who just insist on being treated better than anyone else. You can recognize them from phrases like, "Don't you know who I am?"…or "I've always had it done this way before. What's wrong with you people?"…or "Let me speak to your superior."

For a customer who is profitable and who represents repeat business and referrals, it's easy to overlook minor annoyances in the day-to-day relationship. But if a relentlessly tough customer makes so many demands that his business is no longer profitable—or if he fails to pay bills on time or meet other obligations—it may be time to recommend politely that he take his business elsewhere.

Strategy: "Kill" the customer with kindness as you provide the names of other suppliers, and even offer to call ahead to smooth the way. If the impossible customer can't find satisfaction from competitors, either—which often is the case—he may come back to you with a changed attitude. At that point, you can make a viable arrangement.

Encouraging: When selling to a super-demanding customer who either has come back to you—or simply knows he can't do better anywhere else—you can often boost your price.

Because the customer's order comes with special requirements that take more time or money—or both—to satisfy, you are justified in demanding a higher price. And once you know that the customer isn't switching to the competition, he will probably pay without further fuss.

Timely Profile of a Workplace Menace: What to Look Out For

Martin Blinder, MD, who practices psychiatry in San Francisco and Honolulu. He has done extensive research on workplace violence.

The rise in workplace violence has given psychiatrists enough data to build a psychological profile of employees who are most likely to engage in lethal acts of revenge. *Traits that are reason for considerable concern...*

•**Homicide-prone workers are profoundly narcissistic,** exhibiting an overwhelming sense of entitlement and a predilection for deprecating others. They hold themselves out as superior and may be inclined to make such pronouncements as "Where do you get off criticizing me?"

•**They have what coworkers describe as *sour personalities.***

•**They are repeatedly offended by *slights*** and are "victims of injustice."

•**They are controlling and demanding** and often act obsessively toward coworkers or supervisors despite counseling, admonitions or appeals to reason.

•**They tend to make coworkers uncomfortable, even anxious.**

•**They are devotees of conspiracy theories.**

•**Mistakes are always "someone else's fault."** They file one grievance after another. They may have drawers full of documents that "prove" their position.

•**They harbor persistent and inappropriate anger.** Often they express great interest in, and approval of, violent acts reported in the press.

•**They make cryptic but ominous statements** such as, "Sooner or later, everybody gets theirs."

SELF-DEFENSE

If you recognize this profile in employees, monitor them closely. But observe them in a benign, supportive and nonthreatening fashion.

How to fire: Do so in a matter-of-fact way, with regret and courtesy. Minimize the employee's feelings of humiliation. Provide a compassionate severance package, including medical benefits. In the long run, such beneficence may prove to be an enormous bargain.

Much of the Best Business Software Is Free

Patricia Robison, chief technology officer, Nekema, Inc., an Internet financial services firm, 30 Montgomery St., Jersey City 07302.

Don't overlook new opportunities in free business software. Free doesn't mean "low quality" in the world of software—rather, it often means "state of the art." And you can't beat the price!

HAVE NO FEAR

Business owners who have doubts about using free software may be surprised to learn they already are relying on it—especially if they use the Internet or have a Web site. *Examples...*

•**More than 75% of all E-mail traffic is handled by free Sendmail software.** No commercial product comes close to having its installed base, tested features and security.

•**More than 50% of all Web servers run with free Apache software.** Microsoft is next in market share, with 25%.

•***Linux* is the fastest-growing operating system (OS)**—used on servers that handle Web sites and large databases. The US Postal Service uses hundreds of *Linux* systems nationwide. Distribution of the free *Linux OS* is accelerating—successfully competing with other multiuser operating systems such as *Windows NT* and Sun's *Solaris.*

•**The two leading Web browsers**—Netscape *Communicator* and Microsoft *Internet Explorer*—are given away free, as are a great many Web applications from other corporations that are used with them.

HOW IT WORKS

Free software pays for itself by getting customers to use complementary products or services provided by the software suppliers. *Basically, there are two kinds of free software...*

•**Private company free software.** This is distributed by individual businesses—the way Microsoft distributes the *Internet Explorer* Web browser. Netscape pioneered this strategy, popularizing the Internet by giving away its Web browser to consumers so businesses would buy its server software to host Web pages.

Since then, many leading software firms have adopted their way of doing business, giving away basic versions of their products while enticing users to pay to upgrade to more sophisticated versions or to buy complementary products.

Examples: Eudora Light E-mail program ...*Free Agent* newsreader...and Adobe *Acrobat* document imager, among many others.

These are all high-quality products designed and distributed by reputable companies to enhance their reputations and attract customers. So the old idea that "if it's free, it can't be very good" truly is obsolete in the software market.

Small businesses often need no more than the "standard" free applications for most purposes. They can fully use the basic program ...without paying a penny for any upgrades. A few employees might need a "heavy use" E-mail reader, but most need just a free, standard E-mail program.

A wide and growing range of private company free software is available, and businesses should explore their options before paying for software that may be no better—or not even as good.

•**"Open-source" software.** These programs aren't owned by anybody. They are developed collaboratively by software experts around the world working from businesses, universities and foundations as well as independently. Much of the best and most successful free software available to business is "open-source."

Sendmail, Apache and *Linux* all are open-source, and Netscape *Communicator* is moving to open-source with its next release.

Open-source software is not a simplified, introductory version of a product—it is the best that its creators can make it.

Open-source software is supported by major corporations, such as IBM, and by specialist companies, such as Red Hat and Caldera, which support business applications of *Linux,* its creators and software consultants—all of whom contribute to its further development. Visit their Web sites for more information and downloading instructions *(www.redhat.com* and *www.caldera.com).*

MORE OPPORTUNITIES

Many companies feel more comfortable acquiring free private company software, rather than free "open-source" software.

But state-of-the-art open-source software can offer a business the chance to obtain top performance at no charge. *Advantages of open-source software...*

•**Quality.** Open-source software often is simply better than commercial software for specific applications. *Examples...*

•IBM recently began distributing free Apache Web server applications as part of its own product line—after deciding its own Web server product couldn't compete.

•In a recent user-satisfaction survey of information technology professionals, the free *Linux OS* solidly outscored expensive commercial OSs such as Microsoft's *Windows* and *Windows NT* and Sun's *Solaris.*

Linux is noted for being virtually crash-proof. That is vital for servers hosting business Web sites and databases. It will run on computers much too small to run *Windows NT* (such as a 486 with only 8 megs of RAM). Yet it scored ahead of the expensive commercial

OSs in product functionality, availability, flexibility, Internet readiness and JAVA support—as well as price and cost of ownership.

Peer review: Unlike commercial software, the development of open-source software is "peer reviewed." Its code is openly published and any computer programmer in the world can suggest improvements.

The best improvements are selected by the top experts on the program and are included in each new release.

Result: A leading open-source program may have more developers working on it than even a company like IBM could assign to a competing product.

●**Cost.** Some open-source software isn't entirely free. Although businesses can obtain the code to open-source programs free, they usually choose to buy the software in a package purchased from a commercial firm that includes complementary programs and support. But the cost still typically is only a small fraction of that of commercial software.

Example: Recently, a single-server license for *Linux,* good for an unlimited number of users and bundled with word-processing and business software, was available for $60. A single-server license for *Windows NT,* good for only 50 users, costs more than $3,000.

DRAWBACKS

For businesses, the main drawback of free open-source software is a shortage of user-friendly business applications at the "front end"—for the average employee to use.

Most open-source applications are at the "back end"—such as *Apache* running Web pages...*Linux* as the OS for computers hosting Web servers, databases and fire walls ...*Sendmail* managing E-mail networks, etc. But this is rapidly changing. Top commercial software companies are moving to make their products available to work with open-source software.

●**Support.** IBM, in addition to supporting *Apache,* is now making versions of its top business software products that run on *Linux.* So are other leading commercial firms, such as Oracle, Sun, Sybase, Informix and Hewlett-Packard. Corel's *WordPerfect Office Suite 2000,* which includes a full range of business

software, is available on Linux, as is Sun's Star office suite.

BUYING STRATEGY

Before buying expensive computer software, consider the opportunities in free software.

Explore what's available both in private company free software and open-source software. *Steps to take...*

●**Read reviews of free software in leading computer magazines.** You may be surprised at what's available.

●**Post questions in Internet discussion groups** and newsgroups.

●**Visit the Web site of the Free Software Foundation,** *www.gnu.org,* and the Open-Source Software Organization, *www.open source.org.*

●**Go to Yahoo! or your favorite Web search engine** to search "free software" and "open-source software."

Also—use free software sites on the Web to search for free business application software, such as issue tracking *(Perfect Tracker),* check writing *(Simple Check),* etc. Free software sites include *www.tucows.com* and *www.shareware. com.* Closely examine candidate software purchases, and select the one that will perform best for your business.

How to Ace Your Next Job Interview

Laura Lofaro, founder of Sterling Resources International Inc., an executive search and consulting firm specializing in banking, 666 Fifth Ave., New York 10103.

The hiring process today is very different than it was even five years ago. *Here's how to stand out and become more desirable than your competitors...*

●**Supplement your résumé with a one-page highlight sheet.** Most employers are too busy to absorb the many details that appear in standard résumés.

The points in this highlight sheet should appear in reverse chronological order, with your most recent accomplishment first and an explanation for each. Such highlights not only serve as an easy way for managers to evaluate you, they also demonstrate your instinct for making their lives easier. That's a big plus today.

This sheet also provides the talking points for your interview.

Example: "Reorganized workloads of my direct reports to emphasize communication and efficiency. This move saved the company $200,000 in new staff salaries."

●**Let the interviewer talk for the first five minutes.** Many job candidates become so caught up in selling themselves that they fail to listen to what their potential employer has to say. Nothing is more off-putting to an interviewer than a candidate who doesn't listen.

My advice: Get the interviewer talking by asking easygoing, job-specific questions. *Examples...*

"What is it like to work here?"

"What is your average day like?"

Once the ice is broken, move on to questions such as "Can you tell me more about the responsibilities of this position?" or "Can you tell me what skills the ideal candidate for this position would have?"

An employer who is willing to tell you what kind of candidate he/she is looking for is essentially giving you a script for the rest of the interview.

●**Expect to interview with several people.** These additional people may be at higher or lower levels than the person who originally interviewed you.

Everyone you meet is important—in today's workplace, the opinions of all team members are solicited and valued.

●**If the interviewer wants you to meet someone on a higher level:** Ask several questions about this person before you leave the interviewer's office.

To do this gracefully, mention that you want to be as prepared as possible. Then ask if he would mind sitting with you for a minute to tell you about the person you'll be meeting. *Key questions to ask...*

"What are the person's duties?"

"What is he like?"

"How long has he been with the firm?"

"What is his pet project now?"

The answers will help you frame your responses when you meet the next person and make him more comfortable with you.

People in power like to offer help and advice, so let the person you meet lead the conversation. Keep your answers brief.

●**If the interviewer wants you to meet someone on his level or lower:** The message you want to send is that you do not intend to take the person's job or pose a threat to him.

When introduced, let the person tell you what he does, how long he's done it and anything he wants to share about his background. This will allow the interviewer to establish his turf and feel safe with you.

Then ask him questions that will enhance what he has already told you. *Examples...*

"What do you like about working at this company?"

"What's your favorite part of the job?"

"Are most of the people who work here friendly?"

Thank-You Notes Boost Job Chances

More than three-quarters of executives from the nation's 1,000 largest companies said they consider a post-interview thank-you note to be at least somewhat helpful when they evaluate job candidates. But only about one-third of candidates send the notes. The ones who do tend to stand out—and increase their chances of being hired.

Survey of 150 large-company executives by Accountemps, temporary staffing service, Menlo Park, CA.

On-Line Job Search

Placing a résumé on the Internet is a great way to circulate it among prospective employers. *But:* It may keep circulating long after you want it to. When a document is circulated electronically, it quickly becomes impossible to recall, and you will never know all the places it goes. *Safety:* Date résumés so a prospective employer won't judge you by an old résumé—and your current employer won't mistakenly believe you are looking for a job.

Peter Weddle, career entrepreneur, Old Greenwich, CT, and author of *Internet Résumés: Take the Net to Your Next Job.* Impact Publications.

Big-Time Consulting Resources for Entrepreneurs

Bruce Judson, nationally recognized Internet marketing expert and author of *HyperWars: 11 Strategies for Survival and Profits in the Era of Online Business.* Scribner. He is editor of the newsletter *Grow Your Profits,* www.growyourprofits.com.

More low-cost and free consulting resources are available for small businesses now than ever before—often through the Internet. *Examples...*

●**Small Business Development Centers** provide business and demographic databases for local geographic areas...and offer professional counseling. For the nationwide directory: *http://sbdcnet.utsa.edu.*

●**Ernst & Young's (E&Y) "Ernie" On-Line Consulting** lets one person from the company submit any number of questions to E&Y by E-mail during the year. Questions are forwarded within E&Y to an appropriate expert, who replies. Users also get unlimited access to a "previously asked questions" database. Priced by the kinds of service desired. *http://ernie.ey.com.*

●**Service Corps of Retired Executives (SCORE)** has more than 12,000 business counselors nationwide, 550 E-mail counselors and hosts more than 5,000 workshops annually. *www.score.org.*

●**Management Consulting Network International** is an on-line network of consulting firms as well as related research and

data resources worldwide. A search engine for the site helps you find what you are looking for. *www.mcni.com.*

●**US Small Business Administration** provides extensive free research data and links to valuable outside sources of information. *www.sba.gov.*

More from Bruce Judson...

Yes...There Is Money to Be Made Via the Internet... Here's How

There is a myth that no one is making money on the Internet today. I learned the truth while I was researching my most recent book about business on the Internet. I encountered a surprising number of Internet businesspeople who didn't want to be interviewed. In fact, they didn't want to be mentioned in my book at all. How could this be? In America today, doesn't everyone want to be publicized?

But these people were deliberately avoiding the limelight. It was not just me they were ducking—but anyone or anything that might attract attention to them.

Reason: They were running highly successful cyber-businesses and did not want to attract competition. Part of keeping competition away was a conscious effort not to be boastful about their success.

Reality: Today, there are thousands and thousands of successful businesses with substantial incomes from the Internet. The vast majority of these are not large companies, funded by venture capitalists with seemingly unlimited money to lose.

Rather, they are businesses that, like entrepreneurs in the physical world, are funded with a combination of sweat and limited money. And —it's clear they are making money...because otherwise they would have vanished long ago.

WHO ARE THEY? HOW DO THEY DO IT?

So, what kind of businesses are actually making money on the Internet? Most meet seven essential criteria. *They...*

...find a niche—typically a service—that they can provide using the Internet to meet a specific need.

...are entrepreneurs who were the first to move into their niche. They then worked through the Internet to build and hold their dominant positions. On the Internet, being first is a huge advantage for any business.

...understand how to use the Internet to create value. That, in turn, serves to bolster their control of the niche.

Example: There are some cyber-businesses that provide the same service under two different names—one very serious and one that sounds like fun. This is smart marketing for two reasons—it takes advantage of the Internet's ability to target customers...and it gives potential competitors the illusion that this is already a crowded area.

...understand how to make Internet marketing work for them. *This means two things...*

• **They crystallize their offers and find the best prospects in the Internet's global universe.** Successful cyber-entrepreneurs have learned how to use the Internet's powerful search capabilities to pinpoint their best prospects. And they have fine-tuned their Internet marketing strategies. These efforts may range from studying search engines...to understanding how to achieve the highest possible rank when possible buyers search on relevant keywords...to participating in appropriate Internet chat groups...to fine-tuning the use of purchased opt-in E-mail lists—where customers have asked to be contacted about certain products or services.

Key: They constantly experiment with multiple approaches until they find the approach that will work best for their businesses.

• **They demonstrate credibility.** The biggest challenge in attracting customers on the Internet is demonstrating that you are not a scam or a fly-by-night operation.

Successful cyber-entrepreneurs use customer testimonials or services such as BBBOnline—The Better Business Bureau Online (*www. bbb.org*)—which offers a seal you can put at your Web site if you meet certain ethical criteria.

...study other successful businesses on the Internet. Like any good businessperson, successful Internet businesspeople are constantly looking for new ideas. I found that anyone who seemed to be doing well on the Internet could point to at least 10 Web sites he/she looked at frequently. That wasn't because these sites were run by competitors—but because they often had innovative ideas these people could adapt.

Six sites that do it right...

- *www.nobrainerblinds.com*
- *www.iprint.com*
- *www.efax.com*
- *www.mrtrademark.com*
- *www.estamp.com*
- *www.webex.com.*

...can easily articulate the extra value of what they do.

Example: Internet service businesses that learned how to use the Internet to perform services significantly faster than in the physical world—which customers appreciate...and pay for. Businesses that provide services such as printing business cards that are ordered from their Web site...or that deliver exclusive or specialized information instantaneously.

Similarly, these businesspeople are highly focused on the needs of their customers. They can easily tell you, "Here's why I am doing what I am doing and the value it creates for my customers."

...automate as much as possible. Anything that can be automated is. This limits the number of employees needed to run the business and makes the operation highly efficient...and faster at providing products or services.

Selling on the Web Made Very Simple

Wayne and Shanna Bumbaca, consultants to on-line auction companies through their company, Shanwa-Graphics in Sheridan, WY. They auction off about 1,600 personal items each week through Internet sites.

Every household has hundreds of dollars' worth of collectibles, sporting goods and electronics gathering dust in the closet, attic or basement.

You can sell these items at on-line auctions more easily and for far more money than at a typical yard sale.

Here's how to get the most for items when selling them on-line...

GETTING STARTED

●**Research the Web.** Develop a feel for how sellers conduct their business. *You'll learn how to position your item by answering the following questions...*

●What was it about the item that attracted your attention?

●What words in the headline or description of the item made you want to bid?

●What payment and shipping methods are offered?

●**Register at an auction site as a seller.** For each item you want to auction, you will be given a Web page. *Be prepared to provide the site with...*

●Category in which you want your item listed.

●Description of the item that is accurate and to the point.

●One-sentence "headline" describing the item.

●Opening price to start the bidding.

●Your shipping terms and accepted payment methods.

●**Expect to pay two fees.** The listing fee varies according to the initial minimum bid you set for your auction. It applies whether or not you are able to sell your item.

Typical listing fee: 25 cents for each item that has a minimum bid of less than $9.99...50 cents for each item between $10 and $24.99...$1 for each item between $25 and $49.99...$2 for each item that has a minimum bid of more than $50.

You will also have to pay a *completion fee,* which varies depending on the amount of the winning bid.

Typical completion fee: 5% of the winning bid on items up to $25...2.5% on items that attract $25 to $1,000...1.25% for items over $1,000.

●**Use catchy words in headlines.** Most buyers will come across your item if a key word from your headline winds up in the information they provide to the Web site's search engine.

●**Be specific.** Avoid words such as *special* or *wonderful.* People rarely search for an item

with adjectives. If you have extra room in your headline, try using *holiday gift, bargain* or *still in original box.*

●**Post a digital photo of your item—** even if your description makes it obvious...or your item is not visually interesting. Wary buyers are much more likely to bid on items with pictures. Crop extraneous background ...and avoid add-ons such as fancy graphics, colors or music that slow the time it takes for viewers to download your images.

How to post a photo on-line, and what to do if you don't have scanning equipment: There are on-line tutorials at *www.pongo.com/ howto* and *www.pages.ebay.com/aw/phototut index.html.*

●**Choose the best format for your item.** Most sites give you two choices—a *Yankee Auction* or a *Dutch Auction.*

●*Yankee Auction* is the most popular. It has open bidding, with the item going to the highest bidder. This is best when you are selling a single item or a group of items to one high bidder.

●*Dutch Auction* is better if you have many copies of the same item to sell. There will be multiple winners, and the final per-item price will be determined by the lowest of the winning bids.

Example: We had 10 identical art prints to sell—so the 10 highest bidders were all winners. The highest bid was $100 while the 10th-highest was $80. According to the rules, the top 10 bidders each got one print for $80.

●**Set your opening price as low as possible** to attract bidders. We like to open the bidding at 10% of what we feel our item is worth. *Other pricing strategies...*

●Research the going price of the item you're selling. You can do this at *www.biddersedge.com,* a free service that lets you search across 24 major on-line sites. You instantly receive the past high, low and average selling prices of any item that was ever auctioned on-line.

●Price your items "off-dollar." Bidders respond much better to an opening bid of $19.99... rather than $20.

●Set a hidden price. A Reserve Price Auction lets you set a hidden minimum price.

Example: Start the opening bid at $1. Your hidden price is $24.99. You are not obligated to sell your item unless someone bids at or higher than your hidden price. There may be a service fee involved.

• **Time your auction to end when the most bidders are on-line.** Most on-line sites give you one or two weeks to hold your auction. But you are allowed to specify the hour and minute when the auction ends.

Most of the active bidding takes place during the last three hours.

Best times to end the auction: Lunch hour ...and between 8 pm and midnight during the workweek. Consider the effect of different time zones, too.

Be available to check your E-mail every 10 to 20 minutes during the three hours before the end of the auction. This is when bidders are most likely to have questions.

• **Be honest about damages to items.** Examine items carefully for chips, cracks or excessive wear and tear. Describe the flaws on your Web page.

Your honesty may scare off some bidders. But after the auction, it will save you the headaches of returned items and the demands for refunds.

WHEN ITEMS DON'T SELL

• **Relist them.** An experienced seller may achieve about a 50% success rate. Most auction sites let you relist an item a second time—at no charge.

• **List an item in a different category.** *Example:* No one bid on a Civil War-era gunpowder flask in the *Antiques—Civil War* category. But it sold when relisted under *Military—Memorabilia.*

AFTER THE AUCTION

• **Send a congratulatory note to the high bidder within 24 hours.** Remind him/her of what he bid on...how much he bid for it...and terms of payment. Ask for his shipping address and phone number.

Trap: Sending an item before the bidder's payment has cleared.

• **Be specific about turnover time.** Inform bidders that it may take three weeks or more to receive the item once he mails you a check—because you will have to wait for the check to clear. If a bidder sends a money order, you can send out the item as soon as possible.

BEST AUCTION SITES

For a listing of auctions by category, visit *www.internetauctionlist.com.* It posts a list of more than 1,000 links to traditional auction houses and resources. *Our favorite auction sites...*

• ***www.amazon.com***
• ***www.ebay.com***
• ***www.onsale.com***
• ***www.sportingauction.com***
• ***www.up4sale.com***

Lots and Lots of Jobs Of All Kinds... And the Internet ...And You

Fred E. Jandt, PhD, professor of communication, California State University, San Bernardino, and coauthor of *Cyberspace Job Search Kit.* Jist Publishing.

A new world of employment opportunities is becoming available over the Internet. *What you need to know to find a job on-line...*

INTERNET ADVANTAGES

Employers have good reason to use the Internet to find job candidates. Compared with other methods of recruiting (particularly newspaper advertisements), the Internet is cheaper ...reaches a larger market...and generates faster responses.

Result: Employers in a variety of industries are posting many kinds of positions on the Internet. These jobs aren't just for "techies" and new college graduates. They include jobs ranging from senior positions in nontechnological industries to part-time work for retirees who don't want to fully retire just yet.

Job seekers get similar advantages from an Internet job search.

In a traditional job search you might prepare and send out dozens of résumés—and then hope that one of them reaches the right person with a job to fill. *But in an Internet job search you can…*

●**Go to a specific employer's "careers" page** on its Web site, see the specific jobs that are open and apply for a job on the spot. You know your résumé is going to the right place for a job that exists.

●**Submit a single résumé to an Internet job bank** and have employers search for you. Literally hundreds (or even thousands) of employers will scan your résumé electronically to match your qualifications with their open positions. A much larger number of employers will see your résumé than if you send it out on paper—no matter how many hard copies you send out.

You can also search the job bank electronically through many thousands of job postings by employers to find the ones that best fit your specifications.

And most Internet job searches are *free* to job seekers.

With all these advantages, it's no wonder that both job seekers and employers with jobs to fill are rushing in growing numbers to find each other over the Internet.

HOW TO DO IT

The first step in an Internet job search is getting on-line.

But if you don't have an Internet connection from home, you do not necessarily have to get one. Your local public library probably has Internet service and staff who will explain how to use it.

Once you are on-line, visit the two main sources of job opportunities to be found on-line—employers and Internet employment agencies (also known as "job banks" or "job boards")…

●**Employers.** If there is a specific company you'd like to work for, the first thing to do is visit its Web site. Almost all major companies have their own Web sites these days—with a "careers" section used to recruit new employees.

Advantage: Companies can describe jobs much more comprehensively on their own Web sites than in newspaper ads…and provide exten-

sive extra information about employment practices, benefits, etc.

Example: Visit the "careers" page on the Nortel Networks Web site at *www.nortelnetworks.com.*

List the companies you'd most like to work for and visit all their Web sites. If there's a specific industry you'd like to work in, find the companies in it and visit their sites.

You can find the Web site of any company you are interested in through one of the many Internet directories/search engines, such as Yahoo! at *www.yahoo.com.*

●**Internet employment agencies or job banks.** These are centralized locations where employers and job seekers come to find each other.

At the busiest sites thousands of employers post literally hundreds of thousands of job openings—and thousands of job seekers post their résumés. *Then…*

●Employers use "search engines" to examine electronically all the résumés on file to identify those that best meet job requirements.

●Job seekers use search engines to examine all posted job openings to find those that best match their desires.

Good Internet employment sites…

●**America's Job Bank** at *www.ajb.dni.us.*

●**CareerPath.com** at *www.careerpath.com.*

●**Hotjobs.com** at *www.hotjobs.com.*

●**JobOptions** at *www.joboptions.com.*

●**Monster.com** at *www.monster.com.*

The largest Internet job banks may not be best for your specific purpose. If you are seeking a job in a particular profession or industry, smaller job banks that specialize in that field may be better.

Find these, and professional or industry trade associations that can point you to them, through a Web directory.

Most Internet job banks are free to job seekers. Those that charge a fee usually offer little extra value for the money.

YOUR RÉSUMÉ

Your résumé will be electronic in an Internet job search—and will differ in major ways from paper résumés, which you may be accustomed to using. *How…*

●**Some employers and job banks will provide forms** for you to fill out on their Web sites. You transfer information from your regular résumé to them.

●**In other cases, you will be asked to E-mail your résumé,** or provide a paper résumé that will be scanned into a database. Either way, the result is a plain text file. All the design features you used to make your paper résumé look good will be lost.

Examples: Typefaces, formatting of paragraphs, paper color and design, etc.

Best: Organize your electronic résumé as a simple typed document, with all lines flush left.

Use simple heading lines at the start of sections and paragraphs.

Emphasize important headings in capital letters.

To see how your electronic résumé will look, put it in an E-mail message that you send to yourself.

If you send a paper résumé to an employer or job bank that will scan it, send one that will be easy to scan—use clear black typeface on a white background.

Remember: Your résumé will be filtered through search engines, so be sure to include key words that relate to the skills an employer may be looking for, such as "finance" or "electrical engineer."

This is *different* from the standard advice for paper résumés, which is to emphasize action words that may impress a human reader, such as "took responsibility" or "developed."

SAFE JOB HUNTING

Electronic résumés also differ from paper ones in that they may be instantly copied and forwarded anywhere. *Snag:* You may not want your résumé to go to some places—such as to your current employer. *Safety…*

●**Send your résumé only to reputable firms and job banks.**

●**Check the confidentiality rules of employers and job banks.** *Example:* Some job banks will keep your résumé anonymous unless you agree to be identified to a specific employer.

●**Use job banks that post résumés** for only a limited amount of time, such as for 30 days, unless you renew your posting. Employers prefer these job banks because the résumés posted there are fresher.

●**Clearly date all résumés** so that if an obsolete résumé remains in circulation it won't be confused with a current one.

Better Career Opportunity

Internet companies offer excellent job opportunities for everyone—not just young hotshots. Because the new businesses lack funds for training, they value professionals with management expertise…marketing and teaching experience…writing or graphic design skills …etc. *Better job searches:* Look for on-line postings at employment sites, such as *www. careermosaic.com* and *www.monster.com*. To boost job security, stay away from fledgling start-ups. Choose companies that have been in business at least three years. Salaries at Internet companies are lower than at more established firms—but stock options can be lucrative.

Rose Emerson, president, Career Relocation Corporation of America, a consulting firm, Armonk, NY.

Compare Salaries On-Line

An easy way to find out what other people with your background and skill level are being paid is to check Web sites that give salary information. Try Job Star, *http://jobstar. org/tools/salary/index.htm*…Wageweb, *www. wageweb.com*…Economic Research Institute, *www.erieri.com*…US Bureau of Labor Statistics, *www.bls.gov*…and Compensationlink.com, *www.compensationlink.com.*

On-Line Publishing

Electronic publishers, such as Fatbrain.com, sell your work to Internet users in return for royalties of 50%. Authors publish directly to their sites for a $1 file-storage fee and collect royalties based on how well the material sells to site visitors. Or publish your book in paperback through iUniverse.com. For $99, they will design a cover, print and bind your book, assign an ISBN number and tell you how to market it. You can order books in quantities as small as one copy. Check *www.fatbrain.com* and *www.iuniverse.com.*

Cyber-Directories Save Time—Big Time

Business directories available on-line can quickly locate firms and their phone numbers for free. *Useful...*

●**AT&T Toll-free,** *www.tollfree.att.net/intex .html*, provides the AT&T directory of toll-free business phone numbers.

●**Bigfoot,** *www.bigfoot.com,* is a leading directory of phone numbers and E-mail addresses for individuals.

●**Big Yellow,** *www.bigyellow.com,* provides more than 16 million business listings in the US and links to the Web pages of many.

●**Companies Online,** *www.companies online.com,* provides additional information, such as contact names and Web site addresses.

●**Global Yellow Pages,** *www.globalyp.com,* gives links to the Yellow Pages for more than 40 countries.

Nancy Tanker, managing editor, *Specialty Retail Report,* 293 Washington St., Norwell, MA 02061.

Clever Tax Strategy For Owners of Private Corporations

DeLorean, TC Memo 1995-287, reported by Irving Blackman, CPA, founding partner of Blackman Kallick Bartlestein, LLP, 300 S. Riverside Plaza, Chicago 60606.

Owners of private corporations can now make personal use of any tax losses their companies may incur through a clever strategy that's been approved by the Tax Court. *Previous rules...*

●**A regular corporation's owner could not personally deduct a tax loss** the corporation suffers—the loss belongs to the company.

●**An S corporation's owner could deduct the business's losses on his personal return.** But owners of S corporations often distribute shares among low-tax-bracket family members (such as children over age 13) to reduce the income tax due on the company's income. And this reduces the value of deductions on the owner's personal return for corporate losses as well.

Solution: A smart business owner entered into a compensation agreement with his corporation under which it paid him large bonuses in good years—but he also agreed to reimburse it for losses it incurred in bad years. He then *deducted* the losses he reimbursed to the company.

The IRS challenged the arrangement saying the large bonuses and reimbursements were designed just to offset each other—with the reimbursements only shifting the business's losses to the owner so he could get a personal deduction for them.

Tax Court: The arrangement is permissible and the owner's deduction for reimbursements he makes is allowed.

Result: The owner of a regular corporation moves any company's losses to his personal return. And the owner of an S corporation moves losses from other shareholders' returns to his own return—while other shareholders continue to have their share of company income taxed to them.

Home-Office Deduction Strategy

A home-office deduction is one of the red flag items that can lead to an audit. In most cases, the deduction is modest because the IRS rules require that an allocation of expenses be made based on square foot usage. The tax benefit, consequently, is also modest. *Strategy:* Save the amount of your home-office deduction as a cushion in the event you are audited. At the audit you can pull out your unused home-office expenses to offset any adjustments proposed by the revenue agent.

Ms. X, Esq., a former IRS agent still well connected.

Tax Aspects of "Buy Or Lease" Decision For Business Cars

Alan Zipp, Esq., CPA, 932 Hungerford Dr., Ste. 13, Rockville, MD 20850. Mr. Zipp is an instructor of income tax courses for the American Institute of CPAs. He specializes in the income tax problems of individuals and small businesses.

When it's time to acquire a new business car you have to decide whether to buy or lease one. *The following tax and nontax considerations can help you make your decision...*

WHO SHOULD ACQUIRE IT?

In most cases it is better for a business to acquire a car than for an individual to do so —no matter whether the car is bought or leased.

An individual who is an employee of his/her business must deduct car costs among miscellaneous itemized expenses, the total of which is deductible only to the extent it exceeds 2% of Adjusted Gross Income.

Thus, an individual may not be able to personally deduct the full costs associated with buying or leasing a car.

But businesses are not subject to any such deduction limitation. They can claim full deductions, and often larger deductions overall.

Idea: Even if a car will be used entirely for personal purposes, the business can own the car and let you use it. You will be charged with income—but only based on the lease value (taken from IRS tables). The company can deduct all its costs because they have become compensation to you.

Example: A business buys a car costing $20,000 and lets a key employee use it 100% for personal purposes. The lease value of this car is about $5,600 a year, which is treated as additional compensation. If the employee pays an effective tax of 31%, the after-tax cost to him is only $1,736 a year—much less than acquiring a car for himself.

This method takes into account the value of insuring and maintaining the car, but not the value of fuel.

DEDUCTIBLE COSTS

The costs of using a car for business are deductible. *These are for...*

- **Purchased cars**—depreciation and operating costs.
- **Leased cars**—lease payments and operating costs.

Driving expenses: Instead of actual expenses, the IRS standard mileage rate can be used to claim deductions for either owned or leased cars.

In 2000, the standard rate is 32.5 cents per mile.

Luxury cars: Annual depreciation limits apply to "luxury cars."

The tax law considers any car costing more than $15,500 in 2000 to be a luxury car.

For cars placed in service in 2000, the annual depreciation limits are...

- **$3,060 for the first year.**
- **$4,900 for the second year.**
- **$2,950 for the third year.**
- **$1,775 for each year thereafter.**

Thus, as a general rule, it pays to lease rather than buy a luxury car since all of the lease payments are deductible, while depreciation deductions may be sharply limited.

Note: Those who lease luxury cars are required to include in income an "inclusion amount" taken from IRS tables, which is based on the value of the car when the lease commences.

But the inclusion amount is very modest, even for upper-end cars, so leasing remains attractive.

"Heavy" luxury car loophole: The luxury car depreciation limits do not apply to cars weighing more than 6,000 pounds.

Many large sport utility vehicles fit this weight category. Most luxury car manufacturers—such as Cadillac, Lexus and Mercedes—now make heavy models as well. Depreciation write-offs for these vehicles have no annual dollar limits. *Full depreciation is allowed, which generally is...*

Year 1: 20.00%	**Year 4:** 11.52%
Year 2: 32.00%.	**Year 5:** 11.52%
Year 3: 19.20%	**Year 6:** 5.76%

Payoff: If a heavy luxury business car is owned for only three years, more than 71% of its cost will have been depreciated by the end of that period—far more than allowed for a normal-weight luxury car.

Idea: Where the luxury car limits do not apply, the vehicle is treated like other business equipment eligible for the additional first year expensing election. Under this rule, up to $20,000 can be written off in the first year, in addition to the regular depreciation deduction. Hence, a $25,000 car can be written off almost entirely in the first year.

OTHER FACTORS

The buy/lease decision also will be influenced by nontax factors...

●**How long you keep the car.** If you plan to keep it only a year or two, leasing may be preferable.

●**How much you drive the car.** If you expect to put on high mileage, leasing may not be practical. Leases typically impose a mileage limit of about 15,000 per year, with a cents-per-mile rate for excess mileage.

Buying a car may be preferable to incurring excess mileage costs on lease termination.

When a high-mileage car that is owned is traded in after a year or two, its value for trade-in purposes generally doesn't reflect the extent of this mileage—value is usually based on the blue book figure with some adjustment for mileage.

●**Quality of car.** Leasing may be the only way for some people to get a higher priced car. Buying a high-priced car generally requires a substantial down payment. But leasing usually requires a deposit of only one or two lease payments.

●**Asset protection.** Where there is any concern about getting sued, leasing is better than owning.

Reason: A car that is owned can be attached by creditors while a leased car cannot.

How to Use Life Insurance—for Your Business, For Yourself

David S. Rhine, CPA, partner and national director of family wealth planning, BDO Seidman, LLP, 330 Madison Ave., New York 10017.

Life insurance is a valuable tax and financial planning tool for business. It can help pay for employee benefits...compensate for the unexpected death of key employees...and finance stock buy-back agreements among shareholders.

Here are some of the best ways for companies—especially smaller ones—to take advantage of today's great life insurance opportunities...

●**Use life insurance as a direct benefit.** Up to $50,000 of group insurance can be provided to each employee, tax free. In addition, coverage exceeding $50,000 can be provided to selected employees on a discretionary basis.

The value of the excess is taxed to the employee in an amount determined by the lower of actual cost or rates on special IRS tables. Even when the value of the insurance is taxed, the employee may come out ahead. Paying only the income tax on the insurance benefit may be much less costly for the employees than paying the insurance premium out-of-pocket.

Example: If the employee is in the 40% tax bracket, each $1 of premiums costs him/her only 40 cents in tax.

Additional direct insurance benefit: Life insurance can be an attractive tax-favored perquisite for directors of private companies.

Example: The company can buy insurance on a director's life and let the director choose a favorite charity to be the beneficiary.

The policy benefit will be much larger than any fee the company would pay to the director in cash and will enable the director to make a large gift to a favorite institution if he dies during his term.

Such insurance is deductible by the company and results in no tax bill to the director.

●**Use life insurance to finance benefits.** Life insurance also can be used to finance more-sophisticated compensation packages for selected executives.

Key: Cash-value policies earn tax-deferred investment returns, and the growing value can be borrowed against to obtain tax-free funds. Together with the tax-free policy benefit, this makes insurance an attractive and flexible funding device.

Example: Split-dollar life insurance is a flexible compensation arrangement that can be customized for selected executives on a discriminatory basis. Using it, the company and the executive share the return on an insurance policy. The company buys an insurance policy for an executive but keeps an interest in it in the amount of the premiums that it pays. The executive receives the death benefit and the growing cash value of the policy.

Thus, if the executive dies after the company pays $50,000 of premiums on a $1 million policy, the executive's family will receive $950,000 and the company will be reimbursed for its $50,000.

If the executive doesn't die during his working years, the policy's cash value in time will grow large enough so the executive can borrow against the cash value to buy the policy from the company.

The employee must report the term-insurance value of the death benefit in income. This will be less than the policy's entire pre-mium and the executive gains from the accumulating tax-deferred growth in cash value.

Advantages: Split-dollar arrangements can be designed with great flexibility to meet specific needs. And in the end, the company recovers the cost of its investment.

●**Purchase key-person insurance.** A company may wish to purchase insurance to protect itself from financial hardship that could result from the death of a vital employee. *Strategies…*

●Combine key person protection with benefit planning.

Example: The company can finance a key executive's deferred compensation plan with cash-value life insurance—but keep the death benefit for itself should the executive die unexpectedly.

●Buy "Nth to die" term insurance. It may be that a business will be hurt badly only if it loses more than one key person within a limited time period.

If so, the premium cost of key-person life insurance may be greatly reduced by buying a policy that pays a benefit only if two (or three, etc.) from a list of designated key people die within a specified time period.

●**Finance stock buy-backs.** Privately owned businesses need to plan for the repurchase or transfer of the shares of owners who die.

Life insurance is the natural tool to finance the purchase of shares from a deceased owner's estate—and to finance estate taxes that will be due on the value of the business.

Trap: A company that doesn't plan to meet these future cash needs may face a liquidity crisis when an owner dies.

Option 1: The company can insure each owner, and repurchase a deceased owner's shares. This is the simplest approach, but there's a snag for family businesses—income that results to the owner's estate may be high-tax ordinary income on the entire proceeds instead of low-tax capital gains on only the increase since the date of death.

Generally, a company's redemption of an owner's shares produces capital gains only if no other family member continues to own shares. However, under certain circumstances, attributions can be waived—so this option may not be attractive for family businesses.

Option 2: Owners can insure each other and purchase each other's shares. This allows owners who cross-insure to draw up a plan for holding the company's shares in any proportion they desire. In contrast, if the company buys an owner's shares, each remaining owner's interest will increase pro rata.

This option also results in lower future taxes. When one owner buys another's shares directly, the purchaser's tax basis in his ownership interest in the company is increased by the price he pays. And a higher basis means less gains tax will be due on a future sale of the shares.

In contrast, if the company buys back an owner's shares, the other owners' total share interest in the company is proportionately increased, but their basis in their shares isn't. So if they sell their shares at a future date, they will owe a larger amount of gains tax.

Drawbacks: With several owners involved, cross insurance can become very complex… and the owners must pay the insurance premiums themselves.

In addition, when drafting a stock repurchase agreement, there's often a temptation to over-insure to provide for the financial needs of the owner's family. But this can be a big mistake that leaves the family with less than is expected. *Reasons…*

• **Payment received by the family** will be subject to estate tax at up to a 55% rate.

• **If the company owns the insurance on the owner,** the insurance policy will be subject to the claims of the company's creditors. If other shareholders own the insurance, the policies will be subject to the claims of their creditors.

Bottom line: Either way, there is a risk that insurance will be taxed or subject to creditors' claims and that family members who depend on it will get much less…or nothing.

Much better: Have the stock repurchase agreement pay no more than the true value of an owner's shares. Then provide additional security for owners' survivors by having each owner buy life insurance for himself, placing it in a life insurance trust.

Insurance proceeds received by the trust will escape estate tax and be immune to creditors' claims. So the family will receive them with certainty, and estate-tax free.

The insurance proceeds then can be used to help finance the estate tax due on the real, noninflated value of the owner's share of the business in a way that assures family financial security.

Building Key Employee Life Insurance

Key questions to ask when deciding on the purchase of key-employee life insurance…

• **Which employees are critical to the firm's survival?**

• **How much coverage is needed to protect the firm against losing one or more of them?**

• **Which policies are the most affordable?**

• **What are their tax implications?**

• **Are premiums tax deductible?**

• **Are insurance proceeds received tax free?**

• **Should the proceeds be payable to family members or to the business?**

Also, check the owners and beneficiaries of all life insurance policies.

Thomas Martin, editor, The Business Owner, *16 Fox Ln., Locust Valley, NY 11560.*

Opening Your Own Store…Secrets of Success

Michael Antoniak, author of How to Open Your Own Store. *Avon Books. Mr. Antoniak is a freelance business/ technology writer who has covered retailing for almost 20 years.*

With careful planning and a willingness to put in long hours—possibly evenings, holidays and weekends— you can earn a decent income and work at a retirement business you enjoy.

To minimize risks: Conduct extensive market research, get expert business advice and go slow.

1. MAKE SHREWD CHOICES

Good retail bets always include specialty items such as clothing, pets, hobby supplies, health food, music, books and hardware.

Trends, however, vary greatly from area to area. Focusing on niches within these markets, such as mystery books or LP records, can contribute to success. *Reason:* Niche stores rarely compete with large chains.

Open a store in a field that you *know.* Acquire the knowledge needed *before* going into business. You will be too busy with the business itself once it opens.

2. MARKET RESEARCH

Take several months to research your retail idea. Start by visiting several stores of the type you'd like to open. If possible, develop friendships with owners who won't be in direct competition.

Ask what mistakes they initially made and what they would do differently if they were to open a store today.

Find out which items sell and which sit on the shelf. Inquire about which types of advertising are best for reaching customers.

Next, find out how saturated the market is with the kind of retail operation you want to open. Look in the Yellow Pages to see how many stores are in the area. Visit the stores at different times of the day to see how brisk business is. Talk to local bankers who may have a sense of how businesses are doing in the area.

Try shopping for the items you intend to sell. *To find out more...*

●**Work part-time** in a store similar to the type you want to open.

●**Contact the trade association** for stores in the field you've chosen.

●**Shop on-line** for a better idea of what's available and the pricing.

3. BUILD BUSINESS KNOWLEDGE

Few first-time store owners realize how many components go into a retail business...

●**Fixtures and office equipment.**

●**Legal, accounting, banking and insurance services.**

●**Staffing.**

●**Negotiating with landlords and suppliers.**

●**Advertising.**

●**Fees and licenses.**

Mishandling any of these areas can lead to costly problems and perhaps even to a disappointing failure. *To reduce risk...*

●**Attend training sessions and seminars offered by trade associations** where you can get basic business advice from others in the business.

Local Chambers of Commerce can also be valuable sources of information about local issues, such as getting business licenses and arranging for bank accounts that allow you to accept credit cards.

●**Experience is essential.** Retain professional services only from lawyers and accountants with experience in your specific niche.

●**Talk with suppliers.** They can be helpful about marketing questions, such as how to arrange co-op advertising, the type where the manufacturer or other retailers share in the cost of local ads.

Caution: Suppliers are in business to sell. But be skeptical of a supplier who wants you to place large orders but who can't spend time offering you advice.

4. START SLOWLY

There's no law that says you have to rush into business with a heavy investment. It's almost always best to start slowly and test the water.

Assessing your idea: Try selling inventory at one of the on-line auction houses such as eBay. It's a great way to sample interest in what you plan to sell.

Or sell for a few months at one of the kiosks that many shopping malls now offer at about $400 a month. Or test your product at flea markets. *Your idea is likely to have potential if...*

●**A wide variety of customers are interested in it,** not just a few who habitually drop by to browse.

●**Consumers ask where they can buy products** similar to the merchandise you're selling.

Also look for customer feedback that tells you there's an opportunity for add-on merchandise. Add-on's can give your store a marketing edge and also add to profits.

5. REALITIES IN FINANCING

Unless you already have a relationship with a commercial lender, don't waste time going to banks for start-up capital. Typically, they only lend to owners who have proven track records.

For funding, be prepared to tap into savings, mortgage property or borrow from friends or relatives.

Once your store *succeeds,* develop relationships with banks that may later be a source of capital for expansion.

Expected start-up cost: It all depends on what you sell and where. A store you can start for $25,000 in a small town will cost several times more in a suburban mall and significantly more in a major city.

The local real estate market is one of the main reasons costs vary. A new shopping mall may be hungry for tenants and offer bargain leases to attract retailers. But—an older mall in a booming suburb may have little available space and demand a premium price.

IMPROVING THE ODDS

Despite all the precautions, there's no fail-safe way to open a store. Even large companies make errors. *To improve the odds...*

●**Don't depend on one type of advertising.** There are so many variables in retail marketing that even the best advisers can't always predict the right type of advertising for a new store.

●**Take advantage of customer databases.** Today, computer software customized to track customer buying patterns for specific retail operations is available for several hundred dollars.

Among other advantages, tracking customer sales helps store owners determine which merchandise to stock and which customers to target in advertising campaigns.

●**Time your opening right.** Don't make the mistake of opening a tennis supply shop in the summer in hopes of cashing in on seasonal sales. *Better:* Open in winter or spring so it's running smoothly when summer arrives.

●**Cover yourself.** If you are your business and its sole employee, any emergency or illness will shut things down. Hire and train someone who can fill in should there ever come a time when you can't be there to mind the store.

Home Business Insurance

Home-based business insurance can protect a home-based firm against theft, flood or fire damage and liability for accidents. These problems are not usually covered by a standard homeowner's or renter's policy. For about $200 per year, owners can insure business property for up to $10,000. Higher liability insurance is also available. Contact your insurance agent for more information.

Jeanne Salvatore, vice president, Insurance Information Institute, 110 William St., New York 10038.

Telecommuters Need State-of-the-Art Equipment

Home-based workers need top-quality electronic equipment. Trying to save a few dollars with second-rate equipment will cost work time—cheap equipment operates more slowly...results in more breakdowns... and makes a bad impression on customers. *Needed:* A dedicated phone line for business, a high-quality voice-mail system, the best computer that can be afforded and a printer that produces high-quality documents.

Lisa Kanarek, founder, Everything's Organized, office organization consultants, Dallas, and author of Organizing Your Home Office for Success. *Blakely Press.*

19

Education Smarts

Answers to the Big Questions Parents Have About Paying for College

Many families think they don't qualify for college financial aid—and shortchange themselves by failing to apply. We asked college aid expert Bruce Hammond to answer the questions parents have about paying for college...

How do I figure out what type of aid—and how much—my child can receive? *There are three types of aid...*

●**Merit-based.** Individual schools offer merit-based scholarships, and all applicants are considered. National scholarships are very competitive.

Best bet: Look for local and activity-specific or affiliation-specific programs.

Examples: Clubs—such as Rotary, Civitan, Daughters of the American Revolution, Amer-

ican Legion, Veterans of Foreign Wars—and parents' employers.

Most states also offer a mix of merit and/or need-based scholarships to at least some students.

Helpful resource: The Web site of the Education Commission of the States *(www.ecs. org)* lists eligibility requirements of each state.

Free scholarship searches are available on the Internet—see below.

●**Need-based.** Eligibility is based on parents filling out the Free Application for Federal Student Aid (FAFSA). It uses income and assets to determine how much the family is expected to pay for college. If the costs are greater than you are expected to pay, you qualify for aid.

Money from the *Pell Grant*—the government's largest aid program—is limited to

---

Bruce Hammond, college counselor at Sandia Preparatory School in Albuquerque, and author of *Discounts and Deals at the Nation's 360 Best Colleges.* St. Martin's Griffin. He is college financial aid adviser at iVillage. com *(www.ivillage.com...*click on "Parent Soup").

$3,125/yr. Subsidized loans from *Stafford*—the primary loan program—have a ceiling of $2,625/yr. for freshmen, rising to $5,500/yr. for upperclassmen. The rest comes from private aid supplied by individual schools and student loans, such as unsubsidized Stafford, Federal Parent Loans for Undergraduate Students (PLUS loans) and supplemental loans from private lenders. These are available regardless of need. *Information: www.estudent loan.com.*

For students from families with annual incomes above $30,000, federal aid is generally limited to low-interest loans and work-study jobs.

●**Merit-within-need.** If federal and state aid do not cover your need, the college may or may not cover the gap. It depends upon how much of its own aid money is available and how much the school wants your child to attend.

Note: People assume most colleges have *aid-blind* admissions policies. This is only the case with 20 to 30 schools. In fact, some colleges reject admissible candidates because of financial need...and all use their own aid dollars to "sweeten the pot" for students they really want.

To find out which colleges offer the biggest aid programs, see the Internet resources listed below and contact the colleges in which you're interested.

What are the best aid/scholarship resources? Ask your high school counselor for aid applications and information on local grants and awards.

The Internet offers a wealth of mostly free resources. *The top three financial aid Web sites...*

●**FastWEB** *(www.fastweb.com).*

●**Project EASI** *(www.easi.ed.gov).*

●**FinAid! The SmartStudent Guide to Financial Aid** *(www.finaid.org).*

College Scholarships For All...Almost

Scholarships are available even to students who don't come from lower-income families.

Corporate sponsorships are awarded by businesses, industry groups and unions to children —and sometimes other relatives—of company employees. These full and partial scholarships may be available to students whose parents are not employees but who have shown a special aptitude or interest in a particular field.

Contact the company's personnel or employee benefits manager to see if such a program is available.

Some schools offer merit—or presidential— scholarships to top students, regardless of need.

Examples: Some leading universities award grants to students in the top 10% of their classes with SAT scores in at least the high 1300s and above.

Many smaller schools, such as Denison in Ohio and Grinnell in Iowa, have offered scholarships to attract top students from other parts of the country to expand the geographic mix of their student bodies.

Contact: The school's financial aid department.

Useful resource: College Student's Guide to Merit and Other No-Need Funding: 1998–2000. Reference Service Press.

Frank Leana, educational director of Howard Greene & Associates, a New York–based educational consulting firm.

College Funding Break

Shrewd moves parents can make to qualify for more college financial aid...

●**Accelerate or defer an employer bonus** so you do not get it in the base year—the year before the student enters college.

●**Avoid large capital gains** in the base year if possible.

●**Pay off consumer debt.** Consumer debt does not reduce your net worth. If you have

$1,000 in consumer debt and $5,000 in the bank, colleges act as if you have $5,000 for tuition. Pay off the debt and you have only $4,000.

● **Make a major purchase in the base year** for financial aid if you were planning to make it soon. This reduces your available cash for aid purposes.

Stephanie Gallagher, financial writer based in the Washington, DC, area, and author of *Money Secrets the Pros Don't Want You to Know.* Amacom.

Amazing On-Line Education Opportunities Now ...Much More to Come...How To Get Started

Robert W. Tucker, PhD, president of InterEd Inc., a consulting firm in Phoenix that helps educational institutions innovate to meet the changing needs of the market, *www.InterEd.com.*

On-line education is a convenient way to advance your career or your interests. Many people now take college courses on-line and earn degrees or certificates on-line.

ON-LINE ADVANTAGES

● **Convenient.** You can download lectures to "attend class" at any convenient time. Exams, however, may be at set times.

● **Fast.** Many courses can be completed within eight weeks—half the time of a regular semester.

● **Flexible.** You can often design your own degree.

Example: The University of Phoenix offers a lot of flexibility for working adults and recognizes prior credits and work experience. *http://www.uophx.edu...*800-765-4922.

● **Tuition reimbursement.** Many employers pay employees' tuition for courses taken on-line. *Warning:* Graduate educational benefits paid by employers may be taxable as noncash income—ask your accountant.

ON-LINE DRAWBACKS

● **You need to be a self-directed learner.** On-line learning offers a different kind of interaction with professors and other students. This may work well for students who are too shy to raise questions in person. Also, the answers they receive from peers and teachers may be better thought out.

● **Higher cost than attending in person.** Surprisingly, on-line tuition averages 10% more than traditional school. While the institution may save on brick and mortar, on-line education requires substantially higher marketing costs and higher salaries for technical support people. But you may save that much in commutation costs.

● **Traditional financial aid may not be available to adult students.** Such aid is designed for dependent, full-time learners.

*Financial aid sources for on-line learning: http://scholarships.em.doe.gov/...*and *www.fastweb.com.*

PICKING A PROGRAM

Education via the Internet is still a very young industry that is undergoing change daily. Some places offer courses but not a complete degree.

On-line education is evolving rapidly, but there are some useful resources to get you started...

● **Get Educated** *(www.geteducated.com)* offers an up-to-the-minute directory of on-line colleges, Internet universities and training institutes.

● **Telecampus** *(http://telecampus.edu)* lists thousands of on-line courses in the US and the rest of the world.

● *Bears' Guide to Earning Degrees Nontraditionally* by John and Mariah Bear (Ten Speed Press) includes information about options for getting school credit for what you already know.

● *How to Get a College Degree Via the Internet* by Sam Atieh (Prima Publishing).

HONING YOUR SELECTION

● **Beware of bogus program accreditations.** To check that an on-line program is legitimate, visit the Council for Higher Education Accreditation Web site *(www.chea.org)*... or the Accrediting Commission of the Distance Education and Training Council *(www.detc.org)*.

● **"Sit in" on some on-line classes before enrolling.** Schools use various technological formats—not all of which you may like.

Example: Some schools upload the lectures and provide chat systems for student discussion. Others let you watch a synchronous video of the instructor teaching, then swap group work by E-mail.

Also notice how easily the system operates through your computer.

● **Communicate with the school dean/ program director.** *Questions to ask...*

● **Are all courses for the degree I want offered on-line?** Some programs require occasional on-campus participation.

Examples: At Duke University's Cross Continent program, you study via the Internet and attend class one week per term *(www.fuqua.duke. edu...919-660-7863)*.

At Fordham University's Transnational MBA Program, you have a face-to-face meeting one weekend a month with professors and classmates *(www.bnet.fordham.edu/public/tmba. htm...914-829-5452)*.

● **How many students are enrolled in your program?** How many have already graduated? While more than 90% of on-line bachelor and graduate degree programs have yet to graduate their first student, a reasonable expectation is for the institution to have graduated 20 to 30 on-line students or the equivalent of one class.

● **How are curricula developed?** How are instructors selected and supervised? Many schools simply try to replicate their traditional classrooms with no special training of faculty or development of curricula. The on-line learning environment is very different from the traditional classroom, so there should be differences.

● **Can I get credit for career experience?** Many programs will give credit, but require you to demonstrate career-gained knowledge and provide work samples. *Examples...*

● Antioch University *(www.antioch.edu ...or 937-767-6325)*.

● Rochester Institute of Technology *(www. rit.edu...or 800-225-5748)*.

● Skidmore College *(www.skidmore.edu ...or 518-580-5000, ext. 5450)*.

Harvard's Howard Gardner Teaches Parents To Nurture Children's Natural Gifts for Learning

Howard Gardner, PhD, professor at Harvard Graduate School of Education and creator of the theory of multiple intelligences. He is author of 18 books, including *The Disciplined Mind: What All Students Should Understand.* Simon & Shuster.

The standard view of intelligence is that you are born with a given amount...you can't change it much...and it can be measured with an IQ test.

But recent research into neurology, developmental psychology and anthropology suggests a different view.

Human beings have many different types of intelligence—from logical to musical to spatial.

We're strong in each of them to different degrees, and no two people have the same blend of intelligences.

Although schools tend to value only one or two types of intelligence, many kinds are needed to compete and succeed in the real world.

By stimulating your children's different types of intelligence, you can encourage them to become more passionate about what they're learning, more intuitive and, ultimately, more successful.

INTELLIGENCE STYLES

During more than 15 years of research, I have identified the following different types of intelligence...

● **Linguistic.** This refers to our skill with words—reading, writing and speaking.

● **Logical.** People strong in this type of intelligence enjoy numbers, puzzles, experiments. They are also quick to spot flaws in arguments.

Schools tend to focus on and reward these first two intelligences—linguistic and logical—

because they are so fundamental to communicating and reasoning well in our society. *But there are others...*

●**Musical.** The ability to remember melodies, have a feel for rhythm, enjoy playing instruments and singing.

●**Spatial.** The ability to create or think in images...to manipulate objects and work with spatial relationships either physically (sculpture, crafts, building blocks) or in the mind's eye.

●**Bodily** relates to awareness and movement of the body. This intelligence is used in sports, dance, theater and handicrafts.

●**Interpersonal.** Strong understanding of other people and sensitivity to their needs. This intelligence is essential to leadership as well as for jobs ranging from salesperson to psychotherapist.

●**Intrapersonal.** A strong self-awareness... independent pursuit of goals...and the ability to learn from experience.

●**Naturalistic.** The ability to identify patterns in the natural world, such as the differences between the stars in the sky from one month to the next.

HELPING YOUR CHILD

It's often easy to identify the different intelligences in which your child is naturally strong.

Notice what activities he/she gravitates toward...which ones he excels in...and the ones in which he enjoys watching himself improve.

How to help your child develop his natural intelligences...

●**Determine your child's strongest types of intelligence.** I don't recommend a "blanket" approach—identifying where your child is strong and then building up every other area in which he is weak. This approach takes up too much time and energy and risks marginalizing all of your child's abilities.

It's more productive to think about what interests promote your child's happiness and satisfaction...and then focus on helping him develop those intelligences.

Children love to dabble, and they should be encouraged to try different things. But most children will also return again and again to the same themes—and that's often where their strengths lie.

Examples: A child high in intrapersonal intelligence may sample many experiences. But he will also spend time thinking or talking about how those experiences affected him.

A child with strong spatial skills might doodle, play with blocks, make sand sculptures, work jigsaw puzzles, study charts or diagrams. All these activities involve understanding how things relate to each other in space.

●**Spend time with your children doing many different things.** Take them to children's museums, aquariums, art museums and basketball games...play musical instruments with them...read with them...and let them help you repair things that are broken.

When all you do is shop, watch television or play computer games with your kids, you are limiting their experiences and narrowing the types of intelligences they use.

If your children balk at trying new activities, provide incentives—such as allowing them to participate more or to invite along other people.

Example: When my son didn't want to attend a classical music concert, I suggested he take along a friend. They had a great time.

Whether or not they sat still the entire time and listened carefully to the music being played isn't important. What matters is that they were exposed to this form of music and discussed what they liked and why.

●**Encourage your child's passions.** When your child is excited about something, give him the tools to explore it further.

Example: If he's fascinated by bugs, shop together for books about insects. If she loves watching gymnastics on TV, enroll her in gymnastics class.

On the other hand, if your child is obsessed with one activity to the exclusion of everything else, use his interest as a "bridge" to other areas.

Example: If a child loves math but has no social life, sign him up for chess club...or send him to summer math camp.

Don't spend lavishly on a child's passion until you know that he is committed to it. It is easy to explore interests without breaking the bank. That way, you won't be tempted to push your child to stay involved in something he no longer cares for.

● **Help your child by finding out how he learns best.** When I taught piano, I noticed that some children got better at playing by watching others play. That's using *interpersonal* intelligence.

Others improved by playing the same passage over and over, exercising their bodily intelligence.

And other children focused on musical and rhythmic notation—using their logical intelligence.

The point here is that one type of intelligence can be used to help children embrace other important types of intelligence.

Examples: Kids who have trouble reading or writing often make great strides if they're encouraged to read and write about subjects they're passionate about.

If a child is having trouble with math but is gifted musically, use the beats in a measure of written music to help him understand fractions.

I once saw a teacher use bodily intelligence to teach young students about architecture. The students used their own bodies to create the shapes of Roman arches. Those kids vividly remembered the material.

● **Spark interest by setting an example.** Children pay far more attention to what you do than what you say.

You can urge them to read, to be kind, to appreciate art and to play sports. But they're much more likely to care about those things if they see that you do the same.

Parents Can Really Help College Kids Cope with Those Challenging New Pressures

Wendy Shalit, who graduated from Williams College in 1997. She is author of *A Return to Modesty: Discovering the Lost Virtue* (Free Press) and is now a contributing editor at *City Journal*, a magazine published by the think-tank The Manhattan Institute, New York.

The transition from high school to college is emotionally challenging for almost all teens and their parents.

To help parents help kids adjust, we asked Wendy Shalit, a recent college graduate—and already a well-respected advice-giver—for her suggestions.

Wendy, is there anything parents can do to prepare kids for the stresses of college? Don't be afraid to give advice.

Many parents today hesitate to speak out because they don't want to turn off their children—or sound out of touch with the times.

But teens who are away at college for the first time want at least some guidance from their parents—even if they don't ask for it.

Parental advice helps students shield themselves from any uncomfortable situations to which they may be exposed to on campus.

What to do: Listen carefully for signs of kids' uncertainty or stress. Then ask them questions in a calm, comforting way. Find out as many details about the situation as you can before offering any opinion or advice.

Also, if you have an endearing nickname for your child, use it. It helps to underscore the fact that you are the parent and you know best …and that you are giving this advice because you care about him/her.

How can parents stay in touch with their college kids without cramping their independence? You are not being overprotective if you regularly keep in touch with your children on campus. You're simply being a good parent.

Weekly phone calls and warm letters and/or E-mail messages are important. But so are visits once a semester.

To avoid embarrassing kids: Behave like parents, not like "cool" friends. When you try to be hip, you send the message that you are ashamed to be a parent, which only makes kids ashamed as well.

What's the best way to help kids handle scholastic pressures? Keep children's schoolwork in perspective and encourage them to do so as well.

Help them to realize that college is a time to enjoy intellectual challenges and not to worry too much about grades.

Also remind children that college is a time to discover what they're good at and what they're not so good at.

If children worry about getting top grades all the time, they won't take risks and won't take advantage of new opportunities that come their way.

What can children do when colleges put them in uncomfortable living situations? Coed dormitories—and even coed bathrooms— are common on college campuses these days.

But they're not necessarily right for every student. If your children are uncomfortable with coed living situations, encourage them to switch to a single-sex choice on campus.

It gets tricky because even single-sex floors can be coed by default—members of the opposite sex come and go as they please. Parents should ask whether single-sex floor or dorm rules are actually enforced.

Can kids be modest on campus without seeming like outcasts? Absolutely. Encourage children to speak up.

Remind them that whenever it seems as if everyone is "going along with something," the reality is that at least several of them feel just as uncomfortable. They're just not speaking up.

Tell your children that if they speak up, they may feel silly at first. But in most cases, many of their peers will be relieved that someone articulated what they were feeling. Nothing helps make like-minded friends faster.

Go to College at 60 For Free

Sit in on college courses free or at reduced tuition. Many states have legislation granting free or reduced tuition to seniors—usually requiring you to be 60 years old or older—on a space-available basis. Call colleges near you to find out which free or reduced-tuition courses they have available.

John Howells, travel writer and author of *Where to Retire: America's Best and Most Affordable Places.* The Globe Pequot Press.

Getting Started on Computers: A Grown-Up's Guide

Mary Furlong, EdD, and Stefan B. Lipson, coauthors of *Grown-Up's Guide to Computing.* Microsoft Press. Dr. Furlong is CEO and founder of ThirdAge Media.

Computers offer older and mature Americans tremendous opportunities to enrich their lives.

They already possess the basic skills and experience required for computing.

Those skills will quickly improve as they use a computer as a tool in their personal lives, and explore new channels of communication over the Internet.

Some of the ways in which computers can enhance your life…

●**Help you write letters,** track finances, even draw and paint.

●**Amplify those things you most enjoy—** travel, hobbies, nature, collecting, art, making money.

●**Keep you up-to-date on current events,** politics, your investments, sports.

●**Enable you to trace your family tree.** There are vast genealogy archives and resources now available on-line, and computer software for organizing that information.

●**Let you communicate with friends and family in new and remarkable ways,** wherever they are.

●**Introduce you to like-minded people to share ideas,** interests and experiences as members of a "virtual community."

JUMPING IN

First-time computer buyers are often advised to assess their needs before purchasing a computer. But, if you've never been on a personal computer (PC), that's a tall order.

The best way for a novice to get started is to simply get started! It takes time to learn how to use a computer and explore how it can enrich your life. Consider that time as an investment. The more you invest, the greater your return.

Moneysaver: You can start with a hand-me-down computer from a savvy relative or friend.

In fact, many older computer users are happy working with computers that their children or grandchildren consider obsolete.

BUYING NEW

If you decide to purchase a new computer, don't worry about finding the latest, greatest machine. You will want a printer, but you don't need fancy gizmos.

●**Expect a one-year warranty with the system.**

●**Pay for an extended warranty if one is offered.** It's worth the extra cost.

●**Buy a desktop system (nonportable).** They are easiest to use.

Portable laptops are great, too, but you pay extra for the portability and the keyboard and mouse can be difficult to master.

●**Get a monitor that measures at least 17 inches diagonally.** At that size, images can be viewed comfortably and the screen is easy to navigate.

●**Essential software.** A computer can't do anything without software. Ask which programs are included in your package. *The basics...*

●Word processing software for writing.

●Personal finance software to track expenses and investments.

●An Internet browser to get you on-line.

●**Buy a major name-brand system,** no matter what your budget. You may save a couple of hundred bucks on a no-name computer, but you'll lose those savings when it needs repairs.

●**Good retail sources for your purchase are local computer,** electronics and office discounters.

●**Buying directly from manufacturers over the phone or Internet** is also a smart way to go. Prices are very competitive, so you get a great deal. A system purchased directly arrives preconfigured—plug it in and you're ready to go.

Many of these systems also carry an on-site warranty. If anything goes wrong, the technicians come to you to repair it.

LEARNING

Once you have the equipment, you can start the discovery process.

●**Hone your computer skills the way you learn best.** For some, that's sitting alone reading books and manuals. Others like someone to guide them, step by step. And, still others prefer to learn in groups.

●**Find out which computer classes and resources are available locally.** If you can connect to the Internet, check out *www.senior net.org*. Members are people like you who are already wired. They are eager to help others.

●**Don't be afraid to ask questions.** When you have a problem, turn to an experienced user or friend. Working with them can only improve your skills.

20

Self-Defense

The Privacy Challenge: How to Keep Them From Knowing Too Much About You

New technology allows more scrutiny than ever of your public and private actions—your data are available to everyone from con artists and telemarketers to your bank, employer, insurance companies and more.

You can't prevent disclosure of *some* of your private information. But you can do a personal risk assessment. Often, a small amount of caution can neutralize large risks to your privacy.

ON-LINE ACTIVITY

Every Web site you visit collects information about your surfing habits.

Result: Your E-mailbox is flooded with unwanted solicitations.

With just your E-mail address, anyone can find out your spouse's name, where you live, how much you paid for your house, etc. *Self-defense...*

●**Use a special E-mail address for surfing the Internet**—especially if you visit chat rooms, newsgroups or register on Web sites. That's where junk mailers harvest information. This way, you can more easily sift through undesirable E-mail.

If you want to use your regular E-mail address in newsgroups, insert "no-spam"* when you are asked to give your E-mail address.

 Example: *no-spam-john-doe@isp.com.* If junk mailers try to reach you at this E-mail address, their mail will be returned.

Individuals who really want to reach you can simply strip off the "no-spam" portion of the address when they reply.

*Spam is unsolicited E-mail.

Robert Ellis Smith, publisher of *Privacy Journal*, Box 28577, Providence, RI 02908. He is author of *Ben Franklin's Web Site: Privacy and Curiosity from Plymouth Rock to the Internet.* Privacy Journal.

●**Don't reply to spam or junk E-mail,** even if it's to ask the sender to remove you from its list.

Reason: Responding confirms your E-mail address and invites more spam.

Better: Send a complaint E-mail to your Internet Service Provider (ISP). It should contact the spammer's ISP.

You can also use antispam software. It works in conjunction with your E-mail software to filter out junk E-mail.

Popular: Spamscan97 *(www.webster-image. com)*…and Spam Buster *(www.contactplus.com).*

●**Alter your browser to reveal less information about you when you download files from Web sites.** If you use *Netscape,* choose *Communicator* from the system menu and select *Messenger.*

●Under *Edit* menu, select *Preferences.*

●Scroll down and click *Advanced.*

●Remove the checkmark in the *Send E-mail as anonymous FTP password* box.

●Click on *OK.*

If you use *Microsoft Internet Explorer 5,* go to Tools–Internet Options.

●Click the *Security* tab. Highlight the *Internet* icon.

●Click the *Custom Level* tab.

●Scroll down to *User Authentications/Logon.*

●Click *Anonymous Logon.*

Warning: Don't disable your cookies. Cookies are data strings in your Internet browser that identify you when you visit a Web page. If you turn off this function to remain invisible, most sites will not allow you to enter.

●**Examine the "privacy policy" before you use a Web site regularly.** Some sites enable you to check an "opt-out" box if you don't want to receive E-mail from marketers.

Helpful resource: *http://w3.one.net/~banks /slpriv.htm* for more advice on protecting yourself when you surf the Internet.

●**Investigate yourself on-line**—to see how much about you is available to the public. Type your name into search engines, such as *www.lycos.com* and *www.excite.com.* To check your postings in Internet newsgroups, search *www.dejanews.com.* Ask directories that list E-mail addresses, home addresses, phone numbers, etc. to remove yours. *Big ones include…*

●*www.anywho.com*
●*www.bigfoot.com*
●*http://people.yahoo.com*
●*www.infospace.com*
●*www.switchboard.com*
●*www.whowhere.com*

●**Use a specific credit card only for on-line purchases.** That way you can conveniently cancel the card if it is stolen or misused.

Warning: Purchases made through conventional retail stores may also be monitored if you pay by credit card or check—or if you are a member of the store's "customer club." To keep your purchases anonymous, pay by cash and don't give any personal data—not even a phone number.

YOUR MEDICAL RECORDS

More and more nonmedical employees in the health industry have access to your confidential information. *Self-defense…*

●**Check your medical records the same way you would your credit reports.** Look over HMO, Medicare and Medicaid files twice a year. Check for incorrect, embarrassing or outdated entries.

Example: If you haven't had high blood pressure for five years, ask your health-care provider to remove—or at least segregate—the item.

Helpful resource: The Medical Information Bureau (MIB), a central database of personal medical information on millions of Americans. It is used by many insurance companies.

Get a copy of your file by writing to: MIB, Box 105, Essex Station, Boston 02112…or call 617-426-3660. *Cost:* $8.50, or free if you receive a letter from an insurance company stating that it used MIB information to make a decision about you.

Talk with your physician and his/her staff. Request in writing that the office physician give out the minimum amount of medical information from your file that is required. Many doctors hand over a patient's entire file without thinking about the potential consequences.

Example: If you have an auto accident, the insurance company should get the information that it needs to settle the claim. But it doesn't need to know that you once took antidepressants or that you are diabetic.

In court: If your medical records are ever subpoenaed, they become public record. Ask the court to allow only the relevant portions of your medical record as evidence. A judge will decide what parts should be kept private. After the case is over, ask the judge to "seal" the court records containing your medical information.

●**Never sign a standard "blanket waiver."** It authorizes the release of all information regarding your medical history, symptoms, treatment, exam results or diagnosis.

Better: Edit the waiver. Write in your own specific terms to limit what's released...

I authorize information from my records to be released from hospital X as relates to my condition Y.

Be sure to add an expiration date to the release.

EMPLOYER MONITORING

By law, most employers are allowed to monitor your E-mail, voice mail, computer hard drive and telephone calls, unless they know you are having a personal conversation.

And—many companies routinely share information from personnel files with workers' creditors. *Self-defense...*

●**Find out your office's privacy policy.** *Items to look for...*

●Are you allowed to check your personnel file? How often?

●Are E-mail messages you delete from your computer still in the system?

●If your E-mail system has an option for marking messages "private," does it guarantee they are protected?

●Are there any penalties if you are found using the Internet or E-mail for personal matters?

●Does your company use a technique that allows the employer to see a list of phone numbers that are dialed from each extension and the length of each call?

●**Create your own privacy contract with your employer.**

Example: Attach conditions to sensitive information. If a disciplinary action is recorded in your personnel file, negotiate for it to be removed after a period of time.

FINANCIAL INFORMATION

Large banks and credit card companies routinely sell your financial data—from account balances to payment histories—to marketers. This leads to a deluge of promotional mail and phone calls. *Self-defense...*

●**Find out about the "opt-out" provisions before you use a financial service.**

Example: American Express never gives detailed account information to outside merchants. It also sends customers a notice asking if they want to receive product offers from American Express or other marketers.

●**Diminish mail and dinner-time phone calls from direct marketers.**

●Add your name to the "Telephone Preference Service" and "Mail Preference Service" lists maintained by the Direct Marketing Association, Box 9008, Farmingdale, NY 11735.

●List your telephone number but not your street address in the telephone book. This will foil compilers of many marketing lists.

●Ask each of the four major credit bureaus not to disclose your credit information to marketers. Call 888-5OPTOUT—this number reaches the four credit bureaus.

●**Send a check to yourself if you do electronic banking.** This is an excellent way to test your bank's privacy loopholes. See if the bank sends you as the payee any unnecessary data.

SOCIAL SECURITY NUMBER

Social Security Numbers (SSNs) are commonly used in computer record-keeping.

Your SSN gives a thief access to your entire identity—and all information that is associated with it financially. *Self-defense...*

●**Only disclose your Social Security Number to private companies** when there are tax consequences, such as opening an interest-bearing account at a bank. Most insurance companies and some credit card companies will back off if you refuse to give your SSN. As a fallback position, offer to provide the last four digits.

●**Review your Social Security statement,** which the government now automatically mails annually to every worker over age

25 (about three months before his/her birthday). If needed sooner: *www.ssa.gov.*

●**Never put your Social Security Number on your checks...**or any identifying information.

If your state's Department of Motor Vehicles uses the SSN as the driver's license number, ask for an alternative number. Most states will grant one.

If a private business requests your SSN on an application, simply leave the space blank or write "refused." Most companies will not question this—or will back off when you ask to see a written policy requiring your SSN.

MD, who has received the FDA Commissioner's Special Citation Award for Public Service for his fight against nutrition quackery.

Quackwatch now is on the Web at *www. quackwatch.com.* The Web site utilizes more than 140 medical and legal advisers, contains extensive consumer information, answers visitors' questions and provides links to other useful resources.

If you don't have an Internet connection yourself, you may be able to use one at your local library.

Greenwich Time, 20 E. Elm St., Greenwich, CT 06830.

Beware of Medical Web Sites

Medical Web sites do not protect visitors' privacy—even if they claim they do. Georgetown University's recent study found that most leading health sites share the information they collect with other companies— from health-care providers and direct marketers to manufacturers of drugs or health-care products. The study also found that visitors to health Web sites are not anonymous, even if they think they are. *Trap:* Many medical organizations require on-line registration to access their Web sites. *Self-defense:* Give as little personal information as possible...do not complete surveys.

John Featherman, president of featherman.com (formerly Privacy Protectors), consumer privacy consultants, Philadelphia.

Quack Alert

Protect yourself against medical quacks who profit by exploiting the health concerns of seniors.

Education is the best defense. A valuable resource is *Quackwatch,* a nonprofit organization founded in 1969 by Stephen Barrett,

Thinking of Being A Human Guinea Pig?

Timothy McCall, MD, a New York internist and author of *Examining Your Doctor: A Patient's Guide to Avoiding Harmful Medical Care.* Citadel Press.

Medical research has been in the news lately. But instead of reports of breakthroughs, we've been reading about conflicts of interest and ethical lapses.

The federal government, citing safety concerns, briefly suspended nearly all research trials at a prestigious research hospital. Then a shocking series of articles in the *New York Times* revealed that some doctors receive thousands of dollars from drug companies for each patient they enroll in drug studies.

There can be good reasons for enrolling in a medical study, but before you do, here's what I suggest:

●**Find out who's sponsoring the trial.** Experiments funded by grants from the federal government tend to be of higher quality than those funded by drug companies. And federally funded studies are less likely to be influenced by commercial concerns.

●**Learn the details of the experiment.** How is the experiment set up? Will the treatments be painful? What side effects are expected? Will you still be able to see your own doctor? Will test results be shared with you?

●**Don't assume that all the risks are known.** Medical researchers are required to describe risks associated with participation in any experiment. But when a treatment is brand new, no one knows all the risks. What sounds good in theory could turn out to be dangerous.

●**Make sure you've exhausted other treatment options.** It's one thing to enroll in a trial of an experimental cancer drug when the available treatments aren't working. It's quite another to sign up for a trial of, say, a new headache pill. Since headaches aren't life-threatening—and good headache remedies are available—it makes little sense to risk the new drug. *Rule of thumb:* The more severe your ailment and the less effective the available treatments, the more it makes sense to bet on an experimental therapy.

●**Find out whether other clinical trials might be more appropriate for you.** Two good sources of information on clinical trials are the National Cancer Institute (800-422-6237 or *http://cancernet.nci.nih.gov*) and Centerwatch (800-692-2622 or *www.centerwatch. com*).

●**Be sure you'd be willing to take a placebo.** In many studies, one group of patients is given real medication while the other group—unbeknownst to them—gets sugar pills (or other placebos). That helps doctors determine whether any benefits were really due to the drug. Some patients, though, are unwilling to risk not getting real treatment.

●**Find out who pays.** Who will pay for diagnostic tests used to monitor your response to therapy? What if you develop side effects that necessitate hospitalization? Will your insurance company be billed for anything?

●**Look out for hidden agendas.** Most patients enroll in clinical trials with only one thing in mind—getting better. But drug companies and researchers may be more interested simply in collecting good data. Some studies refuse to enroll patients who are "too sick." Others won't reveal test results to patients, fearing that poor progress will lead some to drop out. Similarly, when doctors are paid to enroll patients, it can affect their judgment about what's best for you.

The reality is that most clinical trials don't benefit the volunteers as much as they help future patients. That's a worthy goal and, of course, some participants do benefit. If the information to be gained by the study seems important and the risk acceptably small, you may want to sign up.

Hospital Cost-Cutter Is Dangerous

Single-use medical devices—such as syringes, cardiac catheters, obstetrical forceps, laser tips and intubation tubes—are increasingly being cleaned, sterilized and *reused* by doctors and hospital workers to cut costs, putting patients at great risk for infection. *Self-defense:* At the time a procedure is to be performed, tell the doctor or nurse that you do not want a resterilized single-use product. Request that only new devices be used for your care.

Charles Inlander, president of People's Medical Society, America's largest nonprofit consumer health advocacy organization, 462 Walnut St., Allentown, PA 18104.

Don't Overlook Cancer-Causing Chemicals in Your Own Home

Moshe Shike, MD, director of the cancer prevention and wellness program at Memorial Sloan-Kettering Cancer Center in New York. He is coauthor of Cancer Free: The Comprehensive Cancer Prevention Program. *Simon & Schuster.*

Cancer is often viewed as a bolt out of the blue—something beyond anyone's control.

In reality, four out of five cases stem from lifestyle choices, such as smoking, drinking excessively, eating a high-fat diet, consuming grilled meats, etc.

Most of these lifestyle choices are well-known to just about everyone. *But few people recognize the role played by carcinogens in the home...*

ASBESTOS

In homes built before the mid-1970s, asbestos is commonly found in pipe insulation, floor tiles, siding, etc.

As long as it remains undisturbed, this material poses little threat. But if asbestos-containing material is damaged in any way, tiny asbestos particles drift into the air...and into the lungs.

These particles are highly carcinogenic. They can cause malignancies of the lung and abdominal cavity.

Self-defense: If you suspect your home contains asbestos, hire an asbestos-abatement contractor. This is *not* a do-it-yourself job.

For referral to a contractor in your area, call the Toxic Hotline at 202-554-1404. This non-profit organization is funded by the Environmental Protection Agency.

RADON

Radon is a carcinogenic gas produced by the decay of uranium, which is naturally present in soil. Exposure to radon is the second-leading cause of lung cancer in the US, after smoking.

Radon rises from soil into houses, usually through cracks in floors or walls. Concentrations are highest in basements and ground-floor rooms, simply because they're close to the soil. Radon isn't much of a concern in upper-floor rooms or apartments.

The higher the concentration of radon, the greater the risk. The average radon level in US homes is 1.5 picocuries per liter of air (pCi/L). This level is safe. But exposure to a level of 4 pCi/L is roughly equivalent to smoking half a pack of cigarettes a day.

Self-defense: If you live in a high-rise, you're fine. Otherwise, test the air in your home using a radon test kit. These sell for about $25 in hardware stores.

Deploy the kit in the lowest lived-in level of your home—the basement, if you spend time there, or the first floor.

If the radon level equals or exceeds 4 pCi/L, take steps to ventilate the room. In some cases, opening a basement window or installing an exhaust fan will do the trick.

Test the air again a few months later. If radon remains a problem, a radon-abatement contractor should be able to install a ventilation system that is more effective.

LAWN CHEMICALS

Herbicides, pesticides and fungicides should be used with extreme caution. Many contain potent carcinogens, such as *2, 4-D,* which has been linked to non-Hodgkin's lymphoma.

Self-defense: Stay off the lawn for at least a few days after applying the chemicals. Better yet, avoid lawn chemicals altogether. A local nursery or landscaper can recommend varieties of grass that do well without the use of chemicals.

Helpful: Keep your grass at a minimum height of two-and-one-half inches. Weeds and lawn diseases pose less of a problem when grass is kept at this height than at lower heights.

PESTICIDE RESIDUES

With the exception of organic produce, most store-bought fruits and vegetables have been sprayed with pesticides.

The risk associated with eating pesticide-tainted fruits and vegetables is low compared with the risk from not eating fruits and vegetables. Still, it's a risk that can be avoided.

Self-defense: Buy organic produce—or grow your own. Whatever kind of produce you buy, rinse it under running water for 10 seconds or so—long enough to rub the entire surface with your fingers. Soap is unnecessary.

Do *not* soak produce. Doing so leaches out water-soluble nutrients.

ORGANIC SOLVENTS

Paint strippers, lubricants and household cleaners often contain carcinogens, such as *benzene* and *methylene chloride.*

Self-defense: Wear rubber gloves when you are using household chemicals. Keep a door or window open to disperse the vapors —or, if possible, take the work outside.

Painful Phone Call

Cradling a telephone between shoulder and head for a long period of time can lead to a "mini-stroke." Recently, a 43-year-old Frenchman experienced temporary blindness, ringing in the ears and difficulty speaking after holding a phone this way for more than an hour. A computed tomography (CT) scan revealed a tear in the carotid artery in his neck. Apparently, the tear occurred when the artery was compressed against a bone in the skull.

The Journal of the American Medical Association, 515 N. State St., Chicago 60610.

Slamming Self-Defense

Slamming—the unauthorized switching of long-distance telephone service—is still common. *Helpful:* Call your local phone company, and ask for a Primary Interexchange Carrier (PIC) freeze. This locks you into your current long-distance carrier so your service cannot be switched unless you call the local phone company. If it is, you don't have to pay your bill.

Holly Anderson, director of communications, National Consumers League, 1701 K St. NW, Suite 1200, Washington, DC 20006.

Cordless Phone Alert

Don't tell your secrets into a cordless phone. Cordless phones broadcast over an unlicensed frequency band that is shared with numerous other radio-operated devices. That means your cordless conversations may be picked up on your neighbor's baby monitor...you may even accidentally open up someone's garage door. You can add a measure of security by switching channels as you talk. But to really keep conversations private,

use another kind of phone. Cellular phones and PCS mobile phones use *licensed* frequency bands. Digital phones provide the best protection due to their encryption capabilities.

Candy Castle, director of external relations, AT&T Wireless Systems, Redmond, WA.

Cyber-Security Alert

Secure Web sites might not be so secure. *Trap:* Computer hackers attack Web servers, which might not be secure—not data transmission. If you give out personal data on the Internet—including credit card numbers—a hacker attack on the server could get to your information. *Self-defense:* Give out as little information as possible...and check your credit card statements *very* carefully.

Yun Choi, PhD, president of Network SOS, computer-security consultants to brokerages, law firms and insurance companies, Ridgefield, NJ.

Computer Safety

Never run an unsolicited computer program that arrives attached to an E-mail unless you know for sure what it is.

Trap: It may be a "Trojan horse," a malicious program that the creator hopes you will naively run. A Trojan is different from a virus in that it does not reproduce by itself—but if you run it, it may destroy files or steal information such as passwords.

Caution: Don't even run programs E-mailed from friends without verifying what they are—a Trojan-infected computer may attach copies of the data on the computer to all E-mail it sends out without the computer owner knowing it.

Safety: Install a good antivirus program on your computer. It will defend against Trojans, too.

Tatiana Gau, vice president of integrity assurance, America Online, 8619 Westwood Center Dr., Vienna, VA 22182.

Airport Scams Are Multiplying... Self-Defense Made Simple

Alvy Dodson, director of public safety at Dallas–Fort Worth Airport, where he oversees more than 300 officers who patrol an area the size of Manhattan. He has been with DFW Airport for 22 years.

Airport thieves have devised very clever schemes to separate you from your valuables...

Scam: Stealing luggage you've left with strangers. It is not a good idea to entrust your property to strangers...ever.

Scam: Stealing luggage in men's rooms. A popular area for theft in airports is at the small, crowded entrance to the urinal area. Thieves wait for travelers to pile up their bags and turn their backs for a moment.

Also popular—the shelf above sinks, where travelers place rings, watches or cell phones while washing their hands.

Self-defense: If possible, wait until an end urinal or stall is available, so luggage can be placed against the wall. At the sink, place valuables in your front pockets while you wash. Put your luggage on the floor between your feet.

Scam: Looting your luggage cart at the airport. Thieves look for a cart loaded with bags and follow it until you stop to hail a cab or buy a magazine. Then one or two of them create a diversion while a third slips one of your bags out from the bottom.

Self-defense: Always push luggage carts —never pull them behind you.

Also, run twine through the handles of your luggage, especially smaller ones. That way a thief trying to grab a bag will make a commotion as he/she pulls the others along with it. If you must stop with your cart, do so in an area away from the flow of the crowd or against a wall where no one can get behind you.

Scam: Cutting your fanny pack. These are the wraparound pouches people wear on their waists.

Thieves follow you up an escalator. One gets on in front of you...the other behind you. The lead person stumbles as he gets off the escalator, causing you to nearly fall over him. The second person sandwiches you and uses a knife or razor to slice the pack's waistband.

Self-defense: If you wear a fanny pack, wear it with the pouch in front and keep it under a jacket or sweater.

Scam: Stealing luggage off the carousel. Thieves take the black, pull-along suitcases that are so common now. If challenged after they grab yours, they claim it was an honest mistake.

Self-defense: If you must use a black pull-along, make it distinctive. Put your initials in reflective tape on the side. Arrive at the baggage claim area as quickly as possible so you can retrieve your luggage as soon as it is delivered.

Scam: The baggage-handler rip-off. Some dishonest airport employees who load and unload bags from planes run their hands through bags looking for valuables. This is hard to prevent—even if you use small locks on your bags. Small locks are easily broken... although they are better than nothing.

Self-defense: If you must carry valuables, keep them in your carry-on bag. If you must pack them, roll valuables in your clothing and place those garments in the middle of the bag. Thieves will open a zippered compartment or rummage through the top of the contents of your luggage. Also, make your bags "tamper-obvious." Thieves avoid luggage that will show obvious signs of pilfering.

Helpful: Many airports have kiosks that will wrap checked luggage in a thick layer of transparent plastic. *Cost:* About $6/bag.

Scam: Picking the pockets of victims at food kiosks. Thieves move in close to see in which trouser pocket or zippered luggage compartment you keep your wallet. They also want to see your money and credit cards.

Self-defense: Remove the money and credit cards you need *before* entering the airport terminal. Keep them in a clip in your front pocket. Women should avoid carrying their wallets in their purses. Instead, conceal them in a coat or sweater pocket where they do not show.

Scam: **Stealing at checkpoints.** A favorite place for distraction is screening checkpoints. When you are presenting your carry-on articles for X-ray inspection, be ready to proceed *immediately* through the magnetometer. This can be accomplished by removing all metal objects—coins, jewelry, keys, etc.—*before* you approach the checkpoint.

Laptop Danger On Airplanes

Tray tables can be dangerous to laptops. On some planes, tray tables stored in seat armrests can be magnetized. Putting a computer on those tray tables can cause the computer to crash and you may lose data. The problem can occur on trains, too. *Self-defense:* Open the tray table, and slide a paper clip or other small metal object against its plastic surface. If the object sticks, do not use your computer.

Travel Holiday, 1633 Broadway, New York 10019.

Go on Vacation Without Worrying

Before taking a vacation, put valuables that you usually keep at home in a safe-deposit box or leave them with a friend or relative. Pay bills before you leave so they are not overdue when you return. Have your burglar and fire alarms checked to be sure they are working properly. Leave an itinerary with a friend, neighbor or relative so you can be reached in case of emergency.

Ira Lipman, president, Guardsmark, Inc., one of the world's largest security services companies, Memphis.

Official Rip-Off Avoidance Strategies

Lori Groen, postal inspector with the US Postal Inspection Service in Washington, DC. If you suspect letters involve postal fraud, contact Postal Inspection Service Operations Support Group, 2 Gateway Ctr., Ninth fl., Newark, NJ 07175.

Americans lose an estimated $100 million a year to scam artists who use the US mail to con them out of money and valuable personal information.

The big postal frauds now—and how to avoid them...

●**Nigerian advance fee.** You receive an unsolicited letter, written in stilted English, supposedly from someone in the Nigerian government. The letter explains that a huge sum of money—usually $25 million or more—has been uncovered during an audit of funds.

The letter writer says he/she needs help transferring money out of Nigeria and promises you a 30% cut if you allow him to wire funds to your bank account.

Before the funds can be transferred, the letter continues, there are government officials, bank officers and taxes that must be paid. The letter says this money has to come from you.

Trap: Even if this offer were legitimate, receiving stolen money is illegal.

●**Chain letters.** These entice you into sending money—usually up to $1,000—to the person named at the top of a list. Then you're asked to add your name to the bottom of the list, cross off the top name and send copies to your friends. The letter promises that you will receive money from others in the chain.

Self-defense: Do not answer any chain letter that requires you to send money or divulge personal information.

●**Phony inheritance.** A letter from an "estate locator" offers to sell you a report that explains how to claim an inheritance. The letter writer may also offer to search for inheritances for a fee.

Self-defense: Legitimate law firms and others named to distribute unclaimed inherited funds normally do not request a fee from recipients, but from the estates.

The Right Locks for Everything That You Want to Protect

Giles Kalvelage, owner of Access Control Lock Service, Paw Paw, IL.

Best deadbolt. *Medeco Maxum Single Cylinder.* Patented design and hardened steel inserts make it drill resistant and practically pick-proof. 877-397-0672.

•**Best doorknob lock.** *Schlage A53PD Series.* Residential doorknob. Corrosion-resistant. Five styles and nine finishes. 888-805-9837.

•**Best lever door handle lock.** *Schlage AL53 Series.* High-quality lever has an exceptionally strong operating mechanism. Three styles and seven finishes. 888-805-9837.

•**Best patio door lock.** *Charles Bar-Lok Charlie-BAR.* Adjustable aluminum tube locks sliding doors 36" to 48" wide. Plastic bracket keeps bar's end in place so it cannot be lifted from the outside. Bar lifts easily and stores out of the way. Aluminum, bronze and white finishes. 708-333-0071.

•**Best padlock.** *Abus Diskus Maximum 24 Series.* Unique design covers most of the padlock shackle, leaving only a small opening that makes it difficult to cut or pry open. Padlock body is made of thick, 2.2-mm stainless steel. Three sizes ($2\frac{3}{8}$" to $3\frac{5}{8}$"). 800-352-2287.

•**Best car steering wheel lock.** *Master Lock 259DAT.* Hardened steel bar with dual locking "fingers" requires two steering wheel cuts to remove. One size (27" length) fits most vehicles, including SUVs, trucks and RVs. Anti-theft guarantee will reimburse up to $3,000 of your insurance deductible. 414-444-2800.

•**Best bicycle lock.** *Kryptonite Evolution 3000.* The locking mechanism on this U-shaped lock is located on the center of the crossbar, not the end. That makes it harder to attack. The crossbar is shielded by a hardened steel sleeve, preventing thieves from tampering with the lock cylinder. Users who register key numbers with the manufacturer receive replacements within 24 hours. 800-729-5625.

Smoke Detector Alert

The most popular type—an *ion detector*—will detect fast-developing fires, such as wastepaper basket or kitchen grease fires. It won't detect the more common smoldering fires, such as those started by cigarettes in mattresses. Every home needs two types—ion and photoelectric.

B. Don Russell, PhD, associate vice chancellor of engineering and deputy director, Texas Engineering Experiment Station, Texas A&M University, College Station. He has researched smoke detectors for more than a decade.

Better Fire Protection

Automatic fire sprinklers quickly control or extinguish home fires, often before the fire department arrives. Recent technology makes fire sprinklers more affordable and easier to install in homes. Only the sprinklers closest to the fire discharge—in most cases, with only one sprinkler operating. They attack a fire before it spreads—with only a fraction of the water needed if the fire department had to fight the fire. Home sprinklers rarely go off accidentally. They can be mounted flush with walls or ceilings to be less visible.

Mike Murphy, spokesperson, National Fire Protection Association, Quincy, MA.

Electrical Cord Self-Defense

Beware: Unsafe electrical cords are far more common than most people think. Nearly three-quarters of the cords, power strips and surge protectors tested by the Consumer Product Safety Commission in 1997 failed to meet safety standards. *Self-defense:*

Buy only cords certified by Underwriters Laboratories (UL) or Electrical Testing Laboratories (ETL). Use cords with polarized or three-prong plugs to reduce shock risk. Use heavy-duty cords for high-wattage appliances, such as air conditioners and microwaves. Never cover cords with rugs or other objects —that increases the risk of fire.

Ken Giles, spokesperson, US Consumer Product Safety Commission, Washington, DC.

Lawnmower Danger

Ride-on lawnmowers injure about 20,000 and kill about 75 people every year. One-fifth of those killed are children. *Self-defense:* Keep children inside while using a riding mower or garden tractor. If kids come into the mowing area, turn off the mower. Be careful when backing up or going around corners, trees or obstacles. Keep kids away from equipment after you turn it off—they could be burned by hot engine parts.

Recommendations from US Consumer Product Safety Commission, Washington, DC.

Laundry Self-Defense

To protect against disease-causing bacteria, wash hands after loading and unloading a washing machine. Dry clothes in the dryer when possible, using the highest heat they can stand. Separate items likely to contain potentially harmful bacteria, such as underwear and kitchen towels, from other laundry, and wash separately in hot water using one-half cup bleach for a medium-to-large load. Presoak items soiled with blood, vomit or other substances in hot water and one-half cup of bleach per gallon of water—then wash separately from regular laundry. If a family member has a skin infection or illness, wash his/her clothing separately with bleach or sanitizing detergent. Use rubber gloves when handling soiled laundry.

Robyn Gershon, DrPH, senior research associate, Johns Hopkins School of Hygiene and Public Health, Baltimore.

Lyme Disease Self-Defense

Spray standard turf insecticides in early fall to kill adult ticks.

Most important: Spray around the edges of the lawn, by stone walls or where lawn interfaces with the woods, directing spray into the woods—not just on the lawn.

Other tick-control measures: Rake leaves back toward the woods...use wood-chip mulch as ground cover to minimize movement of ticks onto the lawn...keep lawn and ground cover well-trimmed.

Plan ahead: Insecticidal turf spray in late spring kills *nymphal* ticks. If you use natural insecticides such as pyrethrins, a second spraying may be necessary.

Kirby C. Stafford III, PhD, chief scientist, department of forestry and horticulture, Connecticut Agricultural Experiment Station, New Haven.

Beware: Danger from Infused Olive Oil— Botulism

Oils infused with garlic or herbs—and contaminated with the bacterium that causes botulism—cannot be identified by smell, sight or taste. Bacteria originate on the garlic and can readily grow in oil stored at room temperature. *Self-defense:* Buy only commercially prepared infused oil that contains phosphoric or citric acid. Store the bottle in the refrigerator after you open it.

LeeAnne Jackson, PhD, science policy analyst, Center for Food Safety & Applied Nutrition, US Food and Drug Administration, Washington, DC.

New Computer Rip-Off

A new scam may affect millions of computer users. You could be a victim without even knowing it. Some computer-savvy crooks buy inexpensive central processing units (CPUs)—which are the "brains" of personal computers—and doctor them to run at higher-than-rated speeds. They then re-mark them to look like faster, more expensive CPUs and sell them.

Example: A Pentium II 300 or 333 chip might be sold as a faster 400 or 450.

Self-defense: These chips are usually sold by middlemen, known as "gray market brokers," who sell excess legitimate CPUs and re-marked CPUs to small computer stores that assemble their own private-label computers. The chips are also sold on-line through little-known mail-order companies, or at local computer shops.

Avoid purchases from these locations unless you can be sure the CPUs are honestly marked.

Christopher Woiwode, supervisory special agent in the FBI's high-tech detail, San Jose, CA, quoted in *PC World*, 501 Second St., San Francisco 94107.

 **Dining Out? Remember...**

Salad bars and buffets are easily contaminated. *Examples:* A child reaches in and picks up something with his/her fingers. An adult fails to wash his hands after using the toilet and then picks up the food tongs. Food in a salad bar may stay out long enough for bacteria to start to grow. The containers may be refilled without being washed. And containers may be stored overnight a temperatures at which bacteria can easily grow. *Bottom line:* When eating out, order food that is prepared just for you.

Michael Doyle, PhD, director, Center for Food safety and Quality Enhancement, University of Georgia, Griffin.

On-Line Scams

On-line stock fraud is increasing as scam artists realize the Internet offers an easy, inexpensive way to reach thousands or millions of people. Scam artists usually send spam—junk E-mail. Or they go into investment chat rooms and talk a stock's value up or down. The Securities and Exchange Commission (SEC) polices on-line scams, but it is challenging to keep up with fraud in a medium of instant communications. *Self-defense:* Never buy or sell a stock based on Internet tips—do your own research. If you suspect a scam, contact *enforcement@sec.gov*.

Richard H. Walker, director of enforcement, Securities and Exchange Commission, quoted in *Kiplinger's Personal Finance*, 1729 H St. NW, Washington, DC 20006.

The Most Dangerous Scams Can Cost You Your Health...or Your Life—Not Just Your Money

Chuck Whitlock, noted scambuster, consumer advocate and speaker on television and radio. Mr. Whitlock is author of *Chuck Whitlock's Scam School*. IDG Books.

Medical fraud is the most dangerous fraud facing older Americans—and it is becoming more prevalent and more dangerous every day.

Experts say health-care fraud costs $100 billion to $250 billion every year. And it is aimed directly at seniors, who use more health-care services than any other group.

Caution: Financial fraud and consumer fraud can cost you only money. Medical fraud can cost you your health...even your life.

SELF-DEFENSE

To protect yourself from medical fraud, first recognize...

●**The risk is growing.** More medical scam artists are operating today than ever before—

in response to the growing population of seniors who are both exhibiting the maladies of advancing age and being squeezed by rising medical costs incurred on fixed budgets.

●**Everyone is vulnerable.** Medical fraud is even more seductive to potential victims than financial fraud.

Financial fraud offers only easy money. Medical fraud offers longer life, better looks, more potency, less weight, greater strength, the return of lost functions and—for the desperate—even life itself. And it often offers an easy way out, such as a pill to "absorb" fat while eliminating the need for diet or exercise.

Everybody wants these things, so everybody is potentially vulnerable to the false promises of medical fraud.

BIGGEST DANGERS

Areas to be wary of and how to protect yourself...

●**Over-the-counter (OTC) drugs and supplements.** The first problem here is that most consumers have no way of verifying the contents of what they buy. Sellers know this and can take advantage of it by selling something other than what is promised. *Examples...*

●Food supplements sold as "97% protein" have been found under chemical analysis to be as little as 4% protein.

●Items that are expensive to produce, such as Vitamin E, occasionally are "shorted," so less is in the product than is promised on the label.

Self-defense: Buy only OTC items that carry the brand of major firms that have had the quality of their products confirmed by testing conducted by independent consumer groups.

Recommended: Drugs and supplements from major firms, such as Twinlab, Rexall and Nature Made.

A second problem is that clerks in stores that sell OTC products often act like doctors. Don't ask them to recommend a product—they don't have the medical training to do so.

Much better: Ask your doctor what to buy, then tell the sales clerk exactly what you want.

●**Prescription drugs.** The same problem exists here as with OTC drugs—the consumer has no way of verifying what's in the product.

Scam: Store pharmacists sometimes cut costs by reselling drugs acquired not from drug companies, but from wholesalers with aging stocks, or from scam artists who sell drugs they've bought cheaply using mass-produced phony prescriptions. As a result, the drugs you buy may be expired or adulterated.

Self-defense: Buy prescription drugs from reputable drugstore chains, such as Rite Aid and Walgreens. These have centralized purchasing departments that assure product quality and eliminate opportunity for store-level fraud.

●**Bogus doctors.** The fact that a person claims to be a doctor doesn't mean he/she is one. A diploma mill in the Bahamas that was recently shut down was selling 1,100 medical diplomas *per month.*

It's also very easy for a fake doctor to adopt the identity of a real one, referring to the real doctor's education and certifications as his own.

When considering a new doctor, check with...

●Your state's Board of Medical Examiners to be sure he is registered in your state. (A fake doctor won't be registered.)

●Your County Medical Association to see if any complaints have been filed against the doctor.

Smart idea: When looking for a new doctor, call your local hospital's head nurse in the area of specialization you are interested in, such as cardiology. Ask whom he/she would go to if he had a medical problem. Head nurses can be a fount of valuable information.

●**Bogus treatments.** If a doctor (or anybody else) offers a medical treatment that sounds too good to be true—or a price that sounds too good to be true—it probably is.

Self-defense: Get a second opinion. Go to another doctor and ask for an opinion about your case. Don't reveal what the first doctor said.

If after getting the second opinion you still feel uncertain, get a *third* opinion. If insurance won't pay for it, pay for it yourself. It's your health and life that are at stake.

●**Bogus medical equipment.** Scam artists make fortunes selling bogus medical equipment that is supposed to alleviate the maladies of advancing age. *Examples...*

●The ACCU-STOP 2000 was an ear piece worn at night to intercept hunger signals going to the brain and help the wearer lose weight. Medically worthless, it cost only 14 cents to produce but was sold for $39.95—and *3.5 million* were sold before the scam artist behind it fled the country.

●The medical alert device sold with the unforgettable, "I've fallen and I can't get up" TV advertisement was sold with a $7,200 two-year service contract, when the same device was available for $50 with *free* service from the phone company. The maker's salespeople made sales calls lasting up to five hours each to intimidate seniors into buying it, until the government shut them down.

Danger: At best, bogus medical devices are expensive and useless. At worst, relying on them could jeopardize your health and life.

Self-defense: Ask your doctor if the claims for a device are legitimate. If he says, "No," believe him. (If your doctor says, "Yes," but you have nagging doubts, get a second opinion.)

MORE DEFENSES

Purveyors of medical fraud often use very persuasive advertising. They can, because they are not constrained by the truth. *Self-defense...*

●**Never believe testimonials.** The vast majority are made by accomplices. But even "honest" ones can be bogus. *How...*

●It may be the placebo effect or power of suggestion that gave someone relief with a worthless treatment.

●Even those suffering the most serious diseases experience a small percentage of remissions due to unknown reasons. These may be touted as "miracle cures," and the patients may believe it, even though the remissions had nothing to do with the treatment.

Example: Those in Mexico who treat cancer with apricot seeds point to their patients who survive—and ignore the vastly larger number who die.

●**Don't talk to telemarketers.** When a telemarketer calls selling a medical product, just hang up. Seniors, especially, have been raised to be polite on the phone, and telemarketers use this to exploit them.

Exception: If you think an offer may be legitimate, get the name and address of the calling firm. Check it out and then call back if you wish.

More from Chuck Whitlock...

Internet Fraud Warning

Use the Internet—but beware of it, too. The Internet gives consumers new access to great quantities of medical information.

Most top medical groups, such as the American Cancer Society, the American Diabetes Association and the National Kidney Foundation, now have Web sites that can be of great value to consumers, as do hospitals, medical schools and government organizations.

Make the most of them—use your local library's Internet connection if you don't have one at home.

Danger: The Internet is unregulated and crawling with scam artists. So be sure you use it to obtain information only from recognized organizations with unquestionable integrity.

21

Very, Very Personal

How to Build a Better Sexual Relationship

hen the impotence drug Viagra (*sildenafil*) became available, it seemed like a miracle. Just by taking a pill, millions of men who had suffered with impotence—in some cases for decades—regained the ability to enjoy sexual intercourse.

But things are rarely as simple as they seem—especially when sex is involved.

Viagra does offer a safe, effective means of restoring erections, but only rarely is it the sole answer to sexual problems.

WHAT VIAGRA DOES

Viagra helps dilate the arteries in the genital area so that spongy tissue within the penis can fill with blood—that's the way an erection is produced—and stay engorged long enough for intercourse.

Viagra can be helpful for most kinds of impotence, including that associated with spinal cord injury or prostate surgery.

The drug works especially well for impotence stemming from performance anxiety. That's a psychological problem that arises when a man begins to fear that *occasional* trouble in achieving an erection—which is normal—means he is impotent. The fear causes muscles to become tense. Muscle tension squeezes blood vessels shut, making it difficult for blood to flow into the penis.

Often, merely having a Viagra pill in his pocket gives a man the confidence he needs to overcome performance anxiety.

WHAT VIAGRA DOES NOT DO

Effective as it is in restoring erections, Viagra does nothing for the underlying cause of impotence. This poses a significant danger.

Gerald Melchiode, MD, clinical professor of psychiatry at University of Texas Southwestern Medical Center in Dallas. He is author of *Beyond Viagra: A Commonsense Guide to Building a Healthy Sexual Relationship for Both Men and Women*. Owl Books.

Reason: Impotence is often an early—or even the sole—symptom of potentially lethal illnesses like diabetes, heart disease or a pituitary tumor.

A man who gets relief for his problem by popping a pill may fail to get more meaningful medical care that could save his life.

Lesson: Any man troubled by impotence should take Viagra only under medical supervision—and then only after undergoing a thorough physical exam to identify the cause of his problem.

Impotence can also be a sign of emotional strife within a relationship. In such cases, Viagra can permit a couple to have intercourse… but it does nothing to address the real problem—anger, resentment, lack of communication, etc.

Even when impotence has a purely physical cause, it's often complicated by psychological problems that have arisen as a result of the problem.

Example: A man is so ashamed about his impotence that he withdraws from his wife. She worries that she might somehow be causing the problem—yet resents his withdrawal from her.

WHOSE PROBLEM IS IT?

For a couple who is in a long-term relationship, impotence should generally be dealt with by both partners.

Key question to ask yourselves: If this problem were resolved, would everything be OK in our relationship? If the answer is "yes," a prescription for Viagra may be all that's needed.

But Viagra cannot supply the intimacy, tenderness or caring that makes sex truly satisfying. In fact, when those are lacking, it's probably counterproductive to rely on Viagra.

INCREASING INTIMACY

With or without Viagra, men can often give their sex lives a boost simply by closely examining their relationships. *Questions to ponder…*

●**Are you angry at your partner—or vice versa?** When couples fail to discuss the negative feelings that inevitably crop up in long-term relationships, these feelings often find expression in the sexual arena. Better to discuss what's bothering each of you.

●**Are the two of you communicating about sex?** Even after decades together, many couples are too inhibited to talk about what they like in bed.

Real sexual satisfaction remains elusive until partners tell one another what they want.

Important: When telling your partner what you like, always use "I" language. Say, "I'd like you to do so-and-so." Do not say, "Why don't you do so-and-so?"

●**Are you in sync?** Many couples rely on nonverbal cues to signal a desire for sex. But these signals can get garbled.

Typical scenario: A husband assumes that by turning off her bedside lamp, his wife is signaling a desire for sex. In fact, she is merely indicating that she is tired…and wants to go to sleep.

●**Do you have a "sex friendly" lifestyle?** Stress, overwork and fatigue can torpedo sexual satisfaction just as well as physical illness.

Typical scenario: For one couple, Friday night has always been the time for sex. But after a recent promotion, the husband is working longer hours…and finds that he is too tired to "perform" on Friday. The couple is able to resurrect their lovemaking simply by waiting until Saturday.

●**Do you act your age?** Beyond age 45, many men find that they can attain an erection only if they're touched. For women, a decline in vaginal lubrication after menopause makes sex uncomfortable and kills desire.

In the first case, Viagra may help. In the second, use of a lubricant may help. In either case, frank communication is also necessary.

●**Are you willing to work on a solution?** If deep-rooted relationship problems stand in the way of sexual satisfaction, professional counseling may be necessary. For couples truly committed to each other, a couples therapist can help sort out what's wrong…and start making it right.

Make Time for Sex

Many couples schedule sex *out* of their busy lives, making ample time instead for work, kids, community activities, exercise, watching TV and seeing friends.

If you want to have a satisfying sex life, you must set aside "sensuality time" for yourself and your partner...

•**Cut back on TV viewing...**wake up earlier...and limit social engagements.

•**Plan one evening a week together** at home—and make the date unbreakable. Turn off the phone. Spend three hours talking... giving each other backrubs...enjoying your senses and being together. You don't have to have sex, but private, relaxed sensuality often leads to sex. Don't rush.

•**Practice turning yourself "on"** by opening yourself up to sexual stimuli. Let yourself be aroused by fleeting fantasies. Many couples enjoy sharing fantasies with each other. Wear sexy underwear to work ...and call your partner and talk about making love later that day.

Once you start to relax and enjoy yourself, you'll find that spontaneously sexy feelings come to you.

Dagmar O'Connor, PhD, a sex therapist in private practice in New York. She is author of the Do It Yourself Sex Therapy Video Packet *(Dag Media Corp., 800-520-5200) and* How to Put the Love Back into Making Love *(Bantam Books).*

Proper Condom Storage

Poor storage of condoms can make them more likely to break. Lubricated condoms are generally good for five years from date of manufacture...spermicidally lubricated ones, for three years. Both types are labeled with expiration dates. But if a condom's seal is broken—exposing it to air, light or heat—it can fail much sooner.

Richard Kline, group vice president, Carter-Wallace, maker of Trojan condoms, Cranbury, NJ.

Bladder Infections Up

Bladder infections are on the rise among older women—because of the impotence drug *sildenafil* (Viagra).

With sildenafil's continuing popularity, many older women who had been having sex infrequently, if at all, are now having sex often.

Infection occurs when genital friction associated with intercourse forces infectious bacteria into the urethra. Older women are at special risk because they produce little vaginal lubrication.

Symptoms of urinary tract infection: A frequent urge to urinate...scant urine flow... burning during urination...passing blood with urine.

Good news: Urinary tract infections can usually be controlled with an oral antibiotic such as *ciprofloxacin* (Cipro) or *doxycycline* (Vibramycin).

Also helpful: Using a vaginal lubricant, such as *K-Y Jelly*...drinking six to eight ounces of water once an hour to help flush out bacteria ...and urinating immediately after intercourse.

Henry Patton, MD, an internist in private practice in Covington, GA.

Sex Boost from Soy

Soy can be sexy for women going through menopause. Soy foods are full of natural plant estrogens. Eating three to four ounces of tofu daily—or drinking one cup of soy milk—can provide an estrogen boost that makes sex more pleasurable.

Julian Whitaker, MD, founder, Whitaker Wellness Institute, Newport Beach, CA, and author of Shed Ten Years in Ten Weeks. *Fireside.*

Lifestyle Change Before Fatherhood

Many things damage sperm function and can make it difficult for a man to father a child. Cigarettes, alcohol and heavy use of marijuana or cocaine depress sperm production. Hot tubs can make a man's body too hot to produce viable sperm. Antibiotics, other drugs and infections can suppress sperm production. Even vitamin C can cause problems—it changes the acidity of semen. Dietary supplements, such as ginseng, and body-building supplements, such as DHEA and androstenedione, can lower levels of naturally occurring male hormones. And sexual lubricants can interfere with the ability of sperm to move. *Bottom line:* If trying to conceive, examine your lifestyle in detail before considering aggressive fertility treatments.

Harry Fisch, MD, director, Male Reproductive Center, Columbia-Presbyterian Medical Center, New York.

Tight Underwear Myth

Tight underwear does not reduce men's fertility. Because high temperatures weaken sperm, there has long been speculation that wearing tight briefs rather than boxer shorts might warm the testicles and reduce men's fertility.

Now: A study of almost 100 men has found that this belief was incorrect, and that underwear has no effect on sperm quality.

Robert A. Munkelwitz, MD, a urologist in private practice in Southampton, NY.

Sex Too Soon After Childbirth Can Be Deadly

Recently, two Englishwomen died after having sex a few days after giving birth. The problem, say doctors, is that pregnancy-related changes make pelvic blood vessels vulnerable to fatal air embolisms.

The Medical Post.

Hysterectomy Is Rarely The Only Solution for Gynecologic Problems

Brian W. Walsh, MD, assistant professor of obstetrics and gynecology at Harvard Medical School and chief of surgical gynecology at Brigham and Women's Hospital, both in Boston.

Each year, half a million American women undergo hysterectomy—surgical removal of the uterus. This drastic procedure requires three to five days in the hospital, followed by up to six weeks of recovery at home.

Hysterectomy can be life-saving in cases of cancer of the uterus, cervix or ovaries. But nine out of 10 hysterectomies are done simply to control excessive menstrual bleeding or other less serious gynecologic problems.

These problems can almost always be controlled with treatments that are safer and less damaging to a woman's self-image than hysterectomy...and which preserve the woman's ability to bear children.

Here are five conditions that often lead to hysterectomy...and how each can be controlled in other ways...

ENDOMETRIOSIS

This condition occurs when cells from the uterine lining begin to grow *outside* the uterus—typically in the ovaries or behind the uterus. With each menstrual period, a woman with endometriosis experiences slight internal bleeding. This causes inflammation and irritates nerve endings, resulting in severe pain.

***Alternative to hysterectomy:* Laparoscopic surgery.** The doctor inserts a flexible, lighted telescope (laparoscope) into the abdomen through a small incision in the navel. He/she then uses the laparoscope to remove endometrial deposits.

Because endometriosis can recur, the surgery may have to be repeated. But only in severe cases of endometriosis is hysterectomy required.

Hysterectomy—plus removal of both ovaries (bilateral oophorectomy)—stops the growth of endometrial deposits and causes existing deposits to shrink.

ADENOMYOSIS

This endometriosis-like condition is common in women who have had several children. It occurs when pregnancy-related changes in the uterine lining cause it to "invade" the walls of the uterus, thereby weakening it.

The uterine walls ultimately lose their ability to contract. It's this ability that lets a healthy uterus stanch the flow of blood at the end of each menstrual period.

Alternative to hysterectomy: **Endometrial ablation.** In this 30-minute outpatient procedure, a balloon inserted through the vagina and into the uterus is filled with water and then heated. Blood vessels collapse and fuse together, sealing them shut and stopping bleeding.

FIBROID TUMORS

These benign uterine growths can be microscopic—or as large as a cantaloupe. Many fibroids—even some that are big—cause no symptoms. But if one presses against the uterine lining, menstrual bleeding can be profuse.

Alternative to hysterectomy: **Hysteroscopic surgery.** Fibroids that measure less than five centimeters (about two inches) in diameter can usually be removed without making any incision.

The doctor inserts a laparoscope-like device (hysteroscope) through the vagina and uses an attached wire loop to slice away the fibroid bit by bit.

Hysteroscopic surgery can usually be done under local or spinal anesthesia.

Larger fibroids require a more invasive procedure known as *myomectomy*. This involves removing the fibroids through an abdominal incision similar to that made in a cesarean section.

About 30% of women who undergo hysteroscopic surgery or myomectomy wind up needing a second operation, since fibroids can recur.

Fibroids tend to shrink after menopause—but never go away entirely.

Caution: Hysterectomy may be required for a fibroid that develops or enlarges following menopause. Such fibroids may be an indication of a malignant growth.

LACK OF OVULATION

Ordinarily, the ovaries secrete hormones that trigger ovulation. If the ovaries fail to secrete the necessary hormones, the lining of the uterus becomes thicker as cells accumulate there.

This process continues until the destabilized lining begins releasing a torrent of blood.

Alternative to hysterectomy: **Hormone therapy.** The hormones found in birth-control pills are often enough to stop the bleeding.

Caution: If you have high blood pressure or are prone to blood clots, progesterone-only therapy may be safer than the Pill.

UTERINE PROLAPSE

Uterine prolapse is a condition in which the uterus drops out of its ordinary position. Most cases do require hysterectomy, but not all.

The ligaments and connective tissue that hold the uterus in place are stretched and weakened by pregnancy.

Over time, gravity stretches the ligaments further, dropping the uterus lower. In extreme cases, the uterus droops through the vagina.

Alternative to hysterectomy: **Wearing a pessary.** This donut-shaped device—which is roughly the size of a diaphragm—is inserted into the vagina and wedged against the pubic bone to hold the uterus in place.

Pessaries can be an especially good idea for frail women who want to avoid surgery.

Sometimes Mammograms Are Not Enough

Mammograms are less accurate in women with dense breasts. Tumors are hard to spot. They show up as white on mammograms—as does dense breast tissue.

Helpful: Mammography plus ultrasound. On an ultrasound exam, tumors show up as black and healthy tissue as white.

Thomas M. Kolb, MD, assistant clinical professor of radiology, Columbia University College of Physicians and Surgeons, New York.

Try Kegels

Urinary incontinence affects 38% of women and 19% of men over 60. A study of almost 200 older women found that practicing simple exercises known as Kegels, together with some behavioral strategies, were significantly better at reducing accidents than drug treatment. Kegel exercises involve repeatedly squeezing and relaxing the pelvic floor muscles that hold the bladder in place—and are the same muscles that are used to slow or stop the flow of urine. It usually takes eight to 10 weeks of exercise to produce results. Then they should be continued as part of the daily routine. *Note:* They also help men.

Kathryn Burgio, PhD, professor of medicine at the University of Alabama at Birmingham.

Natural Treatment for Prostate Enlargement

Prostate enlargement can be treated safely and effectively with *Pygeum africanum.*

An herbal remedy derived from a species of prune tree native to Africa, pygeum has been used for 30 years in Europe. But since the harvesting of pygeum is threatening the prune trees, it's sensible to take pygeum only if the usual treatments for prostate enlargement—the drug *finasteride* (Proscar), alpha-1 blocking agents like *terazosin* (Hytrin) and the herbal remedy saw palmetto—fail to work. Pygeum is sold in health-food stores.

Russell H. Greenfield, MD, director of continuing medical education, Program in Integrative Medicine, University of Arizona Health Sciences Center, Tucson.

Testosterone Supplements

Stephen Winters, MD, professor of medicine and endocrinology at the University of Pittsburgh School of Medicine. He is author of more than 100 scientific articles pertaining to male hormones.

For years it's been known that testosterone levels start to decline as men hit middle age. Lately, a growing number of doctors have begun prescribing testosterone supplements for their older male patients. The hope is that restoring testosterone to youthful levels will boost physical and mental function.

At the same time, many younger men with normal levels of testosterone have been taking supplemental testosterone to enhance athletic performance.

To learn more about testosterone supplementation, we spoke with Stephen Winters, MD, a leading researcher on male hormones…

●**Who stands to benefit from testosterone supplements?** Men with chronically low testosterone levels clearly benefit. This condition—known as *hypogonadism*—is often caused by a disease process affecting the testicles, such as an injury, mumps during childhood or Klinefelter's syndrome. That's a hereditary disorder marked by an extra X chromosome.

Hypogonadism can also result from a pituitary tumor that shuts down testosterone production…or from AIDS or another disease involving poor nutrition and weight loss.

For men who fall into one of these categories, testosterone-replacement therapy brings increases in energy, muscle mass, strength, stamina, bone density, body hair, beard growth and sexual function.

Collectively, these changes bring heightened athletic prowess and self-confidence…and a significantly enhanced sense of well-being.

●**How can a man tell if his testosterone level is low?** Some men have clear symptoms of testosterone deficiency, such as a weak sex drive, erectile dysfunction, fatigue, depression and/or a loss of motivation.

Physical signs of testosterone deficiency include low muscle mass, sparse body hair and beard, abnormally small testicles, enlarged breasts and a boyish appearance.

But testosterone deficiency isn't always obvious. The only way a man can be sure of his testosterone level is to have a blood test.

•Are testosterone levels tested as part of the standard physical exam? No. The test is usually done only if the doctor—or patient—suspects hypogonadism. By the way, if an older man shows no symptoms or signs of hypogonadism, I don't even think he should have his testosterone level tested. His level is likely to be naturally a little low—and this could trigger unnecessary concern.

•What level of testosterone is considered normal? Among young men, peak (morning) testosterone averages 700 to 800 nanograms per deciliter (ng/dL). Any young man whose morning value falls under 350 is likely to have hypogonadism.

The threshold value for hypogonadism is lower for older men. Doctors often recommend testosterone replacement if a 55-year-old man has a morning value of less than 300 ...or if a 65-year-old has a value under 250.

•Might older men benefit from supplemental testosterone if their testosterone level is only moderately depressed? We don't know. We do know that women experience an analogous decline in estrogen at menopause—and most doctors now prescribe estrogen for these women because it helps reduce the risk for osteoporosis and heart disease.

Many ongoing studies, including a large-scale National Institutes of Health study, are addressing the issue of age-related testosterone decline. But some doctors aren't waiting to learn the results of these studies. They are prescribing testosterone for healthy older men.

I consider this premature. Older men given testosterone tend to feel stronger and have a stronger sex drive. But testosterone supplementation may increase the risk for benign prostatic hyperplasia (BPH) and prostate cancer.

•What if the test indicates hypogonadism? If testosterone is found to be low on one test in the morning, a second blood test should be done to confirm the reading. Tests should also be done to measure levels of the pituitary hormones LH and FSH. If these tests also show abnormally low values, the problem is likely to be in the pituitary gland. Magnetic resonance imaging (MRI) tests and additional blood tests should be done.

High levels of LH and FSH, on the other hand, suggest a testicular problem.

If no pituitary problem can be found, testosterone supplements are probably appropriate.

Because testosterone plays a role in BPH and prostate cancer, men who begin testosterone-replacement therapy should be sure to have a digital rectal exam and a blood test for prostate-specific antigen (PSA) each year.

•What's the best type of testosterone supplement? Some doctors prescribe self-injections of testosterone every two weeks. Others prescribe a transdermal patch, which is applied to the skin once a day, usually at night. Testosterone cannot be taken orally, because it breaks down in the digestive tract before it has any effect.

Injections can be painful. Also, some men experience mood swings as their level of testosterone spikes and then gradually declines.

Because of these drawbacks, more men are opting for the testosterone patch. The only major drawback to the patch is that it can cause a skin rash.

•How safe are over-the-counter testosterone precursors like androstenedione and DHEA? We simply don't have enough data to know.

A recent study found that men who took 200 mg of "andro" each day for several months did not experience a rise in testosterone levels. They did, however, experience a slight rise in estrogen levels.

The implication of this research is that andro may not boost athletic performance—but might cause breast enlargement. It is better to steer clear of these supplements until more information is known.

Prostate Biopsy Self-Defense

Have two pathologists—one of whom is an expert in the field—study the results. Up to 2% of biopsies are misread, which could mean that signs of cancer are missed. Having two doctors read the biopsy reduces the chance of error.

Patrick C. Walsh, MD, urologist-in-chief, Johns Hopkins Medical Institutions, Baltimore.

Baldness Linked To Heart Trouble

Men who are losing the hair on the crowns of their heads have a 36% greater risk of heart problems than men who are not going bald...or who have mildly receding hairlines. Going bald at the crown is an inherited characteristic that may be linked to elevated male hormone levels. Any male going bald in this way should carefully watch his blood pressure and cholesterol levels, and be especially careful to exercise regularly, not smoke and eat a heart-healthy diet.

JoAnn Manson, MD, DrPH, chief of preventive medicine, Brigham & Women's Hospital, Boston, and coauthor of a study of 22,000 male doctors, ages 40 to 84, reported in *Archives of Internal Medicine.*

Writing Personal Ads— Here's the Formula That Works Well

Susan Fox, marriage and family therapist. She is founder of Personals Work, an ad-writing and consulting service for people seeking romantic partners, 57 Rutland Sq., Boston 02118

The most effective personal ads are 50 to 80 words long—but no more than 125 words. Here are my rules for writing the perfect personal ad...

•**Write about who you are—*not whom you want.*** Use at least 75% of the ad to describe yourself. Ads that get answered present a portrait of the writer rather than what the writer is seeking.

•**Choose phrases that describe your qualities.** If necessary, take a poll of your friends. Include your best physical characteristics. Be accurate—but this is advertising, so don't underrepresent yourself.

•**Avoid vague words, clichés, cute images and obscure quotes.** Words such as *nice* and *walking on beaches* are meaningless. Phrases such as *lovely lady seeks gentleman* and *enjoys fine dining* are stilted.

Instead, use clear language. Be straightforward when describing yourself. Create a picture with words.

•**Combine opposites to balance your self-portrait.** The order of the words is important.

Examples: Strong but gentle...elegant but earthy...quiet but feisty.

Don't hammer home the same quality over and over again, such as *kind, loving, generous to friends, true-blue.*

•**Only mention serious nonnegotiables.** These could include nonsmoking or smoking, religion, race, age, height, gender, politics, etc.

ADS THAT WORK

•**"Truly stunning woman with rural American roots,** French heart and soul, cosmopolitan spirit, insightful, loyal, filled with passion and life. Very attractive, creative, elegantly gracious, trim. Loves city strolling, café sitting, architecture, boating, swimming. Expressive eyes, irreverent humor. Successful business owner, casual, relaxed style. Seeks bright, health-conscious, financially stable man of integrity, 40–55, 5'8" plus, who can laugh and is interested in others."

•**"Mediterranean soul, Anglo-Saxon head,** passionate heart, inquisitive mind. Goodhearted, forthright, sincere widower, 55, fit with natural warmth and up-front zest for life. Considered the world's best uncle by all three nieces. Enjoys theatre, exploring Manhattan neighborhoods, Asian food, art, hardware stores and baseball. Also biking, volleyball, golf, Nantucket. Nondogmatic, unconventional, works hard, plays hard, but good at unwinding, too. Seeks smart, educated, natural, trustworthy woman, 45 plus, for lasting relationship."

Related Useful Sites

Education

☐ FinAid
www.finaid.org

Link to a searchable database of more than 400,000 private sector *scholarships*, fellowships, grants and loans for college students. Links to resources for *foreign students* studying here in the US. Also includes addresses of student aid offices.

☐ How Stuff Works
www.howstuffworks.com

Fun and educational site for kids and their parents. Learn what makes everyday objects tick: Refrigerators, clocks, air conditioners, computers, cars, even your body. Great information for all.

☐ Family Education Network
www.familyeducation.com

A site rich in advice and expert opinion about teaching, school curriculum, child development, fun learning activities for free time, even child health and safety information.

☐ The Electronic Embassy
www.embassy.org

Get basic information on most foreign countries through the site that lists all of the foreign embassies in Washington, DC. Many of the countries maintain sites for their permanent missions to the United Nations. These can be directly linked to from the list of embassies.

☐ Britannica Online
www.eb.com

Here's the on-line version of the world-famous reference tool. For an annual fee of $50, you get access to more than 72,000 articles and 12,000 illustrations, maps and pictures. You can register for a free 14-day trial.

☐ B. J. Pinchbeck's Homework Helper
www.bjpinchbeck.com

A 12-year-old's Web site with more than 570 links to great research sources to help kids to their homework. Great for social studies, math, history, English and more. The site is the winner of more than 110 Web awards.

☐ The NASA Homepage
www.nasa.gov

NASA's extensive "virtual library," with news and information on current projects from NASA's on-line newsletter *today@nasa.gov*, space flight information, such as when you can see satellites, and links to NASA's *Education Program* on the Web. Answers to the most frequently asked questions about NASA, including jobs and internships.

☐ Discovery Channel Online
www.discovery.com

Excellent educational resource on history, science, nature and technology. Best surveyed through the *site-at-a-glance* page. Offers program schedules for the *Discovery Channel* and *The Learning Channel*. Your family can post and read messages on such topics as nature and dinosaurs.

☐ PBS Online
www.pbs.org

The official Public Television site. It provides national and local programming schedules, a link to Jim Lehrer's Online Newshour and a terrific scroll-and-click menu that takes you to interesting places, including Sesame Street. Be sure the check out *The Point* for the latest viewpoints on today's issues.

☐ The History Channel
www.historychannel.com

The on-line version of Cable TV's History Channel. Click on *Exhibits* and enter the on-line museum, which has wonderful exhibits on Ellis Island, Great Empires, the Great Sioux Nation and more. Or do a search for virtually any history topic you're interested in to get to well-organized and easy-to-read documentation and graphics.

Language

☐ Berlitz
www.berlitz.com

This site is brought to you by Berlitz, the first name in foreign language education. Click *Language Express*, where you can select any language and learn the basics, including key phrases. Check out *Berlitz Kid Talk*, where there are tips for parents, as well as games, puzzles and other fun language-related stuff.

☐ ACI-plus.com

www.aci-plus.com/tips

This is a great site for students, parents or anyone else who wants to have a better command of the written word. There are lots of tools to improve your writing. Check out the *seven tips to better writing* and *secrets of professional writers.*

☐ Acronym Server

www.ucc.ie/acronyms

Do you know what ASEAN stands for? How about NASDAQ? This site will help you find the meaning of an acronym (a word formed from the initial letters of several words). You can also search for an acronym and even submit a new one that doesn't appear in the database.

Computers

☐ Computing Central

www.computingcentral.com

Computing Central is an information resource for people who use computers at work and at home. Lots of PC tutorials and links to chat rooms, where you can ask others for help in solving specific computing problems.

☐ Yahoo!

www.yahoo.com

Yahoo! is a great starting place, allowing you to search according to the category of your inquiry, from government to health to business to science, etc. It will also automatically connect to AltaVista for searches that are too specific for its own search system.

☐ Techpointer.com

www.techpointer.com

Need help with that computer at three in the morning? Need to upgrade your software? Go to Techpointer for free tech support, software patches, games…

☐ MacCentral Online

www.maccentral.com

MacCentral is about information, giving you the tools you need to get more from your Mac. Updated several times a day and published seven days a week, this site offers news, reviews, software updates, tips and tricks, industry information and more, all in a format that is engaging, fun and, most important, easy to use.

☐ Northern Light

www.northernlight.com

A different kind of search engine gives you more options than most others. First, it not only searches the Web, it also looks through thousands of other sources, including magazines, newspapers, wire services, books and more. And it actually categorizes and organizes the search results in neat little folders.

☐ NCSA Mosaic Access Page

http://bucky.aa.uic.edu

An excellent resource for people interested in learning how individuals with disabilities can use the Internet and E-Mail. Select from a menu of specific disabilities, including vision, physical, hearing and cognitive, and you can check out the *list of products and services* available to enable the disabled to access the Web and use E-Mail.

And On to Tomorrow...

■Interview with Edie Weiner, president of Weiner, Edrich, Brown, Inc., consultants specializing in trend analysis, NYC.

I n the midst of the swirling Internet movement and the awesome political scandal hurricanes, it is too easy to overlook the more profound trends that move our personal foundations and transform our individual futures. But there are many important things happening that will affect us in at least the decade ahead.

WOMEN

Significant incongruities...For the first time in modern history, the U.S. will see large numbers of men retiring between the ages of 55 and 75 at exactly the same time their wives are at their peak earning and hierarchical status in the workforce. While the man will expect to travel and play and relax with his wife...the woman will be closing a deal in China or getting home at 8:30 pm thoroughly exhausted.

Downside: Much more matrimonial discord to come.

Upside: A major growth business opportunity for products and services that keep older men busy, and for counseling services that help men make friends, something they generally don't know how to do.

Also for the first time, in little more than half of all U.S. households, women are now the major breadwinner. In a large proportion that's because they're single heads of household. In 1 out of 4 dual-income households, women are the chief income earner.

Women are the primary breadwinners in almost 3 out of 4 households in which women are executives or professionals.

Whether because they are single, or because they out-earn their husbands, this new growth segment of the population will face a new social reality in the next decade. What women used to call "marrying down" will now be recast into "marrying for non-economic reasons." As these women earn enough to support their own lifestyles, it may be that the construction worker or expert male homemaker will become a far more attractive mate than the stockbroker.

BABY BOOMERS

The population of the world is aging rapidly and deeply. In China there are 210 million people over the age of 60. Two years ago, Italy became the first country in the world to cross over the age boundary and have more people over 60 than under 20.

Many other countries are joining that club. And...the U.S. will see hundreds of thousands of people in the next few decades reaching 100 years of age.

But it is important to understand that even though we are extending life, we are not extending it at the end of life—we're extending it in the *middle.* We're living the years 35 to 75 as if they were the same age. Baby boomers, those currently aged 36 to 53, are moving middle age up from 45 to 65.

We stay fitter, become better accustomed to change, think young and, in effect, get stuck in one mental phase for 40 years before we begin to feel our age mentally.

Many more older women will be dating younger men, as age differences in the middle years begin to fade. This means more need for aids to augment the physical beings of both men and women—Rogaine, Viagra, gingko—as well as more need for manufactured transitions to augment our psychological beings—career shifts, remarriages and second/third families, entrepreneurialism, second home purchases, volunteerism, revisiting of religious confirmations, renewal of marriage vows, spiritual retreats and self-help programs, acquiring new hobbies, adventure travel and on and on…

THE GENERATIONS

The Baby Boom, begun at the end of World War II, describes the 17 years in which births exceeded 4 million per year, totaling over 70 million additions to the U.S. population.

The leading-edge Boomers, coming as they did after a smaller age cohort preceding them, and growing up at a time of great economic boom, were very spoiled—schools expanded to accommodate them, the market rushed to sell them everything from TV cartoon decoder rings to sugary breakfast cereals and they went on to colleges in record numbers.

That same leading edge was able to protest everything about authority, create a sexual revolution, fry their brains on drugs, burn their bras, join the Peace Corps and unite under the "Nation of Woodstock." Still, when they entered the workforce, there were jobs aplenty, with good salaries and good prospects for the future.

Their younger brothers and sisters, however, were not so lucky. By virtue of its sheer size, the leading edge of the Boomers soon clogged up all the entry-level positions, filled professional schools to capacity and drove up housing prices as they started their own households in record number. By the time the middle Boomers arrived on the scene, a clean record and a professional degree or an MBA were prerequisite tickets to the good life.

For the "tail-enders," the glory days were gone, and competition was keen for good paying jobs with good prospects, especially in the wake of the oil crisis of the early 1970s, which led to the first major wave of downsizing and layoffs.

Then came Generation X, a *birth dearth* generation, with yearly births over a 15 year period way below that of the Boom. These youngsters were eagerly courted by colleges who faced falling enrollments. And these youngsters eventually came to be in great demand in the workforce.

In the past five years, at the tail end of Gen X's entry into the workforce, it has not been uncommon to see sign-on bonuses and highly competitive offers to attract the best and brightest of this smaller age cohort.

So, despite the fact that they have been graduating higher education with the largest debts ever—because of the skyrocketing costs of college—they have been able to earn enough early enough to pay down that debt rapidly.

Now comes Generation Y, those youngsters age 22 and under. *Gen Y is larger in number than the Baby Boomer population!*

Over the past several years, competition to get into colleges and universities has been brutal. Costs are continuing to skyrocket. In three years' time (four years after the first Gen Yers have graduated), we will once again find entry level positions in good jobs and attractive fields clogged up.

Amassing even higher debts than their predecessors, Gen Y graduates will come to be financially squeezed as no other generation before it—in a healthy economy. *Implications are many, and they include…*

• **Falling 401K contributions by those in their 20s,** as they seek to pay off loans with relatively smaller salaries.

• **More age discrimination at the higher levels** as more younger people vie for jobs.

• **More "Boomerangs"** (children of Boomers returning to live at home) as housing prices escalate.

• **More focus on gaining more and higher credentials** as a competitive edge.

• **More focus on college preparation** as slots in higher education institutions fill up rapidly.

These are just of few of the demographic trends that will profoundly affect our finances, our future prospects, our lifestyles, our well being, and our children over the next decade.

Index

340

medical errors and, 25-26, 30-31
qualification of professionals and, 26-27
Quercetin in preventing cataracts, 10

R

Radon, cancer and, 316
Raloxifene (Evista) for breast cancer, 1
Rebates, 182-183
Rebound headaches, 4
Recovery drinks, benefits from, 76
REITs, investing in, 159
Religion
  heart and, 83
  hospitalization and, 83
Renova, 13
Renovation, preparing for major, 252
Renter's insurance, 110
Resale number, 139
Retin-A, 13
Retirement
  income taxes and, 138-139
  planning for, 189-199
  saving for, 189-191
  selecting place for, 197
Retirement plans, cutting taxes with,
  137-138
Revocable trusts, 92-93
Rose, benefits from, 76
Rosemary in cancer prevention, 49
Roth IRAs, 121, 131, 137
Roulette, 226

S

S-adenosylmethionine (SAM-e), for
  depression, 4, 81
Safety. *See also* Security
  airbags and, 242
  computer, 317
  in cruises, 222
  with electrical cords, 320-321
  fire extinguishers for car, 242
  genetically engineered foods
    and, 56-57
  with lawnmowers, 321
  trunk latch, 242
St. John's wort, 78
  in controlling anxiety, 70
  in fighting depression, 81-82
  shopping for, 71
Salad bars and buffets, food safety
  and, 322
Salaries, comparing on-line, 295
Sales, on the Internet, 291-293
Salt, 5
Sardine Spread, 72
Scholarships, college, 304
Search engine, visit Web site of, 280-281
Secure Web sites, 317
Security. *See also* Safety
  cordless phone and, 317
  in foreign airport, 216
  getting through in airports, 217
  privacy and, 311-314

Selected American Shares, 150
Selenium in cancer prevention, 50
Self-employed, tax deductions for, 134
Self-Help Sourcebook Online, 11
Self-hypnosis, 14-15
Seniors, shopping discounts for, 177-178
Series EE U.S. savings bonds, giving to
  grandchildren, 207
Service Corps of Retired Executives
  (SCORE), 290
Sex
  after childbirth, 328
  making time for, 327
Sex boost, from soy, 327
Sexual relationship, building better,
  325-326
Shaker sets, collecting, 232
Shopping on-line, tips for, 178-179
Short-term investors, investing in bull
  market, 164-165
Skin
  diet effect on, 13-14
  reversing aging of, 13
Skin cancer, 2
Slamming, self-defense for, 317
Sleep habits and migraine headaches, 41
Slippery elm, 3
Slot machines, 226
Small Business Administration, 290
Small Business Development
  Centers, 290
Small-cap mutual funds, investing
  in, 151
Snoring, therapy for, 38-39
Social Security, 197-199
Soda, sugar-free, 56
Software, getting free business, 286-288
Sound, healing power of, 15-16
Soy, sex boost from, 327
Soybean oil in reducing risk of heart
  attack, 55
Soy protein, health claims for, 52
Spatial intelligence, 307
Spielberg, Steven, 249
State-of-the art equipment, needed, for
  telecommuters, 302
State sales tax number, 139
State Street Corp., 150
Stock market
  predicting future, 162-163
  protecting gains from, 128-130
Stocks
  financing buy-backs, 299-300
  giving appreciated, to children, 131
  Internet fraud and, 322
  picking time to buy, 161
Stop-smoking programs as medical
  deduction, 133
Store, success of opening own, 300-302
Strang Center, nutritional approach to
  cancer prevention, 48-50
Streisand, Barbra, 249
Strength training, 61, 64
Stress management, 55

exercise and, 78
for migraine headaches, 40
Stroke, aspirin in preventing, 39
Sugar
  energy level and, 6
  hyperactivity and, 22
Sugar-free soda, 56
Sulfurophane in cancer prevention, 49
Sumatriptan (Imitrex) for migraines, 41
Sunscreen, 13
Supermarket, saving at, 181-183
Surgery. *See also* Anesthesia
  for cancer, 24
  cataract, 10
  in doctor's office, 31-32
  errors in, 25-26
  laser eye, 32-33
  mental preparation for, 27-29
  preventing postoperative anesthesia
    hangover after, 29
  recovering from, 29
  stopping herbal remedies prior to, 27
Swimming, 61

T

Tamoxifen (Nolvadex), for breast
  cancer, 1
Tax audits. *See also* Income taxes;
    Internal Revenue Service (IRS)
  getting information on, 124-125
  and home-office deductions, 297
  preparing for, 118
  use of Internet to gather information,
    125-126
Taxes. *See also* Estate taxes; Income
    taxes; Internal Revenue Service (IRS)
  and e-commerce, 118-120
Tax identification number, 139
Taxpayer Relief Act (1997), 210
Tea tree, benefits from, 76
Technology-stock cycle, 156
Technology stocks, investing in, 154-157,
  163-164
Teenagers, signs of trouble and
  solutions for, 247-248
Telecampus, 305
Telecommuters, need for state-of-the-art
  equipment, 302
Telephone, cradling between shoulder
  and head, 317
Term-life insurance, comparing
  quotes, 107
Testosterone supplements, 330-331
Thank-you notes in getting new job, 289
Theophylline, 3
Thiazide diuretics for blood pressure, 30
Thurow, Lester, lessons from, 273-274
Tickets, getting refunds on
  nonrefundable, 186
Tight underwear and fertility, 328
Tomatoes in preventing cancer, 51
Tonic water for leg cramps, 44
Tools, shopping for, 170